CITY OF SISTERLY AND BROTHERLY LOVES

CITY OF SISTERLY AND BROTHERLY LOVES

Lesbian and Gay Philadelphia, 1945–1972

Marc Stein

TEMPLE UNIVERSITY PRESS
PHILADELPHIA

Marc Stein is the former editor of *Gay Community News* in Boston and is currently Associate Professor in the Department of History, York University, Toronto.

Temple University Press
1601 North Broad Street
Philadelphia PA 19122
www.temple.edu/tempress

Paperback edition published 2004 with a new preface by the author
Cloth edition first published 2000 by The University of Chicago Press

Printed in the United States of America

Portions of chapters 7, 8, and 9 originally appeared as "Sex Politics in the City of Sisterly and Brotherly Loves," *Radical History Review*, no. 59 (Spring 1994): 60–92. © MARHO: The Radical Historians' Organization, 1994. Portions of chapters 7–13 originally appeared as "Approaching Stonewall from the City of Sisterly and Brotherly Loves," *Gay Community News* (June 1994): 14–15, 30

∞ The paper used in this publication meets the requirements of the American National Standard for Information Sciences—Permanence of Paper for Printed Library Materials, ANSI Z39.48–1992

Library of Congress Cataloging-in-Publication Data

Stein, Marc.
City of sisterly and brotherly loves : lesbian and gay Philadelphia, 1945–1972 / Marc Stein ; [with a new preface by the author].
p. cm.
Originally published: Chicago : University of Chicago Press, 2000, in series: Chicago series on sexuality, history, and society.
ISBN 1-59213-130-1 (pbk. : alk. paper)
1. Gay men—Pennsylvania—Philadelphia—History—20th century. 2. Lesbians—Pennsylvania—Philadelphia—History—20th century. 3. Gay liberation movement—Pennsylvania—Philadelphia—History—20th century. 4. Philadelphia (Pa.)—Social conditions—20th century. I. Title.
HQ76.3.U52P57 2004

2004051730

2 4 6 8 9 7 5 3 1

CONTENTS

PREFACE TO THE PAPERBACK EDITION

More than 12 years after I began working on *City of Sisterly and Brotherly Loves*, I welcome the opportunity provided by Temple University Press's publication of this paperback edition to highlight what I see as its main contributions and to reflect on its place within the growing body of works on lesbian, gay, bisexual, and transgender (LGBT) history.[1]

Ask the average Philadelphian today when the city first developed multicultural LGBT communities, when the silence that characterized local public discussions about LGBT issues was first shattered, and when it first became possible to lead happy and fulfilling LGBT lives in Philadelphia, and the likely answers given will fall within the last three decades of the twentieth century. The same is probably true if they are asked when Philadelphians first began marching for LGBT rights and when LGBT movements first accomplished important goals in the city. *City* was written in part to encourage readers to give different answers to these questions.

Ask the typical LGBT studies scholar to characterize the U.S. homophile movement of the 1950s and 1960s, and you will probably hear talk of the Mattachine Society, dominated by white men, and the Daughters of Bilitis, dominated by white women, and the movement's activists will likely be characterized as moderate civil rights reformers who were hostile to radical sexual politics. Ask them to name and describe the most widely circulating LGBT movement periodicals in this period, and chances are that you will hear references to *The Mattachine Review*, *The Ladder*, and *ONE*. Ask them when LGBT movement periodicals first began to feature sexually explicit images, when the movement's first sit-ins took place, and when LGBT leaders first embraced the term *queer*, and they will probably point to the period after New York City's Stonewall riots of 1969. Ask most LGBT experts when people of color first took leadership positions in the LGBT movement and when multicultural LGBT political groups first appeared, and you will likely get responses that focus on the last three decades. Ask where any of these developments first took place, and Philadelphia will not appear high on the list of answers. *City* was also written to suggest different answers to these questions.

In working on *City*, I imagined the book as a contribution to ongoing conversations taking place in academic and non-academic settings; in local, national, and transnational contexts; and among LGBT and non-LGBT people interested in history, geography, social movements, urban studies, and sex, gender, and sexuality studies. Insofar as *City*'s first edition did not dwell at length on these conversations, it may be useful for me to say a little more here about the book's relationship to earlier contributions and to say a few words about how the conversations have developed since the earlier edition was published.

One set of conversations was with all those who act, speak, and write as though LGBT people and phenomena are irrelevant, marginal, and unimportant at best, and sinful, diseased, criminal, and subhuman at worst. For example, of hundreds of books about Philadelphia's history published before *City*, none paid more than passing attention to LGBT topics. And yet as *City* demonstrates, there are vital LGBT elements of important aspects of post–World War II Philadelphia, and when these elements are ignored, our understanding of the past suffers. What damage is done to our perspectives on the history of Philadelphia's downtown, for example, when the emergence of LGBT neighborhoods there is left out? How can we understand the significance of the Walt Whitman Bridge if we ignore the Catholic Church's antigay campaign against naming the bridge for Whitman? When we examine the careers of Mayors Richardson Dilworth and Frank Rizzo, U.S. Senator Arlen Specter, and U.S. Treasurer Kathryn Granahan, is it best to ignore their involvement in anti-LGBT campaigns? Does it not matter that in the period covered by this study Black Panther activist Mumia Abu-Jamal (now on death row and at the center of an international campaign for justice) may have hurled an antigay slur at Frank Rizzo, Jr., now a member of Philadelphia's City Council? Should we just not talk about the contributions of LGBT people to the city's civil rights, student, antiwar, countercultural, and feminist movements? Against those who marginalize Philadelphia's LGBT history, *City* encourages readers to recognize the centrality of LGBT developments.

Beyond Philadelphia, LGBT topics have been similarly marginalized in U.S. history courses, textbooks, and monographs. *City*, along with various other books, helps to show how histories of cities are weakened when they ignore the growth of large and diverse LGBT communities, how histories of social movements are compromised when they overlook LGBT and anti-LGBT activism, and how histories of politics and the law are limited to the extent that they ignore LGBT issues in campaigns and courtrooms. *City* is perhaps at its most directly critical when it takes Jane Jacobs to task for ignoring LGBT dynamics in *The Death and Life of Great American Cities*. Elsewhere the book makes the point more implicitly by showing how these "larger" histories can be enriched when LGBT issues are taken into consideration.

City also joined another set of conversations that began with an inspiring collection of LGBT historians and anthropologists. Although my book was the first historical monograph to examine a U.S. urban community of lesbians and gay men, it entered a larger conversation about LGBT history that had been going on for some time. These works successfully challenged the myths of "silence, invisibility, and isolation," which are still often used to characterize the pre-Stonewall lives of LGBT people.[2] In the 1970s, 1980s, and early

1990s, the first generation of LGBT studies scholars produced groundbreaking national overviews of LGBT history and extraordinary accounts of major LGBT events and developments. But as generations of scholars in fields such as labor history, women's history, and African American history have known, local studies provide opportunities to see things that cannot be seen on a national or transnational scale, and the resulting insights can then change the way we look at the local, the national, and the transnational. As I worked on this book in the first half of the 1990s, George Chauncey, Elizabeth Kennedy and Madeline Davis, and Esther Newton published the first local historical monographs in U.S. LGBT studies. But Chauncey's important book on pre–World War II New York examined only men, Kennedy and Davis's exceptional monograph on twentieth-century Buffalo lesbians explored a relatively small city, and Newton's exemplary account of twentieth-century Cherry Grove focused on resort town dynamics. So I came to see that my contribution would be to examine relations between lesbians and gay men in a major U.S. city. I now view my work as part of a second generation of scholarship that includes local historical studies by John Howard on Mississippi (1999); Peter Boag on Portland, Oregon (2003); Nan Alamilla Boyd on San Francisco (2003); and David Johnson on Washington, D.C. (2003).[3] Together our works revise the portrait of U.S. LGBT history produced by the field's first generation.

What are the revisions suggested by my work? On the most basic level, discovering significant LGBT communities in post–World War II Philadelphia was itself a contribution. With all due respect to the historians who have written illuminating books about New York and San Francisco, the fact that we now know these LGBT meccas and capitals featured large and dynamic LGBT worlds before the 1970s is not nearly as surprising as discovering that such worlds existed in Philadelphia, a city rarely regarded as an important LGBT center. Having described such worlds in Philadelphia, we can now say with greater confidence that *every* large city in the United States likely featured important LGBT communities.[4]

City also helped reconceptualize the relationship between gay geographies and lesbian geographies. Ever since sociologist Manuel Castells used a San Francisco case study to put forward the suspiciously sexist thesis that gay men were territorial but that lesbians were not, various scholars have challenged his view without losing sight of differences between lesbians and gay men. Geographers contributed to the conversation by exploring lesbian spaces in the last three decades of the twentieth century, and Kennedy and Davis's work explored the earlier importance of lesbian bar territories. *City*, which explores residential, commercial, public, and political spaces, shows that multifaceted lesbian urban territories developed long before the rise of lesbian feminism in the 1970s and discusses the ways in which these spaces converged with and diverged from their gay counterparts.

While part 1 emphasizes the history of intersecting lesbian and gay geographies, part 2 challenges historians who argue that these LGBT worlds were invisible to the "general public" and that there was a "conspiracy of silence" that prevented public discussion of same-sex sexualities. Chauncey's *Gay New York*, for example, suggests that the gay world was "forced into hiding" in the 1930s, 1940s, and 1950s, and that gay life was "*less* visible to outsiders" in the second third of the century than the first.[5] In the absence of published LGBT studies of Philadelphia before World War II or New York after World War II, it is difficult to make chronological or geographical comparisons about these cities. But *City*, along with several of the newer local studies mentioned above, demonstrates that LGBT worlds were surprisingly and significantly visible in the post–World War II era. This does not mean that all segments of LGBT worlds (divided as they were by race, class, sex, and gender) were equally and similarly visible or that visibility was necessarily a good thing. But it does indicate that we will likely need to revise our periodization of silence and invisibility.

In parts 3 and 4, which concentrate on organized LGBT movements, *City* engaged in one set of conversations with the local LGBT studies and another with works on national LGBT politics. With the former, the subject of the conversation was how to conceptualize relationships between forms of everyday resistance (for example, claiming space in bars, using coded language, and hiding from public scrutiny) and organized political activism (for example, waging campaigns for civil rights, participating in demonstrations, and engaging in civil disobedience). While some of the first generation studies have been criticized for romanticizing practices of everyday resistance and for suggesting that organized political activism can be regarded as the logical and linear outcome of everyday resistance, *City* develops John D'Emilio's notion that everyday resistance and political activism were most effective when they worked together, which was not always the case.

With the works on national LGBT politics (most notably D'Emilio's), the conversation was more concrete.[6] In discussing a city that featured homophile political groups in which women and men worked together, *City* suggests that we not view the national movement as made up of separate female and male branches. In demonstrating that Philadelphia's *Drum* magazine had a circulation larger than that of the next three largest homophile periodicals combined, *City* encourages readers to look beyond *The Mattachine Review*, *The Ladder*, and *One*. In describing *Drum*'s sexy male physique photographs and analyzing its radical (though arguably sexist) sexual politics, *City* indicates that we should recognize that at least part of the LGBT movement joined the sexual revolution before the Stonewall riots. As for the post-Stonewall era, in highlighting parallels and relationships between gay liberation and lesbian feminism, *City* challenges those who see the two as developing in isolation. In emphasizing the multicultural dimensions of gay liberation and lesbian feminism, *City* argues that it is simplistic to characterize these as "white" movements. In looking at the activities of Kiyoshi Kuromiya, the writings of Anita Cornwell, and roles of LGBT people at the Black Panthers' Revolutionary People's Constitutional Convention, *City* shows that people of color developed distinctive forms of LGBT politics before the 1980s. And in tracing the continued prominence of the respectable strategies that had been used by the movement in the 1950s and 1960s, *City* suggests that Stonewall did not represent as much of a dramatic break in LGBT history as is often imagined.

Most of all, as is outlined in the Introduction, I wanted *City* to focus on relationships between lesbians and gay men and, in so doing, to join the conversation about how to conceptualize the relationship between lesbian history and gay history. In the first generation, several scholars authored major studies that linked the two; others were committed (with good reason) to resisting the incorporation of lesbian history into gay male frameworks; still others, believing that the field was not yet ready to theorize the historical development of lesbians and gay men "in conjunction," focused on men.[7]

Different projects have different aims, and each of us made choices that reflected our goals and our senses of the past. I may have believed that the lesbian past and the gay past were more intertwined than others did, but my reasons for pursuing a project exploring both had as much or more to do with the questions I was asking than with the answers I anticipated finding. I intended *City* to make a statement about the advantages of studying lesbian history and gay history together, but I was also aware that an *insistence* on the conjoined nature of the two has its own risks. Lesbian histories have the virtue of resisting gay male dominance, and separate gay and lesbian histories have the virtue of encouraging heightened attention to same-sex *sexual* cultures. Ultimately, the political convictions that motivated my approach were based on the notion that the best way to promote alliances and coalitions between communities is to acknowledge, respect, and communicate across differences and to resist historical hierarchies within and between communities. My hope for the future is that a history of relationships between lesbians and gay men could take its place within a larger literature that might include intersectional studies of relationships between, for example, African Americans and Asian Americans, Native Americans and Latinos, and Jews and Muslims.

Finally, *City* participated in conversations between lesbian/gay history and *queer* history.[8] I have been asked many times since *City* was published whether I consider it a work of *queer*, as opposed to *lesbian and gay*, history. The term *queer* is not used much in *City*, though it surfaces several times in excerpts from anti-LGBT texts, and the book points out that Philadelphia's gay sex radicals began to reclaim *queer* as a potent political term as early as 1964. The best way to answer the question is to consider the term's multiple meanings. If *queer* is used as an umbrella term that incorporates lesbians, gay men, bisexuals, and transgendered people, then I answer yes (though if I were writing *City* today I would devote more attention to the latter two groups). If *queer* history refers to the history of dissident, subversive, and transgressive sexes, genders, and sexualities, then *City* is partially *queer*. (Much of what I discuss was dissident, subversive, and transgressive, but the book also highlights the conservatism of LGBT cultures.) If *queer* history deconstructs heteronormativity instead of reconstructing LGBT cultures, then *City* is not particularly *queer* (though I take a certain kind of *queer* pride in doing the latter). If *queer* history rejects essentialist LGBT identities and bounded LGBT communities, then *City* is *queer* to the extent that, as Henry Abelove writes, "from historicizing to deconstructing is arguably just a step."[9] If *queer* history is *critical* history, then *City* is *queer*, both because it is critical of Philadelphia and because it is critical of LGBT conservatism. Taking such critically queer perspectives runs the risk of giving Philadelphia a bum rap and taking potshots at LGBT cultures. But I was convinced when *City* was published, and remain convinced today, that we are strong, smart, and savvy enough to recognize the difference between constructive and destructive criticism, and that we need to do so as we imagine queer futures.

Notes

1. For encouraging me to have *City* published in a paperback edition, I am very grateful to the many scholars who have written to ask when the book would be available for classroom use, and especially to Alison Isenberg and Jorge Olivares. Janet Francendese at Temple University Press expressed enthusiastic interest in *City* and I am very pleased to have had this opportunity to work with her.

2. John D'Emilio, *Sexual Politics, Sexual Communities: The Making of a Homosexual Minority in the United States, 1940–1970* (Chicago: University of Chicago Press, 1983), 1.

3. The earlier works are discussed in the Introduction. The second generation monographs include, among others, John Howard, *Men Like That: A Southern Queer History* (Chicago: University of Chicago Press, 1999); Peter Boag, *Same-Sex Affairs: Constructing and Controlling Homosexuality in the Pacific Northwest* (Berkeley: University of California Press, 2003); Nan Alamilla Boyd, *Wide-Open Town: A History of Queer San Francisco to 1965* (Berkeley: University of California Press, 2003); David Johnson, *The Lavender Scare: The Cold War Persecution of Gays and Lesbians in the Federal Government* (Chicago: University of Chicago Press, 2003). For a collection of local studies, see Brett Beemyn, *Creating a Place for Ourselves: Lesbian, Gay, and Bisexual Community Histories* (New York: Routledge, 1997).

4. John Howard has made a convincing case for moving beyond exclusively urban models within LGBT studies, but I would still argue for the primary historical significance of cities in LGBT history (and even Howard's work supports this point to the extent that much of his study focuses on Mississippi's largest cities).

5. George Chauncey, *Gay New York: Gender, Urban Culture, and the Making of the Gay Male World, 1890–1940* (New York: Basic, 1994), 8–9.

6. On this subject, see also Martin Meeker, "Behind the Mask of Respectability: Reconsidering the Mattachine Society and Male Homophile Practice, 1950s and 1960s," *Journal of the History of Sexuality* 10, no. 1 (January 2001): 78–116.

7. Chauncey, *Gay New York*, 27.

8. Henry Abelove, "The Queering of Lesbian/Gay History," *Radical History Review* 62 (1995): 44–57; Lisa Duggan, "Making It Perfectly Queer," *Socialist Review* 22, no.1 (1992): 11–31.

9. Abelove, "The Queering," 55.

ACKNOWLEDGMENTS

I have learned much about Philadelphia lesbian and gay history in the last eight years and yet remain humbled by all that there is still to learn. My 45 oral history narrators have taught me valuable lessons about passion and pain, love and sex, oppression and resistance, and growing older and remembering. I am grateful to have had these wonderful teachers.

Four teacher-scholars guided me and this book project in countless ways. Henry Abelove, my advisor at Wesleyan University, continued mentoring me long after my undergraduate education was complete. At the University of Pennsylvania, Carroll Smith-Rosenberg served as an inspiring graduate advisor and a model of intellectual creativity, theoretical sophistication, and grace of writing. Michael Katz and Mary Frances Berry generously read and constructively reviewed my work, offering much-needed encouragement along the way. Other remarkable teachers and scholars in Greater Philadelphia, including Joan DeJean, Richard Dunn, Drew Faust, Janet Golden, Larry Gross, Evelyn Brooks Higginbotham, Lynda Hart, Lynn Hunt, Emma Jones-Lapsansky, Peshe Kuriloff, Walter Licht, Margaret Marsh, Claire Potter, Eric Schneider, Bob Schoenberg, and Tom Sugrue, supported and strengthened my work as well.

My extraordinary graduate school cohort (and friends) sustained me intellectually, politically, culturally, and socially. Rebecca Bach, Dana Barron, Steve Conn, Anne Cubilié, Judy Filc, Brendan Helmuth, Alison Isenberg, Marie Manrique, Darren Rosenblum, Abby Schrader, Julia Sneeringer, and Kate Wilson deserve special thanks. Along with Rosanne Adderley, Anjali Arondekar, Rose Beiler, Stephen Best, Agustin Bolaños, Rebecca Bulmash, Stephanie Camp, Amy Cohen, Durham Crout, Denise Davidson, Jeannine DeLombard, Sid Donnell, Sherman Dorn, Susan Garfinkel, Greg Goldman, Larry Goldsmith, Herman Graham, Jay Grossman, Tim Hacsi, Liz Hersch, Paul Howard, Lara Iglitzin, Hannah Joyner, Michael Kahan, James Johnson, Suzanne Litke, Jay Lockenour, Jeff Masten, Lisa Myers, John Noakes, Max Page, Liam Riordan, Amy Robinson, Sue Schulten, David Smith, Monica Tetzlaff, Susan Thibideau, Victoria Thompson, Keith Wailoo, Rhonda Williams, and Marion Winship, they created a community that I was proud to call my own.

An overlapping community, this one defined by shared commitments to sexuality studies, made it possible for me to imagine and complete this project. Christie Balka, John Fout, Lori Ginzberg, Ed Hermance, Jorge

Olivares, and Leila Rupp read and reviewed different versions of the manuscript; their comments and suggestions made this a much better book than it otherwise could have been. I am also grateful for the advice and support of George Chauncey, John D'Emilio, Martin Duberman, Lisa Duggan, Jeff Escoffier, Estelle Freedman, Ramón Gutiérrez, Robin Hornstein, Jonathan Ned Katz, Elizabeth Kennedy, and Joanne Meyerowitz. My thanks go out as well to Randy Baron, David Becker, Brett Beemyn, Allan Bérubé, Nan Alamilla Boyd, Jeanne Boydston, Keith Brand, Michael Bronski, Chris Castiglia, David Churchill, Curt Conklin, Caleb Crain, Jill Dolan, Vicki Eaklor, Charlie Fernandez, Timothy Gilfoyle, Katie Gilmartin, Lynn Gorchov, Jim Green, David Halperin, Phil Harper, Lisa Hazirjan, Chad Heap, John Howard, David Johnson, Kevin Kopelson, Gerard Koskovich, Walter Lear, Ian Lekus, Jeff Maskovsky, Steven Maynard, Robert McRuer, Jeffrey Merrick, Laura Murphy, Ray Murray, Joan Nestle, Esther Newton, William Pencak, Donna Penn, Elizabeth Pincus, Chris Reed, Tim Retzloff, David Serlin, Nayan Shah, Frank Smigiel, Jennifer Terry, Rochella Thorpe, Martha Umphrey, David Warner, John Whyte, and Tom Wilson Weinberg.

After leaving Penn, I was fortunate to work for three years with colleagues and students at Bryn Mawr and Colby Colleges. Special thanks to Sharon Ullmann at the former and Cheshire Calhoun, Elizabeth Hutchison, Elizabeth Leonard, Margaret McFadden, and Rob Weisbrot at the latter. I am proud and pleased to finish this book at York University, whose history department has provided a warm welcome.

My work on this project was aided by the institutional support of Penn, Bryn Mawr, Colby, and York. Thanks also to the Center for Lesbian and Gay Studies at the Graduate Center of the City University of New York for selecting me as the first recipient of the Ken Dawson Award; to the American Historical Association Committee on Lesbian and Gay History and the Gerber/Hart Library for awarding me the Gregory A. Sprague Prize; to the American Historical Association for a Littleton-Griswold grant; and to the Andrew W. Mellon Foundation for dissertation and postdoctoral fellowships. *Radical History Review*, *Gay Community News*, and *Creating a Place for Ourselves: Lesbian, Gay, and Bisexual Community Histories* published articles based on the research presented in this book; thanks to Jon Wiener at *RHR* and Stephanie Poggi and Marla Erlien at *GCN*.

It was a great privilege to work with the librarians, archivists, research assistants, and photographers whose efforts are reflected on every page of this book. For their many contributions to the Gay, Lesbian, Bisexual, and Transgendered Library/Archives of Philadelphia, I especially thank Steven Capsuto, Douglas Haller, and Tommi Avicolli Mecca. The research assistance of Meredith Greene, Tracy Nathan, Abby Schrader, Kristi Strauss, Lisa Williams, Kate Wilson, and Nancy Zobl was exceptionally helpful. I also acknowledge, with thanks, Pat Allen, David Azzolina, Mimi Bolling, George Brightbill, Stephen Campellone, Jo Duffy, Harry Eberlin, Degania Golove, Morgan Gwenwald, Jo Hofmann, Margaret Jerrido, Jim Kepner, Brenda Marston, Theresa Snyder, Bill Walker, and the staffs of the Columbia University Oral History Research Office, the Cornell University Human Sexuality Collection, the Free Library of Philadelphia, the Gay and Lesbian Historical Society of Northern California, the International Gay and Lesbian Archives, the June L. Mazer Collection, the Kinsey Institute, the Lesbian Herstory Archives, the New York Public Library Rare Books and Manuscripts Division, the Princeton University Seeley G. Mudd Manuscript Library, the Temple University Urban Archives, and the Penn, Bryn Mawr, and Colby libraries.

Doug Mitchell and Matt Howard at the University of Chicago Press became enthusiastic about my work at an early stage; they have been true comrades ever since. My copyeditor Carol Saller was wonderfully careful and thorough, as was Doug's assistant, Robert Devens. My literary agents, Sydelle Kramer and Frances Goldin, provided expert guidance.

Old friends from Shrub Oak, Middletown, Boston, and New York cared for me and allowed me to care for them through the many years in which I worked on this book. In quiet moments of solitary work and in shared times together, they were always with me. Heartfelt thanks to Brad Bennett and Barbara Schwartz, Linda and Nissan Carmy, Judy and David Drager-Davidoff, LeRoi Freeman, Rachel Hart and Monty Levinson, Stacia Langenbahn, Jack Levinson, Linda Loewenthal, Catharine Reid and Liddy Rich, and Stacy Sterling and Wayne Bendell.

Members of my family supported me emotionally and materially from the start. Thanks to my late grandparents, Adele Kires Fishbein, Morris Fishbein, Freda Newman Stein, and Solomon Stein; my great aunt Jessie Fogelhut and her late husband Joseph; and my Adler, Balavram, Fishbein, Gordonson, Kemeny, Stein, and Yenan aunts, uncles, and cousins. In a book named for sisterly and brotherly loves, I have special thanks to extend to my "real" sister and brother, Gayle and Scott, and to Gayle's partner Dick Hiserodt. I am particularly grateful that Scott applied his proofreading skills to the manuscript. My parents, Rhoda Fishbein Stein and Walter Stein, provided me with the precious gift of secure love, for which they have my deepest gratitude.

I dedicate this book to a man who entered and transformed my life three years ago. Jorge Olivares is the most generous, sweet, and loving person I have ever met, not to mention the fact that he is exceptionally smart and extraordinarily sexy. Being with him makes me happy and that is an accomplishment that deserves a dedication.

INTRODUCTION

> Might it not be better if we asked ourselves what sort of relationships we can set up, invent, multiply or modify through our homosexuality? The problem is not trying to find out the truth about one's sexuality within oneself, but rather, nowadays, trying to use our sexuality to achieve a variety of different types of relationships.
>
> MICHEL FOUCAULT[1]

Not long after Michel Foucault, the author of *The History of Sexuality*, spoke about the "use" of "sexuality" to "achieve a variety of different types of relationships," James O'Higgins asked him in a 1982 interview about the "growing tendency in American intellectual circles, particularly among radical feminists, to distinguish between male and female homosexuality." O'Higgins wondered whether it was "worth insisting on the very different physical things that happen in the one encounter and the other." He also noted that "lesbians seem in the main to want from other women what one finds in stable heterosexual relationships: support, affection, long-term commitment." "If this is not the case with male homosexuals," O'Higgins argued, "then the difference may be said to be striking, if not fundamental."[2]

"All I can do is explode with laughter," Foucault replied, which prompted O'Higgins to ask, "Is the question funny in a way I don't see, or stupid, or both?" Foucault responded, "Well, it is certainly not stupid, but I find it very amusing, perhaps for reasons I couldn't give even if I wanted to. What I will say is that the distinction offered doesn't seem to me convincing, in terms of what I observe in the behavior of lesbian women. Beyond this, one would have to speak about the different pressures experienced by men and women who are coming out or are trying to make a life for themselves as homosexuals. I don't think that radical feminists in other countries are likely to see these questions quite in the way you ascribe to such women in American intellectual circles."[3]

Four years later, Adrienne Rich addressed the topics of differences and relationships between lesbians and gay men when she added a footnote to her 1980 essay "Compulsory Heterosexuality and Lesbian Existence." Rich had written in the earlier version,

> Lesbians have historically been deprived of a political existence through 'inclusion' as female versions of male homosexuality. . . . Part of the history of lesbian existence is, obviously, to be found where lesbians, lacking a coherent female community, have shared a kind of social life and common cause with homosexual men. But this has to be seen against the differences: women's lack of economic and cultural privilege relative to men; qualitative differences in female and male relationships, for example, the prevalence of anonymous sex and the justification of pederasty among male homosexuals, the pronounced ageism in male homosexual standards of sexual attractiveness, etc. In defining and describing lesbian existence I would hope to move toward a dissociation of lesbian from male homosexual values and allegiances.

In her 1986 footnote, however, Rich changed her position, announcing, "I now think we have much to learn both from the uniquely female aspects of lesbian existence and from the complex 'gay' identity we share with gay men."[4]

By 1990, Eve Kosofsky Sedgwick, in *Epistemology of the Closet*, was observing a "refreshed sense that lesbians and gay men may share important though contested aspects of one another's histories, cultures, identities, politics, and destinies." Referring to "the many ways in which male and female homosexual identities had in fact been constructed through and in relation to each other over the last century—by the variously homophobic discourses of professional expertise, but also and just as actively by many lesbians and gay men," Sedgwick argued that "there can't be an *a priori* decision about how far it will make sense to conceptualize lesbian and gay male identities together. Or separately."[5]

Four years later, Joan Nestle dedicated *Sister and Brother: Lesbians and Gay Men Write about Their Lives Together*, a collection that she coedited with John Preston, "to all the lesbians and gay men who honored each other with their love." Preston wrote that the idea for the book had emerged when two friends "asked each other why the recent burst in lesbian and gay publishing didn't reflect the reality of their lives: that most gay men and lesbians had, in fact, warm and often powerful relationships with one another."[6]

As I think about the paths that I have taken to and through this book, I remember that each time I encountered these passages my interest was piqued. What they suggested to me was that lesbians and gay men paradoxically have used *same-sex* sexualities to set up, invent, multiply, and modify *cross-sex* relationships. *City of Sisterly and Brotherly Loves* offers a case study of, an extended meditation on, and a series of tableaux concerned with this phenomenon. Challenging the tendency to conceive of lesbians and gay men as either entirely distinct or completely conjoined, I examine the history of their relationships. I argue that lesbian and gay history, for better and for worse, has much to teach us about the past, present, and future of relationships between what we tendentiously call "the sexes."

My fascination with this subject began when I was an undergraduate student at Wesleyan University in the early 1980s. Intellectually inspired by both radical lesbian feminism and gay liberation and intimately involved with both women and men, I began to see relationships between lesbians and gay men as offering exciting opportunities for thinking in new ways about relationships between the sexes. By the late 1980s, I was working with both lesbians and gay men on the March on Washington for Lesbian and Gay Rights, in the AIDS activist group MASS ACT OUT, and as the coordinating editor of *Gay Community News* in Boston. Intrigued by the alliances and divisions between lesbians and gay men that I witnessed and experienced, I wanted to learn more about their history. In 1989, when I moved to Philadelphia to begin graduate work at the University of Pennsylvania, and in the early 1990s, when I joined ACT UP (AIDS Coalition to Unleash Power) and Queer Action in Philadelphia, I witnessed and experienced a new set of relationships between lesbians and gay men. When it was time to select a topic for extended research, I chose the history of heterosocial relationships between lesbians and gay men.

I had first encountered the term "heterosocial" in Carroll Smith-Rosenberg's 1975 essay, "The Female World of Love and Ritual." Discussing bonds between women in the nineteenth century, Smith-Rosenberg writes that the "heterosocial" and "homosocial" worlds of women were "complementary." Building on Smith-Rosenberg's work, Kathy Peiss argues that "the complex passage from Victorian culture to modernism involved, among many other changes, a redefinition of gender relations, what might be termed the shift from homosocial to heterosocial culture."[7] Thinking about this shift, I realized that twentieth-century women and men have transformed the world of relationships between the sexes. Convinced that changing configurations of same-sex and cross-sex relationships were implicated in some of the most profound transformations of the century; determined to avoid the assumption that the only cross-sex relationships worth considering are sexual and heterosexual ones; committed to placing relationships between lesbians and gay men at the center, rather than the margins, of analysis; and interested in exploring the ways that lesbians and gay men both reproduced and subverted dominant heterosocial paradigms, I embarked on my project.[8]

Before beginning my primary research and writing, I looked to the best books on U.S. lesbian and gay history to see what assistance they might offer. Jonathan Katz's documentary collections, *Gay American History* and *Gay/Lesbian Almanac*, John D'Emilio's work on political movements, *Sexual Politics, Sexual Communities*, Martin Duberman's collection of documents and essays, *About Time*, and Allan Bérubé's analysis of World War Two, *Coming Out under Fire*, were immensely helpful, providing me with first-rate studies of lesbians and gay men. But these books focused on topics other than the history of relationships between the sexes.[9] As my work proceeded, Lillian Faderman's survey, *Odd Girls and Twilight Lovers*, Elizabeth Lapovsky Kennedy and Madeline Davis's study of Buffalo lesbians, *Boots of Leather, Slippers of Gold*, and George Chauncey's analysis of New York City gay men, *Gay New York*, were published, offering extraordinary insights into same-sex sexual cultures. But although these books acknowledged or demonstrated that lesbian and gay worlds overlapped, they were primarily single-sex studies, and with the exceptions of Esther Newton's *Cherry Grove, Fire Island* and Duberman's *Stonewall*, no new historical monographs took up questions about relationships between lesbians and gay men.[10] A number of studies from disciplines other than history and historical anthropology explored related topics, offering provocative theories and insights about sex, gender, and sexuality.[11] But insofar as they rarely set their analyses in particular historical times and places or focused on processes of historical change, their usefulness for my project was limited.[12]

In the initial stages of my work, I made several choices that shaped what followed: I decided to focus first on organized political movements, in Philadelphia, in the period from the 1940s to the 1970s. Why organized political movements? D'Emilio's study of national "homophile" activism successfully challenged the myth that the lesbian and gay movement began with the 1969 Stonewall riots in New York City, but I knew that local studies often reveal dimensions of history missed in national or transnational surveys. And apart from Duberman's *Stonewall*, none of the published local histories examined times and places where organized lesbian and gay political movements existed.

I focused on organized politics for three additional reasons. First, I had been involved in several movements, was interested in learning more about them, and hoped that a historical study might prove useful for my own work, and the work of others, in ongoing struggles. Second, movement activists often produce documents and publications, and often remain publicly visible, which I hoped would make for rich research possibilities. Third, I was convinced that organized movements, and particularly those in which people work collectively in sustained ways to promote justice and equality, have been key agents of historical change. In none of these areas was I disappointed.

Although researching the movement required that I travel around the country to examine the papers and publications of several major activists, help organize the Gay, Lesbian, Bisexual, and Transgendered Archives of Philadelphia to make use of its collections, and rely on the Freedom of Information Act to gain access to government documents, all of this aided my understanding. Moreover, as my work proceeded, I realized that the history of relations between lesbians and gay men was a crucial part of the history of lesbian and gay political movements and vice versa. Parts 3 and 4, which cover the years from 1960 to 1972, developed out of this stage of my work.

After learning a great deal about organized politics, I decided to explore the period immediately before the local movement developed, the 1940s and 1950s. I did this to see whether I could gain a better sense of what conditions helped precipitate the emergence of the movement and what differences it made to have a political movement on the local scene. To focus my work, I concentrated on public debates and discussions and specifically on representations of same-sex sexualities in print culture. Scholars in lesbian and gay studies have argued for years about the influence of medical, legal, religious, and literary texts on same-sex desires, behaviors, identities, communities, and movements.[13] But there has been little work published on local print culture and I was convinced that this was an important area to consider. I also suspected that thinking about local print culture would help me understand local political culture, in part because I would learn about the dominant cultural forces against which the movement later struggled, but also because, by reading dominant cultural texts carefully, I would find traces of how lesbians and gay men resisted these forces in the absence of a local movement.

Here, too, there were more than just historiographic reasons for my decision. I had worked as a journalist, writer, and editor, and loved reading newspapers, magazines, and journals. From a research standpoint, I knew that printed texts are much more likely to survive and be available than other kinds of sources. And I was convinced that print culture mattered—that it exercised powerful influence in mid-twentieth-century U.S. culture. Here, too, I was not disappointed. Although doing research on local print culture in a city whose newspapers are not indexed was difficult, the rewards were well worth the labor. Moreover, I soon realized that the history of relations between lesbians and gay men was very much shaped by local print culture and vice versa. Local print culture represented lesbians and gay men in different but related ways and this influenced and was influenced by the ways that lesbians and gay men represented one another. Part 2 is the result of this dimension of my work.

Long before I finished these chapters, I knew that I wanted to broaden my conception of politics beyond organized movements and public culture. After D'Emilio's study of the national homophile movement was published in 1983, much of the next generation of scholarship concentrated on everyday political resistance and the politics of everyday life. Chauncey, for example, writes that "the history of gay resistance must be understood to extend beyond formal political organizing to include the strategies of everyday resistance that men devised in order to claim space for themselves in the midst of a hostile society." He explains that "the full panoply of tactics gay men devised for communicating, claiming space, and affirming themselves . . . proved to be remarkably successful in the generations before a more formal gay political movement developed." Kennedy and Davis, discussing lesbians who "forged a culture for survival and resistance under difficult conditions," argue that "these were signs of a movement in its prepolitical stage." Noting that "the personal *is* political," they explain that they use the term "prepolitical" "to make distinctions between different kinds of resistance." Highlighting the importance of everyday strategies, they conclude that "both the homophile movement and gay liberation had their roots in the working-class culture of bars and house parties."[14]

I found these approaches compelling, but I was troubled by the implications that everyday resistance was not "political" in its own right and that "political" resistance followed "prepolitical" resistance in a linear historical process. I also encountered scholarship that suggested that everyday resistance not only inspired, supported, and sustained organized movements, but also worked at odds with them. Activists often encountered opposition and apathy in the communities that they purported to represent, and community members often encountered opposition and apathy in the movements that purported to represent them. Newton argues that "gay liberation's fundamental premise, that gay people must openly declare their sexual preference, was a direct challenge not only to the dominant society but also to the old gay survival methods." She also suggests that whereas "camp culture" in Cherry Grove emphasized "gender reversal, theatrical parody, and heightened sensation," lesbian and gay movement culture was "more influenced by the democratic earnestness of the Declaration of Independence and Walt Whitman." Newton concludes that Cherry Grovers were "determined to ignore" the lesbian and gay movement because "for any resort to become politically active works against a fundamental dichotomy in industrial life between leisure time and work time." According to Newton, in a world divided into "the 'male' public sphere, the domain of work and political action, and the supposedly private 'female' sphere of home, family life, and sexuality," Grovers struggled in the latter.[15] As I began pursuing this line of inquiry, I realized that because I had chosen a time and place with ample evidence of both everyday resistance and organized movement politics, I had a unique opportunity to explore dynamic relationships between the two. Soon I saw that the history of these dynamic relationships was itself intertwined with the history of relationships between lesbians and gay men. Lesbians and gay men moved in different but related ways between the realms of everyday resistance, public culture, and organized movement politics.

As was the case with the other dimensions of my project, there were additional reasons for pursuing this one. I knew as an activist about the support, interest, opposition, and apathy that movements can encounter in their communities; and I knew as a member of several communities about the ways that organized movements can succeed and fail in representing those communities. As an activist working in the conservative 1980s and 1990s, I knew that micropolitical resistance can sustain and support macropolitical struggles even in the worst of times but can undermine efforts to build powerful organized movements even in the best of times. I hoped that working in this area would help me think about how everyday resistance and organized political movements could work together more effectively. From a research standpoint, my work on movement documents and print culture provided me with evidence of everyday resistance, but the 45 oral history interviews that I conducted—19 with lesbians, 24 with gay men, and 2 with straights—proved even more valuable. Although researching everyday life is more difficult than researching organized movements and print culture, here, too, I was pleased with what I learned. Part 1, which covers the full period from 1945 to 1972, derives from this work.

Why Philadelphia? As I designed my project, I had a strong sense that the field of North American lesbian and gay history had moved into a stage in which local studies were building on earlier national scholarship. I supported this move in part because finely textured local studies can reveal things that national and transnational studies cannot and in part because local studies offer intriguing possibilities for doing antinationalist and nonnationalist scholarship.[16] I also liked the idea of doing a local study because I had strong attachments to place—to Shrub Oak, New York, where I grew up; to Middletown, Connecticut, where I went to college; and to Greater Boston, Massachusetts, where I lived for several years after that.

Feeling very much part of a cohort of lesbian and gay history scholars who were dividing up the map of the United States and Canada, I chose Philadelphia, where I was then living. Most published work in lesbian and gay history focused on New York City and San Francisco, which were known to have large and visible lesbian and gay communities, but I wondered about other major cities. When I began my research, Philadelphia was probably North America's biggest city *without* a reputation for a sizable lesbian and gay community. I wondered what I would find there and how this would compare to what others were finding elsewhere.

Although in many ways it made sense for me to research Philadelphia, in one particular way I worried at the outset that it did not: I did not like Philadelphia very much. Concerned about what this would mean for my work, I was partially relieved when I read about a study that revealed that Philadelphia had an unusually large percentage of residents who claimed that they would rather live elsewhere. Convinced by this that I had become a Philadelphian, I commenced my study. In the process of doing it, and with the fresh appreciation that developed after I left the city in 1996, I came to respect, admire, and like Philadelphia much more.

Although I selected Philadelphia at an early stage, only later did I set my work into an urban studies framework, exploring the ways that lesbians and gay men affected the city and the ways that the city affected lesbians and gay men. In addition to learning more about urban studies, this involved examining Philadelphia history, politics, and geography, and thinking more about what was distinctive about Philadelphia and what was not. As I worked in this area, I wondered about the ways that Philadelphia's many appellations—City of Brotherly Love, Holy Experiment, Quaker City, Birthplace of the Nation, Workshop of the World, City of Neighborhoods, City of Homes, and Private City—could be linked with lesbian and gay history. I was also curious about the relevance for lesbian and gay history of Philadelphia's oft-celebrated traditions of religious toleration, sex egalitarianism, and racial/ethnic multiculturalism, all of which are said to be rooted in founder William Penn's seventeenth-century Quaker vision.[17] Meanwhile, I encountered helpful new mapping technologies and provocative new scholarship on contemporary lesbian and gay geographies, which led me to organize part 1's discussion of everyday resistance around different types of urban environments.[18]

Why 1945 to 1972? This period long fascinated me, partly because of the powerful roles that social movements played in these years. Given the fact that historians often begin to write about an era approximately 20 years after the era is over, I also thought it would be interesting to take part in the process whereby the recent past becomes history. Born in 1963, I have many memories of the 1970s, 1980s, and 1990s, but not of earlier decades. To me, the years between 1945 and 1972 seem profoundly similar to, yet different from, the years I remember well. This period shaped my world and the historian in me wants to understand more about how this past influenced my present.

Some of my reasons for focusing on these years were more particular to lesbian and gay history and Philadelphia history. Despite the rich scholarship on the pre-Stonewall era, the prevailing view continues to insist that lesbian and gay history began with the New York City riots of 1969, and this makes pre-1969 scholarship especially important. That said, I also thought it would be interesting to cross the Stonewall divide, to explore what differences the riots made by examining the period immediately following them. Another reason for focusing on the 1940s, 1950s, and 1960s was that, to the extent that much lesbian and gay historical research has depended upon oral history, opportunities for learning from lesbians and gay men who remember these decades will decline and then disappear with time. I decided to begin with 1945 because of D'Emilio and Bérubé's convincing arguments that a new era in lesbian and gay history began with the conclusion of World War II.[19] I chose 1972 as my endpoint for three main reasons. First, I recognized that the kind of research that I needed to conduct for the pre-1972 era, which involved pursuing every document that I could find, would be impossible for the post-1972 era, which experienced a lesbian and gay information explosion. Second, I have many memories of the years after 1972 and found that they unproductively complicated my ability to think historically about this period. And third, Philadelphia's first "gay pride" parade, which took place in the summer of 1972, provided me with a way to weave together many of my narrative threads.

I have a number of different audiences in mind for this book: lesbian and gay Philadelphians, lesbians and gay men, Philadelphians, activists, students, historians, and scholars in sex, gender, and sexuality studies. Although my work has been shaped by the interpretive frameworks described above, at times I play the role of the documentarian, offering passages designed to enable readers to pursue their own interests and reach their own conclusions. I follow the conventional historian's practice of using the past tense when referring to materials that I am using as evidence *from* the past and the present tense when referring to materials that I am using as scholarship *about* the past. Because I regard my narrators (my oral history sources) as experts looking back on the past, I use the present tense for their statements. I have edited the oral history narratives for purposes of clarity, which several narrators asked me to do.

While all of the texts that I discuss are representations, I want to call attention to the fact that the oral history narratives were produced 20–60 years after the period under consideration and were created in dialogue with me—a Euro-American, Jewish, middle-class, academic, activist gay man. Before beginning each interview, I described the nature of my project and offered to answer questions about my work, politics, and life. In several cases, narrators asked a question that led me to reveal that I identified as gay (which the others probably assumed) and that I had a history of sexual relationships with both women and men (which the others probably did not assume).[20]

Although the people whom I discuss did not necessarily use the terms "lesbian" and "gay" in the period under study (most narrators say that they commonly used the term "gay" for both women and men before the 1970s), I call the men "gay" and the women "lesbian." In a project concerned primarily with cross-sex relationships, it seemed best to use terms that distinguished between the sexes, even though this risked reinstating the very differences and relationships that I try to historicize. I asked the narrators to decide whether they wanted me to use their real names or pseudonyms. If they requested the latter, I had them choose alternative names. Pseudonyms are placed in quotation marks the first time they are used.

The book is divided into four parts. Part 1, "Everyday Geographies, 1945–1972," explores convergences and divergences in lesbian and gay cultures. Chapter 1 focuses on residential neighborhoods. Chapter 2 examines commercial establishments, including bars, clubs, and restaurants. Chapter 3 focuses on public space, including parks, streets, and parades. In these chapters, I point out that there were significant differences between the sexes; between racial, ethnic, and class groups; and between types of space. For example, lesbians relied more heavily on strategies of public invisibility and more often socialized in the "private" sphere. These differences affected relationships between lesbians and gay men. For example, gay men tended to be more visible to lesbians than lesbians were to gay men. But in spite of these differences, lesbians and gay men concentrated in the same three neighborhoods (Center City, West Philadelphia, and Germantown/Mount Airy) and developed everyday cultures that overlapped. While lesbian and gay geographies partially diverged and partially converged, they together transformed the twentieth-century metropolis and their history together reveals much about the sexing and gendering of urban worlds.

Part 2, "Public Cultures, 1945–1960," examines textual representations of female and male same-sex sexualities before the rise of the local lesbian and gay movement. While the vast majority of these texts focused on male sexualities, I resist fully reproducing this focus by devoting significant attention to the references to female sexualities that did appear and by considering the implications of these representations for both sexes. Chapter 4 provides a survey of popular, legal, and medical publications, focusing on narratives of gay murders, sex crimes, and sexual psychopathologies. Chapter 5 examines debates about the naming of the Walt Whitman Bridge. Chapter 6 focuses on conflicts surrounding coffeehouses.

In these chapters, I argue that same-sex sexuality was a major theme in local print culture, that female and male same-sex sexualities were treated differently, and that discussions of same-sex sexualities tended to focus on male sexualities or derive claims about female sexualities from male counterparts. This section shows that dominant discourse responded to the existence of the vibrant lesbian and gay cultures discussed in part 1 but offered partial, distorted, and generally negative depictions of them. Constructing gay men as public and visible actors and lesbians as private and invisible objects, public discourse influenced lesbian and gay relationships by creating conditions for particular kinds of alliances, identifications, antagonisms, and conflicts between lesbians and gay men. For example, partly because public discourse concentrated on male same-sex sexualities, lesbians more often confronted public invisibility whereas gay men more often confronted negative visibility. Partly because of the public focus on gay men, lesbians simultaneously experienced greater identification and greater conflict with gay men than gay men did with lesbians. Offering a case study of relationships between everyday community culture and public print culture, part 2 shows how these relationships were sexed and gendered for all women and men.

Part 3, "Political Movements, 1960–1969," explores relationships between lesbians and gay men in homophile groups. Here I place everyday practices and dominant cultural representations in the background and bring political activism to the fore. Chapter 7 discusses the founding of the organized lesbian and gay movement in Philadelphia after an unprecedented police raid on a political meeting in 1960. Chapter 8 examines the strategy of heterosocial respectability used by lesbians and gay men in the Mattachine Society of Philadelphia and the Janus Society between 1960 and 1963. Chapter 9 concentrates on two new strategies that emerged between 1963 and 1967: militant respectability, which was employed by allied lesbians and gay men in East Coast Homophile Organizations, and sexual liberationism, which was employed by gay men in the Janus Society. Chapter 10 focuses on the rise of militant respectability, as practiced by the Philadelphia chapter of the Daughters of Bilitis and the Homophile Action League, and the fall of sexual liberationism, as practiced by the Janus Society, between 1967 and 1969. In each of these chapters (and in the chapters of part 4), I focus on synchronic lesbian and gay developments to highlight their conjunctions and disjunctions.

Documenting the roles that Philadelphia lesbian and gay activists played in organizing conferences, sit-ins, and demonstrations, producing the national movement's most widely circulating publications (the *Ladder* and *Drum*), and bringing a major case before the U.S. Supreme Court, these chapters also reveal the state repression that these activists encountered. Exploring heretofore unexamined traditions of mixed-sex organizing and sexual radicalism in the homophile movement, part 3 examines what lesbians and gay men lost and gained in the alliances and divisions that they created. I conclude that while lesbians and gay men experienced both conflict and cooperation in their movement work, they shared fundamental assumptions about the nature of differences between women and men. Exploring both links and gaps between strategies of everyday resistance, which often depended upon public invisibility, and strategies of movement activism, which often depended upon public visibility, I also show how relationships between these two types of strategies were sexed and gendered.

Part 4, "Twin Revolutions? 1969–1972," and the conclusion, "Sexual Pride, Sexual Conservatism," examine relationships between lesbians and gay men in the new movements of the post-Stonewall era. Chapter 11 discusses the continuing strength of militant respectability, as practiced by the Homophile Action League in 1969–1970. Chapter 12 considers the new strategy of gay liberation as employed by the Gay Liberation Front of 1970–1971. Chapter 13 concentrates on the new strategy of lesbian feminism as used by the Radicalesbians of 1971–1972. The conclusion explores two public demonstrations in the summer of 1972—Philadelphia's first "gay pride" parade and Philadelphia's Women's Strike Day march. In addition to tracing the multiracialization of organized lesbian and gay politics, these chapters show that gay liberationists and lesbian feminists developed parallel agendas that reflected countercultural and radical values, challenged the idea that lesbians and gay men were sexual minorities, and put forward the idea that the potential for same-sex sexual desires was universal. Exploring the influences that gay liberationists and lesbian feminists had upon one another, I resist the tendency to see separation as a sign of isolation. In the end, I argue that while the new strategies differed from one another and from the strategies used by the homophile movement of the 1960s, they, too, reinforced the idea that the sexes were intrinsically different.

In the absence of much published research on relationships between lesbians and gay men in other cities, it is difficult to determine how typical or prototypical Philadelphia was. I would speculate that everyday lesbian and gay cultures overlapped significantly in other North American cities during this period and that local print culture generally focused more on male same-sex sexualities and derived claims about female same-sex sexualities from male counterparts. While I would predict, therefore, that my arguments in parts 1 and 2 will be applicable to other cities, I would speculate that parts 3 and 4 discuss aspects of Philadelphia that were more distinctive. Lesbian and gay activists in other cities undoubtedly united and divided; they undoubtedly did so for many of the same reasons and in many of the same ways that Philadelphia's did; and they undoubtedly embraced some of the same homophile, gay liberationist, and lesbian feminist strategies that were used by Philadelphians. But research thus far suggests that Philadelphians were in the forefront of heterosocial lesbian and gay activism, lesbian homophile militancy, gay sexual radicalism, multiracial gay liberationism, and African American lesbian feminism. That said, Philadelphia lesbian and gay activists were probably typical in believing that women and men were profoundly different.

Monique Wittig has argued that "the class struggle between women and men . . . is that which resolves the contradictions between the sexes, abolishing them at the same time as it makes them understood."[21] *City of Sisterly and Brotherly Loves* suggests that while Philadelphia lesbians and gay men were engaging in other important struggles, they were not furthering the goal of abolishing the sexes. Reviewing the many accomplishments of Philadelphia's lesbian and gay communities between 1945 and 1972, I am struck most by the ways in which these communities both challenged dominant cultural ideas about sexuality and reinforced dominant cultural ideas about sex. Criticizing the notion that straights were superior to lesbians and gay men, they embraced the notion that women and men were fundamentally different. Playing unique roles in struggles to reimagine, reconstruct, and deconstruct relationships between the sexes, they performed in ways that reproduced these relationships. Subverting the hegemony of heterosexuality, they strengthened the hegemony of sex. This remains the central paradox of lesbian and gay identities.

PART ONE

Everyday Geographies, 1945–1972

1

Your Place or Mine?: Residential Zones in the "City of Neighborhoods"

New York, Boston, Washington, Chicago, St. Louis, San Francisco, Milwaukee, New Orleans, Philadelphia, are "homosexual capitals."

XAVIER MAYNE, 1908

During a visit to Philadelphia and Boston I noticed almost nothing of homosexuality, but visitors from those cities later assured me that there was "an awful lot going on" within private circles in these centers of Quakerism and Puritanism.

MAGNUS HIRSCHFELD, 1914

Philadelphia is not, like New York, Chicago, San Francisco, or Los Angeles, one of the gay meccas.

JEFF ESCOFFIER, 1972

Crusty old Philadelphia might choke on its soft pretzels, but homosexuals are now calling this town a national center of gay liberation.

JOE SHARKEY, 1973

I'm just so glad that someone is finally dealing with our part of the history. . . . I mean the pre-Stonewall story and the Philadelphia story. Because Philadelphia never gets its fair share. . . . What do you read about? San Francisco, New York, maybe Washington. . . . Philadelphia never seems to be mentioned, except in negative terms.

JOAN FLEISCHMANN, 1994[1]

In 1945, Philadelphia, with two million residents, was the third largest city in the United States. Advantaged and disadvantaged by its proximity to Washington, D.C., the political capital to the south, and New York, the economic and cultural capital to the north, Philadelphia was one of the country's preeminent urban centers. In many ways, however, Philadelphia was the nation's forgotten big city. New York and Washington had claims to primacy; Chicago was the capital of the heartland; Los Angeles was the rising city of the West. Often referred to as the "birthplace of the nation," Philadelphia seemed to symbolize the past, not the present or future.[2]

Lesbian and gay perspectives on Philadelphia incorporate many of the same contrasting elements that characterize other views of the metropolis: big city and small town, cosmopolitan and provincial, exciting and dull. Asked why he left Philadelphia for New York in 1949, "John Taylor" responds, "For the same reason that any self-respecting gay man would. You have to establish a gay life." Asked whether that could be done only in New York, Taylor says, "That could only be done in another city. . . . New York was a mecca. Why not New York for anybody who loved the theater and the arts and the cultural life it afforded and the gay life?" George Axler, who moved from Philadelphia to New York in 1950, says, "It's like night and day. New York is so much more diverse and so much more stimulating. I always thought of Philadelphia as being rather placid and quiet and peaceful. And if you have a life there, then it's not an unpleasant place to be because there's something for everybody there. But I like the excitement of everything here. . . . The most interesting people come to New York to make their lives here."

Arleen Olshan left Philadelphia for New York in the early 1960s. Discussing her "first love," whom she met when she was "dating gay boys," Olshan says, "Gil moved to New York to become a dancer and I moved to New York to become an artist. And we both moved to New York to get gay." Asked why he left Philadelphia in 1967, Richard Gayer responds, "I was wearing out my hand. I was not meeting men. Then I got a job offer [in San Francisco]. . . . There was no hope in Philadelphia. The only thing good about Philadelphia is that it's a relatively cheap big city. . . . I wanted to meet gay men and it was obvious that there was real potential in San Francisco. And there was none for me in Philadelphia. . . . It just seems to be a place that is so horribly dull that you lived in Philadelphia only if you had to."

While many lesbians and gay men left, others remained behind, some joining the city's chorus of critics. Asked about Philadelphia in the 1960s and 1970s, "Paul Schmidt" says that it was "dullsville": "I really believe it's the 'city of neighborhoods.' Everybody knows everybody. . . . Philadelphia may be large population-wise, and it's spread out over a large area, but it's still neighborhoods. And everybody at one time or another will be in town. It's the business section. And if you were out there carrying on or going to a bar, your chances of bumping into someone were real. It's small and it's provincial. . . . When you compare us to New York, forget it. There's no comparison." According to Henri David, "This is a much more closety town. I think it goes in degrees, New York being the most out city and then you go down to Philly and then you go down to Washington where everyone's totally in the closet because they all work for the government. And then you go from New York to Boston and they're still pretty wild up there. And then you go further up and forget it, they're all in the closet. It seems to be this epicenter of gayness in Manhattan. And it just goes down from there."

Philadelphia also had and has its boosters. For many, the point of reference was not New York or San Francisco. Ada Bello, who emigrated from Cuba in 1958 and lived in Louisiana and Mississippi before coming to Philadelphia in 1962, says, "I didn't like the South. When I first came to this country, I was aware of the tremendous discrimination but somehow I didn't think it was real. . . . I felt that as long as I stayed there I was part of their system. So coming north to me was a great liberation in that respect. I remember walking around Germantown and seeing the variety of people. I was so sick and tired of seeing pale, blond people." For others, the point of reference was north. Describing her courtship with Barbara Gittings in the 1960s, Kay Lahusen says, "We traveled back and forth between Philadelphia and Boston for the better part of a year. And then she proposed I come live with her in Philadelphia. I was very tired of Boston winters by then. And she said, 'Philadelphia is just like Boston, only warmer.' " Still others looked favorably on Philadelphia from the west or the east. Elizabeth Terry, who moved from rural Pennsylvania in the early 1970s, talks about why she came to the city: "Find the big time, find women. . . . I wanted to find a community of women who loved women." Asked why she chose Philadelphia, Terry says, "I had some familiarity with it. It was far, but not too far."

For some boosters, the point of reference *was* New York. Jack Adair, who moved from Philadelphia's suburbs to the city in the 1960s, recalls, "New York had not happened yet. They were still really enjoying much more discrimination than we were." Jeff Escoffier's account of moving from New York to Philadelphia in the early 1970s suggests that just as some Philadelphians had to leave their city in order to "come out," some New Yorkers had to leave their city to do the same: "Part of that whole decision of moving to Philadelphia was that once I moved to Philadelphia I would not be in the closet at all." Olshan remembers "running away from the whole scene in New York" and ending up back in Philadelphia several years after she left. Mark Segal moved from Philadelphia to New York in the late 1960s: "My theory was to go to New York since this was where all gay people were, I thought." But in the early 1970s Segal moved back: "I didn't think that anything was getting anywhere in New York. . . . Visiting Philadelphia as often as I did, I thought that I could be more helpful here. I thought there was more opportunity for my voice to be heard. Also I'm a Philadelphia chauvinist. I happen to love Philadelphia."

Then there are Philadelphia boosters who praise its merits without comparative references to other cities. Becky Davidson says, "I think Philadelphia is a good place. It is a big city. I don't feel that I've had lots and lots of problems. I've had some problems, but I've also been, in a lot of cases, very out as a lesbian. I've always felt like I'm in your face. If I want to hold hands with my girlfriend, I'm gonna hold hands. And so I've run into some difficulties, but I'm a West Philly gal and I know how to answer back."

It would be difficult to determine whether the lesbians and gay men interviewed for this study are representative of the lesbians and gay men who lived in Greater Philadelphia between 1945 and 1972: 19 are women, 24 are men; 10 were born in the 1910s and 1920s, 15 in the 1930s, 18 in the 1940s and early 1950s; 1 is Latina, 1 is Asian American, 8 are African American, 34 (including the Latina) are Euro-American. While 27% of Philadelphians and 16% of Greater Philadelphians were designated "non-white" by the census of 1960, 21% of the lesbian and gay narrators would be similarly categorized.[3] What can be said with certainty is that some lesbians and gay men were born Philadelphian, some became Philadelphian, and some stopped being Philadelphian. Of the forty-three lesbian and gay narrators, twenty-four were born and raised in Greater Philadelphia, six moved there as children, and thirteen moved there as adults. Twenty-seven had not left Greater Philadelphia permanently or semipermanently before they were interviewed, sixteen had, and seven of the sixteen had returned.

The narrators who moved to, around, and out of Greater Philadelphia did so in various migration streams—transnational movements from Europe, Canada, and the Caribbean; the "Great Migration" of African Americans and Euro-Americans from the South; migrations of Asian Americans from the West; and movements to and from rural regions, suburbs, small cities, and large urban centers. Narrators moved in the context of various life changes: they ran away from home and flunked out of school; they escaped persecution, prejudice, and poverty; they left and entered familial, marital, cohabitational, and independent households; they were mobilized and demobilized by the military; they were attracted by economic and educational opportunities; they wanted to live in rural, suburban, and urban environments; and they wanted to live in lesbian, gay, and straight communities.

While the dominant paradigm in U.S. urban studies focuses on African American migration from the rural South to the urban North and "white flight" from cities to suburbs, the dominant paradigm in lesbian and gay studies links multicultural lesbian and gay communities with cities. Cities, many claim, offered lesbians and gay men more independence and autonomy; more freedom from oppression; more economic, cultural, political, social, and sexual opportunities; and more chances to form bonds with other lesbians and gay men.[4] While lesbians and gay men also participated in suburbanization, the Philadelphia story suggests that a multiracial Great Gay and Lesbian Migration transformed the twentieth-century U.S. metropolis.

But was this a Great Gay *and* Lesbian Migration? While some scholars argue that lesbians did not concentrate territorially in cities, others suggest that they did.[5] For the most part, the latter have focused either on the post-1970 era or on commercial establishments, creating the impression that complex lesbian territories that included different types of space developed only in the context of the organized lesbian feminist movement. Evidence from Philadelphia suggests that (1) both lesbians and gay men concentrated territorially in the 1940s, 1950s, and 1960s; (2) lesbian geographies converged and diverged from gay geographies; and (3) they did so in residential neighborhoods, commercial districts, public spaces, and sites of organized political action.

Mapping the 1,150 lesbian and gay sites identified in this study confirms the composite picture presented by narrators: in different ways, for different groups, and at different times, three Philadelphia neighborhoods—Center City, West Philadelphia, and Germantown/Mt. Airy—were popular among lesbians and gay men (fig. 1.1). Highlighting the 42 contiguous census tracts that each contained four or more sites suggests that lesbians and gay men concentrated to a lesser degree in four other areas (fig. 1.2). These 42 tracts, 12% of the city's total, contained 79% of the sites, indicating a very high level of concentration. Furthest north were tracts in Germantown/Mt. Airy, where the concentrations were residential. Next came the area near Temple University in North Philadelphia, where the concentrations were political. Southwest of that was the Fairmount/Art Museum district, where the concentrations were residential. To the west of the Schuylkill River were tracts in West Philadelphia, where the concentrations were residential, commercial, public, and political. In Center City, the concentrations were also multifaceted. Just south of Center City was the South Philadelphia border, where the concentrations were residential and commercial. Furthest south were tracts in South Philadelphia, where the concentrations were residential. In these neighborhoods, lesbians and gay men created homosocial and heterosocial cultures.

Center City

Asked about gay residential concentrations, gay narrators most commonly mention Center City, the original site of William Penn's "green country town." Bounded by the Delaware River in the East, the Schuylkill River in the West, Vine Street in the North, and South Street in the South, Center City is divided into four quadrants by Broad and Market Streets. Discussing which parts of Center City were most gay, narrators often point to the southwestern quadrant, where Rittenhouse Square is located, and the southeastern one, which includes Washington Square.[6]

John Taylor remembers that when he was a teenager and living in West Philly in the 1940s, he began going to Rittenhouse Square, where he met

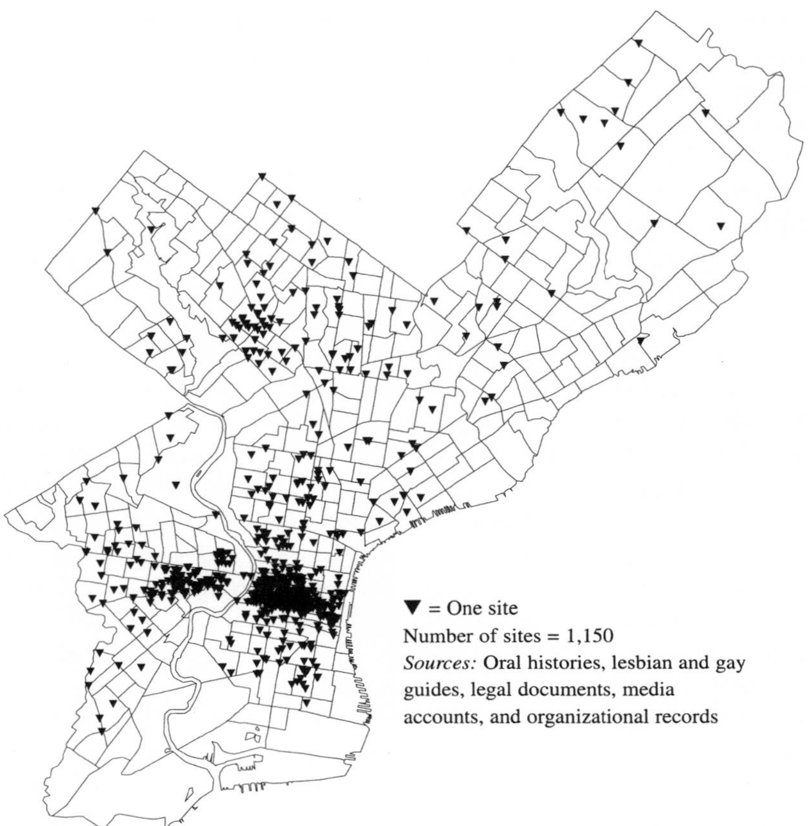

Figure 1.1. Lesbian and gay sites (residential, commercial, public, and political), 1945–1974

"substantial" gay men who had apartments nearby. Asked whether the city had a gay neighborhood, Taylor says, "Rittenhouse Square, very definitely, absolutely, all through there was gay. That's why you could go to Rittenhouse Square, 'cause so many people lived within walking distance." Bill Brinsfield recalls that when he was living in Fairmount in the 1940s and told his aunt that he wanted to be a set designer for the opera or theater, she responded, "What you're going to be is one of those bleach-blonde pansies that live on Spruce Street." In the 1950s, Brinsfield moved to 12th and Spruce in Center City. "Ray Daniels" moved from the suburbs to Center City in the same period: "Spruce Street was the area. We used to call that the street of broken hearts because everybody at one time or another lived on Spruce Street, fell in love, and had their hearts broken." Discussing the 1950s, Tom Malim recalls, "When I moved to Philadelphia, I was told there was a saying: 'Do you live on Spruce Street or are you straight?' "[7] Mel Heifetz, who also

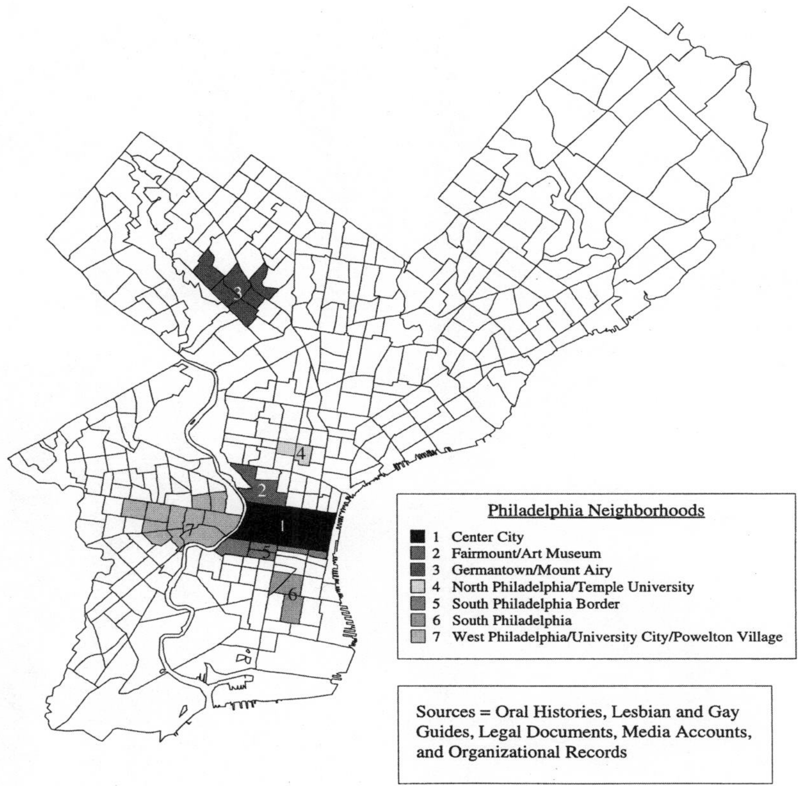

Figure 1.2. Lesbian and gay neighborhoods, 1945–1974. Each shaded census tract has four or more sites identified as lesbian or gay.

moved to Center City in the 1950s, says, "The only part of the city that gay people have ever lived in has been the Center City downtown area or something that's fairly close to it."

"Mark Kendall" remembers an episode from the 1940s that suggests some of the struggles that gay men experienced and the strategies that they used in maintaining their presence in Center City. Kendall was living with his family in an apartment house that they owned when late one night a tenant complained that another tenant, an "obviously gay" man, was entertaining a "dozen men on the fire escape." Kendall called the police, who found the men "in various stages of undress." He remembers watching the men "mincing defiantly out the door" and hearing his mother demand that the tenant move. After several hours in police custody, the tenant returned and gave a "sob story" to the Kendalls' maid, who encouraged the tenant to talk with Kendall's mother. Kendall recalls, "I listened to my mother agree to

Figure 1.3. Spruce Street, 1969. *Philadelphia Evening Bulletin* collection. With the permission of Urban Archives, Temple University, Philadelphia, PA.

have him stay provided he have only one boyfriend at a time. There was an older man, maybe forty, who used to come to visit. My mother suggested he stick with him because he was a gentleman."

Several narrators who first came to know Center City in the 1960s and early 1970s also describe it as gay. Kiyoshi Kuromiya, who moved from West Philly to Center City in the 1960s, says that "in its own way" Center City was "an East Coast San Francisco." According to "Jay Herman," who moved downtown in the same period, Spruce and Pine between Broad and 21st "could be defined as the gay mecca." Harry Langhorne, who moved from New York to West Philly in 1970, says that "Philadelphia's gay neighborhood" was "east and west of Broad," with concentrations on Pine, Spruce, and Locust. Another popular section was the countercultural South Street strip, which, according to a 1967 *Philadelphia Magazine* article, attracted "hippies" and "homosexuals."[8] "Gus Johnson," who moved from South Philly to Center City in the 1960s, says that in part because of the gay presence Center City was "a great, big hiding place" for draft dodgers, AWOL soldiers, and others resisting the war in Vietnam. Johnson recalls, "The gay community should receive a medal because they really went all out to help. . . . And because the gay community was the political underground to the feds, we could hide very well."

One popular residence in the northern half of Center City was the Arch Street Young Men's Christian Association (YMCA). Herman recalls living at the Y when he moved to Philadelphia: "About five o'clock on Friday afternoons, the various odors of cologne would come wafting through the halls and some of this cologne was on the bodies of people who had come down from New York for a weekend in Philadelphia. Some of the cologne emanated from the bodies of Philadelphia people who lived at the Y. I also remember that you could walk down the hall and occasionally there would be a door ajar and some young man would be lying across his bed with only a towel over his backside. . . . It got to be so active that eventually they put a guard at the elevator and anybody who went up in the elevator had to show their key to indicate that they were bona fide residents."

Gay residential patterns in Center City shaped and were shaped by the Philadelphia "Renaissance," which included various "renewal" and "redevelopment" projects undertaken in the 1950s, 1960s, and 1970s.[9] As scholars of other cities have noted, gay men played significant roles in early stages of gentrification. Attracted to areas that had relatively cheap and aesthetically appealing housing; that were near valued social, economic, and cultural institutions; and that were close to other areas of gay concentration, gay men became owners, landlords, and tenants in the gentrification process. As home prices and rents increased, wealthier gay men, most of whom were

Euro-American, displaced poorer residents, many of whom were African American and some of whom were lesbian or gay. In some contexts, gentrification created new downtown living opportunities for less wealthy lesbians and gay men who were lovers, friends, roommates, or preferred tenants of gay landlords. Later, gay men were sometimes displaced by straights newly attracted to living downtown.[10]

Jack Adair is proud of the role that gay men played in gentrifying South Street and Society Hill. "I moved there in 1967," he says, "when South Street was not a place you wanted to be." Henri David, who lived in southern sections of Center City in the 1960s and early 1970s, claims that gay men's role in gentrifying this neighborhood was "a hundred percent." Asked why gay men favored the area, David says, "Because there's safety in numbers. Because gays were smart. And why not live where the theaters are and the restaurants and the movies?" Asked why they were gentrifiers, David says, "Because gays like things nicer, just have better taste. . . . It happens everywhere. Gay boys move in, there goes the neighborhood, there goes the real-estate values. It's great." Pointing to another redevelopment zone, Daniels recalls that Hopkinson House, an apartment building on Washington Square, was called "Pansy Palace." "All the gays flocked to the new buildings," he remembers, "the ones that had the money." Kendall, who lived in Hopkinson House in the 1970s, suggests that while gay men were not always welcomed, they found ways to avoid discrimination: he recalls the manager saying that "he was glad we were taking a two-bedroom apartment" because they "preferred" not to rent a one-bedroom apartment to two men.

As a gay tenant, Daniels was able to take advantage of gentrification: "Landlords tended to like to rent to gay people, strangely enough. And the reasons of course were because they were clean and they would fix the place up. They would paint it, they would wallpaper it, they would decorate it, and they would be great neighbors." Gay landlords also benefited: Heifetz's real-estate business began when he purchased rooming houses on Arch Street in the 1960s. Gentrification, however, was not "great" for those who were displaced and for those with less money. Daniels notes, for example, that the blocks south of Pine were mainly black and low-income until the gay area expanded.

With a significant gay presence, Center City featured many house parties where gay men socialized. Herman remembers having "a set" of 10 gay friends who would host dinner parties in Center City. According to Johnson, "There were parties going on everywhere. All you had to do was walk down the street. . . . It was just a few friends dropping over and a few of their friends dropping over and then the next thing you know by ten o'clock you have a hundred people at your house." Kendall recalls, "There was one party where somebody very baldly invited me into a bathroom, and I hardly knew what was going to happen, and something happened where we had the bathroom door locked to the point that a couple of people got impatient."

Several narrators suggest that parties were as important or more important than bars. Discussing Center City parties, Paul Schmidt says, "That's where I think a lot of the gay life really was." According to Brinsfield, "Everything then was parties and socializing, because the bars closed. . . . And if you didn't want to roam the streets and get arrested and be harassed by the police, then you tried to get invited to a party." Although parties were occasionally raided by police, they were generally perceived to be safer than the bars or streets.[11] Heifetz remembers enjoying parties because, unlike the bars, they did not feature restrictions on "physical contact" and "dancing": "You didn't need the bars. Because every weekend there would be two or three parties." According to Daniels, "Everything just didn't revolve around the bars. . . . There was another aspect of gay life, which was very different from the bars and Rittenhouse Square and that kind of scene. We lived lives, we went to work, we came home, we talked to our friends, we had people come over, we entertained." Daniels tells a story of throwing a party with his roommate: "We agreed that we would invite about twenty-five close friends. . . . But I got carried away and I mimeographed invitations. . . . And I started giving them out in the bars. . . . Well, first the friends came and they brought gifts and everything was going fine. And then all of a sudden more and more people kept coming and coming and coming and coming. And my roommate finally said to me, 'Who are these people?' . . . I had managed to have the party of the year."

Daniels also illustrates some of the ways that social play and display were important dimensions of gay gentrification: "All of the apartments that I went to, and even my own apartment, were *done*. We *did* them. . . . Some of the apartment buildings weren't so great, but you'd walk in and say, 'My god, look at this apartment, it's a knockout.' " Daniels remembers that when he or his friends would move, "We'd say, 'This apartment's going to be great. . . . I'm really going to fag it up.' " Daniels remembers doing one apartment "in blues": "Wanamaker's sold fabric, and I went and I bought this fabric that was so expensive. But I just charged it. . . . We didn't care about things like money. We just went out and we spent it and when we didn't have anymore left we'd say, 'Well we'll have to wait until we get more.' Or we would figure out some way to postpone the rent for another month. We were out, we wanted to party, we wanted to have fun. That's why I guess they called us gay."

While many gay men could not afford these expenses on their own, some found ways to live beyond their individual means. Daniels recalls, "If you wanted a gigantic apartment, you had the salary to support it. There were some people that did, but most of us had other things we wanted to do. . . . One friend of mine lived in a house. It was a three-bedroom house and there were three guys. . . . That house was done to the nines. And I went to a number of parties there. . . . They combined their resources. One person could not have done that."

Sharing neighborhoods and homes strengthened the bonds that gay men felt with one another. According to Daniels, "You'd entertain. There was a sense of community. . . . I retract that—there was a sense of family. 'Cause you have to remember that back then you didn't go to your family and say, 'Hey mom and dad, I'm gay,' and they'd say, 'Oh gee that's great, I'll go and join Gay Parents.' . . . You didn't do that. You just suddenly moved away. . . . So your friends were your family. Your friends became your brothers and sisters. . . . If someone was having a hard time, we'd all chip in and throw some money in the hat and help them out with their rent. And then they in turn would help somebody else out when they got back on their feet."

Although several gay narrators reject the claim that Center City was a gay neighborhood, they do so in ways that clarify the picture presented by those who say that it was. Lewis Coopersmith, who has lived in Center City since the 1930s, says, "The idea that there's an unusual concentration of gay people in the area doesn't occur to people such as myself who have never lived in any other neighborhood." This comment suggests the importance of recognizing that some narrators perceived Center City to be residentially gay without having lived there themselves.

Kendall also rejects the notion that Center City was gay. Kendall lived downtown from the 1920s through the early 1960s and then, after several years in West Philly and Germantown, moved back: "Center City did, even back in the forties, tend to attract gay people, largely because of the density of the population and the ease of remaining anonymous. And also the only gay clubs that I knew of way, way back when were in Center City. Also Rittenhouse Square was well known as a trysting spot." But Center City was "mostly straight." "There was no gay neighborhood per se," he argues. "There were gays who would come to Center City." Kendall's comments suggest that for him to consider a neighborhood gay, it would have to have a gay majority. "They consider Center City, in a sense, the gay ghetto," he says, "but there are still, I think, more heterosexuals living in Center City than gays." While Kendall uses a strict definition of what constitutes a gay neighborhood, others base their designation on the sense that Center City was significantly gay.

Richard Gayer, who moved from New York to Northeast Philly in the 1950s and lived in Germantown for several years in the 1960s, also rejects the notion that Center City was gay. Although he refers to Spruce Street as "notorious" when discussing the apartment where one of his first gay sexual partners took him, he says that "nobody had a gay neighborhood in 1964," not "even" San Francisco. According to Gayer, "The place where there were gay people . . . would be around Rittenhouse Square, between there and Broad Street . . . , but there weren't any high density gay blocks." Like Kendall, Gayer uses a strict definition.

Coopersmith and Kendall also reject the notion that Center City was a gay neighborhood because of other meanings that they associate with this designation. Coopersmith, who has lived his whole life in an area that others point to as Philadelphia's gayest, says, "I do not have any interest in being part of a gay ghetto and personally find the idea of all kinds of ghettos unpleasant." After rejecting the description of Center City as gay, Kendall says that he also does not agree with "the concept of the gay community." "What community?" he asks. "As far as I'm concerned, there is no gay community. It's the same kind of lumping of groups together that is done in general."

While some lesbian narrators also reject the notion that Center City was a gay neighborhood, a larger number think that it was. Barbara Gittings, who shared an apartment with Kay Lahusen near Rittenhouse Square in the 1960s, says that they lived where they did because "it was cheap" and that they "didn't think of it as a gay neighborhood." In contrast, Joan Fleischmann, who visited downtown in the 1950s and lived there in the 1960s, recalls, "Center City was a gay neighborhood for men. . . . Most of the [gay] men I knew who lived in Philadelphia lived in Center City." Marge McCann, who moved from Logan to Center City in the 1960s, says that "to the extent that there was" a gay neighborhood, it was "east of Broad and Walnut to South." According to Laurie Barron, who moved downtown from Mt. Airy in the 1960s, "a lot of queens" lived near Rittenhouse Square and by reputation it was a neighborhood where one would see "gay men walking with poodles." Marcea Rosen, who moved from the suburbs in the early 1970s, says, "I chose to be in Washington [Square] West gay neighborhood because I thought I would be safer. And I was. And I purposely moved into a gay neighborhood." Asked whether she means a gay male neighborhood, Rosen says, "I guess so. Because I knew where they lived." Discussing the 1970s, Elizabeth Terry notes that "the gay ghetto" was on Spruce and Pine and in the area between Rittenhouse and Washington Squares.

Some lesbian narrators suggest that although gay men concentrated in Center City, lesbians did not. Fleischmann says that lesbians "didn't seem to live in any one particular place" and "were just sort of all over the place." "Women never seem to congregate the way men do," she asserts. Discussing the 1960s, Ada Bello says that while she does not think that Philadelphia had any lesbian or gay "neighborhoods," she believes that gay men favored Center City while lesbians favored West Philly and Germantown/Mt. Airy: "Partly for two reasons. Males go to bars more so they feel more comfortable if they're within walking distance. . . . Also it's cheaper out of Center City." Terry says that although some women would socialize in Center City, the "gay ghetto" was "white and male."

In contrast, several lesbian narrators suggest that Center City was gay *and* lesbian. Asked whether Center City was a gay or a lesbian neighborhood, Ann Lynch replies, "Both," and goes on to describe meeting a group of Center City lesbians in the 1940s. Two of these women, who Lynch thought were "old maids" but later realized were "in a relationship," lived next door to her father near Rittenhouse Square. Lynch recalls that while in their apartment one day, "there was a knock at the door, and there was this woman, and she came in, and she was small and bright, and she was the kind of person you meet that a child, a dog, a man, a woman, anyone would just fall in love with her. . . . And I fell head over heels." Several years later, Lynch moved to Center City. Asked which parts of Center City were lesbian and gay, she says, "Around Rittenhouse Square and around 12th, 13th, Broad." Joey Hardman recalls that she and a group of her lesbian friends shared a Spruce Street apartment in the 1940s or 1950s: "We'd use it for kicking off the shoes and just lying around. And so many people had a key for it." Hardman says that she and her friends once had a wedding ceremony at the apartment and that she was the groom, her girlfriend was the bride, and a man performed the ceremony. When the police arrived, Hardman pushed her girlfriend out through a side door: "I said, 'I don't want her getting mixed up in that 'cause then her mother'll holler at me and that would be it.'" Pat Hill, who moved downtown from the suburbs in the 1950s, remembers going with her boyfriend to a party hosted by a Center City lesbian: "I told him to go home. And I stayed. And I also took a small bottle of champagne to that party. 'Cause I knew I was gonna stay. . . . I stayed for three days. And we broke the bed."

Asked whether Center City was a lesbian and gay neighborhood when she moved there from Olney/Oak Lane in the 1960s, Carole Friedman says, "I think that's fair to say. . . . We certainly did socialize in other lesbians' homes." Barron recalls that both lesbians and gay men were drawn to Center City. While noting that "there was a preponderance of gay men" in Center City, she says that there was a "mixture" of lesbians and gay men there. According to Becky Davidson, lesbians and gay men not only lived as neighbors but also as roommates in Center City. Davidson remembers moving downtown from Northeast Philly in the 1960s and shortly thereafter beginning a relationship with a woman who lived in a boardinghouse on 12th Street in Center City. "It had a big, big, big communal kitchen," she recalls, "and a big, big communal living room," both of which were shared by three lesbians and three gay men. After she and her girlfriend decided to live together, they rented a series of Center City apartments. Asked to define the parameters of the lesbian and gay neighborhood, Davidson says that it was "mostly on Spruce" but also between Walnut and Pine. Drawing a southern boundary, she says, "Lombard always seemed like that was the start of another neighborhood, but more a black neighborhood."

While Davidson thinks that lesbians and gay men both were attracted to Center City, she remembers an episode from the 1960s that reveals some of the problems that they encountered there. According to Davidson, she and her lover once returned early from a vacation only to find that "some of our lesbian books were gone." When their landlord tried to "sneak" the books back into the apartment, "he saw us and just put the books down and left." Davidson remembers being "furious," feeling "betrayed," and moving to a new place. Housing discrimination was also a problem. According to a 1971 article in *Thursday's Drummer*, the *Inquirer* refused to accept an apartment ad from a woman who wanted to include the words, "No discrimination based on race or sexual preference." The following year, *Drummer* published an ad from a man who wanted to share a Center City apartment with "No Fags." In 1974, Byrna Aronson testified before the Philadelphia Commission on Human Relations that in 1967 the manager of the Richelieu had been prepared to rent an apartment to "L." until he realized that Aronson would be the other tenant. According to Aronson, "The manager proceeded to get very upset and said, 'I am sorry, we do not rent to two people of the same sex because they may be homosexual.' "[12]

Several narrators suggest that lesbians participated in the gentrification of Center City. Hill has fond memories of a house that she and her friends called "the Barn." In the 1960s, Hill moved into the house, which she "eventually bought . . . from the Redevelopment Authority" and "modernized." Rosen notes that as lesbians aged in the 1970s, "they became more affluent" and sometimes moved to Center City. Barron says that lesbian professionals "tended to migrate from West Philly to Mt. Airy or Center City," but that "lesbians had more of a tendency to be on the outskirts of Center City." Arleen Olshan, who moved downtown from Logan in the 1960s, notes that lesbians did not form ghettos in Center City: "We couldn't afford it." But like Barron, she says that lesbians often lived in "borderline neighborhoods," including southern parts of Center City, which were "cheap." Davidson bought a Center City house with her girlfriend in the early 1970s and benefited from gentrification. "We barely scraped it together. It was $24,500. . . .

But it wound up being really a lucrative thing. Three years later we sold it for $30,000."

Some gay narrators remember a lesbian residential presence in Center City. According to Heifetz, both lesbians and gay men favored Center City. Tommi Avicolli Mecca, who grew up in South Philly and moved downtown in the early 1970s, remembers having "a lot of lesbian friends who lived around Center City." Johnson recalls knowing several lesbians who lived in Center City in the 1960s and early 1970s. Two were older neighbors whom he visited when he was a teenager. One night, he recalls, they were all drunk: "And Peg leaned over the table and she said, 'Do you know what you are? You're a faggot. You are a homosexual.' She starts using all these terms. And I said, 'No I'm not. No I'm not. Yes, I am.' " Describing the significance of the moment, Johnson says, "you always know" but this was the first time he was "admitting it publicly." Referring to other Center City lesbian friends, Johnson says, "They decided that I should have a boyfriend. So they'd go out to the bars and they'd bring home these guys for me to go out with. And it never worked. . . . But I was very thankful."

Several gay narrators refer to lesbians when discussing Center City parties. According to Heifetz, "At some of the parties there was a lot of mixing between men and women." Daniels says, "I was friendly with lesbians at that time. There were two lesbians. . . . They lived on Spruce Street and I was friendly with them. . . . And I was invited to their home and I likewise invited them to my home." Kendall recalls, "Most of the lesbians we knew rarely went to bars, even when there were lesbian bars. They had a very well-developed social network and they entertained in each other's homes." Brinsfield remembers, "I socialized with the gay women that I knew in their homes." He also recalls parties that were organized by a Quaker-affiliated group in the 1940s or early 1950s: "They used to encourage going to houses and mixing lesbians and gays and black and white people together. . . . We used to go to one house, it was a gay woman who had it, and she would make it available. And there would be maybe five or ten lesbians, five or ten gay men, some heterosexual whites and heterosexual blacks, and a couple of gay blacks. . . ." Brinsfield says that the purpose was to show "heterosexuals" that "homosexuals were not going to eat them alive" and to show "whites" that "because a person was black, it wasn't going to rub off if they danced with them."

While some narrators suggest that lesbians and gay men socialized together because of the bonds that they felt toward one another, Heifetz observes that they did so in part for strategic purposes: "The women gave the appearance of being straight. If the neighbors had anything to say, they would see women coming in. If the police were to respond to a party because of noise, and they'd walk in and they'd see women in there, it wouldn't arouse a great deal of suspicion." According to Heifetz, "Today, now you are out of the closet, and you can just entertain a lifestyle that's strictly men or strictly women. It doesn't matter. They can't bother you. Back then . . . you had far more contact with women. It was far more necessary to have a cover, to be part of your seemingly straight lifestyle." Kendall says, "As far as parties were concerned, it was for convenience, I guess, that at first it developed that gay men and lesbians got to know each other and attended parties together. It was good for appearances."

More commonly, gay narrators suggest either that lesbians did not concentrate residentially in Center City, that lesbians did not concentrate as much as gay men did, or that they were unaware of lesbian residential patterns. Although he says that he got to know lesbians (and married one) when he moved to New York, Taylor, when asked whether lesbians lived in Center City, says, "I have nothing to tell you about lesbians. It was another world. . . . I never knew girls. I'm into guys. And I think I'm typical." Langhorne says, "I'm sure there were lesbians here in Center City, too. But one didn't think of it as being quite the concentration." Noting that lesbians concentrated more in West Philly and gay men more in Center City, Langhorne says that this "fits one's general stereotype about the interests and socializing patterns of gay men and gay women." He explains, "Men are more interested in the bars. They're more interested in promiscuity. They're less interested in nest building."

Narrators present a complicated set of answers to the questions of whether the lesbians and gay men of Center City were exclusively, overwhelmingly, or predominantly Euro-American; whether African American lesbians or gay men concentrated in Center City; and how patterns of racial segregation and separation in housing affected and were affected by lesbians and gay men. Center City was growing increasingly racially exclusive in these years, becoming more Euro-American and less African American. Most Euro-American narrators do not explicitly refer to race when discussing the lesbian and gay presence. One who does is Kendall, who recalls that he and his African American lover "never ran into any problem about two men living together," but that when he went to look at an apartment in Hopkinson House, "I didn't want Billy showing up because I thought there would be a problem . . . , because of racism." Schmidt says, "The blacks were segregated in their areas with their life and their social clique. And the whites [were] the Center City crowd."

Several African American narrators who did not live in Center City, including James Roberts, Sharon Owens, and Elizabeth Terry, refer to Center City or parts of it as gay. Noting that the "gay ghetto" was "white and male," however, Terry says, "Most African American gay and lesbian people that I met during that time, if they were from Philly, lived in the neighborhood that they grew up in." Discussing gay parties, Roberts says that "the black ones would be in either North Philly or West Philly primarily and if they were mixed or almost all white they'd be in Center City usually."

Two African American gay narrators who did live in Center City, Herman and Johnson, also recall thinking of Center City as gay. Herman lived alone in Hopkinson House and with a Euro-American lover elsewhere in Center City. Johnson lived with a multiracial group of gay men in a house that they called "Maison Duck." Kendall's, Herman's, and Johnson's accounts all refer to biracial or multiracial households near the southern edge of Center City, a zone of class, race, sex, and sexual transition.

Two older African American narrators, both of whom came from poorer families, migrated from the South, and lived in predominantly African American neighborhoods, share a different set of perspectives. Tyrone Smith, who moved to North Philly in the 1940s and lived there in the 1950s, 1960s, and 1970s, says that he does not recall thinking that Center City was a "gay neighborhood." Anita Cornwell, who moved to West Philly in the 1940s and lived in West, North, and South Philly over the next decades, says that African Americans were "just not as free to move around" as Euro-Americans: "There's a matter of money and there's a matter of 'don't come in our neighborhood.' " According to Cornwell, "White people think when they buy a house they have bought the whole neighborhood. 'It's our neighborhood.' " She adds that "a lot of times we wouldn't want to move there anyhow; we want to stay with our family or friends." Asked whether she thinks that there were neighborhoods that were better for African American lesbians, Cornwell responds, "I never looked at it that way. . . . I was looking for somewhere I could afford . . . [and] a safe place for a single woman." Cornwell concludes, "There's not that many black people in the country period. So you know how many black gay people there are. So if you go around looking for them to move somewhere, it doesn't make sense."

Notwithstanding significant racial and ethnic variations, mapping the residential histories of the 43 lesbian and gay narrators suggests that they did converge in Center City between 1945 and 1974. Of the narrators' adult residences in Philadelphia, 44% of the gay homes and 36% of the lesbian homes were in Center City. (Center City contained 2–3% of the city's population.) Concentrations increased over time. Of the adult homes from 1945 through 1959, 36% were in Center City, as compared to 43% from 1960 to 1974. In terms of race, while 49% of the Euro-American adult homes were in Center City, 6% of the African American adult homes were.[13]

Mapping another data set—the homes of 260 Philadelphia members of the Gay Activists Alliance (GAA), a group founded in 1971 and active through the mid-1970s—also suggests that lesbian and gay geographies converged in Center City: 32% of the total homes, 22% of the homes of female members, and 33% of the homes of male members were in Center City. Concentrations of members' homes varied by race and ethnicity: 18% of the African American homes, 15% of the Italian American homes, 54% of the Jewish American homes, and 29% of the Euro-American homes were in Center City.[14]

Mapping all 582 lesbian and gay residences identified in this study suggests that lesbian and gay concentrations and convergences in Center City were significant: 36% of these sites (38% of the male ones and 34% of the female ones) were in Center City (fig. 1.4). While the gay residents were more concentrated than the lesbian ones were, the heaviest concentrations of both lesbians and gay men were in Center City.

U.S. Census and Philadelphia City Planning Commission reports reveal some of the characteristics of Center City that may have influenced and been influenced by the lesbian and gay presence. In 1960, Center City, as compared to the 11 other Philadelphia neighborhoods defined by the commission, had the lowest average number of people per household, the lowest percentage of households with a married couple, the lowest percentage of residents under 20, the highest percentage of workers in white collar jobs, the highest median numbers of school years completed, the highest median value of owner-occupied housing, and the lowest percentage of owner-occupied housing. While retaining these characteristics in 1970 and 1980, Center City moved from fourth highest median rent in 1960 to first in 1970 and 1980. In a striking index of change, Center City's median family income was below the city median in 1960 but was highest in the city in 1980. While median "household" income, which included the income of "unrelated individuals," "single-person households," and "families," also increased, its relative position lagged behind, remaining much closer to the city median in 1970 and 1980.[15]

Center City was also becoming more Euro-American. In 1940, Center City was 22% non-Euro-American and 21% African American, significantly above the city figures of 13% and 13%. In 1960, the percentages of non-Euro-Americans and African Americans were below the city percentages. By 1980, while Center City was 10% non-Euro-American and 6% African American, the city figures were 42% and 38%. There were, however, significant variations between Euro-American ethnic groups. For example, while Jewish Americans were more concentrated in Center City, Italian Americans were more concentrated in South Philly.[16]

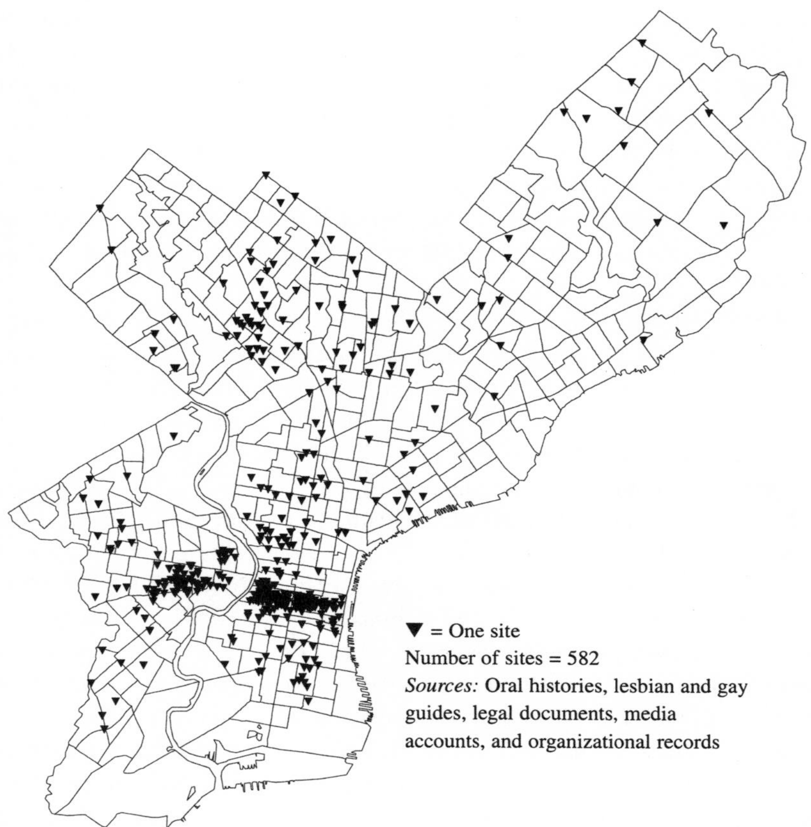

Figure 1.4. Lesbian and gay residential sites, 1945–1974

Center City shared many but not all of the characteristics of lesbian and gay neighborhoods examined by other scholars. Manuel Castells, studying gay men in San Francisco and using the 1970 census, finds that "gay settlement was opposed by property, family, and high class: the old triumvirate of social conservatism." Sy Adler and Johanna Brenner, researching lesbians in an unnamed city and using the 1980 census, argue that " 'property, family and wealth' are barriers to lesbian settlement." With a high percentage of rentals (in a "city of homes" that featured high rates of homeownership) and low percentages of children and married couples, Center City supports the findings about "property" and "family." But with increasingly high housing costs, rents, and incomes, Center City did not lack "wealth" after the "Renaissance."[17]

West Philadelphia

After Center City, West Philly is the neighborhood most commonly identified by narrators as historically lesbian and gay. Located west of Center City, the neighborhood is bounded by the Schuylkill River in the east and north, the city boundary in the west, and Baltimore Avenue and Grays Ferry Road in the south. Narrators often point to two areas close to Center City: University City (near the University of Pennsylvania, commonly called "Penn") and Powelton Village, just north of University City.

Many lesbian narrators say that West Philly was popular among lesbians. Laurie Barron names this one of the city's three lesbian and gay areas in the 1960s and 1970s. Discussing lesbian concentrations, she says that there were "pockets" of West Philly that were "very gay" or "very gay/lesbian friendly." Becky Davidson, who lived in West Philly in the 1950s and 1960s, says that it was popular among lesbians "before" Germantown was. Arleen Olshan, who moved to Powelton in the 1960s, recalls that "the lesbian ghettos were Germantown and West Philly" and that "there were lots of dykes living in Powelton." According to Sharon Owens, who also moved to West Philly in the 1960s, the neighborhood had "a lot of lesbians."

West Philly was popular for several reasons. Describing "huge houses that lent themselves to collectives," Barron mentions an architectural factor.[18] Rosalie Davies says that after she left her husband in the 1960s, she moved from the suburbs to a lesbian and gay collective in West Philly and then to a lesbian one in the same neighborhood. Bello notes that lesbians preferred West Philly and Germantown/Mt. Airy because "it's cheaper out of Center City." Owens says, "The fact that lesbians were living in West Philly and Germantown, as opposed to gay men living downtown, had a lot to do with economics. At the time, West Philadelphia (you wouldn't know it now), was a cheap neighborhood." Olshan links architectural with economic factors: "In Powelton you could get space. You could get one- or two-bedroom places or houses, very reasonably priced. We had a big communal house. And we had six bedrooms in it and at one point we counted and there must have been thirteen women living in that house." A few years later, she and her girlfriend moved to another place in Powelton: "We were still living in a lesbian household, but we had our own apartment."

Lesbians also favored West Philly homes because of their proximity to nonresidential lesbian space. Discussing the neighborhood, several narrators mention the Women's Center, which moved from Center City to West Philly in the early 1970s. Davies says that the collectives concentrated in University City because many residents had links with the feminist community at

Penn. Alvia Golden links architectural, economic, and spatial factors: "West Philadelphia was where all the University-type lesbians lived. And they all had these disgusting, huge houses." "There was a huge commune culture in the sixties and seventies," she explains. "Huge commune culture and huge lesbian commune culture. And the only way you could have a commune was to have one of those big old houses. And those big old houses are in West Philadelphia, Germantown, Mt. Airy, the ones you could buy cheap anyway."

Lesbians were also attracted to West Philly because they fit into its heterogenous population. Elizabeth Terry recalls that many of the lesbian collectives were "intentionally multicultural." Asked about the reaction of her neighbors when she moved there, Bello says, "That was one of the beauties of West Philadelphia. It was fine. There was no problem of any kind, because I think they're accustomed to a lot of variety. . . . I think it was a tolerant environment. . . . There weren't so many families; that's another thing."

Some of the features that attracted lesbians to West Philly distinguished this neighborhood from others. Comparing the lesbians who lived in West Philly to the ones who lived in Mt. Airy, Barron says, "Putatively, the differences were that the West Philly lesbians were more radical in their politics and more vegetarian in their diet." Carole Friedman recalls that while she was living in Germantown in the early 1970s, she "began to sleep over in West Philly" when she became involved with a woman who taught at Penn. Referring to different types of lesbians, she says, "Germantown was more old gay and West Philly, around the University, was more feminist-lesbian."

Lesbian movement in and out of West Philly was shaped by and shaped urban redevelopment.[19] Gentrification in Center City encouraged some lesbian residents to move to West Philly. Barbara Gittings, Kay Lahusen, and Arleen Olshan all left Center City for West Philly in the 1960s. Meanwhile, as Marcea Rosen suggests, some lesbians left West Philly when their new affluence allowed them to move to Center City or Germantown/Mt. Airy. Others participated in the gentrification of University City. Bello remembers that the first time she and her lover explored the possibility of buying a house, a real-estate agent told her that "nobody" would give a mortgage to two women. But later they did buy a house, which they "got involved with fixing up." Bello, who worked at Penn, explains, "It's a neighborhood that had gone through a lot of transformation. I understand it used to be a very fancy apartment building sort of neighborhood and it went down and then they started to gentrify. . . . Penn was bringing people in the neighborhood through a program that I'm sure was thought about for the faculty but then they extended it to everybody." She continues, "I moved to West Philly in 1970. We got the house for $15,000. And only five years later, you couldn't touch it."

With a significant lesbian presence, West Philly featured a number of lesbian house parties. Anita Cornwell remembers parties of African American lesbians in West Philly in the 1950s and says that, although she did not like the way the women categorized one another as "studs" or "femmes," these parties were her primary means of getting to know other lesbians.[20] Olshan says that there were "lots" of lesbian parties in the 1970s and adds that "Philly is a more at-home entertaining town." Owens, who refers to a "lesbian party circuit," remembers that "the hallmark of a good West Philadelphia lesbian party" was "if the neighbors called the police at two in the morning." At one party, "The cop was standing there, seeing if the noise level went down and talking to one of the women at the house. And he was looking at the porch, and saying, 'Aren't there any boys at this party?' And she said 'No.' And he said, 'What is this, a sorority?' And she said, 'Sort of.' "

While many lesbian narrators say that West Philly attracted lesbians, others disagree. In some cases, this may reflect the fact that they are thinking about a period before the 1960s. When Ann Lynch first moved to Philadelphia in the 1950s, she lived in West Philly, which she says seemed like less of a lesbian and gay neighborhood than Center City. "There were more families out that way," she explains. Other lesbian narrators reject the idea that West Philly was a lesbian neighborhood for some of the same reasons that they reject the idea that Center City was. Joan Fleischmann says that she "didn't really notice" a concentration of lesbians when she moved from New Jersey to West Philly in the 1960s. Gittings, Lahusen, and Cornwell, all of whom lived in West Philly, indicate that they did not think of it as a lesbian neighborhood.

While some lesbian narrators reject the notion that West Philly was a lesbian neighborhood, some gay narrators think that it was. Discussing the early 1970s, Mark Segal notes that "the lesbian neighborhoods were in West Philadelphia and Germantown." According to Harry Langhorne, "There were lesbians out in West Philadelphia and some gay men as well." Lesbians, he observes, were "more concentrated out there than downtown." Explaining why this was the case, he says, "Nest building is more readily done in West Philadelphia. It's a quieter, more tree-lined, homey type of neighborhood, as opposed to the apartment houses of Center City."

As Langhorne's comments suggest, some narrators describe West Philly as lesbian *and* gay, although they generally think that it was more substantially lesbian. Barron recalls, "I didn't know of many gay men in West Philadelphia. There were a few but not a whole lot." Owens says, "I didn't really think of West Philly as a gay male neighborhood, although I think there were a fair number of gay men who lived in West Philly." Discussing West Philly, Henri David says, "I knew a lot of guys who lived out there, but only because it was cheap." According to James Roberts, "I knew a lot of black gay men who lived in West Philadelphia but I wouldn't say it was a gay neighborhood." While the estimates in these accounts range from "a few" to "a lot" of gay men, Paul Schmidt goes further, characterizing Powelton as a gay neighborhood.

Davies reveals that proximity could provide protection for lesbians and gay men in West Philly. Referring to her neighbor Byrna Aronson, who she says looked like a "stereotypical dyke," Davies recalls, "One time she knocked on my door because one of the gay men in the building had brought home a trick and the trick was attacking him. And she wanted to call the police. . . . She probably threw him out of the building." Davies also suggests that proximity could create problems. Discussing encounters between lesbians and gay men, Davies mentions stories of Aronson "tossing men out of parties when they were annoying women."

Although only a few gay narrators refer to West Philly as a gay neighborhood, many talk about living and socializing there in the 1960s and 1970s. Mark Kendall recalls that while he was still living with his family and before he moved to Powelton in the 1960s, he and his lover socialized with gay friends in West Philly: "And they were very hospitable. And so much so. One of them, there was a middle bedroom that was always reserved for Herbie and me. . . ." Langhorne, Kiyoshi Kuromiya, and Jeffrey Escoffier all lived in West Philly when they came to the city to study at Penn. Segal, Roberts, and Gus Johnson remember going to lesbian and gay parties in West Philly.

Most gay narrators, however, do not regard West Philly as a lesbian or gay neighborhood. In part, this reflects the same reasoning that leads some to reject the notion that Center City was lesbian or gay. But in addition, gay narrators may have been less likely to recognize areas of greater lesbian concentration. Insofar as they regarded the neighborhood as less significantly lesbian or gay than Center City was, they also may have been less likely to designate it a lesbian or gay neighborhood. Moreover, some narrators, to the extent that they regarded West Philly as an African American neighborhood, may have thought that it therefore could not also be lesbian or gay.

The composite portrait presented by narrators, however, suggests that West Philly was popular among African American lesbians and gay men. While Center City was becoming more Euro-American in these years, West Philly was becoming more African American. African American narrators Cornwell and Owens recall living in West Philly and knowing other African American lesbians who did so as well; African American narrators Roberts and Johnson remember having African American lesbian and gay friends who lived and socialized in the neighborhood; Euro-American narrator Friedman says that she knew African American lesbians who lived there;

Euro-American narrators Schmidt and Kendall remember socializing with a multiracial group of lesbians and gay men who lived in West Philly.[21]

In the 1950s and 1960s, African American lesbians and gay men formed two social clubs that met in private homes, many of which were in West Philly. According to Michael Smith's 1983 lesbian and gay guide, *Colorful People and Places*, the West Set was an African American men's "social group" founded in 1957; Mox-Nix was a "primarily" African American men and women's social group founded in the late 1960s.[22] "Jay Haines," a member of the West Set, says that eight of the group's twelve members lived in West Philly. "That's how we got the name West Set," he recalls. According to Haines, the West Set organized trips to Atlantic City and Puerto Rico; visited similar clubs in New York, Washington, and Baltimore; and sponsored parties and dances in Philadelphia. In the 1960s and 1970s, the club held an annual dance during the Penn Relays (a track and field event) and a "Miss West Set competition." Haines recalls that the dances were held "wherever we could find a hall that would hold from 350 to 500 folks." These included locations in West Philly, Center City, and Cherry Hill, New Jersey.

Discussing the club, Haines suggests a reason that some African American lesbians and gay men might have preferred socializing at home: "In the black community it was not accepted, gaiety. Therefore, it had to be toned down if you were going to be a part of the bigger community." In the West Set, he explains, "You had schoolteachers, you had government workers, you had business people. In those days, it was important that you be about trying to better your condition. And when we got together it was to let the guard down and just relax and be gay, if you will, without worrying about who saw you."

African American clubs provided opportunities for lesbians and gay men to socialize together. Comparing the West Set to Mox-Nix, Haines says that the latter included "gay girls and gay fellas" whereas the former was "totally fellas." While his group, the West Set, was all male, Haines says, "We knew all of the women in the Mox-Nix and we liked them all." Haines also notes, "What we found was that in Washington, the girls and the fellas were much more united than they were here. Here the girls separated themselves from the fellas. So you had the fellas on one side, the girls on the other. And never the twain shall meet. . . . In Washington, after they had that drag on who was gay in the government, they never gave a party without having some women there. Now the women might all be gay, but you couldn't tell." Haines continues, "By going down there to parties as often as we did, we began to become friendly with girls who were friendly with girls up here."

Insofar as several narrators suggest that African American lesbians and gay men were closer to one another than Euro-American lesbians and gay men were, lesbians and gay men may have converged more in African American residential neighborhoods than in Euro-American ones. According to Roberts, "Among black people, we don't have as much of an option to subdivide ourselves. We can't afford really to lessen our power. . . . I see a lot more linkages between black gay men and lesbians than I see between white gay men and white lesbians." Roberts says that in the 1960s and early 1970s these linkages developed "mainly at house parties." Noting that most African American lesbian and gay parties took place in North Philly or West Philly, he recalls that they were "sometimes" hosted by women but "more often by men." Discussing these parties, he says, "There was a sexual tension there, but there was more of a sense that we're all black people and we're all gay or lesbian and even though we're not going to sleep together we can get along together. When you go to an all-male environment, an all gay-male environment, I think there is a lot more cruising. There's a lot more competition going on. But I've noticed the more you introduce women into a social environment, the less that happens." Tyrone Smith also remembers African American lesbians and gay men socializing together at parties in the 1960s. Discussing parties in North Philly, he says, "That's when I really got to know lesbians."

Cornwell presents a more mixed portrait of relations between lesbians and gay men in North and West Philly. On the one hand, she remembers having several African American gay friends in her building in North Philly in the 1950s and 1960s and says, "Most of the time when I had friends over they were women, but I knew that one guy, and I was friendly with him. I went up to his house. I used to come up for a drink or he used to come down to my place." On the other hand, she says that she "never knew many gay men" and describes fundamental differences: "Gay men are more active than gay women. . . . Just looking for partners. Women don't do that sort of thing. Not women of my generation anyway. I mean to some extent you did, but not that . . . ferocious search. . . . Gay women and straight women are socialized the same. How many straight women do you know that just actively go out looking for parties all the time? I mean naturally we're all wanting to meet somebody. And you always got an eye peeled. But you're not going out just relentlessly looking for somebody."

Mapping the residential histories of the lesbian and gay narrators suggests that they converged in an 11-tract zone in the eastern section of West Philly. Of the narrators' adult residences in the city, 25% of the lesbian homes and 14% of the gay homes were in these tracts. (The 11 tracts contained about 3% of the city's population.) Concentrations increased over time. Of the adult homes from 1945 through 1959, 12% were in the zone, as compared to 19% from 1960 to 1974. Concentrations varied by race: 34%

of the African American adult homes and 14% of the Euro-American ones were in these tracts.[23]

Mapping the GAA homes also suggests that lesbian and gay geographies converged in the West Philly zone: 19% of the total homes, 15% of the homes of female members, and 20% of the homes of male members were located there. GAA concentrations were also shaped by race and ethnicity: 18% of the African American homes, 8% of the Italian American homes, 21% of the Jewish American homes, and 27% of the Euro-American homes were in the 11 tracts.

Mapping all of the identified lesbian and gay residences suggests that lesbian and gay concentrations and convergences in West Philly were significant: 19% of these sites (23% of the female ones and 17% of the male ones) were in the West Philly zone (as compared to 36% in Center City). While the lesbian residents were more concentrated in these tracts than the gay ones were, the second heaviest concentrations of both lesbians and gay men were in the West Philly zone.

These 11 tracts shared with the tracts of Center City several significant characteristics. In 1960, 1970, and 1980, the 11-tract zone, when compared to the 12 neighborhoods defined by the Planning Commission, had the second-lowest number of people per household, the second-lowest percentage of households with a married couple, the second- or third-lowest percentage of residents under 20, the second- or third-highest percentage of white collar workers, and the second-lowest percentage of owner-occupied housing. In 1960, 1970, and 1980, a majority of the tracts also had a higher median number of school years completed, a higher median value of owner-occupied housing, and a higher median rent than the city medians.

But in other ways the West Philly zone was different. Some parts of Powelton, for example, had lower owner-occupied housing values and rents. Moreover, all but one or two of the tracts had median family incomes and median household incomes that were lower than the city medians in 1960, 1970, and 1980. And the 11-tract zone was more non-Euro-American and more African American than the city as a whole. In 1960, the zone was 34% non-Euro-American and 33% African American, while the city figures were 27% and 26%. In 1970, the zone was 49% non-Euro-American and 49% African American, while the city figures were 34% and 34%. In 1980, the zone was 52% non-Euro-American and 43% African American, while the city figures were 42% and 38%. With relatively low indices of "property, family, and high class," the West Philly zone shared many of the characteristics identified by scholars of other cities' lesbian and gay neighborhoods, but it differed insofar as the zone was more substantially African American and high-rent.

Germantown/Mount Airy

After Center City and West Philly, Germantown/Mt. Airy is the neighborhood most commonly identified by narrators as historically lesbian and gay. Located in northwest Philadelphia, Germantown and Mt. Airy are north and east of Fairmount Park. Many narrators refer to the two interchangeably, but Germantown is east of Mt. Airy.

Many lesbian narrators point to the lesbian presence in Germantown/Mt. Airy. Ann Lynch says that her two closest friends in the 1950s were lesbians who lived in Germantown. Laurie Barron, who lived in Mt. Airy in the 1960s, says that "pockets" of the neighborhood were "very gay" or "very gay/lesbian friendly." Ada Bello, who moved to Germantown in the 1960s, notes that lesbians were attracted to Germantown/Mt. Airy in this era. Carole Friedman, Arleen Olshan, and Marge McCann all moved from Center City to Germantown in the 1960s. Friedman says that the neighborhood was becoming more lesbian around this time. Olshan describes it as a "lesbian ghetto." Sharon Owens, who lived in Germantown in the early 1970s, recalls that Germantown had "a lot of lesbians." Elizabeth Terry, who also moved to Germantown in this period, says that it was a lesbian neighborhood and remembers that one of its apartment buildings was nicknamed "the Lesbian Arms."

Some narrators say that Germantown/Mt. Airy was popular because of its inexpensive housing costs and large houses. McCann thinks that lesbians were attracted to the neighborhood because it had "big, pretty houses" that were "cheap." Alvia Golden says that lesbians liked the "big, old houses" that were "cheap" in Germantown/Mt. Airy. According to Friedman, "There were apartments in what had been old mansions . . . that were really quite nice. And very reasonably priced. So compared with living downtown, in Center City, you could get much more. You'd have green, too." Asked why lesbians were attracted to Germantown, Terry says, "Lesbians like the great outdoors and it was so close to Fairmount Park and Lincoln Drive and the Wissahickon Trail." Barron recalls, "I liked being on the edge of Fairmount Park. I liked being up where it was a little quieter and greener."

In addition to architectural, economic, and environmental factors, narrators also mention racial ones. McCann points out that Germantown was "a partially black neighborhood" and "housing is always cheaper in an area that's partially black." She also suggests that lesbians were drawn to Germantown/Mt. Airy because it had a reputation for being tolerant. Friedman says that she moved to Germantown because she knew people who lived there and that it therefore "felt safe and congenial." She continues, "Later people were consciously drawn to Germantown because it was racially mixed. I mean to the extent that you really do find that in suburban areas, it was successfully racially mixed and mixed class-wise, if not house by house, then block by block. I think it was an area that people who were consciously trying to create community, gays, straight, lesbian, would move into." Barron adds, "One of the beautiful things about Mt. Airy is that it has for many many years been a really diverse neighborhood, a mixture of mostly black and white, gay and straight."

Although narrators note that some of the same factors that drew lesbians to West Philly attracted them to Germantown/Mt. Airy, they also refer to differences. Remembering a house where six lesbians lived, Barron says, "That was one of a number of lesbian collectives that formed in Mt. Airy. But I think that mostly individuals and couples started moving into Mt. Airy." Terry says that while "there were some collectives in Germantown," there were not as many as in West Philly. Friedman observes that Germantown was more "old gay" and West Philly more "feminist-lesbian," but she also notes that "later Germantown became more a lesbian-feminist place."

While some narrators suggest that Germantown/Mt. Airy, like West Philly, featured inexpensive housing, others see the former as more expensive. This may reflect different stages in processes of gentrification.[24] At an early stage Germantown/Mt. Airy may have attracted poorer lesbians because of cheap housing; at a later stage it may have attracted wealthier lesbians. Moreover, as Barron and Marcea Rosen's comments suggest, some lesbians who were poorer at one stage may have become wealthier at a later stage. Discussing the "flight to Germantown," longtime West Philly and Center City resident Becky Davidson says, "The Germantown dyke crew is very different. I consider them upwardly mobile snotty types. I always feel like they're looking down their noses. They all have kids, they all like to be near the Park, they're professional lesbians. They don't like people who say fuck." Also commenting on why lesbians moved to Germantown/Mt. Airy, Rosen says, "Don't forget the children. 'Cause lesbians are having babies and they don't want to have them at 13th and Locust."

Social and geographic distance from the Center City bar scene appealed to some lesbians. Discussing parties in Germantown/Mt. Airy, Bello says, "Other than the bars, that was the way people got together. And a lot of people couldn't go to the bars because they had jobs that they considered sensitive." Bello remembers "a whole group of lesbians" who were teachers: "They were terrified. At some point in fact they actually sort of distanced themselves from me because they found out I frequented bars. And they did a lot of socializing among themselves. But that was just about the only thing they could do, and then go out together, but to straight places, like restaurants. And they had to go out as a group. Then they would go to one of the apartments and maybe have some cookies and drinks. But they were totally cut off from the community at large."

Very few gay narrators describe Germantown/Mt. Airy as a lesbian or gay neighborhood. An exception, Mark Segal, who lived in Mt. Airy in the 1960s and early 1970s, says "the lesbian neighborhoods were in West Philadelphia and Germantown." Although most gay narrators do not describe Germantown/Mt. Airy as lesbian or gay, quite a few lived in the neighborhood and refer to other gay men who did so. Tyrone Smith remembers that one of his lovers lived there in the early 1960s. When Richard Gayer left his parents' home in Northeast Philly in the 1960s, he moved to Germantown. Asked why he picked Germantown, Gayer says that a gay friend lived there and that he moved nearby. In the late 1960s, Mark Kendall moved from Powelton to Germantown. Paul Schmidt moved from Fairmount to Germantown in the early 1970s and says that the neighborhood was becoming more gay in the 1960s and 1970s. James Roberts also lived in Germantown in the early 1970s.

Some lesbian narrators remember gay men living in Germantown/Mt. Airy. According to Barron, "Mt. Airy was primarily lesbian" but "there were some gay men." Rosen says that gay men concentrated in "Germantown, Mt. Airy, and Center City." Although she does not consider it a "gay neighborhood," Davidson thinks that "a lot" of lesbians and gay men lived in Germantown in the 1960s and 1970s.

Mapping the homes of the lesbian and gay narrators suggests that lesbian and gay residential geographies converged in a six-tract zone in Germantown and Mt. Airy (five tracts in the former, one in the latter). Of the narrators' adult residences in Philadelphia, 12% of the lesbian homes and 3% of the gay homes were in these tracts. (The six tracts contained about 1% of the city's population.) Concentrations increased over time. Of the adult homes from 1945 to 1959, 3% were in the zone, as compared to 7% from 1960 to 1974; 9% of the African American adult homes and 7% of the Euro-American homes were in the zone.[25] Mapping the homes of 260 Philadelphia members of GAA also suggests that residential geographies converged in the six tracts: 2% of the total homes, 7% of the homes of female members, and 1% of the homes of male members were located there. Mapping the combined data set of 582 residences suggests that lesbian and gay concentrations and convergences in Germantown/Mt. Airy were small but significant: 4% of these sites (10% of the female ones and 2% of the male ones) were in the six-tract zone (as compared to 19% in West Philly and 36% in Center City).

These six tracts shared with the tracts of Center City and West Philly several significant characteristics. In 1960, 1970, and 1980, the six-tract zone, when compared to the 12 neighborhoods defined by the City Planning Commission, had the second-lowest number of people per household, the second- or third-lowest percentage of households with a married couple, the second-lowest percentage of residents under 20, the second-highest percentage of white collar workers, and the second-lowest percentage of owner-occupied housing. In 1960, 1970, and 1980, a majority of the tracts also had a higher median number of school years completed and a higher median rent than the city medians.

In other ways, however, the six tracts shared West Philly's greater income, housing, and racial heterogeneity. Depending on the year, one or two of the tracts had lower median rents than the city median. Across the 20 years between 1960 and 1980, the tracts were about evenly divided between those with median occupied housing values that were higher and those that were lower than the city's median. This was also the case with median family incomes. All but one or two of the tracts had median household incomes that were below the city medians. The six Germantown/Mt. Airy tracts were also more non-Euro-American and more African American than Center City and the city as a whole. In 1960 the figures were 34% and 34%; in 1970, they had increased to 48% and 47%; in 1980, they were 58% and 56%. Like the West Philly zone, the Germantown/Mt. Airy area shared many of the characteristics identified by scholars of other cities' lesbian and gay neighborhoods, but was more substantially African American and high-rent.

While lesbians and gay men lived in all parts of Greater Philadelphia, their most substantial residential presences were in Center City, West Philly, and Germantown/Mt. Airy. Notwithstanding significant differences in the ways that narrators define, perceive, and account for lesbian and gay concentrations, their composite portrait suggests that all three of these neighborhoods were popular among both lesbians and gay men. The quantitative evidence considered here suggests that gay men were the most heavily concentrated in one particular neighborhood (38% in Center City). But lesbians were more heavily concentrated in the three neighborhoods combined than gay men were. (While 57% of the gay residences were located in these three areas, 67% of the lesbian residences were.) Perceptions of lesbians as less territorial than gay men may reflect geographic differences between the sexes in general or between lesbians and gay men in particular. But they also may reflect differences in the ways that territoriality is defined and differences in the ways that lesbians and gay men make themselves visible. In terms of the latter, if it is true that gay men were more publicly visible than lesbians were, gay residential concentrations may have been more noticed but not necessarily more significant than their lesbian counterparts. In any event, some lesbians and gay men shared homes in these districts, but many more were neighbors. Creating predominantly divergent households and predominantly convergent neighborhoods, lesbians and gay men mapped the geography of their everyday relationships.

2

"No-Man's-Land": Commercial Districts in the "Quaker City"

The men and women got along reasonably well.
KAY LAHUSEN

The gay guys did not like gay women.
ANN LYNCH

I was interested in meeting men and women, anyone who was gay.
BARBARA GITTINGS

We didn't like them and they didn't like us.
PAT HILL

We're so few, we're friends.
ANITA CORNWELL

Many gay men didn't like women at all and didn't like lesbians.
And many lesbians wanted to have nothing to do with gay men.
MARK KENDALL

There was good friendship. We shared a common bond.
MEL HEIFETZ

The two genders classically were separated.
LEWIS COOPERSMITH

Prejudice is prejudice.
GUS JOHNSON

Lesbians and gays . . . were like strange bulldogs
when they met. There was no camaraderie.
BILL BRINSFIELD

Ask enough lesbians and gay men who lived in Philadelphia between 1945 and 1972 about the history of relations between the city's lesbian and gay communities and the range of responses will be wide. In part, this reflects differences of time, space, class, ethnicity, gender, race, and sex. When lesbians and gay men discuss these relationships, however, they generally agree that many of the most meaningful encounters and lack of encounters took place in the commercialized leisure establishments—the bars, clubs, restaurants, and other businesses—that were central institutions of lesbian and gay urban worlds.[1]

In any given year within this era, lesbians and gay men frequented dozens of Philadelphia commercial establishments with predominantly lesbian, lesbian and gay, or gay clientele. Lesbians and gay men also favored a number of primarily straight establishments with significant lesbian and/or gay patronage. In these places, lesbians and gay man worked and relaxed; they ate, drank, and smoked; they talked, read, listened, watched, and played; they touched, danced, flirted, cruised, and courted; they met friends, partners, and lovers; they fought and made up; and they made love and had sex. Creating homosocial and heterosocial cultures, they developed worlds of same-sex and cross-sex relationships.

Lesbians and gay men gathered in these establishments in spite of the significant risks of antilesbian and antigay prejudice, discrimination, harassment, and violence that they faced there. Verbal and physical attacks were common. Many lesbian and gay commercial sites were owned, operated, and/or protected by organized criminals. Owners and managers, whether or not they were associated with organized crime, often had to pay off police and other officials to avoid legal and extralegal trouble. When owners or managers did not pay, when payoff agreements broke down, when reformers brought these practices to light, when politicians wanted to appear tough on vice, and when any of these parties wanted to act against lesbians and gay men, local police and state Liquor Control Board (LCB) officials were more likely to conduct raids.

Among the more publicized raids were those on Barton in 1954; Allegro in 1958; Artist's Hut, Gilded Cage, Humoresque, and Proscenium in 1959; Club 214 and Uniform Social and Athletic Association (U.S.&A.A.) in 1964; and Rusty's and Hideaway in 1967. Between 1958 and 1971, the LCB suspended the licenses of, revoked the licenses of, and/or fined International Society of Waiters and Bartenders (1959, 1960, 1962, 1963); Allegro (1961); Pep's (1961); Track Seven (1961, 1963, 1966, 1968, 1970); Maxine's (1962); Parker (1962); Barone's (1963, 1967); U.S.&A.A. (1965, 1966, 1967, 1968); 4–6 (1965, 1967, 1968); Zu-Zu (1965, 1966); Golden Griffon (1966); Penrose (1968); Spider Kelly's (1968); Speedie's (1969); and Mask and Wig (1970).[2]

In establishments frequented by lesbians and gay men, there were risks that police would entrap, question, arrest, detain, jail, charge, and imprison owners, workers, and patrons. The most common charge was probably "disorderly conduct," a catchall category that gave police great license to act against lesbians and gay men. Whether or not they were charged, once caught up in the legal system, lesbians and gay men faced additional risks of being bribed, blackmailed, and swindled by police, lawyers, bail bondsmen, and judges; being verbally and physically abused; and being exposed to families and employers. There were other dangers as well. In two cases, establishments frequented by lesbians and gay men—International Society of Waiters and Bartenders in 1963 and Mystique in 1972—burned down under mysterious circumstances.[3] That lesbians and gay men continued to patronize these establishments in spite of the risks is evidence of their collective determination to resist the forces that opposed their worlds of same-sex and cross-sex relationships.

Bonds, Boundaries, and Barriers

When narrators discuss relationships between lesbians and gay men in commercial establishments, they recite, reproduce, reject, and reverse a variety of popular ideas about relationships between the sexes and relationships between lesbians and gay men. Some remember close relationships. Discussing alliances among activists and nonactivists, Kay Lahusen says, "The men and women got along reasonably well in those years, both within the movement and in the larger community." Asked about relations between lesbians and gay men, Mel Heifetz replies, "There was good friendship. We shared a common bond." Noting that he remembers a "real mixture" of lesbians and gay men in certain restaurants, "Pru Chis" speculates, "That might have been the Quaker influence. . . . That whole experience, how Pennsylvania was founded and who it was founded by, the great tolerance of the Quakers, having put up with so much, . . . was embedded in the educational institutions in Philadelphia. It was everywhere."

While some lesbians and gay men report bonding "everywhere," others say they did so in more specific places and times and with more specific groups of lesbians and gay men. Many narrators, for example, remember more cross-sex mixing in after-hours clubs and restaurants than in bars. Many also suggest that relations between lesbians and gay men were closer in certain periods than in others. And many recall bonds that formed between lesbians and gay men with particular class, ethnic, gender, and race identities.

In some contexts, for instance, lesbians and gay men developed bonds based on particular gender and class convergences. Discussing Maxine's, a predominantly gay bar and restaurant, Ann Lynch recalls, "Because we were collegiate looking, clean-cut, and behaved ourselves (we weren't the beer-bottle-breaking diesel dykes that they objected to), we were always welcome." Lynch asserts, "The gay guys did not like gay women. . . . Gay women, especially women who come from poorer families, identify with truck drivers, whereas gay men may come from poorer families but they identify with beauty and art. . . . The dichotomy is just amazing. So I was always more comfortable with the gay men, which is unusual. But then they saw me as more of their peer." Tyrone Smith recalls, "The lesbians that I was around were what we call today lipstick lesbians, 'cause they looked like women." Smith remembers being advised to avoid masculine women and feminine men: "A lot of the older people in my life always said, 'You don't want to be seen with people that look like that. . . .' As effeminate as I was, everybody tried to tone me down." While some lesbians and gay men bonded on the basis of shared femininity, others bonded on the basis of shared masculinity. Discussing butch lesbians, Bill Brinsfield notes, "If I ever saw them being friendly with men, they were extremely masculine men or the bouncer of a bar or the bartender."

Masculine lesbians and feminine gay men formed bonds as well. Carole Friedman, who says that she was more "butch" than "femme," remembers, "The contact I had with drag queens was at the after-hours clubs and the breakfast places. . . . There would be playful interaction, always around the central theme of who's the real woman. And they always won hands down." Barbara Gittings, who recalls dressing as a boy and calling herself "Sonny" when she first went to bars, says that she enjoyed meeting gay men who shared her interests in literature and music: "I remember in particular a couple of gay men that I befriended. . . . They gave Tupperware parties and they had a piano and an organ at home." Asked about relations between lesbians and gay men in this period, Gittings says, "I didn't know any lesbians, or practically none. Mostly gay men I was socializing with. . . . I really thought of myself as a gay person. Just happened to be female, but gay, and I was interested in meeting men and women, anyone who was gay. This was my people, this was for me, this was my home, and that's where I wanted to be."

Some bonds were racially or ethnically specific. Asked about the history of relations between African American lesbians and gay men, Anita Cornwell says, "We're so few, we're friends." According to Elizabeth Terry, "We had a sense of community, whereas there really is no entity 'white folks.' Most white folks will say they're Italian or they're Sicilian or they're Irish or something like that, so there wasn't this togetherness. . . . But with African American people there was always a community." Whether Euro-American lesbians and gay men identified more strongly in terms of race or ethnicity, they also formed bonds with one another based on a "sense of community."

Senses of community based on specific class, ethnic, gender, and racial identities could divide lesbians from gay men as well as unite them. Euro-Americans, for instance, often excluded African Americans from particular bars. Moreover, while lesbians and gay men often bonded on the basis of their sexual identities (as lesbian and gay), they often divided on the basis of their sex identities (as female and male). Brinsfield recalls, "Lesbians and gays in the forties and the fifties absolutely were like strange bulldogs when they met. There was no camaraderie." Discussing bars, Chis says, "Lesbians were very segregated from my group." Asked whether he remembers lesbians in the bars, Smith replies, "They had their own places." Joan Fleischmann remembers, "Women were really not welcome in most of the men's bars." According to Pat Hill, "In my world, they had nothing to do with each other." John Taylor notes that "gay men and gay women did not really mix well."

Narrators account for these divisions in a variety of ways. Some blame the lesbians. According to Lewis Coopersmith, "The two genders classically were separated. . . . And that wasn't all due to the men. Walk around town and see how many lesbian bars you're welcomed to. The social isolation comes more from women than it does from men." Chis says, "I think they were more closeted than I was. And I was pretty closeted. . . . I found them to be kind of an unapproachable group." Paul Schmidt recalls, "It was very separate. . . . I'm sure it's probably distorted, but . . . when I thought of a lesbian in a bar, I would think of someone who was very masculine getting into a fight with another woman. And everyone would duck 'cause a beer bottle was coming." Brinsfield asserts, "Everything that lesbians, in my observation, say that they hate about men, they . . . imitate. All the swaggering and talking out of the side of the mouth. . . . I don't mean all lesbians, but some take on those aspects and build them into their personality. . . . While a lot of gay men who are effeminate imitate women, they don't hate women. They're imitating them because they admire those crazy qualities of overblown things like Joan Crawford and Bette Davis. . . . Somehow this burlesque of womanhood is what they would sometimes begin to actually make into a lifestyle. . . ." Describing the lesbians of this period as "so intense," Brinsfield says that "maybe they saw in the gay men effeminacy or something that they thought wasn't a man." He concludes that "the campy aspect" of gay men "turned off these dead serious lesbians, the daughters of that love which cannot speak its name."

Some narrators blame the gay men. Lynch recalls, "I had no problem, but a lot of women I've seen come into men's bars, I have seen them practically be asked to leave or frozen out—no one talking to them, paying any attention to them. Some of the guys could be really what I would call piss elegant. They'd stand and hold their head up high and look disdainfully down on these dykes that somehow had invaded their territory." Cornwell says, "There are gay men who like women who are similar to women. . . . There are some gay men who are more stud-like who also like women. But there are some who don't like women. I'm of the opinion that most straight men don't like women, but most of them will hide it to certain degrees. But see, a gay man who doesn't like women has no reason to hide it because he doesn't want anything from the woman. So I think the hatred shows more." Marge McCann blames men in the context of discussing how relationships changed over time: "The rise of the women's movement created a wedge between women and men. And it would have been no different in the gay culture. 'Cause we got a sense of our own worth. And gay men were no faster than other men in catching up. . . . I've had higher expectations of gay men. They should understand 'cause they were discriminated against. . . . Being thought of as feminine meant they got the same discrimination. But most of them didn't get that."

Lesbians are not the only ones who blame gay men. According to Gus Johnson, "There were lots of gay men who really were sexist and separatist. And they were open about it. They wanted to exclude women from gay bars. . . . I was going out with someone who made a statement at a party once that he didn't like women and he didn't think that they should be allowed in certain groups. And it ended it for me. Because what I said is, 'If you can call this woman a bitch or whatever you're going to call her, then you can certainly call me in a moment of anger a nigger. . . . Prejudice is prejudice.' "

Some hold both lesbians and gay men accountable. On the one hand, Hill says of particular types of gay men, "They certainly did not act like they thought women even deserved to breathe. . . . There are gay men who don't really know any women, who really don't know what women are." On the other hand, Hill also says, "It could have been my own disdain for them, too, although I'm not aware of that. But now that you're asking me, not only was it their arrogance, which I feel from a lot of gay men of that type even now, that women just don't have brains and shouldn't be allowed to live, but also it probably was a kind of homophobia on our part or my part. . . . I had the same homophobia that the rest of society had, that gay men are hairdressers, ballet dancers, effeminate, less than men, less than real men. . . . I might not have liked them much. I don't think that I thought that I wanted to be close to them at all. I just thought of them as different creatures. . . . So it's kind of a two-way thing, I guess. 'Cause we didn't like them and they didn't like us." Mark Kendall also blames both: "Many gay men didn't like women at all and didn't like lesbians. And many lesbians wanted to have nothing to do with gay men. I think it was just the ordinary type of xenophobia. There was lack of familiarity, lack of contact. . . ."

Then there are those who blame factors of space and time. According to Harry Langhorne, "In a small community it's more necessary for people to bond together. And there may only be one bar in town and it's for men and women and they mix and it's no problem. You come to the big city and there are these social opportunities and people tend to self-segregate." Focusing on time rather than space, Heifetz suggests that once lesbians and gay men rejected the "closet" and no longer needed to appear straight, they developed more single-sex "lifestyles."

While narrators disagree about whether and why lesbians and gay men conflicted in commercial establishments, they agree that there were far more predominantly gay establishments than predominantly lesbian ones. Rosalie Davies offers two explanations for this: "Lesbians don't have the money to spend in bars. Gay men have the highest disposable income in the country. But also a lot of what gay male bars are about is about tricking, is about supporting a promiscuous sex life. I'm not putting a value judgment on that; I'm just making a cultural difference statement. And if you look at it in a bigger perspective, you're going to say gay men are raised as men. Men are taught to screw as many women as they can in order to really be men. And the size of their penis is very important. Gay women are raised as women, and women are supposed to look not for looks but for somebody who can take care of you and somebody who's loving and kind. And they act that out. So gay men screw everything in sight, and lesbian women, it's appalling. They fall in love the first time you sleep with them and they move in. Fuck her and she'll be here for breakfast and she's there two years later."

Whatever the reasons for the greater number of predominantly gay establishments, the disparity affected and was affected by other dimensions of lesbian and gay life. First, to the extent that lesbians predominated in fewer commercial establishments, socializing in residential space was often more important for them. Second, to the extent that commercial establishments were more subject to state surveillance and repression than residential spaces were, lesbians were often less visible to state authorities. Third, to the extent that lesbians went to predominantly gay establishments more frequently than gay men went to predominantly lesbian establishments, lesbians often knew more about gay cultures than gay men knew about lesbian cultures. And fourth, to the extent that they had fewer alternatives, patrons of predominantly lesbian establishments had more to fear from gay encroachments than patrons of predominantly gay establishments had to fear from lesbian encroachments.

Notwithstanding these disparities, mapping the 265 lesbian and gay commercial sites identified for the period between 1945 and 1974 suggests that the vast majority of establishments frequented by lesbians and gay men—74%—were located in Center City (Fig. 2.1). The next largest concentrations were in a strip of South Philly tracts that bordered Center City (8%) and in the

West Philly zone (5%). Although establishments that were popular among lesbians were less concentrated in Center City than were those that were popular among gay men, of the 17 predominantly lesbian sites, 53% were in Center City, 6% were in the South Philly border tracts, and 12% were in the West Philly zone. Although establishments that were popular among African Americans were less concentrated in Center City than were those that were popular among Euro-Americans, of the 28 predominantly African American sites, 43% were in Center City, 18% were in the South Philly border tracts, and 11% were in the West Philly zone.[4]

While the largest percentages of predominantly Euro-American and predominantly African American sites were in Center City, there were significant racial differences *within* this neighborhood. The majority of predominantly Euro-American sites in Center City clustered between Market and

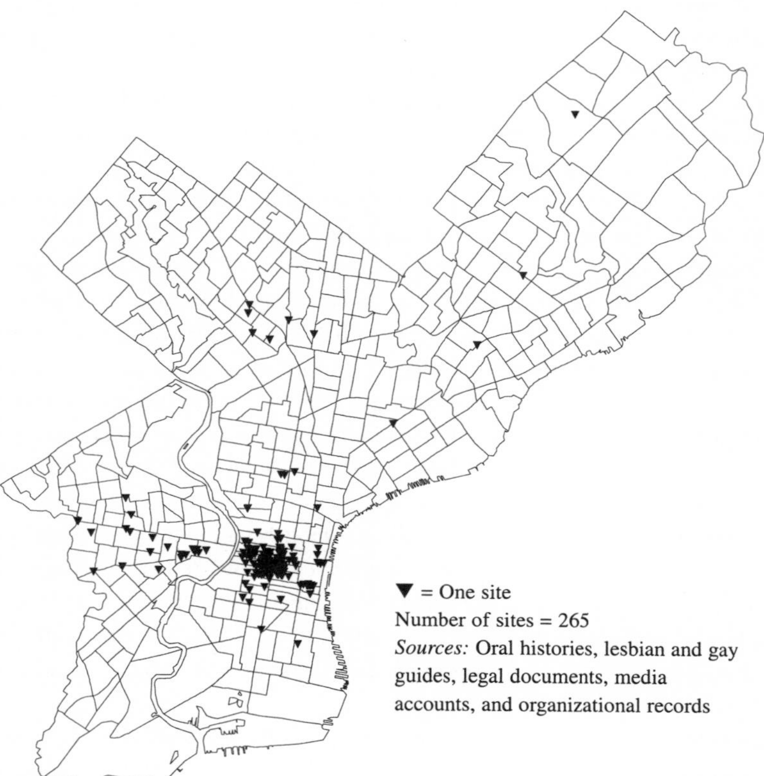

Figure 2.1. Lesbian and gay commercial establishments, 1945–1974. Commercial establishments include bars, bathhouses, bookstores, clubs, hotels, movie houses, restaurants, theaters, and other businesses.

South and especially around 13th and Locust (in southeastern Center City). Here, on or near the "Locust Strip," lesbian and gay establishments shared a neighborhood with prominent hotels, theaters, music halls, and restaurants, as well as gambling dens, striptease joints, massage parlors, and prostitute bars. In contrast, about half of the predominantly African American sites in Center City were located further to the south (on or near South Street, a long-time African American entertainment strip) or further to the north (on or near Market Street).[5]

Lesbian Bars, Clubs, and Restaurants

Lesbians frequented several bars, clubs, and restaurants in which they were in the majority. In the 1950s, these included Barone's Variety Room (near the Locust Strip), which had primarily Euro-American clientele, and Jeanette Dembry's (in South Philly), which had primarily African American clientele. In the 1960s, lesbians also predominated in Businessman's Association (in southwestern Center City) and My Sister's Place (in northwestern Center City), both of which had multiracial patronage. In the early 1970s, Rubery M. Gertrude (in southwestern Center City) joined the list of predominantly lesbian establishments.

Barone's, widely known as Rusty's, was the most well-known spot. Ada Bello recalls, "Barone's fronted on Walnut Street and upstairs was Rusty's. You had to go down the alley and up the stairs." According to Pat Hill, "It was definitely up flights of steps, knock three times. It was very, very sub rosa." In fact Laurie Barron and Marcea Rosen both report that they were not able to find it at first. Although many called the bar Rusty's because Rusty Parisi managed it, the sign outside identified it as the Variety Room. Barron recalls, "It wasn't until a couple of years later that I discovered that Rusty's and Barone's were arguably one and the same." Such obstacles, which helped owners, workers, and patrons avoid unfavorable public attention, often made it necessary for lesbians to act in daring ways to find the bar. Bello remembers getting involved with a New Yorker whom she met in Rusty's: "She had come to Philadelphia, jumped in a cab, and asked the cab driver to take her to a gay bar. It was that brazen. The guy said, 'I don't know of any, but I think I can get somebody from the office who does,' and then called on the radio and got the address."

Having arrived at the entrance, lesbians had to cross a variety of thresholds to join the world inside. Arleen Olshan remembers that when she was a teenager, gay friends tried to take her to Rusty's: "Here's this woman greeting us in full drag, with a suit and tie, looking absolutely handsome and wonderful, totally self-assured, and she said, 'Honey you got age cards?'

Figure 2.2. *Gay Dealer*, 1970. Courtesy of Gay, Lesbian, Bisexual, and Transgendered Archives of Philadelphia, Philadelphia, PA.

And I said, 'No.' She said, 'Come back when you do.' " Joan Fleischmann recalls, "Rusty always stood at the door. And it was a big deal if she spoke to you. . . . I was there every weekend and she would talk to me occasionally."

In many narrators' accounts, the most significant thresholds crossed were related to age, class, gender, race, sex, and time of day. Fleischmann recalls, "Rusty was always like someone from another world. She was very rough and tough and masculine. And I was in awe of her." Pat Hill remembers, "I was very attracted to obvious dykes. . . . The obvious ones, with the men's shirt rolled up and a pack of Camel's stuffed in their shirt, that's somebody that I could be with. . . . This woman that used to come in Rusty's . . . , who carried a gun, she was this South Philly type and was a very, very, very tough woman. And I wouldn't have known what to say to her." Carole Friedman recalls, "I was a nice Jewish girl, I got all A's, I played the piano, and suddenly I was spending Friday and Saturday nights at this bar, drinking scotch and soda, smoking. I mean it was a different world. Staying up, when did they close the bars, two o'clock? Then there were some after-hours clubs. We would sometimes go there, and then wind up somewhere for breakfast at five in the morning, drive home still drunk. I mean I look back, I don't know who that was." Asked about the class backgrounds of Rusty's clientele, Friedman says, "I experienced the bars as being both, as being divided between tougher, working-class, for me the 'other' lesbians, and then more middle-class women who were going to the bars to meet each other because that's where you were able to do that."

Crossing these thresholds was often sexually charged. Friedman recalls, "There was a tremendous sense of sexual electricity in the air, which was the shadow side of everything I'd been brought up with. And that side is always both enticing and threatening in equal parts. So that's the way I remember Rusty's, a sense of excitement, of danger, of possibly having fallen off the edge of the known world. And not knowing what that would mean for the future. Maybe there not being a future. I mean there were a lot of tough-looking women who would hang out at the bar who must have been like, oh my god, 35 or 40. As I sit here I'm 48. These were the oldest women I'd ever seen who were lesbians. It was scary. It was scary and titillating."

African American lesbians had a more difficult threshold to cross. Anita Cornwell remembers going to Rusty's and finding it "very prejudiced." "I could tell they didn't want us there," she recalls. Euro-American narrators remember few African Americans in Rusty's. Olshan thinks that "Rusty's had a mix," but adds, "There weren't many black lesbians coming out to the bars in Center City. There were other black lesbian bars and other black gay bars." By the early 1970s, African American lesbians had begun to frequent Rusty's more regularly. Elizabeth Terry remembers going and estimates that the crowd was "about thirty percent African American and about five percent Latina."

After entering Rusty's, many lesbians found themselves in a space that they learned to love and desire. In a 1974 interview, Parisi talked about what her bar had been like in the 1950s: "When I first opened they were beautiful, fun people. . . . They all got together, they laughed, they joked, they danced with one another. . . . To be in the 'in crowd' you were just in the crowd."[6] Discussing Rusty's in the 1960s, Friedman says, "That's the period in which I really came to know myself and define myself as a lesbian, not only in some private way ('oh my god, oh my god, is this true of me'), but in if not a public sphere then a community sphere. I began to have lesbian friends and go to the bars and make a world around myself." While some stress the importance of residential space for lesbian socializing, Friedman says, "I wouldn't underestimate the importance of the bar. We certainly did socialize in other lesbians' homes. . . . But I would say that the bar was the real spiritual, recreational community center for me." According to Marge McCann, "Rusty's was like old home week, every weekend. It was comfortable. The jukebox was reasonable with enough music to dance. And you could go and sit and put your feet up and just hang out." Bello recalls, "I used to go to Rusty's almost every Saturday. . . . In a way it was like a kid in a candy shop. . . . I had found people like me and there was a world I could just go in anytime I wanted." Fleischmann emphasizes the sexual ambience. Discussing a bar that also attracted gay men, Fleischmann says, "The atmosphere was different from Rusty's because Rusty's was all women. Rusty's atmosphere was kind of frantic, a lot of flirting, a lot of carrying on by people behind their lovers' backs." Friedman adds, "There was always sexual diciness and couple diciness, but that's as much youth as anything else. . . . Generally people cared about and for each other and watched out for each other."

Feelings of solidarity helped lesbians resist repression and harassment. Bello remembers a police raid: "I was back at Rusty's with somebody. . . . We had had dinner and we were going to Rusty's and she was applying for her citizenship. And I said, 'Oh just for a drink.' And they came. And because I was so anxious to protect her, I think they got suspicious, because the minute they came into the room, I just popped up and said, 'She's here as a visitor, she doesn't have anything to do with the place.' So they pulled me out and they made me show my identification and they shouted out loud in my face." According to Olshan, "Dykes used to call each other brothers. 'You're my brother.' And you were family and you protected each other from the police, from the other butches, from sailors who wandered in, from straight guys who were hanging outside to beat you up. . . . Sailors would try to horn in on the femme in couples and the butch would have to try to take him out. And he had no greater pleasure than to beat the hell out of a butch dyke."

Lesbians bonded and battled in other commercial establishments as well. Several generations of narrators remember going with their girlfriends to eateries near Girls' High when they were teenagers. Marge McCann adds, "Every once in awhile, like there was a place that opened at 9th and Washington for awhile, other bars would spring up." Bello remembers Businessman's Association: "There was a woman actually that received everybody on top of the stairs and insisted on kissing them. It was like a ritual." National lesbian and gay guides indicate that Jeanette Dembry's featured "entertainment" and that My Sister's Place was "very popular."[7]

Although the patrons of these bars and clubs were predominantly lesbian, small numbers of men also gathered there. According to Parisi, "There are a number of gay boys that come in and I do like them. . . . We do get fellows;

some are friends of mine. Nice guys. No one could resent them for being here. I wouldn't tolerate anyone who'd get pushy with the girls. . . . The men that I know are fine because they know it's hands off. I've never been with one and I'd never want to be."[8] According to Olshan, "Rusty's was really primarily lesbian with an occasional straight man who was friends with the bartender." Bartenders were "gay and straight" men. McCann says, "There were occasionally gay men, more often straight men, actually, in Rusty's. And the bartender was gay." According to Fleischmann, "There were a few men whom Rusty knew, like johns or something of that sort, and she would let them in there at the bar. But not very often. Most men were told it was a private club." Fleischmann notes that johns were there for "women who were prostitutes who were also lesbians."

Several gay narrators remember going to Rusty's. Jack Adair recalls, "I went in a few times and felt very strange. . . . Everyone looked at me." Also referring to Rusty's, Lewis Coopersmith says, "My first lover and I were able to go to a lesbian bar all the time only because he knew the owner. You had to know somebody to get in. . . . My first lover used to like lesbian bars. . . . John was bisexual, so he liked women sexually as well as men. And lesbians intrigued him." Describing the experience of going to Rusty's, Coopersmith says, "There weren't any reactions. . . . But I was aware of the fact that there was a tendency not to welcome men into lesbian bars."

Lesbians had several reasons for not welcoming gay men. Some lesbians may not have appreciated the sexual attention or sexual competition of gay men. Some may have thought that the gay men were straight. Some may have feared that the entrance of a few gay men was a sign of more to come. Some may have disliked certain aspects of gay culture or male culture. And some may have wanted an all-lesbian or an all-female environment, in part because of the ways in which lesbian sexuality thrived in the absence of men. Parisi attributed the success of her business to the fact that it was "all women." She explained, "This way they feel they have a place they can do what they please when they please." Parisi also stated, "I always felt there are so many gay bars for fellas—let 'em stay there." Asked about her feelings about men in general, Parisi responded, "That's debatable. There aren't many *men* in my estimation. Honey, we can say we're more men than they are. I know I am more of a man than a hell of a lot of them. . . . So that's what I think of men in general. Not much. But there are a few."[9]

Lesbian and Gay Bars, Clubs, and Restaurants

While lesbians and gay men patronized predominantly lesbian and predominantly gay bars, clubs, and restaurants, they also frequented establishments that attracted large numbers of both lesbians and gay men. More often than not, gay men were in the majority but there were enough lesbians to create a mixed-sex milieu. In the late 1940s, Euro-American lesbians and gay men gathered at Bridge Tavern (in northeastern Center City). In the 1950s and 1960s, they met at Surf (near the Locust Strip). In the 1960s, African American lesbians and gay men patronized 4–6 (in West Philly); Euro- and African American lesbians and gay men frequented Hideaway (near the Locust Strip) and Attic (in Germantown). By the late 1960s and early 1970s, Surf had closed; African American lesbians and gay men predominated at 4–6, Hideaway, and Attic; and Euro-American lesbians and gay men gathered at Foster House (near the Locust Strip) and Mystique (in southwestern Center City). African American lesbians and gay men also favored several bars in which they socialized with African American straights. In the 1950s, 1960s, and early 1970s, these included Pep's and Showboat (on and near South), Carver (in South Philly), C&W and Den (in West Philly), and Speedie's (in North Philly). Another Speedie's (on Market) attracted Euro- and African American lesbians, gay men, and straights.[10]

Lesbians and gay men also frequented several primarily Euro-American after-hours private clubs, which were allowed to remain open for an hour after the bars closed at 2:00 a.m. Most of these were on or near the Locust Strip. In the 1950s, these included International Society of Waiters and Bartenders ("Witches and Bitches") and U.S.&A.A. In the 1960s, lesbians and gay men also favored 214, Penrose, Roosevelt Democratic (R.D.), Sports Alliance (S.A), and Zu-Zu. In the early 1970s, lesbians and gay men frequented Penrose, R.D., S.A., and U.S.&A.A., as well as H.C., Mask and Wig, and P.B.L.[11] Discussing these clubs, Mel Heifetz says that their names "came from the licenses that they had to buy." Ray Daniels recalls, "You paid a fee and they gave you a membership card." One club reminded Daniels of Prohibition: "You rang the bell and the guy would open the box and look out to see who was there and then he'd close it and open the door." Richard Gayer remembers joining the Penrose under a pseudonym because his job was "Defense Department–related" and he feared losing the job if his name was linked with a gay club.

Lesbians and gay men also favored several diners, automats, coffeehouses, cafeterias, and restaurants. In the late 1940s, they frequented Dewey's, Horn and Hardart's, and Hamburger Heaven near the Locust Strip and another Dewey's near Rittenhouse Square. These places continued to attract lesbian and gay clientele in the 1950s, as did Artist's Hut, Gilded Cage, Humoresque, Proscenium, and Second Fret, all of which were coffeehouses near Rittenhouse Square. In the 1960s and early 1970s, lesbians and gay men frequented many of these same places, in addition to Day's Deli (near Rittenhouse

Square); Jimmy Neff's (near the Locust Strip); and Horn and Hardart's, Parson's Table, and Tad's Steak (on or near Market).

Surf was among the most popular mixed spots. Ann Lynch remembers finding her way there: "There's an old trick. You can go to a town and go get your hair done. And when you get a hairdresser, you can kind of check him out and say, 'Do you know where any gay bars are in this town?' Or you can even ask a policeman. I was very nervy. I got directed to the Surf." Marge McCann recalls that when she was 16, a gay friend from high school, without a word about same-sex sexualities exchanged beforehand, took her on a night's adventure to Surf.

Some narrators describe Surf as a lesbian bar while others say that it attracted both lesbians and gay men. This conflict may reflect several factors: the clientele may have changed; the clientele may have been different on different days of the week or at different times of the day; and some lesbians and gay men, accustomed to predominantly lesbian or predominantly gay bars, may have exaggerated the lesbian or gay presence. Writing in *Thursday's Drummer*, Greg Lee recalled the confusion that he experienced in 1970 when he encountered women in Mystique: "What's this? There's WOMEN in here! What kind of gay bar is this? Oh, hey, it must be gay 'cause there's two guys over there makin' out. Oh yeah, women, lesbians, that's right! Sorta forgot there was such a thing for a minute."[12]

According to Lynch, Surf was "a women's bar" and "they had a sign on the wall saying women in pants shall not dance." Pat Hill remembers going to Surf "under the pretense of being straight": "I had heard it was a lesbian bar. It was not a gay bar. I mean it wasn't all lesbian, but it was a women's bar. It was not a men's bar. And I can't tell you how many other people I've heard do the same thing. Drag a guy in there, sort of ogle everybody." Hill was aware that she was being ogled as well: "I felt like just this little debutante. I felt like something that had come in from another planet. And this was just this really upsetting shocking world of women who looked like men. And I wanted to fit into it."

Although Mark Kendall also remembers Surf as lesbian, other narrators think that it was more mixed. Bill Brinsfield, after likening conflicts between lesbians and gay men to "gang wars," says that Surf was "no-man's-land": "That was the common place where gay men and lesbians met. And they seemed to get along there fairly well. The lesbians that went there who couldn't stand gay men hung to themselves on one side. . . . There was mixing with a certain group of lesbians and gays and they seemed to tend to the left side of the bar. They had their area and they were social and that's where I socialized with the gay women that I knew." According to Joan Fleischmann, Surf was "a mixed bar, men and women," and "drag queens used to go." McCann, who says that Surf's clientele was "mixed but mostly men," remembers one man in particular: "A black drag queen called 'Sarah Vaughan' taught me how to dance. . . . He just saw me floundering and said, 'I'll teach you to dance.' "

Discussing Bridge Tavern and Surf, Joey Hardman says that she had "a lot" of gay friends. "Not to go to bed with," she jokes, but adds, "I don't think there was any hostility." According to Hardman, there was more likely to be physical conflict between lesbians and between lesbians and straight men than between gay men or between lesbians and gay men: "I never saw two gay fellas fighting. . . . You'd see the girls fighting, but you wouldn't see the men." Hardman says that while she did not get into fights with other women, she did have fights with "straight guys." "Not other gay guys," she notes, suggesting that she considered herself one of the "guys."

Surf was not the only mixed bar. According to Nancy Love's 1967 *Philadelphia Magazine* article, "The Invisible Sorority," "Lesbians often go to the same gay bars where male homosexuals congregate," including "quite a few downtown spots, particularly the Hideaway which is very popular with teenybopper lesbians." *Drum*, a local gay magazine, described the Hideaway in 1968 as "the city's most popular gathering place for hustlers, underage drinkers of both sexes, rough trade, and diesel dikes." Reminiscing about the late 1960s, Victoria Brownworth notes that "older dykes, drag queens, prostitutes, and gay boys" taught "queer lessons" at Hideaway, Rusty's, and Mystique.[13] Arleen Olshan also recalls Hideaway: "There was a woman named Larry that worked at the door who was this massive stone butch in drag, total drag butch. And there were sailors and straight men who did come in regularly. There were drag queens. It was a real mixed bar. It was mostly women, with a lot of drag guys, but not many real straight-appearing gay men."

Narrators also remember Attic. According to Tom Malim, "It was somewhat mixed in the sixties and then later on it became completely black. Just as Germantown had a turnover, there was that turnover." Olshan recalls that Attic was "mostly men" and "mostly black." Jay Haines, who describes Attic as "predominantly black," says, "I think there were some girls who might have gone there, but most every time I went there it was all male." Laurie Barron recalls, "It was upstairs and there was a pool table in the back room and a group of us used to go there pretty frequently." According to Barron, "It was very much mixed black and white. . . . I don't remember there being gay men." She adds, "Some of these hangouts . . . would get a reputation for being one or the other on a particular night of the week." Discussing Attic, "The Invisible Sorority" noted that "the men use the front bar and the girls the back one."[14]

African American lesbians and gay men often favored predominantly African American bars, clubs, and restaurants, partly because of the bonds that they felt with other African Americans, partly because these establishments were often located in predominantly African American neighborhoods, and partly because of the racism that they encountered at predominantly Euro-American spots. Daniels, who is Euro-American, recalls an example of the latter: "I went home with a black person who I met at the U.S.&A.A. . . . If you went to bed with a black person, they would say you were a dinge queen. . . . It was years and years and years before I ever told anyone that I did something with a black person. And then when I told one of my friends about it, my friend said, 'Oh, I'm so glad you told me because I did too.' "

Haines and Tyrone Smith remember predominantly African American bars that were popular among lesbians and gay men, but emphasize that many of these establishments also had straight clientele. These types of bars were particularly appealing to lesbians and gay men who were attracted to straights, to lesbians and gay men who wanted to be thought of as straight, to straights who were attracted to lesbians and gay men, and to people who did not identify themselves as lesbian, gay, or straight. According to Smith, "On South Street you had a different mix, because you had the nightlifers, who might be the prostitute, the gambler, the jazz musician, who would hang out down there too. So you were exposed to a different element of people. It wasn't identified as being gay. It was just nightlife. You could blend in the fabric of African American communities' nightlife and be a lifer and it'd be okay, whereas in the neighborhood you just couldn't do that." According to Smith, gays were accepted by "the nightlife crowd." But he also recalls other reasons for going downtown: "I was always taught that you just don't hang out in bars in your neighborhood. And I got this from what I was hearing my mother say to my sisters: 'If you're gonna go out with a guy, he doesn't take you to a neighborhood bar. He takes you out. You go in town, you go to a movie, you go somewhere, you do something.' So in hearing this, I patterned myself the same way in my own gay world."

Among these bars were Pep's, which Smith describes as a "show bar" past its "heyday." Discussing Carver, Haines says, "It was gay in that there were gay people in it, but also straight." Along similar lines, Haines says that Pep's, Showboat, and both Speedie's "weren't gay" but were "mixed." One gay guide listed Carver and both Speedie's as "men's," "women's," "gay," and "non-gay" bars. Discussing spots where lesbians and gay men both congregated, "The Invisible Sorority" mentioned two bars on Columbia Avenue, one of which was probably Speedie's. William Gardner Smith's 1954 novel, *South Street*, may have used Speedie's as a model for "Ray Cee," a bar on "the North Side" in which men danced with men and women danced with women.[15]

One of the more popular African American spots was 4–6. Smith explains that "downstairs was straight, upstairs was gay." Asked whether both women and men went upstairs, Haines replies, "Anybody who was gay." Paul Schmidt, who is Euro-American, remembers meeting several interracial couples at house parties and then being taken to 4–6, where he saw "some lesbians." Although she does not recall the bar's name, Elizabeth Terry recalls going to a "lesbian and gay" place in the vicinity of 4–6 where there were "very feminine women" with "very butch women." According to Terry, the clientele included about equal numbers of women and men.

In 1973, the local *Gay Alternative* produced a "Gay Guide to Philadelphia," which included a number of "black" bars not listed in national guides. Although some of these bars may not have been open or may not have attracted lesbians or gay men in the period between 1945 and 1972, it is possible that earlier guides failed to list them. While more racially inclusive than other guides, however, the *Alternative* designated each bar's clientele "men," "women," or "black," collapsing differences between African American lesbians and gay men and suggesting that all men and women were nonblack. That said, many of the "black" bars listed may have attracted both lesbians and gay men. These included Brown Bomber and Sam's (on and near South); C&W, Den, and Chestnut Lounge (in West Philly); Mellie's (in South Philly); Saxony North (in North Philly); and Terminal (in Olney).[16]

As for the after-hours clubs, while several male narrators describe them as predominantly male, others remember more mixed clientele. Ada Bello says of U.S.&A.A., "It was mixed and I usually went there after Rusty's closed." Carole Friedman also remembers the clubs: "They were a riot. That was my first immersion in just such another world, a real underworld. Boys looked like girls and girls looked like boys." According to Heifetz, "That's where you used to see the lesbians, in those clubs." Heifetz remembers "friendly exchange" with lesbians: "I used to be friendly with some of the women who worked at the bust-out joints. A lot of them were lesbians. Along Locust Street, for two or three blocks, they used to have bars. They were owned by the Mafia. They used to have B girls who used to hustle the tourists coming in for drinks. They would order drinks, it would be water. You would order champagne, it would be water. . . . But these girls were gay. . . . At night they would skip out the back door and then they'd find them in the clubs."

Heifetz argues that one of the things that drew lesbians and gay men to after-hours clubs, as opposed to bars, was the chance to dance with same-sex partners. "There was no dancing in any of the bars," he explains. "If you stood in front of the jukeboxes and started to move your rear end a little bit, somebody would yell over and tell you, 'You can't do that.' " Daniels remembers, "Two men could not dance together under LCB rules." According to Brinsfield, "Women could dance together in bars. They wouldn't be arrested. But if two men got up, they'd be arrested." Other narrators suggest that same-sex dancing by lesbians was also restricted. In any case, as McCann's story of dancing with "Sarah Vaughan" suggests, lesbians and gay men could dance in cross-sex pairs in mixed bars. Discussing gay men in a bar at 13th and Locust and probably referring to *American Bandstand,* Gaeton Fonzi's 1962 *Greater Philadelphia Magazine* expose "The Furtive Fraternity" observed, "Sometimes, with a lesbian they know, they will display their own dancing talent, an ability a few claimed they developed on a local, nationally broadcast television show."[17] In mixed bars, same-sex couples could exchange partners and form cross-sex pairs if the police appeared. In after-hours clubs, same-sex dancing was less restricted. Heifetz recalls, "In the after hours clubs you could dance. . . . So if the women wanted to dance, one with the other, it would be in the club scene."

Lesbians and gay men also frequented several of the same restaurants. Discussing Dewey's and Day's, Pru Chis says, "The restaurants were really mixed." According to Bello, "everybody" went to Dewey's after the bars closed. Barron remembers that it was called "Fag Dewey's." Daniels recalls that "all the gays" went to 13th Street Dewey's and that when "gay bars started opening on the other side, west of Broad Street, gays started going to the one on 17th Street." Fleischmann says that "you'd find streetwalkers, you'd find drag queens, you would find everybody" in Dewey's. She even recalls encountering Liberace there and getting his autograph for her mother. Heifetz says, "The Dewey's were the biggest hangouts I can remember and I can remember a lot of celebrities coming into Dewey's. . . . Liberace was one of the gay types. We used to see him in there all the time."

Brinsfield remembers that Hamburger Heaven was also popular: "On Saturday night, after the bars, it would just be jammed." Discussing the clientele, Brinsfield says, "You would get the raunchiest kind of gay person and the most elegant, the most haughty Main Line, dressed in suits and ties and hats, and . . . this element that was kind of a fringe, criminal element. . . . That again was like the no-man's-land where nobody got into fights and everybody got along, although there was a lot of bitchery and people looking down their noses at others. But everybody mixed there together. And gay women would come there. Straight people, too, would come to see the show."

Coffeehouses also had significant lesbian and gay patronage. Some narrators emphasize one or the other. Hill says, "They definitely weren't gay. . . . I don't know what the gay men were doing. . . . But there was a very intense sort of network of attraction between several of us that centered around the Gilded Cage. . . . It was a straight-slash-lesbian scene." Heifetz, who owned Humoresque, estimates that his clientele was 60–75% straight, 25–40% gay, 75–80% male, and 20–25% female. Asked about lesbians at Humoresque, Heifetz says, "I don't remember lesbians at that point in my life. I may have been in their company, but I was not quite out yet and I was far more fascinated with the male."

The composite picture presented by narrators suggests that the coffeehouses were popular among both lesbians and gay men. Becky Davidson recalls going to Artist's Hut and Gilded Cage with gay friends. Smith, who remembers several coffeehouses, says, "That was my first exposure to really white gay." According to Heifetz, "All of the coffee shops had some gay people." Olshan says of Gilded Cage, Humoresque, and Proscenium, "There were some lesbians there. There were some gay people there." Daniels, who remembers Artist's Hut, Gilded Cage, Humoresque, and Proscenium, says, "There was a mixture of lesbians, gay men, straight men, and straight women. . . . That was probably, when I come to think of it, the only place where there was that kind of mixture that took place openly."

The mixed clientele of the coffeehouses made them particularly attractive to some patrons. Marcea Rosen remembers regularly meeting a woman with whom she was having an affair at Second Fret and Gilded Cage: "There were lesbians there, but it was my feeling that it wasn't overpoweringly a gay place." "Women weren't as visible," she argues. "We could blend in a little more. I was married, I had children, I had a family, I had a job. And wherever I went I was above reproach in a straight world. And I always enjoyed fooling them. I loved it. Just sort of humming to myself and saying, 'I may be married to a college professor and have three kids and a house in the suburbs, but I'm not what you think I am.' "

In these bars, clubs, restaurants, and coffeehouses, lesbian and gay worlds overlapped. Lesbians and gay men clashed with and ignored one another in these spaces, but they also developed same-sex and cross-sex bonds. These bonds, which expressed and encouraged feelings of solidarity, proved useful in resisting oppression. Lynch remembers helping a woman after an encounter in a mixed bar: "I met a couple, a guy and a gal, and they were not in uniform, and they told me they were in the navy. . . . Months later, I got called down to be questioned by somebody from the navy. They asked me if she was a lesbian. I was shocked. I said, 'What are you basing your assumption upon?' They said, 'Well she only goes to movies with women.' And I sat down, I just gave them a lecture. I said, 'Listen, if you're a small-town girl, you go into the armed service, naturally you're going to go to the movies with your girlfriends.' I said, 'You're away from home for the first time. You really don't know what the score is.' By the time I finished talking I had this man convinced that she was all right and I was all right."

While this account refers to same-sex solidarity, others refer to cross-sex counterparts. Schmidt remembers helping a lesbian during a raid on U.S.&A.A.: "I was standing by a girl one time and the policeman asked her what her age was and what her date of birth would be and she couldn't think of it. And I told her what her date of birth would be and he heard me. Well 'Paul' went out the door with the cops." Discussing raids on bars, Brownworth describes the many times that she was "spirited out the back door" by "an older butch or a drag queen."[18] Lesbians also helped gay men. Barbara Gittings remembers going out with a friend named "Pinkie": "Pinkie got to talking with a couple of young men who were in the bar. The next thing I know, we're outside, and they bring out the brass knuckles and were cutting him up. . . . I was in no position to do anything except to wait for them to go away and then to help him to a hospital."

Schmidt recalls another police raid on U.S.&A.A. in which about 10 lesbians and gay men suffered and resisted together: "They took us downstairs, put us into that wagon, and we all went down to 11th and Winter to the police station. We sat there for about a half hour. . . . And then they released us all and we all hollered, 'Well aren't you gonna take us back?' They said, 'You ought to be glad you're getting the hell out.' . . . But the funny thing was, when we walked back, that place was loaded and jumping like nothing ever happened. I says, 'What is this?' I says, 'We were all roughed,' and we told everybody, 'We just got back from the goddamn police station.' "

Gay Bars, Clubs, and Restaurants

Philadelphia had dozens of predominantly gay bars, clubs, and restaurants. In the late 1940s, gay men frequented Green Dragon (in southwestern Center City) and Maxine's and Venture Inn (near the Locust Strip), all of which had primarily Euro-American clientele. In the 1950s, Euro-American gay men also patronized Allegro, New Look, and Westbury (in southwestern Center City); Essex (in northeastern Center City); and Forrest and Pirate Ship (near the Locust Strip). African American gay men frequented Nick's (on South). Joe's and Pete Hill's (near Market) had multiracial gay clientele. In the 1960s, Allegro, Forrest, Maxine's, Nick's, Pirate Ship, Venture Inn, and Westbury continued to attract gay men. Other primarily Euro-American gay places were Coach Room (near Rittenhouse Square); Mystique and Pen and Pencil (in southwestern Center City); Colonial, Den Room, Drury Lane, Hush Room, Page One, and Parker (on or near the Locust Strip); Teddy's (near South); Track Seven (in northeastern Center City); and Terminal (in Olney).

Other primarily African American gay spots were African Room (near the Locust Strip) and Spider Kelly's (near Market). The Ritz (in northeastern Center City) had multiracial gay patronage. Over the course of the 1960s, Ritz, Terminal, and Track Seven became more heavily African American.[19] Gay guides designated some establishments "'mixed': appears straight but sufficiently active to make it worthwhile." In the 1960s, these included Club 13, Golden Griffon, and H.M.S. Pinafore (near the Locust Strip); Sheraton (in northwestern Center City); and Cedar Cafe (in Northeast Philly). Forrest, Mystique, Ritz, and Track Seven were also listed as "mixed" in some years.[20] In the early 1970s, new predominantly Euro-American gay spots included 247 (near Rittenhouse Square); Steps (in southwestern Center City); Comeback, Living Room, Midway, Peyton Place, and Rendezvous II (near the Locust Strip); Funky Dunky (in northwestern Center City); Harlow's (near Market); and Miss P.'s (near South). New predominantly African American gay establishments included Buddy's (in South Philly) and First Nighter (in northeastern Center City).[21]

Narrators most commonly mention Maxine's, Allegro, and Westbury when discussing gay bars. John Taylor describes Maxine's as "famous." According to Bill Brinsfield, Maxine's was a "national monument." Mark Kendall says it was "*the* bar." Paul Schmidt recalls, "Allegro was *the* place." Henri David notes, "The Allegro was three or four floors of madness." Kiyoshi Kuromiya remembers hundreds of gay men at Allegro and says that "it would take forty-five minutes to get up the stairway." Jay Herman and Mel Heifetz describe Westbury as "most popular." In 1964, Forrest became the first local bar to advertise in the gay press.[22]

While most narrators report first learning about gay bars, clubs, and restaurants via word of mouth, Kendall describes discovering Pirate Ship accidentally: "Before it was the Pirate Ship, it was a place called the Locust House and it was straight. . . . One day I walked in by myself and it was the Pirate Ship. . . . One of the waitresses who still worked there, who had waited on us for years before at the Locust House, came up. And she nearly dropped whatever she was carrying when she saw me there. . . . And I said, 'This place certainly seems to have changed its clientele.' And she said, 'I'll say it has and we don't like it very much and we're going to get rid of them.' And I thought to myself, 'The Locust House never had it so good.'" Leroy Aarons, in a 1993 *Inquirer* column, describes another accidental discovery. In 1955, Aarons was in the navy and "on liberty" in Philadelphia: "I trooped around Locust Street in civvies convincing myself I was interested in the girlie shows. I knew better. Passing through one of those ubiquitous downtown alleys typical of Philadelphia, I found myself drawn to the door of a place called Maxim's [*sic*]. . . . The place was jam-packed with men, only men,

Figure 2.3. "Philadelphia Guide to the Gay Scene," c. 1969. Jay's Place advertised itself as Philadelphia's "only homophile book shop." Jay's was owned and managed by James Mitchell, who was the model featured on the cover of this guide to gay bars, clubs, restaurants, and cruising areas. Courtesy of Richard Schlegel.

well-groomed masculine men in sport jackets and ties. I had stumbled on my first gay bar."[23]

Ray Daniels remembers first going to Maxine's when he was a teenager: "My friend Rose, she liked to run around with gay people. Back then they used the term fag hag, which is a terrible name, but that's what they used to call women and girls who hung out with gay guys. They'd call them fag hags or fruit flies. . . . I knew nothing about the gay bars. I had just started coming into town. I was doing the coffeehouses. I would sit around [Rittenhouse] Square. . . . Rose, however, found Maxine's." One evening, she took him there: "And Rose said, 'Do you see anything unusual?' And I said 'No.' And she said, 'Oh come on. Look around.' So I looked around and I said, 'No, I don't see anything unusual.' I said, 'They have red flocked wallpaper.' . . . She said, 'Look around.' And I said, 'The only thing is that woman. You and

Figure 2.4. Maxine's and Venture Inn, Camac Street, 1950. *Philadelphia Evening Bulletin* collection. With the permission of Urban Archives, Temple University, Philadelphia, PA.

that woman are the only two women in here.' And she said, 'Well what kind of bar do you think this is?' I said, 'A bar where a lot of guys go.' And she said, 'Oh, for crying out loud, you're so stupid! We're in a gay bar!' And I said, 'We aren't.' She said, 'We are.' "

Having found these places in one way or another, patrons quickly learned that they were differentiated by class and race. Gay guides listed Comeback, Drury Lane, Maxine's, Mystique, Peyton Place, and Sheraton as "elegant." Daniels recalls that when he and Rose went to Maxine's, "We sat at tables with tablecloths. . . . This was a special dress-up kind of thing. You wore a suit and a tie or a jacket and a tie." Lewis Coopersmith says, "Maxine's was the upper-class bar. It tended to have a more professional clientele, a better educated clientele, a clientele with greater income and more sophistication. It was the bar at which somebody was sitting at the piano playing Noel Coward songs or Cole Porter songs instead of having a jukebox on." Maxine's, he asserts, was the only "vaguely sophisticated, nonmoronic gay bar perhaps ever to occur in Philadelphia." Describing Drury Lane, Herman says, "It was an elegant bar. . . . It seemed to me and to others that they were trying to control the kind of people who went in there by charging a little more than most places did for their drinks."

As some of these comments suggest, classy bars were sometimes regarded as such not because of the status of the clientele but because of the styles displayed in decorations, music, and clothing. Discussing Maxine's, Schmidt says, "Some people would say, 'Oh it's all those ribbon girls from Wanamaker's [department store] all dressed up in suits and out trying to have people think that they got money. And all they are is ribbon girls in Wanamaker's. . . .' And I said, 'Look, whether they're ribbon girls or not, at least they're dressed up. They're clean and they're buying their own drinks.' I said, 'That's a plus honey.' "

Not everyone liked these class performances. Kendall remembers the first time that he went to New Look: "They were what was later called a bunch of piss elegant queens. And there were affected mannerisms. To me they all seemed clones of one another. They all sounded alike and looked alike. And I was really turned off." He remembers that Maxine's was also filled with "the piss elegant." According to Brinsfield, "the middle range of gay people" called the clientele of Drury Lane "piss elegant." Richard Gayer recalls that some called it "Dreary Lane" because the patrons were "pompous." Pru Chis says Drury Lane was filled with "fancy fags."

Narrators remember Allegro in more varied ways, partly because new owners redesigned it in the early 1960s, partly because its clientele and styles changed, and partly because different people had different standards. Schmidt says of Allegro: "It was a dump. Physically it was falling apart. But when you stepped in there on a Friday and Saturday night, you had better be in a jacket with a necktie and a shirt, or they would have dissed you terribly. 'Cause that was considered class." Coopersmith recalls, "The Allegro was always the melting pot of gay Philadelphia. It had the largest crowd probably and the largest cross section." Heifetz says that while Maxine's and Drury Lane were "dress-up bars," at Allegro "you didn't have to be dressed." More critically, Herman says, "I didn't like the Allegro as much as I liked the Westbury or the Drury Lane. It just seemed to be different kind of people that went there. And I guess I would say that I thought they were rather lower in class status."

While Herman describes Westbury as more classy than Allegro, others remember the two as similar. Discussing Westbury, Coopersmith says, "It was arguably the most democratic bar. . . . It had a broader cross section of people and probably was the most middle-class bar. . . . Democratic isn't the word. Let me just say middle-class or conventional. . . . It had the same quality as a typical neighborhood corner bar does. It's never too crowded, it's never too noisy, and nobody's behaving eccentrically." Heifetz says that "Westbury was not a dress-up."

Narrators also describe the class character of multiracial and predominantly African American bars from multiple perspectives. Tyrone Smith says of the "basically black" clientele of Spider Kelly's, "They were attractive men. They wore suit and tie and sport jacket. That was the thing then. You dressed to go out." Discussing a later period, James Roberts says that Spider Kelly's "seemed like a very dangerous place": "It wasn't uncommon, I was told, for acts of violence to take place there. . . . They seemed to have derelicts, drag queens, people with suits, people on the make." Narrators remember Ritz in various ways as well. Kendall liked Ritz more than Maxine's, Drury Lane, and Allegro: "There was the lack of pretentiousness there. . . . I met people there from all walks of life. . . . Very accomplished people, who didn't have to prove anything to anybody. There were doctors and lawyers as well as ditchdiggers and warehouse people. And there were some ex-convicts." Others were less impressed. Roberts describes Ritz as "a dump." Herman says, "I had a friend at that time who used to go to the Ritz with some frequency and wanted me to go too. Told me I should stop being such a stick-in-the-mud and go to the Ritz with him. So I agreed to go on one occasion and I was very uncomfortable there. And I got particularly uncomfortable and left when this guy walked in and you could see that he had a gun, a shoulder holster I guess it was. You could see the butt of the gun sticking out from his suit. And so I said to my friend, 'Well that's it for me.' "

While some establishments had mixed reputations, others were generally known as "lower" class, which attracted some patrons and repelled others. Brinsfield says Green Dragon was "the scroungiest, most demented place." Gay guides listed Club 13, Pirate Ship, Ritz, and Track Seven as "rough trade" bars and noted that hustlers worked these spots. Kuromiya says that although he liked "sleazy bars," Track Seven was "unpleasant." Speculating that the bar was called this because it was near the bus station, he says "it was almost as sleazy as the bus terminal itself." Brinsfield declares, "Most gay bars that I've been in, and I've been on two continents, have really been cesspools, cesspools with tables."

Living with his mother and grandmother at 11th and Locust in the 1950s and 1960s, Brinsfield had a unique vantage point: "It was this awful strip of sleazy bars. . . . And in the middle of that was the Pirate Ship. . . . This was known as the raunchiest hellhole of any gay bars that ever existed. . . . The bouncer was named Miss Juice and there was somebody called Almost Paradise, a strange man that wore white gloves. Almost, Miss Juice, Chi Chi the African Birdwoman, and all these absolutely insane people that were really demented. . . . There were scenes, like there'd be somebody that came in one night and this guy started screaming because they had been in jail together, and he had been the boy of this tough. And then he grabbed him and dragged him out of there. It was just unreal dramas. Fellini, Ken Russell, and Greenaway combined could not dream up a scenario like this bar."

Gay bars were also differentiated by race. Kendall remembers New Look's clientele as "all white." According to Schmidt, Allegro's patrons were "mostly white." Kuromiya estimates that 90% of the crowd at Maxine's and Drury Lane were white. Jack Adair says Forrest's clientele was "largely" white. According to Daniels, the bars he patronized were "99% white." Asked whether the bars he knew were "all white," Brinsfield says, "Practically completely."

Some African American narrators remember racism in predominantly Euro-American bars. Discussing "racial tension" in Allegro, Herman says, "They . . . apparently . . . had a quota on the number of blacks that they would allow in there. And when they had reached the number, the quota, they would tell subsequent black guys who would try to come in, 'Oh you have to have a photograph identification from the LCB.' " Also referring to Allegro, Gus Johnson recalls, "If you were very dark with real negroid features, they turned you away." According to Roberts, "Many of the bars were very racially segregated." Roberts remembers going to Allegro and Westbury: "Some nights, I guess when they reached their quota of black people, they wouldn't let you in. . . . It was very insulting. I felt very hurt because I had assumed that because gay people were an oppressed minority that there was more solidarity. Then of course I realized that just because you're gay doesn't mean you can't have the prejudices that other white people have."

Some African Americans avoided predominantly Euro-American bars for these reasons. Smith recalls, "I would hear people say, 'You don't go on the other side of Market Street 'cause the white faggots will beat you up.' " Asked whether he remembers any incidents, Smith replies, "I just never took my ass over there. I just didn't. I mean you knew your space." Asked about racism in bars, Jay Haines recalls, "I never put myself in a position to experience it. One, I had a bad temper, and two, why be uncomfortable? And when you've experienced it all of your life, you become sensitive to it. And you can tell when you get into a room whether this is going to be a good scene or not. If it's a bad scene, I'm leaving. . . . Most of the time it might be if you got into a gay bar that was predominantly white and you were the only black there and the bartender had attitude." Haines says, "I was never interested in venturing south of Market Street. And that's where most of the white bars were. And everything I was doing was on the north side, so that's where I stayed." Kendall, who is Euro-American, recalls learning that "there was a kind of line of demarcation for many years even into the sixties where black gays only went north of Market and south of Pine or Lombard."

One of the more popular predominantly African American establishments was Nick's. Haines describes Nick's as "gay at night and mixed during the day." Smith also remembers Nick's: "You would come in the restaurant and you would order and get your food, and then you would slide around to the bar because you weren't of age." African American gay men also sometimes established a more significant presence in predominantly Euro-American gay bars, changing the bar's patronage in the process. Daniels recalls, "When a bar started to get black, then the whites moved over to another bar, kind of like the way when more blacks moved into a neighborhood, the whites moved out. . . . It happened to the Allegro. And people moved to the Westbury." Kendall says, "It wasn't until I guess the late sixties, I'm not sure just when, that blacks started going more to some of the bars. I think the Allegro was the first."

African American gay men also established a more significant presence in several predominantly straight bars. Haines recalls, "I think I was among the first to go over to 13th Street, to what we called the Ritz. . . . We turned that into a gay bar." Asked how this was done, Haines replies, "A few of us went in and we started going back and more started coming. And before you knew it, the regular drunks that used to be into the place just stopped coming. And the crowd changed. The owner of the bar hired a couple bartenders from the crowd. And it just got to be known as a gay bar." Less permanently, African American drag queen "Marvina" changed the atmosphere in Sonny and Lucky's Tavern when, according to the *Tribune*, the West Philly bar celebrated her birthday in 1962 with a party attended by hundreds.[24]

While gay bars, clubs, and restaurants might have primarily Euro-American or primarily African American clientele, they often were not exclusively one or the other. Smith recalls, "You would maybe have a white friend who would say, 'I'm going over,' and they would take you to their club, to a club on the other side of Market Street." Discussing Allegro, Roberts recalls, "The only time I would go would be if I went with some white friends because I noticed that if I was with a white person they'd be less likely not to let me in." Herman remembers going to Westbury: "There were a number of blacks who came in and without any problems as far as the management was concerned. Sometimes if you tried to talk to a white guy you would get some attitude." But Herman also remembers meeting at Westbury a Euro-American man who became his lover. Kendall recalls friends taking him to the Ritz: "It was the first time I was in a truly interracial bar. . . . I thought, 'Ah this is for me.'" He also remembers that the first time he went alone to the Ritz he saw an African American man order two six-packs of beer: "I said, 'Who's gonna drink all that beer?' And he turned and gave me a look and said, 'Why, we are.' "

Predominantly gay bars, clubs, and restaurants were also differentiated by gender. In some establishments, most of the male clientele seemed to conform to dominant gender codes of masculinity. In some, including "rough trade" and "hustler" bars, many men performed gay versions of hyper-masculinity. In some, many men performed gay versions of femininity. Oftentimes men who performed hyper-masculinity and men who performed femininity preferred the same places, particularly if they desired one another or depended upon one another as audiences. In some establishments, men performed a wide range of gay genders.

Gay guides, narrators, and newspaper accounts describe Forrest, Harlow's, Hush Room, Miss P.'s, Pirate Ship, and Spider Kelly's as having drag queens among their clientele and staff. According to Fonzi's "The Furtive Fraternity," a bartender named "Kim Novak" worked at Hush Room. Daniels notes, "The Forrest was a bar where a lot of drag queens went. . . . You'd see the drag queens sitting there with their big piles of hair teased out and lots of rhinestones." Discussing Westbury, Heifetz says, "Eddie Marcus was a bartender and he would be made up. He would have a full face of paint on and be working behind the bar. And he would camp and carry on." Heifetz recalls that "one of the really popular bartenders" was "Patty Page," who worked at Drury Lane and later owned Miss P.'s. Many narrators remember "Mary the Hat Lady" at Maxine's. Some bars also hosted drag shows. According to a 1955 article in the national magazine *Coronet*, "Sedate Philadelphia is the scene of not-too-secret 'drags' where young men adorned with wigs and falsies try to outdo each other in 'female' seductiveness."[25]

Perhaps the best known drag queen in Philadelphia was "Sarah Vaughan." Discussing his first night in a gay bar in Philadelphia, Schmidt recalls going to Westbury: "There was someone over in the corner with a big straw hat on. And she lifted her head and put her head down and someone said, 'That's Sarah Vaughan.' " On his first night at 4–6, Schmidt encountered her again: " 'Sarah Vaughan' was a barmaid. And she jumped up on the table . . . and she was singing 'Mustang Sally.' " Remembering his "first experience of a drag queen," Smith describes meeting the "hostess" at 4–6: "She dressed well, she was attractive, and she was a star. I mean she was 'Miss Sarah Vaughan.' " According to Daniels, who remembers her from Forrest and Allegro, "The thing about 'Sarah Vaughan' was, she *did* drag. She *did* it. She was very realistic. Some of the drag queens really looked draggy. 'Sarah Vaughan' would just wear very plain clothes. I'm sure she had some glittery things, but when she got dressed up, she dressed very ordinary, like a regular woman would dress to go to work, and styled her hair, didn't wear a lot of makeup, and really just looked like a real woman." According to Daniels, "Vaughan" circulated in various bars: "Bouncers at the door, I don't think they ever hassled her. I don't think anybody would have. . . . 'Sarah Vaughan' was tough. I mean it was not easy for her. He was a drag queen and he was a person of color. So he had two things right there. He had a double battle. So he was a strong person."[26]

Creating and crossing boundaries of class, race, and gender, gay men built bonds based on friendship, love, and desire. Daniels says of his first time in Maxine's, "People talked to us, the bartenders were friendly. As I later found out, it was a place where you came together to socialize." Discussing Forrest, he recalls, "As soon as you walked in and sat down, then whoever was sitting there would say, 'Oh hi, how are you? I'm so-and-so.' " Daniels also remembers other forms of friendship: "Then there was the cruising bar. . . . The Allegro was considered the naughty bar. You went there to pick up people." Asked why bars were successful, Schmidt says, "That was the only place that gay people could socialize. . . . And it was safe. It wasn't on the streets and it wasn't in the parks." Summarizing gay life in this era, Brinsfield recalls, "It really was harassment, harassment, harassment. And the only thing that kept you from killing yourself was some of the humorous aspects, some of the colorful people, some of the ludicrous situations you would get into. And the camaraderie."

Camaraderie helped gay men resist the oppression they faced. Drag queens, along with bartenders, were particularly vulnerable and particularly assertive during raids. Daniels recalls a raid on Allegro: "The first ones that went were the drags. . . . The macho guys were the last, but [the police] weren't interested in that because they wanted to stereotype." Daniels remembers one queen: "There was a movie, 'I Want to Live!' with Susan Hayward. It was about a murderess and she went to the electric chair, and there's a line in it where she says: 'I want to live, I want to live!' And she's screaming this. And there was this guy and he called himself Rita Hayworth, this drag queen. And he wore red hair. Of course he no more looked like Rita Hayworth—I mean Rita Hayworth was beautiful; this guy was not. And in the course of the raid, he jumped up on the bar and he said, 'I'm Rita Hayworth, I want to live, I want to live!' And he started running around the bar. And of course he was handcuffed and thrown into the wagon."

Gay men used various strategies of resistance in times of trouble. One strategy was to lie. Discussing raids on Green Dragon when he was a teenager, Brinsfield says, "They would take you to 12th and Pine. And then they'd say, 'How old are you?' And you would say, '33.' And they'd say, 'Get out of here.' " Another strategy was to run and hide. Brinsfield, who worked at Allegro, describes an example of this when discussing the owner, who was married and whose sons tended bar: "A big fight broke out. And of course the sons didn't know that all the gay men were going to scream and run. . . . So the two sons start fighting. And suddenly they're fighting with this bunch of thugs that had come in. And somehow, at one point, one of the sons turned around and just bopped the boyfriend of the father. Boom. Out cold. . . . Three of us were crouching in horror under the piano. And all this glass was flying and people were being punched out. And of course when the police came, the police rebeat all the gay people." In a later period, gay men continued to run and hide. Discussing raids on Allegro, Kuromiya remembers, "You felt safe up on the third floor, because by the time a raid happened, you could jump out the third-floor window."

Some gay men fought back. Discussing Ritz, Haines says, "The fellows would come down and they'd fight the gays and the gays would fight back." He continues, "That's part of the young hotheadedness and the mixture of so-called straights and gays." Asked whether he and his friends ever had trouble of this kind, Haines replies, "Not really, because we were together. And of course cool heads prevail. And we always had to live to fight another day. And after awhile we became the old heads and we got respect so that if we said something they listened."

Still another strategy was to develop early-warning and early-response systems. Discussing raids, Daniels recalls, "Someone would call and say, 'They're on. I've got a tip. They hit such-and-such a bar. They're heading for the Allegro.' " Daniels also remembers bars with "buzzers": "They would hit the buzzer, and there was a light, and the light would flash, and that was the signal that the police or the LCB were in the establishment. The first thing that happened was the bartenders would lock the register. And then they would jump over the bar." Johnson recalls, "When the police were raiding a bar, you would pull the fire alarm, which would just block them up."

Daniels remembers a retaliatory strategy. Describing a raid on Allegro, he says, "The owner of the bar knew there was going to be a raid. . . . So the wife told all the people who she liked to stay away. . . . After the raid was over, the people who had stayed away were very angry because . . . there were people who were friends of theirs who were arrested. . . . There was a group of people who said, 'We will not go back to the Allegro.' . . . It was their own way of protesting what had happened, what they had considered to be a dirty thing to do. And then the Allegro was sold."

The solidarity that supported strategies of resistance in predominantly gay establishments extended to lesbians in some contexts but not in others. Gay narrators suggest that many of these spots had exclusively or overwhelmingly male clientele. When Adair discusses Forrest, when Herman discusses Westbury and Drury Lane, when Kendall discusses Maxine's and New Look, and when Chis discusses Drury Lane and Allegro, they all use the same words to describe the clientele: "all men." According to Kendall, "At the gay bars, the feeling was that women, even lesbians, were not particularly welcome. . . . There was definitely a tightening in the atmosphere if women came in." Discussing lesbians, Herman says, "They didn't come to the gay bars. And I remember people saying that as far as lesbian bars were concerned, they weren't welcoming to men. So it was really, I felt, two different worlds." Herman believes that "indifference would be the best word" to describe the attitude that gay men had toward lesbians.

While gay men may not have noticed or may not remember a lesbian presence in predominantly gay bars, many lesbians recall experiences there. Joey Hardman recalls "good times" at Forrest. Ann Lynch remembers dinners with lesbian friends at Maxine's. Marcea Rosen says that she went to Drury Lane. Barbara Gittings, Marge McCann, and Elizabeth Terry describe going to predominantly gay bars. Enough lesbians went to Forrest and Mystique that lesbian and gay guides began listing them as lesbian spots in the early 1970s. All of this is not to say that lesbians were generally welcomed or were present in large numbers in these establishments. But just as there are more lesbian than gay narrators who recall residential concentrations of the "other" sex, there are more lesbian narrators who recall knowledge of, familiarity with, and experiences in predominantly gay spots than there are gay narrators who recall knowledge of, familiarity with, and experiences in predominantly lesbian spots.

In many ways, gay men's reasons for not welcoming lesbians into predominantly gay establishments paralleled lesbians' reasons for not welcoming gay men into predominantly lesbian establishments. But there were at least two ways in which these two phenomena were not parallel. Whereas gay men could choose from among dozens of spots in which they were predominant, lesbians could choose from among just a few. When lesbians entered predominantly gay establishments, gay men had many other predominantly gay places to go. Moreover, in the context of a culture in which men were advantaged economically, socially, and politically, exclusively or overwhelmingly male institutions often contributed to the oppression of women. Gay bars, clubs, and restaurants helped gay men resist the oppression that gay men faced, but the ones that excluded lesbians or discouraged lesbian patronage contributed to the oppression that lesbians faced.

Other Lesbian and Gay Businesses

Bars, clubs, and restaurants were not the only commercial establishments that lesbians and gay men frequented. A number of pornographic and nonpornographic bookstores carried publications that attracted lesbian and/or gay clientele. In 1969, Jay's Place II (near the Locust Strip) began advertising itself as "Philadelphia's only homophile book shop." Other popular bookstores were Adam and Eve's and Reedmor (in southeastern Center City); Adult Book Shoppe, Book-A-Rama, Book Bin, Bookmark, Edward's, Elster, Hastings, and Robin's (on or near Market); Easy Reader, Jay's Place, and Middle Earth (in southwestern Center City); and David's, Penn Book Center, and University of Pennsylvania Bookstore (in West Philly).[27]

Several movie theaters and bathhouses were popular among gay men. The movie houses, most of which were on or near Market Street, included the Aarde, Arch Street, Center, Family, News, Palace, Pix, and Studio theaters. The bathhouses, most of which were near the Locust Strip, included the Bellevue Health Club, Camac Baths, and Jack Drucker's Baths.[28]

Lesbians and gay men also favored several downtown hotels. Lesbian and gay guides began listing the Bellevue Stratford in the early 1970s. Hotel Philadelphia was the site of annual "Miss Philadelphia" contests, which drew hundreds of spectators from 1965 through 1968. Organized by Jack "Sabrina" Doroshow, Henri David, and Joe Venuti, the winners included "Harlow"

Figure 2.5 Jay's Place, Pine Street, c. 1970. James Mitchell stands in front of his bookstore, which moved from 34 S. 17th Street to 1511 Pine Street in 1969–1970. *PACE!*, Jan. 1970, 21. Photograph by Richard Schlegel. With the permission of Richard Schlegel.

(Richard Finocchio), who was featured in Frank Simon's 1968 film, "The Queen." (In the early 1970s, "Harlow" had a sex-change operation and took the name Rachel Harlow.) In 1969, David hosted his first of many major Halloween events. This one was held at the Adelphia Hotel. In early 1970, "Miss Queen of Hearts" was crowned at the Drake Hotel. Later in 1970, "Gay Halloween" was celebrated with a costume ball at the Drake. In 1971 and 1972, David's Halloween events drew hundreds to the Warwick Hotel. Also in 1972, David hosted a costume ball at the Academy of Music.[29]

In the first half of the 1970s, lesbian and gay publications began listing antique, advertising, art, art supply, clothing, craft, drug, eye care, food, framing, hotel, jewelry, leather goods, medical, music, plant, travel, and other businesses. Whether lesbians and gay men favored particular businesses because their owners were lesbian or gay, because they were located in lesbian and gay neighborhoods, or because they catered to lesbians and gay men, these businesses were part of a substantial lesbian and gay economy that by the 1970s had existed for decades.

In the bars, clubs, restaurants, and other businesses that they patronized, lesbians and gay men forged partially divergent and partially convergent senses of community. Lesbians and gay men diverged when they socialized in differ-

Figure 2.6 Rachel Harlow (formerly Richard Finocchio), 1972. *Philadelphia Evening Bulletin* collection. With the permission of Urban Archives, Temple University, Philadelphia, PA.

ent neighborhoods, different establishments, and different spaces within the same establishments, and when they had conflicts while socializing together. They also diverged to the extent that their leisure cultures differed and to the extent that they encountered different forms of oppression and developed different forms of resistance in the contexts of their leisure cultures. Lesbians and gay men converged when they socialized in the same neighborhoods, establishments, and spaces, and when they formed bonds while doing so. They also converged to the extent that their leisure cultures had important elements in common and to the extent that they encountered similar forms of oppression and developed similar forms of resistance in the contexts of their leisure cultures. Paradoxically paired, lesbians and gay men built cross-sex relationships while pursuing same-sex desires.

3

The Death and Life of Public Space in the "Private City"

In her influential 1961 book *The Death and Life of Great American Cities*, Jane Jacobs argued that "extraordinary governmental financial incentives" had been required to achieve the "monotony, sterility and vulgarity" seen in most U.S. cities. To address this situation, Jacobs suggested that a new vision was needed: that cities require "a most intricate and close-grained diversity of uses that give each other constant mutual support." To "generate exuberant diversity" and make cities "fantastically dynamic," urban planners had to "insure the presence of people who go outdoors on different schedules and are in the place for different purposes, but who are able to use many facilities in common."[1]

One of Jacobs's chapters focused on urban parks and here Jacobs used Center City, Philadelphia, as an example. She began with William Penn's seventeenth-century plan for the city, which placed four residential squares at equal distances from a central square. Noting that the "fates" of the four were "wildly different," Jacobs wrote that the "best known" was Rittenhouse Square, "a beloved, successful, much-used park." Washington Square fared less well. Several decades earlier, it had become "Philadelphia's pervert park, to the point where it was shunned by office lunchers and was an unmanageable vice and crime problem." She continued, "In the mid-1950's it was torn up, closed for more than a year, and redesigned. In the process its users were dispersed, which was the intent. . . . Beyond the rim of offices, it is today designated for large-scale urban renewal."[2]

Jacobs attributed Rittenhouse Square's success to its "diverse rim" and "hinterland," which produced "a mixture of users." To describe the scene, she turned to reporter Joseph Guess's portrait of the square's "ballet":

> First, a few early-bird walkers who live beside the park take brisk strolls. They are shortly joined, and followed, by residents who cross the park on their way to work out of the district. Next come people . . . on their way to work within the neighborhood. . . . In mid-morning mothers and small children come in, along with . . . shoppers. Before noon the mothers and children leave, but the square's population continues to grow because of employees on their lunch hour. . . . In the afternoon mothers and children turn up again, the shoppers and errand-goers

> linger longer, and school children eventually add themselves in. In the later afternoon . . . homeward-bound workers come through. . . . From then on into the evening the square gets many young people on dates. . . . All through the day, there is a sprinkling of old people with time on their hands, some people who are indigent, and various unidentified idlers.

Jacobs offered a compelling contrast with Washington Square: "The perverts who completely took over Philadelphia's Washington Square for several decades . . . did not kill off a vital and appreciated park. They did not drive out respectable users. They moved into an abandoned place and entrenched themselves. . . . The unwelcome users have successfully been chased away to find other vacuums, but this act has still not supplied the park with a sufficient sequence of welcome users."[3]

Jacobs did not point out that one of the "vacuums" that "perverts" filled was Rittenhouse Square, the very park whose virtues she extolled. Blind to the gay men of one square, Jacobs only had eyes for the perverts of the other. But Jacobs was not the only one with blind spots. Many gay men who used Rittenhouse Square did not see the lesbians in their midst. And while lesbians were generally more aware of the gay presence than gay men were of the lesbian presence, some lesbians were as blind about lesbians as gay men were.

Blind to both lesbians and gay men, Jacobs failed to help her readers see that both groups contributed to the successes and failures of Rittenhouse Square, whether as strollers, workers, mothers, children, lunchers, residents, shoppers, young people, old people, and indigents, or as "unidentified idlers." Although lesbians and gay men used the square throughout the day, it is tempting to suggest that Jacobs and Guess may simply have gone to bed too early, after the "young people on dates" had arrived but before the lesbian and gay presence became more obvious. Ironically, recognizing the contributions of lesbians and gay men to the spatial, functional, and temporal diversity of both Rittenhouse and Washington Squares, both before and after urban renewal, might have strengthened Jacobs's argument.

Good park, bad park. Mothers, children, shoppers, residents, employees, and young people on dates in Rittenhouse Square, a veritable showcase of the family, heterosexuality, capitalism, and consumer culture. Perverts in Washington Square, a den of depravity. The busy schedule of work and leisure in the West. The history of abandonment, invasion by perverts, and then a vacuum in the East. The "life" and "death" of great American cities. Sexual perversion functions here as a symptom, source, and sign of urban disaster.

But there are other stories that can be told of Rittenhouse and Washington Squares and of other public places in the "Private City." Lesbians and gay men used public space in all parts of Philadelphia. But the lesbian and gay presence was particularly strong in certain parks, streets, buildings, and restrooms, and at specific times of the day, week, and year. Free from the particular types of protection, safety, security, surveillance, violence, and danger that were associated with residential and commercial areas, public space had its own advantages and disadvantages for lesbians and gay men wanting to meet, socialize, cruise, and have sex. Public space could offer publicity to the butch lesbian walking up 13th Street on Saturday night and the drag queen parading down South Street on Halloween. It could offer privacy to the teenager meeting girlfriends in the showers at Girls' High and the hustler having sex with a married man in the men's room at Broad Street Station.

Paradoxically, lesbians and gay men were often "seen" as "invisible" in public. But visibility was in the eyes of the beholder. Lesbians and gay men often saw things that others did not. And the frequency with which they were said to be invisible suggests that something was being seen, even by straights. Strategically managing their levels of visibility to one another and to others, lesbians and gay men made public space their own. Depending on the perspective, lesbians were either particularly good or particularly bad at this. To the extent that they were more invisible than gay men were, lesbians often had more trouble finding one another but more success in avoiding certain forms of public censure, harassment, and violence. Often regarded as a burden, invisibility allowed lesbians to avoid adding to the considerable dangers that they already faced as women in public space.

Class, ethnicity, gender, race, and place also shaped the public visibility of lesbians and gay men. For example, while lesbians were often less visible than gay men on account of their sex, masculine lesbians, like feminine gay men, were often quite visible because of the ways in which they subverted normative relationships between sex and gender. Moreover, like masculine gay men, masculine lesbians were often visible because of the ways in which they used public space. For another example, African American lesbians and gay men were differently visible in African American, as opposed to Euro-American, neighborhoods.

Lesbian and gay geographies converged and diverged in the public sphere, and these convergences and divergences were linked with those in residential and commercial spheres. Depending on the context, public convergences and divergences made lesbians and gay men more or less visible. For example, by appearing in public space with gay men, lesbians sometimes increased their visibility as lesbians. By appearing in public space with lesbians, gay men sometimes decreased their visibility as gay men. Converging and diverging both helped and hindered lesbian and gay men's efforts to find one another, gain strength in numbers, build community, respond to danger, and claim public space. Reflecting past relationships between the sexes, these convergences and divergences produced future relationships, helping to make Philadelphia "exuberantly diverse" and "fantastically dynamic."

Parks

For gay men, Rittenhouse Square was among the most popular places to meet, socialize, and cruise. As gay diarist Donald Vining wrote in 1948, the square's "reputation as a cruising ground was well deserved." Jess Stearn's 1961 book, *The Sixth Man*, told a story of two gay men watching "a visiting potentate" check into a nearby hotel: "With an expression of utter boredom and distaste one homosexual said to the other: 'Why are these people making all that fuss about a prince, when there's a queen on every corner on the square?' "[4]

Rittenhouse Square's popularity predated World War Two. John Taylor recalls that around 1940 a gay friend in West Philly told him that if he went to the square he would "meet people" and Taylor says that "he was very

Figure 3.1. Rittenhouse Square, 1967. *Philadelphia Evening Bulletin* collection. With the permission of Urban Archives, Temple University, Philadelphia, PA.

right": "You would walk or you would sit on a bench until you made eye contact with somebody and then you'd start talking and very frequently the types that I was interested in would be living near Rittenhouse Square. So that was my first experience going to somebody's apartment." Taylor says that while he had had same-sex sex previously, this was the first time he did so with "substantial" people: "college boys, teachers, guys in the professions." He notes that before this, he did not know that he was "part of a larger community." "But when I met those people," he explains, "it was equivalent to coming out, to understanding that there was a gay life."

Bill Brinsfield suggests that the square's gay population extended beyond the "substantial" men who lived nearby. Declaring that Rittenhouse was "the place to go" in the 1940s, he says that "there was the meeting of all minds" in the square, from "poorest to Main Line," and "the amazing thing, when you discovered it, was that everybody knew everybody." He notes that many people "weren't serious about making out" because Rittenhouse was "a social thing." But "the people who were really out to get down to the nitty gritty walked around the edge, on the pavement, which they called the carriage trade."

By the late 1950s, the gay scene in the square was linked with the neighborhood's coffeehouses. Mel Heifetz recalls that his coffeehouse, the Humoresque, attracted gay men who spent time in Rittenhouse. About the latter, he says,

> The most popular hangout for gay people in Center City was Rittenhouse Square. . . . And at any hour of the day or night, there would be something going on in there. . . . You could sit on the wall adjacent to the center area and you would have 15 or 20 friends near you. Their jokes, the stories, the remarks about people walking through. Something cute would walk through and everybody would light up. You would constantly do a run around the track. The racetrack was the outer rim that had all the benches on it. And there would always be some young queens that would be very aggressive and want to be seen or they would want to pick up somebody. . . . And it was marvelous because if you were not quite out, or if you were a little bit withdrawn or you didn't know how to cruise, all you had to do was sit anywhere on a bench in this park. And within the course of an hour, you'd have 20 people coming by that would be cruising you or looking at you or sitting down next to you. In my whole life, I don't think there's ever been an area that has been quite as gay-friendly or as easy to get picked up. . . . You really felt as if you were on safe ground. . . . There could be two or three hundred gay people in that park on any given night.

> And I couldn't begin to convey to you what a nice feeling and mood it was. . . . It's like being in Provincetown and walking down the street where everyone is gay and hand in hand and you feel as though there is no one to oppress us.

Heifetz says that whereas dancing and touching were constrained in "sinister" bars, there was more openness in the square.

For gay teenagers not old enough to get into bars legally, Rittenhouse was particularly appealing. Henri David says that in the 1960s he knew quite a few young gay dancers on Dick Clark's *American Bandstand*. For many of them, he says, the "only way to be gay was to come to Rittenhouse." Remembering that they would go to the square "dressed to kill," David says, "We would have little birthday parties for each other there and bring cake and sodas because we had nowhere to go."[5]

Over the course of the postwar decades, while Center City became more residentially Euro-American, the square's population became more multiracial. Discussing the 1940s, Brinsfield recalls "no blacks" or "a token" few. Remembering the 1950s, Heifetz says that "it was mostly white, but there were some black queens." David remembers the young gay crowd in the 1960s as "very mixed." Adrian Stanford's poem, "Remembrances of Rittenhouse Square," published in a homophile movement magazine in 1965, showcased "Sarah Vaughan":

> black sarah ruled,
> and we of lesser divinity paid homage to her
> with our pansy smiles,
> we breathed magnolia air,
> dreaming other visions through the velvet of our mascara lashes,
> and blessed ourselves with water from the shallow pond,
> and kissed each handsome boy as he passed by. . . .[6]

While the number of Asian Americans was smaller, Kiyoshi Kuromiya says that he "practically lived" in the square in the 1960s.

Although many narrators say that the square's gay population was racially diverse by the 1960s, few recall seeing any or many lesbians there. Mark Kendall observes that "gay men were much more visible" in Center City and that "one could see groups of what were clearly gay men walking together on the streets, in Rittenhouse Square, in Washington Square." Heifetz notes, "I don't ever remember a strong presence of women." Tyrone Smith says that his "first exposure to white gay men" occurred in the square, but describes the scene as "basically men." James Roberts thinks that the square was "a well-known gathering place" for Euro- and African American gay men but says, "I don't remember that many women being out there. The women I do remember were basically friends of the men. I don't think it was distinctly a lesbian gathering place." David says that there were "quite a few" lesbians but that they were "very separate" from the gay men.

The "fantastically dynamic" world of the square, however, did include lesbians and lesbians did mix with gay men. Ann Lynch recalls that, for a time in the 1940s, she spent afternoons in the square "watching for Ellie," the woman she loved, to come home from work. Arleen Olshan, who describes herself as a "beatnik" in the 1950s, thinks that "lesbian cruising and gay male cruising were slightly different" and that "people teased that you go out with a lesbian and you bring a U-Haul and you live together and that's the end of that." But she thinks that both kinds of cruising took place in the square and offers as an example an experience of meeting "a young dyke" one afternoon: "She was real obviously a lesbian, blond DA haircut, all men's clothes. And we had really good conversations. And we wound up riding home on the subway together."

Olshan suggests that lesbians and gay men not only used the same space but mixed socially: "I used to hang out with gay guys in Rittenhouse Square

Figure 3.2. Arleen Olshan and friend in Rittenhouse Square, c. 1972. Photograph by Jo Hofmann. With the permission of Jo Hofmann.

a lot. . . . And I was very comfortable in their company. They were totally outrageous. It was wonderful." Becky Davidson remembers happening upon the square when she was a teenager in the 1960s and seeing "effeminate men" who she knew were "queer": "And I said, 'Oh my god. I know they're like me. That's what, that's how I am. . . .' I remember saying to myself, 'There's men like that, there's got to be women like that.' " Davidson says that she soon realized that there were "a lot" of lesbians in the square and developed a crush on one named Bobbie. She also remembers from the square a woman named Sonny, a "drag dyke" who pocketed 75 dollars from Davidson's mother in exchange for a promise to find Davidson when she ran away to New York. Later, when she was taken to court for truancy, Davidson promised that she would stop going to the square if her mother would move with her from Northeast Philly to Center City. She remembers thinking, "I'm right down the street from Rittenhouse Square. She must be crazy. Of course I'm gonna hang out." Davidson recalls spending a great deal of time with gay men in the square and that when a friend told her that he was gay and asked her to take him to the square and "introduce him around," she did.

According to Nancy Love's 1967 article, "The Invisible Sorority," "You don't find [lesbians] cruising the street corners and bars, engaging in open relationships in rest rooms or behind bushes in parks the way men have been known to do." But this did not mean that lesbians did not socialize and cruise in public in different ways. Nor did it mean that lesbians did not do so in some of the same places that gay men favored. Love herself described a "wild teenager" who was "haunting" the square. She also wrote about "Renee," who "began to hang out in Rittenhouse Square" but later became involved with a lesbian who provided "advice about how to straighten herself out." According to a student cited by Love, "When I first moved out of home, I was a pretty wild kid and went to clubs with that Rittenhouse Square crowd." Love's claim that "you don't find" lesbians in these places rested in part on who "you" were.[7]

Joan Fleischmann remembers "hanging out" in the square with her best friend, a gay man, in the 1950s, yet says that the crowd there was "just guys." Kay Lahusen notes that "there was a lot of cruising that the guys did late at night" in the square, but adds that "lesbians aren't given to cruising in the park." Nevertheless she recalls that when she and Barbara Gittings lived nearby in the 1960s, "We didn't think a thing about going up there at midnight, or even later, and walking around. . . . We knew that we were among friends." Whether or not these women were visible to other lesbians or include themselves in the scenes they describe, the frequency with which lesbians tell stories about Rittenhouse suggests that they, too, contributed to its "exuberant diversity."

Lesbians and gay men shared not only physical and social space but also the attendant risks of harassment. According to Gaeton Fonzi's 1962 article "The Furtive Fraternity," the square and Suburban Station "rank at the top in the number of complaints to the police." In 1963, the *Inquirer* reported that city representative Fredric Mann had begun a campaign to "bar undesirable loiterers from Rittenhouse." *Il Popolo Italiano*, a local Italian American newspaper, commended Mann for "protesting the appearance of loafers and sex-deviates who represent a potential menace to the well-being of citizens who visit Rittenhouse." In 1970, Robert Crawford, the new president of the Fairmount Park Commission, ordered an investigation into "degenerate type of behavior" and "naughtiness after nightfall" in the square.[8]

Kendall remembers a night at the square when two men approached him, "fishing for sexual activity." After a policeman appeared, the two men left. The cop then asked Kendall about his "friends" and wanted to know what he was doing out so late. After Kendall said that he was just sitting, the policeman "let" him stay. Recalling that he was "well dressed that night with a suit and a tie," Kendall suggests that had he not been, he might have had more trouble.[9] Heifetz says that "during political periods, when elections were coming up, they would start having sweeps of the park and they would chase you out." Discussing the police in the 1950s and 1960s, Ray Daniels says, "I was harassed with my friends in Rittenhouse Square. They would come through the park and they would chase you. They'd say 'Go on, get the hell out. Clear out of here, you queers.' "

Violence was also a risk. Brinsfield remembers that in the 1940s, Euro-American working-class men from South Philly would come to the square and "beat people up and terrorize people." In 1970, *Gay Dealer* noted that "homosexuals in Philadelphia have been subject to increased physical attacks and harassment by the police," that "ten gays were pulled in" on one night, and that "others have been detained overnight." "Long subject to abuse, threats, and assault from straights," *Gay Dealer* declared, "gays are now being forced to submit to totally illegal and unwarranted police brutality—particularly in the Spruce Street, Delancey Place, and Rittenhouse Square areas."[10]

But they did not submit. Daniels recalls that when the police would raid the square, "you'd go somewhere for a cup of coffee or go to one of the coffeehouses; then you'd come back." Heifetz remembers that when there was likely to be trouble, the square's guard, who "probably was gay," would "tell us that we would have to be cool and we would have to get out of there by nine o'clock." Heifetz and Daniels also remember a code word. Heifetz explains, "If you saw somebody on the street and you thought that they might get nasty, right away would be the word 'neshenu.' And no one ever knew what it meant, except gay people, but it meant we better be cool, this guy is bad."

As many of these stories suggest, everyday strategies of resistance enabled lesbians and gay men to continue using and enjoying the square, which challenged those who opposed the public pursuits and pleasures of lesbians and gay men. Using coded language, clothing, hairstyles, and other embodied signs, they managed their levels of visibility to one another and to others. They cultivated particular types of relationships with guards and police. They avoided the square during difficult times and returned when times were better. They warned and stood up for one another and fought back when attacked. And they created and recreated lesbian and gay cultures and communities in public space.

Rittenhouse was not the only park where lesbian and gay geographies converged. As Love's article on lesbians pointed out, "the gay set has its own meeting places," including "certain parks." While Jane Jacobs and Kendall point to the presence of gay men in Washington Square before urban renewal, other narrators suggest that Washington Square was popular among lesbians and gay men in later years. According to Jess Stearn's 1961 book, "homosexuals often make a beeline for stately Rittenhouse Square and Fairmount Park."[11] Laurie Barron and Elizabeth Terry note that Fairmount Park was popular among lesbians as well.

In other parks, lesbian and gay geographies diverged. Parks where female athletes played sports often featured lesbian social networks. According to Irene Wolt, female baseball players formed an exhibition league in Pennsylvania that lasted for two seasons in the 1950s and had two teams: "the Norristown Nifties and the Philadelphia Fillies (formerly the Allentown Chicks)." Wolt quotes Betty Hoy Jetter, a member of one of the teams, as saying that most of her team's members were lesbians. Terry recalls moving to Philadelphia in the 1970s, in part because she was an athlete and had met a group of "field hockey dykes" from nearby West Chester, who gave her "the idea that there was a community" in Philadelphia.[12]

Lesbian and gay geographies also often diverged in parks where men had sex with other men and in parks with particularly dangerous reputations. Taylor remembers regularly having sex in a "wooded area" in West Philly's Cobbs Creek Park in the 1930s and 1940s. League Island Park, near the Philadelphia Naval Yard in South Philly, was also popular. For example, according to court testimony, one evening in 1957, a sailor on the submarine U.S.S. *Sirago* went on shore leave to a club and met a man who drove him to League Island Park, where the two had sex. In the 1970s, gay guides began listing League Island Park as a cruising area with "heavy military patronage," warning readers to proceed "at your own risk." According to Roberts, "Gay Acres," near the railroad tracks between the Art Museum and the Schuylkill River, was also a cruising area. Brinsfield recalls that Reyburn Plaza near City Hall was used by what middle-class gay men would consider "scroungy low-life gays." According to the *Bulletin*, a 1950 gay murder suspect acknowledged meeting the victim on Reyburn Plaza.[13]

Men pursued sex with other men in parks in spite of the risks. The U.S.S. *Sirago* sailor was discovered by a guard and convicted on a sodomy charge, although the decision was later reversed on the grounds that he had been drunk. According to a 1956 *Philadelphia Medicine* article on homosexuality, law enforcement officials "police the public parks and they very carefully police public toilets, especially subway toilets." According to a 1961 study of the Philadelphia Morals Squad by Penn law student Richard Elliott, "Police seeking to arrest homosexuals for solicitation for sodomy restrict their investigative activity to public places and will not enter a private establishment unless the owner requests police aid."[14] Elliott discovered that in one seven-month period, 23 men were taken into custody after being entrapped by "attractive" male officers on the Morals Squad. An additional 14 were arrested on sodomy charges as a result of "routine patrols." Of these, 10 involved "consensual homosexual activity" and most were discovered in "parked cars and public parks." An additional 13 were arrested on the basis of complaints made by persons "solicited by a homosexual on the street or in a park."[15]

Elliott's study reveals not only the risks of park cruising, but also the willingness of men to take the risks and the strategies that they used to increase their chances of success. According to his investigation, "homosexual solicitation in public places" peaked after 1 a.m. and usually began with a man sitting down next to another on a bench. The study noted that while most apprehended men spoke "freely" about their own homosexuality, they would "not reveal the names of partners." This may have been related to the finding that "most persons who cruise public places do not regularly associate with other homosexuals," but it also may have been an example of gay men protecting one another.[16]

Streets

Lesbian and gay geographies also converged and diverged on the streets. While gay men were more often considered visible on the streets, at least by those who knew when, how, and where to look, lesbians were more often thought to be as invisible on the streets as they were in parks. And many lesbians did successfully avoid unfriendly notice. As Nancy Love's article noted, "no one stares if women show affection in public—a kiss goodbye at an airport, two elderly ladies walking hand-in-hand on a street in Chestnut Hill." But many lesbians successfully sought out friendly stares. As one of Love's sources reported, "There's a girl who's been riding down my street in this red sports car and giving me the eye. I'd like to meet her."[17]

Butch lesbians and the lesbians who accompanied them were particularly noticeable. Joey Hardman recalls walking around Philadelphia in her World War Two uniform and says that she was not harassed: "I guess they believed in those days that you were helping do something good for the service." In 1974, Rusty Parisi talked about what it was like to be a butch on the streets in the 1950s and 1960s. "I wouldn't be seen walking down the street with my hair teased," Parisi explained. "Well, if I was supposedly the butch, honey, I had to look it with the shirts and T-shirts."[18] Becky Davidson and Pat Hill recall what it was like to see a butch. Davidson has a "vivid" memory of encountering two women at a bus station when she was eight years old in the 1950s. One of the two was as "butch as the day was long" and Davidson says she asked her mother, "Is that a boy or a girl?" Hill remembers feeling "tortured" in the 1950s when she was living near Rittenhouse Square and "trying not to look at women on the street." One day she saw "a fairly obvious lesbian," who was "butchy looking" and "handsome," watering her flowers. Hill recalls thinking, "Oh, is she cute!" With "a little research," Hill learned that the woman had "a very exotic reputation" and "engineered" an invitation to a party at the woman's house. Discussing Byrna Aronson, who lived in Philadelphia in the 1960s and 1970s, Rosalie Davies describes what it was like to be seen with a butch: "Byrna looks like everybody's notion of a stereotypical dyke. She walks around with t-shirts, a pack of cigarettes in the side of her sleeve turned up. She's a tall woman and a big woman." Walking down the street with Aronson, she says, was "like walking down the street with a drag queen."

The most active areas of lesbian and gay street life were in Center City. Psychotherapist Samuel Hadden, who had an office near Rittenhouse Square, reported that while walking to his car one day he saw two men who had just attended one of his group sessions "meet at a corner and go off arm in arm." Hadden wrote that he "never saw either one again." He also noted that one of his patients claimed that when he began "treatment" in 1964, "whenever he walked the six blocks from his place of business to his apartment in the evening he was good for several approaches." Gaeton Fonzi stated that "male prostitutes" in "wigs and female attire," were known to "regularly cruise the center city streets in search of trade." According to a 1963 article in the *Tribune*, Dr. James Weston, a Euro-American pathologist, told an audience of African American undertakers, "The evidence of increasing homosexuality among Negroes is all around us. . . . All you have to do is to visit Center City Philadelphia at night." Kiyoshi Kuromiya says that his first gay encounter in Philadelphia took place in "a dark alleyway" near City Hall. He remembers thinking, "It's great to be in a big city." Kuromiya also says, "All of Center City was pretty active. It was quite gay and you could pretty much stop and talk to anybody and strike up a conversation and/or relationship."[19]

Within Center City, the most popular streets were on or near the Locust Strip, in the area called the "Merry-Go-Round," and Spruce. Both lesbians and gay men cruised, socialized, and hustled on the Locust Strip. George Axler remembers visiting the area in the 1950s when he was working at the Hedgerow Theater outside Philadelphia: "I saw two gay men and I followed them . . . to a gay bar. I didn't know where to go or how to find a gay place in Center City." Marge McCann remembers forgetting where the Surf was located: "So what I'd do was come in town on the subway on Saturday nights and stand around in the general neighborhood and watch people to try to figure out who to follow to find out where the bars were and the courage to follow somebody. And so finally somebody [female] said 'Come with us.' "

Street life on the Locust Strip was often easier to find than the bars. In 1961, after a visit to the area, Charles Simpson wrote to *Greater Philadelphia Magazine*, "We were all amazed at what we saw on the street, most notably the men dressed as, and acting like, women." In 1969, two policemen took a *Bulletin* reporter, at 1:00 a.m., to 13th and Locust, where they pointed out "men they take to be homosexuals and women they think are lesbians." Kuromiya, who remembers the "constant flow of people" between the bars, wrote in 1970, "You see the beautiful boys and the flamboyant queens, the diesel dykes, the leather queens, and the hustlers on 13th Street."[20]

The Merry-Go-Round acquired its name because cars and pedestrians circled around Spruce, 18th, Delancey, and 21st Streets. James Roberts remembers seeing "license plates from New Jersey and Delaware" and thinking that it seemed like "sharks circling bait." Although it was known primarily as a gay men's cruising area, lesbians had their own reasons for favoring it. A 1974 *Inquirer* article quoted Byrna Aronson as saying that some residents liked the Merry-Go-Round because "there are people on the street all the time" and the area thus had low burglary and mugging rates.[21]

Spruce was also popular. Arleen Olshan recalls spending time with gay men at one of the more popular intersections: "We'd hang on the corner of Broad and Spruce. And it was just outrageous. We'd laugh and cut up and 'Oh, Mary' this and 'Oh, Mary' that." Lewis Coopersmith says that Spruce was "the great meeting ground" in the 1950s and 1960s: "The idea that people were closeted before Stonewall is absolutely nonsense. I mean if you were young and walked down the street in Center City, Philadelphia, it was very difficult not to wind up with a sex partner." Mel Heifetz says, "Spruce Street used to be so gay in those days that to walk up Spruce Street was an evening of entertainment in itself. It could take two hours just to walk four or five blocks, because there would be so many people sitting on doorsteps and there'd be so many people socializing on the street." Barry Kohn, in *Barry and Alice: Portrait of a Bisexual Marriage,* describes walking down Spruce, "the homosexual street," in the early 1970s: "I would see people who, according to the usual stereotypes at the time, I assumed were homosexuals. They were the thin, soft, effeminate men with tight blue jeans, carefully groomed and particularly self-conscious about their appearance. . . . There were plenty of other homosexuals on Spruce Street, but they walked, talked, and dressed just like any other person."[22]

While certain streets in Center City were particularly well-known for lesbian and gay cruising, others in the neighborhood were also popular. Gus Johnson recalls an encounter that took place when he was around 16 years old and living in southeastern Center City in the 1960s: "I had a big standard poodle named Gustave. . . . And I was walking my dog down Pine Street and this man turned the corner. . . . I followed him all the way down to 3rd and Pine and somehow got in front of him and my dog tripped over his laundry and I started helping him up. And then I started apologizing and it was all over after that. I planned this whole thing and I'd never ever been with an adult man in my life. . . . And I said 'Well I'm going your way' and then he invited me in for tea."

Lesbians and gay men socialized, cruised, and had sex on the streets of other neighborhoods as well. Chea Villanueva, a Filipino and Irish American lesbian who lived in Philadelphia in the 1960s and 1970s, writes in her 1995 autobiographical book *Jessie's Song* that in 1969 she ran away from reform school and, looking like a "pretty delinquent boy," met her girlfriend after school: "We enter an alley. We need no words. I lean her against a wall, I put my leg between hers, she drops her book, we kiss long and hard." According to a 1959 story in the *Tribune*, a South Philly minister met two 19-year-old men on the street, invited them back to his house, and "allegedly escorted the youths to the bedroom where he made his immoral offer." Tommi Avicolli Mecca writes that the first time he "touched another boy" was when he was 12 and living in South Philly in the 1960s: "After we shoplifted a copy of *Playboy* from a drugstore (it was the only porn we could find), he took me into an alley at night and pulled down his pants." According to Elliott's 1961 study, "two Morals Squad policemen were anxious to attempt arrests in the vicinity of Broad St. and Olney Ave. where they understood that bold solicitations were being made." Fonzi's article revealed that "a street corner near Old York Road and Champlost in the Fern Rock section was a prime pick-up spot for car-cruising males." Tyrone Smith recalls going with "gay friends" to "see the boys" at civil rights demonstrations at Girard College in North Philly in the 1960s. A 1972 lesbian feminist newsletter referred to "the Market Street, 52nd Street, and 13th Street Queens." According to *City Police*, in a "white working-class neighborhood there lived a man who wore his long hair tied back with a red ribbon. He was a factory worker who . . . shared a house, which he owned, with several men. . . . He was an avowed homosexual, but he was well liked by his neighbors, who had known him most of his life. During the summer months when the neighborhood people spend a good deal of time on the streets, the patrolman would occasionally stop and chat. . . . 'He's a faggot, no question, but the neighbors like him, he lives his own life, and he don't bother nobody. So why should I fuck with him?' "[23]

Lesbians and gay men cruised and socialized on the streets in spite of the risks. In a 1958 incident, Charles Ferro and two friends met two marines, Charles Kernaghan and Richard Taylor, on Camac between Spruce and Locust around 1 a.m. After four of the men went to the nearby apartment of one of the friends, Kernaghan attacked Ferro, who later died. According to Kernaghan's account, "Ferro tries to get funny with me. I never run into anything like that before. Ferro picked up a large kitchen knife. He starts for me. But marines know how to handle this stuff, so I grabbed a rolling pin and we fenced, and I hit him on the head." Kernaghan was later acquitted on manslaughter charges. According to the *Tribune*, the South Philly minister accused the two men whom he had invited back to his home of attacking and "trying to rob him." After he called the police, the men claimed that the minister had propositioned them and the minister was arrested.[24] Roberts remembers seeing people in cars call Center City pedestrians "faggot" and throw things at them. According to Johnson, "straights" would pick up teenagers around 20th and Spruce and "take them down by the railroad tracks and kill them—rob them, rape them, and kill them."

Lesbians and gay men also encountered trouble from one another. Tyrone Smith learned not to go south of Market because "the white faggots will beat you up." Discussing the area around 13th and Locust, Henri David recalls, "I witnessed fights that were very ugly and bloody where lesbians would pummel bisexual men into the ground. I mean it was horrifying. And they did it because they knew that one of their girls had slept with one of the guys." David says "these bulls," "these creatures of the night, would appear and you had better run in terror because they would kill anything that moved." David thinks that lesbians and gay men got along in the streets "as long as there was no hanky panky."

Notwithstanding these conflicts, lesbians and gay men developed ways of using and enjoying the streets that helped them avoid and respond to the risks they faced. Smith remembers having to "cross turfs" within North Philly to visit gay friends in the 1950s and 1960s. To avoid getting beat up, Smith "learned to network": "After awhile you didn't get beat up 'cause this is so-and-so's friend. Miss A. J., that was always the name to mention. And when you came on my side, my name was the name to mention." Mecca recalls that being called "faggot," "queer," and "sissy" was part of his daily routine in South Philly in the 1960s. But he, too, developed strategies of resistance, "scurrying down alleys to avoid groups of boys on corners or walking the back route to school or taking the scenic tour of South Philadelphia's finest abandoned houses to get to the supermarket." *Plain Dealer* reported that in one week in 1970, while several gay men were beaten on Spruce and Delancey and a "gay brother was knifed in Kensington," another gay man, who was robbed at knifepoint, succeeded in "subduing his two rough trade assailants."[25]

Lesbians and gay men also risked and responded to police harassment and violence. Describing the work of the Morals Squad, Elliott's study noted, "The homosexual conduct thought disruptive to good order and morals comes from those who seek new associations in public places. They approach men on streets, in railroad and bus terminal lavatories, in movie houses and in bars." Discussing car-cruising in Fern Rock, Fonzi revealed that "police made some 20 arrests before word got out that the man on the corner was a cop." While Elliott's study reveals that apprehended men would not reveal the names of partners, Fonzi's suggests that gay men managed to get the word out that police were causing trouble in particular times and places. Noting that police decoys were usually unarmed because "an experienced homosexual cruiser will subtly frisk a potential partner," Fonzi revealed another way that gay men tried to avoid trouble.[26] Some lesbians and gay men escaped some aspects of police harassment because of family ties. Pru Chis recalls being pulled over by the police when he was "with this guy." He says that "they knew that we were queer" but at the station, after someone recognized his family name and asked whether he was related to his uncle, who had "connections," they were released.

But it was often difficult to avoid police harassment. Ray Daniels recalls an incident in the 1960s in which "two police officers in the vicinity of 20th and Spruce" picked up a man, took him "to what is now Judy Garland Park, which back then was a parking lot and a wooded area," and "beat him very, very badly." A gay man interviewed for a 1970 story in the *Bulletin* described being arrested: " 'Soliciting, hell,' he said. 'Yes, I was walking on

Locust St. Yes, and I made a pass at another guy. The cop saw it and arrested me. Would he arrest you for whistling at a girl? I call it discrimination.' " According to *City Police*, "When a policeman catches two homosexuals . . . in a car parked on a dark street, he has an almost unrestricted license to act." A gay newsletter in 1972 reported that police were driving around the Merry-Go-Round, "stopping to take identification from randomly selected pedestrians," and jailing some of them. One officer indicated that "the main purpose of the police activity was to rid the streets of homosexuals." In contexts such as these, everyday lesbian and gay life on the streets became everyday lesbian and gay resistance.[27]

Police threatened public safety not only in the ways that they responded to cruising. In a 1967 incident, African American drag queen Joseph Riley locked himself out of his apartment in West Philly and called the police to let them know that he would be breaking into his apartment. Three policemen subsequently arrived, arrested Riley for burglary, beat him with a nightstick, and broke his leg. In another incident the following year, Riley was approached by two policemen outside his apartment, forced at gunpoint to let them come inside, and coerced into having sex with them. Even in these most brutal of circumstances, gay men fought back. In 1971, a common pleas arbitration panel awarded Riley $9,000 in damages for the first incident.[28]

Lesbians also faced risks. According to Rusty Parisi, "you could be picked up by the police just looking gay walking the streets." Asked whether women were "picked up for looking too butch," Parisi responded, "Yes indeed. . . . If the cop on the beat didn't happen to like you, he'd throw you in a cell and leave you there for a couple of hours, overnight or for a week." Ada Bello remembers a woman being arrested "because she was necking with a woman in a car." McCann recalls "cat-calling" and comments such as "You want a real man?" in Center City. One of Love's sources was quoted as saying, "Most men are afraid of women who are obviously male. Their egos get smashed all over the ground. They don't particularly like seeing Billie (her butch partner) and me walking down the street when she's wearing slacks and a man's shirt." In 1968, Spencer Coxe of the Greater Philadelphia American Civil Liberties Union (ACLU) wrote that "female homosexuals" were "being stopped by cops on the street and asked for identification." In 1970, the *Bulletin* quoted Aronson as saying, "Some of us were just walking on the street, not doing anything, not even holding hands, and the cops picked us up. We were taken to three different police stations."[29]

Lesbians also developed strategies to resist harassment and violence. Marge McCann recalls, "Once I learned there were fly-button pants for girls, if I was traveling by myself, I didn't get harassed because I was dressed [as a girl]. If I was traveling with other women, then it became obvious that we were a bunch of lesbians. And if I was traveling by myself on the subway at 3 a.m., I could just kind of slouch down in my coat and pass." Fashioning gendered appearances, traveling alone and in groups, and paying attention to changing styles, times, and places, lesbians and gay men moved from their many points of origin to and through the streets of Philadelphia.

Restrooms and Transportation Stations

While there were significant convergences in the lesbian and gay geographies of parks and streets, these geographies generally diverged in public restrooms ("tearooms") and transportation stations. Public restrooms, unlike parks and streets, were often segregated by sex. And cruising areas in transportation stations were often linked with restrooms. In some contexts, sex segregation encouraged same-sex sexual encounters, but segregation generally kept lesbian and gay geographies separate. Whether lesbian encounters in these types of space were less common or less visible, they diverged geographically from their gay counterparts.

John Taylor remembers the men's rooms in the Market Street elevated train stations in West Philly as "very wild" in the 1940s and says that he "met a lot of nice people" in them, people he knows "to this day." According to a 1956 article in the *Inquirer*, "the labyrinthine turns, blind spots and side alleys" of the subway concourses provided "uncounted lurking spots for the pervert." As the *Inquirer* observed, "Sex deviates use the Broad St. Subway as an 'underground railway,' congregating wherever the Morals Squad is not, making its rest rooms convenient places of assignation, and getting away easily on passing trains when police are called." According to Elliott's 1961 study, "It is difficult to conceive of a naive and innocent heterosexual loitering long enough in the vicinity of the men's room of the Philadelphia Suburban Station to be solicited for a homosexual relationship without speculating as to his innocence and naivete, to say nothing of his pure heterosexuality." Fonzi's 1962 expose referred to gay men walking "in pairs down through the empty subway concourse," cruising "the men's rooms of the railroad and bus terminals," and frequenting the Suburban Station men's room and 30th Street Station. Greg Lee wrote in *Drummer* about having sex in the 69th Street Terminal in the 1960s. A 1972 gay guide joked that one source of information had been "stationed" at Philadelphia's Greyhound Bus Terminal when he was in the navy.[30]

Cruising in transportation stations came with risks. A 1961 correspondent to the ACLU's Spencer Coxe reported that "eight arrests have been made during the past week in the men's rest room of the Chestnut Hill Pennsylvania Railroad Station." According to Fonzi, three dozen men, including "two doctors, a lawyer, and a minister," were arrested in "a railroad station's men's room in Chestnut Hill" after police "hid in the ceiling." Discussing a 1969 incident, the *Tribune* reported that "six teenage boys dolled up in girls' clothing had a surprise date" with police at the 69th Street Terminal at around 3 a.m. on a Sunday morning. On their way home from a "ball for transvestites," the six "got the attention of a policeman" when one "lifted his skirt 'up to here' to fix his glitter stockings." Charged with "female impersonation, disorderly conduct, and disturbing the peace," the six were fined $50 plus $11 court costs each and were remanded to Broadmeadows Prison when they were unable to pay.[31]

As Fonzi noted, most "homosexual arrests" were made in Center City, "for there, as every homosexual knows, is where the 'action' is." Arrests were particularly common in the Suburban Station men's room, but were also made at 30th Street Station and the bus terminals. A 1950 gay murder suspect was identified by the *Bulletin* as having "spent most of his time in Broad Street Station." In 1951, the *Bulletin* reported that a gay extortion suspect was arrested in Broad Street Station. John Dopirak, the victim of a gay murder in 1954, received a three-month sentence in 1951 for disorderly conduct and trespassing in Broad Street Station. In 1953, according to the *Tribune*, two men were arrested after they were found in a "compromising position" on the Broad Street concourse. Whether these stories indicate patterns of police harassment of gay men, crimes against gay men, or both, they suggest that men cruised the stations in spite of the risks.[32]

An incident described in Elliott's study highlights both the risks of cruising the train stations and the ways that some men went about doing this. According to Elliott, "A plainclothes policeman detailed to the Pennsylvania Railroad's 30th Street Station sat on a bench in the vicinity of the men's room. A neatly dressed young man walked over to the policeman, grabbed his arm and told him he wanted fellatio performed on him." After he was arrested, he told the police that he was a married college student, that his wife was in her seventh month of pregnancy, and that he often came to the station and "seldom failed to find the sexual activity he sought." Elliott also reported that "police assume many cruisers will attempt to make contacts in lavatories."[33]

Transportation stations were not the only places with popular restrooms. In 1950, Judge James Crumlish reported on his discovery that "sexual perverts, because of lack of control, had become very bold and were using public toilets and other public buildings as meeting places; they operate and communicate by instincts and signs peculiar to themselves and are ever on the alert for new recruits." According to Fonzi, the men's rooms in the Stephen Girard Garage and Wanamaker's were the sites of frequent arrests. The *Bulletin* reported on the 1963 case of a man who was arrested in Wanamaker's on a morals charge and paid bail bondsman Joseph Nardello $2,500 to have the case discharged.[34] Mel Heifetz says that "all of the department store tearooms were very popular" and that "Wanamaker's and Strawbridge and Clothier were notorious." These restrooms were part of a larger gay scene. Heifetz recalls that Wanamaker's was "a very popular hangout for gay people" and that he "used to walk through Gimbels" and "invariably wind up getting picked up or picking somebody up." He says that "the department stores were all cruising grounds" and that because "a lot of queens worked in them," gay men "didn't feel threatened."

Public restrooms at Penn, Temple, and other schools were also popular. According to a 1970 gay newspaper, the administration at Penn "has conducted raids on men's rooms and lounges and closed facilities in order to harass gays." Another article referred to "the gym scene" at Penn, suggesting that this was also popular.[35] According to Kiyoshi Kuromiya, "the men's room at Houston Hall and at Logan Hall [at Penn] were active all through the 1960s and 1970s." Gus Johnson says that "everybody was screwing everybody else" in the gym and shower rooms at South Philly High in the 1960s. Discussing after-school "race riots" between African and Italian Americans, he says that "the odd thing about it was that a lot of the kids that you were having sex with were the same kids that were fighting you after school."

The YMCA also had popular tearooms. According to a 1960 report by the executive secretary of the Philadelphia-Central YMCA, there were "frequent reports of homo-sexual approaches and activity in two of our semi-public men's washrooms." Men pursued sex so actively that "house officers could not successfully control the problem" and the Y spent nearly $2,000 on closed-circuit television surveillance. Officials claimed that this reduced "traffic in these washrooms by over 50%."[36]

Gay men also cruised at ice-skating rinks. According to Heifetz, the rink at Suburban Station was "a very popular gay hangout" and "the tearoom in the Suburban Station, adjacent to that, was infamous." According to Henri David, the Penn Center ice skating rink was "very cruisy." In 1982, an article in *Harper's* by Taylor Branch described rink and restroom cruising in the 1960s. Branch wrote that Dan Bradley, the president of the Legal Services Corporation and the "highest federal official in American history to declare publicly that he was a homosexual," had been cruised at "an enclosed ice rink in an arcade beneath his hotel" in Philadelphia in 1968. When he "walked quickly upstairs into the hotel bathroom," he was "shocked to see a man standing casually waving an erect penis." Bradley then walked back to the rink and "posed nervously behind his *Inquirer*." Soon "a blond young street urchin in blue jeans and a T-shirt walked up and said, 'I'll let you suck me for five dollars.' " After the hustler repeated the proposition, Bradley accepted.[37]

Responding to harassment and violence in public restrooms and transportation stations, gay men developed strategies of resistance. Taylor remembers that bathroom "peepholes" would allow some warning about the approach of new strangers and "you didn't do anything until you were pretty sure that whoever you were with wanted to do something." According to a 1974 article in the *Inquirer*, the "preferred arrangement" for tearooms involved "two-door entrances" so that "when the outer door opens, occupants have time to cease their activities."[38]

Another strategy involved determining when to tell the truth and when to lie. Of the six queens caught by police at the 69th Street Terminal in 1969, the first two released were a "juvenile," who was turned over to the custody of his parents, and a minor, whose mother told police that he was not 18 years old, as he had claimed, but 14. For minors, telling the truth about age sometimes caused more trouble with parents but less trouble with the law. After the *Tribune* published the names of the other four, who claimed that they were 18, the mother of the 14-year-old "rounded up all the other mothers." Police then learned that all but one were under 18. The younger queens were released to their parents; the older one's mother paid her son's fine.[39]

More generally, gay men who cruised and had sex in public restrooms and transportation stations resisted harassment and violence by communicating and acting collectively. They chose locations that maximized their chances of success. Depending on what was possible and what was advantageous, they traveled alone, in pairs, or in groups. They shared warnings about, avoided, and escaped locations that they believed were too dangerous. If caught by police, they made up stories and offered money if they could and if they thought that these would help. At a basic level, gay cruising and gay sex in public places resisted those opposed to the existence and the practices of gay men and those opposed to all public cruising and public sex.

Reports occasionally surfaced that lesbians, too, were gathering in bathrooms and public facilities. According to Love's 1967 article, "Homosexuals will tell you there are cliques of gay girls and gay boys at every school in this city. . . . Women who are now in their 50s and 60s say they frequently made their first contact with other homosexuals in a Philadelphia school. . . . Run-ins with school authorities . . . are generally kept pretty quiet, but sometimes word leaks out, as it did with a suspension at an all-girls high school last spring involving a coterie that took to meeting in the pink marble shower rooms in the gym."[40] Barron recalls going regularly with "a whole bunch of lesbians" to the pool and sauna at the Germantown YWCA on "skinny-dipping night for women" in the early 1970s. Whether lesbian encounters in public restrooms, transportation stations, and other buildings were less common or less visible, lesbian and gay geographies generally diverged in these public places.

Parades

While lesbians and gay men met, socialized, cruised, and had sex in public space in every corner of the city and on every day of the year, twice a year gay drag queens paraded through the streets of Philadelphia to the cheers of thousands. Flamboyantly challenging everyday boundaries between the "private" and the "public," between "women" and "men," and between "masculinity" and "femininity," drag queens commanded attention on Halloween and New Year's Day. On at least one occasion, they did so as well on Easter; in 1971, "a man in drag won the 'best life-style expression prize' " in the Easter Parade.[41]

By the end of World War Two, Philadelphia had a long tradition of extraordinary parades, the best known of which was the New Year's Day Mummers' Parade. Organized largely by working-class Euro-American clubs, the parade featured outrageously costumed men who marched along Broad Street with extravagant floats. According to La Forest Potter's 1933 book, *Strange Loves: A Study in Sexual Abnormalities*, "for quite a number of years, the first prize has *always gone to a 'fairy,'* made up as a woman."[42] Gay drag queens continued to participate in the Mummers' Parade after World War Two. Pru Chis remembers his father talking in the late 1940s or early 1950s about "how much he enjoyed the transvestites" and about how each year two or three would die of exposure to the cold because "they dressed in these skimpy dresses." Kiyoshi Kuromiya says that the parade was "much more gay" in the 1960s and 1970s than in later years and that "five to ten thousand people, like clockwork, would show up between Pine and Broad and Locust and Broad." Joan Fleischmann remembers "the drag queens coming up Broad Street with the Mummers" in the 1960s and says that "everybody would be cheering and clapping and even the cops would be smiling." She recalls that lesbians and gay men would go to Surf, cross the parking lot to watch the parade, and then return to the bar when it got too cold: "That particular stretch of Broad Street was all gay."

During one year's parade, Fleischmann recalls, she and another woman had an argument and were thrown out of Surf by a bouncer: "And I wasn't ready to leave. And I must have been telling him so, loudly and clearly. And he had us both by the arm and he was taking us out the front door. At that point, [police commissioner Frank] Rizzo drove up. . . . And he said, 'Is this guy bothering you?' And I said something like yes." Fleischmann remembers going with Rizzo to the police station but leaving without pressing charges.

Figure 3.3. Mummers' Parade, 1960. *Philadelphia Evening Bulletin* collection. With the permission of Urban Archives, Temple University, Philadelphia, PA.

Bill Brinsfield tells a Mummers' Parade story of a more brutal Rizzo, "an absolute monster." He says that Rizzo "seemed to have an awful feeling towards lesbians" and that during one parade, "everybody was drinking," but Rizzo pulled bottles out of the hands of several lesbians and "punched" or "slapped" one of them.

While gay drag queens had a place in the Mummers' Parade, their place was preeminent on Halloween. For a number of years, drags paraded through two different neighborhoods in Center City. A predominantly Euro-American parade with predominantly Euro-American spectators took place near 13th and Locust. A predominantly African American parade with predominantly African American spectators took place on South.

According to Fonzi's 1962 article, "the 'Fags in Drag' parade" featured men who "adorned themselves in female attire and paraded in glory along Locust Street on the one night of the year when wearing female costumes was not incongruous nor illegal."[43] Brinsfield, who remembers the Locust "promenade" in the 1940s and 1950s, says that he thinks it became large, with "a hundred or hundreds" of drags, in the early 1950s. Mark Kendall recalls hearing about the parade in the 1940s and seeing it in the 1950s. Ray Daniels estimates that 50–100 drag queens participated in the 1950s. Henri

David remembers the last parade, in the early 1960s, as having "maybe two hundred" drags.

Accounts of the route of the Locust promenade conflict in some respects, but agree that in the central segment drags paraded east from Broad and Locust to 13th and Locust. Brinsfield thinks that Pirate Ship was the "focal point," but that drags would go in and out of other bars, including Allegro, Maxine's, and Forrest. Inside the bars, "They'd all scream, 'You look great' or 'What's that tacky thing you're wearing?' " Kendall remembers the drags parading on Broad, turning down Locust, and going into Maxine's and Pirate Ship. Daniels says, "The part I remember was them coming down 13th. . . . People stood outside and watched and then when the parade was over they went into the bars." He recalls that "there would be another kind of parade" in the bars, which sponsored parties and contests. In 1962, Fonzi wrote that "a number of bars even held contests for the best costume, and each year a 'Queen' was crowned." According to a retrospective 1966 account in *Drum*, "gay bar frequenters were encouraged by bar owners to dress in elaborate costumes for 'bitches Christmas [Halloween].' Some even gave prizes for originality, humor, beauty and drag."[44]

Kendall recalls that some of the outfits were expensive and that "it was not uncommon to see mink coats." Daniels remembers that some of the queens "would be up in their convertibles" and "done up to the hilt" with "piles of hair and jewels and big wide dresses and gowns." He recalls one group in which a man was dressed as a bride and had "bridesmaids, a maid of honor, a groom, the best man, the ushers." The "wedding party" included "good-looking guys" who were not "necessarily gay." Kendall says that "there's no way of knowing" but "the impression was that it was mostly gay men, if not exclusively." According to Brinsfield, "Usually they had these very masculine boyfriends . . . who were really homosexual but another kind of homosexual that never admitted it." *Drum* reported that "many homosexuals and others paraded through the center city area."[45]

Many more watched the parade. According to Kendall, "I think it was known internationally. My understanding is that there were people who came to Philadelphia from all over the world pretty much especially for that." Brinsfield says that his "mother used to go," that "thousands of people" would be there, and that many of the spectators were straight. He says that "it was so good-natured that even the straight people" did not cause trouble. What "heckling" he does remember involved "straight guys" who "would be pretending to be making a date or maybe they did—who knows?" He says, "I didn't see anything but good nature, unless they were tourists who were just there with their mouths open to their shoes and not saying anything, just in total disbelief. And it was the one time, also, that all the gays who went to bars, who still probably looked down their nose at the people who were participating in this, also were part of it. They were out there and cheering." According to Daniels, who remembers there being "about a thousand" spectators, "You stood behind the barricades and the police all stood there. They kept everything in order. And everyone was joking and laughing. There was no hostility or anything like that. And it was really a nice mixture of gay and straight people who were watching it. And people clapped and applauded the person who they thought was the best." Daniels adds, "Everybody got along. There were a lot of women there. It was a very mixed crowd." David, who remembers "a couple thousand spectators," says, "People lined Broad Street and it was mostly straight people and they were perfectly friendly and lovely. And they cheered and yelled and it was very supportive of all these drags."

Meanwhile, there was another parade of mostly African American drag queens on South. Jay Haines recalls the parade in the late 1950s and early 1960s and says that drags would "make their rounds of some of the white gay bars" and then come to the neighborhood near Nick's on South. According to Haines, the drags were "predominantly" black but included some Euro-Americans. He remembers hundreds of spectators: "They were all outside and they'd wait because the limousines would pull over and people would come out in drag. And everybody wanted to see the outfits."

According to Isabelle Fambro, "People used to congregate by Pep's and the Showboat to watch. South Street would be filled with people. All the way down South Street from 3rd or so to 18th, gays were filling the streets, really dressed. It was like the mummers. We called it 'prancing.' They would promenade up the street. And people watching were dressed in finery, too. People walked along playing the blues, everything was blues then. You could hear saxophones all night. It was mostly gay men and people had on some fine clothes."[46]

Tyrone Smith recalls watching and participating in the parades in the 1950s and early 1960s and says that the Locust event was mostly Euro-American while the South one was "basically black." Declaring that "it was like Mardi Gras," Smith says that "people would actually stand on both sides of the street behind police barricades." He remembers queens coming down Broad and parading in and out of Pep's, Showboat, and Nick's: "You'd go down to different bars on South Street, go in and out of them. Just wearing your wear, just carrying on." Smith says that "nobody was really making fun of you" and people would say "how wonderful you looked and how nice your drag was." Asked to distinguish the Mummers' and Halloween parades, Smith says that "the drag on Halloween was more, was real. It was the essence of looking real. . . . We started to see real attractive drag queens in the [Mummers']

Parade when we talk about the 1970s and 1980s. But prior to that it was just like mimicking."

Smith does recall encountering trouble on one Halloween: "I wanted a white gown with an emerald green opera coat. . . . I'd gotten the money together. We'd gotten the material. I'd taken the stuff to this girl to make it for me. And I got dressed. I was absolutely breathtakingly gorgeous and I knew it. I knew it. And I came outside and I started to walk from . . . where I got dressed up to Broad Street. And by the time I got to Broad Street, these boys had ripped everything off of me. I was standing there with nothing on but the shreds. And I cried and I went back." Noting that his attackers were straight and African American, Smith says that he was "devastated, but fierce": "I came home. I went back to this girl's house. And she was a seamstress and she had material. And I took material and draped myself and pinned it. And went out that same night. I was determined." Remembering that he successfully reached Broad and South, he says, "I wasn't gonna let them get my goat."

Accounts of the circumstances surrounding the end of the Halloween parades conflict. According to a 1962 lesbian and gay newsletter, Rizzo, as part of his "campaign against homosexuals," ruled that year that Center City bars that served impersonators would lose their licenses. Fonzi reported in 1962 that "the crowd of spectators and curiosity-seekers was beginning to become unwieldy" and that Rizzo "ordered all the bars in the neighborhood not to serve anyone in costume." While the drags stayed away, "The crowd showed up anyway and spent the evening strolling up and down Locust Street, staring closely at each female and making remarks to the 50 policemen who had been assigned to keep them moving. Some female impersonators went to parties in other parts of the city, others stayed home." In 1972, *Philadelphia Magazine* reported that in the year of the crackdown, "when a genuine transvestite in high heels and blonde wig . . . showed up at 13th and Locust, there was a virtual stampede" and "that was the last year the crowds came to Locust Street on Halloween." In 1966, *Drum* offered an account less critical of the police, who were reportedly "tolerant of the situation until the parade began to attract hostile spectators who were more inclined to hoot and toss debris—some brought just for the occasion—than they were to appreciate the costumers' effort and skill." According to *Drum*, "In 1962, violence and tension rose to near-riot proportions. Not without justification, the Philadelphia Police called for a cessation of the illegal and dangerous activities. The solution to all the problem appeared to be the banning of costumed bar-going."[47]

Gay narrators similarly offer conflicting accounts. Brinsfield recalls that Rizzo "forbade anybody to be in drag on Halloween" and he remembers

Figure 3.4. Tyrone Smith, c. 1962. Courtesy of Tyrone Smith.

"posters in the Allegro that said 'No Drags Allowed.'" Responding to the notion that police were acting in response to violence, Brinsfield says, "Well they had to have some excuse." He adds that he "never saw any street violence": "I never saw anything but good cheer and good will. And maybe late, late at night fights would break out or break out in the bars, but not in the early evenings when these promenades took place." Daniels says that "the rumor was that it had gotten too big and someone in City Hall or the vice squad or whatever had said, 'Hey, this is too much.'"

David's account presents the police in a more positive light. Remembering the last parade, he recalls, "Everything was cool on Broad Street until it turned down Locust. And unfortunately gangs had come down that year looking for trouble. Whereas before it was people looking for a good time, now this was trouble. And what I witnessed as the finale, as the end of the parade, was this gang of kids jumping on a black drag queen with like seven of them or something. Totally unfair. She's fighting for her life and Rizzo steps in. . . . He saved this queen. Sort of shoved her out of the way, kicked all the guys down into the ground, and broke everything up. And that was it." He concludes, "They stopped it for their own good. They stopped it so that there wouldn't be any more trouble."

Despite the best efforts of hostile spectators and police, Halloween lesbian and gay street revelry did not end in 1962. Becky Davidson, who lived on Camac in the early 1970s, remembers, "You could hang out the front window on Halloween and New Year's and just have a show for the evening." On Halloween, she says, "People would show up either walking down the street or coming out of the cab with all kinds of costumes." Also discussing later years, Kuromiya says, "Halloween used to be a real event, every bit as exciting as Halloween is in West Hollywood or in New Orleans. . . . People would dress up or not, do outrageous impromptu parades in cars and convertibles. People would ride around on the hoods of cars and walk down the street kissing strangers." While one set of lesbian and gay public traditions ended, others took their place.

Separately and together, lesbian and gay Philadelphians developed vibrant public worlds, just as they developed vibrant residential and commercial ones. Geographically converging and diverging, they created heterosocial cultures that they shared and homosocial cultures that they did not. Among the more heterosocial elements of lesbian and gay cultures were the cross-sex relationships that lesbians and gay men developed; the residential neighborhoods in which they both concentrated; the parties that they both attended; the commercial districts that they both favored; the bars, clubs, restaurants, and other businesses that they both patronized; and the parks, streets, and other public places that they both frequented. Among the more homosocial elements of lesbian and gay cultures were the same-sex relationships that lesbians and gay men developed; the households that one sex or the other formed; the parties that one sex or the other attended; the bars, clubs, restaurants, and other businesses that one sex or the other patronized; and the parks, streets, and other public places that one sex or the other frequented.

Geographic convergences and divergences shaped and were shaped by ideas about similarities and differences between lesbians and gay men. Geographic proximity was both cause and effect of the idea that lesbians and gay men were similar. Geographic distance was both cause and effect of the idea that lesbians and gay men were different. But proximity could also be linked with difference (as when lesbians and gay men experienced one another as different) and distance could also be linked to similarity (as when lesbian and gay worlds seemed separate but parallel). Lesbians and gay men often thought of themselves as similar insofar as both of their cultures embraced same-sex sexual desires. But they often thought of themselves as different insofar as lesbians were women and gay men were men. They often thought of themselves as similar insofar as gender transgressions were important components of their cultures. But they often thought of themselves as different insofar as these components linked lesbians with masculinity but linked gay men with femininity. Whether they favored the notion that lesbians and gay men were similar or different, they resisted the hegemony of heterosexuality while reproducing the hegemony of sex.

For some lesbians and gay men, the convergences and similarities between their cultures were more significant; for others, the divergences and differences were. For most lesbians and gay men, neither total separation nor total integration was possible or desirable. Whether the occasion was a Halloween party on South Street, a birthday party in Rittenhouse Square, a ballgame in a park, or a game of seduction on Spruce Street, lesbian and gay Philadelphians created "exuberantly diverse" worlds. Using "many facilities in common," though often "for different purposes," they helped build a "fantastically dynamic" city of women and men.

PART TWO

Public Cultures, 1945–1960

4

"The Most Fabulous Faggot in the Land"

"In an examination of attitudes toward the homosexual," University of Pennsylvania psychiatry professor Samuel Hadden declared in 1956, "it might be well to inspect the homosexual's attitude toward himself." Speaking at a meeting of the Pennsylvania Psychiatric Society after nearly 30 years of "treating" homosexuals, Hadden noted that "from recent literature released by homosexual sympathizers it is obvious that the homosexual, like many an alcoholic, hates psychiatrists but, unlike the alcoholic, he rejects the idea of being considered sick or neurotic." Hadden, who was also chief of neuropsychiatry at Philadelphia's Presbyterian Hospital, added that the homosexual "bitterly resents his acts being labeled as criminal, and would prefer being regarded as a special kind of individual, extraordinarily endowed." Granting that "many extremely talented homosexuals have made great contributions to the arts and sciences," Hadden took issue with those who "would have us believe that they are *all* Platos, Andre Gides, or, at least, Oscar Wildes."[1]

The following year, at the annual American Psychiatric Association meeting, Hadden described a similar conflict in perspectives. Three years earlier, he had formed a therapy group with three gay men. According to Hadden, "Ben" announced at the outset that "any psychotherapeutic efforts would be wasted because homosexuality was so attractive to him that nothing could influence him to give it up." He had "set up an 'establishment' in the appropriate zone of the city and entered into the 'gay' life with zest." Ben told the group that his "great ambition" was to be "the most fabulous faggot in the land." "Tom," who was " 'married' to a wealthy young physician," was "equally emphatic about his intention to remain a homosexual" and abandoned Hadden when his friends "issued an ultimatum because they feared exposure."[2]

Although Hadden claimed that Ben and "Bill" became "motivated to change" after "the murder and dismemberment of a sailor by a homosexual" known by all three men, Hadden's account laid bare a dynamic cultural contest over the meanings of same-sex sexualities. In opposition to the views held by Ben, Tom, and their friends, Hadden offered perspectives developed within the psychiatric community. In his therapy groups, Hadden asserted, "the rationalization that homosexuality is a pattern of life they wish to follow is destroyed by their fellow homosexuals." Given the fact that many of his patients had been referred to him by the courts and offered the options of therapy or prison, Hadden's claims of success may have been overstated. Convincing Hadden that they had been "cured" was a good way for his charges to escape the punishments of law and psychiatry.[3]

Neither Hadden nor his patients fought this contest alone. Temple psychiatry professors O. Spurgeon English and Gerald Pearson wrote in 1937 that "treatment for fully developed homosexuality is almost impossible" because "the individual is too content with the homosexuality." In 1945, they noted that the homosexual "complains that society does not give approval to homosexual activity, yet at the same time he is quite satisfied with his means of gratification." In her 1953 book, *The Sex Paradox*, Philadelphia lawyer Isabel Drummond wrote that "most homosexuals don't seek treatment and don't want to be cured." Three years later, Penn psychiatrists Edward Strecker and Vincent Lathbury reported that one of their patients, 25-year-old "Beatrice," told them, "You might as well know the truth! I'm a homosexual and I like it. It doesn't bother me a bit and I don't want any treatment for it."[4]

Although Hadden celebrated his treatment triumphs, his work revealed that "the homosexual's attitude" often challenged dominant society's. As George Chauncey has argued, it is a mistake to place too much weight on the role of elite discourse in shaping lesbian and gay identities and communities. Chauncey writes that "medical discourse did not 'invent' the homosexual; doctors did not create new categories on which people based their identities."[5] More often than not, elites responded to the existence of vibrant lesbian and gay communities, rather than catalyze their creation or direct their development. That said, dominant society's rhetoric, both popular and elite, did influence the conditions of lesbian and gay life. Published texts especially had a breadth of circulation, a level of cultural authority, and a degree of material permanence that most other types of public and private utterances lacked. Offering partial and distorted reflections of lesbian and gay cultures, published texts nevertheless affected lesbians and gay men in significant ways.

The three chapters in part 2 examine publications that emerged from various spheres of public struggle, including science, religion, law, and media. While lesbian and gay voices made themselves heard within these texts, voices that were not specifically lesbian or gay were usually dominant. While the lesbian and gay voices suggest some of the ways that lesbians and gay men publicly resisted their oppression in the years before a locally organized homophile movement took shape, the other voices reveal some of the forces against which lesbians and gay men acted. Together, these chapters show that same-sex sexuality was a frequently discussed topic in Philadelphia print culture between 1945 and 1960. While local print culture focused on a narrow range of same-sex sexualities, rarely presented positive images of lesbians and gay men, and usually presented same-sex sexualities in relation to crime, violence, pedophilia, perversion, subversion, deviance, abnormality, sin, immorality, psychopathology, and/or disease, same-sex sexuality was a significant public issue.

Notwithstanding the case of Beatrice, these chapters also show that same-sex sexualities were constructed in dominant discourse as more male than female. As part 1 suggests, this was not because Philadelphia lacked lesbian cultures. In part, it reflected the ways that lesbian geographies were constituted as more "private," gay geographies more "public." In part, it reflected the tendency of dominant discourse to focus on men and to conceive of sexual agency as male. While cultural links between same-sex sexualities and gender inversion might have led dominant discourse to focus on lesbians as much as or more than on gay men, the primary determinant of public attention was sex, not gender.

The remainder of this chapter presents a collage of images of same-sex sexualities that were perceived and produced in Philadelphia. While the texture of such images differed depending upon whether they were seen in the popular, scientific, or legal press, and while the images took conservative and liberal forms, nearly all shared a fundamental characteristic: same-sex sexualities appeared to be primarily male. As parts 3 and 4 will show, this is not to suggest that such images were not thought to apply to, did not affect, or were not read or seen by lesbians. As Esther Newton has argued, gay men have been on the "lesbian horizon," and "occupy both object . . . and subject positions in American life whenever homosexuality comes up, a near-hegemony which, despite the efforts and effects of separatism, lesbians have not been able to elude or entirely escape."[6] Nor is this to suggest that there were no lesbian images available in nationally and internationally circulating publications that located same-sex sexualities in places other than Philadelphia. These publications were important, but the lesbian images that they offered had much in common with the local images discussed in this chapter.[7] And nonlocal images often allowed Philadelphia readers to place and displace same-sex sexualities outside the local environment. What this chapter does show is that (1) local print discourse on same-sex sexualities in Philadelphia focused primarily on men, and (2) while male same-sex sexualities were often discussed without reference to their female counterparts, female same-sex sexualities were almost always defined in relation to their male counterparts.

Male Same-Sex Sexualities

More than 200 years after Benjamin Franklin helped establish Philadelphia as a colonial publishing capital, the city remained a vital media center. After the demise of the *Record* in 1947, Philadelphia was home to three major newspapers: the *Evening Bulletin*, *Inquirer*, and *Daily News*. In the late 1940s and early 1950s, the *Bulletin*'s circulation was around 700,000, the *Inquirer*'s around 650,000 (except on Sundays, when it doubled), and the *News*'s around 150,000. The twice-weekly *Tribune*, African American owned and oriented, had a circulation around 11,000.[8]

From their earliest post–World War Two coverage of same-sex sexualities, Philadelphia newspapers focused on men and boys. The most dramatic stories concerned a series of gay murders. In 1949, the press reported extensively on the killing of 12-year-old Ellis Simons of West Philly by 16-year-old Seymour Levin of suburban Wynnefield. Several days after the murder, the *Inquirer* stated that Levin's motive was "obscure" but that Simons had been "nude" when the homicide occurred. Linking the case to a 1933 murder that had involved "an act of degeneracy," the *Inquirer* implied that something of this nature was involved in the Simons murder. The *News* quoted officials who said that the killing was "a sex murder" and that their investigation of "Levin's alleged perversion" had linked his case to "the ill-fated Leopold-Loeb case." Soon thereafter, the *News* revealed that Levin had initiated other boys into a "strange flagellation cult." According to the *News*, officials accused "the comic-crime book addict" of having "lured" Simons to his home, subsequently committing "the most sadistic crime in Philadelphia police history" with a knife and scissors "in the climax of a pervert act." Five weeks later, at the beginning of Levin's trial, the *Bulletin* referred to the presence of sperm on Simons's body and the commission of an "unnatural act." After Levin pleaded guilty, a team of psychiatrists declared him a "constitutional psychopathic inferior" with "sadistic, homosexual impulses." The court ruled that the defendant had committed "an act of perverted sexual lust" and sentenced him to life.[9]

Estelle Freedman has described "two major sex crime panics—roughly from 1937 to 1940 and from 1949 to 1955," when, "after a series of brutal and apparently sexually motivated child murders, major urban newspapers expanded and, in some cases, sensationalized their coverage of child molestation and rape." In Philadelphia, the 1949 media frenzy encouraged 10,000 "curious persons," including "souvenir" seekers and a "balloon vendor," to visit the murder scene. Various groups called for action. According to the Junior Chamber of Commerce, proposals ranged from "burning comic books" to "sterilization," and included "permanent imprisonment, better sex hygiene courses in public schools, abolition of crime movies and comic books, issuance of gun permits to women, additional police squads, more playgrounds, abolition of parole or shortening of jail sentences, psychiatric treatment of first offenders and medical treatment."[10]

Shortly after the murder, the press reported that three state assembly members had introduced a bill "to keep sex psychopaths in institutions for life." Three years later, Governor John Fine signed legislation permitting courts to order psychiatric examinations and "indeterminate sentences" for certain types of sex offenders. Further measures were proposed in 1956 after Carl Jackson "pleaded no defense to charges of public indecency and solicitation to commit morals offenses" with "22 victims, mostly young children." Outraged by a reduction in Jackson's bail, 100 residents of Tacony and Mayfair demanded action, prompting a state senator to introduce a measure to deny bail to sex offenders.[11]

Meanwhile, the media strengthened the links that it had made between male same-sex sexualities and murders. In 1950, the press reported that Robert Prado, a police clerk who lived in Center City, had been found "naked" and dead, the victim of an "ice pick slaying." According to the *Inquirer*, Prado, a Mexican-born U.S. citizen, was a "bachelor" and police believed that the case had a "sex angle." Officials soon caught their two "swarthy" suspects, "an unemployed restaurant worker" and "a jobless farmhand." After reporting that both men were "unemployed Puerto Ricans," the *Bulletin* announced that they had been released and that police had turned their attention to "a migratory farm worker from Puerto Rico," who also was soon released.[12]

Even in the absence of an explicit "sex angle," the media hinted that same-sex sexualities were involved in other murder cases. Later in 1950, the *Inquirer* reported that Richard Rosen, a "cripple," had been found dead, the victim of a "vicious beating" in a Center City hotel, where he had gone with another man "to visit two young men." According to the *Bulletin*, police were holding "an unemployed short order cook."[13] Just days after Rosen's death, the papers reported on the "mysterious" murder of John Simpson, who had been found "unclad and dead" in a hotel near the West Philly home that he shared with his wife and son. According to a witness, Simpson had come to the hotel with a man whom he "described" as his "nephew."[14] Early the following year, the *Bulletin* announced that police were questioning a Reading, Pennsylvania, man about Prado's and Rosen's deaths. The suspect had been arrested on the complaint of a man who claimed that the suspect had extorted $750 from him.[15] In 1953, the press reported that former Democratic ward committee chairman and "bachelor" Edgar Clymer had been stabbed to death. Known as the "Mayor of Chinatown," Clymer was killed in the apartment he shared with "another bachelor."[16] Later that year, Philadelphians learned about the beating-murder of Elmer Schroeder, a lawyer and international soccer official, in his West Philly apartment. Repeatedly describing Schroeder as "unmarried" and a "bachelor," the papers traced the investigation of Schroeder's male "roommate" and other "young men" with whom Schroeder had been seen. Witnesses reportedly saw Schroeder in the Forrest bar several days before his body was discovered. The *News* referred to "striking parallels" with the Rosen and Clymer murders: "Circumstances of all three slayings indicate that the murderer of each man had been on fairly intimate terms with each victim." After initial suspicions centered on Basil Kingsley Beck, who was captured after being placed on the FBI's "Ten Most Wanted" list, police arrested Thomas Chester Wetling, Jr., a sailor stationed in Rhode Island. In 1957, Wetling was tried and found not guilty.[17]

These cases were also linked to the 1954 murder and dismemberment of John Dopirak, a Jenkintown, Pennsylvania, restaurant worker, merchant seaman, and Air Force veteran who had lived at the Seamen's Church Institute in Center City. Confessing to the crime was "mad butcher" and "torso killer" Francis X. Ballem of Bywood, Pennsylvania. Describing Dopirak as a "regular" in Center City bars, the press reported that Ballem claimed that he had met Dopirak in Center City and that the two had gone to the Essex Hotel Bar together. After Ballem confessed, police questioned him about the murders of Clymer, Prado, Rosen, and Schroeder. During Ballem's trial, witnesses claimed that they had seen Ballem and Dopirak together in bars in the city's "tenderloin" and in the Gay Nineties Cafe. In 1955, a Delaware County jury convicted Ballem of murdering Dopirak and sentenced him to death. Three years later, Governor George Leader commuted the sentence to life in prison.[18]

Just before Leader did so, the press provided news of yet another gay murder. In August 1958, Charles Ferro, a Bucks County man, was found dead in the Spruce Street apartment of a friend. A marine stationed at the Philadelphia Naval Base, Charles Kernaghan, was charged with the homicide. At his trial, Kernaghan claimed that Ferro had made "immoral advances." Found not guilty of manslaughter on grounds of self-defense, Kernaghan was convicted on charges of assault and battery against Ferro's friend, for which he received a suspended sentence. The California-based homophile magazine *One* concluded that Kernaghan's defenders "could sleep safely in their beds now that one more alleged queer was safely dead."[19]

Throughout this period, the press linked male same-sex sexualities with nonviolent crimes and immoral acts as well. In 1947, the *Inquirer* announced that local hero "Big Bill Tilden, once the greatest tennis player," had been sentenced to nine months at hard labor for contributing to the delinquency of a minor in a California "sex offense." The *News* noted that the "father of pro tennis" had been found in a car with a 14-year-old boy. In a 1948 autobiography, Tilden described his "schoolboy-ish relationship" with the "lad." Admitting only to letting the boy drive his car and "horseplay," Tilden argued that "in all branches of athletics which throw the same sex together constantly and intimately, with strong, close friendships growing up often based at least in part on admiration for physical perfection, an attraction may arise almost like that of love." The result was "occasional relationships somewhat away from the normal," but "in frequent instances creative, useful and even great human beings have known such relationships." "If anything," this was "an illness," which called for psychiatric rather than legal measures. Declaring himself "healed by rehabilitation," Tilden wrote that "greater tolerance and wider education on the part of the general public concerning this form of sex relationship is one of the crying needs of our times."[20]

The following year, the press reported that Tilden had been brought up on another California morals charge for "contributing to the delinquency of a 16-year-old boy" and had been sentenced to a year in jail for violating his probation. According to a 1975 *Sports Illustrated* feature, Tilden was released in December 1949, "just days before the Associated Press half-century poll voted him the greatest athlete in his sport." After his arrests, Tilden's alumni

Figure 4.1. William Tilden and John B. Kelly, Sr., 1945. *Philadelphia Inquirer* collection. With the permission of Urban Archives, Temple University, Philadelphia, PA.

files at Penn were "purged" and his pictures were "stripped from the walls at Germantown Cricket Club," where he had learned to play tennis.[21]

The local African American press also depicted male same-sex sexualities as criminal and immoral. In 1953, the *Tribune* reported on morals charges against a South Philly teacher and an AWOL Fort Dix, New Jersey, sergeant who had been found together in a "compromising position" on the Broad Street concourse. Two years later, the *Tribune* announced that the acting pastor of Nazarene Baptist Church had been "accused of homosexual tendencies" and had resigned. In 1959, the *Tribune* reported that a South Philly minister was being held on bail after "two youths charged he propositioned them immorally." According to the arresting officer, the minister "asked Christ to 'smite these persons who claim a man of God is queer.' "[22]

Meanwhile, the local medical and legal press published articles that discussed male same-sex sexualities in relation to deviance, illness, and crime.[23] In 1956, when *Philadelphia Medicine* published four papers that had been presented at a symposium called "Homosexuality and Sex Deviants" at the College of Physicians in Center City, the focus was on men. In the first, for example, Penn psychiatry professor Philip Roche "sketched some of the patterns of child rearing we find in male homosexuality," which he referred to as a "deviation," a "distortion," a symptom of "passive femininity," and a "neurotic behavior."[24] Three years later, at the annual meeting of the American Psychiatric Association, which was held in Philadelphia, the local medical community learned about the work of South African behavior therapy pioneer Joseph Wolpe. In their paper, "Recovery from Sexual Deviations," Wolpe and Ian Stevenson discussed three male cases, two of which concerned same-sex sexualities. In all three cases, the doctors claimed that they helped their patients "return to normal heterosexual behavior." In 1965, Wolpe became a professor of psychiatry at Temple and the Eastern Pennsylvania Psychiatric Institute. In a 1966 book, Wolpe and Arnold Lazarus described their use of electroshock aversion therapy on men: "The patient is given a painful shock in the presence of a homosexual image on a screen and then a heterosexual picture is flashed onto the screen in temporal contiguity with the cessation of the shock. Homosexual associations thus become anxiety-generating (and result in avoidance response), whereas heterosexual stimuli become conditioned to anxiety relief (and acquire approach valences)." Celebrated for his accomplishments, in 1979 Wolpe won the American Psychological Association's Distinguished Scientific Award for the Applications of Psychology.[25]

Many of the articles in the local legal press concerned sex law reform. Since 1939, Pennsylvania's punishment for sodomy had been 1–10 years in prison and/or a $5,000 fine. Compared to other states, this was relatively liberal. While two states had no penalties for sodomy in the early 1950s, Pennsylvania was among six states that offered the possibility of fines without prison. Pennsylvania also was in a group of 14 states with maximum prison penalties of 10 years (24 states had longer maximum penalties). Section 4501 of the Pennsylvania Penal Code on sodomy stated that "whoever carnally knows in any manner any animal or bird, or carnally knows any male or female person by the anus or by or with the mouth, or whoever voluntarily submits to such carnal knowledge, is guilty of sodomy."[26]

While the sodomy law theoretically applied to both men and women, reports in the local legal press revealed that it was used almost exclusively against men. In 1950, the *Legal Intelligencer* reported on the creation of a neuropsychiatric department in the Quarter Sessions Court. "It seems that the increasing number of sex offenders has caused the Police Department some concern," Judge James Crumlish explained, "and has necessitated the formation of a new squad known as the 'morals squad.' The average number of arrests in cases of this type in Philadelphia per month is about 100 and is said to be on the increase." Assistant district attorney Norris Barratt claimed that arrests of sex offenders had recently doubled, estimating monthly arrests at over 200. Describing procedures that Crumlish had begun using, Barratt reported that more than 100 recent defendants had waived hearings, grand jury indictments, and jury trials. Relying on psychiatrist Winifred Bayard Stewart's recommendations, Crumlish had been able "to intelligently dispose of a large number of cases in a morning." Of the 119 defendants so disposed, 99 were charged with sodomy, 8 with solicitation to commit sodomy, 3 with indecent exposure, 7 with sodomy upon minor boys, and 2 with indecent assault on girls. Eighty-five pleaded guilty, 17 were found guilty, and 15 were found not guilty (the outcomes of the other 2 were not described). Of the 102 who pleaded or were found guilty, 10 received prison sentences, 1 was hospitalized, 27 had their sentences suspended, and 64 were given "probation for neuropsychiatric treatment."[27]

Stewart's report, published in the same issue of the *Intelligencer*, revealed that the 119 defendants were diverse in many ways but that all were men. Their ages ranged from 18 to 76; more than a third were married; 25 were fathers. The 119 included 92 "white," 27 "colored," 54 Protestants, 48 Catholics, 12 Jews. (The percentages of African Americans [23%] and Catholics [40%] were higher, the percentage of Jews [10%] lower, than in the overall population of Philadelphia, which was approximately 18% African American, 33% Catholic, and 12% Jewish in 1950.) The largest occupational group was clerks (24%), followed by skilled mechanics (20%), laborers (13%), students (10%), and waiters or food handlers (10%). Less represented were higher-status groups, such as professionals (7), the arts (2), and business (2). The remainder were categorized as unemployed (6), relief (2), hospital orderlies (5), merchant seamen (2), and tailor (1).[28]

More so than the popular press, the legal and medical press presented challenges to some elements of the popular consensus on same-sex sexualities. For example, Stewart emphasized that 100 of the 119 defendants had been arrested for "consensual" sodomy. She also noted that 82 of them had been eligible for the draft in World War One or Two. Of these, 58–62% had served in the military; 2 had received "blue discharges" for homosexuality. Of the 35 who did not serve, 3 were "classified as 4F for homosexuality," 16 for "physical defects." On this point, Stewart concluded that "the excellent service records of the majority of these men makes one question the wisdom of the inflexible rule of the military services that homosexuality disqualifies a man for service." While stressing that most of the men were fit for the military, however, she made clear that she did not regard them all as fit: she diagnosed more than a third of the 119 with "organic and functional pathology."[29]

By 1956, Stewart's neuropsychiatry program had handled hundreds of men accused of sodomy-related crimes. In one of the 1956 College of Physicians papers published in *Philadelphia Medicine*, Michael von Moschzisker praised the program, which he declared was "in the vanguard of the movement to treat homosexuals with compassion." Between March 1951 and September 1955, 827 people had been processed by Stewart's department (a rate of 15 per month). Of these, 775 had been charged with sodomy, 52 with solicitation to commit sodomy. "Only" 45, the majority "involved with minors" or "chronic offenders," had been sentenced to prison. Only 52 had been found not guilty. A later study revealed that between 1955 and 1965, 2,000 male probationers, 80% of whom were sex offenders, were "treated" in a Philadelphia General Hospital program that was affiliated with the Quarter Sessions Court neuropsychiatry department. In a sample of 92 of these probationers, 44% had committed sodomy or solicitation to commit sodomy; 48% were "white"; 52% were "Negro." African Americans accused of sodomy-related crimes were particularly vulnerable to local psychiatric "compassion."[30]

Meanwhile, in 1952 the *Intelligencer* and *University of Pennsylvania Law Review* published articles on the state's new sex crime legislation (passed after the sensational stories of the Levin-Simons murder). According to the *Law Review*, while 14 states had passed sexual psychopath or related laws since 1938, Pennsylvania's Sex Offender Act of 1951 was different because it provided for criminal rather than civil commitment proceedings. Judges were permitted to order psychiatric evaluations and impose indeterminate life sentences for those convicted on charges of incest, indecent assault, rape, sodomy, assault with intent to commit sodomy, and solicitation to commit sodomy, when "any such person, if at large, constitutes a threat of bodily harm to members of the public, or is an habitual offender and mentally ill."[31]

Even more so than in the case of Stewart's article in the *Intelligencer*, the *Law Review*'s discussion of the Sex Offender Act challenged some tenets of antigay orthodoxy. Arguing against the new law, the journal asserted that "almost all of the foregoing protections against medical, judicial or administrative abuse are wiped out." Pointing out the "very limited extent of present psychiatric knowledge about sexual deviation," the *Review* also challenged the notion that sex crimes were increasing and declared that "the growing concern rather appears to be the product of newspaper publicity." The article condemned in particular the implications for homosexual "consensual sodomists," declaring that in this area the law violated "basic concepts of justice." Although critical of the new legislation, the article declared that "the reduction of the number of homosexuals to a minimum is desirable." To accomplish this, the author favored research and treatment experiments and singled out for praise the Quarter Sessions Court neuropsychiatric program.[32]

After Pennsylvania's new law, which came to be known as the Barr-Walker Act, had been in place for several years, state reports on its results showed that it was being used principally against male sodomites. A 1957 Pennsylvania Bureau of Correction report by John Yeager revealed that the bureau had processed 38 Barr-Walker cases. (An additional 10 had been committed to the Farview State Hospital and a total of 175 had been processed by the Department of Welfare.) Sixty-three percent of the bureau's cases were sodomy-related. Although he noted that "females are eligible for commitment" under the act, Yeager stated that "to date, no female has been received in the Bureau of Correction as a Barr-Walker Case" and only three women had been processed under Barr-Walker by the Department of Welfare.[33]

Like Stewart's report, Yeager's analysis put forward images of sex offenders that varied in many ways but not in terms of sex. Eighty-four percent of the bureau's Barr-Walker commitments were described as "Caucasian," 16% as "Negro." All of the "Negroes" were committed "for acts involving homosexuality." Although Yeager did not present his statistics in this way, 21% of the sodomy-related cases were African American, much higher than the 6–8% of state residents who were African American in the 1950s. Of the sodomy-related cases, 80% were Protestant, 17% were Catholic, and 4% were Jewish; 63% had never been married; 25% were unskilled, 21% were semiskilled, 21% were "confined," 17% worked in clerical/sales, 13% were skilled, and 4% were "youth"; 58% had served in the military. Yeager's report grouped the cases into three types: "habitual sex offenders," the "casual, occasional, personally maladjusted sex offender," and "homosexuals with characterlogical problems." Of the 64 "known victims," 67% were male, but "most of the Sodomy's 'victims' were actually accomplices in homosexual gangs." Yeager concluded that "the male victims essentially were participants in the offenses" while "the female victims were essentially 'accidental.'" Largely because of the homosexual cases, Yeager concluded that "a good 40% of B-W's committed to date are in no way dangerous sex offenders" and "the number of homosexuals processed under the Act seems disproportionate."[34]

In 1960, the College of Physicians joined the Philadelphia Psychiatric Society and the County Medical Society to sponsor "A Symposium on the Problem of the Sexual Criminal." The program attracted an audience of 450 and was chaired by Philip Roche, the president of the Psychiatric Society. John Davis, Pennsylvania commissioner of mental health, analyzed the first 139 Barr-Walker cases that his department had reviewed. Of these, 85 were for sodomy, 25 for solicitation to commit sodomy, and 2 for assault with attempt to commit sodomy. The most common outcome was referral to the penal system (67), followed by court discretion under other statutes (34), county prisons (17), state mental hospitals (13), institution for defective delinquents (7), and industrial school (1). According to Davis, in some counties "the Act was freely invoked in breaking up homosexual coteries" and in several instances superintendents of state mental hospitals were "confronted with 20 to 40 cases at one time." Davis explained that "the Department was inclined to recommend that the cases were not suitable within the intent of the Act" and "practically 50% were screened out." In general, "disposition under other statutes" was recommended for "average passive homosexuals who had no other pathological leanings."[35]

Several speakers at the symposium challenged the Barr-Walker Act. Penn sociology professor Marvin Wolfgang discussed problems in defining the "dangerous" sexual criminal. Limiting that category to those who used force and adults who exploited children, Wolfgang argued that "homosexual acts between consenting males aged at least 21 should no longer be punished." Using the 1957 Bureau of Correction statistics, Wolfgang argued that only 10 of the 39 Barr-Walker cases were dangerous. Critical of "legislation that places so much responsibility on the imprecision and inefficiency of present public administrative agencies," Wolfgang indicted the act for targeting homosexuals. He concluded, "The potential yoke of a life sentence for commission of an act like homosexuality . . . performed without violence or dangerous threat to the community, I think, is excessive punishment." Charles Frazier, chairman of the board of Pennsylvania Mental Health, added that he knew of "no empirical evidence showing that psychiatrists have that high degree of reliability of prediction of future dangerousness which I think we must as a society demand before we turn over the keys to freedom to even so humanitarian a profession."[36]

Later reports revealed that by the end of 1961, of the 94 Barr-Walker cases sentenced to state correctional institutions or mental hospitals, half were sodomy-related. Philadelphia County accounted for the largest number (18); Delaware County, which was in Greater Philadelphia, was second (11). Of the 47 sodomy-related cases, 89% were "White," 11% were "Negro," 68% were Protestant, 30% were Catholic, 2% were Jewish, 49% had a history of military service, 85% had not used force. Commitments under Barr-Walker continued until the Pennsylvania Superior Court ruled the sentencing portion of the act unconstitutional in 1967.[37]

Murderers and murdered, criminals and criminalized, ill and ill-treated, gay men in the press were also subversives and subverted. In May 1950, the *Inquirer* reported on a U.S. Senate resolution calling for an investigation of "the employment of degenerates by the Federal Government." The following month, the *News* referred to "91 'deviates' fired by the State Department." Late in 1950, the *News* reported on the "exposure of a 'sex deviate'" in the office of U.S. Senator Joseph McCarthy, a leading antigay and anticommunist campaigner. The next day, the *Bulletin* stated that a Senate committee "described perverts as easy marks for foreign spies and said many federal agencies have been lax about routing such perverts from government jobs." Three days later, Representative Robert Rich of Pennsylvania announced in the U.S. Congress that he had just read an article about "sexual perverts in the employ of the Government." Having "never thought there were so many homosexuals in the whole United States," Rich called for a "thorough housecleaning." In 1955, the *Bulletin* reported that the Eisenhower administration had dropped from the federal payroll 655 people accused of "sex perversion."[38]

Even when gay men in the local press were not at risk of being murdered, arrested, treated, or fired, they were still in danger of being labeled abnormal or deviant. In 1959, for example, the press reviewed a German film, "The Third Sex," being shown in Center City. According to the *News*, the film told the story of an "artistic youth tottering on the brink of abnormality." The young male protagonist develops a "strong attachment" to a male classmate and is then "attracted into a homosexual orbit surrounding a wealthy art patron." The youth's mother, following a doctor's advice to encourage "a love affair with a woman," seeks the "aid of the family maid, an orphan." When the youth's father complains to the police about the patron, the latter retaliates by bringing "formal charges of procuring" against the mother. According to the *News*, the film avoided "sensationalism" and was "a powerful drama involving very real and human people." The *Inquirer* interpreted the film differently. In its review, the youth, portrayed by a "good-looking youngster" and depicted as "easy prey to misunderstanding," was juxtaposed with "definite deviates," including a "girl-hating, jealous friend." The *Inquirer* concluded that the film was a "courageous effort to deal understandingly with the subject of homosexuality." More critically, the *Bulletin* argued that "the question of whether homosexuality is a suitable subject for the screen earns a negative answer." "All too sensational," the film used a "clinical approach" that was "an obvious attempt at achieving respectability." Suggesting that the film displayed "limited medical knowledge," the *Bulletin* concluded that it was "out to capitalize on the sordid curiosity of a minority audience."[39]

Philadelphians also read about male same-sex sexualities in local social science scholarship. In 1944, C. A. Weslager of the Archaeological Society of Delaware contributed to the long-standing debate about how the Native American Delaware (also known as the Lenni Lenape) had come to be called a tribe of women. According to Weslager, the Delaware's "subjugation" by the Five Nations Iroquois was "linked with sexual connotations, real and symbolical." He continued, "Whether the figurative deprivation of the Delaware of their male accoutrements, both physiological and cultural, had its origin in literal practices remains unknown." Referring to "the institution of the berdache or transvestite," which was "well known" among Native Americans on the Plains, Weslager concluded that "the feminizing of the Delaware, which follows similar lines of thought, is the outstanding recorded instance of its kind in the East" and "probably the only time that the rite was so institutionalized as to affect the status of an entire tribal group."[40]

Two scholars from Penn contributed to this debate as well. In a 1946 issue of the *Pennsylvania Magazine of History and Biography*, Frank Speck argued that since the Delaware believed that women were "superior social and political forces in respect to the making and keeping of peace," they regarded their feminized status as "a mark of the respect they expected" and not of subjugation. The following year, an article by Anthony Wallace in *Pennsylvania Archaeologist* discussed the development of divergent interpretations of the Delaware's status as "women." One of his conclusions was that "etymology and history could easily become opportunities for the rationalization of culturally acquired sentiments." Significantly, these articles did not discuss what the tribe's designation as "women" meant for the Delaware's "real" women.[41] As was the case with most representations of same-sex sexualities in Philadelphia's popular, medical, and legal press, the focus was on men.

Female Same-Sex Sexualities

Representations of female same-sex sexualities in Philadelphia print culture in this period were more rare than their male counterparts. Readers of texts that focused exclusively on male same-sex sexualities could easily have concluded that female same-sex sexualities did not exist, were not visible, were not worthy of attention, or did not constitute a legal or medical problem. When female same-sex sexualities were represented, they were usually considered in the context of earlier and more extensive discussions of their male counterparts. Moreover, while representations of female and male same-sex sexualities had elements in common, there were differences. Rarely depicted in relation to murder, violence, or pedophilia, female same-sex sexualities were more often presented in relation to deviance, sickness, and subversion. (Not until the 1971 killing of Leon Weingrad by Gloria Burnette at the request of her lover Lois Farquharson would Philadelphia's newspapers depict lesbians as murderous.)[42] While female same-sex sexualities were also discussed in relation to crime, they were usually depicted as either noncriminal or as criminally invisible.

Representations of female same-sex sexualities routinely compared them to their male counterparts and did so in ways that emphasized their lack of significance, status, and disapprobation. In another of the 1956 *Philadelphia Medicine* articles, Calvin Drayer examined "homosexuality among animals and modern primitive societies" before turning to "our own cultural ancestry." Drayer's paper was unusual in presenting same-sex sexualities in a relatively positive light. After discussing the great frequency of same-sex sexual behaviors in many species and the many "modern primitive" cultures that "approve of homosexuality," Drayer turned to the ways in which male homosexuality was "idealized" in ancient Greece. Although he referred to "relations between female pigeons" and "domestic fowl"; mentioned that female cats and dogs "will often tolerate masculine activity by another female"; and noted that "sows 'go boarding,' mares are said 'to horse,' and cows are described as 'bulling,' " Drayer declared that "overt homosexual activity . . . is said to be more common among males than among females." While Drayer did not endorse this view, neither did he contest it. He also observed that "homosexual love among women never acquired the status of male homosexuality in Greece even though the home of the poetess Sappho (7th century B.C.) on the isle of Lesbos has given us the commonest name for female homosexuals today."[43]

A month after Drayer's article appeared, *Philadelphia Medicine* published a piece by A. E. Rakoff discussing "endocrine aspects of homosexuality" in both females and males. Arguing that homosexuality was not "a disturbance of endocrine origin," Rakoff for the most part avoided presenting same-sex sexualities in a negative light. While he mentioned that "some male homosexuals may have broad hips or high-pitched voices, and some female homosexuals may be small of bust and have flat hips," he emphasized that "so do many normal heterosexuals." Challenging popular images of both male and female homosexuality, he made his case more emphatically for men: "There are many male homosexuals who in their physical development are the picture of masculinity, pre-eminent athletes even in wrestling and boxing, who by virtue of their muscle-bound physiques might compete for the title of 'male of the year.' " In contrast, he pointed out succinctly that "similarly, some Lesbians are the picture of femininity."[44]

Media stories about cross-dressing also referenced women in the context of discussing men. In 1953, a letter to the *Bulletin*'s legal columnist asked whether Pennsylvania law prohibited males from dressing as women and calling themselves by women's names. Researching the question, "Philadelphia Lawyer" discovered two cases of "transvestitism," one male and one female, in the eighteenth-century records of the Mayor's Court. The answer provided was no, but the lawyer recommended that the writer "consult a psychiatrist."[45]

Masculine women were routinely paired with feminine men. In 1951, the *Tribune* reported on U.S. Representative Adam Clayton Powell, Jr.'s concerns about "an alarming growth of sex degeneracy among clergymen as well as parishioners." "Lash[ing] out" at clergy for "tolerating the 'tiny minority' of degenerate ministers," Powell urged them to "stem the growing influence of abnormal sex practices in youngsters." Citing an example of a minister "who engaged in an unnatural relationship with an officer of his congregation" and who led a church with "a fantastically high percentage of worshippers . . . who blatantly and openly flaunt their sex perversion," Powell demanded "action to check the 'boys with the swish and the girls with the swagger.' " Linked with "swishy boys," "swaggering girls" were led by "degenerate" male clergy. Eight years later, the *Tribune* again paired female and male deviations when Dean Gordon Hancock's column expressed concern about "signs that men are becoming more and more womanish, and the women are becoming more and more mannish." Stressing that "women were too fine to be degraded with the impositions of the so-called emancipated women," Hancock argued that "the womanish man has produced the mannish woman" and declared that "the greater blame can be placed at the door of man."[46]

References to lesbians and crime were also commonly made in the context of more extensive discussions of gay men. This was the case, for example, in "A Psychiatric Evaluation of Laws of Homosexuality," a 1956 *Temple Law Quarterly Review* article by Karl Bowman and Bernice Engle. Pointing to "extreme confusion" in sodomy statutes and "defects" in sexual psychopath laws, the authors argued that laws on homosexuality "disregard the concept that a man is innocent until he is proven guilty" and equate "sexual psychopathy" with "homosexuality." Although theoretically these laws might apply to women, Bowman and Engle observed that "male homosexual offenders bear the brunt of the prosecutions" while "law enforcement against female homosexuals is practically nil." Along similar lines, Michael von Moschzisker declared in his 1956 *Philadelphia Medicine* article, "I have never heard of lesbians being prosecuted for acts committed as such, although I suppose some are arrested from time to time in raids on so-called dirty floor shows."[47]

Some legal commentators proposed to address this disparity. In the 1950s, the Philadelphia-based American Law Institute (ALI) drafted and discussed a Model Penal Code (MPC), the culmination of a broad-based effort to promote law reform. When the three primary drafters of the MPC, including Penn law professor Louis Schwartz, presented to their advisory committee a proposal for decriminalizing consensual adult sodomy, they received endorsement. In March 1955, however, the ALI's council rejected this provision. Some argued that decriminalization was "rational" but "would be totally unacceptable to American legislatures and would prejudice acceptance of the Code." Others argued that "sodomy is a cause or symptom of moral decay in a society and should be repressed." The three authors then proposed an alternative, a measure that would designate consensual "deviate sexual intercourse" a misdemeanor and define it as "penetration by the male organ into any opening of the body of a human being or animal, other than carnal knowledge within Section 207.4, and any sexual penetration of the vulva or anus of a female by another female or by an animal." (Section 207.4 defined "carnal knowledge" as "sexual intercourse, including intercourse per os or per anum, with some penetration however slight of the female by the male sex organ." In other words, sexual intercourse in which a male sex organ "penetrated" the mouth, anus, or vagina of a female was excluded from the deviate intercourse provision.) The revised proposal also stipulated that a person "who in any public place solicits another with whom he had no previous acquaintance to engage in deviate sexual intercourse commits a misdemeanor."[48]

In one way, the MPC drafters called attention to lesbianism. Explaining a proposal regarding nonconsensual "deviate sexual intercourse," they noted that their language was broader than many existing laws because some states made "male homosexuality a grave offense while leaving lesbianism unpunished." In the name of equality between the sexes, penalties for same-sex female behaviors would be made more severe. In other ways, however, the MPC rhetorically linked "deviate sexual intercourse" more with men. Using language that suggested that men penetrated while women were penetrated, the drafters constituted males as more active agents of deviate sex. Moreover, when discussing public solicitation, they noted that they were referring to "principally male homosexual" behavior.[49]

In May 1955, the full ALI overturned the council's decision, voting for decriminalization of private, consensual sodomy. In this decision and in the decision to include female same-sex sexual acts under the nonconsensual "deviate sexual intercourse" provision, the ALI proposed to make more equal the treatment of men and women. However, despite these moves toward "equality," the ALI continued to conceive of deviate sexual intercourse as a crime of males against males, as was clear when the ALI explained why it used an age of consent of 18 rather than 16, which was the age used for statutory rape. One reason was the "belief that emotional instability of adolescence probably is greater and more prolonged among males."[50]

Isabel Drummond's 1953 book *The Sex Paradox* focused more attention on female same-sex sexualities than most local texts did. Drummond, a 1922 graduate of Penn law school and an assistant city solicitor between 1923 and 1928, wrote that her goals were "to guide the voting citizens toward needed reforms in matters pertaining to sex legislation and to effective control and rehabilitation of sexual deviants." In a chapter titled "Sodomy, Exhibitionism, and Other Acts 'Contrary to Nature,'" Drummond surveyed legal and medical perspectives. While for the most part she did not specify whether she was discussing male or female sexualities, in one section she wrote that "lesbianism is a very old sexual practice, which, at many periods in history has been considered quite respectable." Arguing that "female homosexuals fall into two general categories," she first described "women who prefer the society of women" and whose relationships ranged "from harmless friendships to genuine love affairs with or without physical love-making." Drummond asserted that "these relationships, which are sincere, usually faithful in the extreme, and evidence many of the finer attributes of heterosexual love," would not likely "ever become court cases." More rare was the second type, "the promiscuous Lesbians of dominant and forceful personality who pass quickly and lightly from affair to affair, usually indulging in physical sexual relations." These women "seduce the weaker and more pliable women who are ordinarily heterosexual" and "engage in the grosser perversions and in the more elaborate physical practices."[51] Drummond thus constructed three images of female same-sex sexualities—the respectable, loving, and faithful lesbian; the promiscuous, dominant, sexual, and perverted lesbian; and the seduced woman who was "ordinarily heterosexual." While no gay man was presented as respectable, loving, and faithful in local publications, the first image, which was quintessentially feminine, had a counterpart in the image of the masculine gay man. The second image corresponded on the one hand to the image of the promiscuous, dominant, sexual, and perverted gay man but on the other hand to the image of the feminine gay invert. The third image's closest male counterpart was that of the "ordinarily heterosexual" target of a gay man's advances.

While Drummond focused for several paragraphs on women, she did so in ways that encouraged comparisons with men. For example, she began this section by quoting a psychiatrist who claimed that "more men than women get sexual satisfaction from the genital acts with their own sex." In highlighting the respectability of lesbianism, she wrote that "it has never incurred the religious and legal condemnation of its male counterpart." Noting that lesbianism was "generally included in the purview of laws relating to homosexuality," she nevertheless pointed out that "convictions of females are rare." At the end of this section, she wrote, "If genital homosexuality is as common among women as among men, which is doubted, it is less noticeable. Women can publicly indulge in osculation and other love-making without criticism or without running counter to the social and legal strictures affecting male homos. The latter have been heard to complain vigorously about such discrimination made against them." While from some perspectives lesbian invisibility was a disadvantage, from others it was an advantage.[52]

The derivation of depictions of female same-sex sexualities from male counterparts can be seen most clearly in several nationally and internationally significant works by members of Philadelphia's medical community. In *Common Neuroses of Children and Adults* (1937), Temple's O. Spurgeon English and Gerald Pearson wrote that the girl's libido is "not directed as strongly as is the boy's to a love object of the opposite sex, and there is more possibility of unsublimated homosexual trends coming to the fore." These authors thus suggested that female homosexuality might be more common than male homosexuality. In spite of this, the book generally described first the family patterns that led to male homosexuality before depicting "analogous" and "similar" processes that led to its female counterpart.[53] In *Emotional Problems of Living* (1945), English and Pearson again based their assertions about same-sex sexuality principally upon male examples. On this basis, they concluded that adult same-sex sexuality was "neurotic," "immature," and "perverted," and that the homosexual was "ruthless in the seduction of younger children," "easily depressed," "delinquent," "alcoholic," and "criminal." Despite all of this, they encouraged doctors to be "understanding" and counseled society to reject "condemnation" and "punishment." Pessimistic about cures, the authors urged homosexuals to be "discreet."[54]

While English and Pearson took several sentences, pages, or chapters to derive their claims about female sexualities from male counterparts, Edward Strecker took 10 years. Strecker was the chairman of the Penn psychiatry department, a member of George Henry's Committee for the Study of Sex Variants, and the 1943–1944 president of the American Psychiatric Association. While serving as an advisor to the surgeons general of the army and navy and the secretary of war during World War Two, he helped shape policy for millions of "psychoneurotic" men rejected or discharged from military service.[55] Influenced by Philip Wylie's *Generation of Vipers*, Strecker's *Their Mothers' Sons* (1946) blamed male homosexuality on "Mom," "momism," and "matriarchy." In one "pathetic" case the book described, a "frigid" mother taught her teenage "sissy" that he would "never find anyone quite as pretty and worthy . . . as mom" and that "sexual intercourse is a horrible affair in which the husband is the beast." In other cases, "Mom" raised the boy "more like a daughter than a son." Emphasizing the risks that "Momarchies" posed for the very survival of democracy, Strecker wrote that "Naziism *was* (hopefully I am using the past tense) a mom surrogate with a swastika for a heart."[56]

In *Their Mothers' Sons*, Strecker limited his explicit discussion of female same-sex sexuality to one paragraph, explaining that "All these same forces operate against the daughters of immature fathers—pops—as well as against the sons of moms. The pop who mentally seduces his daughter may implant a tendency toward lesbianism." Conceiving of female and male homosexuality as parallel, Strecker derived his analysis of the former from his analysis of the latter. On a less overt level, in condemning frigid and matriarchal mothers, *Their Mothers' Sons* used language historically associated with attacks on lesbians: "deviant" mothers were creating "deviant" sons.[57]

Ten years later, in *Their Mothers' Daughters*, Strecker and Vincent Lathbury developed more fully an explicit analysis of female homosexuality, blaming not "pops" but "moms." Explaining that this book should have been published earlier since "not only in shipwrecks, but also in life, women and children should come first," Strecker and Lathbury began by conjuring up a "possessive" mother of a bride, "stepping between the newlyweds and saying, 'You cannot have my girl. She is mine.' " Warning about "the subjugation of males by females and the establishment of a sex dictatorship," Strecker and Lathbury attacked both "masculine" women and feminism. Suggesting that daughters faced greater dangers than sons because "the daughter is of the same sex as the mother," Strecker and Lathbury stressed that "democratic survival" depended upon recognizing that "woman is the complement of man" and that "the main function of women is to give birth to children and 'make' a home."[58] In Strecker and Lathbury's view, just as woman was the "complement" of man, the lesbian was the complement of the gay man.

Although they argued that *Their Mothers' Daughters* should have been published before *Their Mothers' Sons*, the fact that it was not was both cause and effect of Strecker and Lathbury's tendency to derive claims about female sexualities from male counterparts. Strecker and Lathbury did this mainly in blaming "lesbianism," which they called "biological and psychological treason," on "undissolved and unfulfilled mother-daughter relationships."

But they also did this by linking male and female deviations more directly. In one passage, they noted that "it has been said that normally sexed women can unfailingly detect even carefully masked homosexuality, particularly lesbianism," perhaps because "the biological threat to their survival endows them with extra-sensory perception." Warning that such "loose talk" was "scarcely scientifically provable," they nevertheless offered examples of other "misdirected suspicions": "We have heard men indicted as homosexuals because someone saw them looking into the shop windows of an interior decorator or women accused of lesbianism because they had a strong, overhand tennis serve." Concluding that "female homosexuality, like its opposite male number, seems to be rooted in psychological damage," Strecker and Lathbury suggested that the two phenomena were simultaneously "opposite" and similar.[59]

Unlike English, Pearson, Strecker, and Lathbury's work, Samuel Hadden's almost never veered from its focus on male same-sex sexualities. Like A. E. Rakoff, Hadden often highlighted the masculinity of gay men; in a 1957 *Pennsylvania Medical Journal* article, he wrote of treating "marine sergeants, professional football players, world champion boxers, steeplechase riders, and those whose appearance and public behavior might well be the envy of almost any man." In an uncharacteristic reference to lesbians, Hadden referred in a 1966 publication to the "disruptive office vexations" of "the female employee who is homosexually involved," but he also explained that "the female homosexual is less frequently a social irritant than is the male," that "she is more discreet and far less aggressive," and that "few seek treatment."[60]

On rare occasions, female same-sex sexualities received more attention than male ones. William Gardner Smith's 1954 novel *South Street* contained several passages about same-sex sexuality in Philadelphia and these focused on women. While the novel's central drama concerned interracial cross-sex love, one female character, "The Blues Singer," has a bad experience with a man and declares, "Guess I ought to go out and find me a woman." Shortly thereafter, the singer's bass player shows her a "funny place" on the "North Side" called "The Ray Cee," where same-sex couples dance. When the singer asks the bass player how he knows about the Ray Cee, he tells her, "Don't start no signifying." Filled with self-loathing, the singer regards the people she sees as "poor dumb bastards," but then notices that "a very pretty girl, dressed daintily and with a sweet face, was staring at her." At first, the singer wants to strike the girl, but when she returns to the club the next night, she buys a drink for the girl and kisses her. Later in the novel, the singer is taking heroin and is upset about being friendless. Thinking about going back to the Ray Cee, she says, "What the hell, might as well try everything once," but she also knows that she will not go there again. Exceptional in highlighting African American female same-sex sexualities, *South Street* presented these as filled with pathos. *South Street* also used a gay-coded male character to introduce a female character to the social world of lesbians. This cross-sex trope, common in this period's popular lesbian fiction but not in its popular gay fiction, reinforced the notion that lesbians were linked to gay men in ways that gay men were not linked to lesbians.[61]

In an exceptional 1953 newspaper story that also focused on African American women, the *Tribune* reported that police had raided the "wedding" of two women, aged 21 and 35, in their North Philly home. The younger woman was described as a "tall" and "willowy" "blushing bride." The older woman was "dressed in male clothes" and spoke in a "tremulous contralto." The 50 "odd" guests had planned to enjoy a "five-tiered wedding cake," a "ten-pound turkey," "a large bowl of eggnog," and "an unusual amount of other alcoholic beverages." Brought before a magistrate with "a majority of spectators in the 'better-than-ordinary' dress category," the "principals" claimed that "the affair was merely in the line of entertainment and was not meant to be the 'real thing.' " At first, the *Tribune* reported that police were checking "the possibility of someone having taken out a marriage license" and that the couple was being held on $500 bond for suspicion of sale of liquor without a proper permit. Four days later, the *Tribune* revealed that they had been released on a $300 peace bond. The older woman, whose nickname was "Duke," reportedly "wanted to know how anyone could be so dumb as to think those embossed invitations to a wedding between two women could be other than a 'gimmick' for a 'pay-and-eat' party."[62] Strategically challenging her audience to be smart, "Duke" offered readers the option of playing "dumb."

In the absence of alternative images of same-sex sexualities, readers of these texts either accepted or rejected their depictions of same-sex sexual cultures and either accepted or rejected their relevance for both female and male same-sex sexual cultures. Those Philadelphians who had access to lesbian and gay cultures had more bases on which to evaluate these depictions. Those texts that presented challenges to antilesbian and antigay beliefs provided readers with ways to resist these beliefs. Whether they accepted or rejected these representations, however, all Philadelphians had to deal with the effects that these texts had in shaping attitudes and practices.

In general, whether "the homosexual" in print was arrested, tried, convicted, imprisoned, treated, shocked, or cured, he was primarily male. He might be a child-molester, cross-dresser, criminal, pervert, deviant, degenerate, psychopath, or sinner, but whatever he was, he was almost always male. He might even be "the most fabulous faggot in the land," but he was rarely a lesbian. Reading themselves in and against the representations of one another's sexualities, most lesbians and gay men came to think of themselves as both similar and different. To the extent that their sexualities were represented less extensively, later, and comparatively, lesbians were encouraged to experience both stronger bonds and stronger conflicts with gay men than the other way around.

5

The “Objectionable” Walt Whitman Bridge

On 17 December 1955, the *New York Times* and *Camden Courier-Post* reported that Roman Catholics of the Camden, New Jersey, diocese had just opened a campaign against naming the Delaware River’s new bridge, which would soon provide another link between New Jersey and Philadelphia, for nineteenth-century poet Walt Whitman. On behalf of the Holy Name Societies of six New Jersey counties, Reverend Edward Lucitt had sent a letter to the Delaware River Port Authority (DRPA) protesting its decision to honor Whitman. Lucitt also had announced that children from 58 Catholic schools would be asked to participate in a “great men of New Jersey” essay contest, the winners of which would be forwarded to the DRPA for consideration.[1]

According to Lucitt, “Walt Whitman himself had neither the noble stature or quality of accomplishment that merits this tremendous honor, and his life and works are personally objectionable to us.” “When asked why Whitman was ‘objectionable,’ ” the *Times* noted, “Father Lucitt cited a recent biography, *The Solitary Singer*, by Dr. Gay Wilson Allen,” which had called Whitman a “homo-erotic.” When the press located Allen at his home in New Jersey, he claimed that “he had no intention of implying that Whitman was a homosexual”:

> “I used the term ‘homo-erotic’ rather than ‘homosexual’ because the latter suggests sex perversion,” Dr. Allen declared. “There is absolutely no evidence that Whitman engaged in any perverted practice.”
>
> Dr. Allen said that Whitman’s writings showed “a strong affection for man,” hence were “homo-erotic.”
>
> That affection, he said, has dominated much religious writing. “Many saints show the same feeling,” he added.[2]

Trying to save Whitman from the taint of deviance, Allen carefully distinguished homoerotic “writing,” in which man displayed “strong affection for man,” from homosexual “practice,” which was a “sex perversion.” Allen also likened Whitman’s texts to sacred religious tracts. Despite these efforts, the months of controversy that began with these articles demonstrated that eroticizing the homosocial could also taint saints.

The Whitman Bridge debate of 1955–1956 suggests not only that same-sex sexualities were the subject of extensive public discussion in this era but also that public attention focused on particular types of same-sex sexualities and not on others. As was the case with the texts discussed in the last chapter, much of the controversy surrounding the naming of the bridge linked homoeroticism and homosexuality primarily with men. While commentators disagreed about whether Whitman and his work were homoerotic or homosexual, whether this strengthened or weakened his candidacy, and whether the bridge should be named for him, they collectively made male same-sex sexualities more visible than female ones.

Catholic and Conservative Intersections

The Whitman Bridge conflict was built at a critical juncture in the histories of Catholicism and conservatism. Although William Penn had promoted religious tolerance in his "Holy Experiment," Catholics had long suffered at the hands of Protestant Philadelphians. The middle decades of the twentieth century, however, witnessed change in the status of Catholics. In 1960, U.S. citizens elected their first Catholic president, John F. Kennedy; two years later, Philadelphians had their first Catholic mayor, James Tate.[3]

Along the road to increased power, many U.S. Catholics joined their fellow citizens in anticommunist and antigay campaigns, which were led in the early 1950s by a member of their church, U.S. Senator Joseph McCarthy. As Donald Crosby has argued, "For nearly three hundred years their critics accused them of owing allegiance to a foreign power (the pope), of speaking strange languages, of practicing exotic religious rituals, of maintaining their own peculiar system of morals." Now Catholics turned these same accusations against others. Although Catholic support for McCarthy was never as overwhelming as some claimed, Crosby notes that "with a relish born of their centuries-long status as a despised minority, Catholics eagerly took upon themselves the mantle of patriotism." Among the leading Catholic supporters of McCarthy were members of Catholic War Veterans, the Knights of Columbus, the Ancient Order of Hibernians, and the Holy Name Society, "a social and devotional organization." Surveys indicated that McCarthy's second-largest pocket of strength, after Massachusetts, was New Jersey. According to the church, the counties comprising the Philadelphia archdiocese and the Camden diocese were 32% and 27% Catholic, respectively, in 1955.[4]

The bridge controversy developed where the increase in Catholic political power intersected with the rise of conservatism. Distanced from formal national power during Franklin Roosevelt's and Harry Truman's Democratic presidential administrations, conservatives made gains during Republican Dwight Eisenhower's years in office. In Philadelphia, this process was seemingly reversed. After 64 years of Republican rule in City Hall, in

1952 Democratic reformer Joseph Clark was elected mayor; in 1956 he was succeeded by Democrat Richardson Dilworth.[5] Still, having successfully resisted national trends toward Democratic urban hegemony for decades and with Republicans in power at the national level and gaining power in the suburbs, local conservatives pressed forward.

Building their movement on a foundation of popular anticommunism, conservatives championed sex, gender, and sexual traditionalism. As John D'Emilio has argued, "The antihomosexual campaigns of the 1950s represented but one front in a widespread effort to reconstruct patterns of sexuality and gender relations shaken by depression and war." One place where religious, political, and sexual conservatism came together was Collingswood, New Jersey, home to fundamentalist Carl McIntire's Bible Presbyterian Church. McIntire, who had been expelled from the Presbyterian Church U.S.A. in the 1930s and founded the American Council of Christian Churches in 1941, was strongly anticommunist and anti-Catholic, and later played an important role in antigay campaigns.[6] At odds with their anti-Catholic neighbors, members of the Holy Name Society nevertheless shared with them profoundly conservative values. Opening their campaign against Whitman just one year after the U.S. Senate voted to condemn McCarthy, Catholic conservatives had not given up the fight.

Philadelphia and Jersey Approaches

As the bridge controversy got underway, while the *New York Times* and *Camden Courier-Post* explained why Reverend Lucitt found Whitman "objectionable," major Philadelphia newspapers did not. In fact, in the ensuing conflict, these papers never referred explicitly to allegations about Whitman's homoeroticism or homosexuality. Was this due to Philadelphia provincialism? Was it because of the "respectability" of the *Bulletin* and *Inquirer*? Either of these factors might have encouraged the newspapers to avoid lesbian, gay, and sexual subjects. Were the newspapers pro-Whitman and thus motivated to avoid coverage that might have increased opposition to him? Were New York's and Camden's newspapers exceptionally explicit, the former because of their city's sexual cosmopolitanism, the latter because of the local basis of the anti-Whitman campaign? Whatever the reasons, the character of Philadelphia's newspaper coverage is striking because these papers had started the controversy in the first place.

In 1951, the Port Authority had recommended the building of a new bridge three miles downstream from an existing span. Public discussion about naming the bridge began in April 1954 with Edgar Williams's "The Bridge without a Name" in the *Inquirer*. For Williams, who wrote that the bridge would serve as "another link in the great network of highways vital to the world's busiest industrial area," the new structure was a hopeful symbol of regional optimism. But Williams also described tensions between New Jersey and Philadelphia. While the area's first bridge was "known throughout the world" as the Delaware River Bridge, "no loyal Jerseyite would think of calling it anything but the Camden Bridge." "On this side of the river," Williams continued, there were "certain provincialists . . . who insist that it is the Philadelphia Bridge." Reporting that the DRPA referred to the new span as " 'the new bridge' or 'bridge No. 2,' " Williams noted that Jerseyans were generally calling it the Gloucester City Bridge while most Philadelphians thought of it as the Packer Avenue Bridge.[7]

"The Bridge without a Name" prompted letters to the *Inquirer* suggesting names for the new and old bridges. Some proposals, such as "Ike and Mamie," "Eisenhower," or "Roosevelt," sought to memorialize national political leaders. Others, such as Wanamaker, Franklin, or Penn, celebrated famous local figures. Another group was geographic and included "Philester" (combining Philadelphia and Gloucester), "Penjerdel" (combining Pennsylvania, Jersey, and Delaware), and "Delaware Valley." The majority favored "Penn-Jersey Memorial Bridge." In May 1954, Dr. Henry Butler Allen, executive vice president of the Franklin Institute, wrote to the DRPA suggesting that one of the bridges be named for the institute's namesake in honor of the upcoming 250th anniversary of his birth. The following month, the Port Authority agreed to appoint a special committee to select a name for the new bridge, a mandate later expanded to include choosing a name for the existing one.[8]

As the committee's work began, Philadelphia's newspapers were filled with suggestions. The Poor Richard Club joined Allen in promoting Franklin. Others proposed Betsy Ross; William Penn; U.S. presidents James Buchanan, Woodrow Wilson, and Franklin Roosevelt; and John Lord Berkeley and George Carteret (who were identified as New Jersey's founders).[9]

In June 1955, the committee recommended Franklin's name for the older bridge. Concurring with Allen's suggestion that if one bridge were named for Franklin the other should be named for a South Jerseyan, the committee selected Whitman for the new bridge, a proposal that originated with the DRPA staff. Whitman, the committee noted, lived in Camden from 1873 to 1892 and was buried there. And "although Whitman's poetry was bitterly assailed in the years first following publication of *Leaves of Grass*, Whitman today is recognized as one of the most vital forces in American literature." The DRPA unanimously accepted the recommendations.[10]

Not everyone was pleased. Although the DRPA had selected a South Jerseyan in addition to Franklin, the first objections to Whitman came from Gloucester. "The Bridge without a Name" had explained that tunnel advocates opposed construction of the bridge, in part because it would "shatter Gloucester's taxation base." Long-standing South Jersey resentments soon came to the fore. One letter in the *Bulletin* complained that Gloucester had gained "an unsavory name" because of "Philadelphians that frequented its nationally-known beachfront and racetrack." Philadelphia could make "long overdue amends" by naming the new bridge for Gloucester.[11]

In August, Gloucester City Council voted to protest naming the new bridge for Whitman. Not only had the DRPA failed to consult the city council, declared one councilman, but "Whitman had nothing to do with Gloucester." Since the poet had resided in Camden, which was the location of one of the Franklin Bridge's approaches, Gloucester proposed that the existing bridge honor Whitman and a different name be selected for the new bridge. The *Inquirer* editorialized in support of Gloucester's objections, adding that the two names "do not seem to have made much of a hit in Camden, or Gloucester—or Philadelphia." Challenging the DRPA, Gloucester City Council voted in September to change the name of the Whitman Bridge to Gloucester Bridge and set aside funds for signs with the new name. Soon the Camden County Freeholders joined the campaign, passing a resolution in favor of naming the bridge for Gloucester.[12]

The Anti-Whitman Drive

As far as readers of the *Inquirer* and *Bulletin* could tell, initial opposition to naming the new bridge for Whitman had nothing to do with negative attitudes about Whitman per se. In November 1955, however, the *Catholic Star Herald*, the newspaper of the Camden diocese, published three articles by Reverend James Ryan of St. Anne's Church in Westville, New Jersey, raising new objections to Whitman. The *Catholic Standard and Times*, the Philadelphia archdiocese newspaper, soon reprinted Ryan's pieces.

The first article described Whitman as "unworthy" and a "reluctant citizen" of New Jersey. Ryan explained that "illness made him Camden's captive" and that New Jersey was "never the abode of his free choice." He continued,

> The strongest objection that must come to the mind of any thinking citizen to the use of this name is the fact that it would be an insult to all who cherish the ideals of Church and State. As a poet he is recognized even by his most favorable critics as definitely "second-rate." His two tributes to Lincoln, delicate in their imagery though saccharine in their pathos, are the only ones that appear to be of enduring worth. As a thinker Walt Whitman possesses the depth of a saucer and enjoys a vision which extends about as far as his eyelids.

> A naturalist, a pantheist, a freethinker, a man whose ideas were destructive of usual ethical codes—is this a name we wish to preserve for posterity?

After quoting from Whitman's "As I Lay with My Head in Your Lap Camerado," Ryan argued that the poet's name was particularly unfit for a bridge:

> A bridge is a beautiful, graceful structure that thrusts heavenward and descends again to security on the opposite bank. The philosophy of Walt Whitman crumbles under the destructive egotism that gave it life. Godless and selfish it is powerless to thrust beyond itself. We don't want our new span named after a man whose ideas fell far short of spanning the problems of human existence.

Whitman's transcendentalist aspirations had been perceived, but perceived as failing.[13]

At this point, Ryan's attack relied on a whole series of words and concepts long associated with same-sex sexualities.[14] Labeled "ill" by sexologists, lesbians and gay men were thought to have such uncontrollable desires that they were incapable of "free choice." "Delicate," "powerless," "saccharine," and filled with "pathos," male homosexuality was feminized as weak. "Second-rate" in relation to heterosexuality, homosexuality was thought to be non-reproductive and thus non-"enduring." Lacking in "depth," homosexuality was seen as superficial. Identified as narcissistic, homosexuality was linked with "selfish" "egotism." Permitted to exist, homosexuality would prove "destructive" of church, state, and "usual ethical codes." Irrational and foreign, homosexuality would be opposed by any "thinking citizen." Surely, Ryan seemed to suggest, a structure as phallic as a bridge should not be named for a man whose philosophy failed to "thrust beyond itself" and fell "far short." Thus far, however, Ryan had not explicitly labeled Whitman or his work homosexual or homoerotic.

Ryan's second article declared that "although occasional passages in the writings of Whitman might be considered uplifting, or perhaps even sublime, nevertheless these can never nullify the shocking effect of the baser, irreverent passages." Ryan continued, "A golf course without holes just isn't a good golf course no matter how verdant its fairways or trimmed its greens may be. The tea into which arsenic has been slipped might be quite delectable by itself, but the potion as a whole is something to be avoided." Deceptively poisonous, Whitman lacked appropriate "holes" and displayed "baser, irreverent passages." "With his excessive glorification of the ego," Ryan argued, "one is led to suspect that Walt had not reached that maturity of thought which enables a man to make the subtle distinction between himself and God Almighty." Anal eroticism ("baser, irreverent passages"), narcissism, and immaturity had long been linked with same-sex sexualities. Like the first article, however, Ryan's second did not mention homosexuality specifically.[15]

In the conclusion of Ryan's third piece, published just eight days before the *Times* and *Courier-Post* stories appeared, homosexuality itself was finally named. Almost as an afterthought, Ryan remembered "another strong objection":

> Whitman's major works exhibit a revolting homosexual imagery that is not confined to a few isolated passages but permeates the fetid whole.
>
> The author himself unblushingly admits the presence of this unnaturalness in a letter to Edward Carpenter, one of his English disciples: "It lies behind almost every line, but concealed, studiedly concealed; some passages left purposely obscure."
>
> "There is something in my nature furtive like an old hen!" Would that this furtiveness had kept all his literary eggs concealed from the gaze of the public and confined to the barnyard where they can be best appreciated! It is curious to note that, having failed to divinize men, Walt finds no trouble in reducing them to a plane of sub-animal conduct.[16]

Using metaphors of bodily and geographic contamination, Ryan seemed to suggest that the new "passage" over the Delaware River might enable Whitman's influence to burst out of domesticated confinement and into the region's public sphere, reproducing "like an old hen" laying eggs.

Ryan also again used language that associated homosexuality with anal eroticism. Whitman had left his passages "purposely obscure." He had written that something lay "behind" his writing. His messages were "concealed." Ryan simultaneously attacked Whitman for attempting to hide his homosexuality and for failing to hide it successfully. Ironically, the issue of homosexuality had been concealed in Ryan's first two articles. And Ryan, too, had failed to conceal something—that he was attacking Whitman for "homosexual imagery."

While Ryan named homosexuality in his third article and the *Times* and *Courier-Post* did so in their coverage, "provincialists" at the *Bulletin* and the *Inquirer* continued the indirection that marked Ryan's first two pieces. Enabling Ryan's concealed views to reach a wider audience, the *Bulletin* reported on the first of the *Star Herald*'s attacks on Whitman. Then, on 16 December, one day before the *Times* and *Courier-Post* explained why Lucitt found Whitman objectionable, the *Bulletin* offered its version of the story. In some respects the *Bulletin* provided greater detail than the *Times*. Lucitt was identified as the pastor of Sacred Heart Church in Camden. The six Holy Name Societies in South Jersey were said to have 35–40,000 members. But although the *Bulletin* quoted Lucitt's letter to the DRPA, it did not explain what precisely was objectionable about Whitman. The *Inquirer* also quoted Lucitt's letter but it too left the objection unnamed.[17]

Ryan's articles in the *Star Herald* and Lucitt's letter to the DRPA were only the opening shots in a concerted, grassroots campaign. In December 1955 and the first few months of 1956, almost 1,500 letters, a majority of which were signed, mimeographed form letters opposing Whitman, were sent to the Port Authority. Of the 1,490 letters received by the DRPA, 914 (61%) were anti-Whitman form letters, 246 (17%) were individually written anti-Whitman letters, and 330 (22%) were individually written pro-Whitman letters. Of the anti-Whitman letters, 92% were sent from New Jersey. Of the pro-Whitman letters, 49% came from Philadelphia, 13% from other Pennsylvania locations, and 29% from New Jersey. Although it may have been common for spouses to sign one another's names, 54% of the identifiably male or female names on pro-Whitman letters were female whereas 54% of the identifiably male or female names on anti-Whitman letters were male. While the typical pro-Whitman letter was signed in the name of a Philadelphia woman and the typical anti-Whitman letter was signed in the name of a South Jersey man, geography was a more powerful factor than sex in predicting the stance of a letter writer.[18]

In addition to being sent individual letters, the DRPA received anti-Whitman letters from Camden's Knights of Columbus, Catholic War Veterans, and American Gold Star Mothers; two unions and one chapter of Veterans of Foreign Wars in South Jersey; and Philadelphia's Kerrymen's Patriotic and Benevolent Association. Writing in support of Whitman were a number of college- and university-affiliated scholars, the largest group of whom were University of Pennsylvania English professors. (One of the latter, who signed his letter "Ernest Earnest," must have been familiar with Oscar Wilde's *The Importance of Being Earnest.*) Also endorsing Whitman were a number of Protestant and Jewish leaders and groups; several Ethical Societies; and the Delaware Valley chapter of the Daughters of the American Revolution.[19]

Five reasons for opposition were listed on the anti-Whitman form letter. First, Whitman was "not great enough." Second, he "boasted of his immoralities and published immorality as a personal experience." Third, he "held Christianity in contempt." Fourth, he "attempted to teach rebellion against the Natural Law of God." And finally, "His political philosophy, dusted off the scrap heap during the depression, as the Voice of the Common Man, has proven alien to Jeffersonian democracy and he is now the Poet Laureate of the World Communist Revolution." As was the case with other episodes in this era's anticommunist and antigay campaigns, the bridge controversy linked "personal experience" of "immorality" with "World Communist Revolution."[20] Like the *Bulletin* and the *Inquirer*'s coverage, the form letter did not specifically name the nature of Whitman's "immorality" but relied on a series of words and concepts culturally linked with homosexuality—immoral, contemptuous, anti-Christian, rebellious, unnatural, alien, and antidemocratic.

Many of the individual anti-Whitman letters provide evidence of similar patterns. Mrs. William Russell of Philadelphia wrote that "practically his whole life passed in writing poems which were considered both obscene and unmentionable." Mr. R. J. Peterson of Barrington, New Jersey, also mentioned the unmentionable: "There is no need to elaborate on the reasons for my opposition to Whitman's name, as the subject has been thoroughly covered by the *Camden Courier.*" Mr. A. McIntyre of Cheltenham, Pennsylvania, was more specific: "I need only to name one of this so-called poet's effusions—*Leaves of Grass*—a work of vulgarity, to say the least." Richard Dolan of Upper Darby, Pennsylvania, observed that Whitman was "crude" and "pleasure-bent." Vince L. Burns of Philadelphia quoted the late Agnes Repplier, "Philadelphia's own recent literary light," who had regarded Whitman as an "incurable poseur" who "loved his indecency . . . , clinging to it with an almost embarrassing ardor."[21]

Paul Breig's letter makes it unclear whether those who criticized Whitman did so because of his views on homosexuality, sexuality, or both. "Because his works stemmed from his own character," Breig wrote, "which were and still are offending to all women of the world, my opinion is that Mr. Walt Whitman should not be honored with so great a project." Identifying with, and extending imperial protection to, the women of the world, Breig may have thought that Whitman's work was offensive to women because of its celebration of sexuality, male sexuality, female sexuality, and/or male same-sex sexuality. Also opposing Whitman, New York's Thomas Horace Evans wrote that many people remembered only the poet's "A Woman Waits For Me," which "might dangerously accelerate traffic on the Bridge."[22]

Not all Catholics supported the anti-Whitman campaign. Along with pro-Whitman items in the Jesuit magazine *America* and the liberal Catholic periodical *Commonweal* and pro-Whitman comments in *Newsweek* by a dean at LaSalle College, the Catholic magazine *Ave Maria* editorialized, "Lucitt is on questionable ground in challenging the stature of Whitman's work and the respectability of his life. Scholars and historians have never shown that the 'homoeroticism' of his poetry was a reflection of an immoral life." Like Professor Allen, *Ave Maria* distinguished between "homoeroticism" and "immorality" and between "poetry" and "life." Feminizing Whitman's critics, the editorial also warned that if the church applied its weight in unimportant matters it would be "in danger of being regarded as a nagging wife."[23]

Distinguishing between homoeroticism and immorality did not prove as easy as *Ave Maria* may have hoped. According to *New York Post* columnist Murray Kempton, Reverend Lucitt argued that "Whitman's biographers say he wasn't a sex deviate . . . but they keep hinting around. If there were any such things about him, we don't think he deserves having the bridge named after him." In a letter to the editor in *Ave Maria*, Seattle's Mrs. Phoebe T. O'Neill wrote, "For goodness sake, when using such terms as 'homo-erotic' . . . please define a little for poor lay-folk like me." The magazine's response suggested that upholding the distinction would be difficult. Turning to *Webster's* dictionary, *Ave Maria* explained that homoerotic was "an adjective derived from the noun, homoeroticism, a term used in psychoanalysis, meaning homosexuality."[24]

Although the *Star Herald*, *Standard and Times*, *New York Times*, *New York Post*, *Courier-Post*, *Ave Maria*, and *Newsweek* all mentioned homoeroticism and/or homosexuality, the overwhelming majority of anti-Whitman letters sent to the DRPA did not. While it is possible that the nature of Lucitt's objections were named from Catholic priests' pulpits and in other public and private domains, most of the anti-Whitman letters sent to the DRPA and all of the *Bulletin* and *Inquirer*'s coverage joined a long tradition of constructing homosexuality as the "love that dare not speak its name."[25]

The Pro-Whitman Drive

While Whitman had his detractors, the bridge-naming controversy also mobilized defenders. Most of Whitman's supporters highlighted his literary achievements. Many referred to his celebration of U.S. democracy, common men, and nature, and his service nursing Civil War soldiers.

Some pro-Whitman letters objected to the role the Catholic Church was playing. Of these, a number were anti-Catholic. Harry Brandlee of Philadelphia objected to "this agent from Rome, Italy," who would prefer the bridge to be named for "saint mumbo-jumbo." Suggesting that this "Father-of-What?? get married to some nice girl instead of acting like an old lady," Brandlee advised the "agent of a foreign government" to "keep out of our American way of life." "We don't need advice from Rome or Moscow," he concluded. Mrs. Ottilie Van Allen of Philadelphia wrote, "As a member of the Protestant community I resent this attempt to dictate to us on the part of the Catholic Church." Phillips Endecott Osgood, minister of the First Unitarian Church of Essex, New Jersey, opposed "sectarian pressures" and urged the DRPA not "to capitulate to such ecclesiastical urgency."

Miss Elizabeth Wintersteen Schneider of Bala-Cynwyd, Pennsylvania, was "shocked" to learn of "sectarian objections" to Whitman. "He is not the hero of a small cult," she wrote, "but a figure with a broadly based reputation." Insisting that she was not guilty of "anti-Catholic bias," Schneider explained that she would object to her denomination trying to force the adoption of the name of an unimportant Presbyterian poet or general.[26]

More often than was the case with anti-Whitman letters, pro-Whitman letters openly mentioned homosexuality and homoeroticism. Perhaps because of the coverage in the *New York Times* and *New York Post,* more of these letters originated from outside the Philadelphia area. Several letters critical of Catholics raised the subject of homosexuality within the Church. W. Wagnytz of East Orange, New Jersey, believed that "Catholic objections to the name of Walt Whitman because of his being described as 'homoerotic' are not valid. Similar accusations have been hurled at the Catholic Clergy because the Church forces their clergy into a 'sterile' asceticism. The Church has always defended the virtue of its clergy; good taste alone should dictate to the clergy that these tactics should not be used to besmirch the good name of Walt Whitman."[27] Although it defended Whitman, Wagnytz's letter implied that virtue and homoeroticism were incompatible.

Mrs. Mary Inman of New York was more critical of the antigay rhetoric used to attack Whitman: "If the members of any such group, particularly of the religious brotherhoods, fear to be contaminated with 'homo-eroticism' by using the bridge, perhaps there are other facilities, such as boats or ferries, which they could employ." One of the strongest expressions of outrage came from Fred Feiden of Middletown, Connecticut: "But how dare a group like the Society of Catholic Priests be so sensitive about the existence of homosexuality. Let them clean their own ranks first. I don't think that there are many well-informed people who are not aware of the existence of homosexuality amongst the celibate clergy, and lesbianism in the nunneries." He continued, "Michael Angelo [*sic*] was a homosexual. Why don't they destroy the Sistine Chapel or prevent worship in St. Peter's Cathedral?" One letter in the *New York Post* criticized those who "want to take Whitman's name off that bridge because he may have been abnormal sexually." "If they succeed," the letter declared, "their next job is to remove Michaelangelo's statues from the Vatican, tear down St. Peter's Basilica and throw out all copies of Leonardo's Last Supper."[28]

The bridge imbroglio soon called into question the sexual moralities not only of Catholic priests and nuns but also of some of the other figures whose names had been put forward. Patricia Underwood of New York wrote to complain that instead of Whitman, the DRPA was going to name the bridge for "some clown whose only claim to fame is that he managed to garner a few more votes than the next guy or managed to shoot up a few more of the enemy." She continued, "Only be sure that you investigate *their* sex lives very thoroughly and make certain that they didn't beat their wives and that they wore clean linen daily."[29] Pro-Whitman letters such as those sent by Feiden and Underwood challenged the sentiments of Whitman's detractors. But these letters also could have unintended consequences. Rather than help Whitman by linking his name with Michaelangelo, Leonardo, priests, and nuns, Feiden's letter could have lent support to those calling for antigay campaigns within the church. Underwood's letter was pro-Whitman but it linked Whitman with wife-beaters and dirty-linen-wearers.

Not only priests and nuns were threatened by this contagious process. A number of pro-Whitman letters pointed out that Benjamin Franklin was not exactly a paragon of sexual virtue. Mrs. Richard Miner of Philadelphia wrote that Franklin was "a Deist famous for his amorous adventures—for which, unlike Whitman's—there has been ample evidence!" Miss V. E. Rogers of Philadelphia enclosed a copy of an article by Richard Saunders III in the February 1956 issue of *Philadelphia Forum*, which pointed out that Franklin "loved the ladies." Rogers wrote that it would be a sad world, indeed, if it were bereft of contributions from all "whose so-called 'morals' didn't conform to certain rigid standards." Temple University's Hayden Goldberg asked, "Does anyone today attack Shakespeare's greatness because of his immorality? And what about the drunkenness of Edgar Allan Poe and Mark Twain or the extra-marital love affairs and illegitimate child of Benjamin Franklin?" Mocking the evasive language and the metaphor of contamination used to attack Whitman, Frederick Griffin III of Bryn Mawr, Pennsylvania, wrote, "If we must remove the name of Walt Whitman from the new bridge on grounds of—ah—, then I fear we must also protect our purity from the name of Benjamin Franklin, who was so notably prolific, mentally—spiritually—and—ah—phys—. But alas! We have already been contaminated by this good gentleman!"[30]

Like Griffin, Miss Regina Palmer of Feasterville, Pennsylvania, wrote a pro-Whitman letter that addressed the vague language used by Whitman's opponents. "I would also like to know [and] am in fact very curious as to what the objection to Whitman is, specifically," Palmer declared. "Many things are said but I'd like to know the basic reasons. I think all of us are entitled to know what the objection is. I have sincere doubts that it is because he has been called a homosexual. Many great artists and even great theologians have been accused of this thing, but who is to prove it? I take no one's word for this, I want to see the proof."[31] Palmer first insistently called upon Whitman's opponents to mention the unmentionable. Then she simultaneously implied and expressed doubt that the objection was that Whitman had been called a homosexual. Again linking Whitman to figures accused of homosexuality, she concluded by demanding proof, criticizing the lack of evidence but also suggesting that she might oppose Whitman if such proof were provided.

Ironically, then, it was often Whitman's defenders rather than his detractors who were most negative about same-sex sexualities. Some of Whitman's supporters, for example, strongly disputed allegations of homoeroticism and homosexuality in Whitman's life and work. According to Murray Kempton, when *Leaves of Grass* was condemned as obscene in the nineteenth century, "there was no talk of homo-eroticism then; the widow who moved in as his housekeeper was a fallen woman to her friends." H. David Hammond of New York wrote, "I have read some of the poetry in question. I deny that it is 'homoerotic,' 'homosexual,' or what not. He had a strong and healthy interest in humans—their minds *and* their bodies. Some of his writings are, indeed, vigorously heterosexual in import."[32] Constructing homosexuality and heterosexuality as mutually exclusive, Hammond implied that homoeroticism and homosexuality were not compatible with "strong and healthy interest in humans."

Other letters hinted that even if Whitman had homoerotic desires, he was a master of self-control. Using a very Catholic example, Donald Weeks of Philadelphia wrote, "It is very easy to stir up anxiety, fears, prejudices concerning Whitman's sexual character. If Whitman had a 'thorn in the flesh,' he seems to have lived a life of increasing discipline and increasing sweetness without any of the strain shown by St. Paul." Others argued that Whitman was a good selection in spite of any questions about his sexual character. Cornell University's Clinton Rossiter wrote that "Whitman may have been a queer bird in many ways, but what does that have to do with the fact that he is America's greatest poet."[33]

As far as can be determined from the DRPA correspondence, it scarcely occurred to any letter writers that Whitman's homoeroticism or homosexuality might strengthen the case for naming the bridge after him. Fred Feiden seemed neutral, writing, "Whether he was a homosexual or not is irrelevant. He is remembered for his poetry, not his sex life." Philadelphia's Mary J. Allen came closer to celebrating Whitman's sexuality. "The original choice 'The Walt Whitman Bridge' is good," she wrote. "He was a colorful individual and more so since his colorful past has been dug up." Perhaps proving that Quaker Philadelphia had not stopped comparing itself to Puritan Boston, Jerome Relkin of Philadelphia thought that the Port Authority should not be pressured into rejecting Whitman "just because he didn't think in narrow, dogmatic religious terms, nor behave in strict, puritan, conforming ways."[34]

More often, Whitman's supporters used the same kind of inexplicit homoerotic language used by his opponents. Mrs. Edward J. Stinsmen of

Aldan, Pennsylvania, wrote that Whitman was "a humanist—in love with all people—all men." Mrs. Mary Silverman of Philadelphia wrote, "What fitter name for a bridge than that of a man who in his own person and world-famed poetry has been himself a bridge of love and understanding between man and man and between all races of men?" Although they did not refer to Whitman's writings as homoerotic, these letters celebrated Whitman's capacity for both heterosocial and homosocial love. Along the same lines, under the headline, "But Would He Be a Security Risk?" *Harper's* reprinted an 1863 letter of recommendation for Whitman from Ralph Waldo Emerson, who praised the poet as a "large-hearted man, much loved by his friends; entirely patriotic & benevolent." Similarly bringing to life a historical Whitman who could be useful in contemporary struggles about "national security," Murray Kempton's *New York Post* column presented a compassionate Whitman who worked as a volunteer army nurse but was fired from his civil service job after a "check on his 'loyalty' and 'moral character.' "[35]

Some of Whitman's public defenders may have been transporting strategies of resistance that lesbians and gay men often mobilized in everyday life. Denying that Whitman or his poetry was homoerotic or homosexual, demanding evidence that was difficult or impossible to obtain, and appearing hostile to same-sex desire may have helped secure victory in the bridge controversy. Lesbians and gay men in the 1950s could then feel pride that a historical figure with whom they identified had been honored and they could take pleasure in believing themselves in possession of the "secret" knowledge that Whitman was one of their own. Later generations of lesbians and gay men could do so as well. Ironically, all of this may have been made possible by strategies that encouraged hostility toward same-sex sexualities.

The closest to a progay defense of Whitman came from a safe distance from the local scene. In January 1955, several months before the DRPA selected Franklin and Whitman, the California-based homophile movement magazine *One* reported that some readers had complained that an article it had published about Whitman "didn't say real sure if he was homo." *One*'s response addressed definitional issues:

> All we had was the evidence. Who leaves affidavits? . . . Besides, the term homosexual is matter of degrees and types and much would clear up if that were kept in mind. When using term as noun (now well-established by usage) remember it covers very different sorts of people. Those who live homosexuality night and day are a world apart from those who are casually involved now and then, or those called repressed homos. When referring to someone as homo, a more specific classification would help.[36]

In March 1956, *One* reported on the campaign against naming the bridge for Whitman. In addition to noting many of the details covered above, *One* mentioned that Edward McAuliffe, chairman of the DRPA's special committee, had stated that Whitman had an "honored place in our history" and that the DRPA "found no evidence Whitman was homosexual." *One* also added St. Augustine to the list of famous Catholics touched by the controversy. But unlike McAuliffe, who implied that Whitman might not have been chosen had evidence of homosexuality been found, *One* wrote that Whitman's "greatness was not in spite of, but specifically because of the nature of his love for man." *One* left unanswered the question of whether Whitman was a homosexual, but the magazine proudly defended Whitman as a lover of man.[37]

According to a December 1955 story in the *Courier-Post* and January 1956 stories in the *Bulletin* and *Inquirer*, the Port Authority did consider changing its decision and naming the bridge for Gloucester or the poet Joyce Kilmer. The *Courier-Post* editorialized in favor of Gloucester. Early in the new year, the Camden Holy Name Society issued a statement calling for the bridge to be named for Thomas Jefferson, justifying its proposal on patriotic grounds and in the same spirit of regional optimism that had marked "The Bridge without a Name." Explaining why it rejected names of "only local significance," the society declared, "The growth of the Delaware Valley has pushed beyond city, county and state lines—narrow provincialism has no place in planning for the new life of the valley." Recasting earlier arguments about provincialism, the society explained that Jefferson had written the U.S. Declaration of Independence in the region and that even Whitman had written about the declaration.[38]

The DRPA remained committed to Whitman, however, and the public controversy soon quieted down, at least temporarily. Late in 1956, readers of the *Bulletin* and *Inquirer* learned that Gloucester had not given up the fight. In what the *Bulletin* described as a "formal revolt against the bridge authority," on 6 December the Gloucester City Council approved a motion to place signs around the city directing motorists to the Gloucester City Bridge. This opposition, the newspapers reported, derived from the original selection of Gloucester as the terminus for the bridge, the failure to consult with Gloucester over the bridge's name, and the sacrifices that Gloucester had made during the construction process.[39] No mention was made of the role of the Catholic Church or the antigay campaign against Whitman.

Six months later, the *Bulletin* published a past-tense account of a two-year controversy that had become history. "Naming Span for Whitman Caused Bitter Controversy" referred to both Gloucester and South Jersey Catholic opposition to Whitman. "The 19th Century American poet," the *Bulletin* explained, "an iconoclast in his own time, has never stopped being the subject of dispute." The story reminded its readers of some of the language used in Reverend Lucitt's attack on Whitman, but this time the *Bulletin* failed to mention that Whitman was "personally objectionable" to the church. The story did claim, "His poetry is anything but conventional. It does not rhyme. The lines are not metric in the traditional sense. The words spill out in a torrent of seemingly uncontrolled emotion." While praising Whitman as "one of the first wholly American poets" who "celebrated endlessly the glory, both potential and past, of the nation," the *Bulletin* took him to task because, "He also celebrated himself, a fact that has led many to regard him as a first-class egotist. And the self he celebrated was not restrained by society's conventions on morality, sex, womanhood, humility, religion and even politics."[40] As both the *Bulletin* and the *Inquirer* had done consistently during the struggle over naming the bridge, this story relied on a series of gay-coded words and concepts. Even in victory, Whitman was tagged as unconventional, disorderly, nontraditional, uncontrolled, emotional, egotistical, narcissistic, immoral, unrestrained, antiwoman, prideful, antireligious, and subversive.

Decades later, two narrators, one lesbian and one gay, remember the controversy vividly. Alvia Golden recalls that "everyone" knew about it, that it was "headline news." Lewis Coopersmith says, "There was a whole fuss about it because the Catholic Church as usual became hysterical because of the fact that Whitman was gay." Coopersmith claims, "Everybody knew that Whitman was gay. You'd have to be dead not to know that, and that was the basis, as far as I know, of the objection." Although Golden says she does not remember knowing that Whitman was "queer" until the controversy occurred, she suspects that she was unique among her mostly straight friends in this regard. She also remembers learning that "supposedly he had fucked young men right where the structure was being built."[41]

Both Golden and Coopersmith recall the controversy with a mixture of amusement and anger. "I used to write letters to my friends," Golden remembers, "saying I'm writing to you from Philadelphia, the only city in America that has a banned bridge." She continues, "I just thought it was hysterically funny and everybody I knew thought it was the dumbest fucking controversy. We just considered it to be a typical sort of redneck piece of crap." Coopersmith remembers thinking "how silly of the church as usual." Told that many of Whitman's defenders denied that he was gay, Coopersmith responds, "Oh they still do to this day, and Langston Hughes's heirs deny that he was gay, and Liberace's heirs deny it. That sort of nonsense will never die."

In 1989–1990, the Philadelphia Lesbian and Gay Task Force produced a public service announcement featuring a young man sitting alongside the Delaware River with the Whitman Bridge in the background. The man says,

"I just found out Walt Whitman was gay . . . you know, the guy they named the bridge after. I wish I had known that when I was in high school. Back then, I got hassled all the time by the other kids, 'cause I'm gay—and the teachers—they didn't say anything. Why didn't they tell me Walt Whitman was gay?" Five television stations in Greater Philadelphia refused to air the piece, calling it "controversial" and claiming that it "advocated a particular lifestyle."[42]

Exploring the controversy surrounding the naming of the Whitman Bridge reveals some of the ways that same-sex sexualities were discussed in the public sphere, some of the public voices that made themselves heard on same-sex sexual topics, and some of the public forms of oppression and resistance that developed in 1950s Philadelphia. Significantly, these debates also suggest that while commentators approached the bridge controversy from different directions, they arrived at a destination that linked same-sex sexualities more with men than with women.

6

Rizzo's Raiders and Beaten Beats

"Police Raiders Break up Chess Game, Seize Men in Beards, Girls in Tights," ran the outlandish headline in the *Bulletin* on 12 February 1959. The story began in a tone that mocked the police: "There was last night at the Humoresque Coffeeshop, 2036 Sansom St., the playing of music and chess, the talking of talk, and, of course, the drinking of coffee. There was the growing of beards, the wearing of turtle-neck sweaters and tights and the smoking of pipes and cigarettes." For these crimes, the owner of the coffeehouse, 23-year-old Melvin Heifetz, and 34 of his patrons were "hauled off" in police wagons.[1]

The *Bulletin* explained that two policemen from Captain Frank Rizzo's Center City precinct had gone to the Humoresque "because neighbors were telephoning that it was noisy." Describing what the policemen observed, the story returned to its original tone: "Crescendos of classical music. And when the music went diminuendo the rising babble of voices. Yeah, man! Every once in a while the policemen heard a curious shout, 'Check!' " Some of the men had facial hair, "the kind in which mustache and beard melt into a single composition." All seven "girls" had on "full length tights." The men wore "corduroy trousers, very tight pants," and some had "leather jackets, not the kind worn by rocks, but well-tailored jackets." "A number of chess games were in what is called progress. The talk was loud. The subjects were intellectual. [Officer] Powell distinctly heard the word 'art.' " At the police station at 12th and Pine, those patrons who were under the age of 18, "all seven girls and ten of the boys," were released into the custody of their parents. Heifetz was charged as the proprietor of a disorderly house, the other 17 adult males with breach of peace. The next day, Heifetz was held on $300 bail; the other adults were each fined $12.50.

In part, the *Bulletin* offered a narrative of territorial conflict to account for the raid. According to Gertrude Fitzpatrick, a "neighbor of the Humoresque," patrons "parked their cars on her sidewalk and made so much noise in her back yard she couldn't sleep." When she complained, "all she got was 'a mouthful of sass.' " The patrons, reportedly from "various sections of the city," were represented as unwelcome outsiders.

The *Bulletin* also offered a narrative of cultural conflict. Enjoying elite music and effete games, the patrons were regarded as eccentric by the police. While the male patrons wore facial hair and leather jackets, the authenticity of their embodied masculinity was in question insofar as these were not the types of jackets worn by rock and rollers but were "well-tailored" outerwear, "worth maybe $50" each. The colors of the female patrons' tights, some black or red, none pink or orange, signified rejection of contemporary norms of femininity.[2] In contrast, the police, revealingly garbed in "plainclothes," were represented as working-class buffoons.

In the bridge controversy, media explanations for the anti-Whitman campaign shifted over time. As the coffeehouse raids continued and coffeehouse defenders responded, media accounts also changed. Supplementing, grafting onto, and to some extent displacing the earlier narratives of territorial and cultural conflict were stories about drugs, same-sex sexualities, and interracial mixing. Whether this was due to tactical shifts by coffeehouse opponents, who needed to rally support in the court of public opinion and in courts of law, or new media willingness to discuss these topics, the coffeehouse controversy proved to be a critical episode in the history of public discourse about same-sex sexualities in the "Private City." And in this case, public discourse not only strengthened links between same-sex sexualities and men but suppressed and severed links between same-sex sexualities and women.

Raiding Representations

Four historical developments converged in 1959 to help transform a series of police raids into a major media story. The first was the emergence of the "beat generation" and "hipsters." Calling themselves beats, John D'Emilio and Estelle Freedman observe, a group of San Francisco poets and artists including Allen Ginsberg "broke sharply with the values of Cold War America by rejecting the ethos of career, marriage, and suburban consumerism." The beats achieved national recognition in 1957 with the publication of Jack Kerouac's *On the Road* and the arrest on obscenity charges of Lawrence Ferlinghetti, publisher of Ginsberg's homoerotic *Howl and Other Poems.* D'Emilio and Freedman also comment on the relationship between "beat," "hip," and "gay," noting that beats were inspired by "black hipster[s] of the northern ghettos who moved in a world of jazz, drugs, and sex" and that the beat subculture and gay world "overlapped."[3]

Heightened attention to juvenile delinquency was the second development that transformed the raids into a story. National concern about this problem soon led John F. Kennedy to create the President's Committee on Juvenile Delinquency and the U.S. Congress to pass the 1961 Juvenile Delinquency and Youth Offenses Control Act. Media coverage of the National Association of Secondary-School Principals' convention in Philadelphia in the days immediately surrounding the raids highlighted the problems of delinquency. Meanwhile, local officials reported that "juveniles under 18 accounted for nearly one-fourth of the 1958 city arrests for major crimes."[4]

If San Francisco beats found their worst enemy in Captain William Hanrahan, Philadelphia's coffeehouse aficionados encountered their nemesis in Frank Rizzo, whose rise to power was the third development that made a story out of the raids. Born into an Italian American, Catholic family in 1920, Rizzo grew up in South Philly and joined the police force in 1943. In 1952, police commissioner Thomas Gibbons named Rizzo an acting captain, one result of the local Democratic revolution that put Joseph Clark in the mayor's office. After a brief assignment in West Philly, Rizzo began a seven-year, career-making stint as a Center City captain. Rizzo was appointed acting police commissioner in 1966 and commissioner in 1967. According to one biographer, Rizzo then became the "first cop to run for mayor of a major American city." Winning two mayoral terms as a Democrat (but frequently flirting with Republicans such as President Richard Nixon), Rizzo served from 1972 to 1980.[5]

Rizzo's career was linked with key transformations in the relationship between law enforcement and electoral politics. As Frank Donner has argued, "While practices associated with the term *police state* abound in the United States . . . , beginning in the sixties, police state modes of governance emerged in ominous perspective in urban America. Among such subsequently disclosed police state patterns, Philadelphia's is outstanding. Not merely in a rhetorical sense, Philadelphia became a police city." Donner emphasizes the role played by the media in this process: "Rizzo instinctively knew that there was political gold in his blend of moralizing and law enforcement. But in order to extract it, he needed the help of the media." In Rizzo's city, Donner concludes, "the press was cast in the role of an enthusiastic collaborator in an arrangement by which a continuing supply of 'news' was exchanged for an equal amount of personal publicity."[6]

Rizzo's career was built on the tough reputation he acquired in the 1950s, a reputation that derived from the antivice image he cultivated with raids on bars, clubs, gambling dens, brothels, and strip joints. Pressed by the Greater Philadelphia Movement's campaign to rebuild downtown, the fourth development that turned the raids into a story, reformers were only too happy to have Rizzo celebrated for cleaning up a city voted "cleanest" in the nation while the coffeehouse controversy brewed and boiled over.[7]

Whether Rizzo was clean himself is widely debated. In a city W. E. B. Dubois had described as "one of the worst governed of America's badly governed cities" and Lincoln Steffens had called "corrupt and contented," Rizzo's rise took place in the aftermath of extraordinary revelations of municipal corruption. Police were implicated in these scandals most prominently in 1950, when Craig Ellis, head of the vice squad, and two other policemen committed suicide after U.S. Senator Estes Kefauver, the Senate Crime Investigating Committee, and a federal grand jury began examining Philadelphia. Kefauver concluded that "a paralyzing attitude of *laissez faire* seems to hang like an ether mist over the administration of the Philadelphia Police Department." In the next decade, Rizzo was accused of working with South Philly mob leaders and having an affair with stripper Blaze Starr, "Miss Spontaneous Combustion." In 1973, Jonathan Rubinstein's *City Police* described an extensive pattern of Philadelphia police payoffs by gambling, liquor, restaurant, and business interests during Rizzo's reign. In 1974, the Pennsylvania Crime Commission accused the Philadelphia police of "widespread, systematic" corruption. One of the commission's recommendations was that police resources should no longer be used to "curb prostitution and homosexuality," since this was "ineffective" and produced "a greater moral problem than the one it is seeking to cure, namely corruption."[8]

Although some payoffs protected businesses that served lesbians and gay men, for Rizzo cleaning up Philadelphia meant acting against these groups. In 1954, for example, police from Rizzo's precinct raided three clubs "in a drive against alleged obscene shows." At the Barton Sho-Bar, four "female impersonators," one "strip-tease dancer," and the owner were arrested. At a magistrate's hearing, police displayed a banner from the bar that read "Gay Boy Review—Direct from Hollywood." Against Rizzo's protests, the magistrate ruled that police failed to prove that the shows were more obscene than things shown on television and in magazines. In 1958, Rizzo's men raided a party at the home of painter-illustrator Emlen Etting. Rizzo reportedly told Etting, "Unless you and your goddamn pansy friends get back in the house, quiet down and shut up, I will put you all in the paddy wagon and throw you in with the drunks for the night." Also in 1958, Rizzo raided the Allegro, arresting patrons, bartenders, waitresses, and the owner. According to Joseph Yannone, who was Rizzo's driver,

> He hated all those fag joints. . . . On mischief night, especially, you know the night before Halloween, they'd all dress in drag and he would let them do that. But we got complaints about the clubs from the feds. The sailors when they pulled in the shipyard in South Philly would go to these bars, and when the "girl" would pull her dress down, then boom, he'd see it wasn't a girl. The sailors would want their money back, and they'd get the shit kicked out of them. So, we had to crack down. Rizzo was all for it. He really didn't like faggots.

Rizzo had served in the navy and may have identified with the sailors' experiences of attraction and repulsion. In fact, police in this era were both subjects and objects of antigay crackdowns. At least one policeman was arrested on "morals charges" concerning "teen-aged boys" in the midst of the coffeehouse controversy.[9] Before long, Rizzo would have to confront public allegations that his son, Frank Jr., born in 1943, was gay.[10]

Breaking News

Although all four of these developments were linked with same-sex sexualities, it was not immediately apparent to readers of the city's newspapers that the story of the raids was about lesbians or gay men. The initial narratives positioned neighbors against patrons; an older generation against a younger one; police against beats, hipsters, intellectuals, and artists; and proponents of "law and order" against defenders of civil liberties. On 14 February, for example, two days after the first stories appeared, the *Bulletin* and *Inquirer* reported that police had raided the Humoresque again and that Rizzo had highlighted neighborhood complaints about "noise" and "profanity." In the *News*, Rizzo referred to the concerns of "solid citizens who have lived in the neighborhood for 30 to 40 years." The *Inquirer* of 19 February also showed Rizzo raising neighborhood issues when he asked the city's Departments of Health and Licenses and Inspections and the state's Department of Labor and Industry to investigate four coffee shops: the Humoresque, Proscenium, Gilded Cage, and Artist's Hut. Heifetz responded by insisting that the music was played at low volume and was "classical, not rock 'n' roll." Granting that noise or rock music would be legitimate grounds for complaint, Heifetz fought back by representing himself as a good neighbor.[11]

The newspapers also portrayed the conflict as generational. According to the *Bulletin*, Rizzo stated that eight patrons found at the second raid were 15 years old and that he had gone to the Humoresque "because the parents of some of the youngsters asked him to." Heifetz claimed that Rizzo told these four boys and four girls, "I'm going to take you into the police station and bring your parents there to let them know what kind of people you are associating with." These motifs also appeared in the *Bulletin*'s account of a third night of arrests, when Rizzo visited the Artist's Hut, Proscenium, and Gilded Cage. From the latter, "the policemen took a boy who admitted to being 16 and another who they said looked no older than that." Citing the city's 10:30 p.m. curfew for minors under 16 years of age, the *Bulletin* noted that the boys were "collected" at the station by their parents.[12]

Coffeehouse defenders were not willing to yield the generational narrative. One response was to call attention to respectable adult patrons. According to Heifetz, while "four boys and four girls" were in the Humoresque when the second raid took place, there were 30 patrons in all, including "some married couples." Heifetz also enlisted the support of parents. While police were conducting their third set of raids, Heifetz, a group of patrons, and some of their parents were meeting with the ACLU's Spencer Coxe. Meanwhile, the *Tribune* reported that the parents of an African American man arrested at the Humoresque regarded the coffee shop as a "welcome substitute for 'juice joints' and houses of ill repute." Implicitly siding with coffeehouse defenders, the *Bulletin* mocked the police for targeting "kids who ought to be drinking milk." Similarly, a letter to the *Bulletin* praised Rizzo for attacking "highly suspect activities" that "smack of a subversive plot to lure the youth of the nation away from television watching or street corner lounging."[13]

Linked with the narratives of geographic and generational conflict was a narrative of cultural conflict between police and beats, hipsters, intellectuals, and artists. The first *Inquirer* story described the Humoresque as "a haven for 'beatniks' or followers of jazz music." Unlike the *Bulletin*, which reported that patrons under 18 were released into parental custody and patrons over 18 were arrested, the *Inquirer* distinguished between patrons dressed "in traditional garb of chinos and sweaters," who were released, and "beatniks," who were arrested. Two days later, the *Bulletin* reported that, according to Heifetz, Rizzo had called him a "creep" and the Humoresque "a den of iniquity."[14]

Defenders of the coffeehouses responded in several ways. The *News* editorialized that "maybe Capt. Rizzo doesn't understand why girls wearing leotards and men looking like beatniks want to sit around drinking espresso, listening to classical music on a hi-fi set, playing chess and talking about Art with a capital A." "Neither do we," the *News* noted. "But we don't see why they should be arrested, finger-printed and mugged for doing it." A mocking letter to the *Bulletin* praised the police for their "unflinching heroism." These "fearless crusaders" had encountered "coffee-drinking, playing chess, reading, listening to music and, above all, talking," all of which were "menaces to our nation." Some observers denied that the coffeehouses were filled with beats. One letter asserted that "coffee houses in this city entertain fewer than one 'beatnik' for every 400 customers."[15]

Coffeehouse defenders also used the raids to criticize the police more generally. Several commentators focused on police inefficiency, inappropriate priorities, and a failure to address "real" delinquency. After the second raid, Heifetz stated that Rizzo spoke "very loudly and rudely," an indictment of the captain's cultural style. One letter writer claimed that he had "chuckled" in his "beard" at the *Bulletin*'s original story but that he was "pleased with the detectives' ability to recognize the music as 'classical.' "[16] In these class-marked accounts, coffeehouse proponents depicted a conflict between sophisticated coffee drinkers and ignorant police.

One coffeehouse defender positioned the patrons between and against both working-class police and well-to-do neighbors. Horace Proctor, Jr., wrote that he suspected that "wealthy people" who lived near the Humoresque had applied "political pressure" to bring about the raids. According to Proctor, these elites were "so narrow-minded and intolerant of people that are 'different,' that they might use their influence to deny these people their right to live as individuals." Proctor, however, was no celebrant of "difference" that he perceived to be déclassé: "To discriminate against the type of people who prefer coffee, chess, and classical music over beer, gambling, and women is no better than discriminating against their race or religion." Proctor and his wife did not like "rock 'n' roll, baseball or inane television programs." "Should we for this be harassed?" he asked.[17]

The conflict between police and beats, hipsters, intellectuals, and artists was both cultural and political. While Rizzo and the police depicted the coffeehouses as threats to order, Heifetz and his patrons represented the police as threats to civil liberties. Rizzo, according to Heifetz, "behaved in the manner of one of Hitler's storm troopers." According to the *News*, Manuel Rubin, owner of the Proscenium, was working with other owners to "end these Gestapo raids." Reporting on the involvement of the ACLU, which filed a complaint with the city's new Police Review Board, the papers framed the conflict as one that concerned basic civil liberties.[18]

News Updates

On 19 February, one week after the initial stories appeared, newspaper readers learned that Heifetz had made a bold next move. Using the federal Civil Rights Act enacted during Reconstruction, Heifetz had filed suit in U.S. District Court for $25,000, charging Rizzo and the city with damaging his business. Harvey Walters, who had been arrested in the first raid, also filed suit, asking $15,000 for damage to his reputation. Attorney Theodore Mann asked Judge Thomas Clary for a temporary injunction restraining Rizzo and his men from entering the Humoresque without a warrant, making arrests there "without reasonable basis," "interfering with Heifetz's right to conduct his business and with his right of privacy and with his and Walters' right to assemble peacefully," and "interfering with Walters' right to partake of refreshments" and "play chess." Helping to create an impression that the police were bullies, the *Bulletin* quoted Heifetz as saying that his business had been "permanently damaged" because customers were now afraid to come.[19]

Readers thus learned on 19 February that both Heifetz and Rizzo had escalated their conflict. Heifetz was taking Rizzo to court. Rizzo was asking for local and state investigations. But while the stories concerning Heifetz's action fit neatly into the existing narrative frameworks, other stories did not. The *News*, for example, reported that police had raided the coffee shops "looking for 'known narcotics users or sellers.'" The *Inquirer* referred not only to complaints about noise, "foul language," and "'carrying on' between young girls and boys," but also "a report by an undercover policewoman disclosing how she arranged to purchase 'five sticks of marijuana in one of these shops.'"[20]

Letters to the *Bulletin* suggested other new angles. Walter S. Fraser of Willow Grove, Pennsylvania, wrote that he had been in the Humoresque when Rizzo raided it and declared, "I haven't seen any alcoholics or homosexuals there." Referring to Humoresque patrons, Gertrude Fitzpatrick wrote, "I have been subjected to their loud conversation on perverted sex both from the alley behind my home and from the front of my home."[21] "Homosexuals" and "perverted sex" thus entered print media discourse on the raids in denials of the presence of the former and in opposition to the latter as a topic of conversation. Although Fitzpatrick complained about voices penetrating her domestic sphere from "behind" and "front," no one cited in the newspapers at this point had complained about the actual presence of lesbians, gay men, or same-sex sexual behaviors in or around the coffee shops.

What accounts for the week that elapsed between the initial coverage and the first mention of homosexuality? It is possible that the newspapers had known about complaints about homosexuality but had not reported on them. It is also possible that the police, neighbors, patrons, and owners had not shared these concerns with reporters, at least not on the record. Perhaps some of the language the newspapers used *had* signified homosexuality to some readers. Perhaps, after learning that Heifetz was taking the police to court, Rizzo, the police, and Fitzpatrick decided to use drugs and homosexuality to win their cases and rally public support. Whatever accounts for the change, residents were no longer said to be upset primarily about "'carrying on' between young girls and boys."

Drugs and same-sex sexualities were also highlighted when 300 people, mostly members of the Center City Residents Association, met on 19 February to discuss the coffeehouses. Fitzpatrick handed Commissioner Gibbons a petition signed by 33 people demanding the closing of the Humoresque. Another neighbor, Eugene John Lewis, presented a petition with 22 signatures against the Gilded Cage. According to the *Inquirer*, Gibbons told the gathering that "statements that would shock adults were made by boys and girls, ranging in age from 14 to 17, after they were taken into custody." Gibbons claimed that one 14-year-old said "she had gone to the 'place for the sole purpose of becoming acquainted with sex deviates.'" The *Bulletin* reported that Gibbons said that this student "'admitted she had gone to the place (the Humoresque) to make acquaintances with Lesbians. That's my case,' he said. 'It's the case of all decent citizens in the city.'"

Grafting the new narrative of sexual difference onto the earlier narrative of age conflict, Gibbons constructed homosexuality as deviant and youthful and deviance and youthfulness as homosexual.[22]

A similar process took place with the narrative of territorial conflict. According to the *Inquirer*'s account of the Center City meeting, "housewives living in the area" complained about patrons' "obscene language and immoral conduct." The *Bulletin* reported that Milo MacGoldrick charged that the Humoresque was "a gathering place for homosexuals" and that "it's a hangout for a lot of odd screwballs who live elsewhere." Eugene John Lewis claimed that he had been in the Gilded Cage several times and saw "homosexuals and Lesbians and young girls with old men." According to Lewis, "This place attracts groups of undesirables who, when they are not beating up each other, beat up people living in the neighborhood." Representing lesbians and gay men as violent and pedophilic, these accounts grafted new narrative conflicts between domesticated heterosexuals and disorderly homosexuals onto earlier narrative conflicts between neighbors and outsiders. Homosexuality was constructed as foreign to the neighborhood and foreigners to the neighborhood were constructed as homosexual.[23]

The new attention to homosexuality and drugs also transformed the narrative conflict between police and beats. Displacing language describing the patrons as innocent, the newspapers now put forward more images of them as immoral and obscene. Meanwhile, opponents of the coffeehouses rushed forward to praise the police. According to the *Bulletin*, E. Walter Hudson, past president of the Center City Residents Association, called for "a tremendous vote of confidence for Rizzo." Reverend James Vallely of St. Patrick's Church noted, "We have to keep center-city respectable. . . . I'm on Captain Rizzo's side in that respect." The *Bulletin* reported, "Gibbons was also asked what interest the 'anti-egg head, anti-nonconformist, anti-intellectual feelings of the department played in the raids.' 'No interest at all,' Gibbons replied. 'We have quite a few intellects in the department ourselves.' "[24]

Homosexuality was also linked with drug use. Reporting on the Center City meeting, the *Inquirer* noted that 6 of the 18 people arrested at the Humoresque had police records. The next sentence indicated that Bernard Lemisch, counsel for the Fraternal Order of Police, told residents that "more than 27 narcotics purchases had been made from patrons of the four coffee shops." The implication was that the prior arrests had been drug-related and that drug users were either consorting with "sex deviates" or were sexually deviant themselves.[25]

According to the media, defenders of the coffeehouses at the Center City meeting responded to these new attacks in several ways. The *Inquirer* presented no direct response to the accusations about homosexuality and drugs, focusing instead on civil liberties arguments. Several lawyers condemned the raids and suggested that residents should have obtained a court injunction, which one lawyer then immediately offered to do.[26] The *Bulletin* editorialized that "some patrons of some coffee houses are merely odd; but others are odd to a point offensive to public morality and perhaps dangerous to juvenile acquaintances." However, Rizzo's raids were "the wrong way to handle the complaints," not only because "dragnet technique[s]" were "offensive to normal civil rights," but also because they put "most citizens' sympathies where they may not really belong."[27] While criticizing the police, both the *Bulletin* and the lawyers who called for a court injunction implied that there were reasonable grounds for opposing the coffeehouses.

Another strategy was to promise cooperation with authorities. According to the *Inquirer* and *Bulletin*, Jack Spiller, owner of the Artist's Hut, said he "always cooperated with the police." In the *Bulletin*, Edward Halpern, owner of the Gilded Cage, "disputed charges that homosexuals gathered at his shop." " 'I'm not a doctor,' he said. 'I can't tell the differences.' He said certain undesirables might come to his shop but, he insisted, he always tries to get rid of them." Both Spiller and Halpern seemed to agree with opponents of the coffeehouses that their shops should not serve "undesirables."[28]

In the coverage of the Center City meeting, only one person explicitly supported the coffeehouses for their unique character. Near the end of its story, the *Bulletin* noted that, according to one resident, "The coffeehouses gave center-city a touch of local color. 'It shows that we don't roll up our sidewalks at 7 o'clock at night,' he said. 'We need variety in center-city. These places give us a touch of Greenwich Village.' "[29]

More often than not, coffeehouse defenders stressed their respectability. In "A Visit to the Coffeehouses," *Bulletin* reporter James Smart took his readers on a tour, beginning with the Artist's Hut. Observing a sign "warning teenagers of the curfew" and another that read "No Parking, Temporary Police Regulation," Smart represented the coffee shop as law-abiding. After describing the physical environment and patrons, Smart traced the history of coffeehouses back to the Middle East in the sixteenth century, London and America in the eighteenth, and New York in the early twentieth. Countering the image of coffeehouses as recent creations of troubled youth, Smart's story stressed their long and illustrious history.[30]

Asking "Who goes to coffeehouses?" Smart answered by presenting the narrative conflict in clear terms: "The proprietors and habitues say they are college students, artists and art students, persons looking for a quiet place to spend an inexpensive evening in a nonalcoholic atmosphere. Neighbors of the places and policemen add to that list homosexuals, dope users and various types of odd characters." Conflict was also clear in Smart's answer to the question, "What do they do there?" "Proprietors and habitues" stressed eating, drinking, reading, playing chess and checkers, listening to music, and talking; "neighbors and policemen add that they make noise, park cars on the sidewalk and promulgate narcotics addiction and immorality."

While presenting both sides of the story, Smart offered more support for the patrons' version. Most of the customers described were in mixed-sex couples. Although members of these couples might mix and match gender codes (one man looked "Marlon Brandoish," a "girl" sported "khaki slacks," and another "girl" had on "black tights" under her "wool skirt"), most did not conform to common public images of lesbians and gay men. Although same-sex couples were mentioned ("two heavily made-up college girls in mannish blouses and wool skirts," a "well-dressed man in a derby" who stopped to "chat with a friend," and "two young men" sitting together), most were not clearly marked as lesbian or gay.

Quoting a variety of patrons, Smart lent support to their narratives of respectability. One art student noted, "We don't have a beatnik type in Philadelphia." His "companion" observed, "There are pseudos. . . . Kids who like to smoke a pipe and put on a European hat." But these were "phony." According to Smart, patrons "resent the branding of coffeehouses as hangouts for degenerates and dope users." One student said that while "odd characters" frequented the shops, "the same type, and worse" could be found elsewhere. He also said he had seen Rubin "order people out of the Proscenium because he didn't like the way they act." A "married" man explained that he and his wife did not drink alcohol and so did not go to bars. "If the police don't like some of the people here," he declared, "let them arrest those people. Why bother us?" As for the Humoresque, Smart reported that "the coffeehouse crowd" believed that Heifetz was "not responsible for any of the 'weirdos' who may have come to his place." One customer stated that "Mel's a naive sort of guy. . . . He wouldn't know an oddball if one walked in." Challenging the assault on the coffeehouses, defenders joined the campaign against oddballs.

Smart's biographical information on Heifetz highlighted his respectability. Readers learned that Heifetz had first encountered coffeehouses while in the army and stationed in Europe. On returning to Philadelphia, he began visiting the Humoresque, which opened in March 1958 and which he bought in May. Smart noted that on weeknights, the Humoresque served "neighbors, college students and regulars." On weekends, "Teenagers on dates fill the place from 9:30 to 11:30, clearing out before curfew (midnight). The older set shows up a little later." Smart also revealed a few of Heifetz's "secrets," which included the awards he had received from the Boy Scouts and the

Daughters of the American Revolution. One friend stated that Heifetz "doesn't see why he needs any character references." Representing Heifetz's patrons as neighbors, students, and teenagers on dates, Smart portrayed Heifetz as a patriot who was modest about his civic contributions.

While for the most part Smart's story presented the controversy within the narrative frameworks already established, toward the end of the article the reporter introduced a new one: "Underlying the complaints from some neighbors, coffeehouse regulars say, are questions of race. This produces diametrically opposed protests. One is that Negroes are welcome in several of the coffeehouses, and racially mixed couples have been seen. The other is that folk songs rendered by some customers date to the Civil War and are sprinkled with epithets objectionable to Negroes." While the latter claim was not repeated in the press, the former one was. The local ACLU's newsletter reported that "an illegal raid on an interracial gathering in a Mt. Airy residence was excused by the police on the grounds that the arrested persons were part of the 'crowd from those downtown coffee houses.' " Even when the *Tribune* quoted Rizzo as saying that the "contention that his squad staged the raids because colored and white—especially colored boys and white girls—mixed freely" was "a lie," the narrative link between coffeehouses and interracialism was strengthened.[31]

In a period in which the percentage of African Americans in Philadelphia was increasing but the percentage in Center City was decreasing, the presence of African Americans and interracial couples in Center City coffeehouses served as a reminder of the displacement of African Americans from the neighborhood and a symbol of new African American and interracial transgressions. Although the media never discussed interracialism in same-sex sexual forms or same-sex sexuality in interracial forms, homosexuality and interracial sexuality were linked by association in the coffeehouses.

In the end, just as defenders of Whitman had stressed his respectability, defenders of the coffeehouses stressed theirs. Just as proponents of Whitman sought to strengthen their position by attacking the church, proponents of the coffeehouses sought to strengthen theirs by attacking the police. But while Philadelphia's newspapers never reported explicitly that debates about homosexuality were at the center of the bridge controversy, the newspapers did openly report on homosexuality in the coffeehouse conflict. Perhaps statements by police and neighbors made it more difficult to avoid the issue. Perhaps the papers were more willing to discuss same-sex sexualities in the coffeehouses than in Whitman's life and work. Perhaps police and neighbors opposed to the coffeehouses were more closely linked to the writers and readers of Philadelphia's papers than the Catholic and South Jersey critics of Whitman were. Perhaps something had changed in three years. Whatever accounts for the difference, local coverage of the coffeehouse controversy included explicit and extended public discussions of same-sex sexualities.

Making Sex News

In some ways, these discussions constructed same-sex sexualities as both male and female. For example, a column in the *News* referred to "limp-wristed young men" and "girls in crew cuts" who frequented "Bohemian hangouts."[32] References to "homosexuals," "perverted sex," "obscene language," and "immoral conduct" could have signified male and female deviations. Given a larger cultural context in which same-sex sexualities were more often associated with the former, however, readers may have assumed that most or all of the stories concerned men and/or boys. In addition, as is suggested by the distinction Commissioner Gibbons made between "homosexuals" and "Lesbians," some theoretically sex-neutral words may have not been understood in sex-neutral ways. Moreover, even when patrons were depicted as gender transgressors, the dominant image was that of feminine men rather than masculine women. For example, the *Tribune* described one of the men arrested at the Humoresque as an aspiring "French teacher" and another as an honor society high-school graduate who was working at Miss Adele Reed's "beauty school," teaching ballet, and planning to attend Fisk University.[33] Furthermore, to the extent that both female and male sexualities were discussed, they were discussed differently. Insofar as female adults were not arrested but male adults were, lesbianism was constructed more as a problem of minors. Teenage "girls" apparently were corrupting one another or were being corrupted by gay men. Male homosexuality was constructed as a problem of adult men, teenage boys, and intergenerational association.

After the court proceedings began, some stories again constructed homosexuality as neither specifically male nor female. For example, the *Bulletin* reported that 13 neighbors of the Humoresque asked the Common Pleas Court to declare the shop a "nuisance" because it harbored "boisterous people who use vile and obscene language" and "openly flaunted their homosexuality in public." In other stories, homosexuality was portrayed as male. According to an *Inquirer* article that referred to the Humoresque as "a popular haunt of sex deviates," Sherry Goodman told Judge Clary in District Court that the "foul and obscene language is absolutely horrible." Implicitly suggesting that the objects of her complaints were male, Goodman explained that "the young people . . . see a woman approach on the street and are so insensible they won't stop that objectionable language." More explicitly, the *Bulletin* reported that an undercover policewoman testified that the Humoresque was "a gathering place for homosexuals" and that one "nightly visitor" was a man who "dressed as a woman." Similarly, the *News* reported on testimony about "sex deviates and female impersonators." Although homosexuality was linked with effeminacy here, it was again presented as male.[34]

According to the *Bulletin*, Rizzo testified that he chased away "two men misbehaving outside the Humoresque." Rizzo also told the court that the second raid occurred after he witnessed "four girls enter the coffeeshop," where he then saw "obvious homosexuals." His testimony made clear that while male homosexuality was the main problem, the protection of underage girls was his priority. Rizzo thus cast himself in the role of the male heterosexual defender of young female sexual virtue. Perversely and paradoxically, he was suggesting that these young girls were threatened by male "homosexuals."[35]

Along the same lines, the *Bulletin* reported that two undercover policemen claimed that "narcotics addicts and homosexuals" frequented the Humoresque and that one said that he observed "adult young men keeping company with boys and girls." A woman testified that she saw "two persons in men's clothing kissing each other outside the coffeeshop." While this phrasing raised some question as to whether these were in fact men, readers were more likely to conclude that they were male than to imagine that they were female cross-dressers. Describing the testimony of two neighbors who "heard girls crying outside the place," the *Bulletin* juxtaposed images of kissing men with those of crying girls. These stories simultaneously attacked intergenerational homo- and heterosexuality, constructed homosexuality as male, and heterosexualized the "girls."[36]

How did coffeehouse defenders respond, and how did the media present these responses, after coverage shifted to the court proceedings? Heifetz highlighted the denial of civil liberties and challenged the disorderly image conveyed by the police. According to the *Inquirer*, Heifetz told the court, "I never permitted rock and roll. . . . We played practically all classical music since I wanted to attract a good class of customers." Supporting this respectable portrait, Walters testified that one day before the raid he had been discharged from the army and had gone to the Humoresque to see Heifetz, an "old friend" from the Boy Scouts. The *Bulletin* also noted that while Heifetz admitted that there had been complaints concerning "loud music or parking on the sidewalk," he also claimed that "he was never warned by police or neighbors that there were narcotics users or homosexuals frequenting his place." The implication was that had Heifetz been so warned, he might have excluded these two groups. Several days later, the *Bulletin* reported that six teenagers—three male and three female—testified that there was "neither obscenity nor 'running around' " in the Humoresque on the night of the first raid. One mother "backed up her daughter's account." Constance Matthews testified that "she had gone to the Humoresque three or four times herself 'because I always go to every place my daughter goes. I always investigate to make sure it's a proper place for her to go.' "[37]

Heifetz and his allies also attacked the police. While Philadelphians learned about developments in the federal case against Rizzo and the local case against Heifetz, they also read about the Common Pleas Court appeals filed by eight of the patrons convicted earlier. In March, the *Bulletin* reported that one witness testified that he, too, had been arrested at the Humoresque on 11 February, but that although "one officer threatened to kick him" at the police station, he was "slipped out the back door . . . after mentioning that his brother was a member of the Police Department." Two days later, the *Bulletin* reported that Heifetz revealed that another patron seized at the Humoresque had been released when he mentioned that his brother was a policeman. (This patron was none other than drag queen "Sarah Vaughan.")[38]

In the end, Rizzo's arguments won more than they lost. In the Common Pleas Court appeals, Judge Doty dismissed the charges against one appellant, set aside the convictions of three, and upheld the remaining four (including Walters's). According to the *Bulletin*, two patrolmen testified that when they entered the Humoresque, "three boys were dancing ring-around-the-rosy around a table." The lawyer for the patrons argued that one of his clients (one of the two African American men discussed by the *Tribune*) "had done nothing but sit at a table while two other boys were dancing." Although Doty dismissed the charges in this case, he "reprimanded" the appellant for "taking up the time of those who should be busy solving holdups and robberies." As for the others, when the lawyer argued that "there was not one scintilla of evidence that any of the defendants acted disorderly," the judge responded that if the lawyer "went across the street to the Girard Trust Corn Exchange Bank dancing, singing and shouting," he would "wind up at 12th and Pine Sts., too."[39]

In the three cases he set aside (including the other African American case discussed by the *Tribune*), Doty ruled that "what the young men did, if anything, did not add up to disorderly conduct because it occurred within the shop, not on the public highway." In the cases he upheld, Doty accepted police claims that these four "were in a group of six young men they saw leaving the coffee shop, shouting and yelling, who bumped into two young girls and shouted obscenities at them."[40] The court thus dismissed the cases against the homosocially dancing men whose transgressions took place inside the Humoresque and upheld the cases against the heterosocially offensive men who "bumped" and "shouted" in "public."

Rizzo's victory was clearer in federal court, where Judge Clary declined to grant injunctions against the police because Rizzo had been transferred to Northeast Philly and would not likely raid the Humoresque again. Insofar as Rizzo had been made one of two new inspectors in command of the Northeast, his transfer amounted to a promotion. What's more, Rizzo's exile did not last long. Less than a year after his transfer, Gibbons moved Rizzo to West Philly. And in August 1960, less than 18 months after leaving Center City as a captain, Rizzo was given command of the entire Central Division.[41]

Not long after Clary's ruling, Heifetz's isolation from the other coffeehouse owners became clear. In late March, the *Inquirer* reported that, after meeting with Mayor Dilworth, City Managing Director Donald Wagner, Gibbons, and Rizzo, the owners of the Artist's Hut, Proscenium, and Gilded Cage promised "to police themselves and bar undesirable persons." According to Wagner, "These gentlemen said they wanted to cooperate with the police in every way possible" and would rely on the police to "point out the types of people who should be barred." Around this time, Dilworth wrote to an ACLU leader who had been critical of the police raids, "Places where queers congregate do raise the devil with a neighborhood in very short order, and it is very difficult to break up such groups without some violation of civil rights. I will not say that some of my best friends are queers, or that I completely understand them, but I do know that while they are relatively harmless by themselves, when they get to running in packs they can be really vicious, and louse up a neighborhood in no time flat."[42]

Heifetz's neighbors won their case as well. On 26 September 1959, the Quarter Session Court jury found Heifetz guilty of running a disorderly house. According to the *Bulletin*, neighbors testified about "loud noises, disturbances on the steps and street, and the activities of homosexual patrons." Police testified that "six boys" pushed and exchanged obscenities with "two girls." The *Inquirer* reported that witnesses labeled the Humoresque "a hangout for 'beatniks,' sex deviates, dope addicts and pushers" and that police claimed they observed "a group of young men leave the coffee shop and shout obscenities at several young girls." One month later, Judge Leo Weinrott ordered Heifetz to shut down the Humoresque or go to jail. Heifetz chose the former. Meanwhile, in the aftermath of an incident in which Heifetz was accused of drawing a gun on a patron who he claimed was stealing a coffee pot, the *Bulletin* reported that Heifetz was found guilty on new charges of "carrying a deadly weapon and playfully pointing a firearm." He received a suspended sentence for the first charge, a year's probation for the second, and an extra year's probation for the earlier disorderly house charge.[43]

The final federal court ruling on Heifetz's and Walters's suits also proved to be a victory for Rizzo. In December 1959, Judge Clary dismissed both. In his decision, Clary first referred to complaints about noise, the presence of minors, and "patronage from all parts of the City, rather than the immediate neighborhood." Declaring that he did not believe the statements of two neighbors who testified to the contrary, Clary also wrote that Rizzo had "received complaints from parents of persons of tender age." More prominent in the decision, however, were explanations that centered on homosexuality, drugs, and heterosocial offenses. According to Clary, the Humoresque had become "a gathering place of homosexuals and narcotic addicts." Clary gave credence to Rizzo's observation of "two men immediately after leaving the Humoresque hugging and kissing on the sidewalk," the testimony of a female neighbor who saw "similar occurrences," and evidence that "two of those arrested, boys, 18 and 19 years of age, were found hugging and squeezing each other."[44]

Clary also based his decision on police testimony that six men had left the Humoresque "yelling, singing, and in a loud and raucous tone of voice using profanity." After these men ran back to the coffee shop, they were seen "brushing two young ladies who were leaving the place. When the young ladies protested they were answered profanely and the males then re-entered the establishment." Clary also highlighted male police heterosocial concern in relating that Rizzo had observed "four young girls, whom he judged from appearance to be of a rather tender age, enter the establishment," where they were joined by a 17-year-old "youth." According to Clary, Rizzo had also noted that "there were several people present, whom he knew to be homosexuals." Once again, the police appeared to be concerned about teenage girls associating with male homosexuals.

One story that had been critical in the earlier narratives was missing from Clary's decision and from all coverage of the court proceedings. Commissioner Gibbons had initially justified the raids by calling attention to the 14-year-old girl who had gone to the Humoresque to meet lesbians. Perhaps the most striking proof that the media played an active role in linking same-sex sexualities more with men and boys than with women and girls is the fact that not once did the newspapers again mention the girl whose efforts to meet "sex deviates" had so moved Commissioner Gibbons. Why did her story and the stories of the other six girls arrested in the original raid fail to reappear? Had Gibbons fabricated the story and then dropped it? Did Clary hear testimony about these girls but not refer to it in his decision? Did the newspapers fail to report on this testimony? In the end, it seems likely that the story did not appear because the idea of a young woman seeking out lesbians failed to conform to the narratives offered by police. This was not a girl offended by straight or gay men and in need of Rizzo's protection. This was not a girl in danger of contamination or seduction at the coffeehouses;

she herself was seeking out lesbians. This was not a girl whose "problem" could be blamed upon Heifetz, the Humoresque, or the coffeehouses. So her story disappeared.

In the bridge controversy, few Whitman supporters suggested publicly that the poet was a good selection not in spite of but because of his homoerotic desires and loves. *One*'s coverage was exceptional, demonstrating the difference that an organized political movement could make. Similarly, in the local press, only the man quoted as supporting the coffeehouses for the "touch of local color" and "Greenwich Village" came close to offering a progay view. *One* again proved to be exceptional, offering a campy report that linked the story of the raids with the politics of masculinity:

> Philly cop Captain Rizzo has an awful time trying to keep the center of the city clean and pervert-free. Extra terrible job with this Beat Generation. Imagine a 100%, patriotic, real he-man cop having to see things like grown men playing chess! And men (women too) sitting around arty little restaurants sipping coffee—and reading books yet—talking all that egg-head stuff! And that highbrow music! And those beards, and turtleneck sweaters, and tights and things! A he-man just doesn't have to stand for that sort of thing going on.

One made three additional points. First, "Little evidence was presented that the coffeehouses are actually gay—and readers tell us that only a small percentage of the people in these places are gay." Second, "Homosexuals do have a right—and should exercise that right—to patronize any coffee-house, bar, or other public establishment." And third, "Why not a few gay coffeehouses? Up to now, bars have been almost the only public places homosexuals could gather—and since many homosexuals don't drink—seems to me the coffeehouse would be a good addition."[45] In the absence of a local homophile movement and at a safe distance from the local scene, *One* offered the most progay interpretation of the raids. Significantly, *One*'s interpretation staged a conflict between "he-men" and perverts, with deviant women parenthetically set aside alongside their male counterparts.

Rewriting the News

More than 30 years later, the recollections of narrators reaffirm some elements of the narratives circulating in 1959, modify others, and introduce several new ones. Heifetz remembers the objections of neighbors, but now believes that one of the critics was gay himself. He also recalls the presence of interracial couples. "For a black boy to go out with a white girl," Heifetz explains, "there weren't many places that they would really feel comfortable. But the coffee shops, they were comfortable." According to Heifetz, "politically astute" people have told him that this was what triggered the raids: "The police, being very white and being very conservative, didn't like the idea of seeing black and white couples." While Heifetz remembers interracial mixing, he thinks that the accusations about drugs were groundless.[46]

Heifetz's recollections also modify the narrative of police corruption. Not long after he bought the Humoresque, Heifetz remembers, a police sergeant suggested that he talk to Rizzo. Heifetz recalls Rizzo mentioning "complaints" and saying that "if I would cooperate with him, he was sure that it was no problem." "And I didn't know what he meant," Heifetz explains. "And as we talked, it was suggested that if I were supportive of the patrolmen on the beat, that were in cars, and if I were to make a gesture towards them, they would be very supportive of me." In a second conversation, Rizzo suggested that Christmas would be a "nice time" to show his "appreciation." Describing himself as "a little innocent," Heifetz remembers giving the police small bottles of alcohol. "Apparently that wasn't quite the gesture that he had in mind."

> What precipitated the whole thing was the fact that I didn't understand that there was a system of paying off the police in those days. And that if you had made an arrangement where you gave them 50 dollars a week, you would never be bothered for anything. And bars of the day all paid off. As I got older and as I became familiar with the bars and the people that owned them, I found out that there was an arrangement, that they used to go and pay off money every week, either to the police or to City Hall. I actually, years later, wound up walking with someone who owned a bar, and went into City Hall, and I knew what he was doing. He was paying them off. And he did that every week.

Heifetz also describes backlash. The Humoresque "started to attract an undesirable clientele because the people that had been coming in were now scared away." At one point, "some young neighborhood kids" started to come and one night, after they walked out with his stainless steel pots, Heifetz began yelling. According to Heifetz, when they threatened him, he retrieved his unloaded gun and the troublemakers left. When Heifetz called to report the incident, the police charged him with gun violations, which he considers "payback." He also remembers incidents involving his lover, who was stopped by police a few times while driving Heifetz's car. After police saw Heifetz's name on the registration, his lover was harassed. In one incident, police took the car to Germantown and demanded that Heifetz claim it there. In another, two policemen took his lover to a South

Philly park, where, according to Heifetz, "he had to submit to giving them oral sex . . . or they were going to beat him up."

One part of Heifetz's story that was never mentioned in the newspapers at the time but that he talks about today is that he is gay. In fact, Heifetz suggests that accusations about homosexuality in the coffeehouses contributed to his coming out. Born in 1935 and raised by a Jewish family in Center City and South Philly, Heifetz recalls that he had his first same-sex sexual experiences in the Boy Scouts and the Market Street movie theaters. But he does not think that he was aware, when he was 15 or 16, that there was a "gay society," "gay people," or a "gay lifestyle." After serving in the military and returning to Philly, Heifetz began his "first gay romance" with a man he met at the Humoresque. Discussing police accusations about the coffeehouses, Heifetz says, "That was probably the first time in my life that I was ever face to face with the word publicly: homosexual."

Heifetz now estimates that 25–40% of his patrons and 100% of his staff were gay. Asked why he thinks the Humoresque was singled out, Heifetz suggests that although "all of the coffee shops had some gay people," the Humoresque "probably had visibly more gay people." Moreover, when discussing the presence of gay men in the Humoresque, Heifetz sets the conflict into larger geographic terms. All four coffeehouses were in the vicinity of Rittenhouse Square. Symbols of the area's gay presence, the coffeehouses in general and the Humoresque in particular offered those who opposed that presence a scapegoat. Defenders of the coffeehouses who did not publicly acknowledge that they were popular among lesbians or gay men may have been using the same type of strategic dissembling that often proved effective in everyday life. Denying that there were lesbian or gay patrons, that they knew about lesbian or gay patrons, or that they had been informed by police about lesbian or gay patrons may have been among the most promising strategies available for securing court victories, even though this strategy condoned attacks on lesbians and gay men.

Although Heifetz and several other gay narrators do not recall seeing lesbians in the coffeehouses, many lesbian narrators remember the coffeehouse scene as sexually and socially vital for them as well. Pat Hill, for example, remembers Rizzo raiding the Gilded Cage and says that she "begged to go," but that Rizzo "brushed" her aside. "I wanted to be part of it," she recalls. "I *was* part of it. But I guess I just looked so innocent that he wouldn't take me. I wanted to get in the paddy wagon. Because they were taking everybody else off. And I felt very left behind." This image of Hill, part of the coffeehouse scene but "left behind" by the police, is emblematic of how lesbians and gay men often shared social space but experienced different forms of oppression and resistance.[47]

The roles played by lesbians and gay men in the coffeehouse narratives and the other texts discussed in part 2 point to a number of conclusions about sex, gender, and sexuality in the postwar years. As Wini Breines has argued, " 'Deviants' such as Beats, hipsters, juvenile delinquents, homosexuals, even communists, were almost always males . . . in the scholarly and public mind" in the 1950s.[48] This was in spite of the existence of dynamic "deviant" female cultures, including the ones discussed in part 1. The masculinization of lesbians and effeminization of gay men in public discourse failed to make lesbians any more visible, gay men any less visible, than would be expected given their sexes. And yet the stories of the 14-year-old girl looking for lesbians in the coffeehouses and Pat Hill trying to get arrested at the Gilded Cage suggest not only that lesbians were present in these cultural spaces but that they were visible to one another.

In general, however, media narratives constructed gay men as visible, lesbians as invisible. When representations of lesbians did appear, they often were derived from, or conceived of in relation to, or overwhelmed by, their male counterparts. On the whole, the media constructed gay men as public, independent, and sexually active and lesbians as private, dependent, and sexually passive. In turn, to the extent that public discourse shaped the views of lesbians and gay men, lesbians were more likely to define themselves in relation to gay men than the other way around.

The roles played by lesbians and gay men in the coffeehouse controversy and in other public debates between 1945 and 1960 also point to a number of conclusions about relationships between the politics of everyday life and organized social movement politics. First, both lesbians and gay men were part of an alternative late 1940s and 1950s culture that provided a vital public space for dissent from dominant norms. Second, these spaces were critical in the processes by which a variety of social groups moved from the politics of everyday culture in the late 1940s and 1950s to the politics of organized struggle in the 1960s. For example, a significant number of lesbians and gay men who became active in the homophile movement in the 1960s remember spending time in the coffeehouses in the 1950s. Although Heifetz's 1959 suit was an individual instance of gay resistance not sustained by a political group engaging in ongoing struggle, it helped create conditions that made it more possible to imagine the formation of a Philadelphia homophile movement in 1960. Third, resistance to dominant culture in the late 1940s and 1950s involved a complex nexus of strategies that depended upon different types of visibility for different types of dissidents in different types of publics. Finally, relationships between everyday resistance and organized political struggle across a range of U.S. social movements in the postwar era was sexed and gendered. In moving from the world of the everyday to the world of organized politics, lesbians and gay men encountered different problems and possibilities, even as their histories proved to be as intertwined as were the images of men in beards and girls in tights in the coffeehouse controversy.

PART THREE

Political Movements, 1960–1969

7

"Come Out! Come Out! Wherever You Are!" 1960

Just before 10:00 p.m. on Monday, 22 August 1960, 16 policemen and one postal inspector in the Main Line suburb of Radnor arrived at a meeting organized to discuss forming a homophile political group in Greater Philadelphia. Jack Adair, whose family lived nearby and who helped arrange for the use of a friend's estate for the meeting, remembers thinking, "Well that was very nice of my mother to call the police for traffic control." Joan Fleischmann recalls, "I was standing in the back. It was in a barn. It was on the second floor. And the police came off the steps, and I said: 'Oh my god! It's a raid!' "[1]

The *Main Line Times* called it "the biggest raid of its kind in township history." Eighty-four people were arrested. One homophile newsletter reported that "almost all" of the arrested were men. Adair estimates that 95% were men and most were middle class and Euro-American; Fleischmann thinks that 90% were men and all were Euro-American. According to the *Suburban and Wayne Times*, the charges concerned the showing of "allegedly objectionable films." Officials spent several hours identifying and interrogating the arrested and examining the movies seized. Although the experience was terrifying, Adair remembers the time at the police station as his "coming out party" and "debut": "It was like a gay cocktail hour but there was no booze."[2]

By Tuesday morning, 82 of the 84 people taken into custody had been released. At this point, the owner of the estate and "Albert J. de Dion," the "motion picture operator," were brought up on disorderly house charges and released on bail. De Dion, the chairman of the New York chapter of the national homophile group the Mattachine Society had traveled to Philadelphia to help organize a new chapter. Additional charges against the owner for violating fire regulations and operating a business in a residential zone were pending as the long night ended.[3]

If the story of the Radnor raid constitutes one narrative of the beginning of homophile politics in Philadelphia, the story of lesbian links with the national homophile movement constitutes another. While gay men predominated at the Radnor meeting in 1960, local lesbians took the lead in establishing connections with the national movement in the 1950s. Juxtaposing lesbian leadership in the 1950s and gay male predominance at the Radnor raid in 1960 highlights some of the dynamics of lesbian and gay cooperation and conflict in this period. From one perspective, Philadelphia lesbian contacts with the national movement were growing without state repression until gay men's involvement elicited a police response. From another perspective, local lesbian activism remained invisible to the public until lesbians linked their efforts with those of gay men. Early homophile lesbians in Philadelphia gained greater public visibility and greater public trouble through their collaboration with gay men.

The Radnor Raid

According to Jack Adair, the Radnor raid occurred after postal officials intercepted fliers about the Mattachine meeting and contacted the police because they believed the mail was being used to "promote pornography." He thinks that four "primitive" films with "no graphic sex scenes" were shown on the night of the raid. *One* reported that the movies included Kenneth Anger's *Fireworks* (1947), hastening to add that this was "a film about homosexuality which had previously been cleared by the courts." *One* also noted that the audience included "several married couples and noted professional people" and that "police were astonished that only a few of those present 'looked like homosexuals.' " Joan Fleischmann recalls that she "had been led to believe that they were going to be porno flicks" but that "there was nothing pornographic about any of these films." She remembers *Fireworks*: "I mean porno flicks, my god! People opening drawers and putting scissors in them and a bunch of fireworks going off." Explaining that the films were abstract, Fleischmann notes that "they are so old-fashioned today that I am sure nobody would ever think of showing them as a sexual thing." Barbara Gittings, who lived in Philadelphia but was president of the New York chapter of the national lesbian group, the Daughters of Bilitis, remembers hearing about the raid. She says that the movies "might have been some of the early story films that had come out of Europe with gay characters," but recalls being told that they were "not porn" or "skin flicks." These accounts, which stress the respectable character of the films, are supported by the sanguine report that Mattachine New York leaders gave to their chapter's members: "Due to a misunderstanding, we were visited by the local police, who, under the misapprehension that we were showing obscene films, took the entire crowd to the police station for questioning."[4]

An exchange of correspondence between Mattachine New York leaders and Thomas Brandon of Brandon Films casts different light on the nature of the films shown. Brandon wrote that while he and his company were "opposed to government censorship" and the actions taken by the Radnor police, he would hold Mattachine responsible for misusing a film booked for a showing in New York and for failing to notify the company immediately about the seizure. Responding to Brandon's threats of legal action, Albert de Dion wrote that since the district attorney of Radnor had finally returned all films seized, Brandon's copy of *Muscle Beach* was on its way back. Director Joseph Strick's *Muscle Beach* (1950), an amateur short film that was distributed by Brandon Films, has been described as "a satire on the 'labors of relaxation' of exercise devotees."[5]

De Dion, who says that the films shown were "reputable" and not "obscene," acknowledges that they were "controversial" and "openly discussed homosexuality." He thinks that underground and/or male physique films, possibly with "kissing scenes" and possibly more explicit than *Muscle Beach*, may also have been shown. If one of the movies was *Fireworks*, the Radnor audience witnessed what film historian Vito Russo describes as "the bald sexuality inherent in the images of . . . sailors." Adair recalls that the meeting was designed to raise money for and interest in Mattachine. Sexy films could help do both.[6] In keeping with the efforts of many homophile leaders to maintain a respectable image for both their members and the public at large, all official statements by lesbian and gay leaders at the time (and many statements since that time) emphasized that the films shown were not pornographic but did not name or describe them. Doing so might have revealed the films' sexual, if not pornographic, contents.

Whether the films were scientific documentaries, physique movies, avant-garde works, pornographic films, or some combination thereof, they were shown in the midst of a national antiobscenity crusade. In the late 1950s, Postmaster General Arthur Summerfield, West Philly's U.S. Representative Kathryn Granahan, and Philadelphia district attorney Victor Blanc had joined forces with Catholic conservatives, the Legion of Decency, the National Organization for Decent Literature, Citizens for Decent Literature, and the Churchmen's Commission for Decent Publications. In part because of the power of local conservatives and in part because of the perceived moral traditionalism of the region, Philadelphia became a major battleground in the war on obscenity.[7]

In 1959, Granahan used her position as chair of the House Subcommittee on Postal Operations to organize obscenity hearings around the country. Her first stop was the U.S. courthouse in Center City, where representatives of Catholic, Protestant, and Jewish groups, the American Legion, Knights of Columbus, Veterans of Foreign Wars, General Federation of Women's Clubs, and National Council of Federation of American Citizens of German Descent denounced "profiteering" "peddlers" and "perverted" "purveyors" of "pornographic" "filth," "dirt," and "smut." Linking obscenity with crime, juvenile delinquency, pedophilia, incest, rape, murder, drugs, disease, comic books, communism, nudism, New York, California, Europe, and Asia, Granahan's hearings mapped the war on pornography and put Philadelphia on the antipornography map.[8]

Speaking before the subcommittee, Pennsylvania Supreme Court Justice Michael Musmanno called upon William Penn to "break his bronze bondage and descend from his pedestal atop city hall" so that he could see films with "scenes of outright degeneracy." Nicholas Frignito, chief psychiatrist of the Philadelphia Municipal Court, told the subcommittee that many "lewd" publications described "degenerate sexual behavior, homosexuality, rape, bestiality, and other paraphilias."[9] District Attorney Blanc also spoke before the subcommittee. In 1957, Blanc had encouraged the formation of the City Committee to Control Indecent Literature (later called the Citizens Committee Against Obscenity) to respond to the "flood of filth." In addition to requesting voluntary withdrawals of publications such as *MANHUNT*, he imposed "prior censorship" on films such as *Passionate Summer* and *And God Created Woman*.[10] Offering "the Philadelphia story," Blanc told the subcommittee that "we, in Philadelphia, have faced the problem of 'creeping obscenity' " with "success." After listing examples of his office's prosecutions of possessors, publishers, sellers, distributors, and exhibitors of magazines, films, books, records, and Christmas cards, Blanc expressed concern about "types of objectionable matter" that were "flooding the market" but were not prohibited. These included magazines that "pander to the sexual deviates," including "homosexuals, masochists, and sadists." Possibly using as a model the post office's "Chamber of Horrors" exhibit of intercepted materials in Washington, D.C., Blanc displayed a sampling of magazines along with ads that revealed "the deplorable situation in Pennsylvania concerning motion pictures." "Theaters which show these objectionable films can become havens for degenerates and sex deviates," Blanc explained.[11]

Despite these problems, Granahan concluded that "Philadelphia leads the Nation in effective measures to end the flow of obscenity, as in so many other civic endeavors." Many Philadelphians were similarly proud the following year, when students from Blessed Virgin Mary School and St. Cecelia's School and representatives of Philadelphia's Catholic War Veterans traveled to Washington to present to Granahan, House Speaker Sam Rayburn, and Vice President Nixon an antiobscenity petition containing nearly a million signatures collected by seventh- and eighth-graders and their veteran allies.[12]

While the Radnor raid occurred in the midst of a war on obscenity, it also took place at a moment when civil libertarians and homophile activists were mobilizing their defenses. The *Nation* attacked Summerfield's "war on muck" and called Granahan a "worthy successor" of Victorian antivice activist Anthony Comstock. *One* referred to Summerfield as a "filth-hunting crusader from the GOPorkbarrel" and described 1959 as "a clamorous year for the Vigilantes of the Dirty Mind." Often with the help of the ACLU, various writers, publishers, distributors, and sellers fought back. In a series of decisions concerning James Joyce's *Ulysses* (1934), *Esquire* (1946), *Confidential* (1957), *Sunshine and Health* and *Sun Magazine* (1958), *Playboy* (1958), *One* (1958), and *Lady Chatterley's Lover* (1960), the Supreme Court and other federal courts restricted the scope of obscenity and censorship law.[13]

Pennsylvania Judge Curtis Bok's 1949 decision in *Commonwealth v. Gordon*, which ruled that a set of books by such authors as William Faulkner and Harold Robbins were not obscene, was an important victory in the war on censorship. In 1956, in a case concerning *She Should'a Said No!*, Pennsylvania's Supreme Court ruled the state's motion picture censorship law unconstitutional. Three years later, in a case dealing with *Uncover Girls*, the court struck down the state's motion picture obscenity law. After Governor David Lawrence approved new movie censorship legislation, in July 1960 Dauphin County Court ruled this law unconstitutional as well.[14] With no state film obscenity or censorship laws on the books at the time of the Radnor raid, all charges against the owner of the estate and de Dion were eventually dropped.

Gittings argues that the Radnor raid demonstrates that "the real power of the police is the power to arrest." Emboldened to take action against the perceived obscenity of same-sex sexualities, officials moved against gay speech. Ironically, Adair remembers that one of the reasons the meeting was held outside the city was that the suburbs were thought to be safer than the city. He says that although organizers worried about how people would get to Radnor, "everyone was looking over their shoulders" in Philadelphia and "bars were being watched by Rizzo." Rizzo in fact returned to Center City from his brief exile in Northeast and West Philly just days before the raid.[15]

As Adair learned, suburban repression had its own dangers. Local newspaper coverage of the raid avoided explicit references to same-sex sexualities, offering a territorial narrative instead. The *Main Line Times* noted that those arrested "ranged from as far as Michigan, New Jersey and New York City, that only a few were Main Liners, and that most of the crowd came from Philadelphia." Linking criminality with the city, this Philadelphia story made gay suburbanites differently vulnerable. While at the police station, terrified that his mother would find out or that he would embarrass his brothers, Adair watched a local official who was a family friend participate in the examination of the films. A short while later, New York leaders persuaded Adair to appear at a Philadelphia press conference to talk about the raid. Remembering this as his "first lesson in politics," Adair says that while *he* appeared in public, everyone else associated with Mattachine "disappeared." Shortly thereafter, he moved from the suburbs to Center City.[16]

Further complicating the story of the Radnor raid is the fact that Adair and his friend had been using the latter's estate for the Stables, a gay club. Adair estimates that 400 people, including politicians, priests, and lawyers, mostly male and "a good mix" racially, had been attending on average Saturday nights. He thinks that with "so many affluent people" frequenting the club, the police were "afraid that if they opened the hornet's nest, somebody was going to get stung." Speculating that the homophile meeting compelled the police to take action, Adair remembers that officials subsequently began pressuring the estate owner by forcing him to replace his cesspools. With the atmosphere "too hot," Adair and his friend soon turned the Stables into more of a private club.[17]

If Frank Donner is right in his claim that Philadelphia became a "police city" in this period, it is worth adding that its suburbs were not safe havens. One Philadelphia detective joined 13 Radnor policemen, two Delaware County detectives, and a postal inspector to conduct the raid. With the 1960 census, Greater Philadelphia's seven suburban counties earned the distinction of containing more people than the city for the first time. With the 1960 Radnor raid, these suburbs earned the distinction of being the site of the nation's first police raid of a lesbian and gay political meeting.[18]

Despite the worst fears of Mattachine organizers, the Radnor raid did not prevent the establishment of a new group. In February 1961, several area residents met with Mattachine public relations director Curtis Dewees to establish a chapter, appoint officers, and plan activities for the 150 people whose names were included on an initial mailing list. In March, de Dion wrote a letter of thanks to his Philadelphia friends, informing them that the charges had been dropped. He thanked the ACLU's Spencer Coxe, the men who had put up his bail, and Allen Olmsted, 2nd, his lawyer. (Olmsted and his wife Mildred Scott Olmsted, a leader of the Women's International League for Peace and Freedom and the passionate friend of Ruth Mellor, had helped rebuild the local ACLU in the 1940s.) De Dion's letter was appended to the first Mattachine Society of Philadelphia newsletter, which described the raid and addressed the fears that it inspired: "There is no reason to believe it need ever occur again. This was the first time the police have ever disrupted any Mattachine meeting, and we have confidence it will be the last. To those of you still hiding in the bushes, up in the hay loft, under beds, and behind locked doors, we would like to shout. . . . 'come out! come out! wherever you are!!' "[19]

Homophile Politics

The story of the Radnor raid introduces several themes of homophile politics in the 1960s. Time and time again, police repression and postal surveillance would constrain political organizing, while civil libertarians would work with lesbians and gay men against these forces. Mainstream media would continue to choose when and how to report on lesbian and gay news, while homophile groups would develop new media addressed to their "imagined communities." Lesbians and gay men would persevere in their efforts to create protected spheres of activity. Activists would continue to debate strategies for cultivating "respectability," even as their senses of what constituted respectability changed. And lesbian and gay historical memory would be influenced again and again by desires to reclaim a sexually respectable past.[20]

The circumstances surrounding the Radnor raid also suggest some of the ways that boundaries between organized politics and everyday communities were never clear. Homophile politics grew out of developments in the households, neighborhoods, workplaces, businesses, and public places in which lesbians and gay men lived. But while homophile groups were part of the lesbian and gay communities that they purported to represent, their part, measured in terms of membership numbers, was relatively small. Moreover, activists often found themselves at odds with others in their communities, especially when movement strategies of visibility confronted everyday strategies of invisibility and when activists failed to recognize and respect their diverse constituencies. In time and in turn, movement organizations influenced lesbians and gay men, largely through the power that these groups gained to represent, politically and textually, the "imagined community" of lesbians and gay men.

Inspired by the efforts of other social movements, the work of homophile activists in other cities, and the everyday struggles of lesbians and gay men, a small number of Philadelphia lesbians and gay men came to believe that forming political organizations might be the best way to address the problems their communities faced. Working in political groups was one of many options that lesbians and gay men had for improving the quality of their lives, and their political work required making choices among projects. Activists made decisions about alliances and tactics and they selected their targets from among the institutions that most oppressed lesbians and gay men—the state, religion, science, the family, business, education, and media. Activists also made choices about how to conceive of lesbian and gay identities and how to define the boundaries of their communities. Nothing about this process was inevitable. As it turned out, the very acts of forming groups, meeting in private homes and public places, renting offices, publishing literature, sponsoring events, advertising in newspapers, and engaging in demonstrations forced Philadelphians—lesbian, gay, and straight—to renegotiate the conditions of lesbian and gay life.

The Radnor raid introduces one final theme of homophile politics—the struggle to define relationships between lesbians and gay men. The New York leaders working to organize the Philadelphia chapter were men. The films shown appealed primarily to men. And the overwhelming majority of those arrested were men. Two months before the raid, Barbara Gittings wrote a letter to Mattachine's Curtis Dewees offering him "congratulations for securing films on the Lesbian theme." "Now, how the hell did you do it," she asked, "when I've tried for some time with no success?" Dewees wrote back that two or three of these films were "possibilities" but that they were still in the planning stage. If Dewees had these movies in mind for Radnor, his plans apparently went awry. Joey Hardman, who was present at the raid, recalls that *Muscle Beach* was shown, jokes that she "wasn't too interested" in male muscle movies, and notes that "they didn't have a thing about the lesbians."[21]

Lesbians and gay men came to the homophile movement with a set of ideas about one another that had developed in everyday life and public culture but that were subject to change in the crucible of organized politics. Underscoring how frightened she was at the raid, Joan Fleischmann says that "men, who were more accustomed to those things," were "frantic." She continues: "Men were absolutely out of their minds with fear over the fact that this might reach the newspapers. I had never had any experience with having my name in the paper, but I guess men had." Fleischmann recalls that several men gave her their identifications because "some of them felt that they might be searched, but we wouldn't be."[22] Fleischmann's memories suggest that lesbians and gay men made common cause but perceived one another as different. Her memories also hint at the potential for both cooperation and conflict between lesbians and gay men. Lesbians such as Fleischmann not only paid a price for watching gay films but were asked to protect gay men by hiding their identifications. Moreover, while most men "disappeared" after the raid, lesbians such as Fleischmann and Hardman's lover, Mae Polakoff, became the leaders of the new Mattachine chapter.

Homophile activism began later in Philadelphia than in Los Angeles, San Francisco, and New York, a lag which affected the subsequent history of lesbian and gay political relationships. Although initially inspired by developments elsewhere, Philadelphians quickly struck out in new directions. Homophile politics in Philadelphia did not begin with a male-dominated Mattachine chapter or a female chapter of the Daughters of Bilitis (DOB), which was the pattern in other cities. Organized in the wake of the Radnor raid, Mattachine Philadelphia featured a lesbian president and mixed-sex leadership and membership. Over the course of the next decade, several of the city's most dynamic homophile groups brought together lesbians and gay men, often under lesbian leadership. Moreover, Philadelphians proved to be among the most militant leaders of the lesbian and gay movement.

This is not to say that political relations between lesbians and gay men were better in Philadelphia than in cities with separate groups. After cooperation within the same organization proved difficult to maintain, the legacy of conflict sometimes hindered the ability of separate groups to work together. Political relations between lesbians and gay men in Philadelphia were sometimes cooperative and sometimes ridden with conflict, but they were based on conceptions of lesbian and gay community that differed from those of activists in many other cities.

Why was this the case? Perhaps traditions of sex egalitarianism within Quakerism continued to affect Philadelphia. As Margaret Bacon has argued, the women's movement of the 1960s "caught Quaker women largely by surprise" because many of them believed that "they had been spared any personal experience with patriarchy."[23] Paradoxically, Philadelphia's relatively weak feminist movement in the 1960s may have left lesbians with less attractive alternatives and may have made gay men more responsive to their female counterparts. Perhaps the relatively high level of police repression in Philadelphia brought lesbians and gay men closer together. Converging lesbian and gay geographies may also have done so. And perhaps Philadelphia provincialism made it more like a small city or town, where lesbians and gay men have long been thought to be more bonded than in cosmopolitan cities.

John D'Emilio argues that "activists had not only to mobilize a constituency; first they had to create one." Highlighting the long historical "process through which a group of men and women came into existence as a self-conscious, cohesive minority," D'Emilio suggests that for a "movement" to take shape, some lesbians and gay men had to "perceive themselves as members of an oppressed minority, sharing an identity that subjected them to systematic injustice." While recent scholarship has suggested that lesbians and gay men perceived themselves in some of these ways before mid-century, how "cohesive" an identity lesbians and gay men shared remains an open question.[24]

Lesbians and gay men had vastly different *and* substantially similar experiences in their everyday lives. Most homophile activists came to think of themselves as both members of the same community and members of sex-specific ones. The balance between these two senses of community, however, changed over time. The history of Philadelphia homophile politics demonstrates that lesbian and gay activists might have come to see themselves as either more or less unified than they did. In the end, the conditions of lesbian and gay life were set not only in negotiations with straight society, and not only in negotiations between lesbians and gay men within their communities, but in the ways that these two processes were intricately intertwined.

Lesbian Links

Before moving chronologically forward to explore lesbian and gay political relationships after the Radnor raid, the remainder of this chapter steps backward in time. For while the story of the Radnor raid provides a dramatic introduction to homophile politics in Greater Philadelphia, the story of pre-Radnor links between the national homophile movement and individual local lesbians provides an equally important one.

The national homophile movement began nearly a decade before the Radnor raid. Founded in 1950–1951 by Harry Hay and a group of leftists in Los Angeles, the Mattachine Society developed a secret cell structure, a radical analysis of homosexuals as an oppressed minority, and a strategy based upon organizing a mass movement. By 1953, the society had launched *One* magazine and several thousand Californians were participating in discussion groups. In 1953, however, in a "retreat to respectability," the politics of the society changed. Following reports that linked Mattachine's founders to communism, new leaders took control, putting forward an integrationist analysis and a strategy of seeking help from professional researchers. *One* magazine, formally independent of Mattachine, remained more militant. Mattachine chapters formed in New York and Chicago and the society began publishing the *Mattachine Review*.[25]

Del Martin and Phyllis Lyon established DOB as a San Francisco social club in 1955 and began publishing the *Ladder* the following year. When their goals broadened to encompass public education, DOB's working-class members left and formed another club. D'Emilio argues that although the DOB statement of purpose "bore an extremely close resemblance to Mattachine's language and suggests the influence of the Society," DOB retained distinctive qualities based on the "greater isolation and invisibility of gay women" and the unique problems that lesbians faced.[26]

Both cooperation and conflict marked relations between the exclusively female and primarily male homophile organizations. Joint activities brought together lesbians and gay men and fostered a sense of community. From the start, however, DOB emphasized the value of having a separate group. After pointing out that Mattachine was predominantly male, Martin explained in the *Ladder* that DOB was a "women's organization resolved to add the feminine voice and viewpoint to a mutual problem." "While women may not have so much difficulty with law enforcement," she declared, "their problems are none the less real—family, sometimes children, employment, social acceptance." A short while later, Martin wrote that although DOB and Mattachine had discussed "dissolving the women's group and joining Mattachine or starting a women's auxiliary chapter," both had concluded that "more women would be likely to take an active part . . . through an exclusively women's organization." Trying to explain the reasons for this, Martin argued that the lesbian was "elusive," that she was "less promiscuous and less apt to rely on 'gay bars' for her contacts, and by the very nature of her being a woman she is more interested in her home." She added that lesbians and gay men did not always "accept" or feel "comfortable" around one another, a problem she proposed to address through "mutual social functions and panel discussions keyed to enlighten both groups about the other facet and to bring recognition to our community of interests and aims."[27]

Two years of cooperation failed to put Martin's concerns to rest. At a 1959 Mattachine convention, she was angry:

> At every one of these conventions I attend, year after year, I find I must defend the Daughters of Bilitis as a separate and distinct women's organization. First of all, what do you men know about Lesbians? In all of your programs and your *Review* you speak of the male homosexual and follow this with—oh, yes, and incidentally there are some female homosexuals too and because they are homosexual all this should apply to them as well. *One* has done little better. For years they have relegated the Lesbian interest to the column called "Feminine Viewpoint." So it would appear to me that quite obviously neither organization has recognized the fact that Lesbians are *women* and that this 20th century is the era of emancipation of woman. Lesbians are not satisfied to be auxiliary members or second class homosexuals. So if you people do wish to put DOB out of business, you are going to have to learn something about the Lesbian.[28]

Martin did not reject the idea of putting DOB "out of business" in the long term, but for the time being endorsed the maintenance of an all-female group.

Lesbian and gay activists brought to their relationships many conventional ideas about the femininity of women and the masculinity of men. But because they often viewed one another as masculine women and feminine men, conventional ideas about heterosocial relations were sometimes inverted. In a 1957 discussion between members of DOB and Mattachine in San Francisco, lesbians criticized gay men for assuming that lesbians had "exaggerated masculine mannerisms" while gay men criticized lesbians for believing that most gay men were "pronouncedly feminine." At other times, they criticized one another for following conventional gender norms. Some of the "girls" reported that they had trouble accepting the "promiscuity of the men" and that "several male homophiles" knew "nothing at all about female anatomy." One suggestion was that fraternizing with and dating one another might help lesbians and gay men conform to proper heterosocial expectations. Gay men could help lesbians learn "correct feminine behavior" and lesbians could help gay men by telling them when they were "going off the track" with "feminine mannerisms." One sign of success was a report that revealed "considerably less hostility between the men and women present since the intermingling of the two organizations." Perceived sex differences, however, continued to create problems. In a 1959 discussion, "Should Men and Women Homosexuals Associate?" several women said that the reason that lesbians might not express interest in friendships with gay men was that "where frequently the men were accomplished and able to entertain on a grand scale," most of the women were not and "since they were unable to return in kind what they had so bountifully received, they returned nothing."[29] Ideas about sex differences, then, could bring lesbians and gay men together and keep them apart.

Although they cooperated on many levels, homophile activists formed largely sex-separate groups in the 1950s. DOB established chapters in San Francisco, New York, Los Angeles, Chicago, and Rhode Island. Mattachine groups were set up in San Francisco, Los Angeles/Long Beach, New York, Boston, Denver, Detroit, Chicago, and Washington, D.C. According to D'Emilio, "antihomosexualism" and the narrowness of the homophile vision devastated the movement. Taking on "an impossible burden—appearing respectable to a society that defined homosexuality as beyond respectability," homophile leaders alienated many potential supporters when they criticized popular aspects of lesbian and gay cultures that they saw as disrespectable. By 1960, Mattachine had only 230 members; DOB had 110.[30] At this low point in U.S. homophile history, local activists were more free to strike out in new directions. Philadelphians thus faced choices—affiliate with one of the two national groups or go their own way. At different times, they would choose each of these three options.

In the years between the appearance of *One* in 1953 and the formation of Mattachine Philadelphia in 1960, more than 40 letters from Greater Philadelphia or unspecified Pennsylvania locations were published in *Mattachine Review*, the *Ladder*, and *One*. In 1954, Pennsylvania was home to 70 *One* subscribers, making it the state with the fourth-largest number of subscriptions. In 1957, *Mattachine Review* reported that " 'firm' contacts" had been established with Philadelphians interested in starting a Mattachine chapter.[31]

1957 was also the year that DOB received a letter from North Philly's

Gerry Redcay, the secretary of Bridgeport, Pennsylvania's Ell Club. Describing her group, which was based in an industrial city northwest of Philadelphia, Redcay wrote:

> The Club was formed for the purpose of bringing closer unity between the boys and girls and to help each and everyone understand themselves and make their own adjustment to be accepted and to accept the general public. We feel if we pull together, the "kids" will have a feeling of security and belonging, they will also learn tolerance, patience and respect for each other. We abide by the fact that we are all working for one goal, to be accepted, let's do it together. It was Abraham Lincoln who said, "United we stand, divided we fall."

Redcay noted that the club had 125 members, a "mixed group of 'boys and girls,' " and that its board of directors included three men and three women. Later the same month, the *Ladder* welcomed the club's newsletter, the *Lark News*, in an announcement titled "New Addition to the Homosexual Press!"[32]

Founded in 1956, the Ell Club was based at the Lark Bar. (Ell was for the first letter in Lark.) Bar owner Olga "Adams," who identifies as straight, says that she started the club to help her patrons "socially and psychologically." In time, she thinks that she became "their mother and their doctor." Adams developed a library of lesbian and gay books and held a "psychology hour" on weekday afternoons. Meetings were held twice a month and the club sponsored a variety of holiday and seasonal parties.[33]

Although Redcay wrote to the DOB, the Ell Club never became part of the homophile movement. Perhaps the club's interests were more social than political, although this was sometimes true of homophile groups as well. Perhaps the club's working-class members felt alienated by the predominantly middle-class homophile movement. Perhaps the maternal control exercised by Adams was an obstacle. Whatever the reason, in 1964 East Coast Homophile Organizations (ECHO) rejected a proposal to invite the club to join the regional federation.[34]

While the Ell Club did not take the lead in developing a local movement, its hopes for lesbian and gay unity were shared by the first Philadelphians to take an active interest in national homophile politics. Jody Shotwell, Joan Fleischmann, and Barbara Gittings joined the all-female DOB in the 1950s but were committed to cooperation with gay men. All three women participated in the lesbian and gay bar scene in the 1950s. In this period, Shotwell and Fleischmann were "femmes"; Gittings was a "butch." Shotwell was married and "bisexual"; Fleischmann and Gittings called themselves "gay." Elizabeth Kennedy and Madeline Davis argue that "lesbian homophile organizations grew out of a working-class lesbian tradition—women who were conscious of lesbians as a group, from socializing in the bars—rather than a middle-class tradition of isolated individuals and couples."[35] In Philadelphia, middle-class Euro-American women, who socialized with working- and middle-class lesbians and gay men in bars, inaugurated homophile activism.

Shotwell was born around 1917 and when she became involved in the movement in 1954 was a married housewife with three sons and a history of relationships with both lesbians and gay men. Using the pseudonym "Anita," Shotwell told a *Philadelphia Magazine* reporter in 1967, "I've always been attracted to people as people, not males or females." When Anita was a teenager, she fell in love with another girl but her parents did not approve of her "gay friends, particularly the boys." After "nothing ever materialized with the girl," Anita married but maintained her "gay contacts, mostly with men." Until her mid-thirties, she was "out of the lesbian world," but after several of her stories were published in a "homosexual magazine," her "ancient feelings were re-kindled." Marge McCann thinks that Shotwell had an "understanding" with her husband. According to Fleischmann, Shotwell "was always involved with younger, very boyish women" but "wasn't about to leave her husband." The *Philadelphia Magazine* article suggests that Shotwell had at least three lesbian relationships, one of which threatened her marriage: "I wouldn't leave my children. So *she* left. When she was sure I wouldn't take her back she committed suicide."[36]

Shotwell's prize-winning stories and poems appeared in *One*, the *Ladder*, and the *Janus Society Newsletter* between 1954 and 1968. Much of her work concerned lesbian relationships. In "The Gateway," she wrote of a married femme with sons. In "The Ironing," two married mothers come together. In "Hauviette," a "beautiful" woman regrets turning away from the "tall and handsome" Jeanne d'Arc. In "The Room Upstairs," a married woman follows two women, "short-haired and dressed in slacks," to a bar. In "Love Is Not LOVE," the passion has gone out of a butch-femme relationship but returns. And in "Marquita," a San Juan woman confesses her love to a motorcycle-riding woman named Ron.[37]

Many of Shotwell's stories included gay characters. "The Triangle" features a woman who betrays her gay friend by having sex with the man he loves. In "The Snare," a gay man falls for a married male bartender. "Gay Wedding" describes a lesbian ceremony. The female narrator had heard of "gay weddings," but "in most cases the couples were men." Here, the bride was dressed in "kelly-green chiffon with rhinestone shoulder straps"; the bridegroom, a "fresh-faced youngster with red hair, freckles, and braces," wore black trousers, a white shirt, and a black vest. The guests were women, except for two men, one of whom was a gay bartender and had "performed this ceremony" before.[38]

In 1960, Shotwell became embroiled in a heated debate in the *Ladder* when she discussed the "cold war" caused by "the heterosexually married lesbian." Responding to another writer, Shotwell wrote that "the fact of bi-sexuality" could not be "negate[d]" by criticizing it. "I daresay that the percentage of homosexuals who censure the bi-sexual is as great as the number of heterosexuals who denounce the homosexual," she declared. "Yet, the homosexual, who would wish for more understanding and recognition of his nature, is often the most vehement in his criticism of the bi-sexual." She concluded with a defense of "complete sexual freedom between consenting adults."[39]

Although she lived in Philadelphia, Shotwell became the secretary of DOB's New York chapter (DOB-NY) when it formed in 1958. Gittings recalls, however, that Shotwell "felt more comfortable in the atmosphere of Mattachine" and did not find the all-female DOB "all that appealing." Interested in both women and men, Shotwell often worked with gay activists.[40]

Fleischmann also identified and worked with gay men. Born in 1933 and adopted by Catholic parents in Reading, Pennsylvania, Fleischmann remembers developing bonds with "gay boys" long before she met lesbians and became one herself. In high school, she befriended an "effeminate" boy named Ken and joined his gay circle. Recalling that she had "crushes on a number of gay men," Fleischmann thinks that this afforded her "protection" since "these men were not going to be interested." Usually the only girl in her group and often treated "like a little sister," Fleischmann remembers going to gay bars and the local gay hangout, a coffee shop at the Abraham Lincoln Hotel. When Fleischmann's mother told her that her father thought that Ken was "queer," Fleischmann claimed that he was her "boyfriend."[41]

The summer after completing high school, Fleischmann moved with her parents to New Jersey and Ken began working in Atlantic City. Soon Fleischmann was working there as well, and it was here that she met other lesbians, falling first for a "drag butch" bartender. That fall, Fleischmann enrolled at West Chester University in Pennsylvania. Meanwhile, Ken moved to Philadelphia and Fleischmann began going to Rittenhouse Square to visit him. In 1955, having graduated from college, Fleischmann began working as a high-school teacher in New Jersey. When a man she went out with a few times revealed that he "wanted more than just friendship," Fleischmann told him that she was "gay," which she says was not true at the time but was a "convenient excuse." When he said that he knew another gay woman, Fleischmann's response was "hallelujah"; she had been wanting to meet more lesbians. Fleischmann recalls that when she met the woman, who was a "very butch" lifeguard, there was "immediate chemistry" and she thus "came out," breaking a bed in her parents' home in the process.

Some time later, Fleischmann was summoned by her principal, who had received "disturbing" letters that claimed that Fleischmann was "involved in a homosexual relationship." The letters were written by the man she had dated. Fleischmann recalls denying everything. In the meantime, she had begun frequenting gay bars in New York, where she learned about the DOB chapter. Through the DOB, Gittings helped Fleischmann find a lawyer, and soon her employer offered a deal: if she would go quietly the school would provide her with a good reference. Fearing that Fleischmann could not win in court and that the "notoriety" would destroy her career, the lawyer advised her to accept the offer, which she did. Soon she had another teaching job.

Sometime around 1959, Fleischmann joined DOB-NY, was appointed newsletter editor and acting vice president, and had a relationship with Gittings that lasted several months. Using the pseudonyms "Jan Fraser" and "Joan Fraser," Fleischmann also began writing for the *Ladder.* Asked why she concentrated on DOB activities in New York rather than start a group in her own city, Fleischmann explains that she felt safer being active outside Philadelphia.[42] If New Yorkers felt the same way about being active in their city, this may explain why Philadelphians led New York's lesbian movement.

Although she first worked with an all-female organization, Fleischmann continued to feel strong ties with gay men. Mattachine New York's Albert de Dion, who was in the military and sometimes reported to Fort Dix, New Jersey, remembers that he and Fleischmann occasionally "pretended to be a couple." Soon Fleischmann shifted to mixed-sex work in Mattachine Philadelphia. "DOB was a woman's organization that didn't seem to want to have a great deal to do with men," she explains. "And that was something that at the time I couldn't see, having spent so much of my time with gay men."[43]

Gittings also had a strong sense of community with gay men. Born in 1932 in Vienna, she spent her early years as a diplomat's daughter in Europe, Maryland, and Quebec before moving with her well-off, Catholic family to Wilmington, Delaware. While in high school, Gittings recalls, she "carried the torch" for a girl. When the two double-dated, Gittings was paired with a boy she now suspects was gay.[44] In 1949, Gittings enrolled at Northwestern University in Chicago, where she was accused, falsely she says, of being sexually involved with another female student. After a confrontation with her dormitory director and a visit with a psychiatrist, who told Gittings that she was "a homosexual" but could be "cured," Gittings began reading on the subject. Recalling encyclopedias and medical and psychology books that described homosexuality as a "deviation" and "perversion," she says that she did not "recognize" much of herself in these representations.[45] Discussing one text in a 1974 interview, Gittings says, "The fact that it was about male homosexuals really didn't bother me that much. Most of the material was on male homosexuals." In a 1971–1972 interview, however, she says, "Everything I found was so alien, so remote. It didn't give me any sense of myself or what my life and experience could be. It was mostly clinical-sounding—disturbance, pathology, arrested development—*and* it was mostly about men."[46] Gittings's narratives contradict one another on the question of whether the male focus of these texts alienated her, but they agree that she defined herself in relation to, even if in opposition to, images of male same-sex sexualities. Gittings remembers turning next to lesbian novels, which she thinks made her feel more positively about homosexuality, helping her decide that she was a lesbian.

Having flunked out of college, Gittings returned home to Wilmington, where she embarked on her first lesbian relationship. Following a family confrontation brought on by her father's discovery of the lesbian novel *The Well of Loneliness* in her bedroom, Gittings "ran away" to Philadelphia in 1951. There she found temporary shelter with a lesbian acquaintance at Temple University and then more permanent lodgings in Center City. According to Gittings, when she found herself unable to locate local gay bars, she began dressing as a boy, hitchhiking to New York, and frequenting gay bars there. Soon she found out about the Philadelphia bars, where she came to be known as "Sonny." Gittings "wore drag," she recalls, because this was a way to show that she was gay and because "much was made of differentiating both lesbians and male homosexuals into masculine and feminine types." Since "high heels and makeup" were not her "style," she thought she had to be "the other kind."[47]

Gittings's identification as a butch may help explain her strong bonds with gay men. She recalls, "I had no trouble at all, being my own person, as a girl, as a female, when I was growing up. But the one problem I really did have was coming to terms with being gay." Gittings believes that this is why she is "very strongly gay-identified" and not "what some lesbians call themselves, a woman-identified woman." "I feel very strong amity with gay people of both genders," she says, "that overrides any particular feeling I might have that women are more important as a class to me."[48] In fact, while Gittings recalls developing a number of friendships with gay men whom she met in bars, she remembers having little in common with bar lesbians, who did not share her interests in literature and music. Soon, however, she met a circle of lesbians at Swarthmore College and began a six-month relationship with an African American writer.[49]

Gittings's identifications with gay men were strengthened by the books that she read, including Donald Webster Cory's *The Homosexual in America.* Impressed by this work, she wrote to Cory's publisher and arranged to meet him. These encounters led Gittings to visit *One* and Mattachine's offices while vacationing in California in 1956. Mattachine members told her about the DOB, which was meeting while she was in San Francisco. Remembering this episode, Gittings says, "For the first time, I sat down with 12 other lesbians, not in a bar but in someone's living room," which was "a much more natural setting." In another interview, Gittings recalls that "here, for the first time, I was in the civilized setting of someone's personal living room."[50] Drawing a contrast between uncivilized public bars and civilized private homes, Gittings also describes a transition from the gender transgressions of the former to the gender conservatism of the latter. For Gittings, the homophile movement offered a welcome alternative to the butch/femme bars, one in which gender conformity was more the rule than the exception.

The DOB was also an alternative to Mattachine. In 1957, Mattachine New York tried to correct the "erroneous impression that Mattachine is run exclusively by and for men." Acknowledging that its publications had been male-focused and its officers primarily male, Mattachine's newsletter stated that the chapter was "most anxious for women leaders." Aware that many women would be "shy about attending a meeting where the membership body seems to be predominantly male," the newsletter announced that "a new group is being formed to discuss the problem of the Lesbian."[51] Meanwhile, national DOB leaders Del Martin and Phyllis Lyon arranged with Gittings to hold a lesbian meeting at the 1958 Mattachine convention in New York. About 30 women appeared, which led to the founding of DOB-New York. Gittings recalls that the group formed "with the help and encouragement" of Mattachine New York. She served for three years as chapter president.[52]

Asked in 1974 why a separate women's organization had been established, Gittings responds, "The reason wasn't the sort of thing you get today, when people say, 'Men are male chauvinist pigs; we have to have a separatist organization so women can gain strength from each other.' " She says, "Somehow it was a more comfortable setting to be among ourselves," hastening to add that "there were times when we cooperated with the Mattachine Society in jointly sponsoring particular events." Asking herself "Why the need for a separate group?" Gittings answers, "One had been started; women seemed to enjoy being together." "I won't say that there weren't tensions, for heaven's sake," she declares in a 1993 interview. "But by and large, the turf was so huge and the number of people to take it was so small that there couldn't be any serious problems."[53]

In its early years, DOB-NY met every two weeks, held monthly socials, and produced a newsletter. Gittings recalls that 10 to 40 people attended meetings and that the DOB-NY mailing list had 300 names. Although she remembers that homophile groups denied that they "acted as any kind of agency for social introductions," she believes that "women were showing up in order to meet others." She also recalls a debate early in DOB-NY's existence about a "woman who lived as a transvestite, who was accepted even at her place of work as a woman who chose to live and dress as a young man." DOB, however, discussed whether her appearance was "acceptable." Also in line with the respectable orientation of the homophile movement, Gittings wrote to the ACLU's Spencer Coxe that the DOB was "devoted to the integration of the homophile into society by educating the sex variant, encouraging scientific research on homosexuality, informing the public, and working to change the law."[54]

During these years, Gittings began showing signs of the militance and visibility for which she would later become known. While most homophile activists relied upon pseudonyms, Gittings used her real name. Perhaps referring to her privileged class background, Gittings explains that she felt that the more activists who could "afford" to use their real names, "the better we are." She also risked her clerical job by reproducing DOB-NY materials at her office. Shortly after she used company envelopes for homophile purposes, a parent whose daughter had received a mailing called Gittings's employer and complained about the firm harboring "*pre*verts." Fortunately, Gittings's boss "had been in the military service" and "was not unfamiliar with homosexuality." She "had no strong feelings for it or against it" and cautioned Gittings only to be more careful. Meanwhile, Gittings began contributing articles to the *Ladder*.[55]

Although Gittings has claimed that she was politically inactive in Philadelphia in the late 1950s and early 1960s, in 1960 she wrote to the *Inquirer* about the local antipornography campaign. Published just before the Radnor raid, Gittings's letter denounced the campaign, defiantly insisting on a distinction between "spicy or sex-oriented material" and "outright pornography." Taking a stand at odds with the tenets of homophile respectability, the letter suggests that Gittings's politics were in flux during this period. Gittings also was in contact with Mattachine officials about organizing meetings in Philadelphia and with the local ACLU.[56]

While Shotwell, Fleischmann, and Gittings shared much in common, their paths diverged. Intrasex conflict played a more salient role in early Philadelphia homophile politics than intersex conflict did. For example, in the *Ladder* issue in which Shotwell defended the "married lesbian," Fleischmann presented "The Other Side of the Fable." In this story, the female narrator's lover always returns to her husband and child and then comes back, which "torture[s]" both women. Fleischmann recalls that she "couldn't stand" Shotwell's "so-called bisexuality" and remembers thinking that "in a bisexual relationship, somebody always gets hurt, and it's always the lesbian."[57]

A second conflict divided Fleischmann and Gittings. In August 1959, Gittings wrote to de Dion and Dewees about still being "on the merry-go-round with Joan." According to Gittings, Fleischmann was "indignant" that Gittings had mentioned their difficulties to the two men. Gittings concluded that she could not work with Fleischmann yet could not ignore her. The two men reported to the national DOB's Martin on their efforts to "minimize any friction between these two girls." "Each one is terrific in their own way," de Dion wrote, "yet each has their own faults."[58]

Fleischmann remembers that she and Gittings were both "strong" and "didn't have the same kinds of goals." "Barbara was always, in my opinion, less apt to be tolerant of men, at that time," Fleischmann recalls. "But my feeling always was, well, the old Ben Franklin saying: if we don't all hang together, we will all most assuredly all hang separately. And that was always how I felt about organizations. And that there's no place for this 'Well we're women, so therefore we're not going to deal with you, because you're men' kind of thing." According to Fleischmann, "There probably were a lot of lesbians who didn't want to be bothered with men. My own particular history of being involved from the time I was a teenager with gay men probably made me look at them differently."[59] Developments in the early 1960s support the suggestion that Gittings was more committed to sex-separate organizing than Fleischmann was in this period. Because Gittings turned away from all-female work in the mid-1960s, later interviews with her downplay the extent to which she supported single-sex strategies in her early homophile years. At any rate, Fleischmann soon resigned from DOB-NY. While Gittings and Shotwell remained active in DOB, Fleischmann became a leading figure in Mattachine Philadelphia.

By early 1960, Philadelphia still lacked an organizational affiliation with the national homophile movement. It was at this juncture that the meeting to organize a Mattachine chapter was held in Radnor. Several factors might have led the movement in Philadelphia to be sex-divided from the start. A number of local lesbians and gay men had discovered the largely sex-separate national groups in the 1950s. Philadelphians might have followed suit, forming an all-female DOB chapter, a predominantly male Mattachine chapter, or both. Shotwell, Fleischmann, and Gittings had been active in the DOB; it would not have been surprising if they had taken the lead in forming a local DOB chapter. Lesbians might also have decided that working with gay men exposed them to state repression and male chauvinism and that they would just as soon go their own way. And given the single-sex bases of same-sex sexual relationships and the divergences in lesbian and gay cultures, lesbian and gay activists might have concluded that single-sex political organizing made sense.

A number of factors might also have led the local movement to be male-dominated from the start. Mainstream popular culture in the 1940s and 1950s constructed same-sex sexualities as primarily male. Most political groups in this era were dominated by men. The national Mattachine Society was male-dominated, as was the New York chapter. The overwhelming majority of the people arrested in Radnor were men. With Shotwell, Gittings, and Fleischmann concentrating their efforts in New York, there might have been a lack of local lesbian leadership. And both lesbians and gay men might have expected male predominance in politics, just as they had come to do in some aspects of everyday lesbian and gay life.

As it turned out, the early homophile movement in Philadelphia was neither sex-separate nor male-dominated. Philadelphians chose a third way.

8

"Earnestly Seeking Respectability," 1960–1963

In January 1964, *Confidential* magazine published an "exclusive" report on a "homosexual convention" that had taken place in September at the Drake Hotel in Center City. With about 100 people attending each session, the convention featured speeches by "distinguished" scientific, religious, and legal experts. "Deadly respectability was the keynote," reporter Ken Travis declared. "Everyone was conservatively dressed, the men mostly in Ivy League fashion, the women in dresses or suits. No bottled-in-blond men, limp wrists or lisping here, thank you." Opening the conference was "a Philadelphia schoolteacher, a big but pretty young woman who called herself Joan Fraser." According to Travis, "whatever may have gone on in the hotel rooms or at private parties, no swishing was allowed in public" and "a couple of local queens who sashayed up to one session were told politely but firmly to go home and come back only if they were properly dressed and behaved." "Because they are so earnestly seeking respectability," he explained, "the organizations discourage the obvious effeminates."[1]

While some may not have regarded a sensational magazine as a reliable source, the *Ladder* described the article as "fair-minded" and Philadelphia's homophile newsletter called it "responsible." Joan Fleischmann ("Fraser") recalls that "masculine men and feminine women were good public relations" for the homophile movement and, in part because she did not look like "the stereotypical bulldyke," she was selected as convention chair. "One would think that back in those days, men would have been the obvious choices," she notes, but because "women were less threatening to the heterosexual public," lesbians were sometimes favored as leaders.[2]

The 1963 conference represented the culmination of the homophile strategy of heterosocial respectability. Linking the gender-conforming tactics of DOB and Mattachine, lesbian and gay activists joined together to present themselves as adhering to conventional heterosocial norms. Whatever they might do in "private," activists left butch and queen identities at "home" and "earnestly" sought "public" acceptance. Juxtaposing men in "Ivy League fashion" and women in "dresses or suits," homophile groups hoped to win favor with fashion.

From 1960 to 1963, Philadelphia activists maintained a distinctive commitment to the political integration of lesbians and gay men in the context of a national movement generally divided into predominantly or exclusively single-sex groups. Expressing and encouraging bonds between lesbians and gay men, heterosocial respectability required that activists build a sense of political community that would overcome the separatist tendencies of single-sex sexual cultures. Working with dominant cultural ideas about the bonds that could form across sex differences, lesbian and gay activists in Philadelphia reproduced, adapted, modified, and transformed hegemonic heterosocial meanings in their efforts to advance the interests of lesbians and gay men.

Mattachine and Janus

Despite its inauspicious beginnings, by early 1961 Mattachine Philadelphia was established. Although the organization lasted less than a year under this name, it laid the foundation for a period of cooperation between lesbian and gay activists. Mattachine Philadelphia's first "chairman" was Mae Polakoff. According to her long-time partner Joey Hardman, Polakoff was born in the 1910s, grew up in a Jewish family in Strawberry Mansion, Philadelphia, and was divorced and living with her son in Southwest Philly when she and Hardman became lovers in the 1950s. Hardman also recalls that Polakoff owned Mae's Secretarial Service, a Center City business that employed "mostly gay people." Joan Fleischmann remembers Polakoff as "vibrant, alive, wonderful." "Mae was more like a mother than my own mother was to me," she notes, "because I needed someone as a lesbian to guide me in the right direction." Marge McCann says that Polakoff was a "stereotypic Jewish suburban lady"; Kay Lahusen recalls that she was not a "stereotypical" lesbian.[3]

Hardman was also active in Mattachine. Born in 1918 to a poor Euro-American Catholic family in South Philly, Hardman says that she was a "tomboy" as a child, a butch as a young adult, and a member of the Women's Army Corps during World War Two. During the war, she recalls, her first major sexual relationship ended when she came home to Philadelphia one day and learned that her lover had become involved with a man. After the war, she embarked on a new relationship and, with the help of the GI Bill, bought a house in Southwest Philly. Several years later, this second lover married a gay man and ended her relationship with Hardman. Hardman remembers that she had known Polakoff earlier, but that now, after running into one another at Rusty's, they began an 18-year relationship.[4]

Asked why Polakoff was elected chairman, Hardman says, "Because she was so eager, eager to know everything, learn everything, want to do this, want to do that." In addition, Polakoff's self-employed status made her less vulnerable to job loss and her feminine qualities qualified her as an exemplar of respectable homophile politics. Fleischmann, also a femme, was

Figure 8.1 Joey Hardman and Mae Polakoff, c. 1961. With the permission of Joan Fleischmann.

Mattachine's secretary. The vice chairman was Harold Stern, who worked at the Psychoanalytic Studies Institute and was believed to be straight.[5]

Mark Kendall remembers being taken to his first Mattachine meeting by Stern. Born in 1928, Kendall grew up in a middle-class Jewish family in Center City. In 1950, he recalls, he proposed marriage to his girlfriend "with disclosure" about his "homosexual inclinations." Wanting to marry not "half" but "a whole person," the girlfriend encouraged Kendall, while they were vacationing in Atlantic City, to have sex with a man who had been cruising him, which he did. Kendall and his girlfriend did marry, but the marriage lasted only a few months. The following year, he began going to gay bars, including the New Look, which he says was filled with "piss elegant queens." Kendall also remembers disliking the fact that the patrons were "all men" and "all white." Like Barbara Gittings, Kendall describes feeling alienated from gay bars, but Gittings evokes their working-class character while Kendall refers to their upper-class pretensions and racial exclusivity.[6]

While most homophile narrators recall participating actively in lesbian and gay community life before joining the movement, Kendall emphasizes that political activity helped him "come out." When he joined Mattachine, he had not had many same-sex sexual experiences and was quiet at meetings until a "very rough" lesbian named Rocky pinned him to the wall: "She said, 'Tell us once and for all, are you or are you not gay?' " Kendall remembers hedging and finally saying, "Well, I've been coming here." While a Mattachine lesbian helped him come out in this way, Mattachine gay men took him to multiracial bars such as the Ritz, which he remembers enjoying. Kendall says that the people in Mattachine were "very nice" and "totally different from the pretentious groups" he had met in the bars.[7]

Jack Adair, who was born into a well-to-do Main Line, Euro-American Catholic family in 1938, became involved with Mattachine after helping to arrange the Radnor meeting. Adair describes joining the movement after a difficult childhood, when neighborhood boys called him "sissy," "faggot," "queer," and "dolly" and abused him sexually and physically. He recalls that when he was 18 years old he began working at a Philadelphia hospital, met other gay people, and "swore" to himself that he would do whatever he could "to prevent any other kid from going through the childhood" that he had had.[8]

Ten to thirty people attended most Mattachine Philadelphia functions. According to Kendall, about equal numbers of women and men attended meetings but only a few African Americans participated. Homophile Philadelphians were distinctive in organizing lesbians and gay men together but were typical in failing to organize beyond the Euro-American population.[9]

Mattachine Philadelphia's mixed-sex organizing was shaped by the community experiences of its members. Hardman remembers that lesbians and gay men got along well in bars and at the factory where she worked and that she had many gay friends. Fleischmann was close with gay men before she came out as a lesbian and remembers that Polakoff and Hardman's home was "always full" of lesbians and gay men. Kendall recalls reading *The Well of Loneliness* and says that it was "easy to identify" with the main lesbian character because gay men were also "attracted to members of the same sex."[10]

Marge McCann, who joined the movement a year or two after the others, also forged bonds with gay men before she became politically active. Born in 1939 in New Jersey to a lower-middle-class, Euro-American, Protestant family, McCann remembers moving to Northeast Philly when she was 13 and soon thereafter beginning to have sex with girls. When she was 16, a gay friend took her to Surf for her first gay bar adventure. A few years later, she began a relationship with a fellow female student at Temple. After her roommate reported the relationship to school officials, McCann spent weeks defending her "right to exist" and "denying it." In her last year of college, McCann became involved with another Temple student and began going regularly to Surf, where "Sarah Vaughan" taught her how to dance.

In the bars, McCann also learned how to be "stone butch." She remembers meeting Fleischmann at Surf or Rusty's. "Since I was interested in her, I was interested in the movement," McCann explains, describing how she gained an edge over Fleischmann's girlfriend. Soon the two were living together in Logan and working together in Mattachine.[11]

If mixed-sex organizing in part reflected experiences prior to movement activity, lesbian and gay encounters within the movement affected future ties. Adair does not remember conflicts in Mattachine. Kendall recalls a "feeling of cooperation." "Actually," he notes, "several of the core people in the group were friends anyway. [Two of the men] were good friends of Mae's. And so they saw each other socially. And I think any of the other people who came in to the group just accepted that it was both men and women." Kendall says that he was "happy" that both lesbians and gay men were involved, which was "an exception" to what he found in the bars. Kendall's statement underlines the power that political groups could have to strengthen bonds between lesbians and gay men.[12] But because his description of community-based tensions is at odds with the accounts of early lesbian activists such as Fleischmann, Gittings, and Hardman, it also suggests that lesbians who joined the movement may have initially felt closer to and more identified with gay men than the other way around.

Figure 8.2. Joan Fleischmann and Marge McCann, c. 1962. Courtesy of Joan Fleischmann.

Lesbian Mattachine activists remember close ties with their gay allies. Fleischmann thinks that "Philadelphia seems to be the only place where women were really involved outside of DOB." Asked why local lesbians and gay men worked together, she says, "I think it's because of the lesbians involved. Mae was a very strong person. . . . And I'm a strong type as well." Fleischmann and McCann both think that Mattachine women and men got along well. McCann remembers that she and Fleischmann "hung out with the men and with the women." She argues that becoming an activist "in a mixed-gender organization" influenced her greatly: "If my first organization had been DOB, my philosophy as a growing activist would have been shaped by that. Instead it was shaped by Mattachine and Janus."[13]

Lack of conflict does not mean lack of discrimination. According to McCann, "There wasn't a women's movement yet so there wasn't anything to have a conflict about. We knew our place." She remembers that lesbians were "always the coffeemakers" and "typists." However, she does not think that there was more inequality in the homophile movement than elsewhere. Moreover, "there were so few of us that there was more opportunity for a woman to be in a leadership position."[14]

Led by Polakoff, lesbians and gay men together planned Mattachine's activities. Speeches on such topics as "Homosexuality in History" provided a usable past. Discussions titled "Are Homophiles Too Sensitive?" and "Should We Tell Our Friends, Parents, and Relatives?" concentrated on everyday problems. Meetings to consider "How Can We Better Educate the Public on the Problem of Homosexuality?" and "What We Want Mattachine to Accomplish in Philadelphia" focused on more public matters. Most Mattachine activities took place in homes and workplaces in Center City, Southwest Philly, and West Philly; more public events were held in clubs and hotels in Center City. Philadelphia Mental Health Clinic director James Hayes presented "A Biologist Looks at Sexuality" at the John Bartram Hotel. Robert Veit Sherwin, executive secretary of the Society for Scientific Study of Sex, spoke at the East End Club on "Legal Problems Which Must Be Faced by the Homosexual." Mattachine also sponsored picnics in Fairmount Park (one with a "Wienie Roast"), cultural outings (to the theater and Fire Island), and a Halloween party.[15]

While lesbians and gay men engaged in acts of everyday resistance in all Philadelphia neighborhoods, their formal political work in Mattachine and in all subsequently organized homophile groups concentrated in Center City (fig. 8.3). In part, this reflected the fact that Center City was "downtown," the heart of local political, cultural, and economic power. But it also reflected the fact that Center City was home to the largest concentration of lesbian and gay commercial establishments and Euro-American lesbian and gay residences. This geography of politics meant that whereas Euro-American gay men, and to a lesser extent Euro-American lesbians, built a movement that was based in their own neighborhood, African American lesbians and gay men, and to a lesser extent Euro-American lesbians, often had to travel literal and figurative distances from their residential neighborhoods to engage in homophile politics. Homophile politicization was geographically sexed, classed, and racialized.

In March 1961, Mattachine began producing a newsletter, which published material "pertaining to the homosexual and bisexual ways of life." As was typical in the homophile press, Mattachine writers often defined lesbian and gay problems in psychological terms. "The Homosexual and Society," excerpted from Gordon Westwood's *Society and the Homosexual* and reprinted in the newsletter, asserted that male homosexuality was caused

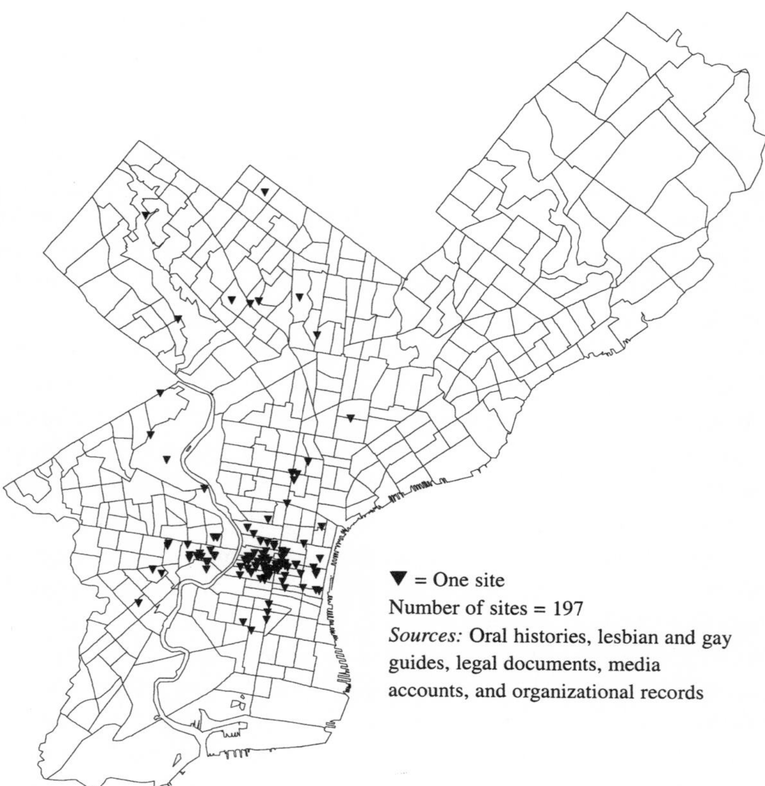

Figure 8.3. Lesbian and gay political sites, 1960–1974. Political sites include locations where activists met, demonstrated, and participated in other organized political activities.

by family disturbances, seduction, and all-male environments. Also using a psychological framework, Adair says that the local group was formed "to assist in helping people adjust to their gayness," "easing that pain." But Mattachine members also conceived of homosexuality as a political issue. Demonstrating the influence of the civil rights movement and its philosophy of racial integrationism, one Mattachine speaker suggested that "other minorities have overcome and corrected prejudices" and that "homosexuals" could do this too, especially "by moving out of exclusively 'gay' circles, by associating with co-workers, and by participating in political, civic and community organizations." Mattachine was also influenced by other political tendencies, including sex radicalism and civil libertarianism. In 1961, the newsletter pointed out that it was not surprising that "tolerance and understanding" were lacking when controversy surrounded "an area of sexuality which is allegedly acceptable to society, that between a man and a woman, i.e. D. H. Lawrence's *Lady Chatterley's Lover*." Progress for "homosexuals," the newsletter argued, depended upon "the efforts, recognition and understanding of men and women as eminent as those who appeared on behalf of Lawrence's book."[16]

Shortly after beginning its activities, the chapter experienced a major blow from its national office. Effective 15 March 1961, Mattachine headquarters in San Francisco revoked all local charters. Struggling with financial and administrative problems, the national office opted for decentralization. "If this is what to expect from organized homosexuality, perhaps we want no part of it," the Mattachine Philadelphia newsletter editorialized. "If we are going to be divided among ourselves how are we to promote better understanding for the homosexual problem?" *Mattachine Review* published a letter from one Pennsylvanian who wrote, "You may rest assured that I have no intention of remaining a member in such high-handed company. I shall remain with our own group here in Philadelphia, and hope for the best. We have advanced so far without your help, and ask no favors from you who are so heartless as to kick a new area council when they are down."[17]

One option was to affiliate with DOB. In late 1961, DOB president Jaye Bell announced that "the time has come for still another step in our growth—especially since we are now the only nationwide organization—that of working our programs to include the male homosexual." As she explained, "This does not mean membership, but it does mean offering them some of the same situations for group enjoyment and acceptance." While the DOB was "re-opening" to men some of its activities, the *Ladder* was "running a special 'Masculine Viewpoint' section" in which contributions from male readers were welcomed "more than ever."[18]

Lesbians and gay men in Philadelphia did not pursue this option. Barbara

Gittings and Jody Shotwell were working primarily with DOB New York. Asked why Mattachine Philadelphia's women did not affiliate with DOB, Fleischmann recalls, "My problem was probably Barbara." In 1963, Gittings wrote another DOB leader, "You informed me on the phone that the Janus Society here had got its impetus at least partly from Joan Fleischmann's desire to embarrass me—this non-DOB organization being right under my nose in Philadelphia." "I am aware that Joan Fleischmann still doesn't like me personally," Gittings explained. "I have *not* been aware that she has carried her resentment so long (about three years) and to such an extent."[19] Meanwhile, Philadelphia's gay activists may have resisted the secondary status that they would have had in DOB and activists of both sexes may have opposed DOB's sex separatism.

Some local chapters, including New York's, retained the name Mattachine, despite threats of legal retaliation by national headquarters. According to Fleischmann, Philadelphians rejected this option because other Mattachine chapters were "more male-oriented" and her group wanted to reject all Mattachine links. Instead Mattachine Philadelphia organized a contest to select a new name. The Janus Society of Delaware Valley was chosen.[20]

Tradition required the gates of the temple of Janus to be opened "when war was to be undertaken," according to a passage in *Bulfinch's Mythology* that was quoted in the new *Janus Society Newsletter* in January 1962. But when one king refused to open them, "Juno herself, descending from the skies, smote the doors with irresistible force." Like Juno, the society would "strive to open doors." The group would "continue to enlighten minds that are in darkness through ignorance, to uphold the rights of minority groups—in short, to illuminate, like the sun, all darkened crevices that breed intolerance, hatred, and bigotry."[21]

Janus was a "god of war" and his gates were rarely closed because there was rarely peace, the newsletter explained. Employing more militant rhetoric than Mattachine Philadelphia had used, the new group declared that "we, as homophiles, are at war with society." But just as Janus was "two-faced" and a god of "beginnings and endings," so too the Janus Society looked forward to "the termination" of "evil and injustice." The newsletter concluded that "like the coin on which Janus was frequently effigized, we ask only to see both sides."

While the group chose a male figure for its name and used a drawing of two bearded male faces for its inaugural newsletter, the selection of Janus was not a sign that men dominated the new group. Lesbians often identified with representations of men. Moreover, Juno was as much the heroine of the story as Janus was the hero. Stressing the literally two-faced nature of Janus, the society created a powerful image for lesbians and gay men who showed one face to their sexual communities and another face to others. The drawing of two bearded faces joined together also presented an image of homosocial coupling and one that may have held special significance for those who identified with bearded beats. More overtly, Janus used the notion of two faces to suggest that the group would be conciliatory as well as warlike.

Janus continued where Mattachine Philadelphia left off, with Polakoff serving as president and Kendall as vice president. In its first two years, the group, which began with 22 members and 53 subscribers, sponsored meetings, parties, open houses, discussion groups, and trips to the opera. Most events took place in members' homes in Center City, West Philly, South Philly, Southwest Philly, and Logan. Kendall recalls that "the most important thing we did was privately among ourselves and what would be considered a support group." But he also says that "in the back of the minds of some of the people was a sense of social consciousness." According to Kendall, Polakoff, Fleischmann, and a few others believed that "if enough people continued doing these things, eventually there would be some impact on society." Toward this end, Janus expanded its series of Center City public events. Psychiatrist Bertram Karon spoke at the East End Club. At the Essex Hotel, Janus played an audiotape of Ed Harvey's "The Talk of Philadelphia" WCAU radio program, which featured two Janus members. Also at the Essex, Janus sponsored speeches by national homophile activists Donald Webster Cory and Robert Wood. By January 1963, Janus was doing well enough to open an office at 34 South 17th Street and attract 125 people to Cory's lecture.[22]

Like other homophile groups, Mattachine and Janus embraced strategies of respectability. At one meeting, Mattachine members agreed that "setting an example for other homophiles is an essential part of our work." Janus's first newsletter declared that the group "encourages medical and social research, sponsors educational programs to promote understanding of the problems of such persons, and encourages high social and moral standards in homosexuals." An editorial argued that Janus had to become a "socially active organization, working with doctors, lawyers and various religious denominations" as well as "organizations already associated with the idea of respectability." Janus regarded the ACLU as its "strongest contact."[23]

Alliances with the ACLU strengthened the links that Gittings and those arrested in the Radnor raid had established. While homophile activists often worked with a discourse of minority rights in these years, they also often turned to a discourse of libertarian privacy rights. In 1961, the ACLU's Spencer Coxe called to Mattachine's attention a YMCA report detailing closed-circuit television surveillance of the men's bathrooms at the Philadelphia Central Y. Convinced that the surveillance, "while offensive," was "not a violation of any constitutional right," Coxe informed Mattachine so that it could "help spread the word." Also in 1961–1962, the ACLU fought a proposed state law providing for "emasculation" of sex offenders; Coxe wrote to Representative Kathryn Granahan asking her to substantiate her charge that in Philadelphia "secret clubs of homosexuals solicited teenage members through the mail"; and ACLU leaders worked with lesbians and gay men to expose police entrapment practices and court corruption.[24]

Janus also hoped to build alliances with scientific experts. Dialogue, however, did not imply agreement. One Janus discussion concluded that homosexuality was not a "sickness of the mind, nor of the body" but a "matter of orientation" and that "a psychiatrist cannot make you a homosexual or a heterosexual." After Bertram Karon's lecture at the East End Club, the newsletter reported that "all the Freudianisms were there in abundance: the breast and the penis, the mouth and the vagina, rivalry of parents, regressive states, and arrested developments." Karon thought the coverage "grossly inaccurate," indicting the reviewer for claiming that he had argued that homosexuality was "incurable" when he had stated that it was "*always* curable."[25]

In late 1962, the newsletter reprinted psychotherapist Robert Harper's "Can Homosexuals Be Changed?" from *Sexology* magazine. Harper's article, which answered in the affirmative, argued that homosexuality was neurotic but not "horrible, sinful, abominable." It also discussed the need to counter homosexual "propaganda," which claimed that "homosexuality is incurable," that homosexuals are "inherently superior to heterosexuals," and that "the homosexual life is more exciting, more romantic, more exhilarating, more wonderful, more 'out-of-this-world' than anything that can be offered by the dull, drab, dreary, deadly world of heterosexuality."[26]

While some may have believed Harper, others endorsed the "propaganda." L. James Benjamin replied to Harper in the newsletter, pointing out that few cases had been documented of "changes from a predominantly homosexual way of life." Moreover, few "mature" homosexuals, "offered a chance to function free of these persecutions and pressures, would choose any other but the homosexual way." Benjamin argued that "since, by Dr. Harper's definition, man is a plurisexual animal and his compulsive exclusiveness indicates sickness, the heterosexual is equally sick." By early 1963, Benjamin was questioning the whole notion of psychiatric expertise. Advancing the view that homosexuality was a product of "predisposition," "environment," and "a conscious realization and desire to follow that path," Benjamin noted that his article was "written without reference to authorities" since "every other theory whether it be half-baked, all-baked, or over-baked" could be supported by "full, documentary evidence."[27]

Working with the police was differently complicated. In some cases, Janus counseled avoidance. A newsletter editorial on venereal disease noted that concerns about police involvement in contact tracing were justified and suggested education, treatment, and checkups by trustworthy physicians for those who were "promiscuous." Janus also criticized police directly. In "Rizzo Rides Again!" the newsletter attacked the new rule that bars serving "female impersonators" would lose their licenses, a regulation designed to suppress the Halloween drag parades. "The captain's longstanding, fervent campaign against homosexuals is familiar to all of us," the newsletter declared. "His past infringements of individual rights are a matter of record. However, we feel that this time he has gone too far. He insinuates that all female impersonators are homosexuals and, therefore, undesirable. He assumes that these people are a menace to the clean, decent folk of Philadelphia. . . . How long will he be allowed to continue his personal vendetta against anyone whom he considers undesirable?" Janus advised readers to complain to city officials.[28]

Sometimes, however, Janus found police more sympathetic than psychiatrists. On Ed Harvey's radio show, Janus president "Marge" and member "Bob" appeared with Lieutenant Shultz of the Morals Squad and Dr. Torney, a psychiatrist. According to Bob's newsletter report, Torney was "fanatically anti" while Shultz said that he and his department were "only doing their job" and seemed "surprised that homosexuals were human beings and not freaks." While Bob wrote that he and Marge "did not come across as a pair of brilliant intellects," he thought that they appeared "more intelligent" than Torney. And Harvey's "compassion and sympathy" increased during the program and made listeners feel "that homosexuals are not ugly or sick."[29]

Lesbian and gay strategies of respectability thus did not require capitulation to dominant attitudes. They did not even require respectability in all contexts. Mattachine's newsletter printed a story about a man attracted to a man dressed in a white evening gown at an outdoor Halloween pageant. The *Janus Society Newsletter* reprinted Shotwell's story about the love of feminine "Marquita" for "boyish" "Ron" and Fleischmann's story about a promiscuous, "jaded" lesbian who had "seen it all: the gay bars, the tough butches, the sophisticated up-towners, the transvestites."[30] The newsletter also discussed venereal disease and drag. Homophile respectability was aimed primarily at those outside lesbian and gay communities. Within lesbian and gay domains, respectability was often cast aside.

"The Furtive Fraternity"

Janus first came to broad public notice in December 1962, when *Greater Philadelphia Magazine* published Gaeton Fonzi's "The Furtive Fraternity," an unprecedented in-depth examination of the local gay community. Fonzi had encountered gay bars while preparing his 1961 expose, "Lurid Locust Street." "In a two-block area from 12th to Broad," Fonzi had reported, "Locust Street is a street of clip-joints, bar-girls, pimps, prostitutes and deviates." Discussing the "slicksters" on the strip, Fonzi had written that one South Philly businessman controlled "at least four different Locust Street establishments (one of which is a hangout for homosexuals)."[31]

Fonzi's 1962 article began with time, place, and characters:

> Saturday night is the gayest night of the week. They come from all parts of the city, from the suburbs, from as far away as Reading and Atlantic City: Handsome young men in natty, continental-style suits, rough-hewn workers in khaki pants and jackets, aging, pot-bellied executives in conservative business suits. Each gravitates to the haunts and spots that fit him best, provide what he's looking for.

The tour of Center City nightspots included "disreputable" bars such as Hideaway, Surf, and Streets of Paris; "higher class" spots such as Maxine's and Drury Lane; and other bars such as Allegro, Venture Inn, Forrest, Westbury, and Hush Room. Fonzi also walked his readers through coffee shops such as Dewey's and Jimmy Neff's; cruising areas along Spruce, in Rittenhouse, and on subway concourses; clubs such as S.A. and U.S.&A.A.; movie houses on Market; men's rooms at railroad and bus terminals; and Bellevue Court Baths. While most of the men discussed were Euro-American, the article described several African Americans, including a bar group of four men, one of whom "swishe[d] a cigarette through the air in wild accenting gestures," and "three very effeminate 'drag queens,'" who were called "Clara," "Madame Fifi," and "Marilyn Monroe." Ignoring predominantly lesbian and predominantly African American gay spaces, however, Fonzi encouraged his readers to imagine that the "fraternity" was primarily male and Euro-American.[32]

In a departure from previous local media stories, Fonzi was critical of antigay legal practices. Using the case of "Edwin," a gay man swindled by a bail bondsman and lawyer after he was entrapped by police in a Market Street movie theater, Fonzi described "a vicious racket." A 1961 police investigation of 337 morals cases, Fonzi reported, had uncovered "systematic mulcting of homosexuals" and "a pattern of a possible conspiracy involving policemen, bondsmen, lawyers and magistrates." In January 1962, district attorney James Crumlish had announced the completion of the investigation. Ten bail bondsmen and "associates" were arrested; four lawyers and six policemen involved were not. According to Fonzi, "the racket apparently still flourishes." Highlighting the use of police decoys, Fonzi also described the geography of "homosexual arrests." In all, nearly 600 people had been admitted to city prisons the previous year on "sodomy and other sex offenses, excluding vice and rape," and "the bulk of sodomy arrests involve homosexuals." Fonzi reported on Rizzo's crackdown on the Halloween parade as well. "Though the great majority of homosexuals have no desire to be female impersonators," Fonzi asserted, "they sympathized with the impersonators' plight, knowing that many had prepared all year and spent hundreds of dollars on costumes."[33]

While Fonzi was critical of antigay legal practices, he endorsed the idea that "homosexuals are sick" and stated that homosexuality was "a manifestation of a neurotic condition" or "arrested emotional development." Homosexuality should be treated, not punished, he argued, noting that "most psychiatrists" believed that sending a homosexual to jail was "like sending away a boy who stole candy to do time in a candy factory." Here Fonzi introduced a "unique program" that had the potential to "blaze a path in reform." In 1956, a program based on Samuel Hadden's methods had been established under the Probation and Parole Department of the Quarter Sessions Court. Instead of reporting to the probation office, a small number of homosexual offenders attended group therapy sessions at Philadelphia General Hospital. After referring to Oscar Wilde's imprisonment for sodomy, Fonzi concluded by writing that "while today there are many judges who look on homosexuality with just as unenlightened an abhorrence, in many areas the curtain of ignorance is rising." But until "man's compassion for man opens his eyes to the fact that much of his attitude toward the homosexual is based on irrational fears and assimilated prejudices," homosexuals would "have to continue to live in fear and isolation, spied on and harassed, intimidated and blackmailed," members of a "furtive fraternity."[34]

In the middle of his article, Fonzi stated, "Bar frequenters make up only a small percentage of Philadelphia's homosexual community. . . . The vast majority of homosexuals in Philadelphia have never been to a gay bar in their lives, nor have they ever solicited anyone in a men's room or movie theatre. They live relatively quiet and outwardly normal lives, suppressing their fears and indulging their sexual inclinations as discreetly and as privately as they can."[35] This was the article's transition to a discussion of Janus, the only section in which lesbians figured prominently. Shifting his focus from leisure to politics, from disrespectable to respectable activities, and from domains in which sex was pictured as publicly lurid to ones in which it was portrayed as privately domestic, Fonzi moved from single-sex gay culture to heterosocial lesbian and gay activism.

Four women and three men from Janus were interviewed for this part of the article. All were "articulate, well-dressed and looked not at all like most people think homosexuals should look like." "Barbara" and "Marge" were identified as secretaries, "Joan" was a teacher, and "Jane" was an assembly-line worker in an electronics plant. Marge, a "smartly dressed blonde," and Jane, a "pleasant-faced smaller woman," were "middle-aged"; Barbara, a "thin, little girl with short black hair," and Joan, a "a hefty but pretty brunette," were in their twenties. The men were identified by their occupations: "Bob" was a store clerk, "Mel" a computer programmer, and "Jack" an insurance salesman. "Marge" and "Jane" were likely Mae Polakoff and Joey Hardman; "Joan" was Joan Fleischmann. Mark Kendall was interviewed as well but was quoted in a section of the article dealing with bisexuality.[36]

Although "The Furtive Fraternity" focused almost exclusively on gay men's lives (and for its title used a homosocial male term), the Janus section highlighted lesbian and gay links. Janus's membership was said to be about 25% female. According to Fonzi, "the number of females" in Janus "may be disproportionate, since most psychiatrists agree that the percentage of lesbians in the population as a whole is far greater—one said five times greater—than the percentage of male homosexuals." (The psychiatric view cited here, while less dominant than Fonzi implied, was embraced by some experts in this period.) While Janus had more male members, however, its early leadership was more lesbian than gay and this was reflected in the group that spoke with Fonzi. Because lesbians hardly appeared elsewhere in the article (and in one passage a gay man complained that "the female in this society has caused more misery to both the heterosexual and homosexual male than you can imagine"), readers might well have gotten the impression that political organizations created an exceptional social space where lesbians and gay men mixed.[37]

The Janus members' comments reveal the respectable assumptions that underlay early homophile activism. Explaining why she was not using her real name, Marge stated that "the stereotype is such that, no matter how well established as an individual I might be, as soon as my sex life is revealed, people would immediately begin to think of the other aspects of the stereotype." Mel worried that if coworkers found out that he was gay, most would stop regarding him as "worthy of respect." Jane noted that her "social life" was "very normal: We go to house parties, we play cards, we go on picnics, we go to the theatre, we watch television, we go to the shore." Fonzi wrote that "the primary point they were all eager to get across was that the majority of homosexuals are, in everything but their sexual inclinations, no different than anyone else." Legitimating their claims to speak on behalf of other lesbians and gay men, Fonzi noted that Janus members "represent, perhaps more than any other segment of the community, what may loosely be termed the 'average' Philadelphia homosexual."[38]

Janus's lesbians discussed respectability in ways that suggest that they thought of lesbians and gay men as sharing a common identity. Responding to the "fallacy" that sexual coercion led to lesbian and gay identity, Jane argued not in female terms but in male ones: "This idea of the old sex deviate preying on the young boy and turning him into a homosexual is ridiculous." Making an equivalence between women and men and between gays and straights, Joan argued that the same reasoning used against her when she was fired from her teaching job could be used to suggest that no one be allowed to teach, since female homosexuals and male heterosexuals might attack girls while male homosexuals and female heterosexuals might attack boys.[39] Neither rejected nor articulated by Janus's gay men, this sense of common identity was expressed and promoted by Janus's lesbians.

Consistent with the strategy of respectability, the Janus members downplayed the sexual aspects of their lives and criticized the "swishy type of homosexual who brought contempt and derision on the majority." Janus "urged all homosexuals to adopt a behavior code which would be beyond criticism and which would eliminate many of the barriers to integration with the heterosexual world."[40] Paradoxically, although these activists identified closely with one another, they thought that their mutual cause would be advanced if their communities adhered to conventional gender norms that distinguished clearly between women and men. Activists were building political community between lesbians and gay men on the ground of sex differences.

Reaction to "The Furtive Fraternity" was mixed. The *Janus Society Newsletter* "commended" it as "informative" and "objective," reporting that "a number of professional people (doctors, lawyers, etc.) have been quite favorably impressed." Mattachine San Francisco's newsletter reprinted the "masterpiece." Mattachine New York thought it "excellent." *Mattachine Review* praised it as "a milestone" and "fair." Reprints of the article were the third most purchased piece of literature sold at a regional homophile conference in 1964.[41]

Not all activists were pleased with the expose. In the *Ladder*, Jody Shotwell attacked Fonzi for violating the lesbian and gay communities' protective boundaries. Describing the "furor accompanying the appearance of this article," she noted that it "sold out on the day of issue." "We accuse the article of sensationalism," she declared, "because of its blatant and unnecessary (we feel) publication of the names and addresses of gay bars and other gathering places." In a sign of conflict between the interests of businesses and political groups, Shotwell reported on "rumors of lawsuits pending against the magazine by some of the bars." In addition, one of the women interviewed by Fonzi had been "rewarded with a punch in the nose by an employee of one of these bars."[42]

Political activists, in promoting public visibility, challenged the everyday strategies of resistance that many lesbians and gay men depended upon for making themselves visible to one another but not to straights. Marge McCann recalls a similar dynamic in the bars: "There were people that were absolutely horrified that we were trying to break the stereotypes down because as long as the stereotypes existed, those of us who didn't fit them were safe. And once the world starts realizing that we are not all stomping bulldykes and screaming queens, then the rest of us become suspect." Pru Chis remembers feeling this way in the 1960s: "The great mass of the American people at that time didn't know anything about us and therefore they couldn't hate us or love us. The only people that really knew us were those that, say lawyers and cops and people like that, would have contact with us. But most people just didn't know us and you sort of were left alone. But I think that I had correctly gauged American common sensibility, fed by the popular media, that if they got to know us, they would really hate us." Asked whether he thought that activists were threatening, Chis says, "Activists were going to change my life and I thought in a way for the bad." Bill Brinsfield remembers that Barbara Gittings "used to stand outside of Maxine's" and "give out pamphlets to gay men." "It had something to do with legal rights," he recalls. "If you're arrested this is what you could do. And that woman would stand out there in the bitterest weather and she couldn't get one gay man to help her." "Activists were somebody that you were almost afraid of during all that suppression," he observes. "Or maybe I was just a pussy. There were still loved ones alive. They would have felt disgraced."[43]

As an activist, Shotwell did not oppose all types of lesbian and gay visibility. She praised Fonzi for granting that "a large percentage of homosexuals live quiet and normal lives apart from public gathering places" and wrote that "we cannot criticize him for not looking further into this aspect, for even a homosexual's home is his castle." She thought that the account of entrapment reminded readers that "sex is a private affair," that the homosexual "cannot be accused of immoral behavior if he refrains from sexual activity in public places," and that "any citizen has the right to be in any public place regardless of his sexual orientation."[44] Shotwell implicitly distinguished here between rights of sexual "activity," which she saw as circumscribed within a private sphere, and rights of sexual "orientation," which she saw as extending into the public sphere. Constituting bars as quasi-public and quasi-private, Shotwell suggested that lesbians and gay men in bars should have all of the rights appropriate to the public sphere but that bars should have the freedom from public visibility ordinarily reserved for private spaces.

Although Shotwell praised many aspects of "The Furtive Fraternity" as "honest," "courageous," and "fair," she criticized Fonzi for "all-too-tritely replacing the sin concept with the sick concept." She concluded that Fonzi was "far too unlearned and new" to this "complex subject." Mark Kendall remembers another critic, future Janus leader Clark Polak, who "made the brilliant comment that it didn't tell him anything he didn't know." Kendall was "chagrined" because "the article wasn't written for him and it wasn't written for gay people."[45]

These disagreements reveal acute sensitivity to questions of audience. Shotwell was angry about the ways in which the article revealed lesbian and gay secrets to a general audience. Kendall thought that the appropriate audience was a general one and was pleased with the results. Polak seems to have wanted Fonzi to write for knowledgeable lesbian and gay readers. Significantly, none of these accounts took into consideration the lesbian and gay readers for whom the article provided a much-needed guide to local gay geography. To the extent that homophile strategies of respectability were oriented toward mainstream audiences, they often encouraged activists to turn away from the very people they purported to represent.

"The Furtive Fraternity" also elicited a set of reactions from Italian American leaders, reactions that further revealed the risks associated with lesbian and gay visibility. In February 1963, Arnold Orsatti's *Il Popolo Italiano*, an Italian American newspaper, began publishing a series of articles on "sex-deviates" and the "night-spots which cater especially to them." Promising to document "illegal liquor operations," the paper reprinted excerpts from "The Furtive Fraternity" and reported that, like *Greater Philadelphia Magazine, Il Popolo* subsequently received threats from "anonymous 'powers behind the street.' " These included "corrupt politicians" and "racketeers and thugs masquerading behind the facades of pseudo-respectability." Alluding to one such "power," *Il Popolo* reported that Al Borden, "publisher and editor of a liquor trade paper called the *Observer*," had called *Greater Philadelphia Magazine* to "point out that Frank Palumbo had no connection with the illegal operations." According to Frank Rizzo biographer S. A. Paolantonio, Palumbo was a South Philly restaurateur and Rizzo's "first political connection." Describing Palumbo as Rizzo's "benefactor," Paolantonio says that Palumbo helped arrange for Rizzo's transfer back to Center City in 1960.[46]

In March, *Il Popolo* revealed that Palumbo, "reputed GOP Boss in South Philadelphia," had a series of familial and personal connections to Cove, Inc., owner of "the building at 13th and Locust Streets which is honeycombed with bars and has been extensively publicized as a hangout for all sorts of degenerates and sex-deviates." Linking Palumbo also with a local judge and a state senator, *Il Popolo* suggested that "maybe it's time the Grand Jury began probing some of the Republican shenanigans." "The tragic part of it," *Il Popolo* noted, "is that these cesspools of degeneracy have become traps for teenagers and young adults who are easy prey for debauched elders and for any blackmail artists who set their snares."[47]

One such tragedy occurred that very month, when John Applegate was murdered in his North Philly apartment. According to *Il Popolo*, Applegate had made "sexual advances" toward two LaSalle College students in a North Philly bar that "sex-deviates have been known to patronize." Depicting the students as innocents, *Il Popolo* wrote that "the boys" were lured to Applegate's apartment "with the promise of female company" and could not have known that Applegate had been convicted of sodomy in 1953 and was awaiting trial on a 1960 sodomy solicitation charge. While *Greater Philadelphia Magazine*'s entrapped "Edwin" had been presented sympathetically, *Il Popolo*'s Applegate was depicted as a villain. While Fonzi had called for psychological treatment for gay men, Orsatti condemned sex deviates. "There is no excuse for Philadelphia becoming a meeting place for sex-deviates who pour into the city from all points of the compass," Orsatti editorialized. "Obviously, the word has gotten out that Philadelphia is a haven for such activities":

> This is a form of social corruption which represents a moral and physical threat to every family, every teenager and every young adult in the community. Nor is it the sex-deviate who deserves our scorn and odium, but those hoodlum vampires who suck financial profit from the misery and degradation of others. While equally deserving of our contempt are those hypocritical and self-serving "leaders" who, by their silence and timidity, permit such practices to flourish unchecked and un-censured. The two-legged lice who grow rich on the sickness of others while infesting the young with a similar sickness are impervious to prosecution simply because of so-called "respectably Christian" men who haven't the intestinal fortitude to speak up.

Linking his Italian American enemies with "sex-deviates," Orsatti put forward many of the very sexual stereotypes that Janus's leaders had challenged in "The Furtive Fraternity." In the end, homicide charges were dropped against one student and charges were never brought against the other.[48]

In the months following publication of "The Furtive Fraternity," *Il Popolo* was not the only local newspaper that linked homosexuality with violence and death. In May 1963, the *Tribune* published Fred Bonaparte's "Homosexuality, Suicides Raising, City Official Tells Morticians," subtitled "Middle-Sexers Most Brutal of Murdering Breed." Dr. James Weston, a Euro-American pathologist with Philadelphia's medical examiner's office, had provided shocking news to an audience of "Negro undertakers and their wives." Weston warned the undertakers that "they can no longer afford to exclude homosexuality as a possible motive for murder or suicide." Using color slides that displayed "tell-tale signs" on the bodies of murder victims,

Weston asserted that "a person who kills for homosexual motives rarely mutilates the genital organs of his mates, but that this is commonplace in heterosexual (man-woman) killings." Although they spared victims' genitals, homosexual murderers were "the most vicious" killers and "homosexuals who kill themselves often mutilate their own sex organs."[49]

The *Tribune*'s story suggests not only that the media continued to favor negative representations of same-sex sexualities but also that such representations were a response to perceptions of greater gay visibility. Moreover, according to Bonaparte, Weston linked the "evidence of increasing homosexuality among Negroes" in Center City to "the Negro's struggle for equality": "As the Negro becomes assimilated into the white society, he will become more involved with the tensions and mental problems of this society." Pointing out that "homosexuality and suicide were rarities within the Negro race two decades ago," Weston noted that "these are the tensions which are causing the increase in Negro suicides and Negro homosexuality." Offering arguments against both cross-race and same-sex bonds, Bonaparte's article displayed the limited extent of positive media change during this era.

Increased gay visibility thus had a host of complicated consequences. While some of these were negative, "The Furtive Fraternity" and support from Janus helped "Edwin" fight his solicitation charge successfully.[50] For Janus, the article yielded unprecedented public attention. Along with the opening of the Janus office and the large audience at the Cory lecture in January 1963, the *Greater Philadelphia Magazine* article marked a new stage in local homophile activism.

Conventional and Unconventional Echoes

The culmination of this period of homophile activism took place on Labor Day weekend in 1963, when the first conference of East Coast Homophile Organizations took place at the Drake Hotel. Discussions about forming a new regional or national grouping began in the aftermath of Mattachine's reorganization in 1961. In January 1963, Mattachine New York, Mattachine Washington, DOB New York, and Janus formed ECHO. One of the federation's first decisions was to sponsor a convention. Philadelphia made sense as a site because it was central, Janus could help with logistics, and the annual American Psychological Association meeting was scheduled to take place there. Mark Kendall was chosen to serve as convention chair and coordinator; Joan Fleischmann soon replaced him. Jody Shotwell attended ECHO meetings as a DOB New York representative.[51]

Barbara Gittings and Kay Lahusen's relationships with the regional and national homophile movement were in flux in this period. Lahusen, who had met Gittings through DOB New York contacts, moved from Boston to

Center City in the early 1960s. Gittings completed three years as president of DOB New York in 1961 and became chapter secretary in 1962. At the national DOB convention that year, she lost in DOB's presidential and vice presidential elections but won the post of corresponding secretary. In February 1963, she became acting editor of the *Ladder* and shortly thereafter was named editor.[52]

In early 1963, Gittings found herself being attacked as a possible candidate for convention coordinator. DOB New York leader Marion Glass circulated a letter to, among others, Gittings and Lahusen, stating that "while it would be desirable to have an 'on-the-spot' Philadelphian as coordinator, some Philadelphians would probably find Miss Gittings unacceptable." Lahusen responded that "one wonders why you have raised her name only to put it down." According to a 1963 letter written by Gittings, Glass had told her that "the ill-feeling of Joan and other unnamed members of the Janus Society is still so pronounced" that they would not want to see her chosen. Gittings responded that she had "not been aware that there is such a mountain of ill-will in Janus Society against me—or that it could have any basis except Joan Fleischmann's personal feeling." "I feel no ill-will towards the Janus Society," she wrote, "and have not felt in competition with it." Opposition also may have arisen because some people thought that Gittings was too butch. Fleischmann recalls that one candidate was rejected because "she was not feminine."[53]

By this time, Gittings and Lahusen were skeptical about ECHO. In April 1963, Gittings wrote to national DOB leaders that, of the four groups in ECHO, "only DOB is totally independent of Mattachine connections. Is this conference partly intended as a springboard for a formal re-affiliation of those 3 Mattachine-spawned groups?" But Gittings also was beginning to show signs of impatience with DOB, asking in reference to a DOB attack on two gay activists, "Can the homophile movement afford to belittle its radical elements???" In the end, neither Gittings nor Lahusen attended the ECHO convention and Gittings nearly balked at covering it in the *Ladder*. In September 1963 they both resigned from DOB New York.[54]

Conference planning was made difficult by actions taken by hotels and newspapers. After arrangements had been made to hold the event at the Adelphia, the hotel backed out just weeks before the convention. ECHO then booked rooms at the Drake, but it, too, tried to cancel. According to one source, the hotel manager told an organizer, "I don't want a lot of people talking about sex in my hotel." This time, a combination of legal action, negotiation, and violent threats made by Janus's Clark Polak kept the conference at the Drake. ECHO also experienced difficulties with newspapers. Three months before the conference, the local ACLU's *Civil*

Liberties Record had taken the *Bulletin* to task for refusing to accept as written an ad for Robert Wood's Janus lecture. The *Bulletin* printed the ad, but only after changing the text to identify Wood as the author of a "controversial" book instead of as the author of *Christ and the Homosexual.* The *Inquirer* printed the ad as submitted; the *News* refused any ad. ECHO conference ads were sent to 10 New York and four Washington newspapers, six national weeklies, and four Philadelphia papers. According to one report, after years of being denied advertising space, activists broke through when the *New York Times* accepted a small announcement. With this as precedent, organizers persuaded the *Inquirer* and *Washington Post* to print ads as well.[55]

The conference, "Homosexuality—Time for Reappraisal," opened on 31 August 1963 with Fleischmann welcoming the participants. Among the presenters were Reverend Edward Lee of Philadelphia's Holy Trinity Episcopal Church, who spoke on "The Church and Homosexuality." Philadelphia lawyer Charles Roisman presented "The Homosexual and Law Enforcement." Local psychologist Irving Jacks spoke on a panel titled "Homosexuality: Research Taboo"; local psychoanalyst Wainwright Churchill presented "The Need for an Objective Approach to Homosexuality." Other participants included Kinsey Institute sexologist Wardell Pomeroy, who moderated a panel, and psychologist Albert Ellis, who spoke on "Sexual Freedom and Homosexuality." R. E. L. Masters, author of *The Homosexual Revolution,* contributed a paper, "The Homophile Movement and the Effeminate Homosexual," which was read by Robert King. Also speaking were Donald Webster Cory, who discussed "The Emergence of the American Homophile Movement"; Mattachine Washington leader Frank Kameny, who presented "The Homosexual and the U.S. Government"; and Artemis Smith, who read from her new novel.[56]

Alliances with professionals were again critical to the homophile strategy of respectability. Noting that "while most of the speakers were not themselves homosexuals, the audience decidedly was," *Confidential* signaled the conference's failure to attract a straight audience but its success in attracting straight speakers. One of ECHO's first decisions had been that the convention should be aimed at both "opinion makers, that is the professional groups," and "the general public." Although the American Psychological Association declined to cooperate with ECHO, homophile organizers "plastered" its meeting with invitations, and one report claimed that 20 to 30 psychologists attended ECHO sessions.[57]

Faith in the promise of such alliances could extend only so far. Shotwell wrote that it was a tribute to audience members that they sat in "well-mannered silence" through an "hour of castigation" by Albert Ellis. Unwilling to maintain silence indefinitely, one guest reportedly responded to

Figure 8.4. Joan Fleischmann (second from left) at ECHO convention, Drake Hotel, 1963. Courtesy of Gay, Lesbian, Bisexual, and Transgendered Archives of Philadelphia, Philadelphia, PA.

Ellis's assertion that the exclusive homosexual is a "psychopath" with a comment greeted by applause: "Any homosexual who would come to you for treatment, Dr. Ellis, would *have* to be a psychopath!" Ellis remembered the exchange differently. He later wrote Gittings that a lesbian audience member had said that any such homosexual would have to be "highly masochistic—since (she very agitatedly implied) I was against homosexuals." Ellis also claimed that only a "vociferous minority" applauded this remark. Still, he acknowledged that "there was a strong undercurrent of hostility against me audible every time I even mentioned the possibility that fixed homosexuals are emotionally ill; and at times there were loud hoots and catcalls." Insisting that he had said that most "exclusive homophiles" were psychotic, not psychopathic, Ellis found it "interesting" that he had gone from being "something of a hero in the homosexual movement" to encountering hostility from "homosexual reporters." He took this "super-vulnerability to criticism" as evidence that "most fixed homosexuals are exceptionally emotionally disturbed." While Shotwell's and Ellis's accounts differ, they both suggest that respectable homophile leaders were not necessarily able to control homophile audiences, that homophile leaders and audiences did not necessarily agree with the views expressed by all of their chosen experts, and that homophile leaders and audiences may have been as interested in influencing their experts as in being influenced by them.[58]

Ellis was not the only speaker criticized. After Edward Lee declared that the Judeo-Christian tradition did not recognize homosexuality but that the church should understand and help homosexuals, a New York lesbian reportedly told him, "You're preaching hate." Referring to Robert Wood's recent Janus lecture, one Philadelphian added, "[Lee] wasn't nearly as bad as that preacher you sent down here to talk to us. Know what his subject was? Homosexuality as an answer to the population explosion!" Activists also criticized the media. The conference was covered on local radio stations WPEN and WCAU but Philadelphia's newspapers "stayed away en masse."[59]

Confidential's report suggests that strategies of respectability were very much in evidence at the conference. However, if reporter Travis is to be believed, this effort by activists to cloak themselves in signs of respectability were not always successful, as he noticed that "a high proportion of the women had very short haircuts." That cultivating respectability was a strategy and not a way of life is suggested in a story told by a hotel elevator operator. "I took a couple of women up to their rooms," he said, "but when they came down, they were men!" Whether these were women perceived as men or men perceived as women, they were presenting themselves differently in different contexts. The strategic nature of respectability is also suggested in Cory's comment that some activists "denounce promiscuity at meetings" and then "cruise all night until they've had three or four affairs."[60]

The strategy of adopting respectable gender norms did not go uncriticized. Masters's paper attacked the homophile movement for opposing male effeminacy. Not only did "the real effeminate" encounter "great difficulty in everyday life," Masters asserted, but the reasons for activist rejection were based on fears of the "effeminate tendencies . . . present in most, if not all, homosexuals." Although he recognized that it could be a "drawback" to "have such people around," Masters wondered if the movement could "retain its good conscience when it rejects those who are rejected by every other quarter."[61]

Although Masters's talk was framed in gay and not lesbian terms, it was precisely the combination of lesbian respectability and gay respectability that strengthened the activists' strategy and made worse the exclusions that this strategy required. Working with gay men, lesbians could gain the public visibility more often afforded gay men and could make use of greater male access to sociocultural resources. In the company of lesbians, gay men could shed their images as sexually predatory perverts not "domesticated" by "female influence." Both lesbians and gay men could use heterosocial visibility to keep the sexual aspects of their lives invisible. Using this accommodationist strategy, otherwise unconventional activists could be seen as conforming to heterosocial gender conventions. This strategy could also challenge expectations that relations between the sexes were necessarily sexual and that same-sex sexualities were linked to hatred or fear of the "other" sex. One cost of this strategy was the exclusion of gender-crossers; another was the acceptance of conventional gender and heterosocial norms. To the extent that such norms were central to the oppression of lesbians and gay men, these strategies of respectability were necessarily limited.

Lesbians and gay men at the ECHO convention joined a tradition that extended back to the eighteenth century, a tradition of meeting in Philadelphia to declare a struggle to achieve rights long denied. Homophile activists also joined a more recent tradition of fighting for rights. The Radnor raid had taken place about six months after four African American students in Greensboro, North Carolina, sparked a nationwide campaign of sit-ins for racial desegregation. The ECHO conference opened just days after the civil rights movement's 1963 March on Washington. "There are 15 million of us in the United States," Bob King of Mattachine Washington told *Confidential*'s Ken Travis. "This makes us the second largest minority in the country, second only to the Negroes." Travis wrote that "the boys and girls aren't quite ready to stage a Gay March on Washington yet, but from the looks of things at their convention, they may work up to it in a couple of years." He concluded, "If we ever do see the day when 200,000 homos march down Constitution Avenue, though, the capital had better watch out. Those handsome Washington cops will be facing a new form of hazardous duty."[62]

In the end, the ECHO conference proved to be a high point for the homophile movement, for its Philadelphia hosts, and for the lesbian and gay alliances that made it happen. Activists in three key East Coast cities got to know one another, worked cooperatively, and enriched one another's efforts. In the coming years, these bonds would sustain activists as they entered a more militant stage.

The period surrounding the conference, however, also revealed signs of what would later become major movement divisions. From the start, DOB's leaders were more tentative in their support for cooperation among the East Coast groups. Barbara Gittings and Kay Lahusen were at odds with national and New York DOB leaders and with Janus's Joan Fleischmann and Marge McCann. Gittings and Lahusen's increasingly close ties with gay militants eventually would lead DOB to remove Gittings from her position as editor of the *Ladder*; their conflicts with Fleischmann and McCann would divide Philadelphia's lesbian militants.

At the time of the conference, Clark Polak was about to become the most important gay activist in Philadelphia. One aspect of Polak's political style was revealed in the violent threats that he made when the Drake attempted to back out of its commitment. ECHO's criticism of Polak would be only the first break in the militants' ranks. This break would deepen as Polak began focusing Janus's attention on publishing the highly successful and highly controversial *Drum* magazine.

Meanwhile, to the extent that the work of political groups reflected broadly and deeply based community developments, the period leading up to the ECHO conference illustrated the promise of lesbian and gay cooperation. To the extent that political groups gained power to effect change in their communities, this period demonstrated the possibilities of an even more cooperative future. Cooperation faltered after 1963 because of divisions within lesbian and gay communities, the failure of political groups to bridge these divisions, and the larger context of power imbalances between women and men in which lesbians and gay men often found themselves and to which they often contributed.

9

"News for 'Queers' and Fiction for 'Perverts,'" 1963–1967

Not long after the 1963 ECHO conference, the Janus Society conducted an unusual presidential election. In the context of a national homophile movement that elsewhere tended to feature overwhelmingly male or exclusively female groups, a lesbian was running against a gay man in Philadelphia. While the fact that Marge McCann and Clark Polak opposed one another was a symbol of Janus's mixed-sex character, only one candidate could win.

Janus's 1963 election marked the beginning of a new era in the history of relationships between lesbians and gay men. Over the next few years, Philadelphians developed two new homophile strategies. Building upon earlier heterosocial traditions, a number of local leaders embraced a politics of militant respectability. Influenced primarily by the civil rights movement and racial integrationism, these activists were militant in their championing of both direct action tactics and minority-group respectability. McCann, Joan Fleischmann, Barbara Gittings, and Kay Lahusen favored this approach, which was used most prominently in a series of July Fourth demonstrations at Independence Hall. A second group, led by Polak, adopted a politics of sexual liberationism. Influenced primarily by the "sexual revolution" and civil libertarianism, these activists expressed themselves most forcefully in Janus's *Drum* magazine and were reviled by respectable militants.

Notwithstanding their conflicts, respectable militants and sexual liberationists shared with one another and with society at large basic assumptions about the nature of differences between women and men. While the former juxtaposed feminine lesbians and masculine gay men in their demonstrations, the latter highlighted differences between asexual women and sexual men. Both emphasized differences between the sexes. Defiantly challenging the doctrines of heterosexual supremacy, they reinforced traditional ideas about sex differences.

Gender Gaps

According to Mark Kendall, Mae Polakoff had decided that she "didn't want the headache of being the president [of Janus] anymore." Joan Fleischmann thinks that Polakoff was "burned out." As announced in the Janus newsletter, "Marjorie Miller" (McCann) faced "Clark P." (Polak) in the election. McCann's platform looked back with pride at the accomplishments of Janus, which was becoming "known in the community" and was "gaining the support of prominent and influential people." Her "Assistance" plank called for expanded legal, medical, and religious services. Her "Instruction" plank proposed lectures, research, work on the Model Penal Code, and a "speaker's bureau of experts." Her "Development" plank urged Janus to strengthen its fundraising and newsletter and form a board of consultants made up of "people of professional and community standing," which would help create a "responsible public image."[1]

Born in 1937 to a middle-class Jewish family, Polak was 26 years old when he ran for election (McCann was 24). Norman Oshtry, Polak's lawyer, thinks that Polak grew up in Oak Lane, Philadelphia, and that his mother committed suicide when he was a child. According to Lewis Coopersmith, "They opened the closet one Christmas day and there was mother. . . . Clark was very disturbed by this. It haunted him the rest of his life." Jim Kepner writes of Polak, "As a child he'd overheard his parents complaining they should have had an abortion, and Clark could never feel that anyone really liked him."[2]

In 1976, Polak told John D'Emilio that he began having sex with boys at age five and that at Central High School he was known as "queer." He also told D'Emilio that when he was a teenager he came across Donald Webster Cory's *The Homosexual in America* and that reading the book was "cataclysmic," helping him realize that "our numbers are legion." After high school, Polak went to Pennsylvania State University but flunked out. Writing to a troubled student in 1964, Polak referred to those years: "Your letter is so very familiar to me in that I could have written something similar when I was nineteen. Aware of my orientation, thinking I was alone and fearing that I must be somehow off my rocker or at least a vicious pervert, I was convinced that therapy or some kind of external flagellation was necessary to either cure me of my wicked ways or let me be resigned to my less than acceptable fate."[3]

After returning to Philadelphia, Polak became a businessman. Coopersmith states, in language that evokes the anti-Semitism that Polak encountered, "Clark was an intuitive genius in the business world. He was the classic Jewish businessman. He was born with the instincts to make money. . . . Few people realize quite how successful Clark was because he lived plainly and he didn't brag." Before he became an activist, Polak owned Frankford Personnel and Northeast Advertising Service in Kensington. Kay Lahusen remembers that Polak was "self-made" and "proud of the fact that he had done so well."

By the late 1950s, Polak had moved to Center City and was going to bars and coffeehouses. Although the details remain a mystery, in 1957 he was arrested and released on charges of disorderly conduct.[4]

Polak told D'Emilio that he first learned about Janus from his lesbian roommate, which suggests both that he knew lesbians in his premovement years and that a lesbian played a role in his politicization. He also noted that when he first began attending meetings in 1962 lesbians were running Janus and he blamed Janus's inactivity on this fact. In early 1963, Polak organized Cory's lecture, which his platform called "the largest single money-making event in Janus history." Polak also attended the ECHO conference, reacting strongly when the Drake attempted to cancel the arrangements. Minutes of an ECHO meeting reveal that Polak "made threats in a somewhat violent manner" and "antagonized the management to the extent that the authorized ECHO representatives had difficulty in reassuring them." ECHO unanimously censured Polak and referred disciplinary action back to Janus.[5]

Polak's platform was more critical than McCann's of Janus's previous efforts. If the group had been a "private business," he wrote, "we would be in Bankruptcy Court." Moreover, because Janus had failed to register its name, it was operating illegally. That Janus had survived at all was a "testament to the interest and perseverance of those who have kept it operating." But the members had failed to respond with "great fervor" because they lacked "direction." For the future, Polak recommended change. His financial plank called for a "Janus $100 Club" and noted that he had already contacted "financially substantial professionals and businessmen." Polak also planned to raise money through an expanded lecture series, increased membership and subscriptions, and revenue from legal and medical referrals. His legal plank stated, "We must operate in a way that is beyond reproach at all times and in all areas. If we want the duly constituted governments to recognize us, we have to recognize the methods proscribed by these governments." Polak also recommended that Janus seek "public recognition and endorsement" through an honorary board including physicians, clergy, and politicians. Signaling his priorities, Polak focused on the newsletter and law reform. "Our newsletter is our voice and we must be able to present it to anyone, regardless of position, with pride," he declared. Last on Polak's list but first on his mind was law reform, but this he thought should wait until money and professional advice were secured.[6]

McCann's and Polak's platforms provide a rare opportunity to compare the agendas of a lesbian and a gay man running for the same office. The similarities are striking. Both planned to increase lectures, referrals, membership, and fundraising. Both favored legal incorporation and legal reform. And both supported the cultivation of respectability and the development of respectable alliances. Nevertheless, there were differences. McCann was less critical of Janus's past. Polak emphasized finances more, essentially using a business model, and his organizational schema was more hierarchical, envisioning a membership that would take "direction." In the end, Polak won the election, receiving 20 votes to McCann's 10. Fleischmann remembers the election as an "insurrection" and that Polakoff was "beside herself." She thinks that Polak "got people, men especially, to vote for him." Polak told D'Emilio that he won because he was male.[7]

Sharing the news with Richard Schlegel, Polak wrote, "Don't congratulate me, please, send condolences because it is a great deal of work." And Polak proved to be very hard-working. In the seven years that he led Janus, some of his campaign pledges were fulfilled, others were tried and discarded, and a few were undermined from the start. Polak certainly made a financial success of Janus, perhaps the wealthiest homophile group in this era. Also as promised, he prioritized the newsletter and legal reform. The new president's plan to operate "beyond reproach," however, was quickly compromised. Sounding like a political boss or a lobbyist, Polak wrote in "the strictest of confidence" to Schlegel that there was a 10% chance of achieving state legal reform in three years and that he had been "given to believe that said change might be

Figure 9.1. Clark Polak, 1965. *Drum*, Mar. 1965, 2. Courtesy of Gay, Lesbian, Bisexual, and Transgendered Archives of Philadelphia, Philadelphia, PA.

possible to BUY, for cold cash" through "donations to the right campaign funds."[8] Moreover, as Polak transformed the Janus newsletter into the sexually controversial *Drum* magazine and developed semiautonomous pornography businesses, he did not maintain a respectable image.

The election of a gay man to lead Janus changed the terms of lesbian and gay cooperation. Janus under Polak's leadership attracted a large but passive following. Most members did little more than contribute financially and receive publications. Hundreds attended Janus events but fewer than 20 participated actively. Former members describe the group as a "one-man show." Cooperation between lesbians and gay men, however, did not initially disappear but shifted to reflect a fragile and unequal division of labor. While Polak took control locally, Fleischmann and McCann served as Janus delegates to ECHO. As Polak began working on Janus's new magazine, Fleischmann contributed articles and a "Woman's Way" column and Barbara "Harris" [Horowitz] became editor of a new Janus newsletter, *For Members Only*.[9]

At times, activists openly discussed their efforts to build unity. One meeting considered the question, "Can Homosexual Men & Women Get Along Together?" Another asked, "Should Male Homosexuals Marry Female Homosexuals?" Harris's first newsletter expressed the hope that "strong male-female stratification" in the homophile movement might decrease. Fleischmann wrote in her first "woman's page" that "homosexual men and women need to know one another better, to understand and to accept their differences." While noting that "some may feel that what I write is a criticism of male attitudes," Fleischmann declared, "Anything I describe here as being characteristic of lesbians is not superior to or more normal than or more correct than an opposite or different male trait. I do not believe that the woman's way is better than the man's. It is not. It is just different, as perhaps it should be."[10]

Although Euro-American lesbians and gay men worked together in Janus through 1964, the group did not attract significant numbers of African Americans or other racial minorities. In an article headlined "Homosexuals See Hope for Selves by Negro Victory in Rights Drive," the *Tribune*'s John Wilder reported on a 1964 Janus lecture given by Mattachine Washington's Frank Kameny at the New Century Club. This was the first time that one of Philadelphia's major newspapers covered a homophile event. Wilder estimated that 150 people attended the lecture and reported that Kameny compared the struggles of homophile groups to those of the National Association for the Advancement of Colored People (NAACP). He also noted that Kameny called homosexuals "the largest minority after the Negro," claimed that homosexuality represented "the last major area where prejudice and discrimination are prevalent in this country," and asserted that "now that it is becoming unfashionable to discriminate against Negroes, discrimination against homosexuals will be on the increase." Observing "no other Negroes among the audience" and only "one distributing pamphlets," Wilder reported that he was told by "Charles Philips" (Polak) that Janus was "open to all persons of both sexes regardless of race."[11]

Several days later, a letter from Philips, applauding the coverage, appeared in the *Tribune*. Noting that the reporter "seemed quite upset that there was a minimum of Negroes present," Polak reiterated that Janus "warmly welcomes any person, regardless of race, religion, or sexual preference." "Now that the Negro press has begun to cover our functions," he wrote, "we hope that we will find an increasing representation." Asking "who better can know the hardship and humiliation that comes from blind prejudice than the Negro," Polak observed that "the Negro, whether he be homosexual or heterosexual, is a natural ally to a cause as vital and basic as adult man's right to express his sexuality privately with other consenting adults." Quoting Kameny, Polak wrote, "The exclusion from virtually all employment of anyone known to be homosexual is well-nigh complete and absolute. It is far beyond anything ever encountered by the Negro in his worst nightmares." Making analogies between sexual and racial oppression, Kameny and Polak downplayed the enduring racism of U.S. society and the particular problems of African American lesbians and gay men.[12]

Nevertheless, the continuing effort to build a sense of community that would encompass lesbians and gay men is striking. This was spearheaded by lesbians. Gay men rarely spoke about lesbians, discussing same-sex sexualities in male or sex-neutral terms that ignored lesbian distinctiveness. In part, this reflected different levels of familiarity with same-sex sexualities in the "other" sex. Janus men such as Kendall, Coopersmith, Schlegel, and Richard Gayer remember few if any significant relationships with lesbians before they became activists. Janus women such as Fleischmann and McCann recall important premovement relationships with gay men. Significantly, even when Philadelphia lesbians became alienated from Janus, they did not give up on cooperation with gay men.

Different Drummers

Relations between lesbian and gay activists were never free from tension. But conflict reached new levels in 1965, a year marked by renewed militancy in the national movement as activists pressed for social change through direct action.[13] One of the most important projects of militants was the annual Fourth of July demonstrations at Philadelphia's Independence Hall (1965–

1969). And two significant national homophile publications were led by militant Philadelphians: *Drum,* edited by Clark Polak (1964–1969), and the *Ladder,* edited by Barbara Gittings (1963–1966).

Four groups contested for power in New York, Philadelphia, and Washington's homophile organizations during these years. A relatively conservative gay old guard lost control of Mattachine New York to militants in 1965. A relatively conservative lesbian old guard controlled the national and New York DOB. A third group consisted of lesbian and gay militants who worked through Mattachine groups in New York and Washington, ECHO, and the North American Conference of Homophile Organizations (NACHO). This group included two Philadelphia lesbian couples: Barbara Gittings and Kay Lahusen, and Joan Fleischmann and Marge McCann. The fourth group, which worked through Janus and was led by Polak, was gay, militant, and misogynist.

The first break in cooperation on the East Coast developed because of conflicts over *Drum*. One of the main activities of the homophile movement was producing periodicals that promoted lesbian and gay causes. Scholars have identified *Mattachine Review*, *One*, and the *Ladder* as the premier homophile publications of the 1950s and 1960s. With circulations in the hundreds and low thousands, these magazines reached a small but significant national audience.[14]

When Polak placed an ad for Janus's new publication in the 1964 ECHO conference program, activists around the country were shocked. "*Drum* presents news for 'queers,' and fiction for 'perverts,'" the ad explained. "Photo essays for 'fairies' and laughs for 'faggots.'"[15] *Drum* combined male physique photography; the raw, risqué, and campy comic strip "Harry Chess"; and hard-hitting news, features, editorials, and reviews. Promoting a radical and entertaining vision of sexual liberation, *Drum* challenged the carefully constructed image of respectability cultivated by much of the homophile movement.

Polak's interest in sexual politics developed before he began publishing *Drum*. Fleischmann remembers thinking that Polak wanted to make Janus "a social group for men to meet men." Richard Gayer recalls that when he first attended a Janus meeting, he "wasn't looking for a gay civil rights organization" and "hoped that this would be some sort of a sex club." "Initially disappointed that there were women there," Gayer later did find male sex partners through Janus.[16]

Meanwhile, several months after the Janus election Polak approached Coopersmith about starting a "personal advertisements publication." Combining the men's first names, Clark and Lewis, Polak called the business LARK Enterprises and began producing a "multipage sheet of personals"

Figure 9.2. *Drum*, 1964–1965. Courtesy of Gay, Lesbian, Bisexual, and Transgendered Archives of Philadelphia, Philadelphia, PA

in which readers "could advertise and also answer advertisements" for a "nominal fee." After a few months of operation, postal officials visited the two men at Coopersmith's home. "They were very pleasant," Coopersmith remembers, "and quick to point out we weren't breaking any laws." However "they indicated that somewhere down the line there could be legal problems" and "were obviously trying to intimidate us."[17]

Government documents confirm that postal agents met with Coopersmith and Polak in September 1964. Using "test correspondence," postal officials had investigated a series of Polak's ads for "a correspondence club" and "booklets on homosexuality, adultery, and other subjects pertaining to sex." Although officials acknowledged that "none of the pamphlets offered for sale appear to be in violation of Obscenity Statutes," Polak decided to discontinue the club after grossing $1,000. While these activities were not directly related to Janus, Polak was identified in postal reports as the group's president.[18]

One month after officials visited Coopersmith and Polak, *Drum*'s first issue was published. Fleischmann remembers coming up with the magazine's name. "We were talking about names," she recalls, "and I said, 'Well you know there's the quote about marching to a different drummer.'" Polak cited Henry David Thoreau's *Walden* in the first issue: "If a man does not keep pace with his companions, perhaps it is because he hears a different drummer. Let him step to the music which he hears, however measured or far away."[19]

Three of *Drum*'s controversial features were its comics, parodies, and photographs. "Harry Chess," drawn by A. Jay, featured its title character, "the rugged, virile, sensuous, clever, top agent of A.U.N.T.I.E.—(Agents'-Undercover - Network - To - Investigate - Evil)"; Mickey Muscle, Harry's teenage assistant; Lewd Leather, the leader of "M.U.C.K.—Maniacal-Underworld-Control-Korp."; and Big Bennie, "girl bartender, bouncer, and informer." *Drum*'s first parody, "Heterosexuality in America," spoofed *Life* magazine's "Homosexuality in America." "Franky Hill: Memoirs of a Boy of Pleasure" rewrote John Cleland's eighteenth-century British novel *Fanny Hill*. "Tropic of Crabs" was a takeoff on Henry Miller's *Tropic of Cancer*.[20]

From the start, Polak believed that he was establishing a genre. "*Drum* is a new concept in magazine publishing," he wrote. "To our knowledge, a balance of top level photography, fiction, news and humor directed specifically to the male homosexual has never before been attempted." Creating a hybrid of homoerotic physique magazines such as *Physique Pictorial* and *Tomorrow's Man* and homophile publications such as *Mattachine Review* and *One*, Polak linked sexuality and politics in new ways. *Drum*'s ads worked with discourses of both sexual and homosexual liberation:

Figure 9.3. Harry Chess comics in *Drum*, Mar. 1965, 7–10 (drawn by A. Jay). Courtesy of Gay, Lesbian, Bisexual, and Transgendered Archives of Philadelphia, Philadelphia, PA.

> *Drum* stands against the common belief that sexual drives may be dismissed like a stray dog—with a shout and a kick. Or that they can be sermonized away or replaced by a veil of beauty. Or that if one does enough gymnastics or knitting, there won't be enough time to think about sex. *Drum* stands for a realistic approach to sexuality in general and homosexuality in particular. *Drum* stands for sex in perspective, sex with insight, and, above all, sex with humor.

Weaving these discourses together, Polak worked to liberate gay men sexually and ally the gay movement with sexual liberationists. In 1965, he wrote that *Drum*'s objective was to be a "gay *Playboy*, with the news coverage of *Time*." Criticizing the word "homophile," he noted that "by putting 'sex' back into 'homosexuality,'" and "by being unequivocally pro-homosexual, we will continue to rock the boat."[21]

Polak's description of his magazine as a "gay *Playboy*" and his correspondence with Hugh Hefner's *Playboy* suggest *Drum*'s place in a larger context. Discussing *Playboy*, which first appeared in 1953, and Helen Gurley Brown's *Sex and the Single Girl*, published in 1962, John D'Emilio and Estelle Freedman argue that "the first major challenge to the marriage-oriented ethic of sexual liberalism" came from "entrepreneurs who extended the logic of consumer capitalism to the realm of sex."[22] While Polak shared with Hefner and Brown an entrepreneurial spirit and an ethos of sexual liberation, he differed from them in presenting only men as sexual.

Polak's prosex and progay messages were not aimed at a general audience. In 1966, *Drum*'s contents page began including a statement that the magazine was "published by male homosexuals for the information and entertainment of other male homosexuals." In one Janus newsletter, Polak declared, "From the very beginning I have attempted to produce a magazine that illustrated—rather than pontificated on—the philosophy that, to use a cliche, it's OK to be gay." He continued, "*Drum* has attempted to be supportive of the view that homosexuality is and should be totally acceptable to homosexuals. In so doing, it flies in the face of those in whom antihomosexual prejudice is most firmly entrenched—homosexuals themselves." Answering the question of why "vast numbers of homosexuals fail to affiliate with the various groups," Polak argued that the movement needed to develop "homosexual directed programs" and be "more responsive to the needs of the homosexual community." One of Polak's goals, in other words, was to redefine the relationship between the gay movement and the gay community.[23]

With the publication of *Drum*, one wing of the homophile movement had come to imagine the existence of a national community of gay men entitled to their own cultural space and a shared network of politics and desire. No longer would all homophile magazines assume readerships that included straights, lesbians, and gay men. Written in gay language with gay photographs for gay audiences, *Drum* confirms Benedict Anderson's argument that language has the "capacity for generating imagined communities, building in effect particular solidarities." As Anderson explains and *Drum* illustrates, print media have played a central role in the development of imagined communities.[24]

To be sure, much of *Drum* consisted of reprints, excerpts, and reviews of mainstream cultural texts. In sections such as "Gay Moments in Advertising," however, these texts were presented in ways that created and affirmed gay perspectives and taught readers particular ways to read mainstream texts. Sometimes, as was the case when the parody "Heterosexuality in America" revealed that "heterosexuality shears across the spectrum of American life," readers were shown how to see dominant discourses of heterosexual supremacy. At other times, as in a photograph of Robert Kennedy being kissed by a man, readers were taught to see homoeroticism in presumptively heterosexual life.[25] Most of the time, *Drum* celebrated gay men's distinctive sexual cultures. Unanswered was the question of whether and where lesbians would fit in this imagined community.

Drum quickly became the largest-circulation homophile publication in the United States, larger than all other homophile publications combined. The *Wall Street Journal* reported in 1968 that the magazine had a circulation of 15,000.[26] Letters to the editor suggest a number of reasons for its success. Although it is likely that *Drum* staffers wrote some letters themselves, these reveal the kinds of readers imagined by Polak. One "aging" man wrote that after watching the homophile movement since it began, he had "given up hope." But "then came *Drum*, and for the first time homosexuals began to treat themselves with respect." Much of the praise focused on *Drum*'s sexual politics. One reader wrote, "I'm glad to see an organization put sex back into homosexuality. Certain other organizations who shall remain nameless try to obscure the fact that we homos like to gratify our sexual desires." Some, however, suggested that Polak's hopes of combining politics and pleasure were not always fully realized. "I don't want to join a 'movement,'" one reader explained. "I just want to subscribe to a groovy magazine. That's why I think you should spend more time making *Drum* bigger and better and much less on legal matters."[27]

Many supported *Drum* because its vision was distinctly male and masculine. One reader wrote, "For too long society has castrated us in order to tolerate us. *Drum* implies we're men with feelings all the way from bawdy sex to great ideas." Another praised *Drum*'s celebration of masculinity:

> Believe it or not, just came by your mag; just shows old Petal Bottom don't get around much no more! Your mag has elements of a masculinity and courage that are exciting. It's High Old Time! I have long contended that the queer's fight will not, and cannot, be won by an approach of either sweet reason or rationalization. We're going to have to come out with it, all of it—no posing, or posing straps before the world, or clouding our own vision. That we stand four-square for Priapus, and are damned proud of it.

The Greek and Roman god of procreation, Priapus was also known as a representation or personification of the phallus.[28]

While tens of thousands of readers embraced *Drum*, homophile leaders lined up solidly against the magazine. Most rejected not the existence of the magazine but its links to the movement. One Florida activist argued that Janus should either stop calling itself a homophile organization or change *Drum*: "I think that thing gets worse and worse with each issue (I'm not talking about its entertainment value . . . for most of the gay kids—they are probably eating it up—I'm referring to the public image it projects for Janus AS a homophile organization." Mattachine New York's Dick Leitsch wrote, "If we had a dime for every time a high-ranking police official in New York has tried to tar and feather MSNY with *Drum*, we'd be wealthy! I don't object to titillating pictures being published; I only reject the right of someone claiming to be a part of this movement doing it."[29]

Leitsch was "exceedingly aware that *Drum* was selling well." However, he expected movement publications to be addressed to a general audience. "It contains nothing likely to reach the public at large and move them to our side," Leitsch argued, "and little that will attract any useful persons to the movement." Drawing a clear line between politics and entertainment, Leitsch concluded, "The only excuse for it is whatever profit it may make for the organization. Its only purpose seems to entertain faggots, which is not one reason for this movement. If we're in business to entertain, then let's go the whole hog and provide drag shows, muscle movies, gay bars, dances and orgies!"[30]

The most comprehensive and public attack came from one of the most militant homophile groups. A statement by Mattachine Washington in *Eastern Mattachine Magazine* announced that no physique photographs would appear in its publications and no Mattachine Washington material would be sent to publications that regularly featured such photos:

> The policy is viewed as the only concrete means which the MSW has to place itself against the rising tide of "combination" magazines which contain both articles of serious homophile interest and photographs

> of naked teenage boys in provocative poses. These magazines, which may sometimes have the best intentions, can easily bolster the public's erroneous image of the homosexual as a child-molesting sex fiend. They try to cater simultaneously to physical and intellectual interests—which should remain separate.[31]

What Polak had identified as a strategy for promoting activism, other homophile leaders saw as the movement's greatest danger.

And *Drum* did pose risks. The Federal Bureau of Investigation (FBI) had begun monitoring homophile groups in the 1950s. In 1963, an FBI special agent, along with Philadelphia Morals Squad members and assistant district attorneys, attended Donald Webster Cory's Janus lecture. The FBI also obtained materials from the 1963 ECHO convention. In early 1964, Barbara Gittings and Kay Lahusen suspected that someone had been tampering with their mail.[32]

Drum was particularly risky because while the Supreme Court and other courts continued to restrict the scope of obscenity and censorship law, law enforcement and postal officials continued their antiobscenity campaigns. In the years following the Radnor raid, the Supreme Court ruled in favor of male physique magazines in 1962 and *Tropic of Cancer* in 1964. Obscenity law was still in flux, however, and in 1966 the Court ruled against *Eros* magazine but for *Fanny Hill.* (The Court's decision in the latter, that a text could be found obscene only if it was "utterly without redeeming social value," proved to be the most stable framework articulated.) Both *Eros* and *Tropic of Cancer* were initially found obscene in Philadelphia courts, a favored first stop in obscenity prosecutions. In 1962, antiobscenity crusader Kathryn Granahan of West Philly acquired new status when she was named U.S. treasurer by John F. Kennedy. Meanwhile, according to figures compiled by the U.S. post office, 4,979 arrests and 4,095 convictions for "obscene" mailings took place from fiscal year 1961 through fiscal year 1968. The numbers peaked in 1965.[33]

Beginning in 1964, Polak, Janus, and *Drum* were targeted by customs, post office, and federal, state, and local law enforcement officials. Government agencies, including the FBI, conducted a campaign of surveillance against not only Janus activists in Philadelphia but also readers of *Drum* around the country. In 1965, Richard Schlegel, founder of a Janus chapter in Harrisburg, lost his job as Pennsylvania Department of Highways director of finance after the results of postal monitoring of his mail were revealed to his superiors.[34] A 1965 postal report reveals that Philadelphia district attorney James Crumlish examined each issue of *Drum* and that copies were sent to the U.S. attorney for the Eastern District of Pennsylvania.[35] Beginning in the same year, U.S. customs blocked Polak's attempts to import a variety of publications.[36] Warned by lawyers that "Tropic of Crabs" would leave *Drum* open to obscenity charges, Polak removed the article from all newsstand copies.[37] In 1966, the Buffalo postmaster temporarily withdrew the entire run of *Drum* from the mails while he forwarded samples to the Department of Justice for possible obscenity prosecution.[38]

Polak did not fail to respond. In addition to providing reports, editorials, and advice on these developments in *Drum*, he published articles titled "How to Handle a Federal Agent," "I Was a Homosexual for the FBI," "Frontal Nudes," and "The Story behind Physique Photography." (Ever-vigilant, postal officials helped the FBI obtain a copy of the parody of the bureau.) Beginning with the December 1965 issue, Polak included nude centerfolds in copies of *Drum* sent to subscribers and Janus members.[39] He worked with the ACLU to mobilize support for Schlegel and others victimized by state repression, a strategy that yielded an article in the *New Republic*, a congressional investigation, and a promise by the postmaster general to end postal surveillance of magazines aimed at gay men (a promise not kept). Ever the profiteer, Polak also began selling "uncut" copies of the *Drum* issue containing "Tropic of Crabs." Labeling this issue "Censored" in ads for old copies of the magazine, Polak ensured that it was one of the first to sell out.[40]

Although investigations and harassment continued, ironically Assistant Attorney General Fred Vinson, Jr., was less offended by *Drum* than many homophile activists were. Vinson wrote to Chief Postal Inspector Henry Montague that Janus "appears to be an 'official' spokesman of proclaimed homosexuality and it would seem, judging by *Drum* magazine, to take a serious position on homosexuality." Although he thought that "it does possess features which may be considered 'pandering' to the prurient interest of homosexuals," he found it to consist "largely of advocacy of and information about homosexuality." Vinson recommended further investigation only if Janus mailed "other homosexual material of a more prurient nature." A Philadelphia postal inspector similarly described some articles as "obscene" and "offensive," but said that "taken as a whole, the magazine does not appear to be in violation of the federal or Commonwealth of Pennsylvania Obscenity Statutes."[41]

Polak was not the only Philadelphia editor of a national homophile publication making controversial decisions in this period. After becoming editor of the *Ladder* in 1963, Barbara Gittings unsuccessfully fought the DOB's policy of labeling each issue "for adults only," which she felt tainted the magazine as obscene. She also opened discussions on using the *Ladder* for lesbian pen pals, a proposal rejected by DOB leaders on the grounds that such "introductions frequently are preludes to the use of the United States mail for either immoral or lewd writings" and that many letters written in a previous experiment had been from men. Early in 1964, Gittings began using the subtitle *A Lesbian Review* on the *Ladder*'s covers. She recalls that she and Kay Lahusen did not like the magazine's name because it was not identifiably lesbian: "We made the letters for the *Ladder* smaller and smaller and the letters for *A Lesbian Review* larger and larger, until they were about the same size. And we were trying to take it even further. We couldn't get rid of the name, the *Ladder*, but at least we could pale it into insignificance."[42]

Before *Drum* appeared, Gittings and Lahusen had begun using photographs on the *Ladder*'s covers. In September 1964 the magazine featured its first photographic cover with human subjects; the November 1964 front cover was the first to use a photograph of a human face. "Most American girls feel they can't risk appearing in a photo if they're recognizable, since the *Ladder*'s circulation is chiefly in the U.S.," Gittings and Lahusen explained in a letter to Ger van Braam, a subscriber from Indonesia. "We've heard that Indonesians feel it's impolite to disappoint someone who asks for something," they wrote, "so we want to beg you never to hesitate to say 'No' to us in your own interests!" But since van Braam was the only subscriber in her country and thus would not run much risk of being recognized, Gittings and Lahusen wrote that they hoped that she would allow them to feature her "appealing face," which she did. According to Gittings, "We wanted to show lesbians and others who might be reading the magazine that lesbians are happy, healthy, wholesome, nice-looking people." Although the photographs that were used in the *Ladder* were more respectable than *Drum*'s, Gittings and Lahusen wrote to one potential contributor that they were "enthusiastic" about the "nude studies" she had proposed. For his part, Polak declared that he favored "artistically rather than sexually oriented" physique photography, made selections primarily on the basis of "aesthetic value," and paid less attention to "erotic value."[43] In another convergence, both publications seem to have first featured photographic images of African Americans in 1966.[44] Juxtaposing these developments, it seems clear that both Gittings and Polak, editors of the nation's most widely circulating lesbian and gay movement magazines, were attempting to embody lesbian and gay identities in visual representations. Lesbian and gay bodies had often been regarded as diseased and disfigured, and these photographic innovations challenged these visions. The human body had become a crucial site for representing positive lesbian and gay identities.

But comparing the magazines' use of photographs also reveals differences between lesbian and gay embodiment. *Drum* used paid models; the *Ladder* relied on unpaid volunteers. *Drum*'s photographic subjects were easily recognizable; the *Ladder* usually featured shots that concealed the subjects'

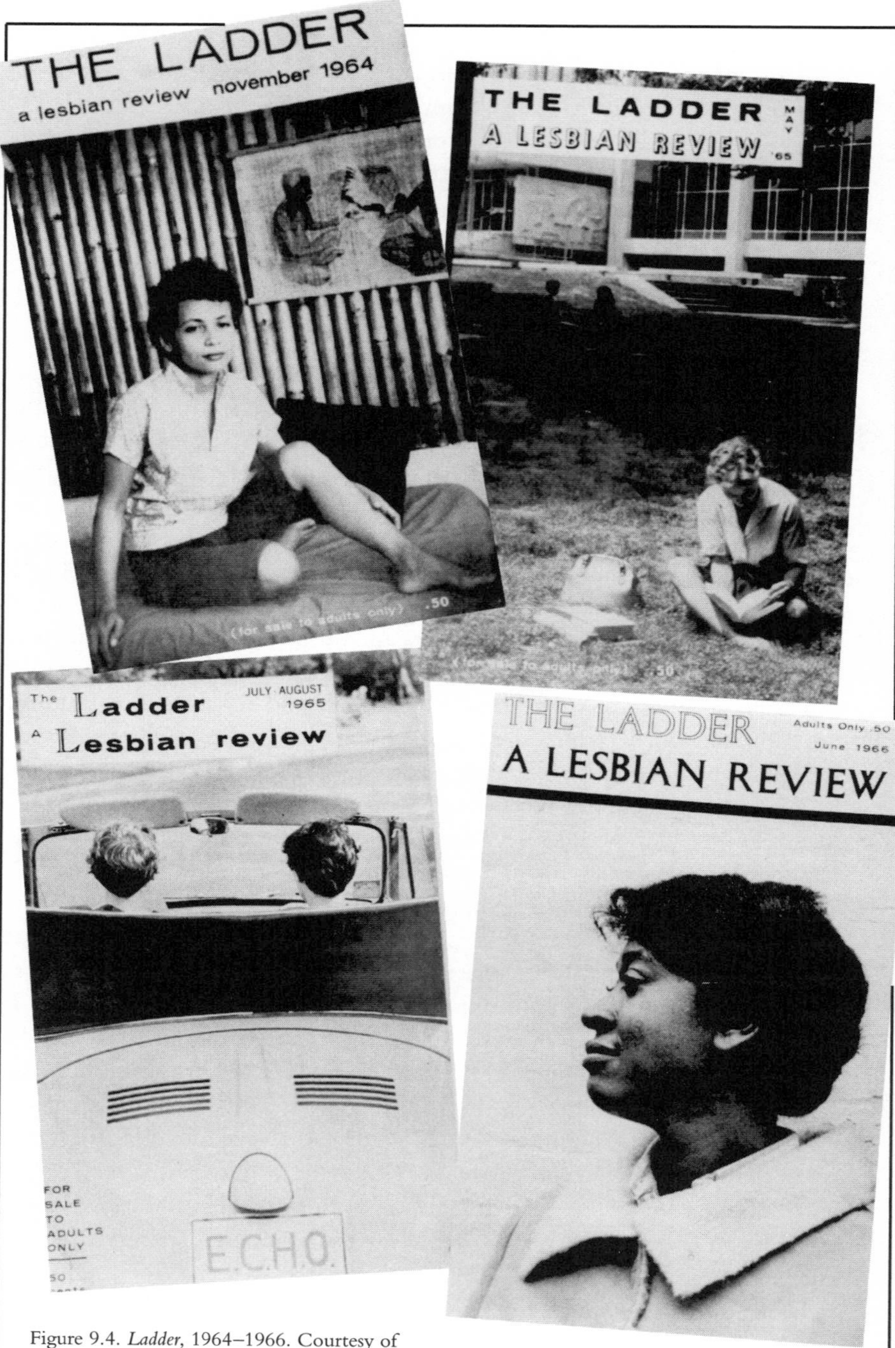

Figure 9.4. *Ladder*, 1964–1966. Courtesy of Barbara Gittings and Kay Tobin Lahusen.

individual identities. *Drum*'s subjects were nearly or fully nude; the *Ladder*'s were more fully clothed. *Drum*'s photographs were rejected by the homophile movement; the *Ladder*'s were celebrated.

Lesbian activists from Philadelphia figured centrally in the isolation of Polak, Janus, and *Drum* from much of the homophile movement. Their actions, however, belie any attempt to interpret this rejection as a simple conflict between lesbians and gay men, accommodationists and militants, or respectables and liberationists. Although opposed to Polak, these lesbians worked closely with gay men. And while they cultivated respectability, they were militant supporters of direct action tactics.

Plotting for the expulsion of Janus from ECHO began in 1964. In a "strictly confidential" letter, Marge McCann, who had become national DOB corresponding secretary, informed DOB founder Del Martin that there would soon be a new Mattachine Philadelphia. Explaining the reasons for breaking with Polak, McCann pointed to *Drum* and argued that Janus had become a "one-man organization" and was looking "less and less like a homophile organization."[45]

While McCann and Joan Fleischmann's decision to leave Janus was a product of lesbian and gay conflict, they were not opposed to working with gay men. McCann explained to Martin that "we have 'subterranean' support for MSP from both Washington and New York Mattachines" and asked for the names of male contacts in Philadelphia. McCann and Fleischmann underlined their desire to work with men by adopting the Mattachine name. Not everyone was pleased by this. Martin wrote McCann that she recognized the need to "break up" Janus. "No one is impressed with *Drum*," she explained, "and I wince at seeing Joan's name in the masthead." But "creating another Mattachine" would not "endear" them to DOB. "DOB is an important cog in the homophile movement," Martin argued, "since the other organizations lean heavily toward the male orientation and neither understand nor pretend to deal with the problems of the female." "You speak of three women starting MSP," she wrote. "Wish it were a Philadelphia Chapter of DOB."[46]

Mattachine Washington's Frank Kameny wrote a letter to McCann that contributed to the climate of intrigue: "I have to keep my homophile movement fences mended and in good order. Clark must not know that this letter was even written." Kameny argued that Mattachine Philadelphia should "steer a course different both from what Janus is now and from what Janus was prior to a year ago," a "lazily-pleasant and cozy group with very little drive." The new group "should not be a showplace of democracy in action, but an effective instrument of purpose." Kameny argued that the group should have "as many men as women" and that because "most of your interest and support are going to come from the male homosexual population," the group's president should be a man. Perhaps anticipating a negative reaction from his lesbian allies, Kameny concluded that this last part was "not really necessary."[47]

While McCann and Fleischmann's subsequent leadership of the new Mattachine demonstrated their independence from Kameny, they also articulated a militant lesbian position against sex separatism. McCann's response to Martin made their commitments clear:

> MSP will not be one of those homophile groups which ignores the existence of the Lesbian. For one thing, we are. For another, I think that all too few Lesbians feel any real "kinship" with male homosexuals, feeling rather that "those nasty boys" deserve whatever they get in the courts and in public opinion. I, for one, do not feel that way. We may not get into legal predicaments as often, but we, too, have to hide, most of the time, our real natures, from society, family, employers, etc. Yes, some of the problems of the Lesbian are unique, and so are some of the problems that male homosexuals have. However, the Janus Society here does not represent either the Lesbian *or* the male homosexual, and there is work to be done.[48]

McCann was opposed to both gay activists who ignored lesbians and lesbian activists who did not feel "kinship" with gay men. Despite their "unique" problems, McCann imagined lesbians and gay men sharing identities, communities, and politics.

In February 1965, ECHO voted to accept the application of Mattachine Philadelphia and expel Janus. Responding to Polak's request for an explanation, Fleischmann drafted a letter that offered four reasons. First, Janus had "little if any membership participation." Second, its efforts to become a national organization were in "direct competition" with other groups. Third, Janus had become a "publishing house" and not a "homophile organization." Finally, ECHO could not accept the inclusion in *Drum* of "certain materials which many, both inside and outside the homophile movement, find offensive at worst, and highly inadvisable, at best." Using a pointed example, the letter explained that "the ACLU, while defending the right of *Playboy* to be published, would not publish a *Playboy*-type of magazine." The letter continued,

> Controversial, unconventional, and unusual ideas and positions have far higher probability of being listened to and accepted, if presented within the framework of, and clothed with the symbols of acceptability, conventionality, and respectability (in the listener's terms, not in the

> speaker's), as arbitrary as we grant most of those symbols to be. Put in the negative: discard those symbols or flaunt them and both the speaker and his ideas will quickly be relegated to the lunatic fringe, to be discounted, rejected, and ignored totally. In short, if one tries to play an avant-garde role in everything, one will succeed in nothing.

Fleischmann stressed the need to "clothe" homophile ideas respectably, much as she would have preferred Polak to clothe the male models in *Drum*.[49]

Ironically, although Janus was kicked out partly because it failed to act as a membership organization, Mattachine Philadelphia was formed primarily as a vehicle that would allow Fleischmann and McCann to continue their activities within ECHO. McCann admitted to Martin that "a move to oust JS from the affiliation would already have been made except that then Joan and I would have no organization to represent." As Mattachine Philadelphia president, McCann made several media appearances, conducted a national survey of sodomy laws and law reform, and met with a representative of the Philadelphia Council of Churches. Fleischmann and McCann also played major roles in the 1964 and 1965 ECHO conferences.[50] But the second Mattachine Philadelphia never accomplished much outside of its role in ECHO.

Direct Action

While *Drum* was the source of one major conflict among homophile activists in these years, the adoption of direct action tactics was another. On 17 April 1965, Mattachine Washington sponsored a demonstration at the White House to protest Cuban and U.S. antigay policies. The following day, Mattachine New York demonstrated at the United Nations building. One week later, Philadelphia featured another demonstration. According to Polak, "a small group of rowdy teenagers" had been patronizing the 17th Street Dewey's until the restaurant's managers instructed its employees to refuse them service. Polak had "no objection" to this, making clear in Janus's newsletter that "we in no way supported those few individuals who were loud and in other ways unreasonable." But as *Drum* explained, "lower level employees became somewhat over-zealous and began excluding large numbers of persons on grounds other than improper behavior." The magazine pointed specifically to "Dewey's refusal to serve a large number of homosexuals and persons wearing non-conformist clothing." According to Janus's Barbara Horowitz, Dewey's claimed that the "gay kids" were "driving away business."[51]

On 25 April, after more than 150 people were denied service, two teenage boys and one teenage girl refused to leave the restaurant after they, too, were not served. *Drum* called it "the first sit-in of its kind in the history of the United States." Police arrested not only the three but also Polak, who had offered to help them obtain a lawyer. According to *Drum*, all four were found guilty of disorderly conduct. Janus then organized a five-day "protest demonstration," distributing 1,500 pieces of literature before 2 May, when the action "climaxed" with another sit-in staged by three people. Police were called again, but this time there were no arrests. The Janus newsletter proudly listed the action's successes, which included "an immediate cessation to all indiscriminate denials of service." Janus was also able to "assure the homosexual community that (a) we were concerned with the day-to-day problems and (b) we were prepared to intercede."[52]

Discussing the sit-in, Janus's newsletter report made clear its alienation from the politics of respectability:

> All too often, there is a tendency to be concerned with the rights of homosexuals as long as they somehow appear to be heterosexual, whatever that is. The masculine woman and the feminine man often are looked down upon by the official policy of homophile organizations, but the Janus Society is concerned with the worth of an individual and the manner in which she or he comports himself. What is offensive today we have seen become the style of tomorrow, and even if what is offensive today remains offensive tomorrow to some persons, there is no reason to penalize such non-conformist behavior unless there is direct anti-social behavior connected with it.[53]

Rejecting more than a decade of homophile coupling involving masculine men and feminine women, Janus momentarily put forward a new heterosocial pair, the masculine woman and feminine man.

Several weeks after the Dewey's affair, on 29 May Mattachine Washington demonstrated a second time at the White House. Shortly thereafter, Frank Kameny proposed to ECHO that it sponsor picketing demonstrations on 26 June at the Civil Service Commission building in Washington and on the Fourth of July at Independence Hall in Philadelphia. The proposal was adopted, 9–3, against the wishes of DOB New York. Reaction was swift. Within days, DOB withdrew from ECHO. A DOB statement explained that "the use of direct action techniques calls for a great deal of thought, preparation and training" and "unilateral picketing by the homosexual community alone would be detrimental to the homophile movement at this particular point."[54]

Activists debated the adoption of direct action tactics in sexed and gendered language. Stressing the importance of preparation, Martin argued in loaded terms, "You don't just send your gals off half cocked and jeopardize

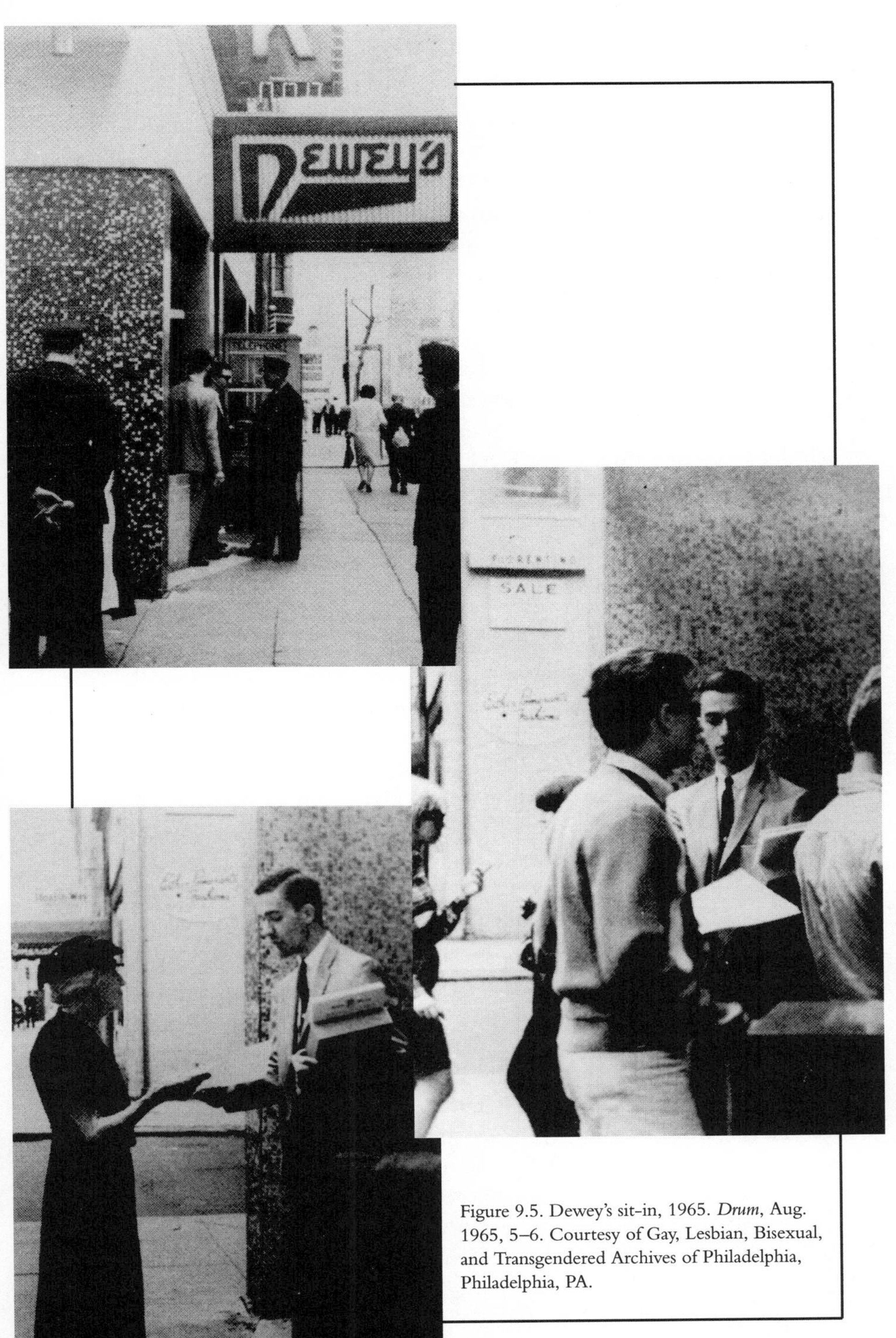

Figure 9.5. Dewey's sit-in, 1965. *Drum*, Aug. 1965, 5–6. Courtesy of Gay, Lesbian, Bisexual, and Transgendered Archives of Philadelphia, Philadelphia, PA.

their future because a few crack pots are impatient." In a letter to DOB that attacked accommodationist "Uncle Tomism," Kameny wrote the "Ladies" that he wondered what image they had of ECHO: "We are not a bunch of male ogres, waiting to pounce upon poor, defenseless, feminine DOB, and submerge it, totally, in a sea of men." He assured DOB that "the women's interests, to the very limited extent that they may possibly differ from the men's, certainly do not go unrepresented." Fleischmann wrote DOB's leaders, "To those ardent feminists in the movement who see no reason why we women should 'stick out our necks' so the men can cruise in freedom, let me remind you that women in government are subject to the same pressures as men and lose their jobs just as quickly." Having emphasized respectable clothing in criticizing *Drum*, Fleischmann now defended direct action by referring to the respectability of demonstrators' clothing. The first picket in Washington "was composed of conservatively dressed people carrying signs." "I mention all of this," she explained, "to allay the fears of those who visualize us as wild-eyed, dungareed radicals throwing ourselves beneath the wheels of the police vans which have come to cart us away from our sit-in in the Blue Room of the White House."[55]

At Independence Hall, homophile activists integrated patriotic, civil rights, and heterosocial discourse. Demonstrating on the nation's birthday in the "birthplace of the nation" strategically identified lesbians and gay men with the highest ideals of the United States. As *Eastern Mattachine Magazine* explained, "July 4th was felt to be the appropriate date for this demonstration, for, as we all know, the most basic rights of Americans are set forth in the Declaration of Independence, signed on that day nearly two hundred years ago." Kay Lahusen reported, "This dignified protest, which startled many a citizen into fresh thought about the meaning of Independence Day, might well have been applauded by our Founding Fathers, who were intent on making America safe for the differences." Among Philadelphia's startled citizens were readers of the *Tribune* and *Inquirer* and viewers of the CBS television affiliate, which covered the event.[56]

The demonstration also strategically identified lesbians and gay men with the highest ideals of dominant heterosocial values. According to Lahusen, picketers conformed to the rules for picketing, which stipulated "conservative and conventional" clothing: "Women wear dresses; men wear business suits, white shirts, and ties." Kameny counted 32 male and 7 female picketers, along with an additional man and 4 women distributing leaflets. Lahusen counted 34 men and 10 women.[57] Outside Independence Hall, lesbian and gay militants marched together on the ground of sex difference.

After the Fourth of July, Philadelphia lesbians, several of whom were members of both DOB New York and Mattachine Philadelphia, tried to

re 9.6. East Coast Homophile Organizations demonstration at Independence Hall, 4 July 1965. *Philadelphia Inquirer* collection.
 the permission of Urban Archives, Temple University, Philadelphia, PA.

force DOB's hand. Descending on a DOB New York meeting on 11 July, militants led by Fleischmann and McCann pushed through a resolution encouraging the national DOB to support ECHO's demonstrations. Their action tapped into long-standing fears about lesbian autonomy. Two DOB New York lesbians wrote to national headquarters about the "Mattachine oriented women" in their chapter. "With the tactics brought to bear at this meeting by Mattachine oriented sympathizers and supporters," they asked, "can DOB continue to remain an autonomously functioning organization? Is there not some sort of insidious strategy afoot by Mattachine members? . . . I can find no reason whatsoever that the N.Y. Chapter of DOB should become the dog following its master's heels in 'echoing' Mattachine policies."[58]

One DOB New York lesbian wrote of her objection to a suggestion made by "Ernestine Eckstein," an African American Mattachine New York and DOB New York member, to make DOB New York "a boy-girl organization." "I re-joined DOB because it is a woman's organization," she explained. Expressing fears that DOB might take the lead of "Dr. Kameny and his willing female exhibitionist disciples," she declared, "I personally have long been averse to male 'authorities': male authors, male researchers, male psychiatrists as spokesmen and leaders for a lesbian or woman's movement or organization. I am and will always remain an 'unreconstructed feminist.' " Raising concerns about "Frank Kameny and the girls from Philly," another DOB New York leader made clear where these "disciples" lived.[59] In these letters, lesbian militancy was sexualized as exhibitionism, lesbian and gay cooperation was equated with male domination, and lesbian and gay alliances were heterosexualized.

Unlike Mattachine, DOB remained nationally centralized and in the end the East Coast militants lost out. By 1966, McCann was no longer a national DOB officer. Gittings, who supported the militant position and published articles in favor of picketing in the *Ladder*, was removed as editor by DOB's board in 1966.[60] Caught between a national lesbian organization that they regarded as insufficiently militant and a local gay organization that was dominated by Polak, Gittings and Lahusen continued their activities unaffiliated with any particular group. Until ECHO disbanded in 1966, Fleischmann and McCann worked through the locally inactive Mattachine Philadelphia. In a striking footnote to her discussion of this period, Fleischmann recalls that when she and McCann broke up around this time, she needed a job and took one in Polak's personnel agency.[61]

"Cocks" and "Cunts"

How did Polak, Janus, and *Drum* respond to these developments? Although isolated within the homophile movement, Polak was the leader of one of the most active gay groups in the country, published the most widely read homophile publication, and owned a successful pornography business, Trojan Book Service. Trojan benefited from the services of Polak's new lover, physique model and photographer James Mitchell, who appeared on the cover of *Drum* in 1966.[62] While *Drum* and Trojan defied the politics of respectability, Polak used his profits to support activities that were more consistent with his commitment to "operate beyond reproach." Janus lectures regularly attracted 100–400 people to Center City auditoriums at the New Century Club, the County Medical Society, the Penn Center Inn, and the Sheraton, Adelphia, and Sylvania Hotels. Speakers included Frank Kameny, Donald Webster Cory, and Wardell Pomeroy in 1964; Samuel Hadden, Kurt Konietzko, Albert Ellis, and Hymen Schwartz in 1965; and Isadore Rubin and Kameny in 1966. Polak also created an advisory board that included Gilbert Cantor, Spencer Coxe, Gaeton Fonzi, and Konietzko.[63]

Between 1964 and 1967, Janus utilized strategies of respectability in breakthrough stories and ads in the *Tribune*, *Inquirer*, *Bulletin*, *Greater Philadelphia Magazine*, *Legal Intelligencer*, *Bucks County Life*, *Civil Liberties Record*, *Temple University News*, *Sexology*, and *Camden Courier-Post*. While antigay media bias continued, progay, antigay, and gay-neutral voices now competed for attention.[64] Janus members also appeared on radio shows and spoke at Penn State, Temple, Beaver College, the Philadelphia Ethical Society, Shiloh Apostolic Temple, the Optimists' Club of Mayfair, Argufiers (a biracial group), and the National Presbyterian Council's Office of Church and Society.[65]

Polak worked through conventional legal channels as well. In 1964, in consultation with the ACLU, he began lobbying state officials for the revocation of sodomy and sodomy solicitation laws and the reform and adoption of the Model Penal Code. Janus's position was that "private sexual acts of consenting adults are matters of individual preference and are not rightfully the concern of the law."[66] In 1965, by threatening legal action, Janus forced the Penn Center Inn to capitulate after it tried to cancel a Janus lecture scheduled to take place there. Janus was less successful when the Sheraton declared after another lecture that it would not allow Janus events to be held there in the future.[67] Janus's advisory brochure, "You're Under Arrest," was reprinted in *Drum* and distributed in bars and men's bathrooms.[68] Polak regularly provided legal aid to gay men; interceded with the police; and reported on bar and club raids, Liquor Control Board actions, and legal and extralegal harassment, arrests, and convictions of gay men.

His support extended beyond Philadelphia to Harrisburg, Reading, and Chester in Pennsylvania; Cape May and New Brunswick in New Jersey; and Rehoboth Beach in Delaware. He also shared news about a nationwide antigay blackmailing ring that included two Philadelphia bail bondsmen. After allegedly extorting millions of dollars from more than a thousand gay men, including a member of the U.S. Congress, the ring was broken in 1966, in part on the testimony of a Philadelphia businessman.[69]

Polak also commented publicly on political candidates. In 1964, he flirted with the idea of endorsing Republican Barry Goldwater for U.S. president. "Extremism in defense of liberty is no vice," Goldwater had declared. Polak responded with a *Drum* editorial, "Liberty in the Defense of Vice is No Extreme." What attracted Polak was Goldwater's libertarianism. "As the Federal establishment supplies more of the goods and services required for daily living," Polak declared, "each of us pays the price in terms of erosion of our private liberties. So Goldwater's cry for limited government is not only appealing, but seems a necessity for the maintenance of the United States as a democratic republic." Describing himself as "one who would prefer to vote for Goldwater" because of this, Polak nevertheless pointed to the ways that Goldwater's opposition to pornography and his defense of "good old morality" contradicted his stands in favor of "freedom." He thus hoped that Goldwater would be defeated, but predicted that freedom would erode "regardless of the outcome." Although the editorial came with a caveat that its opinions did not "necessarily represent those of the Janus Society, *Drum* magazine, or their Boards," Polak's statement suggests some of the ways that civil libertarianism was an important part of the homophile vision.[70]

Meanwhile, Philadelphia district attorney James Crumlish, a Democrat, was running for reelection. In November 1965, in a report on gay bar raids, *Drum* commented, "Observers note the coming of a District Attorney election." Democrat Arlen Specter, who was serving as a Pennsylvania special assistant attorney general, had bolted his party and was running as a Republican against Crumlish. Charged with investigating Philadelphia's magistrate courts, Specter documented "widespread corruption" during the campaign. Among his findings were cases of men who were sexually entrapped by male police and then solicited by lawyers and bondsmen to make payoffs in exchange for having morals charges dropped. One of the bondsmen arrested as a result of Specter's investigation was Joseph Nardello, who was later indicted for his role in the nationwide antigay blackmailing ring. Successfully labeling Crumlish weak on crime, Specter won election, the first major victory for city Republicans since 1953.[71]

Embracing nonpartisan politics as well, Polak could be as patriotic as the Fourth of July demonstrators. In 1964, Janus leaders met with Public Health

Department officials and suggested that "a simple way of cutting down one area of [draft] rejection was to remove 'Homosexual Tendencies' from the list of disqualifications." The same year, Polak released a report derived from sexological data and Selective Service statistics for Philadelphia. Reasoning that 97.5% of all male "homosexuals" entering the armed services did not indicate "homosexual tendencies" on their applications, Polak argued that gay men were serving their country effectively.[72] Polak also took an active role in nationally coordinated demonstrations against the "exclusion of homosexuals" from the military. Although he expressed last-minute reservations because of antiwar demonstrations and declared that Janus was "neutral" on the Vietnam War, on Armed Forces Day in 1966 Janus distributed five to ten thousand leaflets at the Philadelphia Navy Yard.[73] When the Fourth of July picket at Independence Hall became the "Annual Reminder" in 1966, Polak lent his support. Barbara Gittings recalls that Polak paid for professionally produced picket signs, a contribution valued by the 50 marchers.[74] As in other demonstrations of homophile patriotism, the FBI conducted surveillance of the Armed Forces Day and Fourth of July actions.[75]

Juggling antirespectable and respectable projects, harassed by legal authorities, and at odds with much of the homophile movement, Polak considered reorganizing Janus. In mid-1965, the Janus newsletter announced that Polak would resign as president and become executive director. Plans were soon announced to divide Janus into the Janus Trust, Drum Publishing Company, and the Homosexual Law Reform Society (HLRS).[76]

Some had hopes that Barbara Horowitz, Janus newsletter editor, membership chair, and lecture series moderator, would emerge as the new leader. Horowitz had her doubts about Polak. One friend wrote to her, "you yourself have wailed in letter after letter about Clark not allowing you to be privy to membership lists for fear that you would (possibly) call an election." Unlike Joan Fleischmann and Marge McCann, however, Horowitz remained a defender of Janus and Polak. Although she was ambivalent about *Drum*, she believed that the magazine served to "heighten interest in Janus."[77] She speculated that Fleischmann and McCann disliked Polak because of his "essentially masculine orientation," noting, however, that she was "certainly a woman" and got along "wonderfully well" with him. And she insisted that Janus did more than produce *Drum*, that Janus did benefit from *Drum*'s proceeds, and that *Drum* "intended to be a male-oriented magazine, sells widely as such, and would lose enormous business if it diluted itself."[78]

Many activists tried to use Horowitz to turn Polak in more respectable directions. Mattachine New York's Dick Leitsch wrote, "You are quite an attractive and sensible spokesman for the Society. Perhaps a woman's touch in *Drum* would make it less faggot orientated and more community minded."

Figure 9.7. Barbara Gittings at the Annual Reminder, 1966. Photograph by Kay Tobin Lahusen. With the permission of Kay Tobin Lahusen.

Horowitz, however, wrote another activist that she resented getting "used as middle-man in anybody's squeeze-play." She explained that "one reason why Kameny, Leitsch et al. 'love' me is that I make a point of being unobtrusive, inoffensively passive, all over innocuous."[79] At the same time, she defended herself against accusations that she was "wishy-washy" and "a 'puppet' of Clark's." In one letter, she denied that she was "spineless protoplasm."[80]

Sometime in mid-1965, Janus's executive board met and Horowitz summarized the outcome:

> Clark has resigned as president of Janus, pending the immediate election of new officers. Among peripheral reasons given, the major hope is to get the organization successfully separated from *Drum*. He will still of course maintain control of *Drum*, leaving Janus largely to anyone who is strong enough and able enough to fill the void. I can assure you that this is not merely a nominal, de facto resignation; two of us are already groping with the reins.[81]

Leitsch asked Horowitz if she would run for the presidency. "We aren't going to interest anybody but gay boys as long as we cater to them, and as long as we present only male homosexuals to the public," he explained. "This is why I was so glad to see that you are a nonstereotype." Another male activist was as hopeful as Leitsch: "I was so happy to hear the news from Janus and really think that Barbara is the one that can pull Janus up to a real measure of respectability once *Drum* is separated."[82]

Horowitz was aware of the role her feminine appearance could play in appealing to straight audiences. In one report on a speaking engagement, she wrote of how she had often wondered about how to convince the "outside world" that she was "not" homosexual. But in speaking with this group, the problem was convincing them that she "was": "Obviously fully prepared for a high-heeled, nail-polished euphemistic male and a leather-jacketed, crew-cut nominal female to appear, they were—surprisingly?—distressed and a bit frightened that the Janus representative could not be told at a glance, without specific introduction, from the new, unintroduced members of the discussion group."[83]

For reasons that are unclear, Janus remained under Polak's control, but he increasingly worked through HLRS. By 1965, Polak had decided that the movement was wrong to think that reform would be achieved through legislation rather than court decisions. The HLRS became his respectable vehicle for this new strategy. Work on HLRS's most important cases (examined in the next chapter), which reached the New Jersey and the U.S. Supreme Courts in 1967, began in 1966.[84] If some activists believed in respectability as an expression of their identities and aspirations, Polak used respectability selectively, tailoring his messages for specific audiences.

Polak also responded with direct attacks on the homophile movement. And his criticisms increased after respectable activists objected to the inexpensive arrangements he made for a national homophile conference to be held at a Kansas City physique photography studio owned by Troy Saxon, a.k.a. Stu "Pinky" Rosenbloom. In late 1965, Polak used *Drum* to indict the "comic-opera gulf between the unrealistic homophile movement and the realities of homosexual life," the "leadership's lack of information and sophistication in the areas of sex," and the "almost anti-homosexual disdain permeating the various groups."[85]

While various homophile activists had adapted the rhetoric of the civil rights movement in support of their cause, Polak now turned to the language of Black Power. Quoting Philadelphia lawyer Gil Cantor, Polak wrote, "The 'square' believes in organization, negotiation, in the manners and morals and techniques of the dominant culture, which he addresses in its own language. And then we discover in Watts, California, that the hip Negro has nothing to do with the square Negro and his organizations and that those organizations do not speak for him." Criticizing homophile groups for distancing themselves from gay bar culture, Polak declared that "the present homophile movement neither addresses itself to nor speaks for the hip homosexual." With the exception of the new Society for Individual Rights in San Francisco, he concluded, "the 'square' homosexuals of the homophile movement appear to have sold themselves out and stranded the 'hip' to make his happy way."[86]

In August 1966, Polak struck out again at a national conference. This time, he used a campy adaptation of the language used by Black Power advocates to attack "Uncle Toms": "Antihomosexuality is rampant within the organizations and the concern is for the 'good' homosexuals—which I call Aunt Maryism." "Your publications," Polak continued, "besides being often illiterate and poorly edited, are also reeking with antihomosexuality, groveling, obsequiousness and seem almost designed to maintain the homosexual's position of inferiority."[87]

But if Polak was increasingly alienated from the homophile movement, he maintained a large following among *Drum* readers and emphatically articulated broad visions of sexual liberation. In a letter to the *New Republic* and *Time*, for example, Polak assailed the "antisexualism" of laws on "abortion, birth control, obscenity, prostitution, adultery, fornication, and cohabitation." And he wrote in *Drum*, "Sex cannot be 'dirty' because it cannot be 'pure.' It cannot 'enoble' one any more than it can 'debase.' It is not, under some circumstances, 'good' and under others, 'bad.' You in no way change it by calling a 'cock' a 'penis,' or a 'vagina' a 'cunt.' "[88]

Be that as it may, Polak talked and wrote more enthusiastically about cocks than cunts. It is not true that Polak failed to consider lesbians in his political work. But the alliances he imagined between lesbians and gay men were as based in sex differences as were those imagined by respectable militants. In his review of physique magazines, for example, Polak wrote that "interest in visual sexual stimulation is a peculiarly masculine trait as women almost never achieve the same kind of arousal from photographs or artistic representations." "Lesbians," he said, " . . . are no more concerned with the *Playboy* fold out than straight women are with *TM* [*Tomorrow's Man*]." In a 1966 interview, Polak again turned to sex differences:

> It is not that homosexuals, as homosexuals, do not form long term relationships, but that male homosexuals as males do not form them. Female homosexuals, as females, do tend to form more lasting unions than male homosexuals. But that's females for you. If there weren't females in the heterosexual relationship, you wouldn't have the incidence of relationship longevity there either. Males and females, regardless of their sexual orientations, are males and females first. When a male is walking down the street—with either his girlfriend or his boyfriend—he's eyeing everyone who appeals to him. In the heterosexual and lesbian situations, the female's non-concern with a variety of sexual partners acts as a stabilizing influence.

Fleischmann had argued in a 1964 "Woman's Way" column that one of the biggest differences between lesbians and gay men was their "attitudes toward establishing and maintaining a permanent relationship." Lesbians, she noted, "emphasize physical appearance less" and are "less urgent in the immediate consummation." Explicitly or implicitly, both Polak and Fleischmann linked gay men with straight men and lesbians with straight women, establishing strong bases for same-sex bonds.[89]

But just as Fleischmann had hoped that the fact that women's and men's ways were different would not preclude alliances between lesbians and gay men, so too Polak imagined that sex differences need not divide lesbians and gay men. In *Drum* he argued, "The homosexual value system (which for males is largely male and for lesbians is largely female) differs from that of the straight world that uses a compromise between male and female." He later elaborated: "The male homosexual attitude toward promiscuity is quite properly different from the heterosexual attitude because heterosexuality includes women." Because women are less concerned with sex, Polak argued, a "balance" is required in heterosexuality "in which males tone down their sexual interest and females increase their sexual interest." Homosexual men, in contrast, were free to have more sexual partners while homosexual women "tend to be far less promiscuous."[90] For Polak, what lesbians and gay men had in common was that both were more true to their "real" sexes than straights could ever be.

Had Polak built Janus around this idea, paying as much attention to lesbians as he did to gay men, Philadelphia might have produced separate and equal paths for lesbian and gay activism. But Polak's vision functioned more as an excuse to ignore lesbians than as a model for equality and cooperation. If homophile strategies of militant respectability were limited because they failed to challenge conventional links between sex and gender, homophile strategies of sexual liberation were limited because they failed to challenge conventional links between sex and sexuality.

The end of 1966 brought to a conclusion several years of conflicts in the national homophile movement. Lesbian and gay activists had formed a contingent alliance, one that depended on mutual interest and imagined community, not equality. Struggling against oppression from outsiders, lesbians and gay men negotiated the internal boundaries of their convergent and divergent identities and communities. Strategies of militant respectability and sexual liberationism developed in dynamic interaction with everyday forms of resistance, with one another, and with the forces arrayed against lesbians and gay men. With rare exceptions, these strategies worked against the notion that gay men were feminine and lesbians were masculine. Juxtaposing masculine gay men and feminine lesbians, respectable militants and sexual liberationists built upon and promoted particular types of pairings, bonds, and alliances between women and men. Challenging the hegemony of heterosexuality, they reinforced the hegemony of sex.

10

"The Masculine-Feminine Mystique," 1967–1969

In November 1967, several months after a Philadelphia chapter of DOB was established, "The Masculine-Feminine Mystique," an editorial by A. B., appeared in the new group's newsletter. "Are we so concerned with being lesbians," Ada Bello asked, "that we tend to forget the fact that we are also women, and, as such, members of a quite numerous 'minority group?' "[1] Although women did not constitute a numerical minority in the United States, Bello's description established rhetorical links with the racial minorities whose movements occupied center stage in U.S. politics in the 1960s. Claiming status as a minority group at this juncture was a powerful means of asserting that sex constituted a meaningful category of identity and that women might engage in political activity to achieve equality.

Like Betty Friedan's *The Feminine Mystique* (1963), Bello's editorial criticized ideas that placed women at a disadvantage in the workplace.[2] Unlike Friedan's book, Bello's message was directed toward lesbians, and its language suggested that lesbians had failed to identify their interests with those of other women. The editorial's title suggested one reason for this. In the context of a long history of cultural links between lesbianism and masculinity, "The Masculine-Feminine Mystique" encouraged lesbians to embrace female identities.

In many ways, DOB Philadelphia's nascent liberal feminism was consistent with developments that transformed the national DOB in this period. In the early 1960s, *The Feminine Mystique*, along with the Presidential Commission on the Status of Women, had helped galvanize a new women's movement. After feminists secured the prohibition of sex discrimination in Title VII of the 1964 Civil Rights Act, Friedan helped found the National Organization for Women (NOW) in 1966. John D'Emilio has highlighted the influence of the women's movement on lesbian activists in this era. While the homophile movement in the past had most often identified its struggles with those of African Americans, the national DOB now turned to feminism.[3]

In 1968, Philadelphia lesbian activists again struck out in directions different from the ones charted by national DOB leaders. This was the year in which Martin Luther King, Jr., was assassinated, urban riots erupted, students occupied buildings, protesters battled police at the Democratic convention in Chicago, and women's liberationists disrupted the Miss America pageant in

Atlantic City. D'Emilio argues that the national DOB underwent an "abrupt" transformation around this time. DOB president Rita Laporte embraced a "radical feminist perspective," the *Ladder* became a "lesbian-feminist" vehicle, and DOB rejected what Laporte called a "group 'marriage' " to the male homophile movement.[4] In Philadelphia, however, a March 1968 raid on Rusty's bar helped persuade the DOB chapter to join with gay men to form the Homophile Action League (HAL).

Bello's editorial is noteworthy, then, not only because it was consistent with national DOB developments but also because it offered an endorsement of the women's movement otherwise lacking in DOB's and HAL's work in Philadelphia in 1967 and 1968. Moreover, insofar as the DOB chapter lasted only a short time before reconfiguring as HAL, Bello's editorial is the exception that proves the rule that Philadelphia's lesbian activists were committed to working with gay men. Significantly, the lack of feminist rhetoric and the decision to form a mixed-sex group did not signal willingness to yield leadership to men. As had been the case with Mattachine Philadelphia and the early Janus, HAL was a lesbian-led organization with mixed-sex membership.

While HAL emerged as Philadelphia's preeminent homophile group, Clark Polak, *Drum*, and Janus faced political repression. Utilizing both respectable and disrespectable strategies, Polak's various projects supported and endangered one another. By the late 1960s, while heterosocial militancy was radicalized by HAL, sexual liberationism was crushed by the state.

DOB and "The Invisible Sorority"

DOB Philadelphia formed following a May 1967 organizing meeting held by national DOB president Shirley Willer at the Benjamin Franklin Hotel in Center City. According to Ada Bello, an "older" woman named Lindy, the owner of a downtown printing business, was the principal figure behind the chapter's creation. Lindy's lover had died, Bello remembers, and Lindy conceived of DOB as "a social group" that might help her cope with the loss. As was the case with Barbara Gittings and Clark Polak, Lindy may have been willing to take initiative because she was less vulnerable to job loss than many other lesbians and gay men. According to the group's first newsletter, 17 women had joined the chapter and "Edna W." had been elected president. Over the next few months, 13–17 women attended DOB events. Bello and Carole Friedman recall that all were Euro-American; Friedman thinks that they were primarily middle-class.[5]

As was the case with earlier lesbian leaders in Philadelphia, Bello and Friedman's homophile politics were shaped by their prior participation in mixed-sex lesbian and gay communities. Unlike their earlier counterparts, Bello and Friedman were politically active before they joined the homophile movement. And Bello was the local movement's first Latina leader. Born in Cuba in 1933 and raised in a Catholic, middle-class family, Bello remembers having "discreet" relationships with women when she was a student activist at the University of Havana. After transferring to Louisiana State in 1958, she began going to New Orleans bars, where she socialized with both lesbians and gay men. Within this community, Bello was a "sissy butch," which means that she "didn't know anything about baseball or football" and "couldn't fix a car." Discussing the gay men who she knew in this milieu, Bello says that although some were "antifemale" and used "female names or pronouns" when they "wanted to ridicule something," lesbians and gay men generally "got along," partly because "women were more willing to take the way men were."[6]

After a short stay in Mississippi, Bello followed her friend Lourdes Alvarez to Germantown in 1962 and soon began going to Rusty's, Dewey's, the U.S.&A.A., house parties, and the Atlantic City "gay beach." Fearing that she might "sound like the old gay guys sounded about women," Bello recalls that gay men "took the whole apartment to the beach," bringing radios, hair dryers, and other household items. In 1967, Bello and Alvarez attended the local DOB's first meeting. Because she was applying for U.S. citizenship, Bello joined the chapter under the name "Marie Smith." Referring to the fears that many women felt about using their real names, Bello jokes that the chapter had quite a few members named "Smith."[7]

Bello edited DOB's newsletter with her lover, Carole Friedman. Born in 1945 to a middle-class Jewish family in North Philly, Friedman recalls that when she was 16 she "fell in love" and embarked on a two-year relationship with a fellow student at Girls' High. In 1963, Friedman left Philadelphia to pursue piano studies at Oberlin College. Although now certain that she must have been "surrounded" by gay men and lesbians in Oberlin's conservatory, Friedman says that at the time she felt "isolated" and "anguished" by the sense that there was "something terribly wrong" with her. After returning to Philadelphia the next year, she began working in a North Philly settlement house and participating in the civil rights movement. Soon she fell in love again, moved with her partner to Center City, and began going to Rusty's, Dewey's, house parties, and after-hours clubs, where she was more the butch and her lover was more the femme.[8]

In 1967, Friedman went to her first DOB meeting, which was held in a downtown office building:

> I can remember feeling frightened, nauseated, light-headed, as an elevator went up. . . . And I just remember my terror because this was really different from going to the bar. I mean the first times I went to the bar I was scared, too. But this was really different because it was

> daylight, because I was saying something about myself. I was going to engage the world in some way, not just stay within the ghetto of a social life as a lesbian. . . . I just remember that terror. And then feeling more and more confident as I went to future meetings.

Friedman thinks that going to the DOB meeting was more "scary" than later marching in lesbian and gay demonstrations because this involved how she felt "inside." Joining the homophile movement, she says, represented an "essential step" that allowed her to "integrate the knowledge" that she was a lesbian with "everything else" that she "knew" about herself. She remembers this as her "first real contact with the idea that homosexuals constituted a minority movement and could be viewed as having not a psychological problem but a civil rights problem." "That changed everything for me," she recalls, "made everything possible." Somewhere around this time, Friedman broke up with her lover, moved to Germantown, and became involved with Bello. Friedman observes, "For me, the personal, the political, also having a quasi-public forum for working out my own thoughts about all this, that all came together."[9]

Friedman's language works with a series of opposing terms with which she has come to understand a life transition. Before she became involved with DOB, her lesbianism was circumscribed within the "social life" of

Figure 10.1. Carole Friedman and Ada Bello on Fire Island, 1969. With the permission of Ada Bello.

a "ghetto" and she viewed homosexuality as a "psychological problem." In contrast, the lesbianism of DOB was proclaimed in the "daylight" of a "quasi-public forum" and was a "political" issue that concerned "rights." Earlier her "personal" world of "inside" feelings had been divided from her "political" world of "civil rights" activism. DOB integrated the "personal" and "political."

Several months after DOB Philadelphia was established, *Philadelphia Magazine* featured Nancy Love's "The Invisible Sorority," which brought unprecedented attention to the local lesbian community. Published five years after "The Furtive Fraternity," Love's article focused on lesbians, but repeatedly described them with reference to gay men. Breaking with the media's tradition of paying more attention to male same-sex sexualities, the "Sorority" maintained the tradition of exploring female sexualities in relation to male counterparts.

Like other journalistic voyages into urban underworlds, Love's piece began with a visit to an otherwise "invisible" site:

> A small sign over the door on Quince Street, a little alley next to the Forrest Theatre, says "Variety Room." It's very quiet as you go up the old wooden steps to the second floor and down the long corridor. You don't hear the juke box until you're actually in the room. You pay the $2 minimum to a woman in a white button-down shirt and slacks who looks a little like a gym teacher you once had, and she gives you a strip of tickets for drinks. It's a smallish wood-paneled room with a bar at one side and lots of tables clustered around a dance floor. At first, the relaxed atmosphere and informal dress and young girls make you think of a girls college hangout in a small town.

But Love quickly disrupted this impression, describing dancing, talking, and laughing lesbians: a "blond nurse in a blue work shirt and slacks"; "art students in turtleneck jerseys"; a "striking girl with long hair" who was a "model"; and "two off-duty waitresses in identical black uniforms, overburdened with makeup and tortuously teased hair." On the walls, "a blow-up of a sultry, wet-to-the-skin Sophia Loren," "a seductive Jane Fonda," and "paintings of cowgirls." Completing her description, Love wrote, "And now the dance floor is packed. Female bodies pressed together. The guard is down at the Variety Room. At least for tonight, in this small club on the second floor of a tiny alley in Philadelphia, no one is trying to hide."[10]

Love's article offered a series of biographical sketches, references to the geography of lesbian life, and perspectives from psychological, legal, and religious authorities. Lesbians, she emphasized, were "inconspicuous" and "virtually invisible when they want to be." "Surely no other minority group lives with quite this compulsion for secrecy," she wrote. "At least the family of the Negro or Jew knows he's a Negro or a Jew." Making a point of exposing the invisible, Love nevertheless depicted an exclusively Euro-American "sorority." Other types of lesbians remained hidden from view.[11]

Love did describe a few butch lesbians, but noted that the lesbian is rarely "extremely masculine" and "usually wears a mask of makeup and respectability." Most of the article focused on "feminine" lesbians: Italian American Maria, a 19-year-old whose boyfriend and parents did not know the extent of her lesbian relationships; Greek American Helena, who kept a "nice home" for her butch girlfriend; 19-year-old Renee, who dated men "to keep up a healthy image"; 50-year-old Anita (Jody Shotwell), who had been married for 25 years while remaining "an active homosexual"; middle-aged Dora, a divorcee with a son; and 22-year-old Melanie, who described herself as "borderline." The majority of women discussed had had, were having, or planned to have relationships with men. Declaring that "both the homosexual and heterosexual communities of Philadelphia have no difficulty naming married lesbians they know," Love gave as an example "the young crowd in the Northeast who go off to the seashore sans husbands." While Gaeton Fonzi had discussed bisexual men only briefly, Love claimed that "the total homosexual, the one who has never had a relationship with a man and probably never will, is a much rarer bird than one of the varieties of bisexual." One such "bird" was Susie, a "committed" lesbian who was athletic and boyish and who told Love that she had passed as male "because men get paid more than women." "They just thought I was a gay boy," she joked.[12]

Love made lesbianism visible not only by exposing "invisible" femmes and discussing a few butches but also by referring to lesbian geographies in homes and workplaces, single-sex schools, and "parks, clubs and bars." Bars and clubs in Philadelphia, Love asserted, were "relatively free from harassment" compared to those in New York. But risks remained, as was evident for teenagers who had been meeting in shower rooms at an "all-girls high school" but were suspended when caught.[13]

In the process of making lesbian culture visible, Love linked it repeatedly with gay culture. Trying to explain why lesbians were offended by the term "dyke," Love used a gay comparison: "It's kind of like calling a male homosexual a 'fairy' or a 'pansy.' " Discussing invisibility, Love wrote that "like her male counterpart, the female homosexual is usually alienated from her church, estranged from her family" and anxious about losing job, marriage, and children. But lesbians, she argued, were "better at concealment," in part because of society's "different set of standards" for men and women. For examples, Love asserted that "no one thinks anything is wrong with a girl wearing slacks and short hair" or with two women who "show affection in public" or live together. In addition to considering "the camouflage of this double standard," Love wrote that "lesbians generally protect themselves better." Invisibility, she suggested, was a successful lesbian strategy.[14]

Discussing lesbians and the law, Love also made comparisons with gay men. According to the acting head of the Morals Squad, " 'They have their own ways of ferreting each other out.' You don't find them cruising the street corners and bars, engaging in open relationships in rest rooms or behind bushes in parks the way men have been known to do." As a result, "in Philadelphia, it's pretty hard to find any cases on the books against lesbians." Elsewhere in the article, however, Love discussed a Philadelphia County Court case involving custody of five children. Claiming that the mother's lesbian relationship was "having a bad effect on the children," a grandmother had sued for custody. After the case was decided in favor of the mother, the Superior Court ordered a new trial. Although this did not make Love question her notion that lesbians were "rarely in trouble with the law," it suggested that lesbians encountered legal trouble in their private and domestic roles whereas gay men encountered legal trouble in their public and sexual roles.[15]

Love also discussed the incidence and character of female same-sex sexualities comparatively. Referring to Alfred Kinsey's statistics, she wrote that rates of female same-sex contacts were "considerably lower" than rates for men but still provided "ample evidence that lesbians are here among us in some force, especially in an urban center like Philadelphia." Love also invoked Kinsey's claim that lesbians "succeed" more often than gay men in establishing "long-term relationships." Lesbians thus might measure up in relation to gay men but comparative measurements remained central to the portrayal of lesbians.[16]

Fonzi's depiction of the gay world was nearly devoid of lesbians, except in his discussion of Janus. While Love's article focused on lesbians, much of the lesbian world she described was shared with gay men. At one point, she noted that many lesbians are "more comfortable around other gay people—male and female" than around straights. Although she discussed lesbianism in single-sex schools, bars, and residences, she also observed that "lesbians often go to the same gay bars where male homosexuals congregate," including two bars in North Philly, the Attic, and the Hideaway. The only bar described as "exclusively female" was the Variety Room, but even here Love mentioned a male bartender and gay patrons. Beyond the bars, Love described "cliques of gay girls and gay boys in every school" and friendship networks that included lesbians and gay men.

As was the case with "The Furtive Fraternity," Love's article provided its most in-depth coverage of same-sex sexualities in the "other" sex when discussing the homophile movement. The implicit suggestion was that in politics lesbians and gay men came together. Clark Polak, identified as the publisher of *Drum* and founder of the Council on Religion and the Homosexual of the Greater Delaware Valley, was quoted as stating that "modern psychiatry is the greatest enemy." Although her name was not revealed, Barbara Gittings was also interviewed. Described as "one of the most outspoken of the local women leaders in the homosexual community," Gittings attacked the view that "homosexuality is a sickness."[17] Whereas the "Fraternity" suggested that gay activists moved from single-sex social worlds to mixed-sex political ones, the "Sorority" implied that lesbians moved from mixed-sex social worlds to mixed-sex political ones.

Moreover, while Fonzi portrayed activists in very positive terms, Love did not. Criticizing lesbians who gave only "lip-service to the importance of admitting their predisposition," Love used as an example the woman (Gittings) who "refused to give permission to have her name used." Then she introduced DOB:

> Unfortunately, homophile organizations don't seem to get anywhere in Philadelphia. The Janus Society, for male and female homosexuals, is still in existence, but most of the women members left it in a row about the kind of male cheesecake art work that was appearing in the Society's magazine. They started their own group, a chapter of the national Mattachine Society, but that petered out very quickly. Now, a few local women have started a chapter of the Daughters of Bilitis to, among other things, provide a homosexual meeting place outside of bars. This they believe would elevate their image, and it probably would, if they could attract more than the handful of members.

Love thus depicted homophile politics as a mixed-sex world, but described relationships between lesbian and gay activists as conflicted. This was in stark contrast to the close ties she presented between nonactivist lesbians and gay men. So while Fonzi suggested that politics was an unusual sphere insofar as lesbian and gay activists got along, Love suggested that politics was an unusual sphere insofar as they did not. She also portrayed a gap between the "packed" Variety Room and the "handful" of DOB members. Activists in Love's "Sorority" were at odds with their brothers and unpopular with their sisters.[18]

Readers had a variety of reactions. Frank Bemus of a group called U.S. Divorce Reform wrote a letter to *Philadelphia Magazine* that offered "no objection to the straight lezzies" but denounced "part-time lesbians who take excursions into heterosexuality and respectability through marriage." He pointed to one of his group's members whose "lesbian wife dragged him into that fascist hole known as Philadelphia County Court when he attempted to wear the pants." "Naturally," Bemus explained, "the court backed lezzy up," and the woman was awarded custody of their children.[19]

Drum responded with a different kind of hostility:

> Part of the press ritual is that, from time to time, each newspaper and magazine gets daring and explores the invisible, dark, furtive, nether, guilt-ridden, persecuted, blackmailed, lonely, frustrated, transvestistic, bizarre, depraved, despised, feared, fearing, second-rate, substitutive, suicidal, alcoholic, thrill-seeking, sick, uncontrolled, sinful, invisible, bitchy and undesirable-but-here-to-stay-so-we-might-as-well-face-up-to-the-disagreeable-facts of the so-called homosexual underground.

Other elements in the "ritual" were "an aren't-we-courageous stance"; "descriptions of fem men and butch women followed immediately by disclaimers that . . . the overwhelming majority are not like this"; and "smugness about the superiority of heterosexuality." Rushing to the defense of the unnamed lesbian leader (Gittings), *Drum* explained that "she doubted the accuracy with which her comments would be quoted."[20]

In the DOB newsletter, Carole Friedman praised the "fine" article for its "factual, descriptive quality" but criticized it for implying that "the organization's aims are primarily of a social nature." In a letter to *Philadelphia Magazine*, DOB commended Love for helping to "keep before the public eye the image of those of us who must make ourselves invisible." But DOB also wrote that its aims were not "primarily social" and that it was working toward "integrating the lesbian with her society, through research, action, and educational programs." While the mixed-sex Janus had little trouble convincing Fonzi that it was a political group, the all-female DOB had less success with Love. Along similar lines, Bello recalls that the *Bulletin* and *Inquirer* refused to accept ads from DOB because "they claimed that they were personals." DOB struggled to register its concerns as political.[21]

Helping lesbians meet one another in fact was an important function served by DOB. Bello remembers that many members wanted the chapter to be a "social group." Friedman recalls, "We would always joke that women would come to the group when they were looking to find a lover, and become politically or socially involved with the group for a period of time. And then couples would disappear. And when they would break up, they would come back." As far as Bello and Friedman were concerned, however, social and political functions were not mutually exclusive.[22]

Nor did local DOB leaders conceive of bar life and homophile activism as mutually exclusive. Some scholars have argued that DOB was composed of middle-class women who were uncomfortable with the working-class world of bars. However, Gittings and McCann frequented bars before they became national DOB officers and McCann, Bello, and Friedman were regular bar patrons through the 1960s. Bello recalls that bars were not good places to "make friends" and that "it was nice to be in an organization that was all women and gave you the opportunity of meeting other people." Still, she thinks that many DOB members went to bars: "I don't think that there was anybody there who was there because they couldn't go to the bars. . . . People who were deadly scared of being identified as a lesbian weren't going to go and join something called the Daughters of Bilitis." Friedman notes that while the bars contained both middle- and working-class women, DOB was made up of middle-class "bar lesbians."[23]

While DOB members were pleased with some aspects of the new media focus on lesbians, it proved to be just a phase the media was going through. In no time at all, the media returned to its primary focus on gay men. In November 1967, Bello wrote about recent gay-related headlines concerning Penn student John Green, whose body had been found in the Delaware River. Tobacco store owner Stephen Weinstein soon confessed. With a mayoral campaign underway, Democratic incumbent James Tate, Republican challenger district attorney Arlen Specter, and the university traded accusations about ignoring earlier evidence of wrongdoing by Weinstein. "Unfortunately," Bello declared, "every time the public is confronted with the issue it is in relation to some monstrous crime."[24]

Another series of stories on male same-sex sexualities began appearing in the summer of 1968. When an attorney told a common pleas judge that his male client had been sexually assaulted in a sheriff's van, the judge ordered an investigation, appointing Alan Davis, Specter's assistant, to lead it. After interviewing 3,304 inmates and 561 employees at the Detention Center, Holmesburg Prison, and the House of Correction, Davis estimated that during a 26-month period, 2,000 homosexual assaults involving 1,500 victims and 3,500 aggressors had occurred. Reporting that 56% of the assaults involved "Negro aggressors and white victims," Davis's report put forward two images of male same-sex sexuality, one that was African American, older, and aggressive, and the other that was Euro-American, younger, and passive. The report also indicted Penn, which operated a laboratory at Holmesburg in which inmates were used to test drugs and commercial products. With inmates able to earn money by "volunteering," a system of sexual exchange had developed in which inmates traded sex for testing opportunities. Criticizing the *Bulletin*'s coverage, Friedman wrote that it was "regrettable" that the newspaper failed to distinguish "cases involving consensual adults" and "cases involving assault."[25]

Also linking same-sex sexualities with male crime and violence, other media accounts focused on the 1967 murder of Haverford "bachelor" William Thompson, the 1968 murder of North Philly "hairdresser" George Casey, and the 1969 murder of retired seaman Joseph Costello. According to another 1968 story, a group of African American parents and the NAACP claimed that male camp counselors had sexually abused male campers in a program run by the Philadelphia Anti-Poverty Action Committee. In 1969, the media reported that a male former Philadelphia high-school teacher was convicted on charges of solicitation to commit sodomy with male students; six African American teenagers were arrested at an Upper Darby railroad station on charges of female impersonation and disorderly conduct; and African American cross-dresser Joseph Riley accused police of breaking his leg in 1967 and raping him in 1968.[26]

Philadelphia Magazine focused on male same-sex sexualities in two articles in this period. According to a 1967 feature, the City Council of Cape May, New Jersey, passed an ordinance prohibiting bikini bathing suits on men and boys over the age of 12 because "horny" "queers" had been "wearing women's bathing suits on the main beach." In 1968, "Here He Comes, Miss Philadelphia," examined the Miss Philadelphia Affair, which drew 500 guests to the Hotel Philadelphia. Apart from a passing reference to "a girl in a man's tux," this article also focused on men. Meanwhile, Center City audiences encountered male cross-dressers in Frank Simon's film documentary "The Queen," which featured the triumph of Philadelphia's "Harlow" at the 1967 Miss All-America Camp Beauty Contest.[27]

Only rarely did the media focus again on lesbians. One exception was a 1967 *Bulletin* article by Marta Robinet on women in Holmesburg Prison. According to Robinet, the "ever-present threat" of "homosexual problems" meant that "shower stalls, open cells, even workrooms, the sewing room, and laundry" had to be "under the constant vigilance of staff members." Part of the article focused on "Alice," a "true sex deviate" and "butch drag" who displayed "tremendous physical energy" while "smiling her scorn." But according to Robinet, "most women prisoners form homosexual alliances because they miss their men."[28]

Despite the appearance of "The Invisible Sorority," then, "the furtive fraternity" continued receiving greater attention in the press. DOB was more concerned, however, with the negative features of these representations than with the fact that they were predominantly male. Bello and Friedman declared in one newsletter, "Like any group unaccustomed to seeing itself reflected in the mass media, we tend to be overly enthusiastic about any representation which relates to our lives, whether it be accurate or not." But they urged readers to be "more critical" and praised cases in which lesbians and gay men used the media "for our purposes, rather than being used by them."[29]

Friedman recalls, "The media images were there for us to react against and use as a kind of diving board for our own ideas. And in the same way, the crap coming out of the psychiatric establishment provided easy polemical targets." She also remembers criticizing the Free Library for restricting access to books on homosexuality:

> There were so few sources of information about who one was and could be. And that's what I remember best, I guess, looking back. It's not just the absence of positive role models and rhetoric like that. There was such an absence of images of possibility, of how to be a human being, of how to be this kind of a human being. And if you are given at all to learning about the world through books, through movies, through TV, and if you either can't get access to those things or the images presented to you are distorted or are just used for commercial purposes, it's tragic for the individuals whose lives are constrained in that way.

Like the newsletter itself and the criticisms of media and psychiatry, the attack on the library's policy challenged the ways that knowledge about lesbians and gay men circulated but not the fact that most of this knowledge focused on men.[30]

Analogies and Alliances

As the DOB chapter developed, it defined itself in relation to gay men's activism. Announcing the formation of the Philadelphia group, the DOB New York newsletter thanked Janus for offering "assistance and good will" and noted that although the first meeting would be "for women only," the chapter would soon "call upon the local gentry for assistance." Shortly thereafter, the chapter rented an office at 34 South 17th Street, which was also home to Janus. Ada Bello remembers that Clark Polak helped distribute the DOB newsletter, "liked to cooperate," and "might have even contributed some money." Denouncing the state sodomy law, proposals for law reform, and police raids on bars, DOB's newsletter took up many of the same local issues that concerned Janus, even though some of these issues affected gay men more directly. Helping to build the homophile movement by participating in the Eastern Regional Conference of Homophile Organizations (ERCHO) and the Annual Reminder, DOB Philadelphia allied with gay men as well as lesbians.[31]

DOB Philadelphia conceived of lesbians and gay men as linked. Although it focused on women, the newsletter often reprinted and reviewed media representations of gay men. The newsletter also praised Provincetown impersonator Lynne Carter, reported on the Miss All-America Camp Beauty Pageant, and urged society to adopt the kind of "acceptance" of homosexuals that Johns Hopkins University doctors had shown toward transsexuals. In not explaining or justifying their reports on gay men, drag queens, and transsexuals, the newsletter both assumed and encouraged links between lesbians and these other groups. In one case, the newsletter explicitly justified its coverage of gay men. Discussing *Playboy* letters about police harassment of gay men, the newsletter declared, "Heterosexual society and, perhaps, even the female homosexual community tends to feel too safe and out of the reach of such practices. This is a most dangerous mistake. When the rights of one individual are violated, the rights of everyone are jeopardized."[32]

While DOB Philadelphia cooperated with Janus and understood lesbians to be linked with gay men, the group also defined itself as distinct from, and even in opposition to, gay men's groups. For example, DOB criticized a *New York Times Magazine* feature on "homosexuals" for "an afterthought about lesbianism which was condescending at best and downright prejudiced." The article had stated, "In some communities Lesbians maintain association with male homosexual groups, working as their secretaries or club colleagues. It's an intriguing relationship. Since there appears to be no persecution to counteract, the motive must be desire for recognition or status, a new version of female emancipation." According to DOB Philadelphia, the article "presented lesbian organizations as ineffectual groups mimicking the male homosexuals, without serious purpose or motivation."[33]

DOB Philadelphia also distanced itself from local gay activism. According to Bello, *Drum* "represented all the things the women in the Daughters of Bilitis found distasteful: sexual jargon too raw for the times and unabashed emphasis on male genitalia." The chapter also criticized Polak for suggesting in *Temple University News* that both homosexuality and rape were "natural." The "homosexual community" hoped to "erase the illegal stigma that society has attached to homosexuality," the newsletter declared, "and we can hardly expect to achieve it by coupling it with a criminal act." Asked about this confrontation, Bello says it was "the sort of insensitivity" lesbians expected from gay men. She continues, "You might just scream a little but try to dismiss it. You know: 'they just don't know better.' "[34]

Meanwhile, although DOB Philadelphia was overwhelmingly Euro-American, its politics were influenced by other "minority" movements as well. Bello thinks that the "comparison with other minorities" was "natural" and that Carole Friedman was instrumental in making connections between homophile and other civil rights movements. Friedman remembers that "taking a principled stand" was familiar to her because she had been involved in civil rights work. She recalls that when she participated in the Reminder, it "felt good, felt familiar, felt safe in a certain way." Criticizing the use of the word "queer" in *Philadelphia Magazine*'s feature on Cape May, Bello wrote that "there are no differences between words like 'nigger,' 'kike,' 'spic' and 'queer.' " Attacking the "sadistic, tyrannical and pathetic" lesbian portrayed in a production of "The Killing of Sister George," Bello and Friedman argued, "No doubt that there are Negroes who fit the description of the white racist. But . . . who would dare to present that most negative and biased image today?" Like other homophile activists, Bello and Friedman sought to gain advantage by identifying their struggle with "minority" causes and by asserting that lesbians and gay men had it worse.[35]

DOB Philadelphia's politics thus took shape in relation to dominant society, lesbian and gay cultures, lesbian and gay movements, and ethnic and racial movements. But unlike the national DOB, it almost never linked itself with feminism and the women's movement. "The Masculine-Feminine Mystique" was the exception. Asked about the expression of feminism in this article, Bello remembers that she and Friedman "were very much like that" and that she "felt very strong about the feminist issue, even then." Bello adds that she did not know how well this would be received because "there was, at that time, the one-issue approach to social change." Asked where she had encountered feminist ideas, Bello responds that she had always felt this way, that there was something wrong with women who came from Catholic countries who did not feel this way, that she had witnessed sex discrimination while working at Penn, and that maybe she "just was feeling the vibrations in the air" as "women were starting to speak up."[36] Perhaps Bello and Friedman's feminism was not expressed in the newsletter as much as it shaped their convictions. But it is also possible that later developments, including the rise of lesbian feminism in the 1970s, have made Bello remember more feminist consciousness within the DOB chapter than existed at the time. DOB Philadelphia's political vision was distinctly lesbian, but it was not overtly feminist.

The same was true of Barbara Gittings and Kay Lahusen's political vision. The *Ladder* announced shortly after Gittings was removed as editor in 1966, "Certain changes in editorial policy are anticipated. To date emphasis has been on the Lesbian's role in the homophile movement. Her identity as a woman in our society has not yet been explored in depth."[37] This signaled not only the national DOB's turn to feminism but also criticism of Gittings's alliances with men and her failure to take the *Ladder* in a feminist direction.

While Gittings and Lahusen remained active in homophile politics after 1966, the remainder of Philadelphia's first generation of lesbian activists did not. Mae Polakoff and Joey Hardman did not stay involved after Polak was elected to lead Janus. Jody Shotwell's fiction continued to appear in the *Ladder*, but in 1968 she died of cancer. Marge McCann and Joan Fleischmann dropped out of the movement after ECHO disbanded.[38]

By the time DOB Philadelphia was established, Gittings had become a leader in the North American Conference of Homophile Organizations and was working closely with gay men. At a Defense Department hearing in 1967, she and Frank Kameny represented a gay man whose security clearance the department was trying to revoke. Gittings also worked with Polak, joining him on the Council on Religion and the Homosexual and appearing with him on the Murray Burnett radio show in 1967. Discussing her many radio interviews, Gittings says, "Clark Polak took me first. He wanted a woman to go on the air with him, so he asked me."[39]

Gittings remained a supporter of the strategies of militant respectability used in the Independence Hall demonstrations. In 1967, 25–30 women and men picketed; in 1968 there were 75. As in earlier years, the FBI monitored these actions, but the Reminder also began receiving other types of attention. In 1967, the *New York Times* covered the demonstration, Rose DeWolf featured it in her *Inquirer* column, and Gittings was interviewed on two radio stations. Although the national DOB had withdrawn from ECHO because of opposition to picketing, among the demonstrators in 1967 and 1968 were Bello and Friedman and in 1968 the DOB office was used as Reminder headquarters. As was the case in 1965–1966, the marchers wove together discourses of heterosocial respectability, minority rights, and patriotism. According to DeWolf's column, one spectator said, "Are those people all . . . I mean, they look okay . . . do you think they are really . . . that is, both the men and women, too?" A sign used in 1967 read, "Discrimination against Homosexuals Is as Immoral as Discrimination against Negroes and Jews." A 1968 flier asked, "Are we guaranteeing to all of our citizens the rights, the liberties, the freedom, which took birth and first form in the Declaration of Independence?"[40]

While they identified with other social protesters in this era, Reminder leaders also highlighted the ways in which they were different. In 1967, for example, organizers excluded volunteers who did not conform to a dress code. According to Samantha Morse, she and her friends showed up at Independence Hall to join the picket, but because they were "hippies" and were "not dressed appropriately," they were told by Reminder leaders that they would not be allowed to march. She continues, "The organizers felt that hippies had a bad name in the press already and would only hurt their cause: equal rights through social acceptability was the idea." In the end, after speaking to a protest leader and emphasizing that they wanted to be included, Morse and her friends were allowed to march for the last 10 or 15 minutes of the demonstration. Distancing themselves from antiwar activists, the picketers used as their 1967 slogan, "We don't dodge the draft . . . the draft dodges us." Seeking to improve their position by emphasizing their relative lack of progress, they held up a sign that read, "Homosexual American citizens: Our last oppressed national minority." The 1968 flier stated that "even in the South" officials met with "representatives of the Negro community" but that meetings with homosexuals were "almost without exception" refused. The flier continued, "Other of America's minority groups know that they have the active assistance of their governments. . . . The homosexual American citizen meets only with the active, virulent hostility of his government." While capturing some elements of change, homophile activists overstated the progress made by other groups while promoting the interests of lesbians and gay men.[41]

The "Glorious Strike" and the Raid on Rusty's

In the spring of 1968, Carole Friedman announced in DOB Philadelphia's newsletter that "as we move into the second week of our glorious strike," President Lyndon Johnson appeared on television "to urge the 10 million striking homosexuals to return to work." Confronting bare department store windows, shortages of gym teachers, the absence of hairdressers for Lady Bird, and the lack of a Senate quorum, Johnson promised to end all federal practices that discriminated against homosexuals.[42] While readers were unlikely to have missed the April Fool's joke for long, few would have imagined such a strike depending on lesbian window designers, hairdressers, or senators. While teaching gym was an occupation commonly associated with lesbians, two of the other three jobs named were stereotypically associated with gay men. And the Senate, while not known to be gay, was overwhelmingly male. DOB Philadelphia had not forgotten that its members were women, but the language used in "the strike" both assumed and encouraged a strong sense of community with gay men. Within months of Johnson's imagined capitulation, Philadelphia's activist lesbians again decided that their cause would best be served by forming alliances with gay men.

The series of events that led to this decision began on 8 March 1968, when police raided Rusty's. According to Ada Bello, who remembers speaking with women who had been at the bar that night, the police arrived at the door, the jukebox was unplugged, the lights were turned on, and the dance floor emptied. Dramatically reconstructing events, Bello describes "the small posse of trench coat clad figures" who "slowly moved from table to table." When "somebody refused to show identification," angry words were exchanged and screams erupted. Police took into custody a dozen women, who were booked on disorderly conduct charges, held overnight, and brought before a magistrate in the morning, when all charges were dropped.[43]

Among the women arrested was Byrna Aronson, who several hours earlier had visited the DOB office for the first time. According to a 1974 article in the *Inquirer*, Aronson did not see the police when they first arrived: "I leaned down to kiss my girlfriend on the cheek, and Captain Clarence Ferguson, in a pork-pie hat, tapped me on the shoulder and said, 'You're under arrest.' And I said, 'What for?' He said, 'Sodomy.' I just started to laugh." The *Inquirer* stated that "it was alleged (in graphic language) that several women had been making love on the floor, that others were drunk and disorderly, and that some had resisted arrest." DOB women were also in Rusty's that night, and although none was arrested they followed Aronson and the other women to three police stations and were present at their hearing. According to the DOB newsletter, the women experienced "verbal abuse" by the police, who failed to advise the women of their rights and "pressured" them "to fill out a questionnaire."[44]

Bello argues that in raiding Rusty's, "the Philadelphia police made a very valuable contribution." She speculates, "Maybe it was the mood prevailing in the country at that time. Maybe it was because there is such a thing as the last straw. But out of this incident . . . our group got the first clear sense of direction. Some of the women came to us and demanded action. . . . Several women joined the chapter, among them Byrna Aronson." According to a 1975 interview with Aronson, "Police injustice and harassment were not the only things that radicalized Byrna that day. The solid support of the Daughters of Bilitis raised her consciousness and helped her identify with a gay community. She became a gay activist."[45]

Friedman recalls a "sense of crisis" and that this was a "radicalizing event." She remembers the challenge presented to DOB: "Were we going to really try and change the world or were we going to talk among ourselves about how the world ought to change?" She also thinks Aronson challenged DOB in class terms:

> There was this middle-class, more intellectual sort of niceness about DOB. And Byrna, while she, I believe, came from a middle-class, maybe even an upper-middle-class, Jewish background, still seemed to come more from the hard knocks of the street. She was more streetwise. She had defected more than the other women in DOB from middle-class ideas of success. . . . And yet she could speak both languages. She could speak the more structured, intellectual, educated language, so she could challenge more middle-class women. . . . I experienced her as kind of

> coming out of the darkness, out of the darkness of the bar scene. And she was radicalized by this terrible experience. . . . My sense is that that changed the world for Byrna, relatively quickly, really overnight.[46]

Discussing her own transitions earlier, Friedman describes going to her first DOB meeting in the "daylight." Here she refers to Aronson "coming out of the darkness" and changing "overnight." While DOB was made up of middle-class lesbians, the raid increased their identifications with the mixed-class bar clientele who shared with them the dangers of lesbian nightlife.

Like Aronson, the DOB chapter changed overnight. Editorializing against the raid, Bello and Friedman wrote that the "homophile community must become aware of its rights, aroused by these violations, and determined to secure the full and equal protection of the law." On 24 March, Barbara Gittings spoke to the chapter, offered "great help to those involved in the raid," and suggested that the chapter distribute ACLU materials, inform the ACLU of abuses, establish an emergency telephone service, and compile a list of lawyers. Gittings soon helped Bello and her friend Lourdes Alvarez directly. One night shortly after the raid, the three women were at Rusty's when police raided the bar again. Bello and Alvarez were applying for U.S. citizenship and rarely risked going to bars in this period. But Bello remembers saying on this night, "I'm going anyway. There's not going to be a raid." According to Bello, when police asked for identifications, Gittings showed her ACLU card, which encouraged the police to move on.[47]

In May, two DOB representatives and an ACLU observer met with a police inspector. Bello describes the decision to go to the police as pivotal: "We were at the crossroads. Once we had contacted the police there was no going back." Friedman wrote in the newsletter that the chapter had decided to "assume the role of spokesman for those arrested that night and the homophile community they represent." Although the police arranged a meeting with "a fine public relations man—always polite, always friendly, always evasive," DOB claimed success insofar as the group "let the police know that we exist, we are aware of our rights, and we are not afraid to protest violations." By bringing along an ACLU representative, DOB "served notice" that "we are not alone." DOB also obtained a police statement that "homosexuals have been, are now, and will be treated equally with heterosexuals." Moreover, the meeting "affirmed our value as an organization by going to bat for the community we represent."[48]

While Friedman wrote early in her article that DOB was going to "assume the role of spokesman" for those arrested and "the homophile community *they* represent," later in the article she described DOB "going to bat for the community *we* represent" (emphases mine). In the first passage, DOB assumed a "role" and the women arrested "represented" the community. In the second, DOB was the community's representative and Friedman did not pause to highlight the process whereby it had become just that.

HAL and Heterosocial Action

In August 1968, several months after the raid on Rusty's, the DOB chapter unanimously voted to dissolve and regroup as the Homophile Action League. This decision stemmed in part from the difficulties of working as a chapter of a national organization. But HAL also formed because Philadelphia lesbians saw DOB as insufficiently political and militant. In the words of Gittings, "They wanted action in Philadelphia."[49] And the DOB lesbians who created HAL thought that working alongside gay men would help them become more political and militant.

Bello and Friedman's first *HAL Newsletter* described the new group's politics and its hopes for mixed-sex membership:

> This newly formed group, open to both men and women, has adopted the name "Homophile Action League," and has as its main purpose "to strive to change society's legal, social, and scientific attitudes toward the homosexual in order to achieve justified recognition of the homosexual as a first class citizen and a first class human being. . . ." We wish to emphasize that word 'ACTION' in our name. . . . We are *not* a social group. We do *not* intend to concentrate our energies on "uplifting" the homosexual community, for such efforts would be sadly misplaced. It is our firm conviction that it is the heterosexual community which is badly in need of uplifting.

Gittings, who joined HAL, argues that "there hadn't been any really concerted effort on the political scene until HAL was organized and began to attract some men." Friedman explains:

> Some of us wanted the group to become more politically engaged, not only to be a social meeting ground but to be more involved in social change. And it seemed then that the vanguard would be for gay men and lesbians to be working together. Feminism later turned everything on its head. But at the time, DOB seemed restrictive and a little prissy. . . . My feeling is that there was a sense of "ooh men," which wasn't feminist. It wasn't lesbian consciousness. It was some kind of old thing that women had. "Ooh men, ooh they're dirty, aren't they?" So that it seemed that it was more forward looking to work together. . . . I remember the discussions and the sense that in order to do that and

> to be that kind of gay political person in Philadelphia, that we would need to either bring men into DOB or to break away from DOB. . . . Certainly, at that point, we felt an identity as gay people, gay men, gay women, suffering from the same discrimination and needing to fight the same battles.[50]

The women who formed HAL linked politicization, militancy, and heterosocial cooperation for a number of reasons. They identified closely with gay men and the oppression that gay men suffered. Single-sex groups in the homophile movement, and especially women's groups, were often seen as social and not political. And engaging in politics was typically considered a male activity, which meant that working with gay men might help lesbians enter the political arena.

The national DOB was not pleased. The *Ladder* praised the new group's newsletter for its "good hard-hitting content" and noted that "judging only from their first three issues, they intend to slant most of their material to the Lesbian." But the *Ladder* was also skeptical: "However, the organization is open to both men and women, so that slant may soon change. While it lasts, congratulations on your work!"[51]

HAL was not immediately successful in becoming a mixed-sex group. "I don't think any of the males that came at first stayed for too long," Bello recalls. She does not think that there were conflicts between women and men. "But remember," she advises, "they were in the minority and they were new. And the chair was always a woman." According to Bello, after Edna W., Lourdes Alvarez and Byrna Aronson served as chairs. Friedman recalls, "It had been an all-women's group, so that leadership pattern had already begun and that system of relating was already there. So men, like new women, were coming into something that was already established and had its own patterns." Gittings remembers problems attracting men: "The men would walk into a room filled with women engaged in serious discussion and making serious decisions. And either they were looking to cruise or they were looking for fun and they didn't see that in the room. So they walked out." Ironically, although HAL lesbians believed that working with gay men would help them become more political, Gittings suggests that gay men were looking for social opportunities. And although their community worlds overlapped, gay men so often socialized homosocially that they were less likely to see erotic potential in heterosocial environments.[52]

In many ways, HAL picked up where DOB Philadelphia left off. The new group took over DOB's office. Shortly after Clark Polak moved his offices to 1230 Arch Street in 1969, HAL moved a block away at 1321 Arch. The group also participated in NACHO and ERCHO.[53] Although there were important continuities, HAL adopted a more strident tone than DOB had used. Early in 1969, Friedman and Bello wrote that "we are living in an age of revolution" but "confrontation" was the "antithesis of the more comfortable approaches characterizing many homosexuals, and many homophile groups." "The black, the poor, and the student have been actively confronting the systems which deny and demean them," they argued. Meanwhile, "we wait (sometimes) in dread, always in a defensive posture, rarely prepared." Because confrontation was "impossible for the invisible," homophiles would have to rely on "those who do not need to work and those whose careers will not be affected by their aggressive pursuit of equality." Perhaps drawing lessons from Janus, they suggested that the homophile movement employ people, who "would be dependent for their livelihoods on the groups they were employed to serve, and not—like the rest of us—on the system we are attempting to alter."[54]

HAL's rhetoric was particularly militant in relation to psychiatry and the media. Bello and Friedman argued that "the void left by religion's demotion has rapidly been filled; and all too often it is fools who have rushed in where once even angels feared to tread." The fools were psychiatrists, who were providing a "new opiate of the masses." Attacking psychiatrist Charles Socarides, Friedman explained that "we are clearly among those 'certain groups' who have the audacity to assert that homosexuality is fully equal to heterosexuality." HAL also responded to the *Inquirer*'s coverage of the prison sex scandal. "You imply that the operative factor in these incidents has been homosexuality," HAL wrote in a letter to the editor, "whereas it is apparent that the true problems center, rather, around violence, aggression, and brutality, and the prison system which fosters them. When a rape is committed, heterosexuality is not condemned as the culprit."[55]

At times, HAL even hinted at the notion of homosexual superiority. Criticizing novelist James Michener, who had commented on the dangers of young boys being seduced into homosexuality, Bello asked, "Does Mr. Michener really believe that that is all it takes to tilt the balance? Is the case for heterosexuality so flimsy that to be exposed, through reading material, to the existence of homosexuality will automatically change the sexual orientation of the reader? Not even me, Mr. Michener, who at times could be accused of indulging in some biased contemplation of heterosexuality, think so little of it."[56]

HAL's most important action in its first months focused on bars. In late 1968, the *HAL Newsletter* observed that although gay bars were "left alone" on most nights, there were still times "when the patrons of gay bars wish they had been left alone." In December 1968, about six months after the Liquor Control Board revoked the license of the U.S.&A.A., HAL wrote to the LCB and received a response from Pennsylvania assistant attorney general Thomas Shannon. To HAL's question on whether regulations that prohibited liquor licensees from permitting on their premises "persons of ill repute," "known criminals," and "undesirable persons" applied to homosexuals, Shannon answered that the LCB "does not consider homosexuals as a class to be undesirable persons within the meaning of the Liquor Code." He also wrote that "the mere fact that patrons in a licensed establishment may be 'hand-holding,' regardless of sex, would not be considered grounds for Board action."[57]

Gittings worked with HAL and the ACLU on bar issues while maintaining a busy schedule of public speaking and NACHO work. One of her projects involved developing with Spencer Coxe a pamphlet "outlining the rights of persons, particularly homosexuals vis a vis the police in non-arrest (or pre-arrest) situations." "Female homosexuals," Coxe wrote in an ACLU memorandum, needed guidance on four matters:

1. being stopped by cops on the street and asked for identification (happens occasionally with female homosexual couples).
2. "Vice Squad" forays into gay bars. . . .
3. Police refusal to give reason for "check" or for arrest.
4. Police refusal to identify selves.

Coxe noted that "Barbara is not sure whether the publication should be broadened to include discussions of concern to male and not female homosexuals, e.g. entrapment, and blackmail. She will discuss this with some male homosexuals." Meanwhile, HAL distributed an ACLU pamphlet, "If You Are Arrested," and Tom Harvey of the ACLU spoke in a new HAL lecture series.[58]

Although more militant than DOB, HAL remained cautious. In one newsletter, Friedman wrote that "heterosexual friends" may be "amused" by the use of initials instead of full names. Making reference to job vulnerabilities, she explained that "no one looks forward more than we to the day when we can openly proclaim what we unashamedly are and, without fear of discrimination, sign ourselves more meaningfully than—C. F." Initials worked for the newsletter, but there were times when HAL needed to use names. Bello explains that most of HAL's letters were signed by "Ellen Collins," but she warns historians not to "set out on a wild goose chase looking for this woman." "Ellen Collins," who had letters published in *Newsweek* and *Medical World News*, was a name HAL selected out of a telephone directory. In time, Bello recalls, she became "quite popular" and "even got junk mail."[59]

As had been the case with DOB, HAL linked the homophile cause with other movements and highlighted the relative lack of homophile progress. In one instance, Bello criticized a *New York Times* ad that featured the line "Show me a happy homosexual and I'll show you a gay corpse." Bello responded that "if the group in question were one of the minorities that society, in one way or another, has learned to respect, the advertisement would have brought about protest galore." Bello advised boycotting books, plays, and movies that presented "this 'Uncle Tom' attitude." "And as for the civil-righteous heterosexuals," she concluded, "we suggest they re-read the copy of the ad substituting the words Negro or Jew for the word homosexual."[60]

In one instance, HAL defended the analogies that it made. In response to a *Playboy* article, Bello and Friedman argued that "whether Homosexuals do or do not have distinct cultural traits and structures is irrelevant to their classification as a minority." Declaring that "the only inherent quality which all Homosexuals share is their sexual preference," Bello and Friedman stated that "discriminatory patterns have brought into being other attributes which can be found among many . . . but not all homosexuals." To qualify as a minority, homosexuals only needed to share "one attribute," but "many Homosexuals do share other traits," which were a "result" of and not a "criterion" for "minority status."[61]

While HAL compared the status of lesbians and gay men to the status of African Americans, Jews, and other minorities, and while it linked the homophile movement with the student, civil rights, and antipoverty movements, the group did not refer in its newsletter to identifications and links with women and feminism. In fact, returning to the language of "The Masculine-Feminine Mystique," it appears that DOB Philadelphia's and HAL's members *were* "so concerned with being lesbians" that they tended to forget the fact that they were "also women."[62]

If Bello's "Masculine-Feminine Mystique" signaled some level of local lesbian activist identification with feminism, that level remained low through 1969. And if Bello remembers correctly that she and Friedman felt very strongly about feminism, the one-issue approach to social change appears to have guided their work in DOB and HAL. In the case of HAL, perhaps feminist rhetoric was downplayed because the group's lesbian leaders feared that this might conflict with their desires to develop a mixed-sex membership. But perhaps Bello and Friedman have projected back into the 1960s a type of feminist consciousness that they did not develop until the 1970s. Whatever their identifications with feminism, Philadelphia's lesbian activists in DOB and HAL were moving in a direction different from the one charted by the national DOB. That direction was political but it was not explicitly feminist.

Liberation and Repression

While the lesbians of HAL radicalized the politics of militant respectability in the crucible of the late 1960s, government officials set out to destroy Clark Polak's politics of gay sexual liberation. By 1967, Polak was committed to the three projects that would absorb his energies through 1969—legal reform, homophile publishing, and pornography. He pursued the first through the Homosexual Law Reform Society, which had its biggest success in 1967, when the New Jersey Supreme Court in *Val's Bar v. Division of Alcoholic Beverage Control* unanimously upheld the rights of lesbians and gay men to congregate in bars. Employing the politics of respectability, *Drum* noted that HLRS funded this particular case because it concerned "homosexual association" and not allegations of "kissing between two males."[63]

HLRS also funded work on *Boutilier v. the Immigration and Naturalization Service* (INS), which reached the U.S. Supreme Court in 1967. Canadian Clive Michael Boutilier had been living in the United States since 1955 when he applied for U.S. citizenship in 1963 and revealed that he had been arrested in New York in 1959 on a sodomy charge. Using the "psychopathic personality" provisions of the 1952 Immigration Act, the INS began deportation proceedings. With the help of the ACLU and HLRS, Boutilier appealed. *Drum* reported proudly on HLRS's brief, which included "more statements from psychiatrists and psychologists that, in their professional opinions, homosexuality is not psychopathology than were ever brought together before." HLRS-funded lawyers argued the case in respectable terms, emphasizing Boutilier's history of cross-sex sexual activities, his good conduct, and the eminence of gay men in history. For the purposes of this strategy, it helped that Boutilier was Euro-American and Canadian rather than a member of an ethnic, racial, or national group historically less welcomed by dominant U.S. society. By a 6–3 margin, however, the Court upheld the statute. Still, *Drum* proclaimed victory in the "impassioned dissent," which included William O. Douglas's statement that "homosexuals have risen high in our public service—both in Congress and our executive branch—and have served with distinction."[64]

While supporting respectable strategies within courtrooms, Polak elsewhere made legal arguments more consistent with sexual radicalism. For example, he challenged the ACLU when its new statement on homosexuality failed to reject homosexual solicitation statutes. According to Polak, the ACLU was unfairly distinguishing between "good" and "bad" homosexuals. He also reprinted in *Drum* Richard Elliott's critical study of the Philadelphia Morals Squad.[65]

Meanwhile, Polak engaged in extensive public speaking, participated in regional and national homophile conferences, and wrote "What Organized Homosexuals Want" for *Sexology*. In 1967, author John Gerassi delivered an HLRS lecture at the Hotel Sylvania and Janus announced plans for a Philadelphia gay community center. According to Charles Kaiser, in 1968 Polak became television talk show host Phil Donahue's first openly gay guest. In 1968, the 31-year-old Polak was described in the *Inquirer* as the "elder statesman" of the local "homosexual" community.[66]

Polak's second project, *Drum*, continued to integrate homophile activism with sexual liberationism. After 21 issues were published from 1964 to 1966, however, *Drum* began appearing less frequently, coming out nine times in the next three years. Retaining a mix of photography, comics, news, and reviews, *Drum* reported on Janus and HLRS's work and provided a vehicle for selling products associated with Polak's third project.

That project was a set of pornography businesses including the gay-oriented Trojan Book Service, the straight-oriented Beaver Book Service, and three Center City bookstores. Trojan sold books, photographs, films, and magazines, including a number of Trojan's own publications such as *Stud* and *Like Young*. The company's brochure declared that Trojan offered the "world's largest selection of homosexual literature." In 1968, *Philadelphia Magazine* featured Polak in an article on local pornographers. Described as "the most interesting of the dozen dealers in the city today in that he maintains some sort of philosophy toward the business, no matter how iconoclastic," Polak declared that for the first time he was "doing something because of the money." Referring to Beaver, he explained, "For years the homosexual has been the product of heterosexual exploitation. Now it is time for the homosexual to exploit the heterosexual by making a buck on him. It's *gay* power."[67]

In January 1967, chief postal inspector Henry Montague decided that since Polak had ceased all correspondence club operations, the post office should redirect its investigation to focus on his activities as an obscene dealer and publisher. With the cooperation of the Justice Department, the post office began monitoring Polak's mail to determine whether he was violating federal laws. This involved reading his outgoing mail, using test purchases, and examining the contents of "broken" packages. Postal officials and U.S. attorneys also investigated allegations that photographer James Mitchell, Polak's lover, had used underage female models and had advertised for male models in the *Daily Pennsylvanian* and *Distant Drummer*.[68]

The quantity of Polak's mail and the success of his businesses are revealed in postal reports that indicate that Polak purchased $42,478 in postage between June 1967 and April 1969. In 1969, he bought more than $30,000 in postage. In one eight-day period in 1969, Polak deposited an average of 1,585 pieces of mail daily. The post office reported receiving more than 500 complaints about unsolicited ads for Polak's businesses and organizations before the enactment of a new federal law on "pandering" in 1968. In the following year, the post office received approximately 160 additional complaints.[69]

While federal officials continued monitoring Polak's activities, local and state authorities proceeded apace. On 12 March 1967, police allegedly received a report of a burglary in progress at Polak's Center City home. Two policemen found a man and a woman leaving the premises with materials that included gay-related books and films. Police then obtained a search warrant for the house and found approximately 75,000 "homosexual oriented books and periodicals," photographs of male nudes, and a mailing list "conservatively estimated to contain over 100,000 names."[70]

Later that day, Polak was arrested and released on bail on charges of possession of obscene photographs and publications with intent to distribute. District attorney Arlen Specter obtained another warrant to search Polak's premises on 14 March 1967. Although a grand jury indicted Polak, in March 1968 a judge destroyed Specter's case by suppressing evidence seized with a faulty warrant. Photographer Neil Edwards, a.k.a. Elliot McNeil, who was associated with Polak and Trojan, was also arrested on obscenity charges in Philadelphia in 1967 and also had the charges dropped in 1968 when a judge suppressed evidence.[71] Meanwhile, other Philadelphians also struggled with antigay censorship. According to the *Wall Street Journal*, in April 1967 Joseph Brierley, superintendent of the Pennsylvania Correctional Institute in Philadelphia, "killed" an issue of *Eastern Echo*, a prisoners' publication, because it was "devoted entirely to sex in prison" and " 'dealt in specifics' about homosexual affairs." In response, *Eastern Echo*'s 10-man editorial staff resigned.[72]

Although he avoided conviction in 1967–1968, Polak's legal troubles were far from over. On 14 February 1969, he was arrested again, this time for selling obscene publications and permitting peep shows in his Market Street bookstore, Book-A-Rama. On 17 April Polak was found guilty and received a two-year prison sentence, later reduced to one-to-two months, which he appealed.[73]

Less than two weeks later, Polak wrote to Paul Gebhard at the Kinsey Institute: "I've had to redefine priorities in my own activities here and have decided to relinquish all my duties with the Janus Society, H.L.R.S. and *Drum*." In a letter to Janus members and *Drum* subscribers dated 5 May 1969, Polak announced, without explanation, "There will be no further issues of *Drum*." According to Norman Oshtry, Polak was "tired." Richard Schlegel, who had moved to Philadelphia to work with Polak, recalls that *Drum* "never did for him what he wanted it to do," which was to make him a "gay Hugh Hefner with all of the assets, money, notoriety, publicity, and mansions." Schlegel says that Polak's "only question to himself was what to do with the assets" and that Polak at one point "met with some ladies" from HAL and offered to turn over the Janus mailing list and other materials: "I believe that he drew this dichotomy in his mind, *Drum* versus Janus. *Drum* was to be destroyed, chucked. Janus Society, however, could continue." As Schlegel remembers, "The women were wishy-washy; they hemmed and hawed. They didn't know whether they wanted to or not. And they didn't know at the time that that was the only opportunity they had."[74]

Meanwhile, Schlegel joined with Jack Ervin, the sole remaining officer from Janus's 1963 elections, to try to wrest control of the organization. The two also had support from William Damon, who had begun working under Polak's supervision as editor of *Drum*, and Mitchell, Polak's temporarily estranged lover. Assuming the title of acting president, Ervin wrote to Janus's banks, attempting to withhold authorization for Polak to sign checks. On 19 May, Polak's lawyer wrote to Ervin explaining that Polak was "perfectly willing to transfer the Janus Society responsibilities."[75]

Eight days later, police raided two of Polak's bookstores, confiscated peep show machines and a film, and arrested Polak and three of his employees on obscenity charges. On 2 June, a local judge held Polak in contempt for failing to produce additional films allegedly shown at his stores.[76]

On 4 June, Ervin wrote to Schlegel that Polak had threatened legal action if Ervin did not cease his efforts to take control of Janus's bank accounts. Either Polak had changed his mind or he was distinguishing between Janus money and Janus responsibilities. Noting that he had "no intention of becoming involved in any legal action with Clark," Ervin capitulated. Having lost this battle, Schlegel and Ervin wrote to Polak requesting use of Janus resources to distribute a new constitution, by-laws, and slate of candidates for election.[77] By the summer of 1969, Janus's future was in doubt and Polak's troubles were far from over.

Over the course of the 1960s, Philadelphia's homophile activists had used three strategies to improve the conditions of lesbian and gay life. In the early 1960s, Mattachine and Janus activists favored heterosocial respectability, presenting themselves accordingly in "The Furtive Fraternity" and the ECHO convention. In the mid-1960s, Mattachine and ECHO activists turned to militant respectability, which they demonstrated most prominently at the Annual Reminder and in *The Ladder*. Meanwhile, Janus employed militant respectability at the Dewey's sit-in but embraced sexual liberationism in *Drum*. In the late 1960s, while respectable militants gained in strength, sexual liberationists struggled against state repression.

Each of these movement strategies was shaped by the everyday practices discussed in part 1 and the public debates considered in part 2. In turn, these organized movements influenced everyday lesbian and gay cultures and public conceptions of same-sex sexualities. Relationships between the sexes were central in this dialectical process. Just as everyday lesbian and everyday gay practices both converged and diverged, and just as public discussions of female and male same-sex sexualities both converged and diverged, so too lesbian movement and gay movement strategies both converged and diverged. In residential neighborhoods, commercial districts, and public space, lesbians and gay man developed homosocial and heterosocial cultures. Public debate on same-sex sexualities, however, focused almost exclusively on male forms and most of this attention was negative. When female forms were considered, they were almost always derived from or conceived of in relation to male counterparts. Lesbian and gay activists thus approached and interacted with one another with identities and interests that were compatible in some contexts but not in others.

At the most profound level, however, lesbian and gay activists in the 1960s shared two basic characteristics. They were determined to struggle against the oppression of lesbians and gay men. And they were convinced that women and men were fundamentally different. Whether this belief would survive the "revolutions" that were about to occur remained to be seen.

PART FOUR

Twin Revolutions? 1969–1972

11

"Turning Points," 1969–1970

In the August 1969 *HAL Newsletter*, Ada Bello and Carole Friedman predicted that "years from now, when social historians write their accounts of the homophile movement, June 28, 1969 will be viewed as a turning point." Under a threateningly patriotic headline, "Give Me Liberty Or . . . ," the two women explained that "on that date, for the first time in history, masses of homosexuals took to the streets, demanding their rights in an open confrontation with the minions of an oppressive society." Reconstructing events in New York, Bello and Friedman wrote that when police entered the Stonewall Inn, "they had no reason to fear this raid would be different from all the others." But instead of "dissolving into the night," hundreds of people "congregated outside." When police attempted to lead their prisoners to a "paddy wagon," "they were met with a hail of coins, beer cans, rocks, and cries of 'Gay Power.'" Soon the police retreated into the bar, which was then set afire by "angry protesters." In the next few days, thousands rioted in the streets of Greenwich Village.[1]

Today, the Stonewall riots are rarely seen as a turning point in the homophile movement. Nor are they typically seen as transforming the "homophile movement" into the "lesbian and gay liberation movement." Instead, the riots are often viewed as the first act of lesbian and gay resistance *ever*. Younger activists in other social movements distanced themselves from older counterparts in the 1960s and 1970s, but perhaps in no movement was the denial of prior political traditions so complete. Individual narratives that portrayed "coming out" as a revolutionary break with psychological repression were recapitulated in social narratives that depicted the riots as a revolutionary break with political repression. What better way for post-Stonewall activists to represent themselves as having broken with the past than to deny that lesbian and gay politics even had a past?[2]

Bello and Friedman called the riots a "turning point." The "masses" had participated, they wrote, surely a departure from the small numbers active in the homophile movement. They had taken to the "streets," challenging the relegation of lesbian and gay life to the private sphere. And the confrontation had been "open," clearly different from less visible acts of resistance.

A few months later, Bello criticized *Esquire*'s Tom Burke for failing to acknowledge that lesbian and gay politics had a pre-Stonewall history. Burke had written that "the new homosexual of the Seventies" was "an unfettered, guiltless male child" who "thinks that 'Over the Rainbow' is a place to fly on 200 micrograms of lysergic acid diethylamide." Bello complained that it was "a pity that when the straight press finally discovers that 'old Aunties' are dead they still manage to distort the image of the homosexual." "Certainly," she pointed out, "some homosexual youth might smoke pot and drop acid," but that had "more to do with today's youth culture than with homosexuality." "Proud, unapologetic and guiltless homosexuals of all ages have been around for quite some time," she argued. "Pickets and boycotts are not new to the homophile movement," she explained. "The new militancy and radical approaches are the logical result of long years of laborious battles; they did not emerge miraculously from pot and LSD." Still, even Bello and Friedman depicted pre-Stonewall lesbians and gay men as passive. Attacking the "unholy silent partnership" of police and organized crime, Bello and Friedman declared that the riots were a sign that "homosexuals" would not remain "helpless pawns in the hands of these de facto ruling powers."[3]

If one historical debate has focused on whether the riots transformed or began lesbian and gay politics, another has centered on who participated in, identified with, and sought to gain advantage from the riots. Martin Duberman writes that the Stonewall had a "magical mix of patrons ranging from tweedy East Siders to street queens." As for lesbians, Duberman shares conflicting reports that range from accounts of virtually no lesbians in the bar to claims that a "dyke dressed in men's clothing" precipitated the riot by fighting back against police. He concludes that "few women ever appeared in Stonewall" and endorses Craig Rodwell's recollection that "a number of incidents were happening simultaneously."[4]

Although the Stonewall patrons and Village rioters were predominantly male, some gay men did not identify with events at Stonewall and some lesbians did. According to New York homophile activist Randy Wicker, the sight of "screaming queens forming chorus lines and kicking went against everything that I wanted people to think about homosexuals." A sign placed by Mattachine on the Stonewall after the riots read, "We homosexuals plead with our people to please help maintain peaceful and quiet conduct on the streets of the Village." Some lesbian activists shared these views. As Barbara Gittings notes, "Unfortunately, all the good work the movement had done was less remarkable than a riot by homosexuals. It's a shame that you have to do something like that to get really noticed." Bello and Friedman viewed the riots more positively. "No event in history, with perhaps the exception of the French Revolution, deserves more to be considered a watershed," Bello declares.[5]

HAL leaders, like many homophile activists, sought to turn the riots to political advantage and did so by describing events in particular ways. Bello and Friedman's account made no mention of the many drag queens, African Americans, Latinas, and Latinos who rioted, but claimed that New York's homophile groups had "allied themselves with the protestors" and were "attempting to organize the total gay community in order to help channel this newly-released energy."[6] As early as July 1969, homophile groups were not the only ones doing so. A radical new Gay Liberation Front (GLF-NY) had formed, challenging New York's homophile leadership.

Meanwhile, news of the riots spread. For activist Philadelphians, Stonewall's meaning was refracted through the city's position as a center of militant respectability and sexual liberationism. Respectable militants welcomed the opportunities created by the riots but opposed many of their transgressive features. Sexual liberationists had reasons to see the raid that caused the riots as yet another example of state repression. Both groups soon became aware that, while the riots inaugurated a new era in lesbian and gay politics, 1969 witnessed the ending of two Philadelphia traditions—the Annual Reminder and *Drum*.

From 1969 through 1971, Philadelphia's most important lesbian and gay political groups were HAL, Gay Liberation Front Philadelphia (GLF), and Radicalesbians Philadelphia. This chapter examines HAL and the immediate post-Stonewall challenges to militant respectability. Among those challenges was a second revolution, the eruption of radical lesbian feminism in 1970. More militant than homophile groups elsewhere and more lesbian-led than other mixed groups, HAL was in a unique position to respond to the twin revolutions of gay liberation and lesbian feminism. While analyzing the demise of Janus and *Drum* reveals the larger dimensions of state repression and exploring GLF and Radicalesbians suggests the radical significance of the revolutions, examining HAL exposes continuities between pre- and post-Stonewall politics.

The Final Reminder

On the Fourth of July, just days after the riots, somewhere between 45 and 150 activists demonstrated in the fifth Annual Reminder. The contrast between drag queens and bar patrons rioting in Greenwich Village and well-dressed lesbians and gay men peacefully picketing in Philadelphia could hardly have been greater. Demonstration leaders again used a language of patriotic respectability. As Barbara Gittings exclaimed, "We are here today to remind the American public that in its homosexual citizens, it has one large minority who are still not benefitting from the high ideals proclaimed for all on July 4, 1776."[7]

Figure 11.1. Kay Tobin Lahusen at the Annual Reminder, 1969. Photograph by Nancy Tucker. © 1969 LHEF, Inc. With the permission of the Lesbian Herstory Archives, Brooklyn, NY.

Picket leaders also again identified their struggles with those of African Americans. "Gay Is Good" buttons were modeled on the slogan "Black Is Beautiful." Gittings told the *Tribune* that "in many ways the homosexual population is the most persecuted (and prosecuted) minority group." Whether or not this was true, homophile activists now worked with multiple models of African American resistance. Covering the Reminder, the *Ladder* was ambiguous about which model it favored: "Society continues to ignore the homosexual and the demand for civil rights. Is it, therefore, impossible to win your rights without violence? Are the only groups to achieve freedom those who carry guns? We are asking into society, not out of it, and more and more, we are wondering why our cry is not heeded. Can it be that we are using a 'language' that cannot be understood?" Offering a vision of peaceful integration, the *Ladder* threatened a turn to language that might echo with the sounds of violence. Similarly, Bello attacked Philadelphia's major newspapers for ignoring the demonstration, warning that "in the past they also turned a deaf ear on the noises coming from the ghetto—until they couldn't afford to do it anymore."[8]

Judging by the coverage in the *Tribune*, *Ladder*, and *HAL Newsletter*, demonstrators were united in embracing militant respectability. From the start, however, there were signs that this Reminder would be different from the rest. Among the groups represented at the action were HAL, HLRS, DOB New York, and Mattachine Washington. Curiously missing was Mattachine New York.

Just days before the riots, Dick Leitsch asked Gittings to delete Mattachine New York's name from Reminder materials. Leitsch objected to "a demonstration that pretends to reflect the feelings of all homosexuals while excluding many," including "drag queens, leather queens, and many, many groovy men and women whose wardrobe consists of bell-bottoms, vests, and miles of gilt chains." Mattachine New York went public in its newsletter:

> Led by minions of the shiny-faced middle class, these ultra-sweet displays are almost ultra-straight. . . . A "conservative appearance" is demanded, and to make certain that no scraggly beards, mincing gaits or, God forbid, pants suits or bell bottoms sneak into the line, a 3-man committee will be on hand to "rule off the line those not meeting standards!" MSNY is obviously not supporting this exclusive, non-representative affair. Our bitterness and non-support stem from a few years ago when we took down the bulk of the people who marched that day. Two of our men, both clean, neat and "butch," were excluded from the march . . . because they were "improperly dressed." They were wearing neatly pressed and very clean tan cord slacks and clean, well-pressed, but open at the collar white shirts and no jackets.[9]

Political differences were again inscribed on clothing, but now political fashions had changed.

Although Craig Rodwell shared Leitsch's concerns, he recruited about 50 New York volunteers to participate in the Reminder. In an example of how heterosocial cooperation protected gay men, Rodwell says that four "white rednecks" with "baseball bats" spared the activists as they prepared to depart on their bus because "the presence of women and children took them by surprise; they had expected to see 'just faggots,' and as well-indoctrinated macho men felt they had to desist from a physical attack on 'innocents.' "[10]

Conflict did erupt in Philadelphia. According to *Distant Drummer*, a local leftist newspaper, "the only dispute of the day arose between the marchers themselves—over the issue of holding hands." Challenging an older generation that had been responsible for the Reminders since 1965 was a younger group much affected by recent events. *Drummer*'s reporter wrote that while he was talking to demonstration leaders, "who were in their late 30's or 40's," Rodwell "came running up to tell them that two girls had been ordered not to hold hands while marching." According to one participant, Mattachine Washington's Frank Kameny "slapped their hands" and said, "You can't do that!" *Drummer*, noting that Gittings was 37, quoted her as saying, "There is a time and a place for holding hands. . . . On a picket line—no." Rodwell, age 28, objected: "Our message is that homosexual love is good." Declaring that "there's a generation gap among homosexuals, too," Rodwell and his lover, age 21, began "defiantly marching hand in hand," as did two young female couples.[11]

Holding hands threatened the strategy of respectability that had been central to the Reminders since their inception. Challenging the cultural effeminization of gay men, masculinization of lesbians, and pathologization of lesbian and gay bodies, respectable militants presented idealized images of feminine lesbians, masculine gay men, and heterosocial couples. Unlike Clark Polak, whose imagined single-sex community was founded upon sexual desire, these activists imagined a mixed-sex community founded upon a desexualized social identity. Holding hands proved controversial in part because the moment that two bodies sexed as "the same" touched, the asexual lesbian/gay dyad was revealed to be a strategic construction.

Visibly representing the two lesbian political styles on display at Independence Hall, the *Ladder* featured one photograph of Gittings and another of two women holding hands. Two years earlier, "The Invisible Sorority" had suggested that "no one stares if women show affection in public." To whatever extent this was true in situations not perceived as lesbian, it was untrue in the context of a homophile picket line, particularly when lesbians were inspiring gay men to hold hands as well. In a sense, this context established a boundary between the homosocial and the homosexual for women that was equivalent to the stricter boundary that often existed for men. When Gittings said that there was "a time and a place for holding hands," she was implicitly ascribing a sexual meaning to hand-holding and relegating the sexual to the private sphere. But were the lesbian hand-holders making a sexual statement or were they making visible their identities as lesbians? Or was it both? If it was to make themselves more visible, was this because, as the *Ladder* observed, the 1969 picket featured fewer women than had marched in previous Reminders? And when Rodwell linked hand-holding with "homosexual love," was he defending sexual expression or evoking nonsexual love?[12]

While younger radicals clashed with older homophiles at Independence Hall, the generations were joined in embracing national signs and symbols. In a period in which movements against the Vietnam War and for Black Power raised fundamental questions about the nature of U.S. values, these activists were celebrating the national holiday by taking the liberty of walking together before one of the nation's icons of identity. Activists at the "birthplace of the nation" were claiming what they saw as their rightful place in the United States.

The generational break soon deepened. Not long after the Reminder, young lesbians and gay men in New York founded the Gay Liberation Front (GLF-NY). As Toby Marotta explains, "Unlike *homosexual*, the clinical term bestowed by heterosexuals, and *homophile*, the euphemism coined by cautious political forerunners, *gay*, which homosexuals called each other, was thought to be the word that would most appeal to homosexuals who were thirsting to be known as they knew themselves. Hence also *liberation*, intended to suggest freedom from constraint. *Front* implied a militant vanguard or coalition." Initially, that coalition included lesbians and gay men. By 1970 there were more than a hundred gay liberation groups around the country.[13]

When the Eastern Regional Conference of Homophile Organizations (ERCHO) met in Center City in November 1969, gay liberation had not yet found an institutional vehicle in Philadelphia. So when gay liberationists clashed with homophile activists, Philadelphians, who had been on the cutting edge of their movement for half a decade, were attacked as conservative. As the conference began, liberationists tried to block the reading of a letter from Commissioner Rizzo, who "commended the homosexuals on their conduct during the annual Fourth of July demonstration." On this the radicals failed. But they succeeded when homophile activists challenged the accreditation of GLF-NY and three student groups. Meanwhile, radicals raised objections to the presence of a straight woman from Mattachine New York and to the fact that the conference was being held at My Sister's Place, which they believed to be segregated. (Ada Bello says that this actually was "one of the few female gay bars that had a large number of black women.") Additional conflicts erupted over calls for a boycott of *Gay Power*, a New York newspaper that radicals claimed was "exploiting the gay population for the economic benefit of a straight publisher."[14]

Extended debate focused on the Reminder, antiwar demonstrations, and a human rights statement. Craig Rodwell and Ellen Broidy from New York proposed that the Reminder, "in order to be more relevant, reach a greater number of people and encompass the ideas and ideals of the larger struggle in which we are engaged," be moved and have "no dress or age regulations." To replace the Reminder, they proposed an annual Christopher

Street Liberation Day to commemorate the Stonewall riots. On this proposal, radicals carried the day, winning a unanimous vote with one abstention.[15] The symbolism was clear: the movement's largest annual action would no longer be held on the nation's birthday in the nation's birthplace but would instead mark gay liberation's birthday in its birthplace. As had happened so often in the past, Philadelphia lost pride of place to New York.

Radicals were less successful with their antiwar resolutions. The conference approved, 54–6, a call for those lesbians and gay men taking part in the November antiwar mobilization in Washington, D.C., "to do so as homosexuals." But a resolution calling for ERCHO to endorse the mobilization was defeated, 27–35. According to the Los Angeles *Advocate*, what radicals saw as "an overwhelming moral issue," others thought "extraneous." *Gay Power* noted that "more conservative delegates" argued that "no group of organizations could presume to speak for all homosexuals, since homosexuals, like other people, ranged from the most conservative to the most radical."[16]

Radicals were more successful with their human rights statement, which ERCHO passed as amended:

Resolved, that the Eastern Regional Conference of Homophile Organizations considers these inalienable human rights above and beyond legislation:

1. Dominion over one's own body
   a. through sexual freedom without regard to orientation
   b. through freedom to use birth control and abortion
   c. through freedom to ingest the drugs of one's choice
2. Freedom from society's attempts to define and limit human sexuality, which are inherently manifested in economic, educational, religious, social, personal and legal discrimination
3. Freedom from political and social persecution of all minority groups:
   a. freedom from the institutionalized inequities of the tax structure and the judicial system
   b. freedom and the right of self-determination of all oppressed minority groups in our society
   c. we specifically condemn the systematic and widespread persecution of certain elements of these minorities, including all political prisoners and those accused of crimes without victims

Section 1 passed 39–13, section 2 was approved without objection, and section 3 was adopted, 43–16.[17]

Although the decision to replace the Reminders represented a step away from U.S. iconography, the human rights resolution worked within a familiar national idiom. Mobilizing natural rights discourse from the U.S. Declaration of Independence and Constitution, ERCHO declared these rights "inalienable" and "above and beyond legislation." Claiming dominion over not land but bodies, freedom not from England but from dominant society, and self-determination not for colonies but for minorities, these resolutions sexualized the founding discourses of the United States, deploying them against the state.

Integrating libertarian and minority discourse in new ways, the ERCHO statement contained a fundamental tension that would mark the politics of gay liberation. For while the first section defended "sexual freedom without regard to orientation" and the third aimed at securing freedom for "minority groups," the second sought "freedom from society's attempts to define and limit human sexuality." But were not the concepts of sexual "orientation" and sexual "minorities" a product of "society's attempts to define and limit human sexuality"? While the first and third suggested the existence of a minority whose desires were oriented in particular directions, the second implied the existence of universally polymorphous sexual desires.

Discussing the conference, Bello recalls that GLF-NY's delegates "were convinced that we were worse than reactionary." Kay Lahusen remembers radicals asking HAL, "Where are your women, where are your blacks, where are your American Indians?" She and Gittings laugh when recalling that HAL consisted mainly of women, that a Native American member of HAL was there, and that HAL included "all those flaming Cubans."[18]

After the conference, homophile activists reflected on the issues that divided them from liberationists. "We hear the call, the appealing call, to commit ourselves to alliances with other minorities," Carole Friedman wrote, "to throw in our lot with the radical left, to strive not for equality within the system, but for a new liberty to be obtained by destroying the system." Friedman identified three reasons to reject this. First, "the radical, humanist, libertarian principles and guarantees built into the U.S. Constitution are still viable." Second, the movement needed "every tactic, every person, every idea" it could "command"—"from street people to college professors, from drag queens to Ivy-Leaguers, from Goldwaterites to Trotskyites." Putting "all of our eggs in the radical basket" would "alienate the vast majority of those 15 million homosexuals from their own liberation movement." Third, other minorities "have shown not the least interest in the liberation of the homosexual" and to ally with such groups "would be to allow ourselves to be used as pawns." Not opposed to alliances, Friedman wrote that this should be pursued "as long as, and only if, the other groups make a firm commitment to our cause."[19]

The difficulties of forming such alliances were apparent in the issue that Friedman singled out, military exclusions. Radicals, Friedman observed, say that lesbians and gay men should be "delighted" by such exclusions. "It is our role," she countered, "to achieve for the homosexual the right to decide for himself whether or not he cares to enter the army." HAL also saw conflict between its populist concern for the "majority" and revolutionary rhetoric that could alienate the majority. HAL's leaders sought substantive change but not change that would antagonize the communities they claimed to represent.

With the endorsement of its resolutions by ERCHO, gay liberationists appeared to have won the day. However, as the *Ladder* reported, "conservatives" such as Gittings and Kameny won most of the elections at the conference. Moreover, in early 1970, Friedman wrote that "what appeared to be a firm step towards marriage between the ERCHO and the Left was perhaps little more than an impulsive flirtation." Six of the thirteen groups represented at the conference, including HAL, had dissociated themselves from some of ERCHO's decisions. HAL voted to reject sections 1 and 3 of the rights resolution. In another sign of homophile opposition to gay liberation, toward the end of 1969 Lahusen joined with disenchanted GLF-NY members to form the more moderate Gay Activists Alliance (GAA-NY) in New York.[20]

Looking back, Bello and Friedman say they are not bitter about the conflicts. Bello explains, "We just became obsolete overnight, just from the name. After Stonewall anything called homophile was just ready for the dustbin. So in a way I understand. They were part of the making of the future, except that it was somewhat unpleasant." She adds that at times HAL acted as a "bridge to close the ideological gap," mentioning as an example the fact that HAL members went to antiwar protests but did not carry homophile banners. Friedman remembers that for HAL, "like any old guard that's being superceded, there was friction" and "defensiveness." She says that this was bound to happen "when you've been in a leadership role in defining a social change movement and almost overnight you find yourself in the backseat being called conservative." As she explains, "There was the marrying of these different things: Vietnam, the whole countercultural movement, drugs, feminism, Black Power, Gay Power. Putting that together in an entire context of social revolution. And here we are, the gay kids from Philadelphia, where our most radical thing had been that the boys and girls would get together and ask the Gillette Company what its employment policy was."[21]

Gittings and Lahusen have more negative feelings. Gittings remembers, "Suddenly, here were all these people with absolutely no track record in the movement who were telling us, in effect, not only what we should do, but what we should think. The arrogance of it was what really upset me." Asked whether she favored ending the Fourth of July pickets, Gittings says that she "probably felt a little twinge of regret" but adds, "The handwriting was on the wall. . . . They'd served a wonderful purpose. They'd gone on for five years. They'd been effective. They'd done a lot for the community. But the time was up." Lahusen refers to the "heyday of radical chic" at GLF-NY meetings, where she felt like a "plain Jane dinosaur." "Convinced that this was a Communist or a New Left plot," Lahusen admits that she made "an effort to investigate these people." Referring to DOB's earlier opposition to picketing, Lahusen says, "We found ourselves in the old guard, the way the West Coast people must have felt when we were jumping up and down."[22]

In later years, as the Stonewall riots were constituted as the founding event of the lesbian and gay movement, the Reminders were often forgotten. Few of the millions of people who marched in parades commemorating the riots were aware that the origins of their celebrations lay in a small band of respectable militants who picketed at Independence Hall on five July Fourths in the 1960s. Ironically, Philadelphia's post-Stonewall celebrations have been among the smallest of those held in large U.S. cities.

Drummed Out of Philadelphia

The Reminder is not the only forgotten Philadelphia casualty of 1969. In May, Clark Polak announced the end of *Drum*. On 2 July, the last day of the riots and two days before the Reminder, a postal inspector provided a U.S. attorney with evidence that Polak was mailing obscene ads. Nine days later, Polak was found guilty on local charges of displaying obscene films and was fined $550. Around this time, one of Polak's bookstores was torn down because of a redevelopment project. On the brighter side for Polak, lawyer Norman Oshtry, arguing against assistant district attorney Edward Rendell, successfully appealed Polak's contempt conviction before the Pennsylvania Supreme Court.[23]

On 23 October 1969, a federal grand jury returned an 18-count indictment charging Polak with mailing obscene ads, films, and publications. The following day, Polak was arrested and released on bail. In January 1970, Oshtry told assistant U.S. attorney Thomas McBride that Polak "may possibly be interested in the Government's feeling as to a guilty plea and probation term with the provisions that he actually goes out of the mail order business." Meanwhile, the Department of Justice concluded that Polak would be "an ideal target for a test case" to affirm its contention that "commercial advertisements are not protected by the first amendment."[24]

On 19 February 1970, Polak was indicted by a federal grand jury on 21 counts of mailing "obscene, lewd, lascivious, indecent, filthy and vile" ads.

Later that day, McBride and eight postal inspectors removed from Polak's offices approximately 250,000 brochures, 300,000 envelopes, a mailing list of 75,000 names, business records, and office machines. According to a postal report, Polak "had to be restrained by his attorney from abusing the inspectors with obscenities." Oshtry later argued that this "massive" search and seizure "wiped out the defendant's business" and had a "staggering impact on the exercise of First Amendment freedoms." A few days after the raid, Oshtry again told McBride that Polak was "considering liquidating his operation."[25]

On 27 February, U.S. District Court Judge Thomas Masterson ordered police to return the "instrumentalities" seized. At a hearing the next month, Masterson declared that the government's argument concerning the "non-obscene material" was "extremely dangerous because a projection of it would be if a man utters an obscenity you could seize his voice box." As for the ads themselves, Masterson declared that although he was sympathetic to the "attempt to control this sewer effluent" and believed that Polak's ads would "meet any test of obscenity," he opposed the government's methods because there had been no prior adversary determination of obscenity. On 30 April 1970, the District Court thus ordered the remainder of Polak's materials returned.[26]

Meanwhile, Polak had placed a series of ads in the New York–based *Screw, Gay,* and the *Los Angeles Free Press* announcing "Trojan's going back into business sale." *Screw* had been one of the few publications to defend Polak after his indictment, noting that "Clark, in spite of the fact that he appears to be one of the most tactless, grubby, and obnoxious characters we've ever known, has a heart of gold. When issues are at stake and people are in trouble, Clark has been known to dole out dollars (in the thousands) to freedom's cause." The ads declared, "Trojan Book Service threw a fire and everybody burned!!! Where were you at 2:30 in the afternoon on February 19th?" (This was the day that Polak's offices had been raided.) According to the ad, "miraculously, all of our stock of paperbacks, male nudist magazines, gay movies and other specialty items was saved."[27]

While Polak attempted to save his business, other Janus members tried to salvage the organization. In July 1969, Polak's lawyer Gil Cantor wrote to Richard Schlegel in response to Schlegel's request to use Janus resources to conduct an election. Cantor responded that the materials "will not be made available." Circumventing Polak, Schlegel then wrote to Janus members and subscribers on behalf of "the interim board," noting that the letter discontinuing *Drum* "did not represent the feelings of the founding members of the Society." New elections were planned and a new publication, *PACE!* magazine, would "fill the void left by *Drum*'s death." *PACE!*'s first issue, dated January 1970, noted that the title was drawn from the same Thoreau passage that *Drum*'s had been: "If a man does not keep pace with his companions, perhaps it is because he hears a different drummer." Schlegel recalls that after it became clear that Janus was finished, James Mitchell came up with the name for a new group, Philadelphia Action Committee for Equality (PACE). In addition to publishing a magazine, PACE sponsored "That Guy '70," a "sportswear and swimwear competition" emceed by Henri David at the Center City Holiday Inn.[28]

PACE!'s two issues looked like *Drum* but featured "more of a bisexual tone." Schlegel's first editorial explained that "*PACE!* is meant to throw the first rope-bridge, albeit weak and tenuous, over the societal abyss between the homosexual and the heterosexual worlds." He described this "chasm" as "a vast wasteland between the two sexual poles, where there has been precious little interaction." *Drum*'s message had been "beamed to, and received by, only homosexuals" and its "impact on the heterosexual world—across the chasm—was negligible." *PACE!* aimed to replace the "rope-bridge" with a "larger and stronger steel span, with easy two-way traffic."[29]

What kind of "two-way traffic" did the former state transportation official hope to promote? Schlegel remembers that he wanted to "merge the male and female nudie demand." Asked whether the intended audience was male, Schlegel responds, "I didn't draw that line in my mind, but I'm sure it was there. I saw, felt no kinship whatsoever with the females, other than to show the female nude." In other words, nude female photographs would attract straight men, whose "sexual poles" might then "interact" with gay men's. Bisexuality in *PACE!* was a vehicle to encourage straight and gay men to come together. Slowed down by marketing and advertising obstacles and damaged by the bankruptcy of its distributor, that vehicle stopped running in 1971.[30]

Meanwhile, sometime in early 1970, Polak left for California with Mitchell. Traveling across the country, the two had what Schlegel remembers as a "spat" at the Grand Canyon. Mitchell later wrote that when they split, Polak gave him *Swinger* magazine to do with as he pleased. Mitchell came back to Philadelphia, where he operated Jay's Place II bookstore.[31]

The return of Polak's materials in 1970 did not mean that federal charges against him had been dropped. In February 1972, Polak changed his plea to no contest. According to Oshtry, Polak was "worn out." Having decided to "get out of the business" and move to California, Polak allowed Oshtry to arrange a plea bargain in which Polak would receive probation and agree to abandon his pornography businesses. Against the objection of the assistant U.S. attorney, Judge Masterson accepted the plea, fined Polak $5,000, and placed him on probation for five years.[32]

Polak's Philadelphia story ends here, but in California he helped found and support the Stonewall Democratic Club, the ACLU Gay Rights Chapter, and the International Gay and Lesbian Archives. He also ran an art gallery, wrote art criticism, and made a second fortune in real estate. According to the *National Gay Archives Bulletin*, toward the end of his life Polak "invested his emotions in rough hustlers" and "got into street drugs." In 1980, he committed suicide, leaving behind one last controversy—which of two wills that he had written should be honored. An earlier one, dated 1970, left his assets, which were valued at more than two million dollars, to his family. A later one, which was drafted in 1976 but which Oshtry thinks never was completed, left more than half of his estate to lesbian and gay community groups. According to this will, Polak wanted his money to further his life's work serving the lesbian and gay community. He specifically stated that his trustees should not exclude any portion of that community, including lesbians, leather queens, drag queens, hustlers, pedophiles, and others considered undesirable. Declaring that he wanted to return his money from whence it came, he also indicated that he did not want any public acknowledgment for these contributions. The earlier will was honored.[33]

Homophile Action

In the immediate aftermath of Stonewall, then, of the two main strategies developed by Philadelphia homophile activists in the 1960s—militant respectability and sexual liberationism—only the former survived in strong, institutionalized form. For a time after Stonewall, HAL continued to attract predominantly lesbian members, but in 1970 more gay men joined. In their 1972 book *Lesbian/Woman*, DOB founders Del Martin and Phyllis Lyon described HAL as "practically the only group still functioning which has managed to achieve an even membership of men and women." They attributed this to the fact that HAL was "started by women: they were the majority and *then* the men were let in."[34]

According to Barbara Gittings, HAL began attracting men when it started to publicize its activities by leafleting in bars and cruising areas. Two active new members were "Jerry Curtis" and Rick Rosen. In 1970, Curtis was a 27-year-old Air Force veteran who had served in Vietnam. Rosen was a 22-year-old who had come to Philadelphia to go to Penn. Rosen recalls that he first learned about HAL when he was leaving the P.B.L. club one night and encountered activists distributing fliers.[35]

One of HAL's new lesbian members was Rosalie Davies. Like Ada Bello and Carole Friedman, Davies was politically active before she joined the lesbian and gay movement. Born into a lower-middle-class Celtic family in England in 1939, Davies emigrated to Montreal with her husband in the 1950s. There, she recalls, she had two lesbian relationships and got to know the lesbian bar scene. After moving with her husband and two children to New York and then Philadelphia in the late 1960s, Davies learned about HAL from a lesbian partner. While noting that she had been involved in the antiwar movement and the left in the past, she says that getting involved with HAL changed her life and gave her the "courage" to leave her husband.[36]

Davies, Gittings, Lahusen, and Bello agree that women and men worked well together in HAL. According to Davies, men did not take control, as they often did in mixed-sex groups. Pointing to Byrna Aronson as an example of a lesbian who had socialized with gay men and knew how to deal with them, Davies says that HAL's lesbians "were extremely strong women."

> Ironically, no, there weren't going to be the problems in HAL that traditionally happened where the lesbians left the organization because the men weren't fair to women. 'Cause no one was unfair to these women. Jerry and George didn't have a prayer with them. Not that Jerry and George weren't strong men. I'm not saying they weren't. They were. But even though they were strong men (Jerry was a perfect example of someone who'd engage in what I call cock fighting with some other group), he couldn't have run it over Marilyn or Byrna.

According to Harry Langhorne, Aronson and George Bodamer often functioned as a "pair" and a "team" on HAL projects.[37] Historical links between lesbianism and masculinity could promote equality between lesbians and gay men and even support a localized reversal of traditional sex hierarchies.

After Stonewall, homophile activists hoped to expand their movement beyond the small numbers that had been involved. Toward this end, in April 1970 HAL began hosting public forums at the First Unitarian Church in Center City. The first, featuring a lecture by Frank Kameny titled "The Homosexual versus the Federal Government," attracted 85–100 people. The *Daily News* described the audience as "men, women, young, old, white, black." The second, "Gay Problems in Philadelphia," had an audience of 125. The third, "Homosexuals and Politics," drew about 90.[38]

Referring to the difficulties that HAL encountered in trying to attract more members, Friedman wrote in the newsletter that "one would never guess that we are but 90 miles from New York." Noting that several gay bars did not allow HAL activists to leaflet indoors, Friedman complained that when the group did so outside the bars, "too many of our own people laughed ('You mean *we're* organizing now?'); too many of our own people denied the realities of their lives ('Problems? *I* don't have any problems.'); too many of our own people turned away in fear ('No thanks, I don't want one. Good luck to you—but I sure as hell won't be there!')." Bello remembers the "apathy of the bar crowd." HAL activists, who had used populist rhetoric in speaking up for "the vast majority" of lesbians and gay men at the ERCHO conference, now were at odds with the many members of their communities who had different "realities." Social movement strategies were still in conflict with the everyday strategies favored by most lesbians and gay men.[39]

At HAL's third forum, Friedman urged those assembled to "be committed to the entire gay community," "work for change in the political system," and "discuss alternatives to bars." Shortly thereafter, HAL organized a gay dance at St. Mary's Episcopal Church on the Penn campus. Three years before, Bello and Friedman had fought to make DOB a "political" rather than a "social" group. Now, inspired by gay dances in New York, HAL attempted to politicize the social and transform the social basis of politics. HAL's first dance, held in July 1970, was an astonishing success, attracting 400–500 people. According to the *Bulletin*, the crowd, mostly under age 30, was "evenly divided between black and white, with more men than women." Writing about the event, Rosen contrasted "a bar filled with frightened, angry, sex objects" with a dance that had "all kinds of happy people."[40]

By early 1971, HAL had held five dances at St. Mary's and each had drawn 300–500 people. HAL members noted that discrimination had forced lesbians and gay men into "ghettos—in housing, in gay bars." But bars were "dreary, expensive places," and "for kids under 21, there was no place to go." Dances provided an alternative. According to the *Daily Pennsylvanian*, most of the people at the dances were teenagers and most were African Americans: " 'It's not that blacks turn out," one woman observed. " 'It's that whites don't. Black people have been scared for years, and are coming out. Black kids put themselves on the line every time they step out of the house.' For whites the resolution comes harder, and for older whites bars are a more private, protected place than public dances."[41]

HAL's dances were the first activities organized by the local lesbian and gay movement to attract substantial numbers of African Americans. In part, this reflected successful publicity and the popular appeal of dances. Also, St. Mary's was a progressive church, which may have been perceived as more welcoming than the downtown clubs, hotels, and offices where previous homophile events had been held. Moreover, St. Mary's was located in West Philly, a more racially mixed neighborhood than Center City, where most homophile activities had taken place. In a sense, Euro-American lesbians and gay men were moving out of a sexual "ghetto" and organizing activities that did not require African American lesbians and gay men to move out of a racial "ghetto." And they were doing so at a moment when African Americans in various cities were taking leading roles in gay liberation. In terms of youth, while respectable activists had often excluded young people out of concerns about popular associations between same-sex sexualities and child molestation, HAL's dances welcomed minors. Because the city's African American population was younger than its Euro-American population, this also contributed to the African American presence.

HAL's leaders were pleased about the new interest but unprepared for the increased diversity. According to Gittings, HAL temporarily stopped sponsoring dances because of problems related to the people the group had so successfully attracted: "There was simply too much shit work involved in running these and cleaning up after some rather rowdy people who started to come in from parts of the city." She adds, "We really worked hard to get the word out throughout the city. And unfortunately, some very rough types began to come with knives in their pants. And we almost had a couple of fights. . . . Another bad element was that drag queens came and used the women's toilet room and left it a mess."[42] Given the degree of class, racial, and ethnic segregation in Philadelphia, Gittings's references to people who came from "parts of the city," along with her comments about drag queens, suggest that it would not be easy for an organization led by middle-class Euro-Americans to organize a mass movement representing all lesbian and gay constituencies.

HAL's work in this era took place in the context of a national upsurge in lesbian and gay political activity. HAL welcomed "with pride" the formation of GLF-NY and reported on the creation of GAA New York, PACE, the Gay Union League of Philadelphia, GLF Philadelphia, the Philadelphia Christian Homophile Church, Le-Hi-Ho in the Lehigh Valley, Mattachine Pittsburgh, and the Gay Rights Organization of Wilkes-Barre, Scranton. In 1970, HAL marched in the first Christopher Street Liberation Day parade in New York. According to Gittings, HAL carried "the most beautiful banner."[43]

While HAL worked to organize and politicize lesbians and gay men, it also challenged other popular and professional audiences. In 1970, it began a "campaign for equality" by placing stickers on subways, trains, and car bumpers that read, "The person standing next to you may be a homosexual. Why isn't he free?" Gittings, Aronson, and Curtis filled a busy schedule of public speaking. Gittings joined the American Library Association's Task Force on Gay Liberation in 1970, helped plan a "Hug-a-Homosexual" booth at the librarians' 1971 conference in Dallas, and became coordinator of the task force that same year. Around this time, she also took a leading role in the fight against the American Psychiatric Association's classification of homosexuality as an illness. In 1972, she and Frank Kameny organized an exhibit called "Gay, Proud, and Healthy: The Homosexual Community Speaks" at the association's meeting in Dallas. She also spoke on a panel on homosexuality at the meeting, as did "Dr. Anonymous," a masked psychiatrist from Philadelphia. Meanwhile, continuing its "program

Figure 11.2. Homophile Action League members at the Christopher Street Liberation Day march in New York City, 1970. Photograph by Kay Tobin Lahusen. With the permission of Kay Tobin Lahusen.

of answering unfavorable articles in the media," HAL wrote critical letters to authors and editors and published reviews in its newsletter. While "Ellen Collins" continued to sign HAL's letters, in January 1970 Bello and Friedman began using their names in the newsletter, as did Aronson when she became editor in September. By April 1970, the newsletter was available at Jay's Place II and five other Center City bookstores.[44]

While hostile media practices continued with articles that linked same-sex sexualities to crime and violence, and with policies that rejected ads that referred to lesbians or gay men, activists succeeded in making 1970 a year of major media breakthroughs.[45] In April, Tom Fox's *Daily News* column, titled "The Rights of Homosexuals," focused on the "very pretty" Carole, who preferred "emotional, affectual and sexual relationships" with other women, before summarizing Kameny's HAL lecture, which criticized antigay government policies. According to Fox, Carole "has enough looks and body to attract the guys, but the guys mean nothing to Carole because she is a homosexual." Describing local "homosexuals" as "caught up in the nationwide drive for equality," he wrote that many were wearing buttons that read "Gay Is Good" or "Love Is a Many-Gendered Thing." Although

Fox's column emphasized what straight men might find attractive in Carole and missed the fact that "guys" like Kameny did mean something to women like Carole, it featured both a lesbian and a gay man, presented their views in a favorable light, and accepted their claims to speak on behalf of lesbians and gay men.[46]

Three months later, William Speers's *Inquirer* column, titled "Brace Yourself for Another Revolt—The Gay Liberation," addressed "Mr. and Mrs. Straight":

> You say you recently bent your mind just enough to cope with the Black Revolution. And the neighbor's freaky kid feeds sparrows so you're thinking that maybe hippies aren't all that bad. And now you're ready to see what those bitchy Women's Lib types are all about. Well, hold onto your proclivities, Mr. and Mrs. Straight, your psyche is about to be rumbled by bigotry's last frontier—Gay Liberation has arrived.

According to Speers, at least four new groups "intent on achieving equal rights for homosexuals" had been formed in Philadelphia. Focusing on younger "gays," Speers noted that "they prefer that term to homosexual, which is too clinical, or queer, which is equivalent to nigger." This generation was "no longer satisfied with life in the ghettos of bathhouses and bars" and preferred events such as the "homosexual dinner dance" held at the Holiday Inn in June. Emphasizing that "leaders of the movement (most of them women) view such events as political, as well as, social actions," Speers depicted lesbian and gay leaders fighting together on behalf of their communities for a just cause.[47]

On the same day, Hans Knight's *Bulletin* article, " 'Other Society' Moves into the Open," began by declaring that "homosexuals are sick" but immediately explained that they were "sick of wearing masks," sick of being "called queers, faggots and fairies," sick of being "labeled criminals," and sick of being "barred from federal jobs and the armed forces." Focusing on activists, Knight wrote that while HAL posters decorated "walls and tree trunks on Philadelphia university campuses," the new local GLF was passing out pamphlets in Center City and the HLRS was "raising thousands of dollars." Although he noted that "only a fraction of the homosexual population—estimates run from 4 to 10 percent" was "organized," he reported that one activist told him, "The point is that at least some of us are coming out of the closets." Writing that "success in the straight world tends to spoil the homosexual for the militant movement," Knight quoted Clark Polak as saying, "We are a threat to the closet homosexual who has it made in business because he's afraid to stick his neck out." In the "Other Society," activists courageously acted on behalf of their communities.[48]

While Knight cited psychiatrist Samuel Hadden's description of homosexuality as an illness, he also presented Penn psychiatrist Harold Lief's "more sanguine view." While he quoted Rizzo as saying that entrapment was no longer practiced and that police did not "bother" homosexuals unless they were a "public nuisance," he also presented Aronson's statement that she had been arrested for "just walking on the street" and a gay man's claim that he had been arrested for making "a pass at another guy" on Locust. While he wrote that "most homosexuals questioned" agreed that Philadelphia was "pretty tolerant," he also referred to Gittings's criticisms of the church, Kameny's struggles against the state, and Polak's call for "Gay Power." Knight's final words were Aronson's: " 'There is only one gay problem,' she said, softly. 'The problem—no offense—is you.' " In a departure from previous patterns, journalistic "balance" was now weighted toward the lesbian and gay side, activists weighed in heavily, and lesbians and gay men tipped the scales together.

While "The Furtive Fraternity" and "The Invisible Sorority" had considered gay men and lesbians separately, these three articles presented them together. While the 1962 and 1967 exposés focused on gay and lesbian community life, the 1970 articles highlighted the movement. While the "Fraternity" portrayed lesbians as gay men's partners in politics and the "Sorority" depicted the failure of lesbian politics to thrive in the absence of gay men, these three articles returned lesbians to political partnership with gay men and extended the partnership to the social sphere. While the "Fraternity" focused on gay men and the "Sorority" used gay men as a standard of comparison for lesbians, these articles concentrated on lesbians as much as gay men and were largely uninterested in comparisons. Fox, Speers, and Knight presented heroic narratives of allied lesbian and gay activists struggling against dominant cultures and conservative elements within their own communities. In other words, after years of homophile challenges to mainstream media, these articles presented many aspects of HAL's image of itself, an image of heterosocial militant respectability.

While HAL continued to fight media prejudice, the group also struggled against economic and legal discrimination. Before Stonewall, HAL had agreed to conduct a survey on employment discrimination for ERCHO. In March 1970, in a *HAL Newsletter* editorial "On Economic Independence for Gays," Friedman noted that HAL had written to 500 major companies. Of these, only 20 replied, and only one, Bantam Books, "answered unequivocally that the sexual orientation of applicants and employees was completely irrelevant to their suitability for employment and promotion." Several said that "they would employ homosexuals as long as no one knew they were homosexuals." One company said that it would employ homosexuals but requested that HAL not publicize this; Friedman promised, "We will, very shortly."[49]

Friedman's conclusion was that homosexuals needed employment counselors more than psychiatrists and fair employment acts more than mental health ones. She argued that "the one overriding problem we homosexuals face is economic, not emotional, for most of us are financially secure only to the degree that we hide our sexual orientation from our employers." For the future, Friedman recommended "emancipation of homosexuals from economic dependence." On the one hand, activists had to "develop gay capitalism," which could be done by supporting self-employment and "encouraging gay businessmen to hire gays" and "gay consumers to support them." On the other hand, activists had to challenge "laws and customs which deny us equal employment opportunities." Influenced by discussions of African American economics, Friedman hoped to promote gay capitalism while simultaneously integrating open lesbians and gay men into the mainstream economy.

HAL also lobbied for law reform. With the help of the ACLU (Aronson's new employer), HAL focused on two goals: extending Philadelphia's Human Relations Act to prohibit discrimination on the basis of sexual orientation and repealing state sodomy and sodomy solicitation laws. In mid-1970, the group circulated a petition calling on Philadelphia city councilman David Cohen to introduce legislation prohibiting employment and housing discrimination against homosexuals. The petition also asked Cohen to help end police harassment and repeal "laws prohibiting the solicitation for and participation in private homosexual acts between consenting adults."[50]

In August 1970, Gittings, representing HAL, spoke before the Democratic and Republican state platform committees at the Bellevue Stratford Hotel and called for the repeal of these laws and the passage of a sexual orientation amendment to the state Human Rights Act. Gittings testified that there were about 700,000 adult members of Pennsylvania's "invisible minority" who were "forced to 'wear a mask because of their sexual preferences.' " In September, Jerry Curtis, representing HAL, the Gay Union League, Le-Hi-Ho, and Mattachine Pittsburgh, registered as a lobbyist in the state legislature. Donn Teal reports that by late summer in 1970, "American gays had two state lobbyists for homosexual rights"—Robert Vain of Delaware (who had been affiliated with HLRS) and Curtis of HAL.[51]

HAL also entered the arena of electoral politics. Late in 1969, HAL conducted a survey of candidates in Pennsylvania, New Jersey, and Delaware, asking them to indicate their views on laws and policies concerning homosexuality. In what HAL regarded as "an indication that much work needs to be done to impress candidates with the size and strength of the homosexual bloc," only one candidate responded. Judge Paul Dandridge, who was running for municipal court judge in Pennsylvania, declared that he favored "revising the penal code to legalize private, consensual, adult homosexual and heterosexual acts" and "extending state laws and policies which are designed to protect groups from discrimination to include the homosexual minority." Ironically, Dandridge had been the judge in Polak's February 1969 conviction. When Dandridge won, HAL claimed that he was elected "in part through our diligent efforts to publicize his favorable views." However, HAL acknowledged with a joke that the results had not convinced anyone of the power of their voting bloc: "We consider it further demonstration of Gay Power that no one saw fit to oppose Mr. Dandridge." HAL was also disappointed when none of the candidates invited to its forum on "Homosexuals and Politics" appeared.[52]

If candidates would not come to HAL, HAL would go to candidates. At a League of Women Voters forum, Gittings recalls, HAL members asked gubernatorial candidate Milton Shapp a question. "Liberal as he was," she remembers, "he didn't come on strong enough on the gay issue" and Marilyn Sauers and Jerry Curtis went up to the stage at the end of the forum and "they nabbed him before he could get away from the podium and they really gave it to him." "One of our women members," she notes, "actually collared Milton Shapp on the stage when he refused to answer the questions."[53] As 1970 ended, heterosocial militant respectability had survived the Stonewall challenge.

Lavender Menace

On 1 May 1970, as 300–400 women sat in a New York auditorium waiting for the second Congress to Unite Women to begin, the lights suddenly went out. When they were turned on a few moments later, 17–20 women wearing lavender t-shirts with the words "Lavender Menace" stenciled in red were standing. "The lavender menace" is what feminist Betty Friedan had called lesbians. According to Alice Echols, "for two hours the protestors held the floor as they talked about what it was like to be a lesbian in a heterosexist culture." Later, the congress adopted resolutions proposed by the group of protesters, which called itself the Lavender Menace: Gay Liberation Front Women and Radical Lesbians. The resolutions proudly declared that women's liberation *was* "a lesbian plot" and that lesbianism should be affirmed when the women's movement or individual women were attacked as lesbian.[54]

At least one member of HAL, B. B., attended the second day of the congress, reporting in the *HAL Newsletter* that she had gone "to relate gay liberation to women's liberation." Describing GLF-NY's lesbian workshop as "the most popular" of the afternoon, B. B. noted that about two-thirds of the women present were straight. She praised the "sisters" who "seized the opportunity to educate many straight women, to tear down prejudice and to accomplish effective consciousness raising among many of the gay women." Although the straight women were "curious, hypocritical and superstitious, even openly hostile," B. B. believed that they came to realize that "the sexist repression they all ostensibly fought was indeed the very same social force that they used against their gay sisters." Although she endorsed the GLF-NY women's "theatrical techniques," B. B. also was critical:

> Some of us were put off by the fantastic aggressiveness and amateurish arguments implemented by the G.L.F. women; for example: "The only way any of you straight women will be liberated is by breaking off all relationships with men" and "everyone knows men are threatened by dikes because they are better lovers than men will ever be." Someone replied forlornly that, alas, it was *not* true, she had had lousy lovers of both sexes.

Allied with gay men, HAL members were not likely to endorse "breaking off all relationships with men." Still, B. B. concluded that GLF-NY "effected an offensive with pride, dignity and humor."[55]

Although HAL's newsletter did not give the Lavender Menace as much attention as it gave the Stonewall riots, radical lesbian feminism proved to be as important a revolution as gay liberation. Although radical lesbian feminism did not take organized form in Philadelphia until 1971, in 1969 and 1970 HAL strengthened its links with feminism. In late 1969, HAL's newsletter began taking the kinds of feminist positions that Bello and Friedman had called for in "The Masculine-Feminine Mystique." For example, although Ralph Weltge's collection *The Same Sex* included an essay by Barbara Gittings, Ada Bello and Carole Friedman criticized the book because "*The Same Sex* deals too much with only one sex." Responding to Roger Mitchell's *The Homosexual and the Law*, Friedman wrote, "Our friends in Daughters of Bilitis might want to take note of one huge area of ignorance, illustrated by the simple declarative sentence on page 10: 'There is no Mattachine Society for lesbians.' Go get 'em, sisters!" Attacking an *Esquire* article, Bello objected to the "complete omission of the Lesbian" and asked, "Does Mr. Burke not realize that male chauvinism, like Judy Garland's songs, is on the way out?" In a review of *Sticks and Stones*, a film about Fire Island, Bello wrote, "From the Lesbian point of view the film does have one deficiency: it was shot with a clear preference for guys and the male body. To compensate for this one-sided view there is only one solution: Lesbian, get thee behind a camera."[56]

HAL's feminism was influenced by local as well as national developments. In March 1970, the *Bulletin*'s Kitsi Burkhart surveyed the local feminist scene, highlighting a chapter of NOW, more than a dozen women's liberation groups, the Women's Caucus of People for Human Rights, the Abortion Rights Association, and Marxist study groups. While these were mostly "white and middle class," Burkhart mentioned three predominantly African American groups (the women's caucus of the Black Economic Development Council, the Women's Rights Organization, and the women of the Welfare Rights Organization) and one mixed-race group (Sojourner Truth Disciples). On 7 March 1970, to celebrate International Women's Day, "the presence of the Women's Liberation Movement in Philadelphia" was announced in a "guerilla action" organized by the Women's International Conspiracy from Hell (WITCH). Founded in New York in 1968 and inspired by the Yippies, WITCH women in Philadelphia "liberated" Pauline's Bridal Shop, Wanamaker's, and Roamans by circling around a bride in chains who "moan[ed] piteously from the oppression of monogamy and the nuclear family."[57]

About two weeks later, three HAL members met with a women's liberation group for what Friedman described as a "rewarding evening of mutual education and a tentative exploration of the possible relationships between the movements for the liberation of women and of gays." According to Friedman, "We recognized our common burdens stemming from the attitudes and institutionalization of sexism in this society, while also recognizing that the specific situations and obstacles facing women and gay people often are at variance, even conflict, with each other, and that each of our groups must devote its energies primarily to the liberation of our own people." The participants "agreed that it would be valuable to seek out those issues which are of concern to both groups and to work together on such an issue-oriented basis."[58] Friedman's language suggests that HAL lesbians still considered themselves gay first, women second.

Two days later, on 21 March, a HAL member attended a women's liberation conference at the Penn Christian Association. *Women*, the "Newsletter of the Philadelphia Area Women's Liberation Movement," self-critically noted that "the fact that a workshop on homosexuality was organized only at the last minute reflects an overwhelming heterosexual bias (blindness?) on our part." Friedman reported that about 50 of the more than 450 women attending the conference heard the HAL representative speak in two workshops, one of which was the session mentioned by *Women*. In the first, "many women who had never before thought seriously about the position of homosexuals in this society, and several others who were aware of their fears of being called 'dykes' because of their involvement in Women's Lib were positively reached." The second, organized by a "gay woman" from New

York, attracted 15 participants and brought together the two types of women who were forming lesbian feminist groups across the country—women who had been lesbians before they joined the women's movement and women who became lesbians through the women's movement. According to *Women*, some women "spoke of their complete rejection of any relationships with men," while others "spoke of their newly found sense of sisterhood with all women, resulting from their involvement in women's liberation, and their puzzlement, worry or optimism in dealing with an accompanying desire for physical closeness." Friedman concluded that "these contacts offer the promise of deepening the Women's Lib people's commitment to uniting with *all* of their sisters.[59]

By the time B. B. traveled to the Congress to Unite Women in May, then, HAL had established links with women's liberationists. These bonds offered the local lesbian and gay movement its first significant new allies since it had gained the support of civil libertarians in the early 1960s. They also offered analyses of sexism and feminism, the first new ways of conceiving of lesbian and gay oppression and resistance since homophile leaders had woven together minority and libertarian discourse. In June 1970, Friedman's article, "From a Gay Sister," was published in *Women*. Friedman argued that "women and gay people—both those who are women and those who happen to be of that other gender—share a common enemy." That enemy was "sexism." Together, she declared, "we battle . . . pernicious assumptions and prescriptions which seek to define what a woman is, what a man is, and how people should relate to each other both within and across the gender groupings." But, she continued, "we cannot simply and naively join forces without cognizance of our differences." "The rhetoric of sisterhood," she added, "moving and beautiful though it is, will not suffice. . . . Straight women must divest themselves of the heterosexual chauvinism this society fosters. . . . If gay women are not included in the 'sisterhood,' then that word is a sham and your movement . . . a failure."[60]

In the coming months, HAL continued to define its relationship to the women's movement. In July, the Women's Liberation Center's coordinating committee agreed to share its space at 9th and Chestnut with HAL. Just a few months earlier, HAL had joined with NOW, Women United for Abortion Rights, and 13 consciousness-raising groups to establish the center, which was located above a downtown "dirty bookstore." According to *Women*, while some center women "maintained that it could only hurt us to associate ourselves with a group with an even worse press than we have," the majority agreed that "it was definitely in our interests to forge a bond between gay and straight people." (Early in 1971, because of a "security problem," HAL moved its office to a West Philly home shared by five members while the center moved to a new location in West Philly.) On 26 August 1970, HAL ran a booth at the Women's Rights Day demonstration in Rittenhouse Square. In November, HAL and a group of women's liberationists attended and criticized a lecture on homosexuality at the Medical College of Pennsylvania.[61]

Although HAL's turn to feminism was unmistakable, there were limits to its enthusiasm. In June 1970, Kay Lahusen praised GAA New York for its single-issue focus, writing, "When I come in there I don't bring in my women's lib-type grievances." She contrasted this with one of the HAL forums: "All these issues intruded themselves: 'What are encounter groups?' 'How 'bout women's lib?' 'Should all oppressed people hang together?' They were discussing everything else except how to get ahead with gay problems in Philadelphia!" According to a report by Lahusen, Gittings declared at a July forum in New York that "she parts company with those lesbians who feel that somehow the two causes (the gay and the feminist) can be fought together. She said the one is based on gender, the other on orientation." Referring to HAL's female majority as an "historical accident," Gittings claimed that HAL's women had taken advantage of the situation "to show male homosexuals that they are both in the same boat." While she acknowledged that "women had feminist work to do within the gay movement, turning men's heads around, insisting that they be treated as equals," she concluded that "if gay men and women don't get together and fight the gay cause, nobody else is going to do it for us." Donn Teal noted in his 1971 book *The Gay Militants* that while lesbians across the country were "joining forces in independent groups and independent caucuses within co-ed groups," "members of such mixed militant organizations as Philadelphia's Homophile Action League, more than half women," were pursuing an "opposite tactic," giving "first priority to rights for all homosexuals" and "dissociating themselves from all other movements, including women's lib."[62] As had been the case when it responded to gay liberation, HAL changed when it encountered lesbian feminism but did not accept many of the fundamental tenets of the new political orientation.

Like most other homophile groups, HAL would not long survive the challenge of gay liberation and radical lesbian feminism. In 1970, a younger, more radical, and more racially mixed group of gay men rejected HAL and formed Gay Liberation Front in Philadelphia. In 1971, HAL's more feminist lesbians turned to Philadelphia's new Radicalesbians. Then again, Philadelphia's GLF and Radicalesbians would not survive for long either. And after these three groups disappeared and new ones replaced them, the politics of militant respectability, which had been shaped in the pre-Stonewall world, lived on as the dominant tendency in lesbian and gay activism, as it still does.

12

Gay Liberation in the "Birthplace of the Nation," 1970–1971

> Homosexual love is the most complete form of expression between two members of the same sex. Philadelphia Gay Liberation Front is struggling to build self-liberating alternatives to society's channeling and limiting of sexual, personal, and political energies. Our fight against homosexual oppression is one with the revolutionary struggle of all oppressed peoples for life, liberty, and the pursuit of happiness.
>
> GAY LIBERATION FRONT, C. JUL. 1970[1]

In the aftermath of the Stonewall riots and the Lavender Menace, a new generation of leftist, countercultural, and feminist gay men and lesbians in Philadelphia created two new political groups in 1970–1971: Gay Liberation Front and Radicalesbians. Rejecting the politics of militant respectability, these activists adopted the strategies of gay liberation and lesbian feminism. Although GLF was overwhelmingly male and significantly multiracial and Radicalesbians was exclusively female and predominantly Euro-American, the two groups' members shared many beliefs that set them apart from homophile activists. For example, while HAL thought of lesbians and gay men as a sexual minority, GLF and Radicalesbians rejected minoritarian conceptions and argued instead that same-sex desires were universal. GLF's statement of purpose viewed "homosexual love" not as the love of two homosexuals but as "the most complete form of expression" between any two people of the "same sex." While lesbian feminists challenged the boundaries that separated straight women and lesbians, gay liberationists challenged the boundaries that separated straight and gay men.

GLF and Radicalesbians in Philadelphia defined themselves not only in opposition to the homophile movement but also in relation to the gay liberation and lesbian feminist groups that formed elsewhere. While race and sex divisions in GLF-NY led to the founding of Third World Gay Revolution and Radicalesbians in New York, GLF Philadelphia was antiracist and multiracial from the start, embraced feminism, and helped create the local Radicalesbians. As had been the case in the 1960s, Philadelphia gay and lesbian activists in the 1970s were influenced by developments elsewhere, but chose their own paths.[2]

GLF and Radicalesbians also defined themselves in relation to one another. Engaging in partially parallel projects, gay liberationists and lesbian feminists did not always cooperate or get along. While both movements were feminist and antiracist, their relationships to feminism and antiracism differed. Still, gay liberation and lesbian feminism influenced one another. Moreover, they shared the conviction that men and women were profoundly different. Challenging many traditional conceptions of masculinity and femininity, gay liberationists and lesbian feminists reinforced many traditional conceptions of maleness and femaleness. These would not be revolutions to overthrow the categories male and female; the revolutions of GLF and Radicalesbians depended upon them.

Gay Liberation Front

At a May 1970 HAL forum, Kiyoshi Kuromiya and Basil O'Brien asked that announcements be made about the formation of a gay liberation group. A short time later, about 50 people gathered at Gazoo, a gay collective store on South Street. Soon GLF was meeting weekly in the countercultural South Street neighborhood, drawing support from a mailing list of more than 250 names and drawing attention from three local leftist newspapers, the *Free Press*, *Plain Dealer* (which became *Gay Dealer*), and *Distant Drummer* (which became *Thursday's Drummer*).[3]

In theory, GLF operated as a "collective." But as *Thursday's Drummer* noted, if the Front had a "leader," it was Kuromiya. Kuromiya was born in 1943 in a Wyoming concentration camp set up by the U.S. government to intern Japanese Americans during World War Two. After the war, he moved with his family to California, where he remembers encountering state repression again when police caught him having same-sex sex in a park. Sent to "juvenile hall" for three days, he was "treated" by a glandular specialist who tried to make him into "a real man."[4]

In the early 1960s, Kuromiya enrolled at the University of Pennsylvania, became involved with the civil rights movement, participated in campaigns to integrate restaurants in Maryland, met Martin Luther King, Jr., at the March on Washington, and was clubbed while leading a group of students on a march in Alabama. Several years later, he became active in the antiwar movement. In 1968, he distributed an announcement that declared that a dog would be napalmed at Penn. After 2,000 people gathered, he circulated a statement congratulating the crowd for saving the dog and urging it to show similar concern about the use of napalm in Southeast Asia. Later that year, he designed a poster that read "Fuck the Draft" and featured an image of a man watching a draft card go up in flames. After copies were distributed

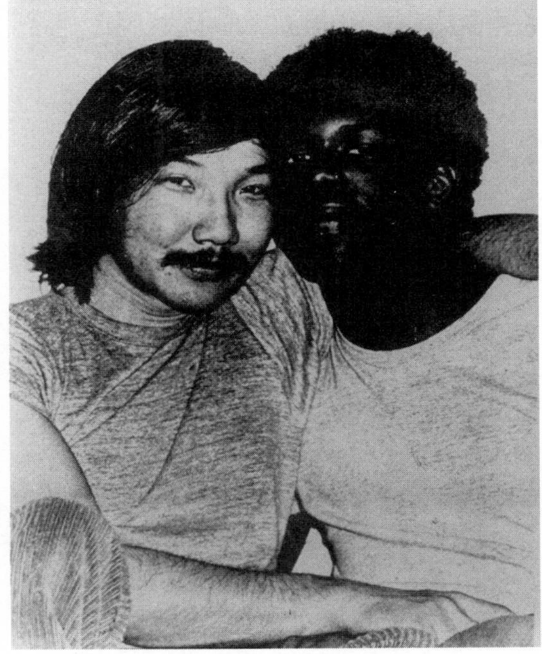

Figure 12.1. Kiyoshi Kuromiya and friend, 1970. *Gay Dealer,* 1970, 16. Courtesy of Gay, Lesbian, Bisexual, and Transgendered Archives of Philadelphia, Philadelphia, PA.

at the Democratic party convention in Chicago, Kuromiya was arrested on obscenity charges. Soon thereafter he was featured in a *Life* magazine article about student activists.[5]

Kuromiya was aware of homophile groups in the 1960s and remembers marching in coat and tie at one of the Reminders. But he recalls thinking of Janus as "pornographic" and "exploitative." By 1970, he was referring disparagingly to the 1965 sit-in at Dewey's as a fight "to return to one of their favorite ghettos." Sarcastically criticizing the Reminder's demand for an end to government and military discrimination, Kuromiya also wrote, "Maybe they should petition Nixon to form a new S.A. as in Nazi Germany."[6]

Younger and more multiracial than homophile activists, GLF narrators talk about relationships between the sexes in ways that differ from their gay predecessors. Earlier local gay activists rarely mention significant relationships with lesbians when talking about their lives before they joined the movement. In contrast, many GLF gay men refer to important relationships with lesbians that shaped their premovement identities. Perhaps lesbian and gay communities had become more heterosocial over time. Perhaps heterosocially oriented gay men were more drawn to gay liberation than they had been to the homophile movement. Perhaps GLF activists were influenced by ethnic and racial communities, including African American ones, that had more substantial lesbian and gay interaction. And perhaps GLF narrators, more profoundly influenced by feminism in the 1970s, 1980s, and 1990s, highlight cross-sex relationships more readily than do earlier gay activists. In any case, while younger lesbian and older gay narrators tend to downplay the significance of community-based cross-sex relationships, older lesbian and younger gay narrators tend to stress their importance.

GLF member Gus Johnson exemplifies this. Born in 1953 to middle-class African American parents, Johnson grew up in Southwark, Philadelphia. Describing his early same-sex sexual experiences, Johnson says that St. Peter's Episcopal School was a "mass orgy" and that at South Philly High he regularly had sex in the gym and shower rooms. Johnson remembers first encountering lesbians when he was a teenager. In one incident, he happened upon two women having sex in a theater dressing room. He also recalls becoming friendly with several Center City lesbians. When one of these pointed out to him that he was "a homosexual," Johnson "admitted" it "publicly" for the first time. Other lesbian friends repeatedly tried to find him boyfriends. In 1969, Johnson left home and moved in with a lover; shortly thereafter, he moved into a "wild" Center City house that was filled with gay liberationists.[7]

Not long after GLF formed, a group of students started GLF Temple, which GLF's newsletter called "the first campus gay organization in Pennsylvania." Kuromiya and Tommi Avicolli Mecca believe that Tom Mantua founded the group. Writing and advertising in the *Daily Pennsylvanian*, Halley Tarr called for the formation of a group at Penn but had less success.[8]

James Roberts was one of GLF Temple's first members. Born in 1950 to working-class African American parents in North Philly, Roberts was a Central High School athlete when he began participating in the gay scene at Rittenhouse Square. Within a few years, he was also going to the Ritz, Spider Kelly's, and lesbian and gay house parties. Discussing the latter, Roberts notes that he socialized with lesbians as well as gay men and as a result developed a sense that African American lesbians and gay men were "linked."[9]

Tommi Avicolli Mecca also joined GLF Temple. Born in 1951 to a working-class, Italian American family in South Philly, Mecca believes that the "strong presence" of women in his ethnic enclave led him to develop important bonds with lesbians and feminists as he got older. He also emphasizes links between his childhood femininity and his adult feminism. Recalling times when he was physically attacked and called "faggot," "queer," and "sissy," Mecca says that he was targeted because he walked, dressed, and played "too much like a girl." In the 1960s, his gender and sexual alienation became intertwined with his political alienation. In a 1991 *Philadelphia Magazine* article, Mecca recalls, "I was against the Vietnam War, I wore love beads and peace symbols, and I didn't believe in [my father's] beloved Republican Party, the military-industrial complex . . . , or Frank Rizzo." But Mecca also writes that among the young, "suddenly it was O.K. to be different" and even "effeminacy" became "more acceptable." In 1969, after finishing high school and breaking up with his boyfriend, Mecca enrolled at Temple. More than 20 years later, he still recalls the day, 16 April 1971, when he joined 10–12 people, mostly men, at GLF Temple's weekly coffee hour at the Student Activities Center.[10]

Gay liberation's strength at Temple reflected its appeal to youth. Tom Ashe and Basil O'Brien observed in the *Free Press* that the movement "thrived on young ideas." *Thursday's Drummer* reported that GLF members were "young," that a few were students, and that most either had jobs or were "scratching out a living on the streets."[11] While homophile activists imposed age restrictions on their groups in order to avoid allegations of pedophilia, gay liberationists welcomed the politicization of youth.

GLF was defined as much by multiracialism as youth. Donn Teal's 1971 book *The Gay Militants* notes that GLF Philadelphia was "50 percent black" and had "active Third World leadership." According to Kuromiya, GLF was

Figure 12.2. Tommi Avicolli Mecca and friend, 1972. Photograph by Jo Hofmann. With the permission of Jo Hofmann.

"about 30% black, 30% Caucasian, 30% Latino, and 10% Oriental." This was at a time when Philadelphia was 34% African American, 66% Euro-American, 2% Latino, and less than 1% Asian American. Influenced by the racial divisions that had occurred in GLF New York, GLF Philadelphia's multiracialism was also shaped by the racial identities and politics of its first leaders and members. Along with racial and ethnic diversity came a geographic base different from that of the homophile movement. While Barbara Gittings refers to people "from parts of the city" causing problems at HAL dances, Kuromiya remembers thinking that those attending GLF's first meeting "seemed like a good group of people" because they were "from all parts of the city."[12]

GLF's social base differed from HAL's not only in the sense that it was young and multiracial but also because it was overwhelmingly male. Kuromiya recalls that "our male/female ratio was not really very representative." Mecca remembers that only a few women were involved with GLF Temple. Roberts says that GLF Temple was "pretty much a male group" and that GLF's first dance at Temple had "some women, but again mostly men."[13] In fact, GLF and GLF Temple were Philadelphia's first lesbian and gay political groups founded and initially led by men.

With a post-Stonewall founding date and a different social base than earlier lesbian and gay groups, GLF politically diverged from its homophile predecessors. And in an age in which radicals often found greatest fault with liberals, GLF attacked homophile groups past and present. In addition to criticizing the Dewey's sit-in and Reminder, Kuromiya wrote that "the history of homosexual protest in Philadelphia is pretty meager" and that homophile groups had been talking about "integrating" for "nearly twenty years" and had "accomplished almost nothing." Referring to HAL's name, O'Brien praised GLF for its "departure from the pattern of operation set by the moderate, church basement 'homophile' groups, whose underground sessions have traditionally been non-productive litanies of self-righteousness, yet to find their translation into 'action.'" While Clark Polak was closing down his operations, GLF was beginning the process through which the earlier history of activism would be forgotten. Claims such as O'Brien's that the Stonewall riots were "the first time homosexuals stood up and fought" would soon become common.[14]

In what must have appeared counterintuitive to homophile integrationists, GLF wanted to change society by turning away from it, to counter culture with counterculture. O'Brien wrote that GLF was "inner-directed —demanding self-acceptance," rather than "outer-directed—demanding acceptance by others." "We don't care what society thinks," he declared, "because we have rejected society." Recalling the centrality of "consciousness-raising," Kuromiya says that GLF "never felt that a group's energies should be applied toward educating the group that oppresses you."[15]

Joining women's liberation groups in referring to "raising" and not transforming consciousness, GLF identified itself as being in possession of knowledge about lesbian and gay life that others did not have. This was a claim that homophile activists had made before. But the consciousness promoted by GLF challenged the very sexual categories that were used by most lesbians and gay men. In one instance, Kuromiya even criticized the word "gay," arguing that although it was less "offensive" than "homosexual," both "came out of our former oppression" and he could not "identify with it." More typically, Kuromiya wrote, "The oppression of homosexuals in America comes from the containment of sexuality within certain narrow roles. Labels, such as homo-, hetero- and bi-sexual show the rigidity of the forms of relating under which we live. Like women, both male and female homosexuals suffer from sex typing. We must break from these narrow roles."[16]

Sexualizing countercultural concepts, GLF counterposed an authentic "self," which was polymorphously sexual, with artificial "society," which channeled and contained sexual desire. Criticizing Mick Jagger's role in the film *Performance*, for example, a *Gay Dealer* review argued that many films were "using the homosexual subculture as a metaphor for the revolt within society":

> Compartmentalized living, performances, the schizoid way of relating to people are only too familiar to the gay scene. The conflicts within the gay person are a miniature form of the conflicts within society. . . . Every gay person has performed. There's the daily act of pretending you aren't gay. And then there's the act of pretending you are gay. . . . The decadent and unproductive life-styles portrayed in the film derive in large part from the oppressive roles (often sexual) laid on us by society. The film doesn't begin to present a viable way of working through the multi-layered masks of social roles and achieving real, live people and honest personalities. What we're confronted with here is not a failure of the film, however. But a failure of society to have ever even considered alternatives to our own performances.

GLF sought not new roles or performances, but authentic selves.[17]

Gay Liberation and Feminism

GLF's opposition to hegemonic sexual categories was influenced by developments in gay liberation elsewhere and by the movement's youthfulness and multiracialism. But it also derived from cross-sex identifications with lesbian feminism. In "The Woman-Identified Woman," which was reprinted in *Gay Dealer*, Radicalesbians-NY argued that "lesbianism, like male homosexuality, is a category of behavior possible only in a sexist society characterized by rigid sex roles and dominated by male supremacy." "In a society in which men do not oppress women, and sexual expression is allowed to follow feelings," the statement declared, "the categories of homosexuality and heterosexuality would disappear." Calling upon straight women and lesbians to think of themselves as "woman-identified," Radicalesbians-NY urged women to "see in each other the possibility of a primal commitment which includes sexual love." GLF applied some of these concepts to men, essentially encouraging everyone to make "primal" same-sex commitments.[18]

Also influenced by lesbian feminism, gay liberationists identified sexism, and not what would later be called homophobia, as the source of gay oppression. For example, *Temple University News* editorialized that GLF Temple's first dance would encourage "serious thought" about "sexism." A *Plain Dealer* article attacked "Straight Man's value system of heterosexual chauvinism, male supremacy, and sex-objectry." "Sexism in the Schools," an article in *Gay Dealer*, argued that "sexist pigs use the schools to perpetuate their sexist ideas," which included "male supremacy and heterosexual chauvinism." Occasionally, gay liberationists discussed gay sexism specifically. One *Gay Dealer* writer described telling a woman he desired that he was struggling with "gay male sexism," which attracted him to "bodies" instead of "the people inside."[19]

Analyses of sexism provided GLFers with conceptual links for their attacks on racism and capitalism. In the *Free Press*, Kiyoshi Kuromiya wrote, "Homosexuals have burst their chains and abandoned their closets. . . . We came battle-scarred and angry to topple your sexist, racist, hateful society. We came to challenge the incredible hypocrisy of your serial monogamy, your oppressive sexual role-playing, your nuclear family, your Protestant ethic, apple pie and Mother." In the *Plain Dealer*, he argued that "acceptance of homosexuality by society threatens the basic unit of capitalism, the nuclear family."[20]

GLF's opposition to sexism was also intertwined with its support for transvestites and transsexuals. Although drag queens figured prominently in the Stonewall riots, they did not always feel welcome in gay liberation groups. In 1969–1970, a number of organizations formed around the country to fight for "transvestite and transsexual liberation." In Philadelphia, however, GLF embraced "trans liberation." A GLF newsletter article headlined "Who Likes Drags?" noted, "Though some other gay organizations may be embarrassed by drags or transvestites, GLF believes that we should accept all of our brothers and sisters unconditionally. Who are we to put up the butch ideal for society when some of our brothers are not, nor do they intend to butch it up for society?" *Gay Dealer* reprinted the "Trans Liberation Newsletter" and a statement of trans demands.[21] How did GLF reconcile its support for trans liberation with its opposition to performances and roles? In part by believing that transsexuals and transvestites were authentic, but also by concentrating its criticisms on the "butch ideal." Gay liberationists urged men to stop performing masculinity.

In part because of this, GLF rejected an earlier generation of sexual revolutionaries. Many aspects of GLF's sexual liberationism likely appealed to Clark Polak and other 1960s sex radicals. But while Polak encouraged liberation from socially imposed sexual *inhibitions*, GLF sought to free sexual selves from socially imposed sexual *roles*. And while Polak celebrated gay masculinity, GLF celebrated gay feminism. Insofar as *Drum*'s world of bars, cruising, and objectification depended upon masculine roles, gay liberationists criticized it. "Dijon," an African American gay man who participated in GLF, recalls that "the most important thing that GLF did, not only here in Philadelphia but across the country, was really smash through role-playing that had been a part of gay culture up to that point, top-man bottom-man." Tom Ashe and Basil O'Brien wrote in the *Free Press* that "StraightMan has forced us into the anti-personal context of bars and street cruising, forcing us to relate to each other as sex objects. Only upon the interaction of full personhoods can our movement be based."[22]

With a feminist analysis of the oppression of lesbians and gay men, how can the absence of women in GLF be understood? Asked why radical lesbians and gay men did not form a mixed-sex group, Tommi Avicolli Mecca says, "It might have been more on the women's part than the men's." When Mecca became secretary of GLF Temple in 1971, he established a "good working relationship" with Women's Liberation at Temple, which he says "helped to bring some women" into the group. But he thinks that "lesbians were drawn to the women's liberation groups." While gay liberationists and lesbian feminists organized separately, Mecca says that GLF and Radicalesbians had "the same philosophy" and that both were "into collectivism, nonstructure, nonpatriarchy, nonhierarchy." Kuromiya notes that he regarded gay liberation as "male liberation" and a "parallel movement to women's liberation."[23]

Gay liberation was parallel to women's liberation not only in the ways it encouraged men to deepen same-sex intimacy and embrace feminist analyses and practices but also in the ways it called for men to be "woman-identified." One article in *Gay Dealer* suggested using the term "women" "generically" and declared that "Feminine Liberation will benefit all 'womankind' including men." Arguing for the "elevation of feminine qualities," the article claimed that "if feminine qualities really have equal status with masculine qualities, men could express their 'feminine' nature in the way that women now, to a limited extent, express their masculine nature, and the result would be a much better balanced society."[24]

The parallels between lesbian feminism and gay liberation, however, could extend only so far, for lesbian feminists did not generally argue in favor of expressing their "masculine nature" and lesbians and gay men did not have the same relationship to "patriarchy." Here was a tension that marked GLF's search to find a place for gay men within a feminist worldview. Although gay liberationists believed that same-sex sexualities could subvert patriarchal power, sexual bonds between men functioned as a foundation for patriarchy in some societies.[25] Were gay liberationists sleeping with feminism's friends or foes? And what about gay liberationists themselves? Many lesbian feminists believed that whereas lesbians were oppressed as women and as lesbians, gay men were advantaged as men even if oppressed as gay men.

Moreover, gay liberation in some ways attempted to masculinize feminism. Challenging straight women *and* men to deepen their same-sex relationships, GLF universalized "The Woman-Identified Woman," evacuating her specifically female identity. For example, while Radicalesbians-NY encouraged women to make a "primal commitment which includes sexual love," for the most part its statement emphasized "commitment" and "love," not "sex." At times, gay liberationists, too, did not emphasize sex in their discussions of homosocial relationships. Halley Tarr, for example, encouraged men to "relate to each other in a loving way." One *Gay Dealer* writer argued, "Gay is something very warm and beautiful that happens between two or more people of the same sex. Gay is love." One GLF member went a step further, describing his "efforts at smashing the 'homoSEXual' definition of crotch mechanics." But gay liberationists often promoted the sexual dimensions of male same-sex relationships. Kuromiya wrote in the *Free Press*, "Personally I don't care what heterosexuals do in bed . . . as long as they stop bothering ME and start loving me as a person, fraternally, emotionally AND physically." The *Gay Dealer* contributor who wrote that "gay is love" concluded his article by declaring "We must have . . . people free to love their sisters and brothers alike. Sexually." While "The Woman-Identified Woman" had called upon women to consider the "possibility" of same-sex sex, GLF issued demands for same-sex sexual action. Dijon argues that "our legacy to the city" was that "for the first time we were presenting the idea that one could be omni-sexual."[26]

What Dijon calls "omni-sexuality" and *Gay Dealer* called the freedom to love "sisters and brothers" relates to another difference between the rhetoric of lesbian feminism and gay liberation. Lesbian feminists had important political reasons for discouraging women from having sex with men. What feminist reasons could GLF offer for discouraging men from having sex with women? As a way of struggling against "gay male sexism"? Gay liberationists did at times point to this. More typically GLF embraced "omni-sexuality," in theory challenging all sexual categories. But GLF rarely if ever called upon gay men to explore cross-sex desires. Dijon recalls that he had been sexually involved with both women and men at the time of Stonewall but that with the advent of gay liberation he felt that it was important to "make a stand with a homosexual relationship."[27]

While GLF never specifically called upon gay men to liberate their cross-sex desires, many would not have responded favorably to the notion that they should do so. Challenging the hard-won sexual identities that gay men had acquired would not only have required a leap from the predominantly same-sex sexual experiences that these men had had, but might also have threatened the special relationship to lesbian feminism that gay liberationists thought they deserved. This relationship often depended upon gay men not displaying sexual interest in women. In effect, GLF encouraged men to liberate same-sex desires and embrace feminist and feminine values while maintaining and promoting distinctions between the "same" and the "other" sex.

Gay Liberationist Action

While GLF concentrated on internal consciousness-raising, it also acted in ways that influenced the external world. In general, GLF focused its efforts on gay, countercultural, and leftist communities. One exception took place late in 1970, when GLF members went to Old St. Joseph's National Shrine, where Father Joseph d'Invilliers and Barbara Gittings were scheduled to speak. Although GLF discussed doing a "guerilla" action by dressing like nuns and priests, members instead decided simply to go and challenge the speakers. While at the church, Basil O'Brien made a point of greeting one of his friends by kissing him "with a loud smack." According to the *Tribune*, GLF also distributed 10,000 leaflets and put up more than 5,000 stickers around the city. Meanwhile, GLF activists spoke at several junior high schools, high schools, and colleges, and GLF Temple participated in the university's student orientation programs.[28]

More commonly, GLF attempted to influence gay cultures and did so by challenging traditional institutions of gay life. In this regard, gay liberationists had more in common with their militantly respectable predecessors than with the gay sexual revolutionaries of the 1960s. Rhetorically populist, GLF criticized popular practices. Tom Ashe and Basil O'Brien wrote that the movement had to liberate the young before they were "caught in the ghetto gay life" and the "mafia-run gay bars." Describing a GLF dance, *Plain Dealer* reported that GLF "turned off the bad trip of gay ghetto bars and street cruising and sitting on the wall in Rittenhouse Square." *Gay Dealer* argued that "the 'gay bar' is the tool by which the oppressor and his underworld cohorts perpetuate their hatred of us." GLF especially rejected bars that restricted "kissing, hugging, slow dancing," prohibited the sale or distribution of gay publications, and carded minors. "The gay bar that is blackmailed by organized crime and neurotic, sadist pigs," *Gay Dealer* concluded, "deprives all gay people of the pleasures and enjoyment of social interaction and basic human rights." Because "gay women and men do not truly desire to relate to each other as prime choices of meat on the market," GLF developed "alternatives."[29]

GLF's youthfulness and multiracialism contributed to its opposition to bars. Kiyoshi Kuromiya remembers that GLF had problems with bars "because of their admission policies, selective carding, the fact that people who didn't drink alcohol or people who were underage were excluded." Dijon recalls bars discriminating against "nonwhites" and that, until HAL and GLF began sponsoring dances, there was "no place for anyone under 21 to go." GLF members also resented bar owners and managers who opposed the use of their premises for political organizing. According to Kuromiya, activists were "thrown out of the Allegro innumerable times trying to leaflet" and were "thrown out of the Steps" as well. In time, GLF began to picket the bars.[30]

GLF also sought alternatives to "the depressing scene at Rittenhouse Square," which was growing more depressing because of the upcoming mayoral election. As S. A. Paolantonio has noted, the "worst kept political secret in America" in 1970 was that "Rizzo was going to run for mayor." It was also no secret that election campaigns often coincided with crackdowns on gay men. According to a GLF leaflet, "homosexuals in Philadelphia's gay ghetto have been subject to an increasing number of physical attacks and intensified harassment by straights and the police."[31]

A September 1970 issue of *Plain Dealer* noted that at least four GLF members had been attacked recently. While one subdued "two rough trade assailants who robbed him at knifepoint," another, Dave Krasnov, was "taunted . . . for being gay" by "a group of blacks" in Rittenhouse Square. When "Joe Covert," also a GLF member, came to Krasnov's aid, he was "beaten for sticking up for his white brother." Covert then "tried to explain to 50 friends of the assailants how gay oppression was linked to the oppression of black people." Noting that "some of the blacks had white girlfriends whom they would defend," Covert challenged them to "see why one of their gay brothers would defend his white boyfriend." They reportedly "responded by threatening his life" and warned that they would "rip apart the whole gay community—'faggot by faggot.' "[32]

GLF's response to antigay violence was based on a new territorial conception of the gay community. Calling for an end to "incursions into the gay ghetto by the police," GLF linked its problems with "the increasing police repression that is hitting oppressed groups in their communities throughout the city." After the courts placed an injunction "against harassment of political organizations and oppressed minorities in Philadelphia by the police," GLF joined an effort to establish "civilian control" over the police. While gay liberationists criticized "gay ghetto" institutions, they also put forward the notion that Philadelphia had a gay ghetto and made the kinds of territorial claims that other "oppressed minorities" had used in their struggles.[33]

Insisting on their "right to meet each other on public land," GLF members at an August 1970 meeting decided to go to Rittenhouse Square to "experience the oppression" of their "sisters and brothers." Arm in arm, they walked to Rittenhouse and then circled it chanting "Gay Power." When a "park pig" ordered the group to stop chanting, one GLFer urged cooperation and GLF complied. But when the policeman demanded that the group move on, GLF refused. The policeman then "viciously grabbed" the arm of the member who had urged cooperation, interrogated him at the guardhouse, and threatened him physically. According to the *Free Press*, this radicalized GLF and motivated the group to "fight back against this police state repression." A GLF leaflet offered assistance to those harassed by police. "Out of the Closets and Into the Streets" and "The Streets Belong to the People," GLF declared. The group discussed forming a "Gay Defense League" and called for gays to gather in the square every evening and on Saturday afternoons. According to Dijon, GLF organized judo classes and patrolled the square.[34]

While taking these actions, GLF and GLF Temple also created social alternatives. In June 1970, Ashe and O'Brien reported that GLF had "overflowed a Germantown coffeehouse, providing the beginnings of an alternative to the dehumanizing gay bars." Discussing coffeehouses, Donn Teal reports that gay liberationists had "gab fests with straights at Hecate's Circle" in Germantown. James Roberts recalls that GLF Temple meetings were "basically a social hour." "People needed to bond," he explains. "You can't have activism until people have socialized together." GLF also discussed the creation of a gay community center, "where people could meet other than the bars or the street." Kuromiya wrote that the "primary purpose of the center" would be to "radicalize and educate the homosexual community towards political action."[35]

In August, less than a month after HAL sponsored its first dance, GLF held a dance at Temple's Student Activities Center. Temple's student newspaper announced that this was "the first gay social event on a Pennsylvania campus" and that the affair would welcome "bisexuals, homosexuals, liberated straights, Lesbians and male gays, blacks, whites." The paper editorialized, "Guys dancing with guys, women with women, women with men, liberated women asking men to dance, group dancing; just think of all the possibilities, or variations on a theme."[36]

Kuromiya and Roberts remember that a number of people had concerns about the dance, some of which were expressed in racially coded references to Temple's neighborhood. "People had discouraged us from it," Kuromiya recalls, "because they said people don't come back onto Temple campus at night because it's a commuter campus. And people don't find the neighborhood a good one to go in at night." Roberts remembers that "some people were even anticipating there would be acts of violence there because, after all, it was in the middle of North Philadelphia."[37]

According to *Temple University News* and *Plain Dealer*, 500–600 people attended the dance. Kuromiya remembers it as a "tremendous success." *Plain Dealer* reported that "women and men, and more Blacks than whites made the dance one of the few well-balanced movement events in Philly." Roberts recalls that "everybody, not just people from the campus, came." Kuromiya says that "it was the first large-scale integrated event they'd had on the Temple campus in the evening" and that GLF "tended to integrate facilities because we were a very integrated group and we drew from all parts of the community and brought them into facilities that were formerly closed to them and closed to gay events." Discussing GLF dances, Tommi Avicolli Mecca recalls, "GLF wasn't afraid to go into the black community and leaflet. It wasn't afraid to go to black events where black issues were being discussed and to stand up and say, 'Hey, we're queer and we're gonna have this event.' " He also notes that "black folks in the group knew other black people who knew other black people." GLF held another dance at Temple in October.[38]

GLF thought of its dances as countercultural and leftist events. As Dijon explains, "These dances were open to anyone that we thought was part of the community, especially part of the revolutionary community." According to *Plain Dealer*, "this dance floor full of freed-up people was the beginning of our community, *us*, people who could groove together without power roles and channeled sexual drive." Declaring that "sisters dancing with sisters, brothers dancing with brothers, touching, kissing and balling people of the same sex is a far loving out expression of living," the article concluded by noting, "Some heteros (Dig it: '*Others*'—out of it, nowhere) came too, and turned on to the scene. Open up. Let go. Hang up your straightjacket and join us."[39]

Although GLF claimed that it did not focus on educating the public, its participation in countercultural and left activities often led it to educate straights. In the spring of 1970, for example, GLF began going to the Belmont

Plateau "Be-Ins" in Fairmount Park. According to Ashe and O'Brien, two days after GLF's first meeting, the front's banner displaced the "star-spangled" one on the plateau. Kuromiya reported that after GLF raised its flag, park guards "ripped" it "off" and GLF had to visit the police to recover it. O'Brien reported that of the 500 people who came to the Flag Day Be-In, 200 "came out" under GLF's banner, drawn in part by GLF's provision of free oranges. According to Teal, "Philadelphia GLFers, more than the New York Front, liked their fun in the sun, and joined straights at music-filled be-ins every Sunday." On one occasion, they provided "one thousand free oranges to the surprised heterosexuals."[40]

According to Ashe and O'Brien, GLF regularly confronted "the sexism of Fairmount Park's Sunday Be-Ins, our 'Think homosexuals are revolting—you can bet your sweet ass we are!' leaflet challenging the heterosexual chauvinism of the counter-culture." O'Brien described one incident in which a "straight boy lead singer" in a "white male rock group" urged the crowd to dance by saying, "The last one up's a faggot." "What's so ironic," O'Brien reported, "is that the GLF people were the FIRST ones dancing at the previous Sunday's Be-In." O'Brien explained that "we let the straight boy finish his song, then put it to him that he had just laid down some heavy sexism." The performer, "in a statement laced with condescension, apologized as best he could." "GLF," O'Brien concluded, "isn't into taking much more of this shit from low conscious straights."[41]

GLF cooperated and struggled with leftist as well as countercultural groups. Kuromiya remembers, "East Powelton Concerned Residents were very surprised when the most support they got from any organization was from Gay Liberation Front. Young Lords found that we were one of the few groups that came out and supported their demonstrations. Black Panthers were very surprised when we were the only organization that brought lots and lots of people out." GLF worked with the Welfare Rights Organization and United Farm Workers as well. At antiwar demonstrations, gay liberationists often provided "entertainment." Kuromiya recalls, "We'd go up to a line of cops with tear gas grenades and horses and clubs. And link arms and do a can-can. Really threw 'em off guard. That was really pretty funny. They'd start approaching us to arrest us. And we'd stop them in their tracks, every time."[42]

Relationships with straight leftists, like those with straight counterculturalists, were not without tension. As Kuromiya noted in the *Plain Dealer*, "We've taken cues from the struggle of Third World people. . . . We've learned to stop pretending from the hip revolution. We've learned tactics from guerilla fighters and student revolutionaries around the world." But he also wrote that "movement people are sometimes among the worst offenders when it comes to refusing to recognize the oppression of the homosexual." Another GLFer reported that an activist had called him "cocksucker" at a Yippie street fair.

"You see the beautiful boys and the flamboyant queens, the diesel dykes, the leather queens and the hustlers on 13th Street," Kuromiya declared in the *Free Press*, "and they fit your image of what we ought to be like. But most of us you won't recognize. And we're the ones you really worry about . . . because in every other way except for our sexual orientation, we're very much like you." He continued, "We've infiltrated every smoke-filled niche of the precious bureaucracy that you call the Movement. We've infiltrated your committees and demonstrations. We've infiltrated your communes and affinity groups." Now, he concluded, "We're ready to . . . shout out our true identities."[43]

At times, alienation from the left led gay liberationists to ally with homophile activists. A *Plain Dealer* writer noted that "the old homophile groups who . . . aren't yet even into chanting, are our sisters and brothers—more so than the cheerleading radical who shouts revolution and identifies with the third person oppression of yellow people, but whose heterosexual chauvinism oppresses our personhood." But gay liberationists also reported progress on the left. For example, *Gay Dealer* noted that although the Puerto Rican Young Lords had said "they have problems relating to gay people," they were "sincere in their aims to become liberated of counter-revolutionary sexism." Moreover, they were "the only straight group to show up at gay dances with their literature and buttons," and they "distributed GLF literature in their community."[44]

The extensive coverage that GLF received in the *Free Press*, *Plain Dealer*, and *Distant Drummer* was another sign of progress on the left. Partly because of this, GLF did not have its own regularly published newsletter. To the extent that the media influenced lesbian and gay cultures in this era, this means that lesbians and gay men were more likely to be influenced by and become leftists and that leftists were more likely to be influenced by and become lesbians or gay men. Gay liberationists actually took over the *Plain Dealer*. Responding to a headline that read "fuck the brass: up the ass of the ruling class," a *Plain Dealer* writer complained that "sexism rears up its ugly head." Declaring that "fucking is ecstasy—up the ass or otherwise," the writer asked, "Why wish it on your enemies?" Kuromiya remembers a number of people on the staff coming out and renaming the paper. Dijon recalls that "we could not as gay people continue to struggle against the subtle sexism" and "very peacefully, very cooperatively, changed the *Plain Dealer* to the *Gay Dealer*."[45]

The Revolutionary People's Constitutional Convention

The culmination of GLF's efforts to cultivate alliances with other leftists took place in September 1970 at the Revolutionary People's Constitutional

Convention (RPCC) in Philadelphia. Sponsored by the Black Panther party, the convention took place in a period that many people today think was marked and marred by African American separatism and leftist sectarianism. To be sure, while the convention was taking place, pan-Africanists and black nationalists, many opposed to alliances with Euro-Americans, were meeting at the International Congress of African Peoples in Atlanta. The convention, in contrast, promoted multiracial alliances. Among the groups present were the Yippies, Students for a Democratic Society, Weathermen, Women's Liberation, Women Strike for Peace, Black Muslims, Resistance, and GLF. While the congress was attended by 2,000–2,500 people, the convention attracted 10,000–15,000.[46]

Founded by Huey Newton and Bobby Seale in California in 1967, the Black Panther party had critics as well as supporters in the lesbian and gay movement. Lesbian and gay liberationists participated in Panther demonstrations but challenged the party on what they considered its antigay sexism. For example, in a July 1970 *Black Panther* article attacking Philadelphia's "Pig Mayor Tate and Fascist Rizzo," Mumia, a local Panther, wrote of Rizzo, "We know that you are a product of perversion, and you have produced perversion. From the leniency shown to the murders on the Philly Pig Force, to your homosexual son." Mumia also called George Fencl, the head of Rizzo's civil disobedience unit, "Georgey boy faggot Fencl." These kinds of comments made alliance-building difficult. HAL's Carole Friedman criticized the Panthers for calling a New York official a "faggot." Kiyoshi Kuromiya declared in the *Free Press*, "We're no longer going to sit back when the Black Panthers call the pigs and rednecks 'faggots and cocksuckers.' "[47] While it criticized the Panthers, GLF came to see the party as the left's vanguard.

The Panthers announced the convention in a widely reprinted "Message to America" released on the anniversary of the Emancipation Proclamation in June 1970. "The Constitution of the U.S.A.," the Panthers declared, "does not and never has protected our people or guaranteed to us those lofty ideals enshrined within it." Calling upon black people to address the question of their "National Destiny," the Panthers explained that "if we are to remain a part of the United States, then we must have a new Constitution that will strictly guarantee our Human Rights to Life, Liberty, and the Pursuit of Happiness." "If we cannot make a new arrangement within the United States," the Panthers warned, "then we have no alternative but to declare ourselves free and independent of the United States." But for the time being, the party would try to remake the United States.[48]

Nearly 200 years before, delegates from 13 British colonies had gathered in Philadelphia, their largest city, to consider independence. After winning that cause, 13 states sent delegates to Philadelphia, their capital, to write the U.S. Constitution. By 1970, although Philadelphia's population had fallen to fourth largest among U.S. cities, its African American population had grown to 34% of the city's total. Recognizing the city's symbolic power as the "birthplace of the nation," the Panthers held their constitutional convention in Philadelphia.

Just weeks before the convention, *Black Panther* published "A Letter from Huey to the Revolutionary Brothers and Sisters about the Women's Liberation and Gay Liberation Movements." Reprinted in Philadelphia's *Plain Dealer, Free Press,* and *Distant Drummer,* Newton's letter referred to homosexuals and women as "oppressed groups" and called upon his followers to "unite with them in a revolutionary fashion." Presuming a straight male readership, Newton admitted that "sometimes our first instinct is to want to hit a homosexual in the mouth and to want a woman to be quiet." But he explained that this was because "we're afraid we might be homosexual" and that a woman "might castrate us, or take the nuts that we may not have to start with." Acknowledging that "we might be homosexual," that men might not have "nuts," and that women could take "nuts," Newton appeared to favor a fluid conception of sex and sexual identities. But he quickly moved to solidify this fluidity by stating that "we must gain security in ourselves and therefore have respect and feelings for all oppressed people." Homosexuals, he argued, "might be the most oppressed."[49]

Modeling his analysis of sexuality on his understanding of race, Newton largely missed or rejected the antiminoritarian impulses of gay liberation and lesbian feminism. The Panther's vision of a transformed U.S. nationalism was based on the rights of groups with clear identity boundaries—blacks, women, homosexuals. In fact the convention's schedule featured Saturday meetings for "social groupings," which included third-world peoples, women, GIs students, workers, female homosexuals, male homosexuals, welfare people, street people, and "head workers." (Topical workshops were to be held on Sunday.) This agenda forced those with multiple identities to choose which one to privilege. Moreover, the schedule failed to recognize that boundaries between social groupings were rarely as clear as they seemed. When an *Inquirer* reporter noticed that 40% of the 6,000 people at one session were white, he observed that apparently "the meaning of the word black has changed radically." The *Tribune* quoted a local African American man who was asked about white delegates at the convention. "I don't consider them white," he replied.[50]

Although Newton may have thought of homosexuals as a distinct minority, this did not prevent gay or straight men from being drawn to him erotically. When Newton's letter appeared alongside a photograph of his shirtless body, as it did in the *Plain Dealer*, the erotic dimensions of his leadership became more visible. Alice Walker has written about the "homoeroticism" that characterized Newton's relationships with other Panthers. She concludes that "these men loved, admired and were sometimes in love with each other," that they might have had sex with men while in prison, and that they were "confused" by all of this. In spite of or because of this confusion, Newton called for "full participation of the Gay Liberation Movement and the Women's Liberation Movement" at conferences, rallies, and demonstrations. He also urged the formation of "a working coalition with the Gay Liberation and Women's Liberation groups." Newton's statement and developments at the conference, however, did little to assure lesbian activists that they, too, would be encouraged to participate fully in making the new nation.[51]

That the Panthers continued to believe in U.S. national ideals is all the more surprising when the state campaign against the party is considered. Just days before the convention, Philadelphia police raided Panther offices in West Philly, North Philly, and Germantown, arresting five women and ten men, some of whom were publicly strip-searched and photographed bare-assed alongside shotgun-wielding police officers for the city's and nation's newspapers. While one African American woman noted in the *News* that this proved that "Black is Beautiful," the more common response was outrage at the police and the papers.[52] After the convention, the FBI concluded that there was "a connection between the Homosexual Movement and the Black Panther Party." And a connection there was—not the least of which was in their common experience of state repression.[53]

On Labor Day weekend, about 60 gay liberationists joined thousands of others at the Constitutional Convention in Philadelphia. The multiracial Male Homosexual Workshop met at the Germantown Presbyterian Church. According to the New York–based *Gay Flames*, "Some of the men dressed in drag the first night and rapped to some Panthers who came over." On Saturday, the convention featured speeches by Newton and Michael Tabor, who had a "deep, beautiful voice, but doesn't come on like a super-butch." Later that day, "Before we went to sleep, we were treated to the vision of two brothers fucking on top of the church's silk AmeriKKKan flag." (For some, this evidently exemplified radical sexual patriotism.) Jim Kepner remembers that workshop members picketed against racism at two gay bars during the weekend. According to the New York–based *Come Out*, on Sunday the workshop met with Panther Afeni Shakur, monitored the situation of two members who had been taken in by police (and were later released), and completed its statement. *Gay Flames* reported that the workshop was influenced by a "Third World" gay statement, which confronted gay Euro-Americans on their racism and their "willingness to criticize the sexism of black men but not that of white men." The Third World participants asked the workshop to "recognize Huey Newton's recently stated position in favor of Gay Liberation as being a tremendous advance in the revolution and that the Black Panther Party holds the most out-front position in terms of the struggle to give power to the people."[54]

As delegates arrived at Temple's gymnasium on Sunday evening to hear the workshop reports, the gay contingent began chanting "GAY POWER TO THE GAY PEOPLE, BLACK POWER TO THE BLACK PEOPLE, RED POWER TO THE RED PEOPLE, WOMANPOWER TO THE WOMEN PEOPLE, CHILDREN POWER TO THE CHILDREN PEOPLE" AND "HO-HO HOMOSEXUAL, THE RULING CLASS IS INEFFECTUAL!" According to *Come Out*, although "snickers" greeted Kuromiya when he announced that he was from the Male Homosexual Workshop, his report was "enthusiastically applauded." Challenging the delegates to question their sexual identities, the workshop declared that "the revolution will not be complete until all men are free to express their love for one another sexually." According to Kuromiya, the statement "was carefully worded not to show or to present gay liberation as being an oppressed minority fighting for rights but more the process of a society in which people can come out and be all that it's possible to be." Most of the delegates, he recalls, "had never thought in terms of coming out themselves." Just as the Panthers wanted to reconstitute U.S. national values, gay liberationists wanted to reconstitute U.S. sexual values.[55]

Using a feminist framework, the workshop stated that "the social institution which prevents us all from expressing our total revolutionary love we define as sexism." Clarifying their position, the workshop declared, "Sexism is a belief or practice that the sex or sexual orientation of human beings gives to some the right to certain privileges, powers, or roles, while denying to others their full potential. Within the context of our society, sexism is primarily manifested through male supremacy and heterosexual chauvinism." The workshop recognized the Panthers as "the vanguard of the people's revolution in Amerikkka," demanded "the right to be gay, any time, any place," declared that gays should be "represented in all governmental and community institutions," and called for the "abolition of the nuclear family because it perpetuates the false categories of homosexuality and heterosexuality."[56]

Dijon remembers that "it was such a beautiful thing to hear Kiyoshi . . . and to be acknowledged by people that we considered to be our peers and even our idols." "Have you ever heard people say to radicals," one gay reporter wrote, " 'You just want to tear things down, but what do you want to replace it with?' The gathering in Philadelphia was designed to get all oppressed peoples together to answer that question. The new America, as spelled out by the various workshops, is a real turn-on." *Distant Drummer* reported that the convention's most important accomplishment was "the cooperative tie forged between the Panthers and the Women's and Gay Liberation movements."[57]

The "new America," however, turned out to turn off the predominantly Euro-American contingent of 20–25 women who formed the Lesbian Workshop. Initially, when the convention was announced, these women had been hopeful, particularly because of the role that Panther women played in forging new alliances. "When Afeni Shakur called the Radicalesbians asking them and Gay Liberation Front to Washington for a planning meeting," New York's Lois Hart wrote, " . . . I was charged with excitement. Afeni Shakur—beautiful Black woman, virile, revolutionary, nickname 'Power'—sexual excitement." Just as men were drawn homoerotically to Panther men, women were drawn homoerotically to Panther women.[58]

Hart later noted that she was a "white woman coming into the Panther presence" at a moment when she was developing "growing consciousness of Women's and Gay oppression . . . questioning the validity of working with gay men and their infuriating unconscious sexism—ruling out straight men categorically as super pig." Hart had difficulties with the "super butch" Panthers, whom she described as "the brown, muscled bare-armed, deep-voiced Afro-American," and "a straight man's trip in cinemascope and technicolor." The very erotic appeal that Panther men held for gay male, straight male, and straight female radicals could turn off lesbian feminists. But as she came to realize that her "connection to the struggle to transform the Black Liberation movement was in the people of the third world gay revolution," Hart helped secure agreement that there would be workshops on women's rights and sexual self-determination, a "chairwoman," and a "heavy woman speaker . . . with a strong Woman's consciousness."

Not long after the planning meeting, Newton's letter was published to mixed reviews by lesbian activists. While a group of New York lesbians wrote in *Come Out* that they had been "excited" by Newton's "written gesture of solidarity," Martha Shelley of New York recalls thinking that the statement was "somewhat patronizing . . . that homosexuals can be revolutionaries, too—something like that. You know, the great Chairman Huey Newton gives his imprimatur. Thank you, Chairman Huey."[59]

For the most part, Newton's letter discussed the women's and gay liberation movements as if they were composed exclusively of straight women and gay men. At one point, however, he admitted that he had "hangups" about male but not female homosexuality. "I think it's probably because that's a threat to me maybe," he wrote, "and the females are no threat. It's just another erotic sexual thing." Newton did not refer to the history of straight male erotic fascination with lesbianism. Moreover, while lesbians might have competed with Newton for women or challenged his "manhood" in various ways (thus representing a real threat), Newton only imagined himself here as the subject or object of male desire. While lesbians might have welcomed Newton's lack of hang-ups about their identities, to the extent that he did not regard them as a threat, he might not have realized the distance he would need to travel to address their concerns.[60]

At the convention, the Lesbian Workshop prepared a statement that in many ways offered a stridently sex-separatist vision. "Women are the revolution," they declared. As their presence at the convention suggests, however, Lesbian Workshop participants were not opposed to working with men. In effect, they were making a bid to be the convention's vanguard. Moreover, the workshop embraced the goals of other movements, declaring that "women's revolution will be the first fundamental revolution because it will do what all the others aspired to." Demanding "complete control by women of all aspects of our social system," the workshop called for "sexual autonomy," "destruction of the nuclear family," "communal care of children," and "reparations" to redress women's status as a "dispersed minority." The statement held out a longer-term hope for "equalization of all power resources, so that someday human beings of all sexes can deal with each other on a more realistic level."[61]

The gay and lesbian statements offer revealing contrasts. Both called upon straights to deepen their same-sex relationships, but the men emphasized the sexual aspect of this. Both pointed to sexism as the foundation of their oppression, but the men indicated that sexism victimized gay men as well as women. While the men asked for "representation," the women asked for "control." Both favored abolition of the nuclear family, but the men justified this on the grounds that the family perpetuated false sexual categories while the women argued that women and children were "owned" by men within families. Finally, the men declared that the Panthers were the revolutionary vanguard, which the women did not support.

Lesbian Workshop members were not pleased with the convention. Called "sex freaks" in one incident, they were also offended by Panther Michael Tabor's speech, which the *Plain Dealer* said used words that "oppress our gay comrades." Lesbian criticisms increased when workshop sessions and an all-women's meeting were canceled at one point and when the "third world woman" scheduled to speak along with Newton was denied access to the building. The group of New York lesbians reported critically that they listened to Newton "declaiming about the declaration of independence for Black manhood and promising to level the earth in pursuit of the goal of the dignity, glory and flowering of this same Black manhood." The New York-based *Rat* noted that "it was a great disappointment to many that he did not follow up on his earlier statements about Women's Liberation and Gay Liberation."[62]

Gendered as masculine, the Panther's new nationalism had little appeal for women-identified women. The *Plain Dealer* reported that "women were righteously angry" about Newton's use of the words "man" and "manhood" and "felt that this just ignored their existence and their oppression." After Newton was followed by a Panther woman whose "rap" they described as "totally devoid of any awareness of women's oppression and merely an echo of male Panther rhetoric," the New York lesbians began to feel that they were being "fucked over." No doubt Panther women were not pleased to have one of their own criticized for "echoing" a man, and Panther men could scarcely have missed language suggesting that Euro-American women were being "fucked over" by African American men.[63]

The next day, at the Workshop on Self-Determination for Women, lesbian concerns increased further. As the New York group described it, the meeting was "presided over by a Panther woman with male Panther guards ringing the room." When some women objected to the "intimidating presence of the men," they were told that they were there to "protect the Panther woman." This provoked more criticism later when it was learned that Afeni Shakur "required no such security" when she met with gay men. Meanwhile, lesbian demands for "the abolishment of the nuclear family, heterosexual-role programming and patriarchy" were met with "charges of racism and bourgeois indulgence." Calls for 24-hour child-care centers, however, were labeled "right-on revolutionary." One Panther woman, Mother McKeever, was said to have issued the "loudest" charges of racism against the lesbians and was criticized for referring to the lesbians as "men."[64]

If Euro-American lesbian activists failed to avoid racism in their interactions with Panthers, Panthers failed to avoid homophobia in their interactions with lesbians. As would happen many times in the coming years, alliances foundered on the question of "the family." In the context of the long tradition of Euro-American attempts to damage and destroy families of color, straight activists of color tended to identify the family as a source of strength and a foundation for liberation. In the context of the long tradition of straight male domination in the family, Euro-American women's liberationists, lesbian feminists, and gay liberationists often pointed to the family as a source of oppression. At the convention, openly gay activists of color supported the Male Homosexual Workshop's indictment of the nuclear family, while women of color at the Workshop on Self-Determination for Women (none of whom was publicly identified as lesbian) opposed a similar proposal.

In the end, falling far short of the lesbian proposals, the Workshop on Self-Determination for Women called for "equal status." On the question of the family, the workshop's statement declared that, within capitalist culture, "the institution of the family" has provided the foundation for "the private ownership of people." The workshop encouraged the growth of "communal households and communal relationships and other alternative forms to the patriarchal family" and demanded the "socialization of housework and child care," "free and safe birth control, including abortion," and "no forced sterilization or mandatory birth control programs." Critical of the family under "capitalism" and "patriarchy" (at a time of heightened attacks on the black "matriarchal" family), the statement avoided indicting the family in all forms.[65]

The workshop also declared that "every woman has the right to decide whether she will be homosexual, heterosexual, or bisexual." This formulation was at odds with the Lesbian Workshop's call for all women to deepen their same-sex relationships. Finally, the workshop demanded "equal participation in government," which fell short of the Lesbian Workshop's call for women to have "control." Martha Shelley soon wrote, "The reason gay males were fairly well treated at the convention was that they simply asked to be allowed to be gay and to fight alongside the Panthers. Women asked for 'that amount of control of all production and industry that would ensure one hundred percent control over our own destinies.' In short, women asked for *real* power, and the Panthers freaked out."[66]

After the Self-Determination Workshop, the radical lesbians from New York decided to "split," attributing their decision to the "threats of violence" and the "atmosphere of sexism." They concluded, "If women continue to struggle for their liberation within contexts defined by sexist male mentalities, they will never be free. . . . Our efforts would be wasted in trying to deal with men without the power to validate our demands. We had attempted to negotiate on enemy territory and found it oppressive and unworkable." Lesbian feminists were issuing their own declaration of independence.[67]

When it came time for the workshops to present reports to the convention, those activists who remained witnessed more problems. One GLF-NY reporter noted that when the representative for the workshop on the military and police referred only to men, a woman in the audience shouted "and women." When he referred again to men, male GLFers "joined the chant, 'and women, and women, and women!'" The next time, "he corrected himself," which earned the crowd's cheers.[68]

When the report for the Workshop on Self-Determination for Women was read, the Lesbian Workshop demands were not included. Promised that their statement would appear in a printed version, lesbian activists later criticized the "tragi-comic compromise they made with our demands," which were revised to state "that women have the right to choose heterosexuality, bisexuality or homosexuality" and that "crash programs in the technology relevant to women be made available to them, i.e., child care." The demand for women to deepen their same-sex relationships had become a call for the right to choose a sexual identity. The demand for the destruction of the family had become a call for child care. Even the "compromise" report that was presented to the convention failed to win support. As the *New York Times* reported, delegates "shouted approval" at most of the recommendations read at the final meeting "but gave cool responses to some that were put forward by members of the Women's Liberation Movement."[69]

At the final plenary, "a woman from Women's Liberation and a Gay brother from GLF . . . called attention to the absence of a Lesbian report, regretting the walk-out of the sisters and urging the inclusion of Gay women as a necessary part of a new Constitution." By this time, it was too late. The New York lesbian feminists soon declared in *Come Out* that "the Black Panthers are sexist" and that "we women of a dispersed nation will build our community, speak in a woman's language born from our woman's oppression, grow strong together and explode in our women's revolution." At the convention, women had been a "dispersed minority" fighting on "enemy territory." Influenced by the convention, women were now a "dispersed nation."[70]

The Panthers left the convention with bitter feelings toward lesbian feminists and women's liberationists. One Panther told a reporter, "We are being used by the whites. . . . They are trying to take over, forcing their mores on us." This Panther and others "were specifically aiming their barbs at the Women's Liberation delegates." A Panther spokesman stated that "the leadership was 'trying to deal with the demands of several different radical white factions, while Women's Liberation is trying to run everything.' " Lesbian feminists were also bitter. Martha Shelley accused the Panthers of believing that women's "function" was to "bear revolutionary babies" and that, "with regard to women, [the party] is indistinguishable from the attitude of the German Nazi Party."[71]

The next meeting of the convention, which took place in Washington, D.C., in November 1970, met with more severe state repression and failed to overcome logistical problems. Still, according to the *Gay Dealer*, the Male Homosexual Workshop was "the largest such gathering to date, with over 150 gay revolutionaries." Seven hundred women met and passed a resolution of support for the Panthers. While endorsing women's liberation, the statement attacked the role played by lesbian feminists in Philadelphia. These women, the resolution stated, "while blatantly overstepping their bounds as whites," sought to "invalidate the experience of black women." "How relevant to Black women's lives are the white middle-class women's demands for 'the abolition of the nuclear family' when Black families are being savagely uprooted." Arguing that black women suffered from male and white supremacy, the statement concluded that "since most Black women choose to struggle for liberation with Black men, can we not then assume that the overriding problem of Black women as they see it is that of white supremacy?"[72]

Not longer after it began, the Panther-led project of reconstituting the nation was over. A party statement explained that the Washington meeting was a gathering of "revolutionary peoples from oppressed communities throughout the world," not the nation. Declaring that U.S. imperialism had "transformed other nations" into "oppressed communities," the Panthers announced that they would no longer conceive of themselves as "nationalists" or "internationalists." Instead, they would embrace "intercommunalism," declaring that "all people from all communities have the right to write their own constitutions for self-governance" and that the Panthers would work on developing "a new constitution for a new world."[73]

Multiracial, youthful, leftist, countercultural, and feminist, gay liberation was a male political formation in Philadelphia. In the 1960s, although some of the city's leading gay activists were misogynist, many lesbian activists wanted to work with gay men. In the early 1970s, although some of the city's leading lesbian activists wanted some level of separation from gay men, many gay activists were feminist. While relationships between gay and lesbian activism had changed, gay liberation and lesbian feminism are best understood not only as episodes in the separate histories of gay men and lesbians but as moments in the history that gay men and lesbians share.

13

Radicalesbian Feminism in "Fillydykia," 1971–1972

In March 1971, *Awake and Move*, the newsletter of the Philadelphia Women's Liberation Center, published "Radicalesbians: Coming Out vs. Coming Home." "For many of us," the anonymous author observed, "joining with other women to form the radicalesbians means coming out—announcing our identity as lesbians for the first time after hiding in the closets for many long, painful years. Others among us, myself included, have been in unsatisfactory relationships with men for many long, painful years. For these women, forming the radicalesbians means not coming out, but coming home." "To women who have been gay for a long time," the article declared, "the word lesbian means pain, guilt, suspicion, fear. To women who are new to the gay world, the word lesbian means joy, trusting other women, and the release of life-long tension resulting from trying to fit society's definitions instead of our own." According to this account, Radicalesbians formed when and where these two types of women came together.[1]

The *Awake and Move* narrative did not describe women who announced their lesbianism before Radicalesbians was created. Nor did it refer to lesbians who experienced joy before lesbian feminism took organized form. Just as post-Stonewall accounts of gay liberation suggested that the riots represented a decisive break with gay oppression, post–Lavender Menace accounts of lesbian feminism suggested that the formation of radical lesbian groups represented a decisive break with lesbian oppression. And in a second parallel development, just as GLF did not accept the concept of a gay minority but instead encouraged all men to come out, Radicalesbians did not accept the concept of a lesbian minority but instead encouraged all women to come out.

Notwithstanding these parallel positions, GLF and Radicalesbians did not have identical social bases or politics. Although both embraced feminism, GLF was overwhelmingly male while Radicalesbians was exclusively female. Although both embraced antiracism, GLF was multiracial while Radicalesbians was predominantly Euro-American. Even in terms of their antiminoritarian positions, while GLF argued for the existence of same-sex desire in all people, Radicalesbians was concerned specifically with women. Lesbian feminists rarely universalized their conceptions of lesbianism to include men or urge men to "come out" or "come home." A narrative in which previously "closeted" gay men welcomed "home" straight men who abandoned "unsatisfactory relationships" with women would have done violence to both the domestic imagery and the feminist contents of *Awake and Move*'s account. In more general terms, while Radicalesbians in some contexts emphasized what lesbians had in common with gay men, in others they highlighted the unique problems and possibilities that lesbians encountered as women.

Another difference between GLF and Radicalesbians is that the latter expressed more ambivalence about sexuality. "When someone asks me if I'm gay, or if I'm a lesbian," *Awake and Move*'s writer explained, "I don't know what to answer. If being a lesbian means having sexual relations with other women to the point of genital contact and orgasm, then I am not. This seems to be the definition used by the 'straight' world and also by the 'gay' world." But this was not the only definition: "I consider myself a lesbian because I love other women. . . . Sex is not an important part of my life; loving other women is." She concluded that "it would be unfortunate if the women in radicalesbians continue to define themselves in the same way that society defines them: according to whether or not, and with whom, they are performing the sex act." Calling for unity, she declared, "Sexual definitions can only separate women: gay women distrust straight women, straight women distrust gay women. We need to come together and enjoy each other."

While in some ways *Awake and Move*'s article used the terms "gay" and "lesbian" interchangeably, it also used them to distinguish sexual identities from loving ones and to distinguish the past from the present and future. To the extent that the term "gay" had been shared by women and men in the past, the article implicitly suggested that "gay women" abandon their bonds with gay men, embrace relationships with straight women, and use the name "lesbian" to signify the new partnership. Whereas homophile women had allied with homophile men because of a shared sense of identity and the perceived utility of heterosocial strategies, lesbian feminists now allied with straight feminists because of a shared sense of identity and the perceived utility of homosocial strategies.

In a variety of ways, however, when Radicalesbians proposed that "lesbians" and "gay women" make a home together, they carried with them the baggage of years of living with gay men. While lesbian feminists broke with gay liberationists, encouraging "gay women" to divorce gay men and make a primary commitment to the women's movement, it was not easy to forget a past and present that they shared with these men. Beneath the rhetoric of separatism lay complex relationships between the sexes. Just as gay liberation was influenced by lesbian feminism, lesbian feminism was influenced by gay liberation.

Radicalesbians

In late 1970, DOB founder Del Martin announced in the *Ladder* that she was saying "Good Bye to All That," to "male chauvinists of the homophile movement," to "washroom sex and pornographic movies," to "publications that look more like magazines for male nudist colonies," and to gay liberationists whose "liberation would only further enslave us." Declaring that she refused to be gay men's "nigger" and that she had never been their "mother," she left each man to his own "device": "Take care of it, stroke it gently, mouth it and fondle it. As the center of your consciousness, it's really all you have." "It is a revelation," she concluded, "to find acceptance, equality, love and friendship—everything we sought in the homophile community—not there, but in the women's movement." Early in 1971, the *Ladder* reported on "the separation of male homosexuals and Lesbians." According to the *Ladder*, the pattern was for women, "disgusted and tired" after working with men in gay liberation groups, to split off and form "lesbian liberation groups."[2]

Miriam Rosenberg's account of the founding of Radicalesbians Philadelphia does not conform to this pattern. In late 1970, Rosenberg began traveling from Philadelphia to go to Radicalesbians-NY meetings. She remembers creating the local Radicalesbians not because she was disgusted with gay men but because she was isolated as a woman within the local GLF. Moreover, Rosenberg recalls that GLF men helped her publicize Radicalesbians' first meeting. The posters they distributed listed GLF's telephone number and announced a dance cosponsored by GLF and Radicalesbians. The meeting took place in January 1971 at the Women's Center in Center City; the dance was held two days later in a Powelton Village warehouse.[3]

Arleen Olshan remembers going to the first meeting. Born in 1945 to a working-class Jewish family in New Hampshire, Olshan moved to Philadelphia as a child and grew up a "tomboy" in West and North Philly and Logan. Discussing her teenage years, she recalls participating in the lesbian and gay scenes of Rittenhouse Square and the coffeehouses. In the early 1960s, she moved to New York, where she began going to gay bars, identifying as a butch, and having sex with women. After living for awhile in California, she returned to Philadelphia in the late 1960s, residing at different times in Center City, Germantown, and Powelton Village. In 1970, Olshan recalls, she went to a lesbian and gay dance at St. Mary's, probably one of HAL's, which she describes as a "miracle." She remembers learning about Radicalesbians from *Drummer*: "You'd run into somebody and you'd say, 'You going to this Radicalesbians meeting?' 'I don't know. Are you going to go?' 'I don't know.' I went to this meeting and there were two, three hundred women."[4]

Victoria Brownworth, who was a Philadelphia high-school student activist in 1971 (until she was expelled for being a "bad moral influence" on the "girls" at her school), writes in her book, *Too Queer*, that there were several hundred women at the first Radicalesbians meeting. Olshan believes that most of the women were in their twenties and that there were "a lot of college students" and "hippie types," "a few older dyke types," and several women "coming out of marriages." Soon Radicalesbians was meeting weekly at the new Women's Center in West Philly. Former members estimate that from 6 to 40 women were present at most meetings. According to Art Spikol's "Gay Today," a 1972 *Philadelphia Magazine* article, Radicalesbians had over 150 members. Rosalie Davies thinks that more than 200 women eventually participated. Discussing the women at the first meeting, Rosenberg recalls that most of the Euro-Americans were "feminists," most of the African Americans were "into butch/femme," and most of the latter did not remain involved.[5]

Anita Cornwell remembers being one of the few African American women and one of the few women over 40 in Radicalesbians. Born in 1923 in South Carolina, Cornwell moved north with her working-class mother in 1939, arrived in West Philly in the early 1940s, and studied journalism at Temple. She recalls that in the 1950s, while living in West and North Philly, she had a series of relationships with African American women. During this period, she also socialized with African American lesbians at house parties. But because she did not like butch/femme roles or bars, both of which were popular among the lesbians she knew, she withdrew from African American lesbian culture in the 1960s. Drawn to the women's movement, she joined Radicalesbians and began writing for the *Ladder* in 1971. In 1983, some of her essays from this period were published in her book, *Black Lesbian in White America*.[6]

Davies, one of several HAL members and one of several mothers who were active in Radicalesbians, remembers finding the group through a women's studies class that she took at Penn. Around this time, Davies's ex-husband remarried, moved to Nova Scotia, and sued for custody of their children. Having been identified publicly as a lesbian in her work with HAL, Davies faced a difficult custody fight. In 1973, a Montgomery County court granted her severely restricted access to her 10- and 13-year-old children. A few years later, however, the children decided that they wanted to live with their mother, which their father did not contest. Meanwhile, Davies became a lawyer and founded Custody Action for Lesbian Mothers.[7]

Laurie Barron learned about Radicalesbians through the Women's Center. Barron's lower-middle-class Jewish family lived in Strawberry Mansion when she was born in 1948 but soon moved to West Oak Lane and then Mt. Airy. Discussing her early years, Barron remembers being a "tomboy" and having

Figure 13.1. Anita Cornwell, c. 1983. Photograph by Tee A. Corinne. With the permission of Naiad Press.

relationships with other students at Girls' High, which was "a hotbed of lesbianism." She also recalls coming across references to One, Mattachine, and DOB and sending away for their publications, which she "devoured." While in high school, Barron and her friends learned about the 1963 ECHO conference and began wearing ECHO buttons that had the words "Ask" or "Ask Me" printed below the acronym. Barron also remembers going to the coffeehouses, Rittenhouse Square, Rusty's, Dewey's, and Jay's Place in the 1960s. After a brief time at Barnard College, Barron returned to Philadelphia, enrolled at Temple, and began going to GLF Temple meetings, where she sometimes was the only woman present, and to Radicalesbians meetings.[8]

Like Barron, Becky Davidson recalls encountering the homophile movement before becoming involved with Radicalesbians. Born in 1948 to a lower-middle-class Jewish family, Davidson grew up in West and Northeast Philly and first met "queers" when she was a teenager and happened upon Rittenhouse Square. Soon she was going to the coffeehouses and Dewey's as well. In 1965 she participated in the Janus demonstration at Dewey's. The following year, she began her first lesbian relationship. Not long after that, she and her lover took an apartment in Center City. Davidson remembers going to the first HAL dance at St. Mary's and participating in the 1970

Figure 13.2. Laurie Barron and Marcea Rosen, 1975. With the permission of Laurie Barron and Marcea Rosen.

women's liberation conference at Penn. Soon thereafter she began going to the Women's Center, where she learned about Radicalesbians.[9]

Pat Hill recalls becoming involved with Radicalesbians through its dances. Born in 1935 in Georgia, Hill moved with her Quaker family to the well-to-do Philadelphia suburb of Huntingdon Valley when she was seven. In high school, she began a relationship with another female student, which ended after her partner went away to college and Hill enrolled at Temple. In the mid-1950s, Hill moved to Center City, joined the coffeehouse scene, and began a series of relationships with women. Over the next several years, she also began going to the Surf and Rusty's. Hill thinks that her first encounter with the lesbian movement took place at a women's dance, which was "very hot and sweaty" and "very exciting."[10]

Most Radicalesbian dances, parties, and meetings were held in Center City, West Philly, or Germantown/Mt. Airy. Olshan recalls that the dances were often held in Powelton Village because "lots of dykes" lived there. Radicalesbians also formed collective households in these neighborhoods. Davies, who remembers living with Jerry Curtis and his lover in a HAL collective in West Philly, says that she subsequently moved to a Radicalesbians collective in the same neighborhood. According to Davies, the HAL collective was "a political collective" insofar as the residents were working on the same political projects, but "it wasn't a political collective in the sense

Figure 13.3. Rachel Rubin and Pat Hill, 1973. Photograph by Joyce Finkleman. *Gay Alternative*, no. 5, 1973, 26. Courtesy of Gay, Lesbian, Bisexual, and Transgendered Archives of Philadelphia, Philadelphia, PA.

of the collective working on itself politically." In contrast, the Radicalesbians collective was "trying to create a new lifestyle."[11]

While Radicalesbians politicized the personal, it also personalized the political. Remembering a Radicalesbians dance, Hill says, "It was so exciting that there was a lesbian event," that it was "political," and that it was "an alternative to Rusty's." Discussing meetings, she says that "part of the point was to meet people, if not the main point." According to Hill, most of the women in Radicalesbians were single. She remembers that after she became involved with another member they "pretty much stopped going" to meetings. Barron says, "You came and you met somebody and then you left." According to a Radicalesbian interviewed by Spikol, "Women use us . . . to come out, to make contacts, to find a group of people to lean on. Some drop out once they've learned to cope. Others stay with it."[12]

In addition to organizing meetings, parties, and dances, Radicalesbians participated in a women's picnic in Fairmount Park, a church social action fair in suburban Lansdowne, a conference on "Reconciliation of the Church and the Homosexual" in suburban Ardmore, the Christopher Street Liberation Day parade in New York, and a lesbian feminist conference in Connecticut. In October 1971, the group demonstrated at the mayoral campaign headquarters of Frank Rizzo and Thacher Longstreth. In November, it began producing a newsletter, called at various times *Getting It Together*, *Joy of Gay*, and *Lesbians Fight Back*. Newsletters in 1972 listed "women-only" meetings, dances, film showings, bike-riding trips, and open houses, as well as mixed-sex gay coffee hours at Temple and Penn, Metropolitan Community Church (MCC) services, baseball games, and picnics. Radicalesbians also spoke on the radio and at high schools, colleges, medical schools, and conferences.[13]

Much of Radicalesbians' work took place in consciousness-raising (c-r) groups. Hill remembers participating in a group of about 20 lesbians who met at the Women's Center. HAL's Carole Friedman joined a predominantly lesbian group of six or seven women who met in West Philly. After her relationship with Ada Bello ended, Friedman became involved with a Penn professor she met through her c-r group. According to Friedman, "The particular genius of a c-r group was that women looked inward and explored in depth difficult personal issues as those issues intersected with ideas of being women in the world. And there was a format, I guess sometimes it became a formula, but there was a structured mechanism for women to hear themselves and each other." In contrast, DOB discussions were "less excavating" and more like "the way friends may throw around ideas." Friedman continues, "I went from being more engaged in a political sense with the outside world and turned more inward to myself, with other women, in a c-r setting." According to Davies, "We did an enormous amount of work on ourselves and an enormous amount of analysis. And the academic women started publishing wonderful work. We were discussing our fear of men, our fear of anger, our relationships with men, man-hating. And then, going away from men, we were talking about where and when patriarchy first took over and we were talking about how women could self-actualize. . . . We were teaching each other to be political."[14]

For Friedman and Davies, Radicalesbians was a single-sex and feminist alternative to HAL. Friedman thinks that she was "more affected by feminism" than Barbara Gittings and Bello were and that they thus "took different paths" in the early 1970s. She says that "realizing that one could be gay and healthy" was "a great kind of earthquake" in her "consciousness," but the "next big earthquake" was "brought on by feminism." Remembering that she began to have "friends who had not been gay-identified" and were "coming out through feminism," she says that she was "quite different from them, but quite interested in what they were going through." She recalls feeling that there was less to learn from the gay movement and more to learn from "rethinking" herself "as a woman." The "gay movement," she says, "was just no longer so alive for me." She remembers "being pulled inside in all of these different directions," feeling "loyalties to people who were not so attracted to the new gay liberation, feminist liberation, women's liberation movements" but feeling "conflicting loyalties to new people and new ideas." She also suggests that there was conflict between "what Ada and Barbara represented," which was "a very acute and developed intellectual kind of social criticism as well as a commitment to civil action," and "the hippie, countercultural liberation movements."[15]

Davies continued to be affiliated with HAL through 1972, but over time her allegiances shifted to Radicalesbians. She thinks that because several HAL women were "so strong" and "weren't particularly womanly," they "hadn't experienced" and "weren't willing to acknowledge the oppressed position of women." Davies describes the women who remained involved in predominantly male groups as "male-identified women" who had "no feminist consciousness whatsoever." "I wouldn't call that a joining of the women and the men," she declares. "I would call it a joining of the men and the men. And anyone who had any sense of herself as a woman wasn't doing that."[16]

Many homophile women, however, were not drawn to radical feminism. According to Bello, "We were aware of the fact all along that whenever you had dealings with organizations that were mostly male, the males would want to be doing all the talking and all that. And at some point I guess women realized that unless they separated and made their own organization, and maybe go back in only after they had found their strength, they would never be treated with any kind of equal footing." Bello says she does not remember "having to leave any organization because of that," but adds that she "stopped being very active in the movement when that had started to happen." In 1970, she left Germantown, bought a house with her new lover in West Philly, and dropped out of HAL. Although Bello now views radical feminism more positively, she still laughs about a New Year's dance in New York where she learned that it was now "out" to stop the music and scream at midnight because "that was tradition." While she thinks that it was a good thing to question tradition, she argues, "Sometimes you look pretty silly. Like at midnight. There's not much gender involved in that."[17]

Gittings says, "I have always characterized the '70s in our movement as the time of greatest separatism, which I never took part in and always opposed." She adds that she had "no patience with those who said that women, as women, have to stick together because frankly most women don't care about lesbians." "I couldn't care less about day care and abortion rights and the other things that women were concerned about," she declares. That said, Gittings did fight for lesbians in their struggles to be treated as the equals of gay men. In 1971, she was part of a group that criticized David Susskind for having gay men but not lesbians on his television show. A short time later, Susskind featured a group of lesbians that included Gittings. *Drummer* reported that all of the lesbians interviewed by Susskind agreed that women's liberation "had been a great help." But the article, titled "Lesbians First; Women Second," noted that "their first allegiance was to gay liberation." Gittings was quoted as saying, "I feel more strongly as a lesbian than as a feminist. . . . As long as prejudice continues to exist against my people, my primary identification will be with them."[18]

While Radicalesbians distinguished itself from HAL, it shared the older group's ambivalence about butch/femme and bars. Spikol reported that a Radicalesbian told him that "male-identified role-playing among lesbians is on the way out" and that what's called a 'male role' or 'female role' is no more than a product of society's conditioning." Davidson says, "Feminism freed me from having to figure out whether I was butch or femme. . . . I felt great about that. I was so excited that they were doing away with role-playing." Olshan argues that Radicalesbians was appealing because many women "didn't fit in the butch or femme category or didn't want to." She says that she now identifies as a butch and a feminist but that "it was very hard" to do so "back in those days."[19]

In an essay published in the 1970s, Cornwell wrote that lesbians assumed, when she was younger, that she was a femme. But when she became older and "heavier," they assumed that she was a "stud," a term that made her "hair stand on end." She regarded it as unfortunate that African American women had not joined the women's movement because "unless they have come across feminist ideas from somewhere, they are apt to remain in the old rut of sexual role-playing that apparently affects all traditional lesbian circles." In the 1990s, Cornwell describes butch/femme culture as "ludicrous," asking, "Why ape the straight world?" especially when most relationships between men and women are "atrocious."[20] If Cornwell is right that African American lesbian culture continued to be organized around butch/femme roles in the early 1970s, Radicalesbian ambivalence about butch/femme may have been racialized and may explain, in part, the group's failure to attract more African American women. And if the same is true of Euro-American working-class lesbian culture, Radicalesbian ambivalence about butch/femme may have had a class dimension and may explain, in part, the group's failure to attract more Euro-American working-class women.

Radicalesbians also was ambivalent about bars. Discussing the group's meetings, Hill says that "it was just such a departure to be having a conversation in a lighted place instead of a dark, smoky place." Davidson recalls Radicalesbian protests at gay bars that discriminated against women and African Americans. A poem published in *Lesbians Fight Back* declared, "I don't belong to Rusty's Bar/I don't know who those people are."[21]

In 1971, *Getting It Together* published "A One Act Bar Scene" by Mike [Marlene "Mike" Miller], Gale [Russo], and Laurie [Barron]. Parodying the Mystique, they set the campy scene in "The Mistaque," which they placed in "Fillydykia." According to the scene, when "Lois Lesbian" and "Simple Burton" stand too close to each other, a male bartender tells them they can pay to dance upstairs. When the two begin dancing downstairs, the German-accented, Nazi-appearing, Argentinian manager tries to throw them out. Just then, "Lavender Menace," also known as "Klarketta Kunt," bursts out of the telephone booth and demands that the "leech" unhand her "sisters." When he says "Der's little place else to go," she responds, "Suppose you gave a bar and nobody came." Then she provides him with a preview of the future in which "Shirley Temple in a mountie outfit leads 3 million gays on horseback across the bar." Making the moral explicit, a statement following the scene declared, "We are tired of watered drinks; we're tired of drink-hustling waiters and waitresses ripping off their sisters and brothers; we're tired of paying a 'fee' to be entitled to dance—especially in the Mystique."[22]

"Klarketta Kunt" saved "Lois Lesbian" in the midst of a campaign season in which the metropolis's underworld was being exposed. In September 1971, in a move that embarrassed both Police Commissioner Rizzo, who was running for mayor, and district attorney Arlen Specter, who was planning to run for governor, governor Milton Shapp approved an investigation of the Locust Strip. After undercover state police were solicited for drinks, prostitution, and sodomy, state officials tried to close 12 bars. Mayoral candidate Thacher Longstreth charged that Rizzo had allowed the strip to flourish. Police were accused of being in cahoots with the bars and Rizzo's campaign coordinator was linked with a company that owned one of the bars. In the end, while a Liquor Control Board examiner was relieved of his duties, the bars remained open. After Rizzo was elected, Specter and Shapp ordered investigations that eventually documented extensive corruption by the LCB, police, and bars. Meanwhile, in February 1972 the Mystique burned down in "mysterious circumstances."[23]

Although members of Radicalesbians expressed ambivalence about bars, butches, and femmes, they knew that many lesbians continued going to bars and continued identifying as butches and femmes. In late November 1971, *Getting It Together* warned that "the heat will be on in the bars during the next 3 weeks (except Mystique and Attic)" and suggested that women be careful. Brownworth remembers "sneaking into gay bars" when she was both a "teenage baby butch" and a member of Radicalesbians. While a *Getting It Together* article asserted that "we are growing in friendship, love, and honesty because we gather in an atmosphere unlike the bar scene," the female author of the article was identified as Mike.[24] While it criticized bars, butches, and femmes, Radicalesbians was claiming to speak and act on behalf of lesbians, many of whom patronized bars and performed butch/femme.

Positioning itself in relation to both HAL and butch/femme bar culture, Radicalesbians located itself spatially within the Women's Center and politically within feminism. That said, its relationship with the feminist movement was conflicted. In 1972, Davies, Friedman, Gittings, and two other women spoke on two panels on lesbianism sponsored by NOW Philadelphia. Davies says that the local NOW was "extremely homophobic." Cornwell remembers hesitating before going to the Women's Center because she had heard that feminists were "casting aspersions on lesbians." According to Hill, "it was very difficult relating to straight women" and "there was a lot of tension between feminists and lesbians." She recalls meeting with a group of straight women and says that it was "a hideous experience" and that "we just might have been meeting with aliens."[25]

Spikol called attention to these conflicts in *Philadelphia Magazine*: "The fact that virtually all lesbians are feminists has given certain elements of straight society a weapon with which to fight the Women's Liberation Movement, although it is clearly hitting below the belt." He explained that "usually the term 'dyke' is enough to cause the moderate woman to back off in fear, feeling that a dyke is somehow a super-lesbian—dominant, aggressive, hard—in a word, masculine." Although Spikol's discussion won praise from the Women's Center, he was not above "hitting below the belt" himself, asserting that "while so much of the writing from the feminist movement has been eloquent, that of Radicalesbians is so dogmatic, so hostile, that it may serve to frighten away many of the very women it hopes to attract."[26]

Rather than moderate its rhetoric, Radicalesbians continued to challenge straight women, in part by linking the concept of the woman-identified-woman with lesbianism. In a 1972 speech at a women's rally, Davies declared that she was proud to be called a lesbian, but that many feminists "are afraid that the number of lesbians in the movement are giving it a bad name." Arguing that "lesbianism has never received priority treatment in the women's movement," Davies insisted that "your gay sister has always been doubly oppressed." She stated that "the lesbian who has a good job may be fired tomorrow, when someone tells her boss that she is gay" and that "landlords frequently refuse to rent to two women." She continued, "We suffer discrimination in public accommodations. If you don't believe me try going to a straight bar and dancing close with another woman! We are ghettoized into gay bars which exploit us with cover charges and high cost watered-down drinks, not to mention police harassment—for our bars are the most frequently raided." Insisting that lesbianism was central to feminism, Davies dared women to embrace it: "Lesbianism is the ultimate challenge to male chauvinism because it tells men they are irrelevant. For this reason we should all be proud to be called lesbians." In an open letter to a friend published in the *Ladder*, Cornwell wrote, "My dear beloved Sister, can't you see the innate horror of your saying that women horrify you? If you are horrified of being you, then what else is there left for you to be?" Cornwell argued that "you are a Lesbian whether you sleep with a woman or not."[27]

Radicalesbians members also signaled that they were woman-identified by highlighting their roles as mothers. Referring to her own story, Davies declared, "Lesbians are the only women whose children are always awarded to the father. Judges consider us unfit to love children because we love other women. . . . Let me tell you sisters, children do not share these judges' biases against their mothers." Davies also noted, "If a child shows homosexual tendencies she is not considered fit for adoption but must remain institutionalized. In other words, lesbians do not deserve children and lesbian children do not deserve mothers." Discussing her children, another Radicalesbian told Spikol, "One day they were out on the porch. . . . At the time, I had short hair, and my lover had long hair, and just as I leaned over to kiss my lover one of the neighborhood kids peeked through the blinds and said, 'Who's that man kissing your mother?' And my kid looked in and said, 'That's no man—that's my mother.' "[28]

Radicalesbians identified most closely with revolutionary feminism. A *Lesbians Fight Back* article, "To Liberate Women Is To Liberate Society," explained that "as we move beyond examining our personal lives and hassles, we look for ways to correct the injustices inherent in the political and economic system" and "recognize total change to be necessary." A Radicalesbians pamphlet cited by Spikol declared that "male supremacy and its primary extension, sexism, is the basis for all forms of oppression, racism, capitalism and imperialism, and can only be destroyed with a feminist revolution."[29]

Indicting male supremacy, many Radicalesbians viewed heterosexual relationships as oppressive. Olshan recalls that she stopped having sex with men in the 1960s. The last man was "sweet," knew that she had had lesbian relationships, and "still proposed" marriage: "And I said I gotta get out of this. It's like no. I gotta get out of this completely! . . . I just pictured myself. This guy lived in the country. I'd be barefoot and pregnant by the stove and going out of my mind. . . . I saw heterosexuality as a jail; it would encase me and I wouldn't be expressive and I wouldn't be myself." Barron recalls that when a boyfriend proposed marriage in the 1960s, "I just freaked out. I just thought to myself, no, no, no, no. I can't live my life as somebody's wife." She says that she then began identifying more as lesbian and less as bisexual. Davidson was not involved with men sexually but remembers that a gay friend proposed marriage: "I avoided that like the poison. I did not want to have any possibility of a man having control over me or my body or anything. I never thought it was safe." Discussing the Radicalesbians era, Hill says, "After having always [had] a steady boyfriend on the side while I was chasing after women and being chased after, then I slept with a man once a year, to remind myself how much I liked women or to just sort of keep my hand in it." She remembers doing this until the late 1970s and then never having sex with a man again.[30]

Cornwell strongly indicted heterosexuality. In the *Ladder*, she asked her friend, "Why in the name of hell do so many of our Sisters continue to let men use and abuse them to death?" She argued that "*any* woman sleeping with *any* man on a fairly regularly basis is prostituting her mind, her body and her spirit." "I've seen your busted jaw and blackened eyes and bruised body," she wrote. "You are living in hell." Contrasting this with her own relationship, Cornwell declared, "I have a person who loves me, who treats me as an equal human being, who respects me and makes every effort to try to understand me."[31]

Cornwell specifically condemned African American men, noting that "some of us can't seem to see just who it is that's standing very flat-footedly on our broken-down backs." She pointedly criticized "nationalism": "So don't get turned off when Blackey starts coming on with all that weird crap about Women's Liberation dividing the black community. Like when were we ever all together with *him* sitting on top of us and Whitey on top of him and everybody giving us black Sisters hell going and coming?" Rejecting calls for unity between the sexes, Cornwell argued in favor of feminist unity against patriarchy: " 'Our' black educators and civil rights leaders (all male, of course) have repeatedly stressed the idea that black men should be advanced at the expense of black women 'if full acculturation is to come about as the patriarchal family is a cherished American institution.' " Responding "bluntly," Cornwell wrote that "patriarchy is the root cause of all the major ills in the world today."[32]

Connecting the oppression of women with heterosexuality, Radicalesbians linked feminism with lesbianism. Insofar as Radicalesbians encouraged all women to reject heterosexuality, the group rejected the minority model favored by homophile activists. But this left open the question of whether the same-sex bonds cultivated by Radicalesbians would be sexual, antisexual, and/or asexual. At times, as in the case of "Coming Out vs. Coming Home," members downplayed the sexual dimensions of same-sex relationships. But Radicalesbian rhetoric often incorporated the sexual. Brownworth recalls that at her first Radicalesbians meeting she "discovered, for the first time, the political side of lesbianism, the sexual side of feminism." Spikol wrote that "there are those radical feminist lesbians who feel that women who are not having sexual relations with other women are copping out." He also quoted a Radicalesbians pamphlet that stated, "We are women whose sense of self and energies, including sexual, center around women. . . . Male society has defined lesbianism as a 'sexual act' and goes no further. But as lesbian women, we say it is more, it is a lifestyle—a political and profoundly revolutionary lifestyle." The pamphlet encouraged women to "make a commitment to each other, which includes sexual love."[33]

Responding to her friend, Cornwell wrote, "I suppose what you're really wanting to know is, am I sleeping with a woman? And the answer, dear Sister, is you can damn sure bet your last dollar I am. And life has *never* been sweeter!" She concluded, "I am doing what you would like to do but are too terrified to even think clearly about." Davies's rally speech also addressed straight women and dealt with sex. "You think we are all just dying to make that first sexual embrace with you," she declared, "and we think you are hoping we will offer that 'first experience' so that you can decide whether you really prefer men or not." She concluded, "sisters unite!"[34]

Members of Radicalesbians sought unity with other women not only in sexual ways. Cornwell's first article in the *Ladder* expressed hope for cross-racial alliances. "[A]ren't we ever going to get it together as to just why he's so afraid of our getting together with *The Girls*?" Cornwell asked. "And especially with the white girls? Which brings me right square to where I want to be which is with our white, brown and black Sisters in Women's Liberation." Her second article linked sexual and racial unity: "With this final step that I have taken," she explained, "that of living with women (of a different race, and this too is crucial . . .), and sleeping with one of them, and enjoying it to the utmost, you are left in the position of either following me vicariously as you've done from the time your life style became a coffin, or, and this is your ultimate horror, you are forced to look down and find a way of your own."[35]

By the summer of 1972, however, Cornwell was writing in the *Ladder* about racism in the women's movement. Referring to a conference of predominantly Euro-American lesbians, Cornwell described learning about the killing of Panther George Jackson and feeling that "*their white Brothers had killed my Black Brother!*" Although Jackson was probably a sexist "pig," she declared, "They didn't shoot him because he was a pig. They got him because he was black. I am black, too, and as James Baldwin is reputed to have said to Angela Davis, 'If they get you in the morning, they will certainly come for me in the night.' " In the coming months, she began thinking more about racism: "I had to admit, yes, there is a difference, it matters like hell. Because as someone has said, 'When things go wrong, all blacks are black, and all whites are whitey.' . . . And the moment I or any other black forget we *are* black, it may be our last. For when the shooting starts *any* black is fair game. The bullets don't give a damn whether I sleep with woman or man."[36]

In a 1974 essay, Cornwell wrote that when she joined the women's movement, she convinced herself that "the color of my skin would have little or no bearing on how Movement women would accept me." But then came "the first major unsettling episode." At a conference, "two white women discussed the actions of several black women, who the white sisters felt were not patriotic enough." When one of the women saw Cornwell, she said "Of course, I can understand why they feel the way they do." Cornwell wrote that "it struck me that she had absolutely no comprehension whatsoever why those aforementioned black sisters were not ardent flag-wavers." Six months after joining the movement, she "faced the truth" that "racism does exist in the Movement." She later noted, "I am not saying that I met racism every step of the way in the womyn's movement. I did not. It was there, however, and is still there."[37] Challenging the movement's racism, Cornwell nevertheless remained a committed feminist.

Lesbian Feminism and Gay Men

Radicalesbians thus defined itself principally in relation to women's movements and communities. In important ways, however, it also defined itself in relation to gay men. Many members shared a past with gay men. Everyday lesbian and gay worlds continued to converge as well as diverge. And lesbians still encountered dominant cultural representations that either focused on gay men or placed lesbians alongside gay men. Although Radicalesbians at times used separatist rhetoric, it also worked with gay activists. To be sure, in some ways Radicalesbians regarded gay men as men, as supporters of male supremacy, and as the beneficiaries of male privilege. In other ways, however, Radicalesbians believed that gay men, too, were oppressed by patriarchy and heterosexuality, that gay men should not be thought of as men, and that lesbians and gay men shared historically vital and politically valuable bonds.

Turning more specifically to Radicalesbians and GLF, while the two did not coincide chronologically or racially, they had similar politics. Both were radical, disdained homophile reformism, and favored alliances with other revolutionaries. Both were countercultural, formed collective households, integrated the personal and political, opposed role-playing, and emphasized consciousness-raising. Both were ambivalent about bars and bar culture. Both regarded patriarchy, male supremacy, and sexism as foundations of oppression. Both embraced sexual and loving identities. And both rejected the minority model and sought new sexual and political partners by urging straights to come out. While Radicalesbians often politically diverged with some of the new gay groups of 1971–1972, it often politically converged with the GLF of 1970.

Gay politics was in flux in 1971. In February, the local People's Fund, which raised money for progressive causes, allocated nearly $12,000 to the Panthers, Resistance, Women's Center, Welfare Rights Organization, and four other groups. When HAL's and GLF's requests were rejected, a spokesman accused the fund of "male chauvinism." Disappointed on the local level, GLF also was affected by developments elsewhere. According to Kiyoshi Kuromiya, shortly after a national lesbian and gay conference was held in Texas in March, "most gay liberation groups around the country disappeared." He links this with the rise of the more moderate Gay Activists Alliance, noting that GAA was more "political," more "structured," and more concerned with "rights" than with "consciousness-raising" and "sexism":

> We would go outside at the national conferences in Atlanta or Austin or wherever they occurred and cry on each other's shoulders. . . . We knew exactly what kind of railroading was going on inside the building. And how people unfamiliar with the gay liberation movement were being made to think it was something very different than what we felt. We felt it as a very liberating experience and that you couldn't make statements this way or that way or define us this way or that way. And you could show people making love. But when you start to say the same words the government was saying, "consenting adults," "in private," etc., who was going to define what is private and what the age of consent is and what acts are legal and what acts aren't legal? The whole idea of legislating sexual behavior was abhorrent to us. And any discussion of that and any setting down of any additional laws we felt was a very big step backwards, as it was when a political organization would sell out its political principles over and over again to maintain its power and gain power by feeling that political promises meant more than human feelings.

According to Kuromiya, gay liberationists came to believe that "the less structure there was to their movement nationally, the better it would be." Asked whether he remembers when GLF disbanded, Kuromiya says, "It's still active. We're still around."[38]

Be that as it may, GLF stopped meeting and acting as Gay Liberation Front around the time that Radicalesbians was established. The GLF that cosponsored Radicalesbians' first dance actually called itself Gay Liberation *Fellows*, a short-lived group with a name that acknowledged its single-sex character. In March 1971, the Fellows invaded WIBG to confront disk jockey Long John Wade, who had used "a lisping falsetto voice" in announcing a song he said he was playing for his friends at Jay's Place. When GLFers telephoned his on-the-air line to protest, Wade replied that it was not as though he had used the word "nigger." According to *Drummer*, "a double-freak combination of a nigger-faggot (a black Gay fellow) then got on the phone." Asked whether he would be willing to share the air, Wade said "sure." Four or five Fellows then went to the studio, chanting "Gay Power" before the microphone was turned off.[39] While gay liberation remained active in Kuromiya's sense, the GLF and the Fellows folded.

For a few months, that left gay activists with two local options: GLF Temple and HAL. As lesbians became more attracted to Radicalesbians, gay men began playing a more significant role in HAL. In August 1971, *Drummer* reported that HAL had 50 members, "evenly divided between the sexes." Although Byrna Aronson remained active, by early 1972 HAL's president was Paul Long and most of its officers were male. In this period, HAL continued working on several projects that it had undertaken earlier, including the Task Force on Religion and the Homosexual. In March 1971, 15–20 members of HAL and the new Philadelphia Christian Homophile Church demonstrated at fundamentalist Carl McIntire's Bible Presbyterian Church in Collingswood, New Jersey. HAL also received money from a second application to the People's Fund, organized another series of forums, and began sponsoring dances again at St. Mary's. According to *Drummer*, the dances were "practically the first activity for gay people of both sexes, which doubles their potential of providing identity and solidarity to a rather nebulous gay community."[40]

With support from Radicalesbians, HAL also focused on electoral and legislative politics. In October 1971, Aronson and Eugene Spotto presented a set of demands at hearings sponsored by the local Fellowship Commission. The primary goal was amending the city's Human Relations Act to forbid discrimination on the basis of sexual orientation in employment, housing, and public accommodations. Aronson and Spotto told the commission that the fire department recently had fired an employee based on "an arrest but NON-conviction on Homosexual charges" and that the school system had fired a teacher when it discovered that he had "declared himself as a Homosexual for the Selective Service." Two other cases of job discrimination were publicized around this time as well. In August 1971, the press reported on John Carfagno's suit against the U.S. Postal Service, which in 1970 had denied him a job in Paoli, Pennsylvania, because he was a "sexual deviate." In September 1971, the *News* reported that Paula Grossman, a male-to-female transsexual, had been suspended from her teaching position in Bernards Township, New Jersey.[41]

After Thacher Longstreth and Frank Rizzo refused to respond to a request that they state their positions on HAL's demands, 20–35 members of HAL, Radicalesbians, the new GAA, and the new Homosexual Information Service (HIS) demonstrated at both mayoral campaign headquarters just days before the election. The candidates did in fact discuss gay issues during the campaign. But when they did so, in allegations and promises concerning the Locust Strip and prison assaults, they mobilized antigay support. After Rizzo won the election, *Getting It Together* offered "condolences" on the "passing of the late Metropolis of Sisterly and Brotherly Love."[42]

HAL's second legislative goal was state sodomy law reform. In April 1971, HAL leaders testified before the state Senate Judiciary Committee, presenting a petition with 4,000 names and criticizing both the existing law and proposals to decriminalize sodomy for married couples only. After the mayoral election, HAL returned to this campaign. In March 1972 the *Daily News* editorialized in favor of eliminating "victimless crimes," including "homosexuality." Later in the year, however, the state replaced its sodomy law with a statute prohibiting "voluntary deviate sexual intercourse," which was defined as "sexual intercourse per os or per anus between human beings who are not husband or wife, and any form of sexual intercourse with an animal." Discriminating against unmarried sexual partners of all kinds, this remained the law until the state supreme court declared it unconstitutional in 1980.[43]

HAL also worked on other projects. In 1971, the group announced that it had persuaded the Penn Sexual Counseling Service to stop using David Reuben's *Everything You Always Wanted to Know about Sex*, which contained "gross distortions and misrepresentations on homosexuality." The same year, HAL reported that it had disrupted an "offensive" performance by Ace Trucking Company at Playhouse in the Park. Early in 1972, HAL praised WIBG, the station that GLF had attacked, for airing a 30-minute segment on antigay discrimination and a public service announcement on antigay harassment. Around the same time, HAL participated in a conference held at the Germantown Community Church to work on improving relationships between lesbian and gay groups. HAL, GLF Temple, HIS, the Metropolitan Community Church, and a contingent from the National Peace Action Coalition sent representatives. The groups agreed to work together on a Gay Children's Committee, Gay Hotline, Gay Pride Week, and Gay Coalition Community Center.[44]

According to Rick Rosen, HAL experienced personal conflicts, political factionalism, financial improprieties, and fears of FBI infiltration in this period. FBI documents reveal that HAL was being monitored under the bureau's women's liberation surveillance program. In addition, while several lesbian members were becoming more active in Radicalesbians, several gay members were turning their attention to the community center project. According to Rosen, after conflict over finances erupted in 1971, a number of men "walked out of HAL in disgust" and started HIS. Criticizing the founders of HIS, Rosen recalls, "And what was Homosexual Information Service going to be? It was going to be all men. Because why did HAL fall apart? Because there were women in it." The *HAL Newsletter* noted that HIS approached "legal reform by conservative (vs. political action in the extreme) structured legal channels." Meanwhile, Aronson continued to speak on behalf of HAL and was identified as HAL chairwoman until the group became inactive in 1973.[45]

While all of this was happening, GLF Temple remained active and new student groups were established. At LaSalle, Students for Individual Rights formed in the fall of 1971. At Penn, a weekly Gay Coffee Hour in Houston Hall was established in late 1971. By early 1973, there were organized lesbian and gay groups at Swarthmore, Bryn Mawr, and Haverford Colleges and students had tried to form one at Villanova.[46]

GAA Philadelphia, which became one of the city's most active lesbian and gay groups in the 1970s, was founded in June 1971 and began meeting at Penn's Christian Association building. Jeff Escoffier, who was a Penn graduate student, recalls that GAA's first president was Tim Woodbury and that Woodbury had been involved with GAA-NY. Escoffier says that when GAA began publicizing its meetings as many as a hundred people would come. He thinks that 90–95% of the early members were male and Euro-American. Tommi Avicolli Mecca remembers going with several GLF Temple members to a GAA meeting at Penn. He says that it was mostly male, mostly Euro-American, and "boring as all hell." According to Mecca, most of the participants were student leftists who were "very intellectual, very academic, and very much into theory, Robert's Rules, constitutions, and endless by-laws." He thinks that he was one of the only GLFers to join GAA at this stage.[47]

Toward the end of 1971, Escoffier became GAA president. In 1972, the group began meeting at Horizon House in Center City, where more than a hundred people would come to weekly meetings. Escoffier recalls that after GAA moved, it attracted more "street people," drags, working-class people, African Americans, and women, but nevertheless remained mostly Euro-American, middle class, and male. Harry Langhorne, a Penn architecture

Figure 13.4. Harry Langhorne, Matthew Grande, and Jeffrey Escoffier at Foster House, 1971. Photograph by Harry Eberlin. Courtesy of Jeffrey Escoffier. With the permission of Harry Eberlin.

student who was elected GAA vice president and then president, estimates that 5% of the participants were women.[48]

According to a 1972 description, GAA was formed by people "who felt that none of the existing organizations were dealing adequately with the political side of Gay Liberation." GAA's statement of purpose declared, "The gay liberation movement is a movement for the right to express one's love freely, without regard to presupposed sexual roles. While this goal can be approached socially and culturally, through consciousness raising groups, gay churches, and educational programs to reduce public hostility to gay women and men, the Gay Activists Alliance Philadelphia stresses the development of gay political power."[49]

In its first year, in addition to sponsoring dances and social events in Center City, GAA undertook four major projects. First, it "zapped" antigay speakers, performers, and businesses. In December 1971, for example, GAA disrupted a talk at LaSalle by antigay psychiatrist Samuel Hadden. In early

1972 it zapped KYW-TV for its "flippant attitude in reporting the beatings of two GAA members in New York."[50]

Second, GAA acted against police harassment. According to Greg Lee, a married bisexual GAA member who wrote a weekly column for *Drummer*, in January 1972, the month of Rizzo's inauguration, "police activity in connection with our town's gay bars was stepped up." In June, GAA members met with police officials to discuss the Merry-Go-Round. According to GAA's newsletter, a police captain stated that "if cruising continues on the merry-go-round, so will police harassment." GAA began distributing a flier with advice on how to deal with the police.[51]

Third, GAA intervened in election campaigns. In October 1971, GAA joined HAL and Radicalesbians at Rizzo and Longstreth headquarters. In March 1972, 50–100 people participated in a GAA and HAL demonstration at a Republican City Committee fundraising event at the Academy of Music. In April, GAA zapped speeches by presidential candidates Hubert Humphrey and Edmund Muskie. In June, Langhorne testified in Pittsburgh before the regional Democratic Platform Committee.[52]

GAA's fourth project was the sexual orientation amendment to the city's Human Relations Act. In April 1972, city council member Isadore Bellis introduced a bill to add "sex" (not "sexual orientation") to the act's antidiscrimination provisions. According to GAA's George Bodamer, council member Thomas Foglietta supported a plan to have GAA offer testimony at hearings on Bellis's bill in June. At the hearings, when Vic Carpenter of the First Unitarian Church mentioned the word "homosexual," Bellis "informed him that any such testimony was not to be allowed, as it was not 'germane.'" Declaring that a sexual orientation amendment would have to be considered separately and that he would never support it, Bellis tried to remove from his list of speakers the eight names submitted by GAA. With Foglietta's aid, some names were restored, but Bellis continued to rule out of order speakers who addressed gay rights. Attempting to circumvent Bellis, GAA put forward "Carole," a "gay woman," who testified that Bellis's bill would not protect all women "as lesbians could still be discriminated against." Bellis ruled her out of order as well. While the "sex" amendment did pass city council in 1972 (the same year that Pennsylvania ratified the federal Equal Rights Amendment and a year after Pennsylvania passed a state ERA), the fight for a local gay rights bill took another 10 years to succeed.[53]

How did Radicalesbians respond to and participate in these developments? Some Radicalesbians approached the men of HAL, GLF, and GAA with expectations of mutual hostility. Pat Hill, for example, thinks that in the years before she became an activist, lesbians and gay men in her world "had absolutely nothing to do with each other." She also remembers that when she first went to HAL dances, the men were "too outrageous" and "took up a lot of space." Men, she says, "either have so much more energy or dance so much more obviously that they sort of crowd women." After Radicalesbians formed, some members continued to experience conflict with gay men. Hill remembers that while leafleting outside bars, she encountered gay men who would say, "Why don't you all just shut up and stop this. You're making things worse." Asked whether Radicalesbians ever talked about gay men, Hill says, "I don't remember any discussions at all about gay men." According to Arleen Olshan, "the gay men were obnoxious in the beginning" and "nobody wanted to relate to specific individuals" because of "the kinds of tactics" they were using, which had "nothing to do with women's issues." Olshan also remembers going to a GAA meeting and feeling "very uncomfortable," particularly when Robert's Rules were used. "I guess it has to do with power," she concludes. Explaining that she does not want "to make any stereotypes" or "say anything that's really hostile," Olshan speculates that "maybe in white, educated, middle-class homes, young men, certainly in the '50s and '60s, were kind of trained toward being heard, to having a voice, to taking leadership roles, more so than women were accustomed to."[54]

Escoffier recalls referring to women as "girls" at a meeting with HAL, GAA, and Radicalesbians and that the Radicalesbians "stormed out," which he describes as a "traumatizing" event but an "effective lesson" that made him realize that he had to learn more about feminism. Laurie Barron went to one or two GAA meetings, but says that it "seemed like a boys' thing" and that she felt more "aligned" with Radicalesbians. According to Barron, "there really was a coming apart in the early '70s." Becky Davidson remembers going to a GAA meeting at Penn: "I decided it was too many men and they were taking over and I wanted something woman-identified so I started with Radicalesbians." She says, "I've gone in and out of man-hating. And that has included gay men at times. When I started with the feminist stuff, I was in a really man-hating kind of place and didn't hang out with gay men. Didn't really hate gay men, but men just became not a part of my life." According to Davidson, "After having gotten this feminist consciousness, if I went to something like a GAA meeting and I'd see gay men taking over, I would see it in a feminist perspective and go, 'Hey! They're men. I mean they're gay, but they're still men.' " Asked whether any gay activists supported feminism, Davidson replies, "No. Gay men as far as I could see were just very hurt. Like, 'Why are we being shunned? We don't understand it.' " Asked whether there were "any gay male counterparts to Radicalesbians, who really wanted to change everything," Rosalie Davies replies, "No. Why would the men want to change anything?"[55]

Although lesbian and gay activists had their conflicts, were these the conflicts of friends or enemies? And precisely when and under what conditions did conflicts develop? Did major conflicts develop in the early 1970s, the mid-1970s, the late 1970s, or none of these? Do lesbian narrators in the 1990s remember more or less conflict than they would have described if asked in the early 1970s? How do their accounts compare to evidence from the early 1970s? And do they report more or less conflict to an interviewer known or assumed to identify as a gay man?

While some Radicalesbians do not recall close ties with gay men in their prelesbian feminist years, others do. Olshan remembers dating "gay boys" and that she "paired off" with them at pajama parties because "there was a lot of sexual pressure" and "gay boys" were "safe." She goes on to describe becoming friends with gay men in the coffeehouses and Rittenhouse Square and then moving to New York with a boyfriend so that both of them could "get gay." Back in Philadelphia, Olshan first encountered the local movement at mixed-sex HAL dances.[56]

Asked whether she related as much to gay men as lesbians when she was a teenager, Barron responds, "In some ways more." Barron recalls that she "didn't see that there was that much of a difference" and that she "just kind of lumped queers together in one category" and knew that she was "one of them." Trying to explain this, Barron says that she identified as androgynous and that she loved "Casper the Friendly Ghost," whom she thought of as "queer" because "the animus and anima were one in Casper."[57]

Davidson's memories of coming upon gay men in Rittenhouse Square and thinking, "There's men like that, there's got to be women like that," also suggest that some Radicalesbians had bonded with gay men before they became lesbian feminists. Discussing the 1960s, Davidson mentions joining gay men at the Janus demonstration at Dewey's and being especially close with an African American gay man who shared her love for folk-dancing. She also remembers that after a childhood friend came out to her, she introduced him to the gay scene in the square and he introduced her to the woman who became her first lover. Asked whether she had problems with the ways gay men talked or thought about lesbians in this period, Davidson says, "Not a whole lot. Occasionally something really biting would be said. . . . They'd be talking about tits and ass and things like that. . . . They would turn themselves into women and then say derogatory things about women." "But for the most part," she adds, "I joked around about it too." When Davidson describes first encountering feminism, she says, "It was like, boing, oh my god, I've thought those thoughts. That's me. . . . That's what I am. It was kind of like the revelation that I had when I went to Rittenhouse Square."[58]

Hill's memories of the word used for lesbians in the 1960s also suggest a degree of common identity with gay men. She recalls that "you didn't use the word lesbian then," that the word was "gay." Likewise, Victoria Brownworth, who remembers bonding with "drag queens," "gay boys," and "queeny gay men" in bars, writes, "I barely knew the word *lesbian* and had only recently learned the word *dyke*. Everything was *gay* then."[59]

The geographies of Radicalesbians' lives, before and after the group was created in 1971, also suggest links with gay men. Lesbian and gay residential and commercial geographies partially converged in Center City, West Philly, and Germantown/Mt. Airy in this period. And Radicalesbian political activities concentrated in the same neighborhoods favored by HAL, GLF, and GAA.

As lesbian feminism developed in Philadelphia, it took complicated positions on gay men. Before Radicalesbians formed, the first lesbian feminist articles in the Philadelphia press expressed some level of identification with gay men. Although an article by New York Radicalesbian Martha Shelley, reprinted in the *Free Press* in 1970, denounced "the male class," she also noted that she did "not mean to condemn all males" and that she had found "beautiful, loving men among the revolutionaries, among the hippies, and the male homosexuals." Radicalesbians-NY's "The Woman-Identified Woman," reprinted by *Gay Dealer* in 1970, argued that "lesbianism, like male homosexuality, is a category of behavior possible only in a sexist society characterized by rigid sex roles and dominated by male supremacy." Although the essay noted that "lesbianism is also different from male homosexuality," it illustrated this by explaining that "the grudging admiration felt for the tomboy, and the queasiness felt around a sissy boy point to the same thing: the contempt in which women—or those who play a female role—are held." In this formulation, dominant society valued masculinity and, while all women were oppressed by this, some men were oppressed by it as well. Meanwhile, gay liberationists supported lesbian feminism not only by publishing "The Woman-Identified Woman" in *Gay Dealer* but also by publicizing the first Radicalesbians meeting and cosponsoring the group's first dance.[60]

Once established, Radicalesbians at times worked with gay activists, demonstrating, advocating reform, and participating in conferences together. A *Getting It Together* report by Carol on the Lansdowne church fair noted that the "most gratifying" aspect of the event was "seeing the representatives from the different gay groups working together for our common cause." Eugene Spotto's account of this event in the *HAL Newsletter* mentioned his "shock and surprise" at seeing an old friend, who was a member of Radicalesbians. Part of the surprise was that both had recently "come out." A *Getting It Together* article by Radicalesbian Mike expressed hopes for "A Gay Community Center uniting all the gay groups in Philadelphia under one roof (but functioning separately from each other)." The *Lesbians Fight Back* calendar listed events for "women and men" as well as events for "women only." In the summer of 1972, Radicalesbians played baseball against GAA in West Philly, joined with men in a "gay unity picnic" in Fairmount Park, and publicized the mixed-sex Penn and Temple gay coffee hours. Radicalesbians also joined GAA, HAL, and groups from other parts of Pennsylvania to sponsor a statewide lesbian and gay convention in Pittsburgh in October 1972.[61]

One index of the changing configuration of relationships between lesbian and gay activists is a set of courses offered at the Free University at Penn. In the fall of 1970, GLF offered a "Gay Liberation Workshop" for "sisters" and "brothers." In the spring of 1971, "Gay Liberation Front—Radicalesbians and Gay Liberation Fellows" offered a "Gay Liberation Workshop." In the spring of 1972, GAA sponsored "Perspectives on Gay Liberation," which was moderated by HAL's Aronson. And in the fall of 1972, GAA sponsored two classes: GAA members Matthew Grande and Dennis Rubini taught "Gay Liberation"; and HAL and Radicalesbians member Davies taught "Lesbianism and Feminism" for "women only." The *Daily Pennsylvanian* reported that these last two classes met at the same time on Tuesdays and that afterward both the men and the women went to the Gay Coffee Hour, which usually drew approximately 150 people, one-third of whom were women.[62]

As this suggests, some Radicalesbians simultaneously worked with mixed-sex groups. Barron was a member of GLF Temple and remembers getting to know Mecca in women's studies classes. She says that "if there weren't the Tommi's around," she would "still be a lesbian separatist." Brownworth and Hill both recall going to GAA meetings. Hill says that her involvement grew out of her friendship with men such as GAA member Tom Wilson Weinberg. Referring to her "Quaker calling," Hill says that she saw herself as a "bridge" between lesbians and gay men. Later, she recalls, she became "a separatist." But even here, she notes that her friends contradict her when she says this: "I always say that I am a very radical separatist type and they don't. They say, 'Oh you've always had men friends and you've always been involved with gay men.' But I don't. That's not how I see myself."[63]

Other Radicalesbians also continued to work with gay men. Olshan says, "I didn't necessarily feel like a separatist, because I had come out, I did have a history, with gay men." She remembers that "there were a number of men, feminist men, who did want egalitarian environments" and "really wanted to hear what women had to say." While still involved with Radicalesbians, she felt "comfortable" working with gay men on the community center project. For a time, Davies continued working with gay men in HAL. In *Lesbians Fight*

Back, she was identified as a member of HAL; on Byrna Aronson's syllabus she was listed as a member of both HAL and Radicalesbians. While she answers "no" when asked whether there were male counterparts to Radicalesbians, when asked specifically about GLF and men such as Kuromiya, she says, "Oh yeah. But they were such a tiny little movement compared to us. Well yeah, they were one extreme end." Even Radicalesbians who stopped working with gay men did not necessarily do this because of conflicts with men. Carole Friedman says that she did not so much move "away from men" but "just became more interested in the conversations going on as a result of feminism." Meanwhile, some lesbians chose to align with GAA and not with Radicalesbians. Cathy McPeek was elected GAA president in the summer of 1972, serving for a short time until she became involved in a sexual relationship with a gay member and left the organization.[64]

All of this is not to say that Radicalesbians did not experience conflict in their work with gay men or that members of Radicalesbians did not experience conflict with gay men after 1972. But in this period the group was not working in isolation from gay men and some members continued to feel bonded with gay men. Moreover, some of the problems with gay men that Radicalesbians describe were experienced by gay men as well. For example, Olshan's account of her alienation at a GAA meeting is similar to Mecca's. Both suggest that working-class lesbians and gay men experienced class conflicts with middle-class lesbians and gay men and that these conflicts sometimes corresponded with conflicts between Temple and Penn. For another example, Hill's account of meeting hostile gay men when she was leafleting at bars parallels the accounts of many gay activists.[65]

Judging by the documents they left behind, Radicalesbians not only worked with gay men but saw their identities as bound up with gay men's. After "Klarketta Kunt" saved "Lois Lesbian," *Getting It Together* got lesbians and gay men together in the play's "moral," which referred to the "ripping off" of "sisters and brothers." A *Lesbians Fight Back* prose poem began, "The jukebox blares the sensuous beats and soft loving words that fall on the ears and lips of the men and women looking at men and women. The bar-tender has not a moment to think about the rhythm of his own breathing or even realize that an hour has past since he last smiled at that nice looking guy on the bar stool in front of him." When the Washington, D.C.–based lesbian feminist newspaper *Furies* reported on Radicalesbian activities in Philadelphia, they noted that "two papers have been given to psychiatry-social worker conventions, 'basically trashing them and their view of homosexuals, female or male.' " When Anita Cornwell wrote about identifying with Panther George Jackson, she cited the words of African American gay writer James Baldwin, who was identifying with African

American lesbian Angela Davis. Finally, when *Lesbians Fight Back* reviewed Kay Tobin [Lahusen] and Randy Wicker's *The Gay Crusaders*, it criticized the coverage of lesbians but affirmed a conjoined sense of lesbian and gay history: "Though this book discusses more men than women it shows us that the roots of the gay liberation movement started well over twenty years ago."[66]

Radicalesbians did indict men as a class and some members in some contexts included gay men in these indictments. Regardless of Radicalesbian intentions, some gay men experienced themselves as indicted in some contexts. Sometimes, however, Radicalesbians did not think of gay men as men. And sometimes gay men did not think of themselves as part of the male class that Radicalesbians was indicting. Hill's memories of lesbians who thought that gay men were not "real men" suggests that when Radicalesbians indicted men as a class they were not always including gay men. On some occasions, Radicalesbians even signaled its willingness to ally with radical nongay men, as when Nikki Francis wrote in *Lesbians Fight Back* about prison issues and declared "Attica Brothers: We Shall Overcome!"[67]

Radicalesbians' bonds with gay men affected not only their political activities and identities but their sexualities as well. Davies notes that after leaving her husband she became "involved with a variety of women" and that "the lesbian movement at that time was very open to nonmonogamy." She says that this was revolutionary for women, whereas gay men had been "doing that forever." She continues, "That's a perfect example of how we were on entirely different tracks politically. So at that time, there was no real possibility, except in the most minimal level, I think, of gay men and lesbian women doing a major thrust for changing the society together."[68] Lesbians and gay men may have been on "different tracks," but these tracks were partially parallel. And lesbian feminists' track sometimes diverged from straight women's and moved toward gay men's. While the major "thrust" of Radicalesbians' work may have been in the direction of women, lesbian feminists and gay liberationists often thrusted together in the same direction.

With historical links, political alliances, conceptual identifications, and sexual affinities with gay men, Radicalesbians routinely called themselves both gay and lesbian in their newsletters. The author of "Coming Out vs. Coming Home" referred to "gay" women in most of the instances in which she was talking about lesbians in the past. But some Radicalesbians remained "gay" in the present. For example, Barron recalls that some of Marlene "Mike" Miller's "closest friends were gay men" and that Miller "probably had more gay male friends and was more gay-male-identified than many of the other women in Radicalesbians." Discussing "dissonance . . . between gay women and lesbian feminists," Barron reveals that she, too, felt bonded with gay men:

> There were gay women who would come to check out Radicalesbians and who might be made to feel very unwelcome because their politics were gay politics. Their consciousness was not feminist. They were not seen as women-loving women. Mike would have been an example of someone who was seen initially as kind of old gay, although I can see where she evolved way beyond that. I felt myself right on the cusp between the two because at the time when I came out it was the beginning of the women's movement. I felt a pull towards feminism. And yet I also, from growing up as a tomboy and feeling in *The Well of Loneliness* an identification with Stephen Gordon, felt a pull toward gay liberation. . . . It was a little bit schizy. I struggled because people like Gale Russo, who came to Philadelphia from Radicalesbians in New York, never seemed to have had that identification with gay liberation. They were coming out of the women's movement. And they had very little to do with gay men whereas I still felt some allegiance. I remember a straight male friend who was like a brother at that time. We went camping together, we did everything together. I brought him to a Radicalesbians meeting. Talk about naive! I thought I was going to be ripped to pieces. I thought they were going to feed me to the wolves. But we were hanging out together and I said, 'Listen, I've got a Radicalesbians meeting that I don't want to miss.' And he said, 'Well that's cool, I'll wait in the car.' I said, 'No, you can come in there with me.' And can you imagine? We walked into the Women's Center and it was like 'What's *he* doing here'? But he was really fine. He was really cool. He was comfortable with the whole idea of women's space and lesbian space. It just had never occurred to me.

Barron says she thought her male friend was "cool" and deserved to be treated as "an honorary lesbian."[69]

In August 1972, one *Lesbians Fight Back* writer issued a striking call for unity. In an article titled "On Putting Your Own Kind Down," Christa observed, "Often we listen and laugh about, or put down other gays who don't see things our particular way." Taking both lesbians and gay men to task, she wrote that "gays of both sexes put down the more obvious members of either group (dyke, swish, transvestite, etc.) by saying we have nothing in common with these people, just can't relate to them, and would prefer not to be around them." She pointed specifically to the tendency of gay political groups to "put down" one another, which she believed was "destructive to gay solidarity." She concluded, "Our liberation will come as a result of group solidarity, group power. Let's all get together and fight our common oppressors, not each other. How about it brothers and sisters?"[70]

Just as GLF was influenced by lesbian feminism, Radicalesbians was influenced by gay liberation. And just as GLF disbanded after an important but brief period of existence in 1970–1971, Radicalesbians disbanded after an important but brief period of existence in 1971–1972. While many lesbian and gay activists went their separately sexed ways in this period, separation should not be mistaken for isolation or segregation and it should not be seen as necessarily incompatible with integration. In dialogue with both feminism and gay liberation, lesbian feminism came out and came home.

CONCLUSION: SEXUAL PRIDE, SEX CONSERVATISM

On 11 June 1972, Philadelphia's first "gay pride march" took place. After the 1969 Annual Reminder, homophile activists and gay liberationists had replaced the demonstration at Independence Hall with an annual march in New York to commemorate the Stonewall riots. Philadelphians participated in Christopher Street Liberation Day activities in 1970 and 1971. During these years, lesbians and gay men around the country began to sponsor their own parades, celebrations, marches, and demonstrations on or near the anniversary of the riots. Several activists recall a Philadelphia commemoration in 1971 but say that it was quite small and did not receive much attention.[1]

The more successful 1972 march was very much a product of cooperation between lesbians and gay men. Byrna Aronson and Jerry Curtis played leading roles in organizing the event. According to B. Hill, a member of the Gay Pride Committee, at least half of the march's approximately 20 planners were women. Carole Friedman, who was also a Gay Pride Committee member, recalls that many of the main organizers were members of HAL. According to the Pride Committee, the purpose of the march was "to celebrate the growing sense of pride and unity among Gay people and to signal our determination to end the discrimination we face." Other groups planned events for the week following the march. GAA held a film festival, party, and dance; GAA and GLF Temple cosponsored a Gay Pride Festival at Temple and a picnic at Belmont Plateau.[2]

In the weeks leading up to the march, Philadelphians learned about it in the *News*, *Bulletin*, *Tribune*, *Drummer*, *Gay Alternative*, and *Tell-A-Woman*. On 11 May, the *News* published "Air Force Vet Risks Job to Proclaim He's Gay." According to the *News*, Curtis would not permit his real name to be used but allowed his photograph to be taken. The article also featured a lesbian named "Dian," who was portrayed as "a slender, attractive lab technician," and Aronson, who was described as "an administrative secretary at the American Civil Liberties Union." Accompanied by photographs of Curtis, Dian, and Aronson, the article reported that "1,000 homosexuals" had "applied for a permit to march through center city June 11 in what will be the first such parade ever staged in Philadelphia." The *Bulletin*'s advance article similarly highlighted heterosocial cooperation. But lesbians and gay men were not the only pairs mentioned in premarch coverage. In late May, the *News* featured an editorial titled "Strange Bedfellows." In this case, the odd couple was "Frank Rizzo and gay liberation." Praising Rizzo for permitting the march to occur, the editorial declared that the mayor was "living up to his promise to be a 'man for all of the people.' "[3]

The march was also publicized with a button that featured two intersecting female symbols (circles with external crosses pointing down) and two intersecting male symbols (circles with external arrows pointing upward at 45 degree angles). To highlight the heterosocial politics of the march, one of the female symbols intersected one of the male symbols. According to the *Drummer*'s Greg Lee, this configuration caused controversy in New York, where "many women and some men, too, felt that being associated, however symbolically, with the opposite sex was bad news." Lee wrote that this "raised the ugly spectre of gay separatism" and that "gay women and men MUST work together to effect their liberation." The following week, he declared that "the sex-symbols, interlocked as they are, demonstrate our unity." Referring to "a gay man who persisted in referring to a lesbian sister as a 'girl' rather than a 'woman,' " Lee wrote, "The problem is that many lesbians, when confronted with this type of stupidity, choose to desert all men completely. Conversely, many gay men in similar situations divorce themselves from contact with any women, their lesbian sisters included." Against these tendencies, Lee argued that "our motto must be 'united we stand.' " One week later, while praising the *News* for "Strange Bedfellows," Lee criticized it for using two interlocking male symbols for a graphic. According to Lee, this was "sexist" because it did not "take into account the millions of female homosexuals (lesbians) in our society."[4]

On the morning of the parade, marchers did not know what to expect. According to B. Hill, "On Sunday morning I was afraid—we all were afraid—of the real and unreal. . . . What if there were only 20 of us walking arm in arm?" Writing about the march a year later, Matthew Grande referred to his fear that "there would be no one there." Pat Hill, who describes the march as "scary," remembers "not knowing if you were going to get stoned." Friedman recalls that it was "the kind of thing you didn't know would be a success until you actually were in the midst of doing it." Consistent with this memory of risk, postmarch media accounts included a number of rearview images of individuals and couples. As B. Hill explained, "My back became famous. Unfortunately, too many backs and not enough faces were photographed for TV and newspapers." In spite of these fears, march turnout exceeded expectations. Reports on the number of participants ranged from 1,000 to 10,000. Friedman remembers feeling "a tremendous high." Pat Hill recalls "how exciting it was." Grande wrote that what he had feared would be an "ordeal" turned out to be "a joy."[5]

The march began at Rittenhouse Square with speeches by Barbara Gittings and Curtis and chants and songs led by Laurie Barron. According to the

Inquirer, Gittings declared, "Gay is good, it's right, positive, healthy, natural and moral. . . . This march may not be a revolution, . . . but it certainly is a revelation." Also at the square, Lige Clark and Jack Nichols, authors of *I Have More Fun with You Than Anybody*, and Kay Tobin [Lahusen], coauthor of *The Gay Crusaders*, autographed and sold their new books. According to a Pride Committee press release, "many well-known figures in the Philadelphia Gay community," including "Johnny Scarlett and the Fabulous Fakes and Patty Page, owner of Miss P's," participated in the march. Along the Chestnut Street route several marchers carried coffins to symbolize "the many Gay people who have lost their lives as a result of society's hostility, and the death of constitutional rights for the 10% of this country's citizens who are homosexual." Others dressed as "doctors, hardhats, policemen, secretaries, judges, clergy, servicemen, and businessmen" and wore chains to symbolize "the restrictions imposed on homosexuals in every walk of life." Several wore masks "to dramatize the fact that in this country Gay people must mask their homosexuality or suffer indignities ranging from insults, to unemployment, to imprisonment." Across the street from the Liberty Bell, marchers ripped off their masks and threw them in a coffin "to celebrate the emergence of Gay pride." The parade concluded at Independence Mall, where an open-air dance and a "liberation ceremony" were held.[6]

According to the *News*, "the gays came in all sizes, shapes, and sexes," 40% were African American, and "many were in drag." Lee reported on the presence of "street queens, transvestites, lesbians, males, females, young, old, blacks, whites, Chicanos, Orientals." The *Tribune* featured a photograph of five "men," three of whom appeared to be African American and one of whom appeared to be in drag. According to *Philadelphia Magazine*, most of the marchers were "faggoty fags" and a quarter were African American.[7]

Many accounts of the march exemplified the tendency of Philadelphians to compare their city, positively and negatively, with others. The *News* reported that one "gawker" asked, "Is this Philadelphia or San Francisco?" To the tune of "From the Halls of Montezuma," marchers sang, "From the streets of Philadelphia / To the streets of Hollywood / There are people marching gay and proud / Proclaiming Gay is good." Discussing the march, Friedman recalls, "You know how Philadelphia is in relation to New York? It was Philadelphia saying we can do it too, in a much more provincial environment than New York. We can take this risk; we can put ourselves out there." Henri David, who describes a feeling of "jubilation" at both the New York and Philadelphia marches, says that the latter was "a we're gonna try really hard kind of parade."[8]

Lee, who described Gay Pride Week as "a first in this conservative town," compared the march favorably to the one held a short time later in New York.

Figure 14.1. Barbara Gittings at Gay Pride Day rally, Rittenhouse Square, 1972. Photograph by Kay Tobin Lahusen. With the permission of Kay Tobin Lahusen.

Figure 14.2. Gay Pride Day march, 1972. Photograph by Harry Eberlin. Courtesy of Gay, Lesbian, Bisexual, and Transgendered Archives of Philadelphia, Philadelphia, PA. With the permission of Harry Eberlin.

Having traveled to New York on a GAA-sponsored bus with members of GAA and Radicalesbians, he declared, "Our own parade here two weeks previous was bigger than that!" Referring to hostile spectators in New York, he wrote, "These were the oh-so-liberal cosmopolitan New Yorkers? Well, thank you but I'd rather live in Philly." *Gay Alternative* reported that turnout in Philadelphia "proportionally exceeded" that of New York, and that Philadelphia's march "can go far in dispelling that persistent fatalism that pervades Philadelphia gay life, that feeling that the city is but a collection of small towns producing a sheeplike breed of don't-rock-the-boat, do-nothing gays." *Philadelphia Magazine*'s comparison focused more on the queens than the size: "Apparently, Philadelphia is not like New York, where their parades feature manly marchers who display their gayness with an elan bordering on machismo. Our man, though, was impressed by a new fashion note displayed by several marchers who combined fur coats with hardhats."[9]

Several months after the march, Jeff Escoffier wrote in *Gay Alternative* (now independent of GAA) that, unlike New York, Chicago, San Francisco, and Los Angeles, Philadelphia was not "one of the gay meccas to which many women and men move." According to Escoffier, the "specific social patterns" of the "Private City" shaped its lesbian and gay politics. Given that many lesbians and gay men feared exposure to family and employers, "highly centralized Philadelphia, with the short distance between the gay ghetto and the main business district, may have kept and still may keep others from joining the movement." This, he argued, explained why many local activists were college students and were not native to Philadelphia. Escoffier also suggested that while the early homophile movement's moderate aims "did not seem to conflict with the already existing social patterns of Philadelphia," the post-Stonewall "new style of gay liberation" did. " 'Coming out' is an essential political act," he declared, and involved "proclaiming publicly that one is gay and proud." In the "Private City," "coming out is more difficult than in other, more developed gay communities." Despite all of this, Escoffier noted that "the new gay movement has taken effect here," and that this was "evident when thousands of Philly Gays marched down Chestnut Street." Still, he cautioned that "new and creative strategies for Gay Liberation in the city must be found before the Philadelphia gay community can be truly liberated." Years later, Escoffier remembers the march as "one of the most exhilarating things" that he has ever done and attributes this to the fact that Philadelphia's downtown was small and that it was not possible to be as anonymous as one could be in New York's parade.[10]

March organizers faced four threats to unity at the march. In the planning stage, some GAA members objected to the wearing of masks, arguing that this was "contrary to the meaning of gay pride." In response, the Pride

Committee decided to have those wearing masks also carry "appropriate placards to dramatize the plight of thousands of gays who for their own security and careers must wear false fronts every day." At the march, organizers clashed with Kiyoshi Kuromiya. According to the Pride Committee, Kuromiya and others were "asked not to sell things because we wanted for once an event untainted by commercialism." The committee continued, "Even gays selling gay revolution buttons can detract from the meaning of the day and appear to be exploitative if the crowd is inundated with vendors." According to *Drummer*, two "officials-for-the-day" wanted to be "better cops than the cops," but the conflict helped Kuromiya sell so many buttons that the "officials" finally went away. March organizers also struggled with crowding around the band platform, which led to delays at Independence Mall.[11]

Perhaps the most serious conflict concerned the participation of lesbians in, and the feminist politics of, the march. While Lee reported in advance that GAA, HAL, and Radicalesbians, along with a contingent of "Straights for Gays," would participate, the *Bulletin* reported that the sponsoring organizations included GAA, HAL, and groups from Penn State and Temple. Whether or not Radicalesbians was an official sponsor, members of the group participated in march planning and the march itself. Exemplifying the double consciousness of lesbian feminists, *Lesbians Fight Back* presented two views of the parade. Brooke, whose last name was not identified, reported that "as a radical feminist-lesbian," she had "mixed and largely critical reactions." Attacking the parade for being largely "a celebration," she complained that "there was very little political or feminist content," though she noted that "since the march was Philadelphia's first and Philadelphia is not one of the more political cities, the non-political and reformist tone of the march was probably unavoidable." Criticizing the march for failing to acknowledge the greater oppression of women, she wrote, "The tone of the rally was best expressed in the chant, 2–4–6–8, gay is just as good as straight. Well, it may be that way for men, but I would say that for women gay is twice as good as straight, since heterosexuality is a bastion of male supremacy and messes women over." Brooke also noted that "lesbians were hassled a great deal, not only by straight male spectators, but by some gay men who seem to think that women's things are cute." "Much of the march," she wrote, "seemed to be a male drag show for the straights."[12]

Brooke was not the only lesbian concerned about drag queens. Although "ashamed" to say this today, Pat Hill remembers feeling "embarrassment" at the presence of drag queens and "the fringes of society." Wondering whether this was her "little deb, Huntingdon Valley self" reacting this way, she recalls thinking that certain people could afford to be radical because they did not have "a lot to lose." Quick to insist that she does not mean to "take away from anybody's courage or strength" and that perhaps many marchers did have a lot to lose, she notes that she was not aware of this at the time. Presenting a different perspective in *Drummer*, a letter signed by "Frank Femia" argued against "trying to present us (gays) as respectable to the straight community." "We are NOT respectable by straight standards, have never been and hope never to be," Femia declared. Responding to another letter writer, Femia wrote, "Your straight world is something that very few of us want. . . . Faggots and dykes are perhaps the only people around who can successfully smash the sexual roles thrown on all of us by straights—usually men."[13]

Brooke also criticized lesbians for bonding with gay men. Although she noted that "the one positive thing for lesbians in Philly was that Barbara Gittings was the main speaker and that Laurie Barron led the chants and songs," her praise ended there. "Lesbians were not particularly together (with individual exceptions)," Brooke argued, "and seemed to be more into supporting their gay brothers than into radical feminist lesbianism." Pointing to an upcoming event, Brooke concluded that "a women's march with a strong lesbian presence will, perhaps, start us on our way to strike out male supremacy."[14]

Although she took this position, Brooke demonstrated that she was not completely opposed to working with gay men by going to the gay pride parades in both Philadelphia and New York. Comparing the two, she observed of New York's, "Women were at the forefront of the march not only in placement but in togetherness and militancy. Philadelphia Radicalesbians made up one of the most militant sections of the gay women at the march." Praising the New York march for being "more militant," she pointed to gay as well as lesbian examples: "Gay men chanted: 'Ho, Ho, Homosexual—the Ruling Class is Ineffectual!' Lesbians chanted . . . 'Hey, Hey, Ho, Ho—Male Supremacy's Got to Go!' "[15]

The next issue of *Lesbians Fight Back* featured an article by B. Hill, who pointed to the large number of women on the Pride Committee and presented a much more positive evaluation of Philadelphia's march. Unlike Brooke, she was pleased about the presence of drag queens: "The street people came in hordes, the Market Street, 52nd Street, and 13th Street Queens were there with bells and bangles in luscious overripe gorgeous drag, strutting, preening, noses in the air, smiles and talk ready and inviting. 'You can't touch me, honey,' they seemed to say. 'I've given it all, I've got it all and I *know* who I am.' " While noting that drag queens were visible, B. Hill asked, "Where oh where were the movement people? Some were afraid. Several wore masks. . . . Perhaps everyone like myself awakened scared shitless Sunday and because they didn't *have* to show, they looked at the day and decided it was a perfect day for the shore."[16]

B. Hill did not ignore inequality between lesbians and gay men. She noted that although "one woman and one man were prepared to speak to the press," the "newsmen chose to stress the male's statement." Hill thought that this might have been related to "the 70–80% male majority in the march." But Hill blamed lesbians more than gay men for this disparity: "The men I worked with on the march seemed to be proud to support a project we worked on together—perhaps prouder than the Lesbians of the community, if representation at the march was indicative of gay pride." Hill concluded with language that suggested that gay drag attitude influenced lesbian pride: "It was a celebration larger and more exciting than I had ever hoped for. It was a ball—it was up the ass of the straights. I am what I am honey and nobody not anyone could put me down. We all had noses in the air, heads high—we were together, we were strong."[17]

Philadelphia lesbians marched in not one but two major public actions in the summer of 1972. After parading with gay men in June, they did so with straight women two months later. On Women's Strike Day, 26 August, 100–400 women and a few men marched from Independence Mall to Rittenhouse Square. According to *Lesbians Fight Back*, on the eve of the march, city council rushed to pass an amendment to the Human Relations Act that prohibited discrimination on the basis of sex. *Lesbians Fight Back* also reported, "Plans for the rally were initiated by Radicalesbians. This is the first time anywhere in the U.S. that a Lesbian group has initiated a march like this. But this is not surprising, for we have herstorically been the most determined fighters against male supremacy and for women's freedom." The first words of the *Inquirer*'s report also gave lesbians pride of place: "Gay women, straight women, housewives and professional women, children, and even a few sympathetic males marched . . . , all chanting 'Power to the Sisters.' " *Lesbians Fight Back* described the presence of "black, brown, white, gay, straight, middle class and working class women." According to *Philadelphia Magazine*, "many women wore a purple-and-white DYKE button," using the term "for its shock value and as a badge of courage and frankness—gay pride."[18]

While Radicalesbians played a prominent role, the day's events drew on the support of a broad array of women's groups. Before Women's Strike Day, *Lesbians Fight Back* noted that women would strike "for free abortion on demand, free health care, free child care, and freedom of sexual expression" and "against sexism—gay oppression, racism, imperialism and the Vietnam War, job discrimination, the oppression of female prisoners, prostitutes, children, older women, high school women, and working class women." After the march, *Lesbians Fight Back* stressed the theme of unity, noting that the lead banner read "Sisters Black and Brown and White—We Can Win If We Unite." The newsletter also reprinted speeches by Linda Byron of the Attica Brigade and Radicalesbians; "Judy," a "radical feminist lesbian" who spoke about racism; Rosalie Davies, who was identified as a member of HAL; and Marilyn Buggey, who spoke about women as workers.[19]

While the rhetoric of the march stressed unity, conflicts between lesbian and straight feminists did not disappear in this period. According to a January 1973 article by Elizabeth Scofield in *Philadelphia Magazine*, many members of the local NOW and Women's Political Caucus criticized the Women's Center for being "lower-class and lesbian-oriented." Scofield continued,

> Those who denigrate the movement say dykes run the show; other pro-movement people say gays have grabbed on to an esteemed women's movement and have perverted it with their own demands. But Philadelphia's homosexual males resentfully feel the gay females are more allied with the women's movement than with gay liberation.
>
> NOW's official position is supportive of gays. But some active Philadelphia NOW members can only mumble, "We tolerate them. They do a lot of work, but they're not after what we're after." Another active member and business executive says, apologetically, "I hate to talk about my sisters this way, but the lesbians shouldn't be running the organization or the committees. They're in delicate positions as liaisons between women and a hostile business community. Women in these posts should be beyond reproach."

Although tensions continued, in the summer of 1973 the NOW chapter elected as its president a publicly identified lesbian named Jan Welch.[20]

Meanwhile, all was not unified within Radicalesbians. In its final issue, dated September/October 1972, *Lesbians Fight Back* published a set of conflicting reports on recent developments. "RL Restructures!" outlined a reorganization plan that had been put into effect and that involved the formation of a steering committee. A second article, this one by Brooke, countered "rumors concerning Philadelphia Radicalesbians, to the effect that one member of Radicalesbians *is* Radicalesbians." According to Brooke, the group was currently led by a four-person steering committee. A third piece, "Philadelphia Radicalesbians Disbands!" described the organization as "always a small group with a huge mailing list" and stated that it was "isolated from the gay community" and was "haunted by a reputation that apparently could not be overcome." Still another article announced that "a small group of independent feminist lesbians" had "opened an office in the Women's Center" and was developing a "gay women's hot line switchboard," a weekly

"Lesbian Open House" at the Women's Center, and a "Peer Counselor Program." In December 1972, a month after Art Spikol's article in *Philadelphia Magazine* belatedly brought Radicalesbians to widespread attention, a Women's Center letter to the magazine praised Spikol for his "lack of pigginess" but noted that "Radicalesbians is unfortunately defunct."[21]

Retrospective accounts of the demise of Radicalesbians also conflict. In 1973, Rachel Rubin wrote that while Radicalesbians "started off as a serious political group," it eventually succumbed to "a lot of bullshit from the inevitable ego-trippers and spotlight-grabbers looking for power and followers." She continued, "Splits developed, arguments continued, people dropped out, new people changed direction, the 'radical' waned, and the leftovers floundered and the whole thing died." According to Laurie Barron, as more and more women joined Radicalesbians, several members wanted the group to be more "respectable," which "diluted" its "radical" and "political edge." Becky Davidson recalls that during this period Radicalesbians and other groups were infiltrated by people who would "come into these organizations and try to take control." She remembers rumors that certain Radicalesbians were members of the Socialist Workers party, had been paid to come to Radicalesbians meetings, and were not lesbians. She also says that these political matters became entangled with attractions and desires between members of the group and that "finally we just said that's it, we're dissolving it, final."[22]

The dissolution of Radicalesbians brought to a close more than two years of radical, countercultural, and feminist work by GLF and Radicalesbians. Rejecting the minority models adopted by the homophile movement, gay liberationists and radical lesbian feminists advanced the position that same-sex desires were universal. Challenging boundaries between cross-sex and same-sex sexualities, GLF and Radicalesbians engaged in parallel projects. As gay liberation and lesbian feminism found new institutional vehicles in the coming years, they continued to develop in dialogue with one another, even when they did not seem to be speaking.

While radical lesbian feminism changed after 1972, it remained dominant within Philadelphia lesbian politics through the 1970s. In contrast, radical gay liberationism struggled after 1972 against increasingly dominant reformist tendencies within Philadelphia gay politics. While many local gay activists embraced militant tactics, their goals were more moderate. GAA, the largest gay group in Philadelphia through much of the 1970s, exemplified this phenomenon. Radicals did find a place within GAA, but the group's dominant political orientation had more in common with HAL's than with GLF's or Radicalesbians'.

In the months following the Gay Pride March, GAA, working at times with the new Gay Raiders, a predominantly male group led by Mark Segal, and the new Gay Youth, achieved a new level of local, regional, and national visibility. In August, the Raiders began staging dramatic disruptions of television programs and political events. The first Raiders "zap" took place after Segal and John Stevens ("Sagittarius") Powell were ejected for dancing together on Ed Hurst's "Summertime on the Pier" television program, which was taped in Atlantic City and shown on WPVI. Several days later, the Raiders disrupted WPVI's *Action News* program while it was on the air. In September, GAA members sought to block the path of Democratic presidential nominee George McGovern as he was leaving the Bellevue Stratford Hotel. In October, Segal and another Raider zapped a campaign appearance at Temple by Democratic vice presidential nominee Sargent Shriver. Later the same month, while President Nixon was delivering a speech at Independence Hall, Harry Langhorne, George Bodamer, and Segal chained themselves for three hours to the doors at Nixon's Center City campaign headquarters. Early in November, Segal disrupted a Republican City Committee dinner at the Civic Center. Over the course of 1973, GAA and the Raiders disrupted Walter Cronkite and the *CBS Evening News,* Johnny Carson and the *Tonight Show,* Mike Douglas and the *Mike Douglas Show,* Frank Blair and the *Today Show,* and a host of other targets.[23]

Meanwhile, in August 1972 the *Advocate* reported that the Pennsylvania State Advisory Committee of the U.S. Commission on Civil Rights had drafted a report that called the Philadelphia Police Department "a paramilitary institution" and described "Blacks, the young, and Philadelphia's homosexual community" as "suffering the most" from police "misconduct, harassment, and brutality." That same month, Barry Kohn, the new director of the Community Advocate Unit of the Pennsylvania attorney general's office (and later the coauthor of *Barry and Alice: Portrait of a Bisexual Marriage*) met with Philadelphia lesbian and gay community representatives. According to the *Advocate*, Kohn stated that the unit would "officially and aggressively work on the area of homosexual civil rights." The *Advocate* reported that "it is believed to be the first time Gays have been specifically named as a minority group whose civil rights must be protected by a state law enforcement agency."[24]

In October 1972, 200–250 people attended the first Pennsylvania lesbian and gay conference, which took place in Pittsburgh and included HAL, Radicalesbians, and GAA among its sponsors. One of the conference's achievements was a Pennsylvania gay rights platform, which declared, "Our states (and especially the Commonwealth of Pennsylvania) have always been a refuge for those who have undergone persecution for their beliefs and

Figure 14.3. Mark Segal at Republican City Committee Dinner, 1972. *Philadelphia Evening Bulletin* collection. With the permission of Urban Archives, Temple University, Philadelphia, PA.

practices in less free environments. With the emergence of new styles of living in our time, this Commonwealth has the opportunity to carry on the 'holy experiment' of William Penn by recognizing that any society is enriched by diversity of opinion and action."[25]

Also by the end of 1972, *Philadelphia Magazine* published two more major stories on lesbians and gay men. In October, Carol Saline's "Trick or Treat?" featured Henri David's "costume balls." In November, Spikol's "Gay Today" focused on both lesbians and gay men, integrating what the magazine had once called "the furtive fraternity" and "the invisible sorority." However, in a sign that movement strategies of public visibility continued to conflict with everyday strategies of resistance, Spikol's article created problems for student groups at LaSalle and Penn. According to the *Bulletin*, LaSalle suspended the "privilege" of Students for Individual Rights to hold meetings on campus after Spikol's article mentioned the group. According to the *Daily Pennsylvanian*, Penn officials told the Gay Coffee Hour's organizers "to stop advertising in off-campus publications." When they did not, they were not allowed to meet in their regular room until organizers discontinued the advertising. Responding to Spikol's description of the Gay Coffee Hour as "open to the public," a Penn official, in a letter to the editor published in *Philadelphia Magazine*, declared that "coffee hours, dances and social activities of that kind held in University facilities and sponsored by University organizations are limited to students and staff of the University."[26] As 1972 ended, lesbians and gay men continued to struggle.

Reporting on the Gay Pride March in 1972, *Philadelphia Magazine* provided an interesting historical perspective: "In the old days, like ten years ago, a rather remarkable event used to take place on Halloween on Locust Street. With absolutely no printed publicity at all, thousands of people would line Locust Street to watch an annual parade. The paraders were transvestites. With its costumey tradition, Halloween was the one day of the year when the city's more adventuresome homosexuals left their closets and appeared in drag for a promenade on Locust Street, then adjourned to private parties, where prizes were given for the best gowns." After describing Rizzo's crackdown in 1962, the article continued: "Things have changed in ten years. Back then *Philadelphia Magazine* did a story on homosexuals called 'The Furtive Fraternity,' a subject taboo in the rest of the local and much of the national press. The fraternity is still around but it is hardly furtive anymore. That fellow Rizzo is now mayor and his administration issues parade permits for homosexual groups—not for Halloween night on sleazy Locust Street, but for Chestnut Street on a Sunday afternoon." The reporter did not think that the pride march would "replace the Mummers Parade as the time for Philadelphia to incarnate its otherwise totally suppressed penchant for exhibitionism." He regarded it instead as "just another of those rapidly proliferating signals that times have changed."[27] As "times" continued to "change," even this type of historical perspective, with all of its limitations, would rarely appear in print. Lesbians, gay men, and straights would too often share the conviction that Philadelphia had no lesbian or gay history worthy of exploration.

If one way of thinking about change is to ponder the meaning of the 10 years that passed between the Halloween parade crackdown and the first gay pride march, another is to consider the distance traveled between the Radnor raid in 1960 and the Center City marches in 1972. In 1960, nearly 100 lesbians and gay men assembled in Radnor to organize a local chapter of the Mattachine Society. The meeting was held in the suburbs because Philadelphia was in the process of becoming Rizzo's "police city." In an era in which the law criminalized same-sex sexual behaviors and law enforcement officials used legal and extralegal means to oppress lesbians and gay men, organizers had good reasons to fear that few people would come to the meeting if it was held within Rizzo's domain. Despite the best hopes of organizers, however, police raided the meeting and arrested 84 people, most of whom were Euro-American, middle class, and male.

Twelve years later, thousands of lesbians and gay men participated in the city's first gay pride parade. The multiracial and class-mixed group of marchers gathered in Rittenhouse Square, which had long been a social and cultural center of the lesbian and gay city within the city. Marchers then proceeded through Center City, Philadelphia's preeminent lesbian and gay neighborhood, to Independence Hall, the site of five Annual Reminder demonstrations in years past. The summer of 1972 witnessed not one but two major public events for lesbian and gay Philadelphia. Led by lesbians on the anniversary of women's suffrage, hundreds of feminists marched from Independence Hall to Rittenhouse Square, reversing the route of the pride parade but traveling on the same ground. Allied with a broad array of women's groups working on a wide variety of issues, lesbians rallied in the heart of the city.

The distance traveled by lesbians and gay men between 1960 and 1972 can be measured in the journey from the suburbs to Center City and from the privacy of the Radnor barn to the publicity of the city streets. In 1960, prospective homophile activists were jailed; 12 years later, lesbian feminists spoke out for the rights of prisoners. In 1960, no major newspaper carried news of the Radnor raid and only the ACLU and the national homophile movement supported those who were arrested. In 1972, all major papers provided coverage; lesbian, gay, and feminist publications did so as well; and lesbians and gay men had many allies. Advance publicity for the Radnor meeting tipped off the police in 1960; in 1972, the media helped produce large turnouts by providing sympathetic coverage in the days leading up to the march. In 1960, organized lesbian and gay activism was Euro-American and predominantly male; by 1972 racism and sexism remained strong but the lesbian and gay movement was multiracial and had powerful male and female components. In 1960, the organized movement was fragile and new; by 1972, the organized movement was strong and had a past.

Lesbians and gay men traveled an even longer road between 1945 and 1972. In the period from the end of World War Two to the first gay pride march, lesbians and gay men in Philadelphia constituted themselves in relation to one another and had important successes in so doing. Transforming the geography of the city, they created residential, commercial, and public enclaves where lesbians and gay men could find sex, love, friendship, work, leisure, and community. Responding to acts of everyday oppression, they performed acts of everyday resistance. Reading themselves in and against cultural representations of same-sex sexualities, they used dominant and oppositional discourse to define what they were and what they were not. Creating organized, collective, and sustained movements, they fought for lesbian and gay rights and liberation.

Movement activists were particularly influential. They formed alliances with religious, legal, and medical "experts"; challenged widely held views of same-sex sexualities as sinful, criminal, and diseased; and demanded that lesbians and gay men be free to represent themselves. Pressing the press, they increased the public visibility and public acceptance of lesbians and gay men. Criticizing dominant cultural representations of same-sex sexualities, they created alternatives in widely circulating publications. Fighting discrimination in public accommodations, they secured increased access to public space. Opposing police harassment and legal corruption, they made lesbian and gay life more safe and secure. Taking action in the judicial, legislative, and executive branches of local, state, and federal governments, they improved the status of lesbians and gay men. Hosting, organizing, and participating in conferences and demonstrations, they built local, regional, national, and transnational movements. Working with other groups and on other causes, they fought for social change.

Each of the organized political strategies examined here was based on ideas about relations between the sexes and relations between lesbians and gay men. Strategies of respectability juxtaposed feminine lesbians and masculine gay men as a way of securing acceptance through conformity to conventional heterosocial norms. Strategies of sexual liberation, which were based on the notion that lesbians and gay men were committed to the sexual values of their respective sexes, essentially feminized lesbians and masculinized gay men. Gay liberation and lesbian feminism rejected the reformist and minoritarian strategies of the homophile movement in favor of revolutionary sexual universalism. Breaking down barriers between gay and straight men and between lesbians and straight women, these strategies challenged boundaries between homosociality and homosexuality and between homosexuality and heterosexuality. Like their homophile predecessors, however, they did not aim to break through the categories of sex. Engaging in parallel projects, lesbian feminists and gay liberationists embraced the notion that women and men were fundamentally different. To the extent that gay liberationists and lesbian feminists continued to distinguish between the "same sex" and the "other sex" in defining their sexual identities, they, too, reified sex differences. In this regard, even the most radical lesbians and gay men were conservative.

How do this book's interpretations of Philadelphia lesbians and gay men contribute to new narratives of U.S. history and lesbian and gay history? How does the past look different after these conclusions are considered? First, this book lends strength to the position that lesbian and gay history should be far more central to the narrative of U.S. history than it is at present. As more and more work in lesbian and gay history is published, it becomes clear that twentieth-century urban geography, society, culture, and politics have been shaped by lesbians and gay men in profoundly significant ways.

Second, there is a new city on the map of U.S. lesbian and gay history, a city with a history of dynamic lesbian and gay residential neighborhoods, commercial districts, and public spaces; a city with a history of extensive public debates about same-sex sexualities; and a city with a history of strong lesbian and gay movements. In terms of the latter, Philadelphians organized some of the country's first lesbian and gay political demonstrations, produced some of the country's most widely circulating lesbian and gay publications, and were in the forefront of innovative political tendencies, including heterosocial lesbian and gay activism, homophile lesbian militancy, gay sexual radicalism, multiracial gay liberationism, and African American lesbian feminism.

Third, lesbian and gay worlds have intersected and overlapped in ways not often revealed by scholarship in lesbian "or" gay studies or by scholarship that situates lesbians exclusively within women's history and gay men exclusively within men's history. Lesbian and gay cultures have diverged as well as converged, but in both cases they have influenced one another, they have been in dialogue with one another, and they have defined themselves in relation to one another.

Fourth, lesbian and gay resistance to oppression has developed in everyday worlds, in public culture, and in organized movement activism; resistance in each of these domains has been sexed and gendered; and relationships between resistance in one domain and resistance in another domain have been sexed and gendered. Lesbians and gay men have developed different but related strategies of everyday resistance. They have developed different but related ways of responding to representations of same-sex sexualities in public culture. And they have developed different but related organized political movements. Not surprisingly, then, lesbians and gay men have moved in different but related ways between struggles in everyday worlds, public culture, and organized movements.

Finally, while lesbians and gay men have challenged many dominant values, they have participated in and contributed to a conservative consensus about the nature of differences between women and men. Rather than represent a "queer" alternative, lesbians and gay men, by and large, have reproduced the dominant system of relations between the sexes. Social, cultural, and political discourses and practices that produce differences between women and men and that produce the categories "women" and "men" are powerful and tenacious. Although lesbians and gay men are often thought of as marginal to or free from dominant values of sex and gender, the history of lesbians and gay men suggests just how strong these values have been. Philadelphia lesbians and gay men courageously challenged the primacy of heterosexuality and offered new visions of heterosocial relationships in the years from 1945 to 1972. In the end, however, to the extent that lesbian and gay identities depended upon distinguishing between same-sex and cross-sex desires, lesbians and gay men not only left binary sex oppositions in place but reinforced their strength. Whether feminist opposition to the categories of sex can be reconciled with lesbian and gay identities remains an open question.

ABBREVIATIONS

ACLU	American Civil Liberties Union
ACLUA	American Civil Liberties Union Archives (Seeley G. Mudd Manuscript Library, Princeton University, Princeton, NJ)
ACLU-GPB	American Civil Liberties Union, Greater Philadelphia Branch
ACLU-GPBP	American Civil Liberties Union, Greater Philadelphia Branch Papers (Urban Archives, Temple University, Philadelphia, PA)
ALI	American Law Institute
BP	*Black Panther*
CCPP	Crime Commission of Philadelphia Papers (Urban Archives, Temple University, Philadelphia, PA)
CLR	*Civil Liberties Record*
DD	*Distant Drummer*
DN	*Philadelphia Daily News*
DOB	Daughters of Bilitis
DOB-NY	Daughters of Bilitis, New York
DOBP	Daughters of Bilitis Papers (June L. Mazer Collection, West Hollywood, CA)
DOBPN	*Daughters of Bilitis Philadelphia Newsletter*
DP	*Daily Pennsylvanian*
DRPA	Delaware River Port Authority
EB	*Philadelphia Evening Bulletin*
ECHO	East Coast Homophile Organizations
ECHOM	East Coast Homophile Organizations Minutes (GLBTA)
ECHOP	East Coast Homophile Organizations Papers (GLBTA)
EMM	*Eastern Mattachine Magazine*
ERCHO	Eastern Regional Conference of Homophile Organizations
FBI	Federal Bureau of Investigation
FOIA	Freedom of Information Act
GA	*Gay Alternative*
GAA	Gay Activists Alliance–Philadelphia
GAA-NY	Gay Activists Alliance–New York
GD	*Gay Dealer*

GLBTA	Gay, Lesbian, Bisexual, and Transgendered Archives of Philadelphia, William Way Community Center, Philadelphia, PA
GLF	Gay Liberation Front, Philadelphia
GLF-NY	Gay Liberation Front–New York
GLFPN	*Gay Liberation Front Philadelphia Newsletter*
GLHSNC	Gay and Lesbian Historical Society of Northern California, San Francisco, CA
GPM	*Greater Philadelphia Magazine*
HAL	Homophile Action League
HALN	*Homophile Action League Newsletter*
HIS	Homosexual Information Service
HLP	Harry Langhorne Papers (HSC)
HLRS	Homosexual Law Reform Society
HSC	Human Sexuality Collection (Rare and Manuscript Collections, Carl A. Kroch Library, Cornell University, Ithaca, NY)
IGG	*International Guild Guide*
IGICA	International Gay Information Center Archives (Rare Books and Manuscripts Division, New York Public Library, New York, NY)
IGLA	International Gay and Lesbian Archives (West Hollywood, CA)
Inq.	*Philadelphia Inquirer*
INS	Immigration and Naturalization Service
JS	Janus Society
JSN	*Janus Society Newsletter*
KI	Kinsey Institute for Research in Sex, Gender, and Reproduction, Bloomington, IN
LB	*Lavender Baedeker*
LCB	Liquor Control Board of Pennsylvania
LFB	*Lesbians Fight Back*
LI	*Legal Intelligencer*
MCC	Metropolitan Community Church
MPC	Model Penal Code
MR	*Mattachine Review*
MS	Mattachine Society
MSNY	Mattachine Society of New York
MSNYN	*Mattachine Society of New York Newsletter*
MSP	Mattachine Society of Philadelphia
MSPN	*Mattachine Society of Philadelphia Newsletter*

MSR	Mattachine Society Records (IGICA)
MSW	Mattachine Society of Washington
NAACP	National Association for the Advancement of Colored People
NACHO	North American Conference of Homophile Organizations
NMALGH	National Museum and Archives of Lesbian and Gay History, New York, NY
NOP	Norman Oshtry Papers, Philadelphia, PA
NOW	National Organization for Women
NYT	*New York Times*
PACE	Philadelphia Action Committee for Equality
PD	*Plain Dealer*
PFP	*Philadelphia Free Press*
PI	*Il Popolo Italiano*
PM	*Philadelphia Magazine*
R.D.	Roosevelt Democratic (Club)
RL	Radicalesbians, Philadelphia
RSP	Richard Schlegel Papers (HSC)
RPCC	Revolutionary People's Constitutional Convention
RPPI	Report of the Philadelphia Postal Inspector
S.A.	Sports Alliance (Club)
TD	*Thursday's Drummer*
Trib.	*Philadelphia Tribune*
TUN	*Temple University News*
U.S.&A.A.	Uniform Social and Athletic Association
WITCH	Women's International Conspiracy from Hell
WWC	Walt Whitman Collection, Special Collections, Van Pelt Library, University of Pennsylvania, Philadelphia, PA
YMCA	Young Men's Christian Association

NOTES

Introduction

1. "Friendship as a Lifestyle: An Interview with Michel Foucault," *Gay Information*, Spring 1981, 4, trans. of Jean Le Bitoux et al., "De l'amitié comme mode de vie: Un entretien avec un lecteur quinquagénaire," *Le Gai Pied*, Apr. 1981, 38–39.

2. James O'Higgins, "Sexual Choice, Sexual Act: An Interview with Michel Foucault," trans. James O'Higgins, *Salmagundi*, nos. 58–59 (Fall 1982–Winter 1983): 14. See also Michel Foucault, *The History of Sexuality,* vol. 1, *An Introduction*, trans. Robert Hurley (New York: Random House, 1978).

3. O'Higgins, "Sexual Choice," 14.

4. Adrienne Rich, "Compulsory Heterosexuality and Lesbian Existence," *Signs* (Summer 1980): 649–650; Adrienne Rich, "Compulsory Heterosexuality and Lesbian Existence," in *Blood, Bread, and Poetry: Selected Prose, 1979–1985* (New York: Norton, 1986), 53.

5. Eve Kosofsky Sedgwick, *Epistemology of the Closet* (Berkeley: University of California Press, 1990), 36–38.

6. Joan Nestle and John Preston, eds., *Sister and Brother: Lesbians and Gay Men Write about Their Lives Together* (San Francisco: HarperCollins, 1994), v, 8.

7. Carroll Smith-Rosenberg, "The Female World of Love and Ritual: Relations between Women in Nineteenth-Century America," *Signs* 1, no. 1 (1975): 8; Kathy Peiss, *Cheap Amusements: Working Women and Leisure in Turn-of-the-Century New York* (Philadelphia: Temple University Press, 1986), 6.

8. See Ann DuCille, " 'Othered' Matters: Reconceptualizing Dominance and Difference in the History of Sexuality in America," *Journal of the History of Sexuality* 1, no. 1 (July 1990): 102–127; Henry Abelove, "The Queering of Lesbian/Gay History," *Radical History Review*, no. 62 (Spring 1995): 44–57.

9. Jonathan Katz, *Gay American History* (New York: Crowell, 1976); Jonathan Ned Katz, *Gay/Lesbian Almanac* (New York: Harper and Row, 1983); John D'Emilio, *Sexual Politics, Sexual Communities: The Making of a Homosexual Minority in the United States, 1940–1970* (Chicago: University of Chicago Press, 1983); Martin Bauml Duberman, *About Time: Exploring the Gay Past* (New York: Gay Presses of New York, 1986); Allan Bérubé, *Coming Out under Fire: The History of Gay Men and Women in World War Two* (New York: Free Press, 1990).

10. Lillian Faderman, *Odd Girls and Twilight Lovers: A History of Lesbian Life in Twentieth-Century America* (New York: Columbia University Press, 1991); Elizabeth Lapovsky Kennedy and Madeline D. Davis, *Boots of Leather, Slippers of Gold: The History of a Lesbian Community* (New York: Routledge, 1993); Esther Newton, *Cherry Grove, Fire Island: Sixty Years in America's First Gay and Lesbian Town* (Boston: Beacon, 1993); Martin Duberman, *Stonewall* (New York: Dutton, 1993); George Chauncey, *Gay New York: Gender, Urban Culture, and the Making of the Gay Male World, 1890–1940* (New York: Basic, 1994). On relationships between lesbians and gay men, see Kennedy and Davis, *Boots of Leather*, 3, 380–384; Chauncey, *Gay New York*, 27, 228; Newton, *Cherry Grove*, 203–206; Elizabeth

Lapovsky Kennedy, "Telling Tales: Oral History and the Construction of Pre-Stonewall Lesbian History," *Radical History Review*, no. 62 (Spring 1995): 71–72; Esther Newton, " 'Dick(less) Tracy' and the Homecoming Queen: Lesbian Power and Representation in Gay-Male Cherry Grove," in *Inventing Lesbian Cultures in America,* ed. Ellen Lewin (Boston: Beacon, 1996), 161–193.

11. See Gayle Rubin, "The Traffic in Women," in *Toward an Anthropology of Women*, ed. Rayna R. Reiter (New York: Monthly Review Press, 1975), 157–210; Gayle Rubin, "Thinking Sex: Notes for a Radical Theory of the Politics of Sexuality," in *Pleasure and Danger: Exploring Female Sexuality*, ed. Carole S. Vance (New York: Routledge, 1984), 267–319; Luce Irigaray, *This Sex Which Is Not One*, trans. Catherine Porter with Carolyn Burke (Ithaca: Cornell University Press, 1985); Diana Fuss, *Essentially Speaking: Feminism, Nature and Difference* (New York: Routledge, 1989); Judith Butler, *Gender Trouble: Feminism and the Subversion of Identity* (New York: Routledge, 1990); Teresa de Lauretics, ed., "Queer Theory: Lesbian and Gay Sexualities," *differences* 3, no. 2 (Summer 1991); Monique Wittig, *The Straight Mind and Other Essays* (Boston: Beacon, 1992); Michael Warner, ed., *Fear of a Queer Planet: Queer Politics and Social Theory* (Minneapolis: University of Minnesota Press, 1993); "More Gender Trouble: Feminism Meets Queer Theory," *differences* 6, nos. 2–3 (Summer–Fall 1994).

12. See Lisa Duggan, "Making It Perfectly Queer," *Socialist Review* 22, no. 1 (Jan.-Mar. 1992): 11–31; Marc Stein, "The City of Sisterly and Brotherly Loves: The Making of Lesbian and Gay Movements in Greater Philadelphia, 1948–1972" (Ph.D. diss., University of Pennsylvania, 1994), 1–61; Lisa Duggan, "The Discipline Problem: Queer Theory Meets Lesbian and Gay History," *GLQ* 2, no. 3 (1995): 179–191; Abelove, "The Queering of Lesbian/Gay History"; Donna Penn, "Queer: Theorizing Politics and History," *Radical History Review*, no. 62 (Spring 1995): 24–42.

13. See Jennifer Terry, "Theorizing Deviant Historiography," *differences* 3, no. 2 (Summer 1991): 55–74; Lisa Duggan, "The Trials of Alice Mitchell: Sensationalism, Sexology, and the Lesbian Subject in Turn-of-the-Century America," *Signs* 18, no. 4 (Summer 1993): 791–814; Chauncey, *Gay New York*, 10; Steven Maynard, "Through a Hole in the Lavatory Wall: Homosexual Subcultures, Police Surveillance, and the Dialectics of Discovery, Toronto, 1890–1930," *Journal of the History of Sexuality* 5, no. 2 (Oct. 1994): 207–242.

14. Chauncey, *Gay New York*, 5; Kennedy and Davis, *Boots of Leather*, 2, 390, 150. See also D'Emilio, *Sexual Politics*, 4–5; James C. Scott, *Weapons of the Weak: Everyday Forms of Peasant Resistance* (New Haven: Yale University Press, 1985); James C. Scott, *Domination and the Arts of Resistance: Hidden Transcripts* (New Haven: Yale University Press, 1990).

15. Newton, *Cherry Grove*, 236–239. See also Robin D. G. Kelley, " 'We Are Not What We Seem': Rethinking Black Working-Class Opposition in the Jim Crow South," *Journal of American History* 80, no. 1 (June 1993): 75–112; Robin D. G. Kelley, "The Black Poor and the Politics of Opposition in a New South City, 1929–1970," in *The "Underclass" Debate: Views from History*, ed. Michael B. Katz (Princeton: Princeton University Press, 1993), 293–333; Donna Penn, "The Present and Future of Recuperating the Past: A Review Essay," *GLQ* 2, no. 3 (1995): 279–305.

16. See Penn, "The Present and Future of Recuperating the Past"; Abelove, "The Queering of Lesbian/Gay History," 53–54; Brett Beemyn, ed., *Creating a Place for Ourselves: Lesbian, Gay, and Bisexual Community Histories* (New York: Routledge, 1997); Marc Stein, " 'Birthplace of the Nation': Imagining Lesbian and Gay Communities in Philadelphia, 1969–1970," in *Creating a Place*, 276–278.

17. See Nathaniel Burt, *The Perennial Philadelphians: The Anatomy of an American Aristocracy* (Boston: Little, Brown, 1963); E. Digby Baltzell, *Puritan Boston and Quaker Philadelphia: Two Protestant Ethics and the Spirit of Class Authority and Leadership* (New York: Free Press, 1979); Richard S. Dunn and Mary Maples Dunn, eds., *The Papers of William Penn,* vol. 2, *1680–1684* (Philadelphia: University of Pennsylvania Press, 1982), 130; Mary Maples Dunn and Richard S. Dunn, "The Founding, 1681–1701," in *Philadelphia: A Three-Hundred-Year History*, ed. Russell F. Weigley (New York: Norton, 1982), 1–2; Margaret Hope Bacon, *Mothers of Feminism: The Story of Quaker Women in America* (San Francisco: Harper and Row, 1986); Jean R. Soderlund, "Women's Authority in Pennsylvania and New Jersey Quaker Meetings, 1680–1760," *William and Mary Quarterly* 44, no. 4 (Oct. 1987): 722–749; Jean R. Soderlund, "Women in Eighteenth-Century Pennsylvania: Toward a Model of Diversity," *Pennsylvania Magazine of History and Biography* 115, no. 2 (Apr. 1991): 163–183.

18. See David Bell and Gill Valentine, *Mapping Desire: Geographies of Sexualities* (New York: Routledge, 1995); Aaron Betsky, *Queer Space: Architecture and Same-Sex Desire* (New York: Morrow, 1997); Gordon Brent Ingram, Anne-Marie Bouthillette, and Yolanda Retter, eds., *Queers in Space: Communities, Public Places, Sites of Resistance* (Seattle: Bay Press, 1997).

19. See D'Emilio, *Sexual Politics*, 23–39; Bérubé, *Coming Out under Fire.*

20. The oral history interviews were conducted from 1993 to 1997 in Pennsylvania, New York, California, and Massachusetts. With the exceptions of Joseph McGrory and Lola Reed, all narrators are cited in the text. I found narrators through direct contacts in Philadelphia lesbian and gay communities, recommendations by other narrators and sources, advertisements that I placed in lesbian and gay publications, communications that resulted from newspaper and newsletter references to my work, and information derived from documentary research.

21. Monique Wittig, "The Category of Sex," *Feminist Issues* 2, no. 2 (Fall 1982): 64.

Chapter One

1. Xavier Mayne [Edward Irenaeus Prime Stevenson], *The Intersexes: A History of Similisexualism as a Problem in Social Life* (1908; New York: Arno, 1975), 640; Magnus Hirschfeld, *Die Homosexualitat des Mannes und des Weibes* (Berlin: Louis Marcus, 1914), 550–554, trans. James Steakley, cited in Katz, *Gay American History*, 50; Jeff Escoffier, "Styles of Gay Liberation in Philadelphia, 1960–72," *Gay Alternative* (*GA*), Dec. 1972, 2; Joe Sharkey, "Phila.—A Capital of the Gay World," *Philadelphia Inquirer* (*Inq.*), 1 Oct. 1973, 1; Interview with Fleischmann. Unless otherwise indicated, all quotations in part 1 are from my oral history interviews. On everyday geographies in Philadelphia, see also David S. Azzolina, "The Circle Always Grew: Folklore and Gay Identity, 1945–1960" (Ph.D. diss., University of Pennsylvania, 1996); Laura Murphy, " 'The Changer(s) and the Changed': Activism, Community, and Lesbian Identity in Seven Women's Lives, Philadelphia, 1972–1983," typescript, 1994.

2. Bureau of the Census, *Census of Population: 1950*, vol. 1, *Number of Inhabitants* (Washington, DC: GPO, 1952), 38–37. See also Burt, *The Perennial Philadelphians*, ix–x, 3–40, 70–77, 595–598; Allen F. Davis, "Introduction," in *The Peoples of Philadelphia: A History of Ethnic Groups and Lower-Class Life, 1790–1940*, ed. Allen F. Davis and Mark H. Haller (Philadelphia: Temple University Press, 1973), 3–12; Edwin Wolf 2d, *Philadelphia: Portrait of an American City* (Harrisburg: Stackpole, 1975), 318–346; Peter

O. Muller, Kenneth C. Meyer, and Roman A. Cybriwsky, *Metropolitan Philadelphia: A Study of Conflicts and Social Cleavages* (Cambridge: Ballinger, 1976), 1–33; Baltzell, *Puritan Boston and Quaker Philadelphia*, ix–xii, 1–15; Margaret B. Tinkcom, "Depression and War, 1929–1946," in *Philadelphia: A Three-Hundred-Year History*, 601–648; Joseph S. Clark, Jr., and Dennis J. Clark, "Rally and Relapse, 1946–1968," in *Philadelphia: A Three-Hundred-Year History*, 649–703; Stephanie G. Wolf, "The Bicentennial City, 1968–1982," in *Philadelphia: A Three-Hundred-Year History*, 704–734; Sam Bass Warner, Jr., *The Private City: Philadelphia in Three Periods of Its Growth* (1968; rev. ed., Philadelphia: University of Pennsylvania Press, 1987), ix–xxvi; Carolyn Adams et al., *Philadelphia: Neighborhoods, Division, and Conflict in a Postindustrial City* (Philadelphia: Temple University Press, 1991).

3. Bureau of the Census, *Censuses of Population and Housing: 1960*, Census Tracts, Final Report PHC(1)–116 (Washington, DC: GPO, 1962), 95.

4. See John D'Emilio, "Gay Politics, Gay Community: San Francisco's Experience," *Socialist Review*, no. 55 (Jan.-Feb. 1981): 77–104; John D'Emilio, "Capitalism and Gay Identity," in *Powers of Desire: The Politics of Sexuality*, ed. Ann Snitow, Christine Stansell, and Sharon Thompson (New York: Monthly Review, 1983), 100–113; D'Emilio, *Sexual Politics*, 10–13, 22–39, 176–186; Judith Schwarz, *Radical Feminists of Heterodoxy: Greenwich Village 1912–1940*, rev. ed. (Norwich, VT: New Victoria, 1986); Eric Garber, "A Spectacle in Color: The Lesbian and Gay Subculture of Jazz Age Harlem," in *Hidden from History: Reclaiming the Gay and Lesbian Past*, ed. Martin Bauml Duberman, Martha Vicinus, and George Chauncey, Jr. (New York: New American Library, 1989), 318–331; Bérubé, *Coming Out under Fire*, 106–108, 123, 244–245; Newton, *Cherry Grove*; Kennedy and Davis, *Boots of Leather*; Trisha Franzen, "Differences and Identities: Feminism and the Albuquerque Lesbian Community," *Signs* 18, no. 4 (Summer 1993): 891–906; Chauncey, *Gay New York*; Maynard, "Through a Hole," 207–242; David K. Johnson, " 'Homosexual Citizens': Washington's Gay Community Confronts the Civil Service," *Washington History* 6, no. 2 (Fall/Winter 1994–1995): 44–63, 93–96; Kath Weston, "Get Thee to a Big City: Sexual Imaginary and the Great Gay Migration," *GLQ* 2, no. 3 (1995): 253–277; John Howard, "The Library, the Park, and the Pervert: Public Space and Homosexual Encounter in Post–World War II Atlanta," *Radical History Review*, no. 62 (Spring 1995): 166–187; Rochella Thorpe, " 'A House Where Queers Go': African-American Lesbian Nightlife in Detroit, 1940–1975," in *Inventing Lesbian Cultures*, 40–61; Katie Gilmartin, " 'We Weren't Bar People': Middle-Class Lesbian Identities and Cultural Spaces," *GLQ* 3, no. 1 (1996): 1–51; John Howard, ed., *Carryin' On in the Lesbian and Gay South* (New York: New York University Press, 1997), 1–12; Beemyn, ed., *Creating a Place for Ourselves*.

5. See Manuel Castells, *The City and the Grassroots: A Cross-Cultural Theory of Urban Social Movements* (Berkeley: University of California Press, 1983), 138–172; Sy Adler and Johanna Brenner, "Gender and Space: Lesbians and Gay Men in the City," *International Journal of Urban and Regional Research* 16, no. 1 (1992): 24–34; Tamar Rothenberg, " 'And She Told Two Friends': Lesbians Creating Urban Social Space," in *Mapping Desire*, 165–181; Ingram, Bouthillette, and Retter, eds., *Queers in Space*, 7–12, 171–175, 213–232, 301–337.

6. William Penn to William Crispin, John Bezar, and Nathaniel Allen, 30 Sept. 1681, in *William Penn and the Founding of Pennsylvania, 1680–1684: A Documentary History*, ed. Jean R. Soderlund (Philadelphia: University of Pennsylvania Press, 1983), 85. See also Arno Karlen, *Sexuality and Homosexuality: A New View* (New York: Norton, 1971), 513.

7. Audiotape, Tom Malim interview with Tommi Avicolli Mecca, c. 1982, Gay, Lesbian, Bisexual, and Transgendered Archives of Philadelphia (GLBTA).

8. Mary Louise Oates, "Flower Children," *Philadelphia Magazine* (*PM*), Sept. 1967, 58–59.

9. See Chester Rapkin and William G. Grigsby, *Residential Renewal in the Urban Core* (Philadelphia: University of Pennsylvania Press, 1960); Robert B. Mitchell, ed., "Planning and Development in Philadelphia," *Journal of the American Institute of Planners* 26, no. 3 (Aug. 1960); Edmund N. Bacon, "Downtown Philadelphia: A Lesson in Design for Urban Growth," *Architectural Record*, 129, no. 5 (May 1961): 131–146; Burt, *The Perennial Philadelphians*, 539–540, 555–562; Sidney Hopkins, "Requiem for a Renaissance," *Greater Philadelphia Magazine* (*GPM*), Nov. 1964, 32–35, 54–59; *Time*, 6 Nov. 1964, 60–75; Nancy Love, "Paradise Lost," *PM*, July 1968, 72–75, 87–99; Wolf, *Philadelphia*, 321–346; Muller, Meyer, and Cybriwsky, *Metropolitan Philadelphia*, 3–5, 23–29; Paul R. Levy and Roman A. Cybriwsky, "The Hidden Dimensions of Culture and Class: Philadelphia," in *Back to the City: Issues in Neighborhood Renovation*, ed. Shirley Bradway Laska and Daphne Spain (New York: Pergamon, 1980), 138–155; Conrad Weiler, "The Neighborhood's Role in Optimizing Reinvestment: Philadelphia," in *Back to the City*, 220–235; Meredith Savery, "Instability and Uniformity: Residential Patterns in Two Philadelphia Neighborhoods, 1880–1970," in *The Divided Metropolis: Social and Spatial Dimensions of Philadelphia, 1800–1975*, ed. William W. Cutler, III, and Howard Gillette, Jr. (Westport, CT: Greenwood, 1980), 193–226; John F. Bauman, *Public Housing, Race, and Renewal: Urban Planning in Philadelphia, 1920–1974* (Philadelphia: Temple University Press, 1987), 90–208; Adams, *Philadelphia*, 15–16, 66–123.

10. See Bell and Valentine, *Mapping Desire*, 325–353.

11. See, for example, *Drum*, Sept. 1965, 5.

12. "HAL Is Gay and No 2001 Computer," *Thursday's Drummer* (*TD*), 26 Aug. 1971, 6; *Drummer*, 10 Feb. 1972, 19; Byrna Aronson, Philadelphia Commission on Human Relations Hearings, 5 June 1974, Harry Langhorne Papers (HLP), #7441, Human Sexuality Collection (HSC), Division of Rare and Manuscript Collections, Cornell University Library, Ithaca, NY (box 1/f48). See also *Drummer*, 17 Feb. 1972, 2.

13. I use 1974 because this is the approximate date of the data from the Gay Activists Alliance (GAA) described below. Insofar as 10% of the gay childhood homes and 6% of the lesbian childhood homes (through age 17) in Philadelphia were in Center City, the high rates of concentration reflect movement to Center City rather than continuities from childhood residence.

14. GAA membership list, GLBTA. I thank Ed Hermance, Harry Langhorne, Tommi Avicolli Mecca, Robert Schoenberg, Tom Wilson Weinberg, and John Whyte for helping me identify the GAA members.

15. See Philadelphia City Planning Commission, *Population Characteristics: 1960 and 1970 Philadelphia Census Tracts; Housing Characteristics: 1960 and 1970 Philadelphia Census Tracts; Socio-Economic Characteristics: 1960 and 1970 Philadelphia Census Tracts; Population and Housing Statistics for Philadelphia Census Tracts, 1970 Census; Socio-Economic Characteristics* (for 1970 and 1980 Philadelphia Census Tracts); *Population and Housing Characteristics* (for 1970 and 1980 Philadelphia Census Tracts).

16. In most cases, the commission provided figures for the "White," "Negro," and "Other" populations. The non-Euro-American figures are derived from adding the "Negro" and "Other" numbers.

17. Castells, *The City and the Grassroots*, 153; Adler and Brenner, "Gender and Space," 29; Adams, *Philadelphia*, 70.

18. See Oates, "Flower Children," 58–59; William J. Speers, "Philadelphia's Communes," *Inq. Magazine*, 21 Feb. 1971, 6–8, 16–20, 24.

19. See Rapkin and Grigsby, *Residential Renewal*, 9; Muller, Meyer, and Cybriwsky, *Metropolitan Philadelphia*, 7; Wolf, *Philadelphia*, 325, 339, 342; Savery, "Instability and Uniformity," 193–194; Bauman, *Public Housing*, 105–106, 112, 114, 127–129, 144–208; Adams, *Philadelphia*, 73–79, 82–83, 90.

20. See also Anita Cornwell, "From an Autobiography: First Love and Other Sorrows," *GA*, no. 9, 1975, 18–21; Anita Cornwell, *Black Lesbian in White America* (Tallahassee, FL: Naiad, 1983), 90–99.

21. See also Stephen Fried, "Private Lives," *PM*, Oct. 1983, 165–166.

22. Michael J. Smith, *Colorful People and Places* (San Francisco: Quarterly Presses of Black and White Men Together, 1983), 91.

23. Four percent of the narrators' childhood homes in Philadelphia were in these tracts.

24. See Rapkin and Grigsby, *Residential Renewal*, 9; Muller, Meyer, and Cybriwsky, *Metropolitan Philadelphia*, 7; Wolf, *Philadelphia*, 321, 325, 342; Savery, "Instability and Uniformity," 193–226; Bauman, *Public Housing*, 111–114, 116, 127–128, 147–208; Adams, *Philadelphia*, 74–78, 83.

25. None of the narrators' childhood homes was in this zone.

Chapter Two

1. See chapter 1, n. 4.

2. See, for examples, *Philadelphia Evening Bulletin* (*EB*), 28 Oct. 1962, 26; 23 Jan. 1963, 17; *Janus Society Newsletter* (*JSN*), Apr. 1964, 4, 17; *Drum*, Apr. 1966, 23; *Inq.*, 13 Mar. 1967, 31; 22 Nov. 1967, 23; *EB*, 22 Nov. 1967, 27; *Drum*, Jan. 1968, 23; *Daughters of Bilitis Philadelphia Newsletter* (*DOBPN*), Jan. 1968, 2–3; *Drum*, Mar. 1968, 8; Liquor Control Board (LCB) reports, Mar. 1959 to July 1971, Crime Commission of Philadelphia Papers (CCPP), Urban Archives, Temple University, Philadelphia, PA (box 19).

3. See, for examples, *EB*, 3 Nov. 1967, 43; 9 Nov. 1967, 4; 22 Nov. 1967, 27; 13 Sept. 1968, 8; *Drummer*, 22 June 1972, 4.

4. For locations, years of operation, and clientele, see my interviews; Gaeton J. Fonzi, "Lurid Locust Street: A Shocking Report on Philadelphia's Sin Center," *GPM*, Oct. 1961, 18–21, 40–45; Gaeton J. Fonzi, "The Furtive Fraternity," *GPM*, Dec. 1962, 20–23, 48–56, 61–65; Nancy Love, "The Invisible Sorority," *PM*, Nov. 1967, 66–71, 84–93; Gaeton Fonzi, "Locust Street Revisited," *PM*, Oct. 1970, 74–81, 124–138; Art Spikol, "Gay Today," *PM*, Nov. 1972, 124–127, 160–172; Rod Townley, "Gay Philadelphia," *Inq. Today Magazine*, 12 May 1974, 10–18, 22–30; Tony Green, "The Wild Side of Midnite," *PM*, May 1977, 146–151, 238–249; Jerry "Jai" Moore, *The Lady Jai Recommended List*, c. 1954, in the possession of Hal Lawson, MI; *Lavender Baedeker* (*LB*), c. 1962, Gay and Lesbian Historical Society of Northern California (GLHSNC), San Francisco, CA; *International Guild Guide* (*IGG*), 1965, GLBTA; *Directory 43*, 1965, GLHSNC; *In Guide*, 1966, GLHSNC; *Bob Damron's Address Book*, 1966, National Museum and Archives of Lesbian and Gay History (NMALGH), New York, NY; *IGG*, 1966, International Gay Information Center Archives (IGICA), New York Public Library, New York, NY; *IGG*, 1967, GLHSNC; *International Vagabond World Travel Address Guide*, 1968, GLHSNC; *IGG*, 1968, GLHSNC; *IGG*, 1969, HSC; Jay's Place, "Philadelphia Guide to the Gay Scene," c. 1969, Philadelphia file, International Gay and Lesbian Archives (IGLA), West

Hollywood, CA; *LB*, 1970–1971, IGICA; *Spartacus IGG*, 1970, IGICA; *IGG*, 1970, IGICA; *Double Exposure*, 6 July 1970, 4, GLBTA; *Gay Guide*, 1971, GLHSNC; *IGG*, 1971, GLBTA; *IGG*, 1972, University of Illinois at Champaign-Urbana; John Francis Hunter, *The Gay Insider* (New York: Stonehill, 1972); *IGG*, 1973, NMALGH; *Gay Yellow Pages*, 1973, IGICA; "1973 Gay Guide to Philadelphia," *GA*, no. 2, 1973; *Barfly*, 1974, GLHSNC; *Girls Guide*, 1974, IGICA; *Tomcat's Gay Guide*, 1974, Kinsey Institute (KI), Bloomington, IN; *Bob Damron's Address Book*, 1974, IGICA; *Gay Yellow Pages*, 1974, NMALGH; Smith, *Colorful People*.

5. On the Locust Strip, see n. 4. On South Street, see Oates, "Flower Children," 56–59, 72–83; *EB*, 3 June 1969, 1, 26; Daniel Grotta, "Bad Year for the Underground," *PM*, Feb. 1971, 82–85, 158–162; *Philadelphia Daily News* (*DN*), 20 Mar. 1972, 5; *Drummer*, 23 Mar. 1972, 1, 3; *EB*, 22 Oct. 1972, sec. 4, p. 4; Roger D. Abrahams, *Deep Down in the Jungle: Negro Narrative Folklore from the Streets of Philadelphia* (1960; rev. ed. Chicago: Aldine, 1970); Dan Rose, *Black American Street Life: South Philadelphia, 1969–1971* (Philadelphia: University of Pennsylvania Press, 1987).

6. "Rusty," *Wicce*, Summer 1974, 4. See also Chea Villanueva, *Jessie's Song and Other Stories* (New York: Masquerade, 1995), 23.

7. Audiotape, Marge McCann interview with Tommi Avicolli Mecca, 3 Dec. 1984, GLBTA; *IGG*, 1971.

8. "Rusty," 5.

9. Ibid.

10. On Foster House and Mystique, see *GA*, no. 5, 1973, 26–27.

11. On H.C., see *Drummer*, 13 July 1972, 2.

12. Greg Lee, "The Gay Bar Jitters," *Drummer*, 22 June 1972, 4.

13. Love, "The Invisible Sorority," 67; *Drum*, Mar. 1968, 8; Victoria A. Brownworth, *Too Queer: Essays from a Radical Life* (Ithaca, NY: Firebrand, 1996), 42. See also Villanueva, *Jessie's Song*, 69.

14. Mecca interview with Malim; Love, "The Invisible Sorority," 67.

15. Smith, *Colorful People*, 95; Love, "The Invisible Sorority," 67; William Gardner Smith, *South Street* (Chatham, NJ: Chatham Bookseller, 1954), 117.

16. "1973 Gay Guide to Philadelphia."

17. Fonzi, "The Furtive Fraternity," 21. See also Harry Langhorne to LCB, 15 Jan. 1973, HLP (box 3/f5).

18. Brownworth, *Too Queer*, 43.

19. On Allegro, see *Gay*, 20 Apr. 1970, 20. On Drury Lane, see *Inq*., 26 Nov. 1967, 1.

20. See n. 4. See also Jess Stearn, *The Sixth Man* (Garden City, NY: Doubleday, 1961), 60.

21. On Harlow's, see *Drummer*, 13 Apr. 1972, 7, 8.

22. See *Drum*, Oct. 1964, 25.

23. Leroy Aarons, "For the Gays, It Is One Step Ahead," *Inq*., 6 Aug. 1993, A23.

24. See *Philadelphia Tribune* (*Trib*.), 29 Sept. 1962, 4.

25. Fonzi, "The Furtive Fraternity," 20; Ted Berkman, "The Third Sex—Guilt or Sickness?" *Coronet*, Nov. 1955, 129.

26. See Nancy Love, "Here He Comes, Miss Philadelphia," *PM*, Aug. 1968, 18.

27. *Distant Drummer* (*DD*), 18 Dec. 1969, 8. See also *Mattachine Review* (*MR*), Dec. 1961, 31; Feb. 1963, 31; *JSN*, Apr. 1964, 8; *Drum*, Oct. 1965, 38; Mar. 1968, 42;

Homophile Action League Newsletter (*HALN*), Mar. 1970, 7; *Drummer*, 10 Aug. 1972, 10; *HALN*, Nov. 1972, 4.

28. See n. 4; *EB*, 12 Feb. 1969, 11; *Inq.*, 12 Feb. 1969, 43; *DN*, 12 Feb. 1969, 3, 38; 14 Feb. 1969, 11; 10 July 1969, 19; *Inq.*, 11 July 1969, 11; *Drummer*, 29 June 1972, 14; 7 Dec. 1972, 4.

29. See *Drum*, Sept. 1965, 5–6; Love, "Here He Comes," 14–24; *DD*, 19 Mar. 1970, 1; *Inq.*, 28 Oct. 1971, 43; *Drummer*, 13 Apr. 1972, 7, 8; 1 June 1972, 1, 3; Carol Saline, "Trick or Treat?" *PM*, Oct. 1972, 215–223; *Drummer*, 2 Nov. 1972, 4, 20; *DN*, 6 Aug. 1973, 27.

Chapter Three

1. Jane Jacobs, *The Death and Life of Great American Cities* (New York: Random House, 1961), 7, 14, 150. See also Warner, *The Private City*.

2. Jacobs, *The Death and Life*, 92–93. See also *Holiday*, Apr. 1969, 78, 102; *Inq.*, 2 June 1974, B1–2.

3. Jacobs, *The Death and Life*, 96–98.

4. Donald Vining, *A Gay Diary*, vol. 2 (New York: Pepys, 1979), 126; Jess Stearn, *The Sixth Man* (Garden City, NY: Doubleday, 1961), 52–53. See also Barry Kohn and Alice Matusow, *Barry and Alice: Portrait of a Bisexual Marriage* (Englewood Cliffs, NJ: Prentice-Hall, 1980), 58.

5. See John A. Jackson, *American Bandstand: Dick Clark and the Making of a Rock 'n' Roll Empire* (New York: Oxford University Press, 1997).

6. Adrian Stanford, "Remembrances of Rittenhouse Square," *One*, Aug. 1965, 13. See also Adrian Stanford, "Rememberance of Rittenhouse Square," *Black and Queer* (Boston: Good Gay Poets, 1977), 15.

7. Love, "The Invisible Sorority," 66–67, 70–71.

8. Fonzi, "The Furtive Fraternity," 23; "Rittenhouse Sq. Area Cleanup Asked by Mann," *Inq.*, 12 Mar. 1963, 6; "The Cancer among Us," *Il Popolo Italiano* (*PI*), 20 Mar. 1963, 4; Donald A. McDonough and Leonard J. McAdams, " 'Blanket' Probe Is Ordered of Nights on Rittenhouse Sq.," *Inq.*, 5 June 1970, 35. See also *EB*, 12 Mar. 1963, 13; *Drum*, Apr. 1966, 6; *Civil Liberties Record* (*CLR*), Aug. 1967, 6; *Inq.*, 6 June 1969, 33.

9. Audiotape, Tommi Avicolli Mecca interview with "Marvin Fleischner," GLBTA. Kendall and Fleischner are the same person.

10. "Legal First Aid," *Gay Dealer* (*GD*), c. Dec. 1970, 6.

11. Love, "The Invisible Sorority," 67; Stearn, *The Sixth Man*, 51.

12. Irene Wolt, "Take Me *Out* to the Ballgame," *In the Life*, Summer 1993, 6.

13. *Commonwealth v. Streuber*, 185 Pa.Super. 369, 137 A.2d 825, 21 Jan. 1958; *IGG*, 1971–1972; *EB*, 5 Sept. 1950, 3.

14. *Commonwealth v. Streuber*; Michael von Moschzisker, "Homosexuality and Sexual Deviants—A Legal Viewpoint," *Philadelphia Medicine*, 1 June 1956, 1427; Richard H. Elliott, "Homosexual Enforcement," 1961, p. 43, typescript in Elliott's possession, Doylestown, PA.

15. Richard H. Elliott, "The Morals Squad," *Drum*, Sept. 1967, 10, 12–13. See also *One*, Dec. 1955, 11; Fonzi, "The Furtive Fraternity," 23, 48–50; Harold Jacobs, "Decoy Enforcement of Homosexual Laws," *University of Pennsylvania Law Review*, 112 (1963), 259.

16. Elliott, "The Morals Squad," 10–12, 28.

17. Love, "The Invisible Sorority," 66, 68.

18. "Rusty," 4.

19. Samuel Hadden, "Homosexuality: An Experientially Determined and Treatable Condition," manuscript, c. 1981, 106, 114, Samuel Hadden Papers, University of Pennsylvania Archives, Philadelphia, PA; Fonzi, "The Furtive Fraternity," 52; Fred Bonaparte, "Homosexuality, Suicides Raising, City Official Tells Morticians," *Trib.*, 25 May 1963, 3. See also Jonathan Rubinstein, *City Police* (New York: Farrar, Straus and Giroux, 1973), 182.

20. Charles G. Simpson, letter to the editor, *GPM*, Nov. 1961, 6; Peter H. Binzen, "Most City Dwellers Are Peaceful," *EB*, 14 Jan. 1969, 49; Steve [Kiyoshi] Kuromiya, *Philadelphia Free Press* (*PFP*), 27 July 1970, 6.

21. Townley, "Gay Philadelphia," 15. See also *IGG*, 1968–1972.

22. Kohn and Matusow, *Barry and Alice*, 52–53. See also Fonzi, "The Furtive Fraternity," 20; *IGG*, 1968–1972.

23. Villanueva, *Jessie's Song,* 11–12; "South Philly Minister Held on Morals Charge," *Trib.*, 14 July 1959, 1; Tommi Avicolli Mecca, "Memoirs of a South Philly Sissy," *PM*, Oct. 1991, 112; Elliott, "Homosexual Enforcement," 48–49; Fonzi, "The Furtive Fraternity," 23; B. Hill, "The Gay Pride March," *Lesbians Fight Back* (*LFB*), Aug. 1972, 3; Rubinstein, *City Police*, 187.

24. "Two Marines Held in Youth's Death," *DN*, 5 Aug. 1958, 4; "South Philly Minister Held on Morals Charge." See also *DN*, 23 Sept. 1958, 6.

25. Mecca, "Memoirs of a South Philly Sissy," 61; "Gay Brothers Attacked in Philly," *Plain Dealer* (*PD*), 3 Sept. 1970, 16.

26. Elliott, "The Morals Squad," 10, 12; Fonzi, "The Furtive Fraternity," 23.

27. Hans Knight, " 'Other Society' Moves into the Open," *EB*, 19 July 1970, sec. 2, p. 6; Rubinstein, *City Police*, 380; "Police Harassment at Merry-Go-Round," *GA*, July 1972, 1.

28. See *DD*, 3 Apr. 1969, 10, 11; *Drummer*, 4 Nov. 1971, 3.

29. "Rusty," 6; Love, "The Invisible Sorority," 68; Spencer Coxe note, 19 Nov. 1968, American Civil Liberties Union, Greater Philadelphia Branch Papers (ACLU-GPBP), Urban Archives, Temple University, Philadelphia, PA (box 7); Aronson, cited in Knight, " 'Other Society.' "

30. "Corridors of Crime," *Inq.*, c. 1956, cited by *One*, Apr.-May 1956, 16; Richard H. Elliott, "Control of Homosexual Activity by Philadelphia Police: A Study of Enforcement and the Enforcers," 1961, p. 3, typescript in Elliott's possession, Doylestown, PA; Fonzi, "The Furtive Fraternity," 21, 23; Greg Lee, "Becoming a Human-Sexual," *Drummer*, 13 Apr. 1972, 4; Hunter, *The Gay Insider*, 551. See also Townley, "Gay Philadelphia," 18; Fried, "Private Lives," 166.

31. Correspondence with Coxe, 29 Aug. 1961, ACLU-GPBP (box 7); Fonzi, "The Furtive Fraternity," 23; "Boys in Girls' Clothing Have Police as Escorts," *Trib.*, 1 Apr. 1969, 3; "Moms Retrieve Female-Impersonating Sons from Jail," *Trib.*, 8 Apr. 1969, 5.

32. Fonzi, "The Furtive Fraternity," 23; "Cook Held in Probe of Hotel Murder," *EB*, 29 Dec. 1950, 3; "Teacher Is Held Here on Morals Count," *Trib.*, 11 Apr. 1953, 2. See also *EB*, 7 Jan. 1951, 3; *DN*, 3 May 1954, 3; *Inq.*, 3 May 1954, 8; Clark Polak to Allen Greenough, 16 Apr. 1965, ACLU-GPBP (box 7); Barbara Horowitz to Dick Leitsch, 27 Apr. 1965, Mattachine Society Records (MSR), IGICA (box 7/f18).

33. Elliott, "The Morals Squad," 26–27, 11.

34. James C. Crumlish, report reprinted in "Judges Approve Neuropsychiatric

Department in Quarter Sessions Court," *Legal Intelligencer* (*LI*), 11 Dec. 1950, 1; Fonzi, "The Furtive Fraternity," 23; "Affidavits in Report of Investigation Allege Payoffs and Gunplay," *EB*, 19 Sept. 1965, 11.

35. "Sexism in the Schools," *GD*, c. Dec. 1970, 5; Halley Tarr, "Penned-in Gays," *GD*, c. Dec. 1970, 5. See also Townley, "Gay Philadelphia," 18.

36. Norman L. Fuller, "The Use of Closed Circuit Television for the Study and Elimination of Homo-Sexual Activity in the YMCA," 1 Sept. 1960, ACLU-GPBP (box 7). See also Fonzi, "The Furtive Fraternity," 23; *Time*, 6 Nov. 1964, 11; *Drum*, Dec. 1964, 30.

37. Taylor Branch, "Closets of Power," *Harper's*, Oct. 1982, 35–37.

38. Townley, "Gay Philadelphia," 18.

39. "Boys in Girls' Clothing"; "Moms Retrieve Female-Impersonating Sons."

40. Love, "The Invisible Sorority," 69.

41. Nora Sayre, *Sixties Going on Seventies* (New York: Arbor House, 1973), 114.

42. La Forest Potter, *Strange Loves: A Study in Sexual Abnormalities* (New York: Robert Dodsley, 1933), 183. See also Robert Scully, *A Scarlet Pansy* (New York: Faro, 1932), 198–199.

43. Fonzi, "The Furtive Fraternity," 23. See also *Welcomat*, 9 Feb. 1983, 1, 18; "Summer Mummers," *PM*, July 1972, 36; Mecca interview with Malim.

44. Mecca interview with Fleischner [Kendall]; Fonzi, "The Furtive Fraternity," 23; *Drum*, no. 22, 1966, 6.

45. *Drum*, no. 22, 1966, 6.

46. Isabelle Fambro, cited in "Testimonies," *Philadelphia Folklore Project Works*, Spring 1993, 6.

47. " 'Rizzo Rides Again!' " *JSN*, Nov. 1962, 1, 3; Fonzi, "The Furtive Fraternity," 23; "Summer Mummers," 36; *Drum*, no. 22, 1966, 6.

Chapter Four

1. Samuel B. Hadden, "Attitudes toward and Approaches to the Problem of Homosexuality," *Pennsylvania Medical Journal* 60, no. 9 (Sept. 1957): 1195.

2. Samuel B. Hadden, "Treatment of Homosexuality by Individual and Group Psychotherapy," *American Journal of Psychiatry* 114, no. 9 (1958): 811–812.

3. Ibid., 812, 814.

4. O. Spurgeon English and Gerald H. J. Pearson, *Common Neuroses of Children and Adults* (New York: Norton, 1937), 175; O. Spurgeon English and Gerald H. J. Pearson, *Emotional Problems of Living: Avoiding the Neurotic Pattern* (New York: Norton, 1945), 381; Isabel Drummond, *The Sex Paradox* (New York: Putnam, 1953), 138; Edward A. Strecker and Vincent T. Lathbury, *Their Mothers' Daughters* (Philadelphia: Lippincott, 1956), 164. I thank Terry Snyder for helping me identify Drummond.

5. Hadden, "Attitudes," 1195; George Chauncey, Jr., "From Sexual Inversion to Homosexuality: The Changing Medical Conceptualization of Female 'Deviance,' " in *Passion and Power: Sexuality in History*, ed. Kathy Peiss and Christina Simmons (Philadelphia: Temple University Press, 1989), 109.

6. Newton, " 'Dick(less) Tracy,' " 168.

7. See Edward Alwood, *Straight News: Gays, Lesbians, and the News Media* (New York: Columbia University Press, 1996), 1–26; Stein, "The City of Sisterly and Brotherly

Loves," 82–121; Marc Stein, "Politics, Histories, and Theories of Lesbian/Gay Heterosociality," paper presented at the 1992 Graduate Student Conference on Lesbian and Gay Studies at the University of Illinois, Champaign-Urbana.

8. See Clark and Clark, "Rally and Relapse," 690–691. The circulation figures come from clipping notebooks at KI.

9. "Levin Boy to Face Tests," *Inq.*, 14 Jan. 1949, 1; "Simons Tragedy Recalls Similar Murder Case," *Inq.*, 15 Jan. 1949, 3; Frank Toughill and Jay Apt, "Police Reveal Morals Motive in Sadistic Scissors Slaying," *DN*, 12 Jan. 1949, 3; Frank Toughill, "Probe Theory Levin Flagellation Cultist," *DN*, 20 Jan. 1949, 2; Frank Toughill and Jay Apt, "D.A. to Receive Mental Report on Levin Today," *DN*, 25 Jan. 1949, 2; Adolph Katz, "Levin Pleads Guilty to Murder," *EB*, 28 Feb. 1949, 3; "Experts Ask Study by Panel of Similar Cases in Future," *Inq.*, 18 Mar. 1949, 2; "Text of Court Opinion Sentencing Levin Boy," *EB*, 17 Mar. 1949, 1. See also *EB*, *Inq.*, and *DN*, 10 Jan.–18 Mar. 1949.

10. Estelle B. Freedman, "'Uncontrolled Desires': The Response to the Sexual Psychopath, 1920–1960," *Journal of American History* 74, no. 1 (June 1987): 92; "10,000 Visit Murder Scene in Wynnefield," *Inq.*, 17 Jan. 1949, 1, 3; Edward A. M. Foley, "Jr. C. of C. Fosters Drive," *DN*, 13 Jan. 1949, 3.

11. Herbert D. Reis, "Bill Seeks 'Life' for Psychopaths," *DN*, 19 Jan. 1949, 3; "Sex Crime Bill Signed by Fine," *Inq.*, 9 Jan. 1952, 12; Meric Legnini, "No Bail in Sex Crimes Aim of New Bill," *DN*, 21 Feb. 1956, 2. See also *LI*, 7 Mar. 1956, 6; *One*, June-July 1956, 24.

12. Ray Zacharias, "Robbery Seen Cause in Police Aide Slaying," *DN*, 21 Aug. 1950, 5; "Two Swarthy Strangers Sought in Ice Pick Killing," *Inq.*, 21 Aug. 1950, 17; "2 Men Held in Killing of Police Clerk," *Inq.*, 24 Aug. 1950, 19; "2 Held in Probe of Clerk's Death," *EB*, 23 Aug. 1950, 3; "Farmhand Held in Clerk Slaying," *EB*, 5 Sept. 1950, 3. See also *EB*, *Inq.*, and *DN*, 20–27 Aug., 18 Sept. 1950; *EB*, 6 Mar. 1960, 27.

13. "Cripple Beaten to Death in Midcity Hotel Room," *Inq.*, 25 Dec. 1950, 1; "Cook Held in Probe of Hotel Murder," *EB*, 29 Dec. 1950, 3. See also *Inq.*, 26 Dec. 1950, 18; *EB*, 26 Dec. 1950, 3.

14. Ray Zacharias, "Hunt Man in Mystery Inn Death," *DN*, 26 Dec. 1950, 2, 32. See also *EB*, 26 Dec. 1950, 1, 56; *DN*, 27 Dec. 1950, 6; *Inq.*, 27 Dec. 1950, 31.

15. See "Extortion Linked to Reading Man," *EB*, 7 Jan. 1951, 3.

16. Ray Zacharias, "Police Feel Parolee Likely Clymer Killer," *DN*, 19 Feb. 1953, 2, 16. See also *EB*, *Inq.*, and *DN*, 18–20 Feb., 19–20 Mar. 1953; *DN*, 20 Feb. 1956, 4.

17. "Hunt Friend in Slaying of Attorney," *Inq.*, 22 Sept. 1953, 1, 16; Ray Zacharias, "Probe Att'y Slaying Link With 2 Others," *DN*, 23 Sept. 1953, 2, 6. See also *EB*, *Inq.*, and *DN*, 21–26 Sept., 10 Oct. 1953; 1–4 Mar., 10 Apr. 1954; 24, 28 Sept., 30 Oct.–2 Nov., 22 Nov. 1955; 18 Feb. 1956; 19–26 Sept. 1957; 16–17 Oct. 1958; *One*, Dec. 1955, 11.

18. Jay Apt and Ray Zacharias, "Quiz Torso Killer about Holdups," *DN*, 1 May 1954, 3; "Torso Slayer Identifies Former Seaman as Victim," *Inq.*, 3 May 1954, 1; "Victim in Grisly Torso Murder May Be Missing Ex-Seaman," *Inq.*, 2 May 1954, 1; Rex Polier, "2 Say Ballem, Torso Victim Were Friends," *EB*, 18 Jan. 1955, 3. See also *EB*, *Inq.*, and *DN*, 28 Apr.–11 May, 21–22 May, 2–3 June, 24–25 Sept., 1 Oct. 1954; 10–28 Jan., 16–17, 30–31 Dec. 1955; 12–13 Nov. 1958.

19. "Whole Town Turns Out to Back Marine on Trial," *DN*, 23 Sept. 1958, 6; *One*, Feb. 1959, 12. See also *EB*, *Inq.*, and *DN*, 4–6 Aug., 23 Sept. 1958.

20. "Bill Tilden Gets 9 Months in Jail for Sex Offense," *Inq.*, 17 Jan. 1947, 3; "Tilden

Starts Morals Term," *DN*, 17 Jan. 1947, 5; William T. Tilden, 2nd, *My Story: A Champion's Memoirs* (New York: Hellman, Williams, 1948), 12, 307–311.

21. "Tilden Is Held on Morals Charge," *Inq.*, 9 Feb. 1949, 3; Frank Deford, "Out of the Sun, Into the Shadows," *Sports Illustrated*, 20 Jan. 1975, 36. See also *EB*, *Inq.*, and *DN*, 1, 9–11 Feb. 1949; 6 June 1953; Burt, *The Perennial Philadelphians*, 310–311; *Sports Illustrated*, 13 Jan. 1975, 50–58; Frank Deford, *Big Bill Tilden: The Triumphs and the Tragedy* (New York: Simon and Schuster, 1975); E. Digby Baltzell, *Sporting Gentlemen: Men's Tennis from the Age of Honor to the Cult of the Superstar* (New York: Free Press, 1995), 165–218.

22. "Teacher Is Held Here on Morals Count," *Trib.*, 11 Apr. 1953, 2; "Cleric Accused of Immoral Charges Resigns Nazarene Church Pastorate," *Trib.*, 8 Nov. 1955, 1; "South Philly Minister Held on Morals Charge," *Trib.*, 14 July 1959, 1. See also *Trib.*, 25 July 1959, 14.

23. See Ronald Bayer, *Homosexuality and American Psychiatry: The Politics of Diagnosis* (New York: Basic, 1981), 41–66; Henry Abelove, "Freud, Male Homosexuality, and the Americans," *Dissent* (Winter 1986): 59–69.

24. Philip Q. Roche, "Psychodynamics of Homosexuality," *Philadelphia Medicine*, 9 Mar. 1956, 1009–1013. See also William Drayton, Jr., "The Cats of Society: Some Leaves from a Psychiatrist's Notebook," *Philadelphia Medicine*, 3 Sept. 1949, 119; *Inq.*, 19 Mar. 1953, 20; Philip Q. Roche, *The Criminal Mind: A Study of Communication between the Criminal Law and Psychiatry* (New York: Farrar, Straus and Cudahy, 1958), 25.

25. Ian Stevenson and Joseph Wolpe, "Recovery from Sexual Deviations through Overcoming Non-Sexual Neurotic Responses," *American Journal of Psychiatry* 116 (Feb. 1960): 742; Joseph Wolpe and Arnold Lazarus, *Behavior Therapy Techniques* (1966; New York: Pergamon, 1968), 151–152. See also Joseph Wolpe, *The Practice of Behavior Therapy* (New York: Pergamon, 1969), 205–209, 215, 255–262, 390; Michael Serber and Joseph Wolpe, "Behavior Therapy Techniques," in *Treatment of the Sex Offender*, ed. H. L. P. Resnik and Marvin E. Wolfgang (Boston: Little, Brown, 1972), 53–67. For reports on Wolpe's work, see *New York Times Magazine*, 4 June 1967, 38; *Drum*, no. 29, Mar. 1968, 32–33; *New York Times* (*NYT*), 28 Feb. 1971, 1; *Temple Free Press*, Mar. 1973, 6; Karlen, *Sexuality and Homosexuality*, 588–589; *NYT*, 8 Dec. 1997, A29.

26. Pa. Stat. Ann., tit. 18, sect. 4501. See also Robert C. Bensing, "A Comparative Study of American Sex Statutes," *Journal of Criminal Law, Criminology and Police Science* 42, no. 1 (1951): 63–64.

27. James C. Crumlish, report reprinted in "Judges Approve Neuropsychiatric Department in Quarter Sessions Court," *LI*, 11 Dec. 1950, 1; Norris Barratt, report reprinted in "Judges Approve Neuropsychiatric Department in Quarter Sessions Court," *LI*, 11 Dec. 1950, 1, 6. See also *One*, Dec. 1955, 11.

28. Winifred Bayard Stewart, report reprinted in "Judges Approve Neuropsychiatric Department in Quarter Sessions Court," *LI*, 11 Dec. 1950, 6. See also *One*, Dec. 1955, 11; *U.S. Census of Population: 1950*, vol. 3, chap. 42 (Washington, DC: GPO, 1952), 8; Morris Fine, ed., *American Jewish Yearbook: 1950*, vol. 51 (New York: American Jewish Committee, 1950), 73; National Council of Churches of Christ in the U.S.A., *Churches and Church Membership in the United States* (New York: National Council of Churches, 1956), ser. D, table 134.

29. Stewart, report reprinted in "Judges Approve."

30. Von Moschzisker, "Homosexuality and Sexual Deviants," 1426–1427; Joseph J. Peters, James M. Pedigo, Joseph Steg, and James J. McKenna, Jr., "Group Psychotherapy of

the Sex Offender," *Federal Probation* 32, no. 3 (Sept. 1968): 41–45. See also Joseph J. Peters and Hermann A. Roether, "Group Psychotherapy for Probationed Sex Offenders," in *Treatment of the Sex Offender*, 69–80. Sodomy-related crimes included sodomy, solicitation to commit sodomy, and assault with intent to commit sodomy.

31. Pennsylvania Act of 8 Jan. 1952, P.L. 495; Pa. Stat. Ann., tit. 19, sect. 1166 (1964). See also Pennsylvania Joint State Government Commission, Subcommittee on Sex Offenders, *Sex Offenders*, 1951; *LI*, 10 Jan. 1952, 1; "Pennsylvania's New Sex Crime Law," *University of Pennsylvania Law Review* 100 (1952): 727–750.

32. "Pennsylvania's New Sex Crime Law," 727–750. See also "The Legal Disposition of the Sexual Psychopath," *University of Pennsylvania Law Review* 96 (1947–1948): 872–887; John A. DeMay, "The Pennsylvania Sex Crimes Act," *University of Pittsburgh Law Review* 13 (Summer 1952): 739–749.

33. John G. Yeager, "Characteristics of 'Barr-Walker' Cases in the Bureau of Correction," Pennsylvania Department of Justice, Bureau of Correction, 23 Oct. 1957, 4, KI.

34. Ibid., 5–6, 9–10. See also Donald B. Dodd, comp., *Historical Statistics of the States of the United States* (Westport, CT: Greenwood, 1993), 78.

35. *A Symposium on the Problem of the Sexual Criminal*, 8 Apr. 1960, Philadelphia College of Physicians (Philadelphia: Pennsylvania Mental Health, 1960), 6–7.

36. Ibid., 9–13, 16. See also Marvin Eugene Wolfgang, "Criminal Homicide with Special Reference to Philadelphia, 1948–1952" (Ph.D. diss., University of Pennsylvania, 1955), 212, 263; Marvin E. Wolfgang, "Victim-Precipitated Criminal Homicide," in *The Sociology of Crime and Delinquency*, ed. Marvin E. Wolfgang, Leonard Savitz, and Norman Johnston (New York: Wiley, 1962), 388–396; *Ladder*, Nov. 1964, 4–8; H. L. P. Resnik and Marvin E. Wolfgang, "New Directions in the Treatment of Deviance," in *Treatment of the Sex Offender*, 211–226; *NYT*, 18 Apr. 1998, A14.

37. William L. Jacks, "A 10-Year Study of Barr-Walker Cases," Pennsylvania Board of Parole, 25 May 1962, KI. See also Arthur T. Prasse, " 'Barr-Walker' Cases or Special Sex Offenders in the Bureau of Correction as of December 31, 1959," Pennsylvania Department of Justice, Bureau of Correction, 14 Jan. 1960, KI; *LI*, 19 Aug. 1963, 1, 5, 6; 26 Aug. 1963, 1, 8; *U.S. ex rel. Gerchman*, U.S. Court of Appeals for the Third Circuit, 355 F.2d (302); *Commonwealth v. Dooley*, Pa. Super., 232 A.2d 45 (1967); Robert L. Sadoff, "Sexually Deviated Offenders," *Temple Law Quarterly* 40, nos. 3–4 (Spring-Summer 1967): 305; *EB*, 10 July 1967, 9.

38. "Senate Is Asked to Vote Inquiry on Degenerates," *Inq.*, 20 May 1950, 2; "Inside the Dome," *DN*, 17 June 1950, 4; "? Is: Where Did McCarthy Poke Pearson," *DN*, 14 Dec. 1950, 5; "U.S. Easy Marks Found by Spies," *EB*, 15 Dec. 1950, 25; Robert F. Rich, *Congressional Record*, 18 Dec. 1950, 16715, A7755; "8,008 Dropped from Federal Rolls as Risks," *EB*, 3 Jan. 1955, 1, 2. See also *One*, Apr. 1964, 18; D'Emilio, *Sexual Politics*, 40–53; John D'Emilio, "The Homosexual Menace: The Politics of Sexuality in Cold War America," in *Passion and Power*, 226–240; Eric A. Gordon, *Mark the Music: The Life and Work of Marc Blitzstein* (New York: St. Martin's, 1989); Johnson, " 'Homosexual Citizens,' " 45–63.

39. " 'The Third Sex' at the Studio," *DN*, 13 Mar. 1959, 60; Mildred Martin, "Film Has Delicate Theme," *Inq.*, 13 Mar. 1959, 22; E. S., " 'The Third Sex,' German Film, at the Studio," *EB*, 13 Mar. 1959, 34. See also *DN*, 11 Mar. 1959, 44; *Inq.*, 11 Mar. 1959, 34; *EB*, 12 Mar. 1959, 26.

40. C. A. Weslager, "The Delaware Indians as Women," *Journal of the Washington Academy of Sciences* 34, no. 12 (15 Dec. 1944): 381, 388.

41. Frank G. Speck, "The Delaware Indians as Women: Were the Original Pennsylvanians Politically Emasculated?" *Pennsylvania Magazine of History and Biography* 70, no. 4 (Oct. 1946): 385; Anthony F. C. Wallace, "Woman, Land, and Society: Three Aspects of Aboriginal Delaware Life," *Pennsylvania Archaeologist* 17 (1947): 31.

42. See *EB*, 30 Aug. 1971; 25 Jan. 1973; *Inq.*, 25 Jan. 1973; *DN*, 25 Jan. 1973; 2 Apr. 1974; *Gay*, 12 Mar. 1973, 8; *Commonwealth v. Farquharson*, 467 Pa. 50, 354 A.2d 545.

43. Calvin S. Drayer, "Homosexuality and Sexual Deviants," *Philadelphia Medicine*, 30 Mar. 1956, 1103–1105.

44. A. E. Rakoff, "Endocrine Aspects of Homosexuality," *Philadelphia Medicine*, 27 Apr. 1956, 1256–1257. See also William H. Perloff, "Role of the Hormones in Human Sexuality," *Psychosomatic Medicine* 11, no. 3 (May-June 1949): 133–139; Karl E. Paschkis, Abraham E. Rakoff, and Abraham Cantarow, *Clinical Endocrinology* (New York: Hoeber-Harper, 1954), 569; William H. Perloff, "Hormones and Homosexuality," in *Sexual Inversion: The Multiple Roots of Homosexuality*, ed. Judd Marmor (New York: Basic, 1965), 44–69.

45. "Is Transvestitism Legal?" *EB*, 21 Aug. 1953, 6.

46. "Adam Powell Blasts Sex Degenerates," *Trib.*, 9 Oct. 1951, 13; Dean Gordon B. Hancock, "Womanish Men Leaders Fail American Society," *Trib.*, 7 Mar. 1959, 4.

47. Karl M. Bowman and Bernice Engle, "A Psychiatric Evaluation of Laws of Homosexuality," *Temple Law Quarterly Review* 29 (1956): 278–281, 315; von Moschzisker, "Homosexuality and Sexual Deviants," 1426–1427. See also Freedman, " 'Uncontrolled Desires,' " 87–88.

48. American Law Institute, *Model Penal Code Tentative Draft no. 4* (Philadelphia: American Law Institute, 1955), 90, 93, 243, 276–281. See also Frank P. Grad, "The ALI Model Penal Code," *NPPA Journal* 4, no. 2 (1958): 127–138; American Law Institute, *Model Penal Code Proposed Official Draft* (Philadelphia: American Law Institute, 1962), 236–237; Louis B. Schwartz, "Morals, Offenses, and the Model Penal Code," *Columbia Law Review* 63 (1963): 669–686; Louis B. Schwartz, "The Model Penal Code: An Invitation to Law Reform," *American Bar Association Journal* 49, no. 5 (May 1963): 447–455.

49. American Law Institute, *Model Penal Code Tentative Draft no. 4*, 279–281.

50. Ibid., 280. See also Grad, "The ALI Model Penal Code," 137–138; *American Law Institute Proceedings*, 18–21 May 1955, 127–132; American Law Institute, *Model Penal Code Proposed Official Draft*, 237; Schwartz, "Morals, Offenses, and the Model Penal Code," 675.

51. Drummond, *The Sex Paradox*, x, 125–126.

52. Ibid.

53. English and Pearson, *Common Neuroses*, 41, 56, 280. See also 145, 173–175, 279–283.

54. English and Pearson, *Emotional Problems*, 370, 375–383. See also 109–110, 138, 253, 377–378, 380–381.

55. Eugene Meyer, foreword to Edward A. Strecker, *Their Mothers' Sons: The Psychiatrist Examines an American Problem* (Philadelphia: Lippincott, 1946), 5–6. See also Edward A. Strecker, *Beyond the Clinical Frontiers: A Psychiatrist Views Crowd Behavior* (New York: Norton, 1940), 206–209; George W. Henry, *Sex Variants: A Study of Homosexual Patterns* (New York: Hoeber, 1941); Edward Strecker, *Fundamentals of Psychiatry*, 4th ed.

(Philadelphia: Lippincott, 1942), 9–10, 153–154, 208, 229–229; *EB*, 17 May 1945, 9; 21 Nov. 1946, 18; *Inq. Everybody's Weekly*, 27 Apr. 1947, 11; *EB*, 23 Sept. 1948, 30; William C. Menninger, *Psychiatry in a Troubled World* (New York: Macmillan, 1948), 228–229; Edward Strecker, *Basic Psychiatry* (New York: Random House, 1952), 133, 148, 152, 197, 222, 231, 241, 267–268, 307, 322; *EB*, 7 Oct. 1956, sec. 4, p. 9; 3 Jan. 1959, 20; Bérubé, *Coming Out under Fire*, 169.

56. Strecker, *Their Mothers' Sons*, 13, 30, 128–131, 133. See also Philip Wylie, *Generation of Vipers* (New York: Rinehart, 1942).

57. Strecker, *Their Mothers' Sons*, 131.

58. Strecker and Lathbury, *Their Mothers' Daughters*, 11–12, 27–30, 36, 40, 144.

59. Ibid., 158–160.

60. Hadden, "Attitudes," 1196–1198; "Newer Treatment Techniques for Homosexuality," *Archives of Environmental Health: Preventive, Occupational, and Aerospace Medicine* 13, no. 3 (Sept. 1966): 284. See also "Group Psychotherapy of Male Homosexuals," *Current Psychiatric Therapies: 1966*, ed. Jules H. Masserman (New York: Grune and Stratton, 1966), 177–186; "Treatment of Male Homosexuals in Groups," *International Journal of Group Psychotherapy* 16, no. 1 (Jan. 1966): 13–22; "Etiologic Factors in Male Homosexuality," *Proceedings of the IV World Congress of Psychiatry*, Madrid, 5–11 Sept. 1966, International Congress Series no. 150 (New York: Excerpta Medica, 1967–1968): 3067–3069; "Male Homosexuality," *Pennsylvania Medicine* 70 (Feb. 1967): 78–80; "A Way Out for Homosexuals," *Harper's*, Mar. 1967, 107–120; "Group Psychotherapy in Homosexuality," *Psychiatric Opinion* 4, no. 2 (1967): 9–12; "Group Psychotherapy for Sexual Maladjustments," *American Journal of Psychiatry* 125, no. 3 (Sept. 1968): 83–88; "Rehabilitation of the Sexual Delinquent," *Pennsylvania Medicine* 72 (Mar. 1969): 49–51; "Group Psychotherapy in the Treatment of Homosexuality," *Linacre Quarterly* (Aug. 1971): 149–156; "What Outcome Can Be Expected in Psychotherapy of Homosexuals?" *Medical Aspects of Human Sexuality* (Dec. 1971): 96–100; "Group Psychotherapy with Homosexual Men," *International Psychiatry Clinics* 8, no. 4 (1972): 81–94; "Group Psychotherapy with Homosexual Men," in *Treatment of the Sex Offender*, 81–94; "The Homosexual Group: Formation and Beginnings," *Group Process* 7 (1976): 81–92. For reports on Hadden's work, see "Help for Homosexuals," *Sexology*, Mar. 1958, 528; *EB*, 29 Jan. 1965, 29; *NYT*, 31 Jan. 1965, 61; *MR*, Jan.-Feb. 1965, 11–18; Karlen, *Sexuality and Homosexuality*, 583, 593, 599–603; *NYT*, 28 Feb. 1971, 1, 47; "The Problem of Treating Homosexuality," *Medical Tribune*, 18 Nov. 1975, 19, 24–27. Hadden's papers are at the University of Pennsylvania Archives and Records Center.

61. Smith, *South Street*, 106, 116–118, 124–126, 288. See Stein, "Politics, Histories, and Theories."

62. " 'Wedding' Entertainment Female 'Groom' Tells Judge," *Trib.*, 14 Apr. 1953, 1, 2; " 'Wedding' Figures Are Held under $300 Peace Bond," *Trib.*, 18 Apr. 1953, 1, 3. See also *Jet*, 16 Apr. 1953, 16.

Chapter Five

1. "Catholics Decry Whitman Bridge," *NYT*, 17 Dec. 1955, 16. See also *Camden Courier-Post*, 17 Dec. 1955, 3; Janice Rowan, "Walt Whitman and the Battle of the Bridge," typescript, Walt Whitman Collection (WWC), Special Collections, Van Pelt Library, University of Pennsylvania, Philadelphia, PA.

2. "Catholics Decry." See also Gay Wilson Allen, *The Solitary Singer: A Critical Biography of Walt Whitman* (New York: Macmillan, 1955); Robert K. Martin, *The Continuing Presence of Walt Whitman: The Life after the Life* (Iowa City: University of Iowa Press, 1992); Betsy Erkkila and Jay Grossman, eds., *Breaking Bounds: Whitman and American Cultural Studies* (New York: Oxford University Press, 1996).

3. See James Reichley, *The Art of Government: Reform and Organization Politics in Philadelphia* (New York: Fund for the Republic, 1959), 75–76; Burt, *The Perennial Philadelphians*, 573–578; Bernard McCormick, "The Troubled See," *PM*, Oct. 1967, 52–57, 80–93; Weigley, ed., *Philadelphia: A Three-Hundred-Year History*, 50, 309, 331, 352, 356–358, 556; *Proceedings from Philadelphia's Political Reform Movement, 1946–1961* (Philadelphia: Historical Society of Pennsylvania, 1988), 3–4; S. A. Paolantonio, *Frank Rizzo: The Last Big Man in Big City America* (Philadelphia: Camino, 1993), 70; Charles R. Morris, *American Catholic: The Saints and Sinners Who Built America's Most Powerful Church* (New York: Random House, 1997), 60–67, 113–115, 129–130, 165–195; Michael W. Cuneo, *The Smoke of Satan: Conservative and Traditionalist Dissent in Contemporary American Catholicism* (New York: Oxford University Press, 1997), 3–14.

4. Donald F. Crosby, S.J., *God, Church, and Flag: Senator Joseph R. McCarthy and the Catholic Church, 1950–1957* (Chapel Hill: University of North Carolina Press, 1978), 158–159, 195, 244–245; *The Official Catholic Directory* (New York: P. J. Kenedy and Sons, 1954), 181, 198, 326, 329. See also John T. McGreevy, *Parish Boundaries: The Catholic Encounter with Race in the Twentieth-Century Urban North* (Chicago: University of Chicago Press, 1996), 64–66, 105–106, 175; Godfrey Hodgson, *The World Turned Right Side Up: A History of the Conservative Ascendancy in America* (Boston: Houghton Mifflin, 1996), 72–84, 159–176, 228; Morris, *American Catholic*, 228–254.

5. See Reichley, *The Art of Government*; Joseph D. Crumlish, *A City Finds Itself: The Philadelphia Home Rule Charter Movement* (Detroit: Wayne State University Press, 1959); Burt, *The Perennial Philadelphians*, 549–555; Joseph Richard Fink, "Reform in Philadelphia: 1946–1951" (Ph.D. diss., Rutgers University, 1971); David Rogers, *The Management of Big Cities: Interest Groups and Social Change Strategies* (Beverly Hills: Sage, 1971), 75–104; Kirk R. Petshek, *The Challenge of Urban Reform: Policies and Programs in Philadelphia* (Philadelphia: Temple University Press, 1973); *Proceedings from Philadelphia's Political Reform Movement*; Clark and Clark, "Rally and Relapse," 649–703.

6. D'Emilio, "The Homosexual Menace," 236. See also Ralph Lord Roy, *Apostles of Discord: A Study of Organized Bigotry and Disruption on the Fringes of Protestantism* (Boston: Beacon, 1953), 141, 165–168, 174, 185–246, 331; Ralph Lord Roy, *Communism and the Churches* (New York: Harcourt, Brace, 1960), 228–230, 234, 264, 419; Louis Gasper, *The Fundamentalist Movement* (The Hague: Mouton, 1963), 16–81, 119–120, 142; Leo P. Ribuffo, *The Old Christian Right: The Protestant Far Right from the Great Depression to the Cold War* (Philadelphia: Temple University Press, 1983), 259–260, 270; Sara Diamond, *Roads to Dominion: Right-Wing Movements and Political Power in the United States* (New York: Guilford, 1995), 52, 93–96, 247; Hodgson, *The World Turned Right Side Up*, 62, 161.

7. Edgar Williams, "The Bridge without a Name," *Inq. Today Magazine*, 4 Apr. 1954, 9–11.

8. See *Inq.*, 7 Apr. 1954, 33; 12 Apr. 1954, 19; John M. McCullough, Secretary, "Summary for Special Committee on Bridge Names," DRPA, June 1955, WWC.

9. See *EB*, *Inq.*, *DN*, and *Camden Courier-Post*, 31 Oct., 17 Nov., 18–19 Dec. 1954;

14 May, 19 May, 6 June, 30 Nov., 3 Dec., 15 Dec., 21–23 Dec. 1955; 1 Jan., 4 Jan., 12 Jan., 21 Jan. 1956.

10. McCullough, "Summary." See also *EB*, 20 July 1955, 1, 22; 21 July 1955, 44; *Inq.*, 21 July 1955, 15.

11. Williams, "The Bridge without a Name," 10; Noah Little, letter to the editor, *EB*, 9 Jan. 1956, 16.

12. "Gloucester Council Protests Whitman Name for Bridge," *EB*, 5 Aug. 1955, 7; " 'A Bridge by Any Other Name,' " *Inq.*, 6 Aug. 1955, 6. See also *EB*, 2 Sept. 1955, 1; 30 Dec. 1955, 19; Albert Agar, Gloucester City Clerk, to DRPA, 30 Dec. 1955, WWC; Vincent Gallaher, County Counsel, Camden County Board of Chosen Freeholders, to DRPA, 18 Jan. 1956, WWC.

13. James Ryan, "Walt Whitman Was Reluctant Citizen," *Catholic Star Herald*, 11 Nov. 1955, 9. See also *Catholic Standard and Times*, 18 Nov. 1955, 11; 23 Dec. 1955, 1; Jay Grossman, "Emerson, Whitman, and the Politics of Representation" (Ph.D. diss., University of Pennsylvania, 1992).

14. See Sedgwick, *Epistemology*, 11.

15. James Ryan, "Emerson Was Disappointed in Writings of Whitman," *Catholic Star Herald*, 25 Nov. 1955, 11. See also *Catholic Standard and Times*, 25 Nov. 1955, 9; Leo Bersani, "Is the Rectum a Grave?" *October*, no. 43 (Winter 1987): 197–222.

16. James Ryan, "Whitman Gave up Claim to Thinker Reputation," *Catholic Star Herald*, 9 Dec. 1955, 11. See also *Catholic Standard and Times*, 16 Dec. 1955, 17.

17. See *EB*, 23 Nov. 1955, 3; 16 Dec. 1955, 17; *Inq.*, 17 Dec. 1955, 9.

18. Ninety percent of the New Jersey writers were anti-Whitman; 71% of the non-Philadelphia Pennsylvania writers were pro-Whitman; 77% of the Philadelphia writers were pro-Whitman; 86% of the letters from elsewhere were pro-Whitman.

19. See WWC.

20. Signed form letters, Jan. and Feb. 1956, WWC. See also D'Emilio, "The Homosexual Menace"; D'Emilio, *Sexual Politics*, 40–53; Elaine Tyler May, *Homeward Bound: American Families in the Cold War Era* (New York: Basic, 1988).

21. Mrs. William C. Russell, 20 Jan. 1956; R. J. Peterson, 10 Feb. 1956; A. McIntyre, 6 Feb. 1956; Richard Dolan, 13 Feb. 1956; Vince L. Burns, 7 Feb. 1956, WWC.

22. Paul V. Breig, 7 Feb. 1956; Thomas Horace Evans, 16 Dec. 1955, WWC.

23. "What's in a Name?" *Ave Maria*, 7 Jan. 1956, 6. See also *America*, 5 Nov. 1955, 157–159; *Commonweal*, 6 Jan. 1956, 346; *Newsweek*, 2 Jan. 1956, 7.

24. Murray Kempton, "One of the Roughs," *New York Post*, 19 Dec. 1955, 4, 32, reprinted in *Camden Courier-Post*, 28 Dec. 1955, 8; Letter to the editor and editorial response, *Ave Maria*, 4 Feb. 1956, 30.

25. Alfred Douglas, cited in Richard Ellmann, *Oscar Wilde* (New York: Knopf, 1988), 386.

26. Harry Brandlee, 20 Jan. 1956; Ottilie Van Allen, 12 Feb. 1956; Phillips Endecott Osgood, 11 Feb. 1956; Elizabeth Wintersteen Schneider, 10 Feb. 1956, WWC.

27. W. Wagnytz, 11 Feb. 1956, WWC.

28. Mary L. Inman, 24 Jan. 1956; Fred L. Feiden, 20 Dec. 1955, WWC; *New York Post*, cited in *One*, Mar. 1956, 7.

29. Patricia Underwood, 21 Dec. 1955, WWC.

30. Mrs. Richard Miner, 12 Feb. 1956; V. E. Rogers, 12 Feb. 1956; Hayden Goldberg, 13 Feb. 1956; Frederick Griffin III, 14 Feb. 1956, WWC.

31. Regina M. Palmer, 9 Feb. 1956, WWC.

32. Kempton, "One of the Roughs," 32; H. David Hammond, 21 Dec. 1955, WWC.

33. Donald Weeks, 12 Jan. 1956; Clinton Rossiter, 19 Dec. 1955, WWC.

34. Fred L. Feiden, 20 Dec. 1955; Mary J. Allen, 15 Feb. 1956; Jerome J. Relkin, 11 Feb. 1956, WWC.

35. Edward J. Stinsmen, 12 Feb. 1956; Mary Silverman, c. Feb. 1956, WWC; "But Would He Be a Security Risk?" *Harper's*, Feb. 1956, 71; Kempton, "One of the Roughs," 32.

36. *One*, Jan. 1955, 35. See also *One*, July 1954, 4–15.

37. *One*, Mar. 1956, 7.

38. "Why Not Just Let It Be 'Gloucester Bridge'?" *Camden Courier Post*, 24 Jan. 1956, 10; "Urge Naming New Bridge for Jefferson," *Catholic Star Herald*, 6 Jan. 1956, 1, 2. See also *Camden Courier-Post*, 22 Dec. 1955, 2; *Inq.*, 7 Jan. 1956, 13; *Catholic Star Herald*, 13 Jan. 1956, 1; *Inq.*, 19 Jan. 1956, 21; *Catholic Star Herald*, 20 Jan. 1956, 1; *Catholic Standard and Times*, 20 Jan. 1956, 1; *EB*, 22 Jan. 1956, sec. 2, p. 2.

39. "Gloucester City Shows Anger at Port Authority—Votes to Order 'Gloucester City Bridge' Signs," *EB*, 7 Dec. 1956, 46; "Gloucester City Claims New Bridge as Own," *Inq.*, 8 Dec. 1956, 22.

40. Stuart Brown, "Naming Span for Whitman Caused Bitter Controversy," *EB*, 12 May 1957, 27.

41. Interviews with Golden and Coopersmith.

42. Cited in Betsy Erkkila, "Introduction: Breaking Bounds," *Breaking Bounds*, 6–7. See also Jay Grossman, "Epilogue: Whitman's Centennial and the State of Whitman Studies," *Breaking Bounds*, 254; Telephone interview with Rita Addessa, 23 Jan. 1998.

Chapter Six

1. "Police Raiders Break up Chess Game, Seize Men in Beards, Girls in Tights," *EB*, 12 Feb. 1959, 3. The newspapers generally used "Haifetz," but Heifetz says he used and uses "Heifetz." Except in legal citations, I have standardized the spelling.

2. See Wini Breines, "The 'Other' Fifties: Beats and Bad Girls," in *Not June Cleaver: Women and Gender in Postwar America, 1945–1960*, ed. Joanne Meyerowitz (Philadelphia: Temple University Press, 1994), 399–400.

3. John D'Emilio and Estelle Freedman, *Intimate Matters: A History of Sexuality in America* (New York: Harper and Row, 1988), 275–276. See also Bruce Cook, *The Beat Generation* (New York: Scribner's, 1971), 24–27, 92–98; D'Emilio, *Sexual Politics*, 176–182; D'Emilio, "Gay Politics," 461–462; Catherine R. Stimpson, "The Beat Generation and the Trials of Homosexual Liberation," *Salmagundi*, nos. 58–59 (Fall 1982/Winter 1983): 373–392.

4. "City Teeners Account for 1/4 of Crime in 58," *Inq.*, 25 Feb. 1959, 12. See also Allen J. Matusow, *The Unraveling of America: A History of Liberalism in the 1960s* (New York: Harper and Row, 1984), 107; James Gilbert, *A Cycle of Outrage: America's Reaction to the Juvenile Delinquent in the 1950s* (New York: Oxford University Press, 1986).

5. Paolantonio, *Frank Rizzo*, 110. See also Greg Walter, "Rizzo," *PM*, July 1967, 43, 71–89; Charles MacNamara, "The Tactics of Counterinsurgency," *PM*, Mar. 1968, 50–53, 120–137; Charles MacNamara, "The Collected Love Letters of Frank Rizzo and Dick Nixon," *PM*, July 1972, 86–88; Fred Hamilton, *Rizzo* (New York: Viking, 1973); Sayre, *Sixties Going on Seventies*, 66–78, 112–132; Joseph R. Daughen and Peter Binzen, *The Cop Who Would Be King* (Boston: Little, Brown, 1977); Frank Donner, *Protectors*

of Privilege: Red Squads and Police Repression in Urban America (Berkeley: University of California Press, 1990), 197–244.

6. Donner, *Protectors of Privilege*, 197, 200.

7. "Phila. Wins 3d Title of Cleanest U.S. City," *Inq.*, 13 Mar. 1959, 29.

8. W. E. B. Dubois, *The Philadelphia Negro: A Social Study* (1899; New York: Schocken, 1967), xix; Lincoln Steffens, "Philadelphia: Corrupt and Contented," *McClure's Magazine*, July 1903, 249–263; Estes Kefauver, *Crime in America* (Garden City, NY: Doubleday, 1951), 218; Rubinstein, *City Police*, 393–433; Pennsylvania Crime Commission, *Report on Police Corruption and the Quality of Law Enforcement in Philadelphia*, Mar. 1974, 1, 827. See also Senate Special Committee to Investigate Organized Crime in Interstate Commerce, 82nd Cong., 1st sess., 1951, S. Rept. 307, 46–49; Senate Committee on Government Operations, Permanent Subcommittee on Investigations, 87th Cong., Hearings, 12 June 1962, 57–81; Crumlish, *A City Finds Itself*, 5–22, 51–53; Reichley, *The Art of Government*, 3–11, 57, 78–79, 89–92; Sayre, *Sixties Going on Seventies*, 123–125, 128–129; Blaze Starr and Huey Perry, *Blaze Starr: My Life as Told to Huey Perry* (New York: Praeger, 1974), 89–101; Clark and Clark, "Rally and Relapse," 650–652; Paolantonio, *Frank Rizzo*, 43–44, 47–48, 59–63, 69–70, 175–178.

9. "10 Are Freed after Club Raids," *EB*, 28 Apr. 1954, 3; "3 Dancers, 4 Men Held in Midcity Nightclub Raids," *DN*, 28 Apr. 1954, 3; Rizzo, cited in Walter, "Rizzo," 78; Joseph Yannone, cited in Paolantonio, *Frank Rizzo*, 61; "Policeman Fired in Morals Case," *Inq.*, 15 July 1959, 9. See also *Inq.*, 28 Apr. 1954, 44; *EB*, 3 Oct. 1958, 3; *Inq.*, 3 Oct. 1958, 46; *DN*, 3 Oct. 1958, 4.

10. Mumia, "Occupation: Philadelphia, PA," *BP*, 4 July 1970, 9; *DN*, 8 May 1973, 4.

11. "Rizzo's Raiders Strike Again at Midcity Coffee House," *EB*, 14 Feb. 1959, 1, 3; " 'Beatnik' Place Raided by Police," *Inq.*, 14 Feb. 1959, 9; Rizzo, cited in "Coffee House Steaming to Halt Rizzo's Raiders," *DN*, 17 Feb. 1959, 4; Heifetz, cited in "Rizzo's Raiders Strike Again." See also "2 City Departments, State Agency Probe 4 Midtown Coffee Shops," *Inq.*, 19 Feb. 1959, 13.

12. "Rizzo's Raiders Strike Again"; Heifetz, cited in "Rizzo's Raiders Strike Again"; "Rizzo the Raider Tours Coffee Spots," *EB*, 18 Feb. 1959, 1, 19.

13. Heifetz, cited in "Rizzo's Raiders Strike Again"; Ruth Rolen, "Did Mixing of Races Spur Coffee Shop Raids?" *Trib.*, 21 Feb. 1959, 11; "Rizzo the Raider Tours Coffee Spots"; C. A. S., Jr., letter to the editor, *EB*, 19 Feb. 1959, 14.

14. " 'Beatnik' Center Raided by Police," *Inq.*, 12 Feb. 1959, 9; "Rizzo's Raiders Strike Again."

15. "Cisco vs. Espresso," *DN*, 17 Feb. 1959, 23; C. A. S., Jr., letter to the editor; Letter to the editor, *EB*, 19 Feb. 1959, 14.

16. Heifetz, cited in "Rizzo's Raiders Strike Again"; Letter to the editor, *EB*, 19 Feb. 1959, 14. See also letters to the editor, *Inq.*, 18 Feb. 1959, 16; *DN*, 20 Feb. 1959, 29.

17. Horace Proctor, Jr., letter to the editor, *EB*, 19 Feb. 1959, 14.

18. Heifetz, cited in "Rizzo's Raiders Strike Again"; Rubin, cited in Stewart Klein, "Coffee Houses Hint Suit for 100Gs," *DN*, 19 Feb. 1959, 5. See also "Rizzo the Raider Tours Coffee Spots"; "2 City Departments"; "Coffee House Steaming to Halt Rizzo's Raiders"; *CLR*, Mar. 1959, 1; May 1959, 2; Dec. 1969, 2; Coxe to Byrna Aronson, 14 May 1971, HLP (box 1/f2).

19. "Coffee House Owner, Patron Sue Police over Raids," *EB*, 19 Feb. 1959, 2. See also "Residents Protest Immoral Conduct at Coffee Houses," *Inq.*, 20 Feb. 1959, 25; " 'Shocking Talk' Laid to Coffee Shop Patrons," *DN*, 20 Feb. 1959, 4.

20. Dave Racher and Jim O'Brien, "Fergy's Turn to Beard the Beatniks," *DN*, 18 Feb. 1959, 3; "2 City Departments, State Agency Probe 4 Midtown Coffee Shops."

21. Letters to the editor, *EB*, 19 Feb. 1959, 14. See also letter to the editor, *DN*, 19 Feb. 1959, 17.

22. "Residents Protest Immoral Conduct," *Inq.*, 20 Feb. 1959, 25; John H. Gordy, "Steamed-up Residents Argue Coffee Shop Raids," *EB*, 20 Feb. 1959, 1, 3. See also *EB*, 19 Feb. 1959, 2; " 'Shocking Talk' Laid to Coffee Shop Patrons."

23. "Residents Protest Immoral Conduct."

24. Ibid.

25. Ibid.

26. Ibid.

27. "Turning Down the Flame," *EB*, 21 Feb. 1959, 6.

28. Gordy, "Steamed-up Residents"; "Residents Protest Immoral Conduct."

29. Gordy, "Steamed-up Residents."

30. James Smart, "A Visit to the Coffeehouses," *EB*, 22 Feb. 1959, 1, 16.

31. Ibid.; "Postscript on Coffee Houses," *CLR*, May 1959, 2; Rolen, "Did Mixing of Races Spur Coffee Shop Raids?"

32. Jerry Gaghan, "Locust St. after Dark," *DN*, 19 Mar. 1959, 39.

33. Rolen, "Did Mixing of Races Spur Coffee Shop Raids?"

34. "Thirteen Want Coffeehouse Ruled Nuisance by Court," *EB*, 25 Feb. 1959, 21; "Coffee Shop Patrons Rowdy, Residents Say," *Inq.*, 28 Feb. 1959, 13; "Coffeehouse Witness Tells of Dope 'Buy,' " *EB*, 2 Mar. 1959, 3; "Coffee House Brief Ordered," *DN*, 3 Mar. 1959, 4. See also *Inq.*, 25 Feb. 1959, 1; *DN*, 25 Feb. 1959, 41.

35. "Rizzo Tells Federal Court of Coffeehouse Complaints," *EB*, 27 Feb. 1959, 42.

36. "Narcotics Addicts Found in Coffeehouse, Police Say," *EB*, 28 Feb. 1959, 3.

37. "Coffee Shop Asked to Cite Raid Ban Data," *Inq.*, 3 Mar. 1959, 29; "Police Showed No Warrant, Coffeehouse Owner Says," *EB*, 27 Feb. 1959, 3; "Teenage Witnesses Deny Disorders at Humoresque," *EB*, 3 Mar. 1959, 11. See also *Inq.*, 27 Feb. 1959, 23; *DN*, 27 Feb. 1959, 3.

38. "Youth in Coffee Shop Raid Says Police Helped Him Flee," *EB*, 7 Mar. 1959, 3; "3 Youths Freed of Charges in Coffee Raids," *EB*, 9 Mar. 1959, 2. See also *Inq.*, 11 Mar. 1959, 45.

39. "Youth in Coffee Shop Raid."

40. "3 Youths Freed of Charges"; "Judge Upholds 4 Fines, Roasts Coffee Shop Set," *Inq.*, 10 Mar. 1959, 29.

41. See *EB*, 20 Mar. 1959, 13; 26 Mar. 1959, 42; Stewart Klein, "An Espresso of Sad Parting," *DN*, 27 Mar. 1959, 4; *Haifetz v. Rizzo* 171 F. Supp. 654; Paolantonio, *Frank Rizzo*, 68–69; Hamilton, *Rizzo*, 59–60.

42. "3 Coffeehouses Vow to Police Themselves and Bar Undesirables," *Inq.*, 27 Mar. 1959, 21; Richardson Dilworth to Henry W. Sawyer, III, 29 Mar. 1959, in the possession of Spencer Coxe, Philadelphia, PA. See also Klein, "An Espresso of Sad Parting." I thank Fred Mogul for sharing Dilworth's letter with me.

43. "Coffee Shop Man Convicted," *EB*, 26 Sept. 1959, 3; "Jury Convicts Owner of Raided Coffee Shop," *Inq.*, 26 Sept. 1959, 11; "Close Place or Go to Jail, Coffee Shop Owner Is Told," *EB*, 28 Oct. 1959, 32. See also *EB*, 23 May 1959, 1; *Inq.*, 24 May 1959, B2; *EB*, 27 May 1959, 58; *DN*, 23 May 1959, 3; *Inq.*, 28 Oct. 1959, 43; *DN*, 29 Oct. 1959, 10.

44. *Haifetz v. Rizzo* 178 F. Supp. 828. See also *EB*, 9 Dec. 1959, 52; *Inq.*, 10 Dec. 1959, 41; *DN*, 10 Dec. 1959, 19.

45. *One*, Apr. 1959, 17–18. See also June 1959, 13.

46. Interview with Heifetz.

47. Interview with Hill.

48. Breines, "The 'Other' Fifties," 383.

Chapter Seven

1. Interviews with Adair and Fleischmann. See also Telephone interviews with Dorothy Adair, 8 Dec. 1996 and 23 Apr. 1998.

2. "Barn Raid Corrals 84 in Radnor," *Main Line Times*, 25 Aug. 1960, 1, 21; *Mattachine Society of Philadelphia Newsletter* (*MSPN*), Mar. 1961, 2; "84 Persons Arrested in Raid on Home by Police, Detectives," *Suburban and Wayne Times*, 25 Aug. 1960, 1, 2; Interview with Adair.

3. "84 Persons Arrested," 1.

4. Interview with Adair; *One*, Nov. 1960, 17–18; Interview with Fleischmann; Audiotape, public forum with Ada Bello and Barbara Gittings, 1983, GLBTA; Interview with Gittings; *Mattachine Society of New York Newsletter* (*MSNYN*), Sept. 1960. See also Vito Russo, *The Celluloid Closet*, rev. ed. (New York: Harper and Row, 1987), 97–98, 118–119; *Mattachine Society Interim*, July 1960, 2.

5. Brandon/de Dion correspondence, 5–10 Oct. 1960, MSR (box 6/f2); OCLC 7949580. See also Ira Wallach, *Muscle Beach* (Boston: Little, Brown, 1959); *One*, Feb. 1959, 13; Christopher Lyon, ed., *The International Dictionary of Films and Filmmakers*, vol. 2, *Directors/Filmmakers* (Chicago: St. James, 1984), 520–521; F. Valentine Hooven, III, *Beefcake: The Muscle Magazines of America*, 1950–1970 (Koln, Germany: Benedikt Taschen, 1995), 112–118. I thank Ray Murray for helping me identify *Muscle Beach*.

6. Telephone interview with Albert de Dion, 21 Aug. 1993; Russo, *The Celluloid Closet*, 97–98. See also Interview with Adair.

7. See James Jackson Kilpatrick, *The Smut Peddlers* (Garden City: Doubleday, 1960), 4–9, 255–257, 273; Robert W. Haney, *Comstockery in America: Patterns of Censorship and Control* (Boston: Beacon, 1960), 82–96, 109–131; James C. N. Paul and Murray L. Schwartz, *Federal Censorship: Obscenity in the Mail* (New York: Free Press of Glencoe, 1961), 176–178, 187, 195, 301, 310–311; Terrence J. Murphy, *Censorship: Government and Obscenity* (Baltimore: Helicon, 1963), 96–100; Bernard McCormick, "The Smut Establishment," *PM*, Mar. 1967, 54–57, 97–101; Dorothy Ganfield Fowler, *Unmailable: Congress and the Post Office* (Athens: University of Georgia Press, 1977), 168–179; Edward de Grazia and Roger K. Newman, *Banned Films: Movies, Censors, and the First Amendment* (New York: Bowker, 1982), 13–14, 40–45, 65–67, 197–198; D'Emilio, *Sexual Politics*, 19, 109, 130–133; D'Emilio and Freedman, *Intimate Matters*, 277–285; Edward de Grazia, *Girls Lean Back Everywhere: The Law of Obscenity and the Assault on Genius* (New York: Random House, 1992), 275–279, 302; Frank Walsh, *Sin and Censorship: The Catholic Church and the Motion Picture Industry* (New Haven: Yale University Press, 1996), 9, 24, 43–44, 95–117, 127, 135, 152, 198, 211; Morris, *American Catholic*, 165–167.

8. See U.S. House Comm. on Post Office and Civil Service Hngs., *Detention of Mail for Temporary Periods*, 86th Cong., 1st sess., 1959; U.S. House Comm. on Post Office and Civil Service, Subcomm. on Postal Operations Report and Hngs., *Obscene Matter Sent through the Mail*, 86th Cong., 1st sess., 1959; U.S. House Comm. on Post Office and Civil

Service, Subcomm. on Postal Operations Hngs., *Self-Policing of the Movie and Publishing Industry*, 86th Cong., 2d sess., 1960; U.S. House Comm. on Post Office and Civil Service, Subcomm. on Postal Operations Hngs., *Circulation of Obscene and Pornographic Material*, 86th Cong., 2d sess., 1960; U.S. Senate Comm. on the Judiciary, Subcomm. on Constitutional Amendments and Subcomm. to Investigate Juvenile Delinquency Hngs., *Control of Obscene Matter*, 86th Cong., 1st and 2d sess., 1959–1960.

9. *Obscene Matter Sent through the Mail*, 139–140, 174.

10. *CLR*, Mar. 1957, 2; Mar. 1958, 1. See also *Kingsley International Pictures Corp. v. Blanc*, 396 Pa. 448 (1959); McCormick, "The Smut Establishment," 56, 99; de Grazia and Newman, *Banned Films*, 256–258.

11. *Obscene Matter Sent through the Mail*, 147–151.

12. Ibid., 230. See also *EB*, 24 Feb. 1960, 10; 14 Mar. 1960, 2.

13. *Nation*, 5 Dec. 1959, 411; *One*, Jan. 1960, 18. See also *Nation*, 10 Oct. 1959, 202–203, 207–210; Kilpatrick, *The Smut Peddlers*, 194–195; Haney, *Comstockery*, 26–81; McCormick, "The Smut Establishment," 55–57, 97–101; Fowler, *Unmailable*, 168–169, 175–178; Paul and Schwartz, *Federal Censorship*, 110, 115–116, 187; Murphy, *Censorship*, 162; de Grazia and Newman, *Banned Films*, 100–114; D'Emilio, *Sexual Politics*, 115, 131–133; D'Emilio and Freedman, *Intimate Matters*, 279–280, 287; Hooven, *Beefcake*, 58–74.

14. See *Commonwealth v. Gordon et al.*, 66 District and County Reports 101 (1949); *Inq.*, 23 Sept. 1954, 17; 30 Dec. 1955, 9; *Hallmark Productions, Inc. v. Carroll*, 384 Pa. 348 (1956); *CLR*, June 1957, 1, 4; *Commonwealth v. Blumenstein*, 396 Pa. 417 (1959); *Kingsley International Pictures Corporation v. Blanc*, 396 Pa. 448 (1959); *CLR*, Aug. 1959, 2; Oct. 1959, 1; Kilpatrick, *The Smut Peddlers*, 191–194, 273; Haney, *Comstockery*, 32; *EB*, 23 Jan. 1960, 2; *Goldman Theatres, Inc., et al. v. Dana, et al., Dauphin County Reports* 75 (1960): 300–341; *CLR*, Aug. 1960, 1; *EB*, 7 Aug. 1960, 3; *CLR*, Oct. 1960, 1; Apr. 1961, 2, 4; Dec. 1961, 2; Murphy, *Censorship*, 105–106; de Grazia and Newman, *Banned Films*, 101, 250–252; de Grazia, *Girls Lean Back*, 215, 251, 290, 308, 318.

15. Public forum with Bello and Gittings; Interview with Adair. See also *Inq.*, 11 Aug. 1960, 25; Paolantonio, *Frank Rizzo*, 69; Daughen and Binzen, *The Cop*, 83–89; Hamilton, *Rizzo*, 50–55, 62.

16. "Barn Raid Corrals 84"; Interview with Adair.

17. Interview with Adair.

18. Donner, *Protectors of Privilege*, 197. See also "Barn Raid Corrals 84"; "84 Persons Arrested"; *One*, Nov. 1960, 17; Paolantonio, *Frank Rizzo*, 71.

19. *MSPN*, Mar. 1961, 3; Albert J. de Dion to Friend, appended to *MSPN*, Mar. 1961; *MSPN*, Mar. 1961, 2. See also Margaret Hope Bacon, *One Woman's Passion for Peace and Freedom: The Life of Mildred Scott Olmsted* (Syracuse: Syracuse University Press, 1993), 60–61, 251.

20. See Benedict Anderson, *Imagined Communities: Reflections on the Origin and Spread of Nationalism* (New York: Verso, 1983); George L. Mosse, *Nationalism and Sexuality: Respectability and Abnormal Sexuality in Modern Europe* (New York: Howard Fertig, 1985), 1–22, 181–191; Evelyn Brooks Higginbotham, *Righteous Discontent: The Women's Movement in the Black Baptist Church, 1880–1920* (Cambridge: Harvard University Press, 1993), 185–229.

21. Gittings to Dewees, 15 June 1960; Dewees to Gittings, 3 July 1960, MSR (box 7/f8); Interview with Hardman.

22. Interview with Fleischmann.

23. Bacon, *Mothers of Feminism*, 222.

24. D'Emilio, *Sexual Politics*, 4–5.

25. Ibid., 75. See also Katz, *Gay American History*, 406–420; Toby Marotta, *The Politics of Homosexuality* (Boston: Houghton Mifflin, 1982), 3–21; D'Emilio, *Sexual Politics*, 57–91; Stuart Timmons, *The Trouble with Harry Hay: Founder of the Modern Gay Movement* (Boston: Alyson, 1990), 129–190; Eric Marcus, *Making History: The Struggle for Gay and Lesbian Equal Rights, 1945–1990* (New York: HarperCollins, 1992), 2, 26–69, 76–77; Harry Hay, *Radically Gay: Gay Liberation in the Words of Its Founder*, ed. Will Roscoe (Boston: Beacon, 1996), 3–8, 37–79, 130–132, 139, 331–349.

26. D'Emilio, *Sexual Politics*, 103–104. See also Del Martin and Phyllis Lyon, *Lesbian/Woman* (San Francisco: Glide, 1972), 219–233; Faderman, *Odd Girls*, 148–150, 190–191.

27. Del Martin, "President's Message," *Ladder*, Oct. 1956, 6–7; Del Martin, letter to the editor, *MR*, Aug. 1957, 34.

28. Del Martin, cited in *Ladder*, Oct. 1959, 19.

29. *San Francisco Council Mattachine Newsletter*, Sept. 1957, 10–11, reprinted in *MR*, Sept. 1957; *Ladder*, Aug. 1957, 7; Mar. 1959, 15.

30. D'Emilio, *Sexual Politics*, 124–125. See also 115.

31. *One*, Dec. 1954, 28; *MR*, Sept. 1957, 9. See also Rodger Streitmatter, *Unspeakable: The Rise of the Gay and Lesbian Press in America* (Boston: Faber and Faber, 1995), ix–xiii, 17–50.

32. Redcay to *Ladder*, 9 Aug. 1957, Daughters of Bilitis Papers (DOBP), June L. Mazer Lesbian Collection, West Hollywood, CA; *Ladder*, Aug. 1957, 30. See also Interview with Adams; M. Elliott to Ell Club, 18 Aug. 1957, DOBP.

33. Interview with Adams.

34. ECHO Minutes (ECHOM), 18–19 May 1963, 8 Feb. 1964, ECHO Papers (ECHOP), GLBTA.

35. Kennedy and Davis, *Boots of Leather*, 138.

36. Anita [Shotwell], cited in Love, "The Invisible Sorority," 84–85; Interviews with McCann and Fleischmann. See also *Ladder*, Apr. 1968, 13.

37. "The Gateway," *One*, Dec. 1954, 4–10; "The Ironing," *One*, Sept. 1955, 24–25; "Hauviette," *One*, Oct. 1958, 13–15; "The Room Upstairs," *One*, Mar. 1959, 10–11; "Love Is Not LOVE," *Ladder*, Apr. 1959, 8–13, 21–23; "Marquita," *One*, Oct. 1960, 6–9; "Marquita," *JSN*, Feb. 1962, 2–5; "Marquita," *JSN*, Mar. 1962, 3–7.

38. "The Triangle," *One*, July 1954, 21–24; "The Snare," *One*, Nov. 1954, 14–17; "Gay Wedding," *Ladder*, Feb. 1963, 4–5.

39. Jody Shotwell, "Letter to Meredith," *Ladder*, Aug. 1960, 17–18. See also *One*, Jan. 1956, 19; Oct.-Nov. 1957, 12; *Ladder*, May 1960, 5–6; Aug. 1960, 15–16; Oct. 1960, 6–11; Apr. 1963, 20; Oct. 1963, 21; *One*, May 1964, 14–18.

40. Interview with Gittings. See also *Ladder*, Nov. 1958, 8; ECHOM, 22 June–24 Aug. 1963.

41. Interview with Fleischmann. See also Fonzi, "The Furtive Fraternity," 54–55.

42. See Interviews with Fleischmann and Gittings; Letter from Gittings, n.d., DOBP; *Ladder*, Apr. 1959, 14–16; Mar. 1960, 14; Apr. 1961, 14; *JSN*, Feb. 1962, 5; Apr. 1962, 2–3; *Ladder*, Feb. 1963, 6; Nov. 1963, 19–21.

43. Interviews with de Dion and Fleischmann. See also *MSPN*, Mar. 1961, 3.

44. Gittings in Marcus, *Making History*, 104–105. See also Kay Tobin [Lahusen] and Randy Wicker, *The Gay Crusaders* (New York: Paperback Library, 1972), 205–224; Katz,

Gay American History, 420–433; Joseph R. DeMarco, "Barbara without Politics," *New Gay Life*, Apr. 1977, 15–18; Tommy Avicolli, "Barbara Gittings," *Advocate*, 9 July 1981, 24–27; Troy Perry and Thomas L. P. Swicegood, *Profiles in Gay and Lesbian Courage* (New York: St. Martin's, 1991), 153–178; Marcus, *Making History*, 106–126; Interview with Gittings; Public forum with Bello and Gittings; Videotape, Tommi Avicolli Mecca interview with Barbara Gittings, GLBTA.

45. Gittings, cited in Katz, *Gay American History*, 421.

46. Ibid.; Gittings, cited in Tobin and Wicker, *The Gay Crusaders*, 207–208.

47. Interview with Gittings; Gittings, cited in Marcus, *Making History*, 106; Gittings, cited in Tobin and Wicker, *The Gay Crusaders*, 209–210.

48. Mecca interview with Gittings.

49. See Tobin and Wicker, *The Gay Crusaders*, 211.

50. Mecca interview with Gittings; Interview with Gittings. See also Donald Webster Cory, *The Homosexual in America* (New York: Greenberg, 1951); *One*, Dec. 1955, 28–29.

51. *MSNYN*, Sept. 1957, 3.

52. Gittings, cited in Tobin and Wicker, *The Gay Crusaders*, 211. See also *Ladder*, Oct. 1956, 10; May 1957, 24–25; Nov. 1957, 20–21; Minutes, DOB—San Francisco, 8 Oct. 1958, DOBP; "D.O.B. News," c. 1958, MSR (box 7/f8); *Ladder*, Nov. 1958, 8; Interview with Gittings.

53. Gittings, cited in Katz, *Gay American History*, 430; Interview with Gittings.

54. Gittings, cited in Katz, *Gay American History*, 428–429; Gittings to Coxe, 17 May 1960, ACLU-GPBP. See also Tobin and Wicker, *The Gay Crusaders*, 212.

55. Forum with Bello and Gittings. See also *Ladder*, Apr. 1960, 21–22.

56. Barbara Gittings, letter to the editor, *Inq.*, 16 June 1960, 10. See also *EB*, 28 Jan. 1960, 14; Gittings/Coxe correspondence, 17 May–18 July 1960, ACLU-GPBP; Gittings to DOB, 16 June 1960, DOBP; Gittings to San Francisco Friends, 8 Feb. 1961, DOBP; Dewees to Gittings, 3 July 1960; de Dion to Gittings, 25 July 1960, MSR (box 7/f8); Interview with Gittings.

57. Jan Fraser [Fleischmann], "The Other Side of the Fable," *Ladder*, Aug. 1960, 15–16; Interview with Fleischmann.

58. Gittings to de Dion and Dewees, 19 Aug. 1959; de Dion to Martin, 17 Nov. 1959, MSR (box 7/f8). See also Gittings, "Background Note," n.d.; Kay Lahusen (and Gittings) to Cleo Glenn, 2 June 1964, DOBP.

59. Interview with Fleischmann.

Chapter Eight

1. Ken Travis, "Confidential Reporter Attends First Homosexual Convention in U.S. History," *Confidential*, Jan. 1964, 26–27, 48–51.

2. *Ladder*, Jan. 1964, 7; C. Philips [Clark Polak], letter to the editor, *Confidential*, Apr. 1964, reprinted in *JSN*, Mar. 1964, 7; Interview with Fleischmann.

3. *MSPN*, Mar. 1961, 3; Interviews with Hardman, Fleischmann, and Lahusen; Audiotape, Tommi Avicolli Mecca interview with Marge McCann, GLBTA.

4. Interview with Hardman. See also Bérubé, *Coming Out under Fire*; Leisa D. Meyer, *Creating GI Jane: Sexuality and Power in the Women's Army Corps during World War II* (New York: Columbia University Press, 1996), 148–178.

5. Interview with Hardman. See also *JSN*, Jan. 1963, 1; Interview with Kendall.

6. Interview with Kendall.

7. Ibid.; Mecca interview with Fleischner.

8. Interview with Adair.

9. See *MSPN*, Mar. 1961 to Nov. 1961; Interviews with Kendall and Fleischmann.

10. Interviews with Hardman, Fleischmann, and Kendall.

11. Interview with McCann.

12. Interviews with Adair and Kendall; Mecca interview with Fleischner.

13. Interviews with Fleischmann and McCann.

14. Interview with McCann.

15. See *MSPN*, Mar. 1961 to Nov. 1961.

16. *MSPN*, July 1961, 4; Interview with Adair; *MSPN*, Mar. 1961, 1–2. See also Gordon Westwood [Michael George Schofield], *Society and the Homosexual* (New York: Dutton, 1953), 39–55; *MSPN*, July 1961 to Sept. 1961.

17. *MSPN*, Aug. 1961, 1; *MR*, Dec. 1961, 26. MSP's status as a chapter never was formalized. See also *One*, May 1961, 14–15; June 1961, 5–11, 19; *Ladder*, June 1961, 13; *MSPN*, July 1961, 1; *MR*, Aug. 1961, 26–27; *Ladder*, Sept. 1961, 7; *MR*, Apr. 1962, 2, 27–29; Oct. 1962, 11–20; D'Emilio, *Sexual Politics*, 123.

18. *Ladder*, Oct. 1961, 9.

19. Interview with Fleischmann; Gittings correspondence, 5 Feb. 1963, DOBP.

20. Interview with Fleischmann. See also *MSPN*, Oct. 1961, 2.

21. *JSN*, Jan. 1962, 1–2.

22. Mecca interview with Fleischner. See also *JSN*, Jan. 1962 to Oct. 1963; *MSNYN*, Feb. 1963, 6; *Ladder*, Mar. 1963, 5–7.

23. *MSPN*, Oct. 1961, 4; July 1961, 4; *JSN*, Jan. 1962, 1; May 1962, 1.

24. Coxe to Catherine Roraback, 2 Feb. 1961; Coxe to Granahan, 29 Jan. 1962; *Catholic Standard and Times*, 1 Dec. 1961, ACLU-GPBP. See also *CLR*, Dec. 1960, 1, 3–5; Minutes and Reports, ACLU-Greater Philadelphia Branch (ACLU-GPB), 9 Mar.–26 Sept. 1961, ACLU Archives (ACLUA), Seeley G. Mudd Manuscript Library, Princeton University, Princeton, NJ (vol. 49/fA4); Coxe correspondence, 1961–1963, ACLU-GPBP.

25. *JSN*, Feb. 1962, 7; *JSN*, Feb. 1962, 8–9; Bertram Karon, letter to the editor, *JSN*, Apr. 1962, 3–4.

26. Robert A. Harper, "Can Homosexuals Be Changed?" *Sexology*, Apr. 1960, 548–553, reprinted in *JSN*, Sept. 1962, 1–2; *JSN*, Oct. 1962, 3; Nov. 1962, 2–3.

27. L. James Benjamin, "Discussing Dr. Harper," *JSN*, Dec. 1962, 2–5; L. James Benjamin, "From the Darkness," *JSN*, Jan. 1963, 1–3.

28. *JSN*, Oct. 1962, 1–2; Nov. 1962, 1, 3.

29. *JSN*, Feb. 1963, 2–3.

30. Emory, "Threshold," *MSPN*, Oct. 1961, 5–8; Jody Shotwell, "Marquita," *JSN*, Feb. 1962, 2–5; and Mar. 1962, 3–7; Jan Fraser [Joan Fleischmann], "Letter to a Girl Who Said I Love You," *JSN*, Apr. 1962, 2–3.

31. Fonzi, "The Furtive Fraternity," 20–23, 48–65; Fonzi, "Lurid Locust Street," 20, 42. See also *GPM*, Oct. 1961, 1; Nov. 1961, 1, 6; Fonzi to Coxe, c. Dec. 1962, ACLU-GPBP. For other gay-related stories, see *Temple University News* (*TUN*), 2–9 May 1962; *EB*, *Inq.*, and *DN*, 11–23 Sept. 1962; *Trib.*, 29 Sept. 1962.

32. Fonzi, "The Furtive Fraternity," 20–21, 52–53, 62–63.

33. Ibid., 22–23, 49–51. See also *EB*, *Inq.*, and *DN*, 14 Jan., 9–13 Feb., 28 Oct. 1961; 23 Jan. 1962; *One*, Dec. 1961, 5–6; June 1963, 29–30.

34. Fonzi, "The Furtive Fraternity," 63–65.

35. Ibid., 53.

36. Ibid., 54–56, 62.

37. Ibid., 54, 56, 61. On comparative rates of female and male same-sex sexualities, see English and Pearson, *Common Neuroses,* 41; Wainwright Churchill, *Homosexual Behavior among Males: A Cross-Cultural and Cross-Species Investigation* (New York: Hawthorn, 1967), 57–58.

38. Fonzi, "The Furtive Fraternity," 54–56.

39. Ibid., 55.

40. Ibid., 56.

41. *JSN,* Jan. 1963, 3–4; *Mattachine Interim,* Jan. 1963, 2; *MSNYN,* Mar. 1963, 5; *MR,* Apr.-Sept. 1964, 21; ECHO 1964 Conference, Interim Treasurer's Report, 6 Nov. 1964, ECHOP.

42. Jody Shotwell, "Magazine Review: 'The Furtive Fraternity,' " *Ladder,* Mar. 1963, 17.

43. Mecca interview with McCann; Interviews with Chis and Brinsfield.

44. Shotwell, "Magazine Review," 17–18.

45. Ibid., 16–18; Mecca interview with Fleischner; Interview with Kendall.

46. "GPM Exposes Illegal Liquor Joints Ignored by State," *PI,* 20 Feb. 1963, 1; Paolantonio, *Frank Rizzo,* 47, 69, 84. See also Reichley, *The Art of Government,* 57, 78–79, 89–92; *PI,* 20 Feb. 1963, 4; Sayre, *Sixties Going on Seventies,* 123–124; Walter, "Rizzo," 79.

47. "Alessandroni Puts Palumbo on Court Payroll," *PI,* 13 Mar. 1963, 1; Eugene Armao, "Palumbo Linked to Cove Inc., Center-City Dives," *PI,* 6 Mar. 1963, 1. See also *PI,* 27 Feb.–15 May 1963. One of *PI*'s articles led James Buchanan of the *Observer* and the S.A. Club to charge Orsatti and Armao with libel. Although they were found guilty, the Supreme Court of Pennsylvania overturned the ruling. See *EB,* 28 June 1968, 16; Fonzi, "Locust Street Revisited," 129; *Commonwealth v. Armao et al.*, Supreme Court of Pennsylvania, 446 Pa. 325, 286 A.2d 626 (1972).

48. "Morals Offender Meets Under-Age Boy in Bar," *PI,* 20 Mar. 1963, 1; "The Cancer among Us," *PI,* 20 Mar. 1963, 4. See also *EB, Inq.*, and *DN,* 4 and 14 Mar. 1963.

49. Fred Bonaparte, "Homosexuality, Suicides Raising, City Official Tells Morticians," *Trib.*, 25 May 1963, 3.

50. Shotwell, "Magazine Review," 17.

51. See *MSPN,* July 1961, 1; *Ladder,* Sept. 1961, 7; ECHOM, 26 Jan.–1 Sept. 1963; Interview with Kendall; Mecca interview with Fleischner.

52. See DOB General Assembly Minutes, 24 June 1962, DOBP; *Ladder,* Jan. 1963, 24; Mar. 1963, 4; Interviews with Gittings and Lahusen.

53. Glass to Gittings and Lahusen, c. 4 Feb. 1963; Lahusen to Glass, 5 Feb. 1963; Gittings to Glass, 5 Feb. 1963, DOBP; Interview with Fleischmann.

54. Gittings to Jaye Bell, Marge Heinz, Ev Howe, and Del Martin, c. Apr. 1963, DOBP. See also Gittings/Lahusen correspondence, 22–28 Sept. 1963, DOBP.

55. Travis, "Confidential," 48; *CLR,* June 1963, 3. See also ECHOM, 18 May 1963–18 Jan. 1964; *Ladder,* July 1963, 19; *MSNYN,* Oct. 1963, 3–5; Jody Shotwell, "ECHO Convention '63," *Ladder,* Dec. 1963, 8–10; Travis, "Confidential," 27; *CLR,* Apr. 1964, 3.

56. ECHO Conference Program, 31 Aug.–1 Sept. 1963, ECHOP; *JSN,* Sept. 1963, 1–3; *Ladder,* Dec. 1963, 8–10; Travis, "Confidential," 27, 51. See also Churchill, *Homosexual Behavior among Males*; Wainwright Churchill, "Homosexuality from Greek Times to

Modern Times," *Sexology*, Oct. 1969, 18–21; Wainwright Churchill, "How Sex 'Perversions' Started," *Sexology*, Dec. 1969, 51–54.

57. Travis, "Confidential," 27; ECHOM, 23 Feb. 1963; Travis, "Confidential," 49. See also Alan Reitman to Coxe, 28 Aug. 1963, ACLU-GPBP; *MSNYN*, Oct. 1963, 3–5.

58. Shotwell, "ECHO Convention '63"; Ellis to Gittings, 24 Dec. 1963, DOBP.

59. Travis, "Confidential," 51; Shotwell, "ECHO Convention '63." See also *MSNYN*, Oct. 1963, 3–5.

60. Travis, "Confidential," 49–50.

61. Ibid., 50. See also *JSN*, Sept. 1963, 2.

62. Travis, "Confidential," 27, 51.

Chapter Nine

1. Interviews with Kendall and Fleischmann; *JSN*, Oct. 1963, 1–5. See also Interview with McCann; Lahusen correpondence, 17 Nov. 1963, 2 June 1964; DOB Minutes, 21 June 1964, DOBP; Notes, John D'Emilio interview with Polak, 5 Oct. 1976, in D'Emilio's possession, Chicago, IL.

2. Interviews with Oshtry and Coopersmith; Jim Kepner, "A Farewell to Friends Departed," *National Gay Archives Bulletin*, Fall 1983, 16. See also Philadelphia Police Dept., "Extract of Criminal Record" for Polak, 20 Oct. 1969, Norman Oshtry Papers (NOP), Philadelphia, PA; D'Emilio interview with Polak.

3. D'Emilio interview with Polak; *Drum*, Dec. 1964, 32.

4. Interviews with Coopersmith and Lahusen. See also Polak to Schlegel, 24 Jan. 1964, Janus file, IGLA; *EB*, 19 July 1970, sec. 2, p. 1, 6; Philadelphia Police Dept., "Extract of Criminal Record" for Polak; Interviews with Oshtry, Schlegel, and Gayer; William Damon Papers, GLBTA.

5. D'Emilio interview with Polak; *JSN*, Oct. 1963, 1; ECHOM, 1 Sept. 1963.

6. *JSN*, Oct. 1963, 1–3.

7. *JSN*, Jan. 1964, 1; Interview with Fleischmann; D'Emilio interview with Polak.

8. Polak to Schlegel, 26 Dec. 1963, Janus file, IGLA.

9. Schlegel to author, 1 May 1993. See also *Janus*, Apr. 1964, 16, 20; May 1964, 8; June 1964, 12, 14; McCann to Martin, 19 Aug. 1964, DOBP; Polak to Janus Board, 28 Oct. 1964, Janus file, IGLA; *Drum*, Oct. 1964, 23–24; *JSN*, Nov. 1964, 1; Horowitz to Leitsch, 9 Nov. 1964, MSR (box 7/f18). *JSN* became *Janus* in stages; I see the definitive shift in Feb. 1964. When *Janus* became *Drum* in Oct. 1964, *For Members Only* was created to serve as Janus's newsletter; I cite *For Members Only* as *JSN*.

10. *Janus*, Apr. 1964, 2; *JSN*, Nov. 1964, 1; *JSN*, Nov. 1964, 3; *Janus*, Apr. 1964, 16.

11. John Wilder, "Homosexuals See Hope for Selves by Negro Victory in Rights Drive," *Trib.*, 25 Feb. 1964, 3.

12. Charles Philips [Polak], letter to the editor, *Trib.*, 3 Mar. 1964, 5.

13. See D'Emilio, *Sexual Politics*, 149–175.

14. D'Emilio, *Sexual Politics*, 110. See also Streitmatter, *Unspeakable*, 17–115.

15. 1964 ECHO Conference Program, 14, ECHOP.

16. Interviews with Fleischmann and Gayer. See also *Gay*, 15 Mar. 1970, 2.

17. Interview with Coopersmith.

18. Report of Philadelphia Postal Inspector (RPPI), 30 June 1965, NOP.

19. Interview with Fleischmann; *Drum*, Oct. 1964, 2.

20. A. Jay, "Harry Chess," *Drum*, Mar. 1965, 7–10; P. Arody, "Heterosexuality in America," *Drum*, Oct. 1964, 18–22; "Franky Hill: Memoirs of a Boy of Pleasure," *Drum*, Dec. 1964, 6–7, 26; P. Arody, "Tropic of Crabs," *Drum*, Apr. 1965, 11–12, 31–32. See also A. Jay and Clark Polak, *The Uncensored Adventures of Harry Chess* (Philadelphia: Trojan Book Service, 1966); "Homosexuality in America," *Life*, 26 June 1964, 66–80; John Cleland, *Memoirs of a Woman of Pleasure* (c. 1750; New York: Putnam, 1963); Henry Miller, *Tropic of Cancer* (New York: Grove, 1961).

21. Polak to Friend, c. Nov. 1964, Janus file, IGLA; 1964 ECHO Conference Program, 14, ECHOP; *JSN*, Feb. 1965, 2. See also *MSNYN*, Oct. 1964, 21; Nov. 1964, 18; D'Emilio, *Sexual Politics*, 133, 136; Michael Bronski, *Culture Clash: The Making of Gay Sensibility* (Boston: South End, 1984), 160–174; Allen Ellenzweig, *The Homoerotic Photograph: Male Images from Durieu/Delacroix to Mapplethorpe* (New York: Columbia University Press, 1992), 123; Jackie Hatton, "The Pornography Empire of H. Lynn Womack," *Viewing Culture* 7 (Spring 1993): 9–32; Tracy D. Morgan, "Pages of Whiteness: Race, Physique Magazines, and the Emergence of Public Gay Culture," in *Queer Studies: A Lesbian, Gay, Bisexual, and Transgender Anthology*, ed. Brett Beemyn and Mickey Eliason (New York: New York University Press, 1996): 180–297; Hooven, *Beefcake*.

22. D'Emilio and Freedman, *Intimate Matters*, 302. See also *Playboy*, Oct. 1964, 63; *Drum*, Nov. 1964, 34; May 1965, 23; *Playboy*, Nov. 1965, 12; *Drum*, Nov. 1965, 18; *JSN*, no. 24, 1967, 2.

23. *Drum*, Sept. 1966, 4; *JSN*, Dec. 1966, 1; Clark Polak, "The Responsibility," *Drum*, Aug. 1965, 3.

24. Anderson, *Imagined Communities*, 133.

25. P. Arody, "Heterosexuality in America," 18; *Drum*, Mar. 1965, 4.

26. Charles Alverson, "A Minority's Plea," *Wall Street Journal*, 17 July 1968, 1, 23, reprinted in *Ladder*, Oct.-Nov. 1968, 38–40. See also Polak to Janus Board, 28 Oct. 1964, Janus file, IGLA; *JSN*, Nov. 1964, 1; Press release, n.d., Polak to Leitsch, 11 Dec. 1964, MSR (box 7/f18); McCann to Martin, 29 Jan. 1965, DOBP; *Sexology*, Jan. 1967, 378. In 1965, Polak reported that "thousands of copies of *Drum* were 'mysteriously' appearing on book stands and in shops" and accused Guild Press of printing extras. *JSN*, June 1965, 3. A rival noted in 1966 that "*Drum* has a circulation of 10,000." Letter to Robert Walker, 6 Jan. 1966 [misdated 1965], MSR (box 2/f6). In 1966, Polak reported on "the largest expansion move ever undertaken by a homophile organization"; 100,000 brochures had been mailed; another 100,000 were planned. *Drum*, Jan. 1966, 4; *JSN*, 4 Oct. 1965, 4. According to *JSN*, this tripled Janus's membership. *JSN*, Nov. 1965, 2. In July 1966, *JSN* reported that *Drum* circulation had doubled in six months (p. 1). Three sources indicate that *Drum* circulation was 15–17,000 between 1966 and 1969. See *Drum* ad rate sheet, 9 Nov. 1966; *PACE!* prospectus, c. 1970, Richard Schlegel Papers (RSP) (box 4/f41, 48), HSC; *Camden Courier-Post*, 17 Jan. 1967, 15.

27. *Drum*, Dec. 1964, 35; July 1965, 33; no. 22, 1966, 34. See also Interview with Coopersmith.

28. *Drum*, Sept. 1965, 33; July 1965, 34. See also *The Compact Edition of the Oxford English Dictionary*, vol. 2 (Oxford: Oxford University Press, 1971), 2295.

29. Richard Inman to Julian Hodges, 25 Mar. 1965, MSR (box 1/f9); Leitsch to Elver Barker, 27 May 1966, MSR (box 1/f12). See also Edward Sagarin, "Structure and Ideology in an Association of Deviants" (Ph.D. diss., New York University, 1966), 232–233, 353, 426.

30. Leitsch to Horowitz, 7 Apr. 1965, MSR (box 7/f18).

31. *Eastern Mattachine Magazine* (*EMM*), Nov.-Dec. 1965, 19.

32. See *Advocate*, 8 July 1982, 16–24; SAC Philadelphia to FBI Director, 4 Feb. 1963, FBI Mattachine Society (MS) file (HQ100–403320); *Ladder*, Apr. 1963, 15; SAC Philadelphia to FBI Director, 27 Sept. 1963, FBI MS file (100–33796); Gittings to Glenn, 23 Mar. 1964; Lahusen to Glenn, c. Apr. 1964, DOBP. I rely on three sources for FBI and post office documents: public materials at the FBI in Washington, DC; the results of a Freedom of Information Act (FOIA) request that Polak filed (in Oshtry's possession); and the results of a FOIA request that I filed.

33. *A Book Named "John Cleland's Memoirs of a Woman of Pleasure" v. Massachusetts*, 383 U.S. 413 (1966); U.S. Commission on Obscenity and Pornography, *Technical Report*, vol. 3 (Washington, DC: GPO, 1971), 158. See also *Manual Enterprises v. Day*, 370 U.S. 478 (1962); *Grove Press v. Gerstein*, 378 U.S. 577 (1964); *Ralph Ginzburg v. United States* 383 U.S. 463 (1966); *EB*, *Inq.*, and *DN*, 8 Feb. 1961, 23–24 Jan. 1962, 15 Mar. 1963, 23 Sept. 1965, 3 Mar. 1966; *CLR*, Dec. 1961 to Oct. 1962, Oct. 1965; *Ladder*, Apr. 1963, 15; *Publishers Weekly*, 1 Feb. 1965, 63; 19 Apr. 1965, 69; Murphy, *Censorship*, 30, 66, 212–215, 229–230; McCormick, "The Smut Establishment," 54–57, 97–101; Fowler, *Unmailable*, 180–182; D'Emilio, *Sexual Politics*, 132–133; D'Emilio and Freedman, *Intimate Matters*, 287; Hatton, "The Pornography Empire," 19–20; de Grazia, *Girls Lean Back*, 366–443, 496–524; Hooven, *Beefcake*, 106–124.

34. See RSP; Richard Schlegel file, IGLA; *One*, Oct. 1962, 21–22; *MR*, Nov. 1962, 13–26; *Ladder*, Nov. 1962, 4–7; Polak to Schlegel, 24 Jan. 1964 and 31 Mar. 1965, Janus file, IGLA; *Janus*, Feb. 1964, 6; Apr. 1964, 2; May 1964, 4, 14; RPPI beginning 6 Jan. 1965, NOP; ACLU correspondence, 1965–1966, ACLUA (1965 vol. 29/fQ8000 and vol. 1/fA1000–1001, 1966 vol. 1/fA1001); Wulf/Coxe correspondence, 23–30 Apr. 1965; Polak to F. R. Ruskin, 27 July 1965, NOP; *JSN*, Aug. 1965, 1; Coxe to Alan Reitman, 21 Jan. 1966, ACLU-GPBP; *Richard L. Schlegel v. The United States*, U.S. Ct. of Claims, no. 369–63, 1969; *Gay*, 15 Dec. 1969, 3; 15 Mar. 1970, 2; Interview with Schlegel.

35. See RPPI, 30 June 1965, NOP.

36. See Coxe to Polak, 28 Jan. 1965, NOP; Hymen Schwartz to Janus, 19 Apr. 1965, ACLUA (vol. 1/fA1000); *Drum*, Nov. 1965, 7; Correspondence and documents, 18 Nov. 1965–28 Oct. 1966, ACLUA (vol. 3/fA1003); *Drum*, Apr. 1966, 4; nos. 18–19, 1966, 30–31.

37. See Janus press release, c. Feb. 1965, MSR (box 7/f18); *JSN*, Feb. 1965, 1–2; Polak to Schlegel, c. Apr. 1965, Janus file, IGLA; *Drum*, May 1965, 2.

38. See Saul Mindel to Chief Postal Inspector, 18 Feb. 1966; H. Montague to Fred Vinson, Jr., 11 Mar. 1966; RPPI, 15 Mar. 1966; Montague to Vinson, 30 Mar. 1966, NOP; Correspondence, 17 Mar.–10 May 1966, ACLUA (vol. 1/fA1001, vol. 3/fA1003); *JSN*, Mar. 1966, 1.

39. See "How to Handle a Federal Agent," *Drum*, Dec. 1964, 15–16; P. Arody, "I Was a Homosexual for the FBI," *Drum*, Mar. 1965, 14–15; Clark Polak, "Frontal Nudes," *Drum*, July 1965, 2, 22; Clark Polak, "The Story behind Physique Photography," *Drum*, Oct. 1965, 8–15; Brennan to Dunn, 22 Jan. 1965; Jones to DeLoach, 10 Feb. 1965, FBI MS file, HQ100–403320; *Drum*, Dec. 1965, 27.

40. See *Drum*, June 1965, 33; Polak to Ruskin, 27 July 1965, NOP; *JSN*, July 1965, 3; Aug. 1965, 1; Camden Postal Inspector to Montague, 5 Aug. 1965; Polak to Bernard Fensterwald, 5 Aug. 1965, NOP; *New Republic*, 21 Aug. 1965, 6–7; Polak correspondence, 1 Sept. 1965; Philadelphia Postal Inspector to San Francisco Inspector in

Charge, 7 Sept. 1965, NOP; *Drum*, Oct. 1965, 5; *U.S. News & World Report*, 6 Dec. 1965, 68–70; *Nation*, 20 Dec. 1965, 496–501; Letters to the editor, *Playboy*, Dec. 1965–Aug. 1966; *Newsweek*, 13 June 1966, 24; McCormick, "The Smut Establishment," 100; *Drum*, Dec. 1968, 38; *Playboy*, Apr. 1969, 68.

41. Vinson to Montague, 4 Apr. 1966; RPPI, 30 June 1965, NOP.

42. Kenneth Zwerin to Gittings, 18 Oct. 1963, DOBP; *Ladder*, Mar. 1964, cover; Interview with Gittings. See also Gittings correspondence, 25 Sept. 1963–25 Feb. 1965, DOBP.

43. Gittings to Ger van Braam, 14 Aug. 1964, DOBP; Interview with Gittings; Lahusen correspondence, 14 Aug. 1964, DOBP; Polak to Friend, c. Nov. 1964, Janus file, IGLA; *JSN*, Dec. 1966, 1. See also *Ladder*, June 1964 to Jan. 1965; Interview with Lahusen.

44. *Drum*, Jan. 1966, 39; *Ladder*, June 1966, cover.

45. McCann to Martin, 19 Aug. 1964, DOBP. See also DOB General Assembly Minutes, 21 June 1964, DOBP.

46. McCann to Martin, 19 Aug. 1964; Martin to McCann, 27 Jan. 1965, DOBP.

47. Kameny to McCann, 30 Jan. 1965, MSR (box 7/f24).

48. McCann to Martin, 29 Jan. 1965, DOBP.

49. ECHOM, 6 Feb. 1965; Frazer [Fleischmann] (for ECHO) to Polak, c. Feb. 1965, ECHOP. This letter was modified and sent. The second and fourth points were deleted and the final paragraph reworded. See also ECHOM, 5 June 1965; Sagarin, "Structure and Ideology," 292–293.

50. McCann to Martin, 29 Jan. 1965, DOBP. See also *MSNYN*, Feb. 1965, 2; ECHOM, 1964–1965; Hodges to Inman, 26 Feb. 1965, MSR (box 7/f1); *EMM*, Mar. 1965, 23; Mattachine Society of Philadelphia (MSP) Minutes, 7 Mar. 1965; MSP Statement of Purpose, c. 1965, MSP Papers, GLBTA; MSP Constitution, MSR (box 3/f17); *Ladder*, July-Aug. 1965, 24; Sept. 1965, 22; *EMM*, Sept.–Oct. 1965, 4; 1965 ECHO Conference Program, 24–26 Sept., MSR (box 1/f11); *EMM*, Jan. 1966, 2; *Ladder*, Jan. 1966, 8; Feb. 1966, 4, 8–9; Mar. 1966, 4; Interview with McCann; Mecca interview with McCann.

51. *Drum*, Aug. 1965, 5–6; *JSN*, May 1965, 1–2; Horowitz to Leitsch, 27 Apr. 1965, MSR (box 7/f18). See also D'Emilio, *Sexual Politics*, 164–165; *EMM*, Mar. 1965, 5–7; Janus flier, "To the Customers of Dewey's Restaurant," c. 27 Apr. 1965, NOP; *Drum*, Nov. 1965, 36.

52. *Drum,* Aug. 1965, 5–6; *JSN,* May 1965, 1–2. See also Interviews with Brinsfield and Davidson.

53. *JSN*, May 1965, 2.

54. ECHOM, 5 June 1965; Statement of DOB Policy, 7 June 1965, DOBP. See also McCann to DOB Governing Board, 13 June 1965, DOBP; DOB-NY Minutes, 6 June 1965, DOB-NY file, GLBTA; *Ladder*, July-Aug. 1965, 25; D'Emilio, *Sexual Politics*, 171–173; Johnson, " 'Homosexual Citizens.' "

55. Martin to Glenn, 7 June 1965; Kameny to DOB President and Governing Board, 8 June 1965, DOBP; Fraser to Glenn, Martin, Lyon, and McCann, 6 June 1965, ECHOP.

56. *EMM*, Aug. 1965, 5; Kay Tobin [Lahusen], "Picketing: The Impact and the Issues," *Ladder*, Sept. 1965, 8. See also *Trib.*, 6 July 1965, 4; *Inq.*, 5 July 1965, 1.

57. Tobin [Lahusen], "Picketing," 4; Frank Kameny, "Homosexuals Picket," *EMM*, Sept.–Oct. 1965, 20. See also correspondence and documents, June 1965, MSR (box 3/f21); *Ladder*, Oct. 1965, cover; Marcus, *Making History*, 134; D'Emilio, *Sexual Poli-*

tics, 165; Interviews with Gittings and Kuromiya; Mecca interviews with Gittings and Kuromiya; Public forum with Gittings and Bello.

58. DOB-NY Minutes, 11 July 1965, DOB-NY Papers, GLBTA; DOB-NY members to Glenn, 15 July 1965, DOBP. See also D'Emilio, *Sexual Politics*, 171–173.

59. DOB-NY member to Glenn, 9 August 1965; DOB-NY member to Glenn, Lyon, and Martin, 6 Nov. 1965, DOBP. See also D'Emilio, *Sexual Politics*, 172–173.

60. See *Ladder*, Oct. 1966, 3, 15, 24. See also correspondence, 25 Aug. 1964–16 June 1965, DOBP; D'Emilio, *Sexual Politics*, 168–171.

61. See ECHOM, 11 Mar. 1966; *JSN*, Mar. 1966, 2; Interview with Fleischmann.

62. See *JSN*, 4 Oct. 1965, 4; *Drum*, Dec. 1965, 35–36; no. 20, 1966, cover; no. 22, 1966, 36; H. Lynn Womack Papers (#7441/box 1), HSC.

63. See *Janus*, Mar. to June 1964; Press release, c. Mar. 1964, NOP; *JSN*, Apr. 1965 to Mar. 1966; Janus flier, 1 Apr. 1965, Janus file, IGLA; *Ladder*, May 1965, 20–21; Janus fliers, May 1965 and Feb. 1966, NOP; Janus flier, c. 30 Oct. 1965, MSR (box 7/f18); *Trib.*, 2 Nov. 1965, 3; *One*, Feb. 1966, 25; *Ladder*, Apr. 1966, 20–22; *HALN*, Feb. 1972, 2; Karlen, *Sexuality and Homosexuality*, 567–571.

64. In addition to coverage cited elsewhere, see *Inq.*, 16 Feb. 1964, D4; *LI*, 17 Feb. 1964, 2; *GPM*, Mar. 1964, 106; *Inq.*, 15 Mar. 1964, D5; *EB*, 15 Mar. 1964, sec. 5, p. 10; 17 Mar. 1964, 52; *Inq.*, 18 Mar. 1964, 42; *CLR*, Apr. 1964, 2–3; *Saturday Review* correspondence, 13 Apr.–29 July 1964, ACLUA (box 790/f11); *Trib.*, 26 May 1964, 5, 6; *Bucks County Life*, July-Aug. 1964, 12–15; *Bucks County Life*, Sept. 1964, 12–15; *TUN*, 25 Feb. 1966, 4; *EB*, 11 Oct. 1966, 88. See also gay-related stories on the Cape May Coast Guard, *Inq.* and *EB*, 14–15 Apr. 1966; a Germantown pastor, *Trib.*, 5 July 1966; and Glassboro State College, *Inq.* and *EB*, 22 Sept.–19 Oct. 1966.

65. See *Janus*, Mar. to June 1964; *JSN*, Nov. 1964 to July 1966; Janus flier, Apr. 1965, Janus file, IGLA; *Drum*, Mar. 1966, 5; nos. 18–19, 1966, 7, 16–17, 34–46.

66. *Janus*, Feb. 1964, 2. See also Philips/Oshtry correspondence, 10–14 Jan. 1964, NOP; *Janus*, Feb. to July 1964; Janus brochure, c. 1964, NOP; *CLR*, Apr. 1964, 3; Polak to Janus Board, 28 Oct. 1964, Janus file, IGLA; *Drum*, Oct. 1964, 15–16; *JSN*, Jan. 1965, 2; June 1965, 2; *Drum*, Aug. 1965, 3; Oct. 1965, 7, 22; Polak to Cantor, Coxe, Levitan, Oshtry, 12 June 1966, ACLU-GPBP; Council on Religion and the Homosexual, et al., *The Challenge and Progress of Homosexual Law Reform* (San Francisco: Council on Religion and the Homosexual, 1968), 15, 46.

67. See *CLR*, Apr. 1964, 3; *JSN*, Apr. to Nov. 1965; *Drum*, July 1965, 4; Dec. 1965, 24.

68. See Janus, "You're under Arrest" flier, Janus file, IGLA; *Drum*, Apr. 1965, 29–31; Horowitz to Leitsch, 27 Apr. 1965, MSR (box 7/f18).

69. See *Janus*, Apr. to July 1964; *JSN*, Nov. 1964 to Jan. 1966; *Drum*, May 1965, 21; Aug. 1965, 20; Sept. 1965, 5–6, 23; Oct. 1965, 7; Polak to Oshtry, 27 Oct. 1965; Oshtry to Ruth, 3 Nov. 1965, NOP; *Drum*, Nov. 1965, 5; Jan. 1966, 23; Apr. 1966, 23; nos. 18–19, 1966, 27; no. 20, 1966, 6, 25; no. 21, 1966, 23; no. 22, 1966, 24; no. 23, 1967, 5; Mar. 1968, 31; *HALN*, Feb. 1969, 3. See also *NYT*, *EB*, *Inq.*, and *DN*, 4–8 Apr. 1964; 18 Feb., 3 Mar., 2 Apr., 12 May, 1 June, 1 July, 17 Aug., 23–24 Aug., 29 Sept., 4 Nov., 1 Dec. 1966; 17 May 1967; 16 May, 21 May, 23 May 1968; 13–14 Jan. 1969; 1–2 June 1970, 10 Nov. 1974; FBI Homex documents, 24 Mar. 1966 to 13 Jan. 1978; *Ladder*, Apr. 1966, 14; *Time*, 26 Aug. 1966, 14; *Sexology*, Mar. 1967, 554–556; *America*, 3 June 1967, 802–803; *NYT Magazine*, 12 Nov. 1967, 44; Interview with Daniels.

70. Clark Polak, "Liberty in the Defense of Vice Is No Extreme," *Drum*, Nov. 1964, 2, 16.

71. *Drum*, Nov. 1965, 5; Arlen Specter, "Summary of the Report on the Investigation of the Magisterial System," 1965, 19–20, 29–33, CCCP (box 3, Magistrate's Court file). See also *EB*, *Inq.*, and *DN*, 13–18 Sept. 1964; 24 Mar.–27 May, 19–20 Sept. 1965; 5 Jan. 1966; Coxe correspondence, 4 May 1965; Arlen Specter, "Statement for the Senate Judiciary Subcommittee on Improvements in Judicial Machinery," 2 Aug. 1966, ACLU-GPBP (box 9); *Drum*, Apr. 1966, 23; *U.S. v. Nardello*, 393 U.S. 286 (1969); Paolantonio, *Frank Rizzo*, 70–86; Clark and Clark, "Rally and Relapse," 661–662.

72. *Janus*, Feb. 1964, 6; Apr. 1964, 5–6, 15. See also June 1964, 4, 16.

73. Janus press release, 18 Apr. 1966, ACLU-GPBP. See also National Planning Conference of Homophile Organizations Minutes, 19–20 Feb. 1966, DOBP; *Drum*, Apr. 1966, 25–26; *Ladder*, Apr. 1966, 4–5; Memos and correspondence, Apr. 1966, MSR (box 3/f2); *EB*, 17 Apr. 1966, 35; *NYT*, 17 Apr. 1966, 10; Leitsch to Lyon, 13 May 1966, DOBP; *Drum*, nos. 18–19, 1966, 27–28; Polak Memo, 2 June 1966, MSR (box 7/f18); *JSN*, July 1966, 2; *Police Chief*, Nov. 1966, 20; Leitsch to War Resisters League, 5 Dec. 1966, MSR (box 1/f13); *Time*, 9 Dec. 1966, 57; *Drum*, no. 23, 1967, 25.

74. See *Mattachine Midwest*, Aug. 1966, 9, IGLA; Second Annual Reminder press release, 30 June 1966; flier, 4 July 1966, MSR (box 3/f21); Kameny to Rodwell, 21 June 1966, MSR (box 2/f6); Interview with Gittings; Mecca interview with Gittings; Public forum with Gittings and Bello.

75. SAC Philadelphia to FBI Director, 6 May 1966; FBI Philadelphia to FBI Director, 22 May 1966; SAC Philadelphia to FBI Director, 23 May 1966; FBI Philadelphia Report, 23 May 1966; FBI Philadelphia to FBI Director, 21 June 1966; SAC Philadelphia to FBI Director, 28 July 1966; FBI MS file, HQ100–403320; Teletype, 3 July 1967, FBI MS file, 100–33796.

76. See *JSN*, May 1965, 1; *Drum*, nos. 18–19, 1966, 52; *JSN*, no. 24, 1967, 1.

77. Inman to Horowitz, 28 Apr. 1965; Horowitz to *MSNYN* editor, received 22 Mar. 1965, MSR (box 7/f18).

78. Horowitz to Leitsch, 27 Apr. 1965, MSR (box 7/f18).

79. Leitsch to Horowitz, 7 Apr. 1965; Horowitz to Inman, 25 Apr. 1965, MSR (box 7/f18).

80. Inman to Horowitz, 7 May 1965; Horowitz to Leitsch, 11 May 1965, MSR (box 7/f18).

81. Horowitz to Leitsch, 11 May 1965, MSR (box 7/f18).

82. Leitsch to Horowitz, 12 May 1965, MSR (box 7/f18); Inman to Leitsch, 28 May 1965, MSR (box 1/f11).

83. *JSN*, Dec. 1965, 2–3.

84. See ECHOM, 5 Dec. 1964; *Drum*, May 1965, 6; *JSN*, July 1965, 1; *Drum*, July 1965, 2, 22; Sept. 1965, 4; Polak to Leitsch, 29 Nov. 1965, MSR (box 5/f2); *JSN*, Dec. 1965, 3; *EMM*, Jan. 1966, 1–3; *Drum*, Feb. 1966, 4, 21; *JSN*, Feb. 1966, 1–2; *Drum*, Apr. 1966, 4, 23; *Ladder*, June 1966, 20; *Drum*, no. 20, 1966, 8; *NYT*, 9 July 1966, 12; *Time*, 22 July 1966, 45–46; Barker to Boutilier Fund, 2 Oct. 1966, MSR (box 1/f1); *NYT*, 8 Nov. 1966, 24; Polak correspondence, 25–28 Nov. 1966, MSR (box 1/f12); *JSN*, Dec. 1966, 2; *One Eleven Wine and Liquors Inc. v. Division of Alcoholic Beverage Control* 235 A.2d 12 (NJ 1967); *Boutilier v. Immigration and Naturalization Service* 387 U.S. 118 (1967).

85. Clark Polak, "The Homophile Puzzle, Part One," *Drum*, Dec. 1965, 14–15. See also correspondence, 29 Nov. 1965–5 Feb. 1966, MSR (box 2/f6, box 5/f2); Minutes,

National Planning Conference of Homophile Organizations, 19–20 Feb. 1966, DOBP; *Drum*, Apr. 1966, 25–26; *Ladder*, Apr. 1966, 4–5.

86. Polak, "The Homophile Puzzle, Part One," 15, 27. See also *Drum*, Aug. 1965, 3, 30; Gilbert Cantor, "Anticipations—Legal and Philosophical," ECHO Conference Address, 25 Sept. 1965, ECHOP.

87. *JSN*, Sept. 1966, 1–2. See also *Drum*, nos. 18–19, 1966, 52; no. 21, 1966, 10–11; Hubert Stewart, " 'Gay Is Good,' Or Is It?" *Inq.*, 4 Nov. 1968, 33.

88. *JSN*, Jan. 1965, 2; Clark Polak, "The Legacy," *Drum*, May 1965, 2.

89. *Drum*, Oct. 1965, 11; nos. 18–19, 1966, 41–42; Joan Fraser [Fleischmann], "The Woman's Way," *Janus*, Apr. 1964, 16. See also Churchill, *Homosexual Behavior among Males*, 57–58.

90. Fraser [Fleischmann], "The Woman's Way," 16; Clark Polak, "The Homophile Puzzle, Part Two," *Drum*, Jan. 1966, 11; *JSN*, Dec. 1966, 2. See also *Drum*, May 1965, 17; Mar. 1967, 41.

Chapter Ten

1. A. B., "The Masculine-Feminine Mystique," *DOBPN*, Nov. 1967, 1.
2. See Betty Friedan, *The Feminine Mystique* (New York: Norton, 1963).
3. D'Emilio, *Sexual Politics*, 228. See also *Ladder*, Nov. 1966 to Aug. 1967.
4. D'Emilio, *Sexual Politics*, 229; Rita Laporte, "Of What Use NACHO?" *Ladder*, Aug.–Sept. 1969, 18. See also Sara Evans, *Personal Politics* (New York: Random House, 1979), 213–214; Alice Echols, *Daring to Be Bad: Radical Feminism in America, 1967–1975* (Minneapolis: University of Minnesota Press), 92–96.
5. Interviews with Bello and Friedman. See also *DOB-NY Newsletter*, Apr. 1967 to May 1967; *DOBPN*, Aug. 1967 to May 1968.
6. Interview with Bello.
7. Ibid.; Public forum with Bello and Gittings.
8. Interview with Friedman.
9. Ibid.
10. Love, "The Invisible Sorority," 66.
11. Ibid., 89.
12. Ibid., 67–71, 84–93.
13. Ibid., 67, 69.
14. Ibid., 66–67.
15. Ibid., 66, 90–92. See *Commonwealth ex rel. Ashfield v. Cortes* 210 Pa. Superior Ct. 515 (1967).
16. Love, "The Invisible Sorority," 67, 90.
17. Ibid., 67–69, 89–93.
18. Ibid., 93.
19. Frank Bemus, letter to the editor, *PM*, Dec. 1967, 4.
20. *Drum*, Mar. 1968, 25–26.
21. C. F., "The Invisible Sorority," *DOBPN*, Nov. 1967, 3; DOB-Philadelphia, letter to the editor, *PM*, Dec. 1967, 4; Public forum with Bello and Gittings.
22. Interviews with Bello and Friedman.
23. Ibid.
24. A. B., *DOBPN*, Nov. 1967, 3. See also *Daily Pennsylvanian* (*DP*), *EB*, *Inq.*, and

DN, 30 Oct.–8 Dec. 1967; 23–25 Jan., 13–17 May 1968; 3–4 June 1969; *Time*, 10 Nov. 1967, 28.

25. Alan J. Davis, "Report on Sexual Assaults in the Philadelphia Prison System and Sheriff's Vans," Biddle Law Library, University of Pennsylvania, 1968; C. F., *DOBPN*, Aug.–Sept. 1968, 5. See also Lawrence Nathaniel Houston, "An Investigation of the Relationship between the Vocational Interests and Homosexual Behavior of Institutionalized Youthful Offenders" (Ed.D. diss., Temple University, 1963); *EB*, *Inq.*, and *DN*, 5 July–3 Oct. 1968; 4 June and 10–11 July 1969; 19 July and 21 July 1970; 13 Oct. 1971; 30 Sept. 1973; *NYT*, 12 Sept. 1968, 31; *Time*, 20 Sept. 1968, 54; *HALN*, Nov. 1968, 5; Alan J. Davis, "Sexual Assaults in the Philadelphia Prison System and Sheriff's Vans," *Trans-Action* 6, no. 2 (Dec. 1968): 8–16; *Drum*, Dec. 1968, 30–31; *Playboy*, Jan. 1969, 50; *HALN*, June 1969, 3–4; *DD*, 16 July 1970, 1, 4; *Drummer*, 21 Oct. 1971, 1, 5, 6; Peter C. Buffum, *Homosexuality in Prisons* (Washington, DC: National Institute of Law Enforcement and Criminal Justice, 1972); Daniel Lockwood, *Prison Sexual Violence* (New York: Elsevier, 1980), 4–8.

26. See *EB*, *Inq.*, *DN*, *Trib.*, and *DD*, 7–9 Feb. 1965; 24 Nov.–10 Dec. 1967; 27 July–27 Aug., 25 Sept. 1968; 14 Jan., 12–14 Feb., 1–10 Apr., 10–11 July 1969; *Commonwealth v. William Martin Campbell, III*, 445 Pa. 488, 284 A.2d 798.

27. Bernard McCormick and Gaeton Fonzi, "My, What a Quaint Place!" *PM*, Aug. 1967, 42, 69–70; Love, "Here He Comes," 20. See also *DN*, 21 Aug. 1968, 36; *EB*, 22 Aug. 1968, 14; *Inq.*, 22 Aug. 1968, 20; McCormick, "The Smut Establishment," 57, 97; Greg Walter, "Incest Is In," *PM*, Oct. 1968, 78–79, 144–151; *Advocate*, Sept. 1969, 18.

28. Marta Robinet, "The Need to Love and Be Loved Is Strong—Even in Prison," *EB*, 14 Nov. 1967, 58. See also Estelle B. Freedman, "The Prison Lesbian: Race, Class, and the Construction of the Aggressive Female Homosexual, 1915–1965," *Feminist Studies* 22, no. 2 (Summer 1996): 397–423.

29. A. B. and C. F., "Homosexuality in the Mass Media—Acknowledged or Defamation?" *DOBPN*, June 1968, 1; A. B. and C. F., "The Homosexual Voice," *DOBPN*, Aug.–Sept. 1968, 2.

30. Interview with Friedman. See also *EB*, 16 Jan. 1949, 3.

31. *DOB-NY Newsletter*, May 1967, 1; Interview with Bello. See also *DOBPN*, Aug. 1967 to Sept. 1968; Council on Religion and the Homosexual, et al., *The Challenge and Progress,* 15, 46.

32. *DOBPN*, Feb. 1968, 2; Mar. 1968, 3. See also Aug. 1967, 2; Sept. 1967, 3–4.

33. C. M., *DOBPN*, Jan. 1968, 2; Webster Schott, "A 4-Million Minority Asks for Equal Rights," *NYT Magazine*, 12 Nov. 1967, 49.

34. Ada Bello, "Early Period, 1967–70," typescript, HAL file, GLBTA; *DOBPN*, Aug. 1967, 2; Interview with Bello. See also *TUN*, 13 Apr. 1967, 1, 4.

35. Interviews with Bello and Friedman; A. B., *DOBPN*, Sept. 1967, 2; A. B. and C. F., "Homosexuality in the Mass Media," 2.

36. Interview with Bello.

37. *Ladder*, Oct. 1966, 24.

38. Shotwell's novella *The Shape of Love* was serialized in the *Ladder*, May to Nov. 1967. For an obituary, see *Ladder*, Apr. 1968, 13. See also Interviews with Fleischmann and McCann.

39. Public forum with Bello and Gittings. See also Audiotape, Murray Burnett Show, 8 Feb. 1967, Barbara Gittings Collection, GLBTA; Memo from Kameny and Gittings, 30 May 1967, Frank Kameny file, IGLA; *Drum*, no. 23, 1967, 24; *Inq.*, 5 Jan. 1968, 29;

ERCHO Address List, 27 Oct. 1968, MSR (box 3/f26); *HALN*, Jan. 1969, 3; *NYT*, 20 Aug. 1969, 38; D'Emilio, *Sexual Politics*, 197–199, 216.

40. Rose DeWolf, "Another Minority Bids for Equality," *Inq.*, 6 July 1967, 33; Schott, "A 4-Million Minority," 45; Fourth Annual Reminder Day flier, 4 July 1968, MSR (box 2/f1). See also *MSNYN*, July-Aug. 1967, 1–2; FBI Philadelphia to FBI Director, 3 July 1967, FBI MS file 100–33796; FBI Philadelphia to FBI Director, 4 July and 10 July 1967, FBI MS file HQ100–403320; *Drum*, no. 26, 1967, 7; *NYT*, 5 July 1967, 5; Kameny Memo, June 1968, MSR (box 3/f26); Kameny to Herman Slade, 15 June 1968, MSR (box 1/f16); HLRS press release, 30 July 1968, RSP (box 4/f 22); *DOBPN*, July 1968, 4; Public forum with Bello and Gittings; Interviews with Bello and Friedman.

41. Samantha Morse, "Refusing to Assimilate," *Au Courant,* 15 July 1997, 10, 15; DeWolf, "Another Minority"; *Drum*, no. 26, 1967, 7; Fourth Annual Reminder Day flier.

42. C. F., *DOBPN*, Apr. 1968, 1.

43. Bello, "Early Period." See also *Ladder*, May-June 1968, 22–23.

44. Townley, "Gay Philadelphia," 28; A. B. and C. F., *DOBPN*, May 1968, 1 [misdated Apr. 1968]. See also Janet Cooper, "An Interview with Byrna Aronson," typescript, Walter Lear Papers, GLBTA.

45. Bello, "Early Period"; Cooper, "An Interview with Byrna Aronson."

46. Interview with Friedman.

47. Interviews with Bello and Friedman; A. B. and C. F., *DOBPN*, May 1968, 2 [misdated Apr. 1968]; Public forum with Bello and Gittings.

48. Interview with Bello; C. F., *DOBPN*, July 1968, 1–2.

49. Mecca interview with Gittings. See also Bello, "Early Period"; Interview with Bello.

50. A. B. and C. F., *HALN*, Nov. 1968, 1–2; Mecca interview with Gittings; Interview with Friedman. See also Byerly, "HAL Is Gay," 6.

51. *Ladder*, Apr.-May 1969, 40. See also Karlen, *Sexuality and Homosexuality*, 538.

52. Interviews with Bello and Friedman; Public forum with Bello and Gittings.

53. See *HALN*, Mar. 1969, 1; May 1969, 4–5; Interviews with Bello and Fleischmann.

54. C. F. and A. B., "A Suggested Policy: Confrontation and Implementation," *HALN*, Feb. 1969, 1–2.

55. A. B. and C. F., "A New Opiate of the Masses," *HALN*, Mar. 1969, 1–2; C. F., *HALN*, May 1969, 5–6; Ellen Collins, letter to the editor, reprinted in *HALN*, Nov. 1968, 5.

56. A. B., *HALN*, Feb. 1969, 3–4.

57. C. F., *HALN*, Dec. 1968, 4; C. F., *HALN*, Feb. 1969, 4. See also *Drum*, Jan. 1968, 23; C. F., *DOBPN*, Jan. 1968, 2–3; *Drum*, Mar. 1968, 8.

58. Coxe Memo, 19 Nov. 1968; Coxe to Gittings, 21 Nov. 1968, ACLU-GPBP. See also *HALN*, Jan. to June 1969.

59. *HALN*, Dec. 1968, 3; Public forum with Bello and Gittings. See also *Newsweek*, 17 June 1968, 10; *Inq.*, reprinted in *HALN*, Nov. 1968, 5; *Medical World News*, 30 May 1969, 8.

60. A. B., *HALN*, Dec. 1968, 4.

61. A. B. and C. F., "Homosexuals as a Minority," *HALN*, May 1969, 1–3.

62. A. B., "The Masculine-Feminine Mystique," 1.

63. *Drum*, no. 24, Mar. 1967, 6. See also *One Eleven Wines and Liquors, Inc. v. Division of Alcoholic Beverage Control* 235 A. 2d 12 (N.J. 1967) [*Val's* was consolidated with this

case]; *EB*, 3 Sept. 1967, sec. 7, p. 8A; *Drum*, Oct. 1967, 26; *EB*, 6 Nov. 1967, 2; *Inq.*, 7 Nov. 1967, 34; *Drum*, Jan. 1968, 4, 23; Council on Religion and the Homosexual, et al., *The Challenge and Progress*, 24–25.

64. *Boutilier v. Immigration and Naturalization Service* 387 U.S. 118 (1967); *Drum*, no. 23, 1967, 3; Aug. 1967, 25. See correspondence, 19 Jan.–21 Dec. 1967, MSR (box 1/f14–15); *JSN*, no. 23, 1967, 2; no. 24, 1967, 2; *DOB-NY Newsletter*, Mar. 1967, 2; *Drum*, Mar. 1967, 3, 10–19, 36; *EB*, 23 May 1967, 13; *MSNYN*, June 1967, 2–3; *Drum*, Aug. 1967, 38; *Sexology*, Aug. 1967, 71; *Drum*, Sept. 1967, 33–34; Schott, "A 4-Million Minority," 54, 59; *DOB-NY Newsletter*, Jan. 1968, 4; *Drum*, Jan. 1968, 4; *Sexology*, Jan. 1968, 387–388; Council on Religion and the Homosexual, et al., *The Challenge and Progress*, 8–9; *Ladder*, June-July 1969, 41; *HALN*, July 1969, 3–4; *Psychology Today*, July 1969, 43–44. HLRS also supported cases in Florida and Delaware. See *Drum*, Jan. 1968, 9; Mar. 1968, 21–22; *JSN*, no. 28, 1967, 1–2; Correspondence, 9 Nov. 1967–12 Feb. 1968, ACLU-GPBP; HLRS press release, 30 July 1968, RSP (box 4/f22); *Drum*, Dec. 1968, 40; Alverson, "A Minority's Plea," 23.

65. Clark Polak, typescript, c. Aug. 1967, ACLUA (vol. 5/fA1600); Elliott, "The Morals Squad." See also correspondence, 31 Aug.–18 Sept. 1967, ACLUA (vol. 5/fA1600); *Drum*, Sept. 1967, 4; Coxe to Jacob Kreshtool, 24 Jan. 1968, ACLU-GPBP; *Drum*, Jan. 1968, 5.

66. *Drum*, Jan. 1968, 4; Clark Polak, "What Organized Homosexuals Want," *Sexology*, Jan. 1967, 378–380; Charles Kaiser, *The Gay Metropolis, 1940–1996* (Boston: Houghton Mifflin, 1997), 206–208; Stewart, " 'Gay Is Good,' " 33. See also *EB*, 3 Apr. 1967, 20; *TUN*, 13 Apr. 1967, 1, 4; *JSN*, Aug. 1967, 1–2; C. F., *HALN*, Dec. 1968, 4; *Ladder*, Apr.-May 1969, 39.

67. Trojan Spring 1966 brochure, Womack Papers (box 1); Walter, "Incest Is In," 144–145. See also McCormick, "The Smut Establishment," 97; Womack Papers (box 1).

68. See H. B. Montague to Philadelphia Inspector in Charge, 9 Jan. 1967; RPPI, 11 Jan. 1967–16 Apr. 1969; K. Similes to Drew O'Keefe, 5 May 1969, NOP; U.S. Commission on Obscenity and Pornography, *Technical Report* 3:99–176.

69. See Similes to O'Keefe, 5 May 1969; Philadelphia Postal Inspector to Louis Bechtle, 5 Feb. 1970; RPPI, 24 Feb. 1970, NOP.

70. RPPI, 22 Mar. 1967, NOP. See also *EB*, 13 Mar. 1967, 32; *Inq.*, 13 Mar. 1967, 31; *DN*, 13 Mar. 1967, 20.

71. See RPPI, 22 Mar. 1967 and 10 Aug. 1967; Philadelphia Postal Inspector in Charge to Chief Postal Inspector, 27 Mar. 1968, NOP.

72. A. Kent MacDougall, "The Penal Press: It Gives All the News That's Fit to Print," *Wall Street Journal*, 2 Nov. 1967, 1.

73. See Similes to O'Keefe, 5 May 1969; RPPI, 19 June 1969, NOP; Philadelphia Police Dept., "Extract of Criminal Record" for Polak; *EB*, 22 Nov. 1968, 3.

74. Polak to Gebhard, 30 Apr. 1969, RSP (box 3/f15); Polak to Janus members and *Drum* subscribers, 5 May 1969, Janus file, IGLA; Interviews with Oshtry and Schlegel.

75. Gil Cantor to Ervin, 19 May 1969, RSP (box 3/f13). See also Ervin and Schlegel correspondence, 3 May–21 Aug. 1969, RSP (box 3/f13–15); Damon Papers; Interview with Schlegel.

76. See *EB*, 28 May 1969, 17; *Inq.*, 28 May 1969, 53; *DN*, 28 May 1969, 6; *EB*, 3 June 1969; *Inq.*, 3 June 1969, 31; *DN*, 3 June 1969, 26.

77. Ervin to Schlegel, 4 June 1969; Schlegel, Ervin, and William Muldowney to Polak, 11 June 1969, RSP (box 3/f13).

Chapter Eleven

1. A. B. and C. F., "Give Me Liberty Or . . . ," *HALN*, Aug.–Sept. 1969, 1.

2. See D'Emilio, *Sexual Politics*, 2–3, 240.

3. Tom Burke, "The New Homosexuality," *Esquire*, Dec. 1969, 178; A. B., "Enter the New Homosexual," *HALN*, Jan.-Feb. 1970, 2–3; A. B. and C. F., "Give Me Liberty Or . . . ," 2.

4. Duberman, *Stonewall*, 182, 190, 196–197.

5. Wicker and Mattachine New York sign, cited by Duberman, *Stonewall*, 207; Mecca interview with Gittings; Bello, "Early Period, 1967–70." See also Faderman, *Odd Girls*, 196.

6. A. B. and C. F., "Give Me Liberty Or . . . ," 2.

7. Gittings, cited in "150 Homosexuals Parade before Independence Hall to Protest Maltreatment," *Trib.*, 12 July 1969, 5. See also *HALN*, Dec. 1968, 5; May 1969, 4; Correspondence, June 1969, MSR (box 2/f1, box 3/f26); *HALN*, July 1969, 6; *Trib.*, 15 July 1969, 9, 28; *Ladder*, Oct.-Nov. 1969, cover and back, 39–40; Bill Wingell, "A Time for Holding Hands," *DD*, 10 July 1969, 8; *Gay*, 29 June 1970, 5.

8. Wingell, "A Time for Holding Hands"; Gittings, cited in "150 Homosexuals Parade"; *Ladder*, Oct.-Nov. 1969, 39–40; A. B., "The Second Largest Minority," *HALN*, Aug.–Sept. 1969, 3.

9. Leitsch to Gittings, 24 June 1969, MSR (box 2/f1); *MSNYN*, July 1969, 9. See also Duberman, *Stonewall*, 217; Marcus, *Making History*, 177, 179, 182.

10. Craig Rodwell, cited in Duberman, *Stonewall*, 209.

11. Wingell, "A Time for Holding Hands"; Bill Weaver, cited in Donn Teal, *The Gay Militants* (New York: Stein and Day, 1971), 30.

12. *Ladder*, Oct.-Nov. 1969, cover; Love, "The Invisible Sorority," 66; Gittings, cited in Wingell, "A Time for Holding Hands."

13. Marotta, *The Politics of Homosexuality*, 91. See also Teal, *The Gay Militants*, 38–60, 273; D'Emilio, *Sexual Politics*, 232–233; Duberman, *Stonewall*, 211–221, 226; Terence Kissack, "Freaking Fag Revolutionaries: New York's Gay Liberation Front, 1969–1971," *Radical History Review*, no. 62 (Spring 1995): 104–134.

14. J. Bradley, "Report on the Fall Homophile Conference," RSP (box 4/f25); Interview with Bello; Bob Martin, "ERCHO Meeting Adopts Radical Manifesto," *Advocate*, Jan. 1970, 24. See also *Gay*, 1 Dec. 1969, 3, 10; C. F., "ERCHO Report," *HALN*, Jan.-Feb. 1970, 5–7; Teal, *The Gay Militants*, 86–87; Marotta, *The Politics of Homosexuality*, 115–119; Duberman, *Stonewall*, 227–229.

15. Resolution cited in Teal, *The Gay Militants*, 322; Marotta, *The Politics of Homosexuality*, 164–165. See also Martin, "ERCHO Meeting"; "ERCHO Spring Conference," *Gay Power*, no. 7, 1969, 6; C. F., "ERCHO Report," 6.

16. Martin, "ERCHO Meeting"; "ERCHO Spring Conference." See also C. F., "ERCHO Report," 6; *Playboy*, May 1970, 236–237.

17. ERCHO resolution, cited in Martin, "ERCHO Meeting"; Teal, *The Gay Militants*, 87. See also *Come Out*, 10 Jan. 1970, 16; C. F., "ERCHO Report," 7; *Playboy*, May 1970, 236–237.

18. Interviews with Bello, Gittings, and Lahusen. See also Marcus, *Making History*, 213.

19. C. F., "Whither the Movement," *HALN*, Nov.-Dec. 1969, 1–3.

20. *Ladder*, Feb.–Mar. 1970, 36; C. F., "ERCHO Report," 7. See also *Playboy*, Aug.

1970, 47; Teal, *The Gay Militants*, 75, 106–107, 126–153; Tobin [Lahusen] articles in *Gay*, beginning 13 Apr. 1970.

21. Public forum with Bello and Gittings; Interviews with Bello and Friedman.

22. Gittings, cited in Marcus, *Making History*, 214; Interview with Gittings; Lahusen, cited in Marcus, 213–214; Interview with Lahusen.

23. See Philadelphia Postal Inspector to Louis Bechtle, 2 July 1969, NOP; *EB*, 12 July 1969, 3; *DN*, 12 July 1969, 8; *Commonwealth v. Polak*, 438 Pa. 67, 263 A.2d 354; *Commonwealth v. Polak*, 217 Pa.Super. 764, 268 A.2d 245.

24. Grand jury indictments, *U.S. v. Clark P. Polak*, U.S. District Court for the Eastern District of Penn., no. 69–329, 23 Oct. 1969; RPPI, 24 Feb. 1970, NOP. See also *Advocate*, Mar. 1970, 5; *Gay*, 1 Mar. 1970, 3.

25. Grand jury indictments, *U.S. v. Clark P. Polak*, no. 70–57, 19 Feb. 1970; Philadelphia Postal Inspector in Charge to Chief Postal Inspector, 19–20 Feb. 1970; RPPI, 24 Feb. 1970; Memo in Support of Defendant's Motion to Suppress Evidence and Return Property, *U.S. v. Polak*, no. 70–57, U.S. District Court for the Eastern District of Penn.; Brief for the Appelant, *U.S. v. Polak*, U.S. Court of Appeals for the Third Circuit, NOP. See also *Inq.*, 20 Feb. 1970, 42; *EB*, 20 Feb. 1970 (not microfilmed but see clipping in NOP).

26. Hearing on Defendant's Motion to Suppress Evidence and Return Property, *U.S. v. Polak*, 20 Mar. 1970; *U.S. v. Polak*, 30 Apr. 1970, NOP. See also *EB*, 1 May 1970, 27; *Inq.*, 2 May 1970, 23; *DN*, 2 May 1970, 5; *HALN*, 25 Sept. 1970, 2. The government's appeal was denied on 12 May 1970 by the U.S. Court of Appeals for the Third Circuit.

27. Lige [Clark] and Jack [Nichols], "Poor 'Ol Clark," *Screw*, 16 Feb. 1970, 13; 15 Mar. 1970, 22; *Los Angeles Free Press*, 20 Mar. 1970, 20; *Screw*, 22 Mar. 1970, 26; 29 Mar. 1970, 26; *Gay*, 29 Mar. 1970, 20; 13 Apr. 1970, 20; 20 Apr. 1970, 20.

28. Cantor to Schlegel, 9 July 1969; Schlegel to Janus members and subscribers, Sept. 1969, RSP (box 3/f14); *PACE!*, Jan. 1970, 2; Interview with Schlegel; PACE, "That Guy '70" flier, 6 June 1970, RSP (box 4/f22). See also *HALN*, Jan.-Feb. 1970, 8; *Screw*, 6 June 1970, 13.

29. Schlegel to Janus members and subscribers, Sept. 1969, RSP (box 3/f14); *PACE!*, Jan. 1970, 2.

30. Interview with Schlegel.

31. See Interview with Schlegel; Mitchell to Schlegel, Dec. 1970, in Schlegel's possession.

32. Interview with Oshtry. See also Philadelphia Postal Inspector in Charge to Chief Postal Inspector, 14 Feb. 1972, NOP.

33. Kepner, "A Farewell to Friends Departed." See also wills and probate documents in Schlegel's and Oshtry's possession; Polak FOIA materials, 27 Mar. 1975–17 Apr. 1976, NOP; Polak file, IGLA; Interviews with Schlegel and Oshtry.

34. Martin and Lyon, *Lesbian/Woman*, 251.

35. See Forum with Bello and Gittings; Mecca interviews with Gittings and Rosen; Interviews with Gittings, Friedman, Davies, and Lahusen; Larry Fields, "Air Force Vet Risks Job to Proclaim He's Gay," *DN*, 11 May 1972, 5.

36. Interview with Davies. See also *Au Courant*, 13 Mar. 1989, 1, 7, 12.

37. Interviews with Davies and Langhorne. See also Interviews with Gittings, Lahusen, and Bello.

38. Tom Fox, "The Rights of Homosexuals," *DN*, 30 Apr. 1970, 4. See also *HALN*, Mar.–Apr. 1970, 3; May-June 1970, 2, 5–6; *DD*, 14 May 1970, 4; "Homosexuals to

Tell Story on Posters," *DN*, 25 June 1970, 20; *Double Exposure*, 6 July 1970, 1; Knight, " 'Other Society.' "

39. *HALN*, May-June 1970, 2; Forum with Bello and Gittings.

40. "Homosexuals to Tell Story"; Knight, " 'Other Society' "; Rick Rosen, "Reflections," *HALN*, 25 Sept. 1970, 1. See also Vestry of St. Mary's Church statement, June 1970, HLP (box 1/f70); *Double Exposure*, 6 July 1970, 3–4; *Gay Liberation Front Philadelphia Newsletter* (*GLFPN*), c. July 1970; Teal, *The Gay Militants*, 58–60, 263.

41. Arnold Eisen, "HAL Activists Move for Gay Liberation," *DP*, 1 Feb. 1971, 3. See also *HALN*, 26 Nov. 1970, 4; *DP*, 2 Feb. 1971, 3.

42. Forum with Bello and Gittings; Mecca interview with Gittings.

43. *HALN*, Oct. 1969, 8; Forum with Bello and Gittings. See also *HALN*, Oct. 1969 to Nov. 1970; *Gay*, 20 July 1970, 4.

44. "Homosexuals to Tell Story"; *HALN*, July 1969, 6. See also *Double Exposure*, 6 July 1970, 1; Teal, *The Gay Militants*, 77, 270; *HALN*, Aug. 1969 to Nov. 1970; *Gay*, 20 Apr. 1970, 15; Bayer, *Homosexuality and American Psychiatry,* 107–111; Marcus, *Making History*, 217–225; Mecca interview with Gittings; Lahusen to author, c. July 1998.

45. See, for example, Coxe correspondence, 27–28 July 1970, ACLU-GPBP; *EB*, 30 Aug., 19 Nov. 1971; 4 June, 28 Sept. 1972; 25 Jan. 1973; *Inq*., 13 Aug., 20 Aug. 1970; 28 Feb., 31 Oct., 25 Nov., 9 Dec. 1971; 25 Jan. 1973; *DN*, 2 June 1970; 8–24 Sept., 18 Nov. 1971; 24 Aug. 1972; 25 Jan. 1973; 2 Apr. 1974; *Trib.*, 21 Mar., 21 July, 29 Aug. 1970; 9–19 Jan. 1971; *PM*, Nov. 1970, cover; Dec. 1970, 6; *Gay*, 12 Mar. 1973, 8; *Commonwealth v. Farquharson*, 467 Pa. 50, 354 A.2d 545.

46. Fox, "The Rights of Homosexuals."

47. William J. Speers, "Brace Yourself for Another Revolt—The Gay Liberation," *Inq*., 19 July 1970, 7.

48. Knight, " 'Other Society.' "

49. C. F., "On Economic Independence for Gays," *HALN*, Mar.–Apr. 1970, 1–2. See also Harold I. Lief, Joseph F. Dingman, and Melvin P. Bishop, "Psychoendocrinologic Studies in a Male with Cyclic Changes in Sexuality," *Psychosomatic Medicine* 24, no. 4 (1962): 357–368; Peter Mayerson and Harold I. Lief, "Psychotherapy of Homosexuals: A Follow-up Study of Nineteen Cases," in *Sexual Inversion*, 302–344; *HALN*, May-June 1969, 4; Jan.-Feb. 1970, 8; Coxe to Niel Thomas, 28 July 1970, ACLU-GPBP; *PACE!*, no. 2, 1971, 2, 63; *DP*, 3 Feb. 1971, 3; Karlen, *Sexuality and Homosexuality*, 583; Bayer, *Homosexuality and American Psychiatry*, 167–172; Interview with Friedman.

50. *HALN*, May-June 1970, 2, 7. See also Coxe correspondence, 27–28 July 1970, ACLU-GPBP; *HALN*, 25 Sept. 1970, 2; Coxe to Aronson, 14 May 1971, HLP (box 1/f2).

51. "Homosexuals Seek 'Complete Equality,' " *Inq*., 11 Aug. 1970, 24; Teal, *The Gay Militants*, 263. See also *EB*, 10 Aug. 1970, 4; *DN*, 10 Aug. 1970, 12; *Gay*, 7 Sept. 1970, 12; *EB*, 18 Sept. 1970, 11; *DN*, 18 Sept. 1970, 40; *NYT*, 20 Sept. 1970, 56; *HALN*, 25 Sept. 1970, 2; *Gay*, 26 Oct. 1970, 3.

52. *HALN*, Oct. 1969, 9; Nov.-Dec. 1969, 8–9. See also Aug.–Sept. 1969, 7; Philadelphia Police Dept., "Extract of Criminal Record" for Polak; "Homosexuals to Tell Story."

53. Forum with Bello and Gittings; Interview with Gittings.

54. Friedan, cited in Susan Brownmiller, "Sisterhood Is Powerful," *NYT Magazine*, 15 Mar. 1970, 140; Echols, *Daring to Be Bad*, 215. See also *Rat*, 8–21 May 1970, 12; *Gay*, 25 May 1970, 17; Radicalesbians, "The Woman-Identified Woman," *Come Out*, June-July

1970, 12–13; *Come Out*, June-July 1970, 14–15; Dec. 1970–Jan. 1971, 10; Teal, *The Gay Militants*, 179–194; Sidney Abbott and Barbara Love, *Sappho Was a Right-On Woman: A Liberated View of Lesbianism* (New York: Stein and Day, 1972), 113–116; Marotta, *The Politics of Homosexuality*, 229–255; Duberman, *Stonewall*, 266–267.

55. B. B., "Congress to Unite Women," *HALN*, May-June 1970, 5.

56. A. B. and C. F., "The Same Sex," *HALN*, Oct. 1969, 3; C. F., *HALN*, Nov.–Dec. 1969, 7; A. B., "Enter the New Homosexual," *HALN*, Jan.-Feb. 1970, 3; *HALN*, May-June 1970, 3. See also Barbara Gittings, "The Homosexual and the Church," in *The Same Sex: An Appraisal of Homosexuality*, ed. Ralph W. Weltge (Philadelphia: Pilgrim, 1969), 146–155.

57. Kitsi Burkhart, "WITCH and NOW Tackle Male 'Oppressors,'" *EB*, 10 Mar. 1970, 42, 43; Gill Barthold and Linda Pincus, "WITCH Has Come to Philadelphia," *PFP*, 9 Mar. 1970, 3. See also *DD*, 12 Mar. 1970, 1; *PD*, 12 Mar. 1970, 13; Echols, *Daring to Be Bad*, 76, 96–98; *Women*, 30 Mar. 1970, 8.

58. C. F., *HALN*, Mar.–Apr. 1970, 5.

59. *Women*, 30 Mar. 1970, 6; C. F., *HALN*, Mar.–Apr. 1970, 6. See also *PFP*, 30 Mar. 1970, 2; *PD*, 2 Apr. 1970, 6; Interview with Davidson.

60. C. F., "From a Gay Sister," *Women*, June 1970, 5–6.

61. "WLC Opens to Women, Groups," *DD*, 18 June 1970, 16; *Women*, July 1970, 2; *HALN*, 26 Dec. 1970, 1–2. See also *Women*, 1 May 1970, 1–2; *EB*, *Inq.*, *DN*, *Trib.*, *DD*, *PFP*, 20–31 Aug. 1970; *Ladder*, Apr.-May 1971, 38; *EB*, 13 Sept. 1970, sec. 6, p. 12; *HALN*, 25 Sept. 1970, 2; 26 Nov. 1970, 3–4; *Ladder*, Dec. 1970–Jan. 1971, 40; *Awake and Move*, Jan.-Feb. 1971, 2–3; Mar. 1971, 1.

62. Kay Lahusen, cited in Teal, *The Gay Militants*, 129; Kay Tobin [Lahusen], "Daughters of Bilitis Confronts Feminist Issue," *Gay*, 3 Aug. 1970, 12; Teal, *The Gay Militants*, 188.

Chapter Twelve

1. *PFP*, 27 July 1970, 1. See also Audiotape, Tommi Avicolli Mecca interview with Kuromiya, GLBTA.

2. See Teal, *The Gay Militants*, 158, 179–194, 212–214.

3. See Steve Kuromiya, "Just a Kiss Away," *PD*, 4 June 1970, 5; *GLFPN*, c. July 1970; *HALN*, 25 Sept. 1970, 1; Stan Luxenberg, "Is 'Gay' an Accepted Word?" *TD*, 31 Dec. 1970, 1; Interview with Kuromiya; Mecca interview with Kuromiya. Kuromiya used the name Steve in this period but now favors Kiyoshi.

4. Luxenberg, "Is 'Gay' an Accepted Word?" 1; Mecca interview with Kuromiya. See also *Life*, 18 Oct. 1968, 90, 92; Spikol, "Gay Today," 169–172; *Au Courant*, 26 Apr. 1993, 1, 11, 14–20; *Philadelphia Folklore Project Works*, Spring 1998, 10–13; Interview with Kuromiya.

5. See previous note.

6. Mecca interview with Kuromiya; Kuromiya, "Just a Kiss Away."

7. Interview with Johnson.

8. *GLFPN*, c. July 1970. See also *PFP*, 27 July 1970, 6–7; Halley Tarr, "Penned-in Gays," *GD*, c. Dec. 1970, 5; Halley Tarr, "The Gay Revolution," *DP*, 4 Dec. 1970, 4; Luxenberg, "Is 'Gay' an Accepted Word?" 1; *DP*, 1–4 Feb. 1971; Interview with Mecca; Mecca interview with Kuromiya.

9. Interview with Roberts. See also *New Gay Life*, Nov. 1977, 17–18.

10. Interview with Mecca; Mecca, "Memoirs of a South Philly Sissy," 113–114.

11. Tom Ashe and Basil O'Brien, *PFP*, 27 July 1970, 6–7; Luxenberg, "Is 'Gay' an Accepted Word?" 1.

12. Teal, *The Gay Militants*, 158; Mecca interview with Kuromiya; Forum with Bello and Gittings. See also Philadelphia City Planning Commission, *Population and Housing Characteristics*, 1983.

13. Mecca interview with Kuromiya; Interviews with Mecca and Roberts.

14. Kuromiya, "Just a Kiss Away," 4–5; Basil O'Brien, "Gay Liberation Front Doesn't Want Your Acceptance," *DD*, 18 June 1970, 5.

15. O'Brien, "Gay Liberation Front Doesn't Want Your Acceptance"; Mecca interview with Kuromiya. See also Teal, *The Gay Militants*, 162–163.

16. Kuromiya, cited in Luxenberg, "Is 'Gay' an Accepted Word?" 5; Kuromiya, "Just a Kiss Away," 5.

17. "What Makes Mick Perform?" *GD*, c. Dec. 1970, 14.

18. Radicalesbians, "The Woman-Identified Woman," reprinted in *GD*, c. Dec. 1970, 18–19.

19. "Gay Lib Sets Dance," *TUN*, 11 Aug. 1970, 2; "Homosexualiberationnow," *PD*, 2 July 1970, 15; "Sexism in the Schools," *GD*, c. Dec. 1970, 4; "Gay Day," *GD*, c. Dec. 1970, 13.

20. Steve Kuromiya, *PFP*, 27 July 1970, 6; Kuromiya, "Just a Kiss Away," 5.

21. "Who Likes Drags?" *GLFPN*, 9 Aug. 1970, cited in Teal, *The Gay Militants*, 212; "Transvestite and Transsexual Liberation," *GD*, c. Dec. 1970, 9.

22. Audiotape, Tommi Avicolli Mecca interview with Dijon, GLBTA; Ashe and O'Brien, *PFP*, 27 July 1970, 6–7.

23. Interview with Mecca; Mecca interview with Kuromiya.

24. "On Feminine Qualities and Emotional Liberation," *GD*, c. Dec. 1970, 11.

25. Interview with Mecca. See also David M. Halperin, *One Hundred Years of Homosexuality* (New York: Routledge, 1990).

26. "The Woman-Identified Woman," 19; Tarr, "The Gay Revolution"; "Sexism in the Schools," 4; "Gay Day"; Kuromiya, *PFP*, 27 July 1970, 6; "Sexism in the Schools," 5; Mecca interview with Dijon.

27. Mecca interview with Dijon.

28. Luxenberg, "Is 'Gay' an Accepted Word?" 1, 2. See also *PFP*, 27 July 1970, 6–7; "Gay Day"; *Trib.*, 22 Sept. 1970, 6; *HALN*, 26 Nov. 1970, 3–4; *Gay Flames*, no. 12, 1971, 6.

29. Ashe and O'Brien, *PFP*, 27 July 1970, 6–7; "Gay Soiree," *PD*, 3 Sept. 1970, 10; "Bar-rooom!" *GD*, c. Dec. 1970, 3.

30. Mecca interview with Kuromiya; Mecca interview with Dijon.

31. GLF leaflet, c. 1970, cited in Teal, *The Gay Militants*, 215; Paolantonio, *Frank Rizzo*, 103; GLF leaflet, c. Sept. 1970, GLF file, GLBTA. See also *Inq.*, 6 June 1969, 33; 5 June 1970, 35; Luxenberg, "Is 'Gay' an Accepted Word?" 1; "Legal First Aid," *GD*, c. Dec. 1970, 6.

32. "Gay Brothers Attacked in Philly," *PD*, 3 Sept. 1970, 16.

33. GLF leaflet, c. Sept. 1970, GLF file, GLBTA. See also "Legal First Aid"; *Advocate*, 16 Aug. 1972, 10.

34. "Gay Liberation Front," *PFP*, 31 Aug. 1970, 11; GLF leaflet, c. Sept. 1970, GLF file, GLBTA; "Gay Brothers Attacked in Philly"; Mecca interview with Dijon.

35. Ashe and O'Brien, *PFP*, 27 July 1970, 6–7; Teal, *The Gay Militants*, 156; Interview with Roberts; Kuromiya, "Just a Kiss Away," 5. See also *Gay*, 13 July 1970, 12.

36. "Gay Lib Sets Dance."

37. Mecca interview with Kuromiya; Interview with Roberts.

38. "Gayla Affair," *TUN*, 18 Aug. 1970, 2; "We're Not Gonna Take It!" *PD*, 3 Sept. 1970, 7; Mecca interview with Kuromiya; "Gay Soiree"; Interviews with Roberts and Mecca. See also *PD*, 17 Sept. 1970, 6; *HALN*, 25 Sept. 1970, 1; Luxenberg, "Is 'Gay' an Accepted Word?" 1.

39. Interview with Dijon; "Gay Soiree."

40. Ashe and O'Brien, *PFP*, 27 July 1970, 6–7; Kuromiya, "Just a Kiss Away," 5; O'Brien, "Gay Liberation Front Doesn't Want Your Acceptance"; Teal, *The Gay Militants*, 168–169. See also Oates, "Flower Children," 58–59; *Gay*, 13 July 1970, 12; *PD*, 23 July 1970, 4; Grotta, "Bad Year for the Underground," 83.

41. Ashe and O'Brien, *PFP*, 27 July 1970, 6–7; Basil O'Brien, "Gay Liberation," *PD*, 30 July 1970, cited in Teal, *The Gay Militants*, 169. See also "We're Not Gonna Take It!"

42. Mecca interview with Kuromiya.

43. Kuromiya, "Just a Kiss Away," 4; "We're Not Gonna Take It!"; Kuromiya, *PFP*, 27 July 1970, 6.

44. "Homosexualiberationnow"; "Palante," *GD*, c. Dec. 1970, 8. See also *PFP*, 27 July 1970, 6; *GLFPN*, 9 Aug. 1970, cited in Teal, *The Gay Militants*, 167.

45. "We're Not Gonna Take It!"; Mecca interview with Kuromiya; Mecca interview with Dijon. See also *PD*, 13 Aug. 1970, 5; *GD*, c. Dec. 1970, 2.

46. On the RPCC, see *Black Panther* (*BP*) beginning 31 May 1970; *NYT*, *EB*, *Inq.*, *DN*, *Trib.*, *DD*, *PD*, Aug.–Sept. 1970; Philip S. Foner, ed., *The Black Panthers Speak* (Philadelphia: Lippincott, 1970), xxvii–xxviii, 50–66, 267–271; Franz Schurmann, ed., *To Die for the People: The Writings of Huey P. Newton* (New York: Random House, 1972), xviii–xx, 20–43, 156–162, 178–181, 207–214; Sayre, *Sixties Going on Seventies*, 66–78; Huey Newton, *Revolutionary Suicide* (1973; New York: Writers and Readers, 1995), 294–298; G. Louis Heath, ed., *Off the Pigs!* (Metuchen, NJ: Scarecrow, 1976), 5, 21–23, 148–188, 219–229; Dick Cluster, ed., *They Should Have Served That Cup of Coffee* (Boston: South End, 1979), 45–46; Assata Shakur, *Assata* (Westport, CT: Lawrence Hill, 1987), 216; Elaine Brown, *A Taste of Power: A Black Woman's Story* (New York: Pantheon, 1992), 277–285; John T. McCartney, *Black Power Ideologies: An Essay in African-American Political Thought* (Philadelphia: Temple University Press, 1992), 133–150; Angela Y. Davis, "Black Nationalism: The Sixties and the Nineties," in *Black Popular Culture*, ed. Gina Dent (Seattle: Bay Press, 1992), 317–324; David Hilliard and Lewis Cole, *This Side of Glory: The Autobiography of David Hilliard and the Story of the Black Panther Party* (Boston: Little, Brown, 1993), 11, 302–321; Hugh Pearson, *The Shadow of the Panther* (Reading, MA: Addison-Wesley, 1994), 226–227, 234–235, 253. On the congress, see *Inq.*, 6 Sept. 1970, 9; *Time*, 14 Sept. 1970, 13–14; *U.S. News & World Report*, 21 Sept. 1970, 82–83; *BP*, 3 Oct. 1970, 15.

47. Mumia, "Occupation: Philadelphia, PA," *BP*, 4 July 1970, 9; Carole Friedman, "Between the Devil and the Deep Blue Sea," *HALN*, Mar.–Apr. 1970, 7; Kuromiya, *PFP*, 27 July 1970, 6. See also Eldridge Cleaver, *Soul on Ice* (New York: McGraw-Hill, 1968), 110; *PFP*, 6 Apr. 1970, 12; Teal, *The Gay Militants*, 165–168; *DN*, 8 May 1973, 4; Marotta, *The Politics of Homosexuality*, 78–82, 113, 126–143; Duberman, *Stonewall*, 216–228, 250–260.

48. Black Panther Party, "Message to America," *BP*, 20 June 1970, 12–13, reprinted in *PFP*, 22 June 1970, 7.

49. Huey Newton, "A Letter from Huey to the Revolutionary Brothers and Sisters about the Women's Liberation and Gay Liberation Movements," *BP*, 21 Aug. 1970, 5, reprinted in *PD*, 3 Sept. 1970, 16; *PFP*, 31 Aug. 1970, 3; *DD*, 27 Aug. 1970, 5. The text of Newton's letter varies; I use the *PD* version.

50. *BP*, 29 Aug. 1970, 9; David Umansky, "Whites Constitute 40 Pct. Attendance at Black Convention," *Inq.*, 6 Sept. 1970, 9; Len Lear, "New 'Constitution' for Poor Last Thing on Minds of Many Panther Delegates," *Trib.*, 8 Sept. 1970, 2.

51. *PD*, 3 Sept. 1970, 16; Alice Walker, "Black Panthers or Black Punks? They Ran on Empty," *NYT*, 5 May 1993, A23.

52. Janie Conwell, letter to the editor, *DN*, 10 Sept. 1970, 23. See also *NYT*, *EB*, *Inq.*, *DN*, *Trib.*, *DD*, *PD*, Aug.–Sept. 1970; *Newsweek*, 14 Sept. 1970, 30–31; *Time*, 14 Sept. 1970, 14–15; *Commonweal*, 2 Oct. 1970, 6–7; *Nation*, 12 Oct. 1970, 332–336; *NYT Magazine*, 18 Oct. 1970, 25, 97; *BP*, 20 Feb. 1971, 4; U.S. Commission on Civil Rights, Pennsylvania State Committee, *Police-Community Relations in Philadelphia* (Philadelphia, 1972); Sayre, *Sixties Going on Seventies*, 66–67; Frank Donner, *Protectors of Privilege*, 213–217; Interview with Reggie Schell, in *They Should Have Served That Cup of Coffee*, 64–66; Ward Churchill and Jim Vander Wall, *Agents of Repression: The FBI's Secret War against the Black Panther Party and the American Indian Movement* (Boston: South End, 1988). On the Philadelphia Panthers, see also Heath, *Off the Pigs!*, 121, 148, 185; Interview with Reggie Schell, 47–69; Brown, *A Taste of Power*, 3.

53. SAC to FBI Director, 21 Aug. 1970, GLF, HQ Cross Reference; Philadelphia to Director, 5 Sept. 1970, Case 100–65673-12, cited in Duberman, *Stonewall*, 312; SAC Buffalo to SAC New York, 13 Nov. 1970, Case 100–14970; FBI Memo, 30 Nov. 1970, Case 100–52208; FBI Report, 18 June 1971, GLF, HQ Cross Reference.

54. "Gay People Help Plan New World," *Gay Flames*, 11 Sept. 1970, 1; Kepner, cited in Duberman, *Stonewall*, 312; "Gay Man in Philadelphia," *Come Out*, Dec. 1970–Jan. 1971, 15. See also Donald Cox, "On to Washington! Panther's New Battlecry," *DD*, 10 Sept. 1970, 3; *PD*, 17 Sept. 1970, 10–11; Teal, *The Gay Militants*, 173–177; Marotta, *The Politics of Homosexuality*, 129; Duberman, *Stonewall*, 251, 259–260.

55. "Gay Man in Philadelphia"; "Statement of the Male Homosexual Workshop," *Gay Flames*, 11 Sept. 1970, 2; Mecca interview with Kuromiya. See also *PD*, 7 Oct. 1970, 17.

56. "Statement of the Male Homosexual Workshop," 2, 7.

57. Mecca interview with Dijon; "Views," *Gay Flames*, 11 Sept. 1970, 8; Cox, "On to Washington!" 3.

58. Lois Hart, "Black Panthers Call a Revolutionary People's Constitutional Convention: A White Lesbian Responds," *Come Out*, Sept.–Oct. 1970, 15.

59. "No Revolution without Us," *Come Out*, Dec. 1970–Jan. 1971, 17; Martha Shelley, cited in Marcus, *Making History*, 185. See also Martha Shelley, "Subversion in the Womans Movement: What Is to Be Done," *off our backs*, 8 Nov. 1970, 5–7.

60. Newton, "A Letter from Huey."

61. "Lesbian Demands," *Come Out*, Dec. 1970–Jan. 1971, 16. See also *PD*, 7 Oct. 1970, 17; Echols, *Daring to Be Bad*, 222–224.

62. "Gay Man in Philadelphia"; *PD*, 17 Sept. 1970, 10–11; "No Revolution without Us"; "Philly Convention," *Rat*, 11 Sept. 1970, 17.

63. *PD*, 17 Sept. 1970, 10–11; "No Revolution without Us."

64. "No Revolution without Us." See also Shelley, "Subversion in the Womans Movement."

65. "Demands of the Workshop on Self-Determination of Women," *PD*, 7 Oct. 1970, 16. See also Daniel P. Moynihan, *The Negro Family: The Case for National Action* (Washington, DC: U.S. Department of Labor, Office of Policy Planning and Research, 1965); *PD*, 3 Sept. 1970, 6; *off our backs*, 30 Sept. 1970, 4–5.

66. "Demands of the Workshop on Self-Determination of Women"; Shelley, "Subversion in the Womans Movement."

67. "No Revolution without Us."

68. "Gay Man in Philadelphia."

69. "No Revolution without Us"; Paul Delaney, "Panthers to Reconvene in Capital to Ratify Their Constitution," *NYT*, 8 Sept. 1970, 5.

70. "Gay Man in Philadelphia"; "No Revolution without Us."

71. Cox, "On to Washington!" 3; Delaney, "Panthers to Reconvene"; Shelley, "Subversion in the Womans Movement."

72. Photo caption, *GD*, October 1970, 17; "YAWF Women's Statement," *PFP*, 7 Dec. 1970, 6–8. See also *Gay Flames*, no. 12, 1971, 6.

73. *BP*, 5 Dec. 1970, after 8. See also *PFP*, 7 Dec. 1970, 6.

Chapter Thirteen

1. "Radicalesbians: Coming Out vs. Coming Home," *Awake and Move*, Mar. 1971, 4. On later developments in Philadelphia lesbian feminism, see Murphy, " 'The Changer(s).' "

2. Del Martin, "If That's All There Is," *Ladder*, Dec. 1970–Jan. 1971, 4–6; Feb.–Mar. 1971, 45. See also Robin Morgan, "Goodbye to All That," *Rat*, 6 Feb. 1970, 6; Teal, *The Gay Militants*, 179–194; Abbott and Love, *Sappho Was a Right-On Woman*, 135–158; Faderman, *Odd Girls*, 204–209; Echols, *Daring to Be Bad*, 210–241; Marotta, *The Politics of Homosexuality*, 229–303.

3. Telephone interview with Rosenberg, 14 May 1994; Radicalesbians Philadelphia (RL) and GLF flier, c. Jan. 1971, GLF file, GLBTA.

4. Interview with Olshan.

5. Brownworth, *Too Queer*, 31; Interview with Olshan; Spikol, "Gay Today," 160, 162; Interview with Davies. See also *Tell-A-Woman*, Feb. 1972, 4; Interviews with Davidson and Barron.

6. Interview with Cornwell. See also Cornwell's "Open Letter to a Black Sister," *Ladder*, Oct.-Nov. 1971, 33–36; "Letter to a Friend," *Ladder*, Dec. 1971–Jan. 1972, 42–45; "From a Soul Sister's Notebook," *Ladder*, June-July 1972, 43–44; "A Black Lesbian Is a Woman Is a Woman," *Los Angeles Free Press*, 24 Nov. 1972, 23, reprinted as "Black/Lesbian/Woman" in *Gay Liberator*, Feb. 1973, 7, and as "Black Lesbian Woman" in *Lesbian Tide*, Sept. 1973, 11–12; "Notes from a Third World Woman," *Wicce*, Early Spring 1974, 2–3; "From an Autobiography," *GA*; "To a Bamboozled Sister," *Sinister Wisdom*, Spring 1977, 46–48; " 'So Who's Giving Guarantees?' An Interview with Audre Lorde," *Sinister Wisdom*, Fall 1977, 15–21; "The Black Lesbian in a Malevolent Society," *Dyke*, Winter 1977, 14–17; "Three for the Price of One: Notes from a Gay Black Feminist," in *Lavender Culture*, ed. Karla Jay and Allen Young (New York: Jove, 1978): 466–476; "To the Sisters of the Azalea Collective and Lesbians Rising," *Sinister Wisdom*, Spring 1980, 43–44; "Backward Journey," *Feminary*, no. 1, 1982, 86–105; *Black Lesbian in White America*.

7. Interview with Davies.

8. Interview with Barron.

9. Interview with Davidson.

10. Interview with Hill.

11. Interviews with Olshan and Davies.

12. Interviews with Hill and Barron; Spikol, "Gay Today," 160, 162.

13. See *Getting It Together*, 8 Nov., 22 Nov. 1971; *Joy of Gay*, c. Dec. 1971; *HALN*, Jan. 1972, 1–2, 4–5; *LFB*, July 1972; Aug. 1972; Sept.–Oct. 1972; *Furies*, Jan. 1972, 15; Spikol, "Gay Today," 166. On MCC, see Byerly, "HAL Is Gay"; *Drummer*, 21 Oct. 1971, 17; 10 Aug. 1972, 4.

14. Interviews with Hill, Friedman, and Davies. See also *GA*, no. 5, 1973, 27.

15. Interview with Friedman.

16. Interview with Davies. See also *HALN*, Jan. 1972, 3; *LFB*, Sept.–Oct. 1972, 6–7.

17. Interview with Bello.

18. Interview with Gittings; Ruth Rovner, "Lesbians First; Women Second," *Drummer*, 16 Dec. 1971, 4.

19. Spikol, "Gay Today," 160; Interviews with Davidson and Olshan.

20. Cornwell, "Three for the Price of One," 471; Interview with Cornwell.

21. Interviews with Hill and Davidson; "I Don't Belong," *LFB*, Aug. 1972, 4.

22. Mike, Gale, and Laurie, "A One Act Bar Scene," *Getting It Together*, 8 Nov. 1971, 6–8. See also Interview with Barron; *GA*, no. 5, 1973, 26–27; Harry Langhorne to LCB, 15 Jan. 1973, HLP (box 3/f5).

23. Greg Lee, "The Gay Bar Jitters," *Drummer*, 22 June 1972, 4. See also Fonzi, "Locust Street Revisited"; *EB*, *Inq.*, and *DN*, 19 Sept.–15 Oct., 24 Oct., 21 Nov.–12 Dec. 1971; 21 Jan., 6 Feb., 16 July, 27 Sept. 1972; 23 Feb., 15 June, 6 Aug., 30 Dec. 1973; 16–22 Aug., 10 Nov., 20 Dec. 1974; 2 Aug. 1975; Rubinstein, *City Police*; Pennsylvania Crime Commission, *Report on Police Corruption*.

24. *Getting It Together*, 22 Nov. 1971, 4; Brownworth, *Too Queer*, 41–42; Mike [Marlene Miller], "Stand up and Be Counted," *Getting It Together*, 8 Nov. 1971, 4, 9.

25. Interviews with Davies, Cornwell, and Hill. See also *Drummer*, 4 May 1972, 3; *Tell-A-Woman*, Feb. 1972, 2, 5; *Philadelphia N.O.W. Newsletter*, Feb. 1972 to May 1972.

26. Spikol, "Gay Today," 160, 164. See also *PM*, Dec. 1972, 10.

27. Rosalee Buck [Rosalie Davies], "I Am a Lesbian, I Am Proud," *LFB*, Sept.–Oct. 1972, 6–7; Cornwell, "Letter to a Friend," 42–43.

28. Buck, "I Am a Lesbian," 7; Spikol, "Gay Today," 162.

29. "To Liberate Women Is to Liberate Society," *LFB*, July 1972, 1; Spikol, "Gay Today," 164.

30. Interviews with Olshan, Barron, Davidson, and Hill.

31. Cornwell, "Letter to a Friend," 42–45.

32. Cornwell, "Open Letter to a Black Sister," 33–35.

33. Brownworth, *Too Queer*, 31; Spikol, "Gay Today," 162–163, 166, 164.

34. Cornwell, "Letter to a Friend," 43–44; Buck, "I Am a Lesbian," 7.

35. Cornwell, "Open Letter to a Black Sister," 34; Cornwell, "Letter to a Friend," 44.

36. Cornwell, "From a Soul Sister's Notebook," 43–44.

37. Cornwell, "Notes from a Third World Woman," 2; Cornwell, "Three for the Price of One," 471.

38. Clemson N. Page, Jr., "Homosexuals Lose Share in $11,900 'People's Fund,' " *EB*,

21 Feb. 1971, 21; Mecca interview with Kuromiya. See also *Advocate*, 28 Apr. 1971, 13; *Awake and Move*, June 1971, 3.

39. RL and GLF flier, c. Jan. 1971, GLF file, GLBTA; "Philly Disc Jockey Zapped When Remarks Rile Gays," *Advocate*, 28 Apr. 1971, 4; "Gays Invade WIBG Studio Following Insults," *TD*, 18 Mar. 1971, 3. See also *EB*, 16 Mar. 1971, 5; *TD*, 25 Mar. 1971, 3, 6; *Advocate*, 13 Sept. 1972, 14.

40. Byerly, "HAL Is Gay." See also *HALN*, 1971–1973; *EB*, 3 Jan. 1971, 19; *Inq.*, 16 Jan. 1971, 4; *DP*, 2 Feb. 1971, 3; *EB*, 3 Mar. 1971, 36; *Advocate*, 17 Mar. 1971, 9; *Inq.*, 29 Mar. 1971, 4; *EB*, 29 Mar. 1971, 1; *Advocate*, 28 Apr. 1971, 3; *Ladder*, Aug.–Sept. 1971, 39; *EB*, 25 Sept. 1971, 5; "A H.A.L. Perspective," Oct. 1971, HLP (box 2/f60); *EB*, 9 Oct. 1971, 8; 17 Oct. 1971, 32; "HAL Makes a Plea," *Drummer*, 21 Oct. 1971, 14; *Inq.*, 28 Oct. 1971, 43; Correspondence, lists, and press releases, 3 Nov. 1971–28 Feb. 1973, HAL file, GLBTA; HAL dance flier, 28 Apr. 1972, HLP (box2/f60); Teal, *The Gay Militants*, 318; *GA*, June 1972, 1; *Crusader*, Dec. 1972, 2; typescript, GAA history, n.d., HLP (box 2/f3).

41. "HAL Makes a Plea"; "Homosexual Sues for Job Refused by Postal Service," *EB*, 5 Aug. 1971, 13; Felicia Stitcher, "Sex-Change Teacher Fights Ouster in New Jersey," *DN*, 20 Sept. 1971, 29. See also *Ladder*, Apr.-May 1971, 38; Coxe to Aronson, 14 May 1971, HLP (box 1/f2); *DN*, 5 Aug. 1971, 5; *Inq.*, 6 Aug. 1971, 7; "HAL Is Gay"; "A H.A.L. Perspective."

42. *Getting It Together*, 8 Nov. 1971, 5. See also *TD*, 8 Apr. 1971, 1; GAA and HAL, "Discrimination against Homosexuals in Philadelphia," 19 Aug. 1971, HLP (box 2/f60); Byerly, "HAL Is Gay"; "A H.A.L. Perspective"; *EB*, 9 Oct. 1971, 1, 2; *Inq.*, 28 Oct. 1971, 43; *EB*, 31 Oct. 1971, 9; *HALN*, Jan. 1972, 1–2; Feb. 1972, 2.

43. "More Cops for Free," *DN*, 22 Mar. 1972, 27; Act of Dec. 6, 1972, P.L. 1482, no. 334, section 1, 18 Pa.C.S.A. sections 3101 and 3124. See also Barbara Gittings, "HAL Presentation at Public Hearing," 29 Apr. 1971, HLP (box 2/f60); Coxe to Aronson, 14 May 1971, HLP (box 1/f2); "A H.A.L. Perspective"; "HAL Makes a Plea"; *HALN*, Jan. 1972, 1; *DN*, 6 Apr. 1972, 23; *Drummer*, 1 June 1972, 4; *Crusader*, Dec. 1972, 2; *Commonwealth v. Bonadio*, 490 Pa. 91, 415 A.2d 47 (1980).

44. "A H.A.L. Perspective"; Byerly, "HAL Is Gay." See also GAA, HAL, and HIS flier for Ace Trucking Company demonstration, n.d., HLP (box 2/f60); *HALN*, Feb. 1972, 1, 3; *Trib.*, 30 Dec. 1972, 20; *Crusader*, Dec. 1972, 2.

45. Mecca interview with Rosen; *HALN*, Feb. 1972, 3. See also FBI-Philadelphia Report, 20 Oct. 1970, HQ-1065894; *HALN*, Jan. 1973 to Feb.–Mar. 1973; Correspondence and press releases, 6 Jan.–29 Feb. 1973, HAL file, GLBTA; "1973 Gay Guide to Philadelphia"; *Ms*, June 1977, 76.

46. See *La Salle Collegian*, 22 Feb. 1972, 1, 3; *TUN*, 24 Feb. 1972, 4–5; "1973 Gay Guide to Philadelphia"; *DP*, 6 Feb. 1973, 1, 5; *EB*, 18 Feb. 1973, 42.

47. Interviews with Escoffier and Mecca. See also GAA Minutes, 1971–1972, GAA file, GLBTA; *Crusader*, Dec. 1972, 4; "1973 Gay Guide to Philadelphia"; typescript, GAA history, n.d., HLP (box 2/f3); Audiotape, Tommi Avicolli Mecca interview with Tom Wilson Weinberg; Interview with Langhorne.

48. Interviews with Escoffier and Langhorne.

49. *Crusader*, Dec. 1972, 4; GAA statement of purpose, c. 1972, GAA file, GLBTA.

50. Richard A. Frank, "Phila. Comes Out of Its Closet!" *GA*, July 1972, 2. See also GAA flier, 9 Dec. 1971, GAA file, GLBTA; GAA press release, c. 10 Dec. 1971, HLP (box 2/f7); *HALN*, Jan. 1972, 2–3; *Advocate*, 5 Jan. 1972, 4; GAA newsletters, 8 Feb. to 22 Feb. 1972, HLP (box 2/f3); *Crusader*, Dec. 1972, 4.

51. Greg Lee, "Open Letter to Mayor Rizzo," *Drummer*, 5 Oct. 1972, 4; *GA*, July 1972, 3. See also fliers, c. 1972, GAA file, GLBTA.

52. See GAA press release, c. 2 Mar. 1972, HLP (box 2/f7); *Drummer*, 9 Mar. 1972, 5; 20 Apr. 1972, 1, 6; Harry Langhorne, "To the Democratic Delegates of Pennsylvania," 25 May 1972, HLP (box 1/f35); Langhorne, "Presentation at the Regional Democratic Platform Committee Hearing in Pittsburgh," 3 June 1972, HLP (box 2/f59); *Advocate*, 11 Oct. 1972, 20; *Drummer*, 9 Nov. 1972, 4; *Crusader*, Dec. 1972, 4.

53. George Bodamer, "Bellis Kills Gay Rights Amendment," *GA*, July 1972, 4. See also *Drummer*, 18 May 1972, 4; *GA*, June 1972, 1; *PM*, Jan. 1973, 90, 92; Mary Frances Berry, *Why ERA Failed: Politics, Women's Rights, and the Amending Process of the Constitution* (Bloomington: Indiana University Press, 1986), 98.

54. Interviews with Hill and Olshan.

55. Interviews with Escoffier, Barron, Davidson, and Davies.

56. Interview with Olshan.

57. Interview with Barron.

58. Interview with Davidson.

59. Interview with Hill; Brownworth, *Too Queer*, 42, 49.

60. Martha Shelley, *Come Out*, reprinted in *PFP*, 27 July 1970, 7; Radicalesbians, "The Woman-Identified Woman," reprinted in *GD*, Oct. 1970, 18–19.

61. Carol, "Gays Travel to St. Paul's," *Getting It Together*, 8 Nov. 1971, 2; E. Spotto, "Spotlite on Lansdowne," *HALN*, Jan. 1972, 5; Mike, "Stand up and Be Counted," *Getting It Together*, 8 Nov. 1971, 9; *LFB*, July 1972, 4; Aug. 1972, 6; Sept.–Oct. 1972, 10. See also "A H.A.L. Perspective"; *Getting It Together*, 8 Nov. 1971, 1; 22 Nov. 1971, 3; *Joy of Gay*, c. Dec. 1971, 1; *Advocate*, 11 Oct. 1972, 10; 22 Nov. 1972, 5; *Crusader*, Dec. 1972, 1; RL et al., "Constructive Changes for Church Adoption," n.d., HLP (box 2/f60).

62. Free University course descriptions, Fall 1970–Fall 1972, HLP (box 1/f79); Tom Candor, "Weekly Gay Coffee Hour," *DP*, 6 Feb. 1973, 1. See also *Tell-A-Woman*, Nov. 1972, 4.

63. Interviews with Barron and Hill. See also Brownworth, *Too Queer*, 33, 42.

64. Interviews with Olshan, Davies, and Friedman. See also *HALN*, Jan. 1972, 3; Buck, "I Am a Lesbian, I Am Proud"; Aronson syllabus, HLP (box 1/f79); *TD*, 20 July 1972, 4; Spikol, "Gay Today," 125; Interview with Langhorne.

65. Interviews with Olshan, Mecca, and Hill.

66. Mike, Gale, and Laurie, "A One Act Bar Scene," 8; "An Alternative?" *LFB*, July 1972, 2; *Furies*, Jan. 1972, 15; Cornwell, "From a Soul Sister's Notebook," 43; *LFB*, Aug. 1972, 5.

67. Nikki Francis, "Sisters in Jail," *LFB*, Sept.–Oct. 1972, 4.

68. Interview with Davies.

69. "Radicalesbians: Coming Out vs. Coming Home"; Interview with Barron.

70. Christa, "On Putting Your Own Kind Down," *LFB*, Aug. 1972, 2.

Conclusion

1. See Interviews with Barron, Hill, and Friedman.

2. B. Hill, "The Gay Pride March," *LFB*, Aug. 1972, 3; Interview with Friedman; Philadelphia 1972 Gay Pride Committee press release, 2 June 1972, Philadelphia file, IGLA. See also Greg Lee, "The March for Gay Pride," *Drummer*, 8 June 1972, 4; "First Phila. Gay Pride March," *GA*, June 1972, 1.

3. Larry Fields, "Air Force Vet Risks Job to Proclaim He's Gay," *DN*, 11 May 1972, 5; B. Douglas Gile, "Homosexuals, Friends Plan Parade down Chestnut St.," *EB*, 6 June 1972, 58; "Strange Bedfellows," *DN*, 25 May 1972, 25. See also *Drummer*, 11 May 1972, 4; *Tell-A-Woman*, June 1972, 5; *Trib.*, 10 June 1972, 6; "First Phila. Gay Pride March," 1.

4. Greg Lee, "This, That, and Other Things," *Drummer*, 18 May 1972, 4; Greg Lee, "Should Gays Be Separatists?" *Drummer*, 25 May 1972, 4; Greg Lee, "Media-ocrity," *Drummer*, 1 June 1972, 4.

5. B. Hill, "The Gay Pride March"; Matthew Grande, "Philadelphia Gay Pride 1973," *GA*, no. 5, 1973, 5; Interview with Friedman. See also " 'Gay' Liberation Parade Draws Crowd of 10,000," *EB*, 12 June 1972, 5; " 'Gay Pride' Marchers Shed Symbolic Chains in Liberation Drive," *Inq.*, 12 June 1972, 31; Larry Fields, "1,000 Gays Proclaim Freedom in March," *DN*, 12 June 1972, 3; *Trib.*, 13 June 1972, 2; Greg Lee, "The Day of the Coming Out," *Drummer*, 15 June 1972, 4; "Summer Mummers," 36, 38; *Advocate*, 5 July 1972, 1; Greg Lee, "Remember, Tom Fox, Gay Is Delicious," *DN*, 7 Sept. 1972, 28.

6. " 'Gay Pride' Marchers Shed Symbolic Chains"; Philadelphia 1972 Gay Pride Committee press release, 2 June 1972.

7. Fields, "1,000 Gays Proclaim Freedom"; Lee, "The Day of the Coming Out"; *Trib.*, 13 June 1972, 2; "Summer Mummers," 36, 38.

8. Fields, "1,000 Gays Proclaim Freedom"; Lyrics in Barron's possession; Interviews with Friedman and David.

9. Lee, "The March for Gay Pride," 3; Greg Lee, "Auntie Sam Wants You," *Drummer*, 29 June 1972, 4; Frank, "Phila. Comes Out of Its Closet!" 2; "Summer Mummers," 38.

10. Escoffier, "Styles of Gay Liberation," 2–4; Interview with Escoffier.

11. "First Phila. Gay Pride March"; Philadelphia Gay Pride Committee, letter to the editor, *Drummer*, 29 June 1972, 5; Jim Quinn, "Marching with Gay Pride: Don Juan in Hell," *Drummer*, 15 June 1972, 12. See also "Phila. Comes Out of Its Closet!" 2.

12. Lee, "The March for Gay Pride," 4; " 'Gay' Liberation Parade Draws Crowd of 10,000"; Brooke, "Women—Get It Together," *LFB*, July 1972, 3. See also *Tell-A-Woman*, Summer 1972, 3.

13. Interview with Hill; Frank Femia, letter to the editor, *Drummer*, 6 July 1972, 2.

14. Brooke, "Women—Get It Together."

15. Ibid.

16. Hill, "The Gay Pride March."

17. Ibid.

18. "Got Them Job Discrimination Blues?" *LFB*, Sept.–Oct. 1972, 8; "Strike! March! Rally!" *LFB*, Aug. 1972, 1; Lillian Williams, "300 March for 'Power to the Sisters,' " *Inq.*, 27 Aug. 1972, B1; "Phila Women March on Strike Day," *LFB*, Sept.–Oct. 1972, 4; Spikol, "Gay Today," 160. See also *Drummer*, 24 Aug. 1972, 4; *DN*, 25 Aug. 1972, 55; *Inq.*, 26 Aug. 1972, 6; *EB*, 27 Aug. 1972, 28; *Drummer*, 7 Sept. 1972, 4; Elizabeth Scofield, "The Soft Underbelly of Women's Lib," *PM*, Jan. 1973, 93.

19. "Strike!"; "Phila Women March on Strike Day"; Linda Byron, "Power to the Sisters," *LFB*, Sept.–Oct. 1972, 5; Judy, "Racism: A Feminist Analysis," *LFB*, Sept.–Oct. 1972, 5–6; Buck [Davies], "I Am a Lesbian"; Marilyn Buggey, "As Women, As Workers," *LFB*, Sept.–Oct. 1973, 6–7.

20. Scofield, "The Soft Underbelly," 93, 150. See also *GA*, no. 5, 1973, 6–7; *Advocate*, 19 Dec. 1973, 1, 23; *EB* and *Inq.*, 18–27 June 1973.

21. "RL Restructures!" *LFB*, Sept.–Oct. 1972, 2; "Clarification of Leadership Roles in a Radical Feminist Organization," *LFB*, Sept.–Oct. 1972, 9; "Philadelphia Radicales-

bians Disbands!" *LFB*, Sept.–Oct. 1972, 10; "Lesbian Office Opens," *LFB*, Sept.–Oct. 1972, 10; The Women's Center, letter to the editor, *PM*, Dec. 1972, 10. See also *GA*, Aug. 1972, 2; *Tell-A-Woman*, Summer 1972, 3; Sept. 1972, 2; Nov. 1972, 1, 5; *Wicce*, Fall 1973, 4.

22. Rachel Rubin, "Just Try Being a Lesbian in Philadelphia!" *GA*, no. 5, 1973, 27; Interviews with Barron and Davidson.

23. See *Ladder*, Feb.–Mar. 1970, 8–13; Teal, *The Gay Militants*, 214; *GA*, Aug. 1972, 2, 3; *EB*, *Inq.*, *DN*, *Drummer*, 16–24 Aug. 1972; *Variety*, 30 Aug. 1972, 36; Lee, "Remember, Tom Fox"; *Advocate*, 13 Sept. 1972, 14; *TUN*, 10 Oct. 1972, 4; *Drummer*, 12 Oct. 1972, 4; *TUN*, 16 Oct. 1972, 3, 5; *Inq.*, 21 Oct. 1972, 12; *DN*, 21 Oct. 1972, 4; *EB*, 21 Oct. 1972, 22; *Advocate*, 25 Oct. to 6 Dec. 1972; *Drummer*, 26 Oct. 1972, 4; Spikol, "Gay Today," 126, 167; *EB*, 2 Nov. 1972, 2; *DN*, 2 Nov. 1972, 1, 3; *EB*, 27 Nov. 1972, 3; *Inq.*, 16 Dec. 1972, 13; Roxanne Patel, "In and Out," *PM*, July 1998, 21–28; Interviews with Segal and Langhorne.

24. Richard A. Rusinow, "Philly Panel Urges Control of Police," *Advocate*, 16 Aug. 1972, 10; "Philly Gays Get Pledge by 'Community Advocate,'" *Advocate*, 13 Sept. 1972, 12. See also U.S. Commission on Civil Rights, Pennsylvania State Committee, *Police-Community Relations in Philadelphia*, 58; Kohn and Matusow, *Barry and Alice*; *Gay Community News*, 28 June 1987, 7.

25. "Meet Produces Rights Platform for Pennsy Gays," *Advocate*, 22 Nov. 1972, 5. See also *Advocate*, 11 Oct. 1972, 10; *HALN*, Nov. 1972, 1–2; *Gay*, 11 Dec. 1972, 20; *Crusader*, Dec. 1972, 1, 4.

26. Saline, "Trick or Treat?" 215–223; Spikol, "Gay Today"; Walter F. Naedele, "Gay Activists Organize at 2 Catholic Colleges," *EB*, 18 Feb. 1973, 42; Tom Candor, "Weekly Gay Coffee Hour," *DP*, 6 Feb. 1973, 1; Grace E. Grillet, letter to the editor, *PM*, Dec. 1972, 10, 12.

27. "Summer Mummers," 36, 38.

INDEX